Professional Review Guide for the RHIA and RHIT Examinations 2009 Edition

Patricia J. Schnering, RHIA, CCS
Debora J. Butts, EdD, RHIA
Debra W. Cook, MAEd, RHIA
Marjorie H. McNeill, PhD, RHIA, CCS
Toni Cade, MBA, RHIA, CCS, FAHIMA
Lisa Delhomme, MHA, RHIA
Anita Hazelwood, MLS, RHIA, FAHIMA
Carol A. Venable, MPH, RHIA, FAHIMA
Nanette B. Sayles, EdD, RHIA, CCS, CHP, FAHIMA
Barbara W. Mosley, PhD, RHIA
Robert L. Garrie, MPA, RHIA
Kathy C. Trawick, EdD, RHIA
Mary Teslow, MLIS, RHIA
Irene L. E. Mueller, EdD, RHIA
Sheila Carlon, Ph.D., RHIA, FAHIMA

PRG Publishing, Inc.
Professional Review Guides, Inc.

DELMAR
CENGAGE Learning

Professional Review Guide for the RHIA and RHIT Examinations, 2009 Edition
Patricia J. Schnering, RHIA, CCS

Vice President, Career and Professional Editorial:
Dave Garza

Director of Learning Solutions:
Matthew Kane

Managing Editor:
Marah Bellegarde

Senior Acquisitions Editor:
Rhonda Dearborn

Product Manager:
Jadin Babin-Kavanaugh

Vice President, Career and Professional Marketing:
Jennifer McAvey

Executive Marketing Manager:
Wendy Mapstone

Senior Marketing Manager:
Nancy Bradshaw

Marketing Coordinator:
Erica Ropitzky

Production Director:
Carolyn Miller

Content Project Manager:
Kenneth McGrath

Senior Art Director:
Jack Pendleton

2009 Current Procedural Terminology © 2008 American Medical Association. ALL RIGHTS RESERVED.

For product information and technology assistance, contact us at
Cengage Learning Customer & Sales Support,
1-800-354-9706

For permission to use material from this text or product, submit
all requests online at **www.cengage.com/permissions**

Further permissions questions can be emailed to
permissionrequest@cengage.com

Library of Congress Cataloging-in-Publication Data
ISBN 10: 1-4354-8536-X
ISBN 13: 978-1-4354-8536-5

Delmar
Executive Woods
5 Maxwell Drive
Clifton Park, NY 12065-2919
USA

Cengage Learning products are represented in Canada by Nelson Education, Ltd.

For your course and learning solutions, visit
delmar.cengage.com

Purchase any of our products at your local college store or visit our corporate website at **cengage.com**

Notice to the Reader

Publisher does not warrant or guarantee any of the products described herein or perform any independent analysis in connection with any of the product information contained herein. Publisher does not assume, and expressly disclaims, any obligation to obtain and include information other than that provided to it by the manufacturer. The reader is expressly warned to consider and adopt all safety precautions that might be indicated by the activities described herein and to avoid all potential hazards. By following the instructions contained herein, the reader willingly assumes all risks in connection with such instructions. The publisher makes no representations or warranties of any kind, including but not limited to, the warranties of fitness for particular purpose or merchantability, nor are any such representations implied with respect to the material set forth herein, and the publisher takes no responsibility with respect to such material. The publisher shall not be liable for any special, consequential, or exemplary damages resulting, in whole or part, from the reader's use of, or reliance upon, this material.

Printed in Canada

1 2 3 4 5 6 7 11 10 09

ABOUT THE AUTHORS

Patricia J. Schnering, RHIA, CCS

Patricia J. Schnering founded PRG Publishing, Inc. and Professional Review Guides, Inc. Mrs. Schnering is a 1995 graduate of the Health Information Management program at St. Petersburg College in St. Petersburg, Florida. In 1998 she was certified as a CCS and in 1999 she received her RHIA certification. Her education includes a Baccalaureate degree from the University of South Florida in Tampa, Florida, with a major in Business Administration. Her HIM experience includes working as Health Information Services supervisor, as a HIM consultant, and as an adjunct HIM instructor at St. Petersburg College. Pat received the Florida Health Information Management Association (FHIMA) Literary Award in 2000 and 2005.

Debora J. Butts, EdD, RHIA

Debora J. Butts is a 1979 graduate of the Health Information Management (formerly Medical Record Administration) program of Clark Atlanta University in Atlanta, Georgia. Ms. Butts received her Master's degree in Management from Webster University in St. Louis, Missouri, in 1983. Her HIM experience includes:

- Twelve years as HIM Program Director and Assistant Professor in the Baccalaureate RHIA program at Texas Southern University, College of Pharmacy and Health Sciences in Houston, Texas
- Three years as Evening Supervisor for Medical Records at Sierra Medical Center in El Paso, Texas
- Two years as Coding Analyst at Grady Memorial Hospital in Atlanta, Georgia
- Numerous consultant and other positions in Health Information Management
- Director of Health Information Management Department at North Harris College in Houston, Texas
- Currently, she is the Document Specialist at Triumph Health care in Houston. Texas.

Debra W. Cook, MAEd, RHIA

Debra W. Cook is a graduate of the Medical Record Administration and the Adult Education programs at East Carolina University in Greenville, North Carolina. Her HIM experience includes:

- Five years in acute health care practice in a variety of positions, including management, utilization management, coding, and consulting
- Over 19 years in HIM education at Alderson-Broaddus College and Marshall University in West Virginia, and Catawba Valley Community College in Hickory, North Carolina. Currently, she is the Department Head of Health Information Technology at CVCC.
- Currently serves on the Panel of Accreditation Reviewers for the Commission of Health Informatics and Information Management Education

Lisa M. Delhomme, MHA, RHIA

Lisa Delhomme is an Instructor in the Health Information Management Department at the University of Louisiana at Lafayette located in Lafayette, Louisiana. She has a bachelor's degree in Health Information Management and a master's degree in Health Services Administration. She teaches several courses, including CPT coding, legal aspects for health care, and computers in health care organizations. Prior to teaching, she held a management position at a physician practice and ambulatory surgery center. Mrs. Delhomme has been an active member of the American Health Information Management Association for nine years. Additionally, she has been involved with committees and projects for the Louisiana Health Information Management Association and Louisiana Medical Group Management Association.

Nanette B. Sayles, EdD, RHIA, CCS, CHP, FAHIMA

Nanette B. Sayles is a 1985 graduate of the University of Alabama at Birmingham Health Information Management (formerly Medical Record Administration) program. Nanette completed her doctorate in Adult Education at the University of Georgia. She is currently the Program Director and Assistant Professor for the Health Information Management and Technology programs at Macon State College in Macon, Georgia. She has a wide range of Health Information Management experience in hospitals, consulting, system development and implementation, and now in education. She is currently President of the Middle Georgia Health Information Management Association and Education Chairperson for the Georgia Health Information Management Association.

Marjorie H. McNeill, PhD, RHIA, CCS

Marjorie McNeill is a graduate of the Health Information Management (formerly Medical Record Administration) program at the Medical College of Georgia in Augusta. She received her M.S. degree in Health Education at Florida State University and her PhD in Educational Leadership at Florida A&M University. Her experience in health information management includes:

- Twenty-four years as an HIM educator. She is the director of the Health Information Management program at Florida A&M University in Tallahassee, Florida.
- Former Director of the Health Information Management program at Armstrong State College in Savannah, Georgia
- Nine years of management and consulting experience in various health care facility practice settings (mental retardation, ambulatory surgery, and nursing home) including acute care hospital experience as Associate Director of Medical Records at St. Joseph's Hospital in Savannah, Georgia.

Marjorie was the recipient of the 2008 Florida Health Information Management Association Distinguished Services Award.

Anita Hazelwood, MLS, RHIA, FAHIMA

Anita Hazelwood is an Associate Professor in the Health Information Management Department at the University of Louisiana at Lafayette located in Lafayette, Louisiana. She has a Bachelor's degree in Medical Record Science, a Master's degree in Library Science and has been a credentialed Registered Health Information Administrator (RHIA) for 27 years.

Some of the courses she teaches include: coding and classification systems including ICD-9-CM and CPT coding; reimbursement methodologies such as DRGs and RBRVS; fraud and abuse; principles of health information management and alternative delivery systems. She is also the Clinical Experience Coordinator.

Anita has actively consulted in hospitals, nursing homes, clinics, facilities for the mentally retarded, and in other educational institutions. She has conducted numerous ICD-9-CM and CPT coding workshops throughout the state for hospitals and physicians' offices.

On a professional level, Anita has been a member of the American Health Information Management Association (AHIMA) for several years. She is also a member of the Society for Clinical Coding (SCC) and served on the SCC board as Secretary in 1998. Anita has been the Internet Task Force Chair for several years. She is a member of the AHIMA's Assembly on Education (AOE) and has served as Membership Chair, a member of the Nominating Committee, and on the Board of Directors.

Anita is a member of the Louisiana Health Information Management Association and was selected as its 1997 Distinguished Member.

Toni Cade, MBA, RHIA, CCS, FAHIMA

Toni Cade is a tenured Associate Professor in the Health Information Management Department at the University of Louisiana at Lafayette. She teaches several courses including health care reimbursement methodologies (MS-DRGs, APCs, RUGs, etc.), hospital statistics, case management, performance improvement, medical terminology and health care risk management. Mrs. Cade is also the Management Internship Site Coordinator coordinating affiliation sites throughout the United States.

Mrs. Cade has 30 years experience with previous positions including Data Analyst for the QIO, Utilization Review Supervisor and Coding Supervisor in a large acute care hospital. Mrs. Cade holds a Bachelor's degree (B.S.) in Medical Record Science and a Master's degree (MBA) in Business Administration. Her credentials include: RHIA (Registered Health Information Administrator) and CCS (Certified Coding Specialist). She was also awarded the designation of "Fellow" (FAHIMA) by the American Health Information Management Association.

She is listed in Marquis' *Who's Who in Medicine and Health Care*. Mrs. Cade serves on the Editorial Advisory Board of *Health Information Management Manual* and *For the Record*. She has reviewed and authored publications on topics including medical terminology, billing, and reimbursement, and health care statistics.

As an independent consultant, Mrs. Cade has extensive experience conducting seminars and workshops in coding (ICD-9-CM, CPT, Evaluation and Management Documentation Guidelines) and reimbursement (DRGs and APCs) to participants in various health care settings throughout the United States. In addition to educational presentations, she also consults at acute care hospitals (e.g., conducting inpatient DRG audits) and works with attorneys involved in medical malpractice cases as an expert health care data analyst and expert witness.

Mrs. Cade has served AHIMA in various positions, including Delegate, Nominating Committee, and Fellowship Review Committee. She was nominated for AHIMA's *Champion Award* and *Educator's Award*. She has served her state association, the Louisiana Health Information Management Association, in many capacities, including serving on the Board of Directors, as President, Secretary, and Project Manager of various projects. She was awarded the *Distinguished Member Award* in 2003. She also received the *Outstanding Volunteer Award* for her efforts as Coding Roundtable Coordinator in Louisiana in 2003–2004.

Robert L. Garrie, MPA, RHIA

Robert L. Garrie is a 1977 graduate of the Health Information Management Program at the University of Louisiana at Lafayette, Louisiana, and is credentialed as a Registered Health Information Administrator (RHIA). He received his master's degree in Public Administration with concentrations in Health Care and Non-Profits from Roosevelt University in Chicago, Illinois, in 1990. Mr. Garrie is currently an Assistant Professor and Academic Coordinator of Clinical Education in the Health Information Management Program at Alabama State University in Montgomery, Alabama. He has a wide range of health information management experience, ranging from acute care and specialty facilities to consulting. Prior to joining the faculty at Alabama State University, he was the Director of Education and Accreditation at the American Health Information Management Association.

Carol A. Venable, MPH, RHIA, FAHIMA

Carol A. Venable is a Professor and Department Head of Health Information Management at the University of Louisiana at Lafayette (ULL). She has a Bachelor's degree in Medical Record Science, a Master's degree in Public Health and Tropical Medicine, and has been a credentialed Registered Health Information Administrator (RHIA) for over 29 years. Prior to teaching at ULL, Ms. Venable held the position of Director of Medical Records at Lafayette General Medical Center and has actively consulted in hospitals, nursing homes, clinics, home health agencies, educational institutions, physicians' offices, and facilities for the mentally retarded. She has written numerous articles and co-edited several coding publications. She has coauthored the books *ICD-9-CM Diagnostic Coding and Reimbursement for Physician Services* and *ICD-10 Preview*. She was coauthor of a chapter in the book, *Health Information: Management of a Strategic Resource,* 2nd Edition. She has been a member of the Louisiana Health Information Management Association and has served as President, President-elect, Treasurer, Delegate, and a member of the Board of Directors, as well as serving on various committees and projects. Carol has also been active in the American Health Information Management Association. She has served on the Item Writing Committee, Benchmarking the Best Practices in HIM Education Project, Council on Education, and the Council on Certification's Roles and Functions Committee. She also serves as a member of the Panel of Accreditation Surveyors. In addition, Carol was awarded the Legacy Award by the American Health Information Management Association. She was elected to serve on the Assembly on Education's (AOE) Board of Directors and has served as chair of the Membership and Nomination Committees of the AOE. She also serves on the Editorial Review Board for Educational Perspectives in Health Information Management, the journal of the Assembly on Education of the American Health Information Management Association.

Mary Spivey Teslow, MLIS, RHIA

Mary Teslow is a 1981 graduate of the University of Illinois at Chicago program in Health Information Management (formerly Medical Record Administration) and has been a credentialed RHIA for over 27 years. She received her first bachelor's degree from Governors State University in Women's Studies in 1976 and her master's degree in Library and Information Science from the University of South Florida in 1994. In 1998 Ms. Teslow was awarded an Endowed Teaching Chair in the Health Sciences. Her HIM experience includes:

- Nineteen years as an HIM educator. She is currently Assistant Professor in HIM at Western Carolina University in North Carolina.
- Fifteen years at Broward Community College in Ft. Lauderdale, Florida, where she developed and directed the Health Information Technology program.
- Seven years in HIM practice, including various management positions in acute care in both an academic medical center and community hospital, as well as managed care.
- Ongoing consulting and publication projects, including creation of the PRG Quick Notes series with Patricia Schnering, and editing and authoring several titles.

Irene L. E. Mueller, EdD, RHIA

Irene L. E. Mueller is a 1992 graduate of the Health Information Administration (formerly Health Information Management) program at Western Carolina University in Cullowhee, North Carolina, where she now serves as Program Director. She received her master's degree in Library Science at Florida State University in 1974. In 2001 she earned her doctorate degree in Adult and Higher Education at Montana State University. Her experience in health information management includes outpatient coding, 12 years as health information management educator (including serving as Program Director for HIT and HIA programs), and consulting experience for physicians' offices and small hospitals in Montana. She is a CAHIIM Panel Reviewer.

Barbara W. Mosley, PhD, RHIA

Barbara W. Mosley is a 1976 graduate of the Health Information Management (formerly Medical Record Administration) program at the University of Tennessee Center for the Health Sciences in Memphis, Tennessee. She received her master's degree in Public Administration with a concentration in Health Services Administration from the University of Memphis (formerly Memphis State University) in 1980. She earned her doctorate degree in Adult Education in 1990 from Florida State University. In 1996 Dr. Mosley was chosen Teacher of the Year at Florida A&M University. In 1998 she was chosen as the Advanced Teacher of the Year at Florida A&M University. Her experience in health information management includes:

- Twenty-four years as Health Information Management educator. Currently, she is a Professor in the Health Information Management Program and the Associate Dean for the school of Allied Health Sciences at Florida A&M University in Tallahassee, Florida.
- Nineteen years of consulting experience at several long-term care facilities in Tallahassee, Florida, and surrounding cities.
- Formerly, Assistant Director of Medical Record Department at the City of Memphis Hospital and the VA Medical Center in Birmingham, Alabama, and Director of Medical Records at the Southeast Memphis Mental Health Center.

Kathy C. Trawick, Ed.D, RHIA

Kathy C. Trawick is the Chairman and Associate Professor of Health Information Management at the University of Arkansas for Medical Sciences in Little Rock, Arkansas. She is a 1985 graduate of the University of Alabama at Birmingham, Health Information Management (formerly Medical Record Administration) program. Dr. Trawick has expertise in higher education and in the allied health sciences. Her basic research interests include higher educational administration effectiveness, institutional effectiveness, and student satisfaction. Dr. Trawick has been a practitioner for ten years in acute care facilities as well as an educator since 1995, and chairman since 1999. Topics of instruction include health care statistics, legal issues, HIM systems, and the CPR, health administration, quality improvement, and cancer registry principles. She is a contributing author of texts in medical terminology and medical law and ethics. She is a consultant to various types of health care facilities. In addition to holding offices at the state level in HIM, HIMSS, and Cancer Registry associations, she also serves on the CAHIIM Panel of Reviewers for HIT/HIA program accreditation.

Sheila A. Carlon, Ph.D., RHIA, FAHIMA

Dr. Carlon has a Ph.D. in Organizational Development and Systems, a master's degree in Health Services Administration, and bachelor's degrees in Broadcast Journalism and Health Care Management. She is a Fellow of AHIMA and received the Educator of the Year Award in 2006 and Cypress College's Distinguished Alumni Award in 2008. Dr. Carlon has been a Program Director and Degree Chair in Regis University's College for Health Professions for the past eight years, where she administers and teaches in four degree programs. She also has extensive hospital and physician office management experience and has been a Health Care Consultant for Deloitte, Touche International.

She is a frequent meeting facilitator and speaker both locally and nationally on such topics as technology, HIPAA, the Global EHR, E- HIM, leadership and management theory and development, HIM advocacy, education trends, and organizational assessment. Dr. Carlon volunteers as an Ombudsman for the Aging Services Division of the Denver Regional Council of Governments, serves as a Board Member of the Golden Gate Fire Department in Golden, Colorado, and volunteers for the Ronald McDonald House, Project Homeless, Quarters for Kids, and Project Mercy in Yetebon, Ethiopia, and is currently helping to launch the field of HIM into the country of Ethiopia.

ACKNOWLEDGMENTS

First and foremost, I wish to express my gratitude to the contributing authors who created and revised the various chapters. They are wonderful people and have graciously provided whatever is needed at the right time while the work is in process. Each of the authors is a seasoned professional and an excellent educator. I can only say that they inspire me to work harder to produce a better product for each edition. With their assistance, we have been able to provide a broad overview of content from both the RHIA and RHIT programs. I am honored to call them my friends and associates.

There are very special people in my life who always knew I could do it when I wasn't sure I could. My husband, Bob, as always, continues to keep me grounded while I spin off in space working on the book. My mother, Emma Miller, is my role model for perseverance leading to success. She embodies grace, courage, strength, and endurance.

My thanks would not be complete without acknowledging all the HIM/HIT educators and students who support our efforts by using PRG products. I am grateful for having met such wonderful people in the HIM profession.

My reward is knowing that the materials you study here may assist you in preparing for the challenge of your examination. Thank you for the letters and words of encouragement.

Whichever credential you seek, I wish you the very best now and throughout your career.

Until we meet....

Patricia J. Schnering, RHIA, CCS
PJSPRG@AOL.COM

TABLE OF CONTENTS

Introduction

Patricia J. Schnering, RHIA, CCS

Although we have no way of knowing what exactly will be on the examination, the authors tried to cover as many HIM concepts as possible. We have carefully selected questions that are generic enough to cover the broad topic categories. Researching the questions as you study should expand your knowledge such that, when you encounter similar questions, you can arrive at the correct answer. We believe this review material will jog your memory and serve to help you build on information you have already gained through your education.

With the collaboration of Health Information Administration and Technology educators, many questions have been updated and new questions added to enhance topic categories in this edition of the book. The more advanced questions for RHIA candidates are at the back of the chapters, where appropriate.

Professional Review Guide for the RHIA and RHIT Examinations by Content Areas

This review guide is arranged by content sections much as you studied in your classes. See Table 1 for content areas and the number of questions in each content area. The number of questions does not indicate the importance of any one subject; it is merely an accounting of the questions in each section of this book.

Table 1 Professional Review Guide for the RHIA and RHIT Examinations, 2009 Edition Content Areas and Number of Questions

Professional Review Guide for the RHIA and RHIT Examinations, 2009 Edition Content Areas and Number of Questions	
Health Information Content Topic	Number of Questions
Health Data Contents and Standards	98
Information Access and Retention	100
Classification Systems and Secondary Data Sources	110
Medical Billing and Reimbursement	113
Medical Science	115
ICD-9-CM Coding	211
CPT-4 Coding	205
Informatics and Information Systems	102
Health Information Privacy and Security	100
Health Law	100
Health Statistics and Research	100
Quality and Performance Improvement	95
Organization and Management	86
Human Resources	95
Mock Examination	180
Total Questions	1810

Examination Content and Insights

The test uses competency categories known as domains, subdomains, and tasks that have been shown to be essential entry-level competencies for HIM practice.

Before you begin your review for the examinations, we suggest that you obtain the RHIA/RHIT Examination Candidate Handbook. The handbook can be downloaded from AHIMA's Web site at www.ahima.org.

The entry-level tasks are grouped into five domains, as shown in Table 2.

Table 2 Entry-Level Domains for RHIA and RHIT

RHIA	RHIT
1. Health Data Management	1. Health Data Management
2. Health Statistics, Biomedical Research, and Performance Improvement	2. Health Statistics, Biomedical Research, and Performance Improvement
3. Health Care Services Organization and Delivery	3. Health Care Services Organization and Delivery
4. Information Technology and Systems	4. Information Technology and Systems
5. Organization and Management	5. Organizational Resources

These five domains are divided further into subdomains which modify the domains. Weights for each domain and subdomain are assigned by the number of questions in the domain or subdomain. Thus, each weight correlates to the degree of emphasis, or importance, given to each domain and subdomain statement as it relates to the HIM practice.

The examinations are based on the competencies. The competencies are aligned with knowledge clusters. On the following pages, you will find additional information on the competencies and their corresponding knowledge clusters listed for the RHIA and RHIT examinations.

Look at the differences in the level of knowledge needed for the RHIA and RHIT examinations. It may help you understand what is expected in each examination by competency. For instance, you can tell by the tables showing the competencies and number of questions with weights that the RHIT examination questions weigh more on domain 1 (especially in coding). However, you can expect a higher level of knowledge in research for the RHIA questions in domain 2. In addition, the RHIA weights are higher in domain 4 and 5. It also helps point the way to where you learned the information in various content areas.

COMPETENCIES FOR THE RHIA EXAMINATION

The RHIA examination has 180 questions (160 questions scored and 20 that are not scored for the exam). The 160 scored questions are the basis for scoring your examination. The 20 unscored questions on the RHIA examination are to be used in obtaining statistical information to help in the construction of questions for future examinations. These 20 questions will not be identified in the exam, nor will they count toward the examination pass/fail score. Table 3 present s the domains and equivalent weights for the RHIA examination. Review the current RHIA and RHIT Examination Candidate Handbook from AHIMA.

Table 3 Domains and Equivalent Weights for the RHIA Certification Examination

Domains and Equivalent Weights for the RHIA Certification Examination			
Domain	DOMAIN AND SUBDOMAINS	QUESTIONS	WEIGHT
1	**Health Data Management**	**40**	**25%**
	Subdomain:		
	A. Health Data Structure, Content, and Standards	13	8%
	B. Health Care Information Requirements and Standards	11	7%
	C. Clinical Classification Systems	8	5%
	D. Reimbursement Methodologies	8	5%
2	**Health Statistics, Biomedical Research, and Quality Management**	**16**	**10%**
	Subdomain:		
	A. Health Care Statistics and Research	8	5%
	B. Quality Management and Performance Improvement	8	5%
3	**Health Services Organization and Delivery**	**32**	**20%**
	Subdomain:		
	A. Health Care Delivery Systems	16	10%
	B. Health Care Privacy, Confidentiality, Legal, and Ethical Issues	16	10%
4	**Information Technology and Systems**	**32**	**20%**
	Subdomain:		
	A. Information and Communication Technologies	8	5%
	B. Data Information and File Structure	5	4%
	C. Data Storage and Retrieval	6	5%
	D Data Security	5	3%
	E. Health Care Information Systems	8	3%
5	**Organization and Management**	**40**	**25%**
	Subdomain:		
	A. Human Resource Management	12	7.5%
	B. Financial and Resource Health Information	12	7.5%
	C. Strategic Planning and Organizational Development	6	3.75%
	D. Project and Operations Management	10	6.25%
Total		**160**	**100%**

COMPETENCIES FOR THE RHIT EXAMINATION

The RHIT examination has 150 questions (130 questions scored and 20 that are not scored for the exam). The 130 scored questions are the basis for scoring the examination. The 20 unscored questions on the RHIT examination are to be used in obtaining statistical information to help in the construction of questions for future examinations. These 20 questions will not be identified in the exam, nor will they count toward the examination pass/fail score. Table 4 presents the domains and equivalent weights for the RHIT examination. Review the current RHIA and RHIT Examination Candidate Handbook from AHIMA to verify the competencies.

Table 4 Domains and Equivalent Weights for the RHIT Certification Examination

Domains and Equivalent Weights for the RHIT Certification Examination			
DOMAIN	DOMAIN AND SUBDOMAINS	QUESTIONS	WEIGHTS
1	**Health Data Management** Subdomain:	39	30%
	A. Data Structure, Content, and Standards	8	6%
	B. Health Care Information Requirements and Standards	9	7%
	C. Clinical Classification Systems	14	11%
	D. Reimbursement Methodologies	8	6%
2	**Health Statistics, Biomedical Research, and Quality Management** Subdomain:	16	12%
	A. Health Care Statistics and Research	7	5%
	B. Quality Assessment and Performance Improvement	9	7%
3	**Health Services Organization and Delivery** Subdomain	22	17%
	A. Health Care Delivery Systems	9	7%
	B. Health Care Compliance, Confidentiality, Ethical, Legal, and Privacy Issues	13	10%
4	**Information Technology and Systems** Subdomain	33	25%
	A. Information Communications Technologies	9	7%
	B. Data Storage and Retrieval	10	8%
	C. Data Security	8	6%
	D. Health Care Information Systems	6	4%
5	**Organizational Resources** Subdomain:	20	15%
	A. Human Resources	14	11%
	B. Financial and Physical Resources	6	4%
	Total	**130**	**100%**

In creating the review guide, we wanted to cover the competencies for both the RHIA and RHIT. The questions in the chapters of this review guide relate to the competencies according to the breakdown of content for both the RHIA and RHIT exams. Table 5 provides a crosswalk between the questions in the chapters to the domains and subdomains.

Table 5 Crosswalk of Domains and Subdomains to Chapter

Crosswalk of Domains and Subdomains to Chapter			
Chapter	Questions	Domains and Subdomains	
		RHIA	RHIT
Health Data Contents and Standards	All	1-A, B	1-A, B 3-A
Information Retention and Retrieval	All	4-C	4-B
Classification Systems and Secondary Data Sources	All	1-C	1-C
Medical Billing and Reimbursement Systems	All	1-D	1-D
Medical Science	All	1-A	1-A
ICD-9-CM Coding	All	1-C	1-C
CPT Coding	All	1-C	1-C
Informatics and Information Systems	1-56		4-A, B, C, D
	All	4 A, B, C, D, E	
Health care Privacy and Security	1-45		3-B 4-C
	All	3-B 4-D	
Health Law	All	3-B	3-B
Health Statistics and Research	All	2-A 3-A	2-A
Quality and Performance Improvement	All	2-B	2-B
Organization and Management	1-25		5-B
	All	5-B, C, D	
Human Resources	1-56		5-A
	All	5-A	
RHIT Mock Examination	1-150		All
RHIA Mock Examination	1-180	All	

Table 6 and Table 7 provide crosswalks between the mock examination questions and the competencies for the RHIA and RHIT.

Table 6 Crosswalk for the RHIA Mock Examination Questions and the Competencies for the RHIA

Crosswalk for 2009 edition of the Professional Review Guide mock examination questions and the competencies for the 2009 Certification Examinations for the RHIA	
COMPETENCY	Mock Exam Question
I.A	3, 4, 5, 7, 8, 13, 17, 19, 20, 21, 22, 23, 24, 25, 26, 27, 28, 29, 30, 31, 32, 33, 34, 36, 37, 38, 39, 40, 41, 42, 43, 44, 45, 46, 68, 76, 85, 99, 106, 107, 108, 109, 110, 111, 112, 113, 117, 122, 123, 126, 127, 128, 129, 130, 158, 159, 161
I.B	3, 7, 8, 14, 15, 16, 17, 20, 21, 22, 35, 62, 68, 74, 75, 76, 78, 85, 87, 88, 89 90, 93, 96, 97, 108, 109, 110, 111, 112, 117, 121, 122, 123, 126, 127, 128, 129, 130
I.C.	13, 18, 19, 21, 22, 23, 24, 25, 26, 27, 28, 29, 30, 31, 32, 33, 34, 36, 37, 38, 39, 40, 41, 42, 43, 44, 45, 46, 68, 76, 78, 90, 93, 96, 97, 107, 108, 125, 167
I.D	6, 9, 10, 11, 12, 18, 19, 21, 22, 23, 24, 25, 26, 27, 28, 29, 30, 31, 32, 33, 34, 35, 36, 37, 38, 39, 40, 41, 42, 43, 44, 45, 46, 62, 68, 76, 78, 90, 93, 96, 97, 107, 108, 112, 167
2.A	1, 18, 19, 20, 47, 48, 49, 50, 51, 52, 53, 54, 55, 56, 57, 58, 59, 60, 64, 65, 66, 67, 68, 69, 70, 71, 72, 73, 76, 78, 80, 81, 92, 98, 101, 102, 103, 104, 105, 113, 116, 117, 118, 119, 120, 121, 122, 125, 132, 133, 135, 138, 142, 143, 146, 147, 149, 150, 154, 157, 158, 159, 161, 162, 163, 164, 165, 166, 167, 169, 170, 171, 173, 174, 175, 176, 177, 178
2.B	11, 12, 47, 48, 49, 50, 51, 52, 53, 56, 57, 58, 59, 60, 63, 65, 66, 67, 68, 69, 70, 71, 72, 73, 78, 80, 81, 92, 98, 100, 101, 102, 103, 104, 105, 108, 113, 116, 118, 119, 120, 122, 125, 126, 129, 132, 133, 135, 138, 142, 143, 145, 146, 147, 149, 150, 154, 157, 158, 159, 161, 162, 163, 164, 165, 166, 167, 169, 170, 171, 173, 174, 175, 176, 177, 178,
3.A	7, 15, 16, 17, 18, 19, 35, 62, 68, 75, 82, 94, 95, 101, 103, 104, 112, 113, 116, 117, 119, 120, 121, 122, 123, 126, 132, 157, 158, 159, 161, 162, 165, 170, 172, 173
3.B	16, 35, 77, 79, 82, 83, 84, 86, 87, 88, 89, 94, 95, 99, 108, 111, 114, 115, 117, 118, 119, 120, 128, 168
4.A	16, 19, 51, 112, 113, 121, 124, 125, 128, 129, 130, 148, 173,
4.B	5, 15, 16, 80 , 121, 124, 126, 128, 129, 130, 158, 159, 161, 162, 168, 170, 173,
4.C	5, 74, 81, 106, 119, 126, 128, 129, 130, 132, 138, 173
4.D	15, 77, 84, 87, 87, 89, 91, 94, 95, 110, 111, 114, 120, 127, 138, 168, 180
4.E	51, 76, 113, 121, 125, 126, 132, 148, 151, 159, 161, 170
5.A	2, 56, 61, 131, 135, 137, 139, 140, 141, 142, 143, 144, 145, 146, 147, 148, 149, 150, 152, 153, 154, 155, 156, 157, 165, 167, 170, 171, 172, 174, 177, 179
5.B	6, 9, 10, 11, 47, 50, 56, 125, 129, 137, 138, 139, 141, 142, 143, 144, 145, 148, 157, 160, 165, 171
5.C	65, 119, 120, 121, 134, 136, 148, 159, 161, 162, 170, 173, 177
5.D	65, 119, 120, 126, 132, 133, 134, 136 , 159, 161, 162, 168, 170, 172, 173, 177

Table 7 Crosswalk for the RHIT Mock Examination Questions and the Competencies for the RHIT

Crosswalk for 2009 edition of the Professional Review Guide mock examination questions and the competencies for the 2009 Certification Examinations for the RHIT	
COMPETENCY	CHAPTER AND QUESTION NUMBER
I.A	3, 4, 5, 7, 8, 13, 17, 19, 20, 21, 22, 23, 24, 25, 26, 27, 28, 29, 30, 31, 32, 33, 34, 36, 37, 38, 39, 40, 41, 42, 43, 44, 45, 46, 63, 64, 68, 76, 85, 99, 106, 107, 108, 109, 110, 111, 112, 113, 117, 122, 123, 126, 127, 128, 129, 130
I.B	3, 7, 8, 14, 15, 16, 17, 20, 35, 62, 63, 68, 74, 76, 85, 87, 88, 89, 90, 93, 96, 97, 108, 109, 110, 111, 112, 117, 122, 123, 126, 132
I.C	13, 18, 19, 21, 22, 23, 24, 25, 26, 27, 28, 29, 30, 31, 32, 33, 34, 36, 37, 38, 39, 40, 41, 42, 43, 44, 45, 46, 68, 76, 78, 90, 93, 96, 97, 107, 108, 109, 125
I.D	6, 9, 10, 11, 12, 18, 19, 21, 22, 23, 24, 25, 26, 27, 28, 29 ,30, 31, 32, 33, 34, 35, 36, 37, 38, 39, 40, 41, 42, 43, 44, 45, 46, 62, 68, 76, 78, 90, 93, 96, 97, 107, 108, 112
2.A	1, 18, 19, 20, 47, 48, 49, 50, 51, 52, 53, 54, 55, 56, 57, 58, 59, 60, 65, 66, 67, 68, 69, 70, 71, 72, 73, 78, 80, 81, 92, 98, 101, 102, 103, 104, 105, 113, 116, 118, 119, 120, 122, 125, 132, 133, 135, 138, 142, 143, 145, 146, 147, 149, 150
2.B	11, 12, 16, 47, 48, 49, 50, 51, 52, 56, 57, 58, 59, 60, 65, 66, 67, 68, 69, 70, 71, 72, 73, 75, 78, 80, 81, 92, 98, 100, 101, 102, 103, 104, 105, 116, 117, 118, 119, 120, 122, 125, 126, 132, 133, 135, 138, 142, 143, 145, 146, 147, 149, 150
3.A	7, 15, 16, 17, 18, 19, 20, 35, 68, 74, 75, 77, 82, 94, 95, 99, 108, 112, 113, 116, 117, 119, 120, 122, 123, 126, 127
3.B	35, 68, 77, 79, 82, 83, 84, 86, 87, 88, 89, 94, 95, 114, 115, 117, 118, 119, 120, 122, 128, 129, 132,
4.A	5, 16, 18, 19, 20, 51, 76, 111, 112, 120, 124, 128, 132
4.B	74, 81, 106, 113, 124, 126, 128, 129, 130, 132, 138
4.C	15, 16, 77, 80, 84, 91, 94, 95, 110, 111, 114, 119, 120, 123,127, 129, 130, 132
4.D	87, 88, 89, 127, 138
5.A	2, 47, 56, 61, 65, 82, 119, 120,126, 131, 132, 133, 134, 135, 136, 137, 139, 140, 141, 142, 143, 144, 145, 146, 147, 148, 149, 150
5.B	6, 9, 10, 11, 47, 50, 56, 125, 129, 130, 134, 136, 137, 138, 139, 141, 142, 143, 144, 145, 148, 149

Table 8 shows the breakdown of the Mock Examination questions by competencies for the RHIA and RHIT.

Table 8 RHIA and RHIT Mock Examination Competency Crosswalk by Question

RHIA and RHIT Mock Examination Competency Crosswalk by Question						
Questions		Competencies				
		I	2	3	4	5
1	RHIA		A			
	RHIT		A			
2	RHIA					A
	RHIT					A
3	RHIA	A, B				
	RHIT	A, B				
4	RHIA	A				
	RHIT	A				
5	RHIA	A			A, B	
	RHIT	A			A	
6	RHIA	D				B
	RHIT	D				B
7	RHIA	A, B		A		
	RHIT	A, B		A		
8	RHIA	A , B				
	RHIT	A, B				
9	RHIA	D				B
	RHIT	D				B
10	RHIA	D				B
	RHIT	D				B
11	RHIA	D	B			B
	RHIT	D	B			B
12	RHIA	D	B			
	RHIT	D	B			
13	RHIA	A, C				
	RHIT	A, C				
14	RHIA	B				
	RHIT	B				
15	RHIA	B		A	B, D	
	RHIT	B		A	C	
16	RHIA	B		A,B	A, B	
	RHIT	B		A, B	A, C	
17	RHIA	A, B		A		
	RHIT	A, B		A		
18	RHIA:	C, D	A	A		
	RHIT	C, D	A	A	A	
19	RHIA	A, C, D	A	A	A	
	RHIT	A, C, D	A	A	A	
20	RHIA	A, B	A			
	RHIT	A, B	A	A	A	
21	RHIA	A, B, C, D				
	RHIT	A, C, D				

Table 8 RHIA and RHIT Mock Examination Competency Crosswalk by Question (continued)

Questions		I	2	3	4	5
RHIA and RHIT Mock Examination Competency Crosswalk by Question						
Questions		Competencies				
22	RHIA	A, B, C, D				
	RHIT	A, C, D				
23	RHIA	A, C, D				
	RHIT	A, C , D				
24	RHIA	A, C, D				
	RHIT	A, C, D				
25	RHIA	A, C, D				
	RHIT	A, C, D				
26	RHIA	A, C, D				
	RHIT	A, C, D				
27	RHIA	A, C, D				
	RHIT	A, C,D				
28	RHIA	A, C, D				
	RHIT	A, C, D				
29	RHIA	A, C, D				
	RHIT	A, C, D				
30	RHIA	A, C, D				
	RHIT	A, C, D				
31	RHIA	A, C, D				
	RHIT	A, C, D				
32	RHIA	A, C, D				
	RHIT	A, C, D				
33	RHIA	A, C, D				
	RHIT	A, C, D				
34	RHIA	A, C, D				
	RHIT	A, C, D				
35	RHIA	B, D		A, B		
	RHIT	B, D		A, B		
36	RHIA	A, C, D				
	RHIT	A, C, D				
37	RHIA	A, C, D				
	RHIT	A, C, D				
38	RHIA	A, C, D				
	RHIT	A, C, D				
39	RHIA	A, C, D				
	RHIT	A, C, D				
40	RHIA	A, C, D				
	RHIT	A, C, D				
41	RHIA	A, C, D				
	RHIT	A, C, D				
42	RHIA	A, C, D				
	RHIT	A, C, D				
43	RHIA	A, C, D				
	RHIT	A, C, D				

Table 8 RHIA and RHIT Mock Examination Competency Crosswalk by Question (continued)

Questions		Competencies				
		I	2	3	4	5
44	RHIA	A, C, D				
	RHIT	A, C, D				
45	RHIA	A, C, D				
	RHIT	A, C, D				
46	RHIA	A, C, D				
	RHIT	A, C, D				
47	RHIA		A, B			A
	RHIT		A, B			A, B
48	RHIA		A, B			
	RHIT		A, B			
49	RHIA		A, B			
	RHIT		A, B			
50	RHIA		A, B			B
	RHIT		A, B			B
51	RHIA		A, B		A, E	
	RHIT		A, B		A	
52	RHIA		A, B			
	RHIT		A, B			
53	RHIA		A, B			
	RHIT		A			
54	RHIA		A			
	RHIT		A			
55	RHIA		A			
	RHIT		A			
56	RHIA		A, B			A, B
	RHIT		A			A, B
57	RHIA		A, B			
	RHIT		A, B			
58	RHIA		A, B			
	RHIT		A, B			
59	RHIA		A, B			
	RHIT		A, B			
60	RHIA		A, B			
	RHIT		A, B			
61	RHIA					A
	RHIT					A
62	RHIA	B, D		A		
	RHIT	B, D				
63	RHIA		A, B			
	RHIT		A, B			
64	RHIA		A			
	RHIT		A			
65	RHIA		A, B			C, D
	RHIT		A, B			A

Table 8 RHIA and RHIT Mock Examination Competency Crosswalk by Question (continued)

Questions		Competencies				
		I	2	3	4	5
66	RHIA		A, B			
	RHIT		A, B			
67	RHIA		A, B			
	RHIT		A, B			
68	RHIA	A, B, C, D	A, B	A		
	RHIT	A, B, C, D	A, B	A, B		
69	RHIA		A, B			
	RHIT		A, B			
70	RHIA		A, B			
	RHIT		A, B			
71	RHIA		A, B			
	RHIT		A, B			
72	RHIA		A, B			
	RHIT		A, B			
73	RHIA		A, B			
	RHIT		A, B			
74	RHIA	B			C	
	RHIT	B		A	B	
75	RHIA		B	A		
	RHIT		B	A		
76	RHIA	A, B, C, D	A		E	
	RHIT	A, B, C, D			A	
77	RHIA			B	D	
	RHIT			A, B	C	
78	RHIA	B, C, D	A, B			
	RHIT	C, D	A, B			
79	RHIA			B		
	RHIT			B		
80	RHIA		A, B		B	
	RHIT		A, B		C	
81	RHIA		A, B		C	
	RHIT		A, B		C	
82	RHIA			A, B		A
	RHIT			A, B		A
83	RHIA			B		
	RHIT			B		
84	RHIA			B	D	
	RHIT			B		
85	RHIA	A, B				
	RHIT	A, B				
86	RHIA			B		
	RHIT			B		
87	RHIA	B		B	D	
	RHIT	B		B	D	
88	RHIA	B		B	D	
	RHIT	B		B	D	

Table 8 RHIA and RHIT Mock Examination Competency Crosswalk by Question (continued)

Questions		Competencies				
		l	2	3	4	5
89	RHIA	B		B	D	
	RHIT	B		B	D	
90	RHIA	B, C, D				
	RHIT	B, C, D				
91	RHIA				D	
	RHIT				C	
92	RHIA		A, B			
	RHIT		A, B			
93	RHIA	B, C, D,				
	RHIT	B, C ,D				
94	RHIA			A, B	D	
	RHIT			A, B	C	
95	RHIA			A, B	D	
	RHIT			A, B	C	
96	RHIA	B, C ,D				
	RHIT	B, C, D				
97	RHIA	B, C, D				
	RHIT	B, C, D				
98	RHIA		A, B			
	RHIT		A, B			
99	RHIA	A		B		
	RHIT	A		A		
100	RHIA		B			
	RHIT		B			
101	RHIA		A, B	A		
	RHIT		A, B			
102	RHIA		A, B			
	RHIT		A, B			
103	RHIA		A, B	A		
	RHIT		A, B			
104	RHIA		A, B	A		
	RHIT		A, B			
105	RHIA		A, B			
	RHIT		A, B			
106	RHIA	A			C	
	RHIT	A			B	
107	RHIA	A, C, D				
	RHIT	A. C, D				
108	RHIA	A, B, C, D	B	A		
	RHIT	A, B, C, D		A		
109	RHIA	A, B				
	RHIT	A, B, C				
110	RHIA	A, B			D	
	RHIT	A, B			C	

Table 8 RHIA and RHIT Mock Examination Competency Crosswalk by Question (continued)

Question		Competencies				
		I	2	3	4	5
111	RHIA	A, B			A, D	
	RHIT	A, B			A, C	
112	RHIA	A, B, D		A	A	
	RHIT	A, B, D		A	A	
113	RHIA	A	A, B	A	A, E	
	RHIT	A	A	A	B	
114	RHIA			B	D	
	RHIT			B	C	
115	RHIA			B		
	RHIT			B		
116	RHIA		A, B	A		
	RHIT		A, B	A		
117	RHIA	A, B,	A	A, B		
	RHIT	A, B	B	A, B		
118	RHIA		A, B	B		
	RHIT		A, B	B		
119	RHIA		A, B	A, B	C	C, D
	RHIT		A, B	A, B	C	A
120	RHIA		A, B	B	A, D	C, D
	RHIT		A, B	A, B	A, C	A
121	RHIA	B	A	A	A, B, E	C
	RHIT	A	A	A, B	A, B	A
122	RHIA	A, B	A, B	A		
	RHIT	A, B	A, B	A, B		
123	RHIA	A, B		A		
	RHIT	A, B		A	C	
124	RHIA				A, B	
	RHIT				A, B	
125	RHIA	C	A, B		A, E	B
	RHIT	C	A, B			B
126	RHIA	A, B	B	A	B, C, E	D
	RHIT	A, B	B	A	B	A
127	RHIA	A, B			D	
	RHIT	A		A	C, D	
128	RHIA	A, B			A, B, C	
	RHIT	A,		B	A, B	
129	RHIA	A, B	B		A, B, C	B
	RHIT	A		B	B, C	B
130	RHIA	A, B		B	A, B, C	
	RHIT	A			B, C	B
131	RHIA				A	
	RHIT				A	
132	RHIA		A, B	A	C, E	D
	RHIT	B	A, B	B	A,B,C	A

Table 8 RHIA and RHIT Mock Examination Competency Crosswalk by Question (continued)

Question		\multicolumn{5}{c}{Competencies}				
		1	2	3	4	5
133	RHIA		A, B			D
	RHIT		A, B			A
134	RHIA					C, D
	RHIT					A, B
135	RHIA		A, B			A
	RHIT		A, B			A
136	RHIA					C, D
	RHIT					A, B
137	RHIA					A, B
	RHIT					A, B
138	RHIA		A, B		C, D	B
	RHIT		A, B		B, D	B
139	RHIA					A, B
	RHIT					A, B
140	RHIA					A
	RHIT					A
141	RHIA					A, B
	RHIT					A, B
142	RHIA		A, B			A, B
	RHIT		A, B			A, B
143	RHIA		A, B			A, B
	RHIT		A, B			A, B
144	RHIA					A ,B
	RHIT					A, B
145	RHIA		B			A, B
	RHIT		A, B			A, B
146	RHIA		A, B			A
	RHIT		A, B			A
147	RHIA		A, B			A
	RHIT		A, B			A
148	RHIA					A, B
	RHIT					A, B
149	RHIA		A, B		A, E	A, B
	RHIT		A, B			A, B
150	RHIA		A, B			A
	RHIT		A, B			A
151	RHIA				E	
152	RHIA					A
153	RHIA					A
154	RHIA		A, B			A
155	RHIA					A
156	RHIA					A
157	RHIA		A, B	A		A, B
158	RHIA	A	A, B	A	B	
159	RHIA	A	A, B	A	B ,E	C, D

Table 8 RHIA and RHIT Mock Examination Competency Crosswalk by Question (continued)

RHIA and RHIT Mock Examination Competency Crosswalk by Question (continued)						
Question		Competencies				
		I	2	3	4	5
160	RHIA					A
161	RHIA	A	A, B	A	B, E	C, D
162	RHIA		A, B	A	B	C, D
163	RHIA		A, B			
164	RHIA		A, B			
165	RHIA		A, B	A		A, B
166	RHIA		A, B			
167	RHIA	C, D	A, B			A
168	RHIA			B	B, D	D
169	RHIA		A, B			
170	RHIA		A, B	A	B, E	A, C, D
171	RHIA		A, B			A, B
172	RHIA			A		A, D
173	RHIA		A, B	A	A, B, C, E	C, D
174	RHIA		A, B			A
175	RHIA		A, B			
176	RHIA		A, B			
177	RHIA		A, B			A, C, D
178	RHIA		A, B			
179	RHIA					A
180	RHIA				D	

Information on the competencies was tied to the latest AHIMA Candidate Handbook available at printing (2008 AHIMA Candidate Handbook).

KNOWLEDGE CLUSTERS for the RHIA and RHIT

In addition to the competencies, AHIMA and the COC have identified the knowledge clusters that emerged from the Roles and Function Study for the RHIA and RHIT. Mastery of these knowledge clusters is necessary to successfully perform the competencies. Table 9 lists the knowledge clusters by domain for the baccalaureate degree program (RHIA). Table 10 lists the knowledge clusters by domain for the associate degree program (RHIT).

The biomedical sciences won't just fit into a domain or subdomain since they are an integral part of any medically oriented profession. These biomedical sciences subjects include medical terminology, anatomy, physiology, pathophysiology, pharmacology, and laboratory testing.

Table 9 Knowledge Cluster Content—RHIA

Domain I: Health Data Management
1. Structure and use of health information (individual, comparative, aggregate)
2. Health information media (paper, electronic/computer-based; e-health-personal, web-based)
3. Type and content of health record (paper, electronic, computer-based, e-health-personal, web-based)
4. Data quality assessment and integrity
5. Secondary data sources (registries and indexes; databases examples: MEDPAR, NPDB, HCUP)
6. Health care data sets (examples: OASIS, HEDIS, DEEDS, UHDDS, UACDS, NEDSS, NMMFS)
7. Health information archival systems
8. National Health care Information Infrastructure (NHII)
9. Data collection tools (such as forms; computer input screens; other health record documentation tools)
10. Standards and regulations for documentation (such as JCAHO, CARF, COP, AAAHC, AOA)
11. Health information standards (such as HIPAA, ANSI, ASTM, LOINC, UMLS, MESH, Arden Syntax, HL-7)
12. Health care taxonomies, clinical vocabularies, terminologies/nomenclatures (such as ICD-9-CM, ICD-10, CPT, SNOMED-CT, DSM-IV)
13. Medicare Severity Diagnosis Related Groups (MS-DRGs)
14. Clinical data and reimbursement management
15. Compliance strategies and reporting (e.g. National Correct Coding Initiative)
16. Chargemaster management
17. Case mix management
18. Audit process (such as compliance and reimbursement)
19. Payment systems (such as PPS, DRGs, APCs, RBRVS, RUGs)
20. Commercial, managed care and federal insurance plans

Table 9 Knowledge Cluster Content - RHIA (continued)

Domain 2: Health care Statistics, Biomedical Research and Quality Management
1. Statistical analysis on health care data
2. Descriptive statistics (such as means, standard deviations, frequencies, ranges, percentiles)
3. Inferential statistics (such as *t*-tests, ANOVAs, regression analysis, statistical process control, reliability, validity)
4. Vital statistics
5. Epidemiology
6. Data reporting and presentation techniques
7. Computerized statistical packages
8. Research design/methods (such as quantitative, qualitative, evaluative, outcomes)
9. Knowledge-based research techniques (such as Medline, CMS, libraries, web sites)
10. National guidelines regarding human subjects' research
11. Institutional review board process (IRB)
12. Research protocol data management
13. Quality assessment and management tools (such as benchmarking, ORYX, SQC)
14. Utilization and resource management
15. Risk Management
16. Disease management process (such as case management, critical paths)
17. Outcomes measurement (such as patient, customer satisfaction, disease-specific)
Domain 3: Health Services Organization and Delivery
1. Components and operation of health care organizations including e-health delivery
2. Accreditation standards (such as JCAHO, AOA, NCQA, CARF, CHAP, URAC)
3. Regulatory and licensure requirements (such as COP, state health departments)
4. Legislative and legal system
5. Privacy, confidentiality, security principles, policies and procedures
6. Health information laws, regulations, and standards (such as HIPAA, e-health, JCAHO, state laws)
7. Elements of compliance programs
8. Professional and practice related ethical issues
Domain 4 Information Technology and Systems
1. Computer concepts (hardware components, systems architectures, operating systems and languages, and software packages and tools)
2. Communications technologies (networks-LANS, WANS, VPNs; data interchange standards – NIST, HL-7)
3. Internet technologies (Intranet, web-based systems, standards – SGML, XML) (4)
4. Data, information and file structures (data administration, data definitions, data dictionary, data modeling, data structures, data warehousing, database management systems)
5. Data storage and retrieval (storage media, query tools/applications, data mining, report design, search engines)
6. Data security (protection methods – physical, technical, managerial, risk assessment, audit and control program, contingency planning, data recovery, Internet, web-based, and e-Health security)
7. Leading development of health information resources and systems
8. Brokering of information services

Table 9 Knowledge Cluster Content—RHIA (continued)

Domain 4 Information Technology and Systems (continued)
9.   Clinical, business and specialty systems applications (administrative, clinical decision support systems, electronic health record and computer-based health record systems, nursing, ancillary service systems, patient numbering systems at master and enterprise levels)
10. Systems development (planning, analysis and design, customization, selection/procurement, implementation, integration, support, testing and evaluation, auditing and monitoring)
11. Human factors and user interface design
12. Systems Life Cycle (systems analysis, design, implementation, evaluation, and maintenance)

Domain 5 Organization and Management	
1. Principles of management	
2. Negotiation techniques	
3. Communication and interpersonal skills	
4. Team/consensus building	
5. Professional development for self and staff	
6. Problem solving and decision making processes	
7. Employment laws	
8. Principles of human resources management (recruitment, supervision, retention, counseling, disciplinary action)	
9. Workforce education and training	
10. Performance standards	
11. Health care finance (payer mix, bond rating, investment, capitalization)	
12. Accounting principles	
13. Budget process (capital and operating)	
14. Cost/benefit analysis	
15. Strategic leadership, management and planning	
16. Organizational behavior	
17. Business building (entrepreneurialism – building your own business; championing best practices, processes, services within your organization)	
18. Change management	
19. Organizational assessment and benchmarking	
20. Strategic leadership, management and planning	
21. Process reengineering and work redesign	
22. Project management	

Table 10 Knowledge Cluster Content—RHIT

Domain I Health Data Management
1. Data versus information
2. Structure and use of health information (individual, comparative, aggregate)
3. Health information media (such as paper, computer, web-based)
4. Health record data collection tools (such as forms, screens, etc.)
5. Data sources (primary, secondary)
6. Data definitions, vocabularies, terminologies, and dictionaries
7. Data storage and retrieval
8. Data quality and integrity
9. Health care data sets (such as OASIS, HEDIS, DEEDS, UHDDS)
10. Data monitoring and compliance reporting
11. National Health care Information Infrastructure (NHII)
12. Type and content of health record (paper, electronic, computer-based, e-health-personal, web-based)
13. Health record documentation requirements (such as accreditation, certification, licensure)
14. Health record monitoring and compliance reporting
15. Classifications, taxonomies, nomenclatures, terminologies, and clinical vocabularies
16. Principles and applications of coding systems (such as ICD-9-CM, ICD-10, CPT/HCPCS, DSM-IV)
17. Diagnostic and procedural groupings (such as DRG, APC, RUGs, SNOMED-CT) (5)
18. Case mix analysis and indexes
19. Medicare Severity Diagnosis Related Groups (MS-DRGs)
20. Coding compliance strategies, auditing, and reporting (such as CCI, plans)
21. Coding quality monitors and reporting
22. Commercial, managed care and federal insurance plans
23. Payment methodologies and systems (such as capitation, prospective payment systems PPS, RBRVS)
24. Billing processes and procedures (such as claims, EOB, ABN, electronic data interchange)
25. Chargemaster maintenance
26. Regulatory guidelines (such as LMRP, peer review organizations)
27. Reimbursement monitoring and reporting
28. Compliance strategies and reporting

Table 10 Knowledge Cluster Content—RHIT (continued)

Domain 2: Health Statistics, Biomedical Research and Quality Management
1. Indices, databases and registries
2. Vital statistics
3. Health care statistics
4. Descriptive statistics (such as means, frequencies, ranges, percentiles, standard deviations)
5. Statistical applications with health care data
6. Institutional Review Board (IRB) processes
7. National guidelines regarding human subjects research
8. Research protocol monitoring
9. Data selection, interpretation, and presentation
10. Knowledge-based research techniques (such as library, Medline, web-based)
11. Quality assessment and improvement (such as process, collection tools, data analysis, reporting techniques)
12. Utilization management, risk management, and case management
13. Regulatory quality monitoring requirements
14. Outcomes measures and monitoring
Domain 3 Health Services Organization and Delivery
1. Organization of health care delivery in the United States
2. Health care organizations structure and operation
3. External standards, regulations, and initiatives (such as licensure, certification, accreditation, HIPAA)
4. Payment and reimbursement systems
5. Health care providers and disciplines
6. Legislative and regulatory processes
7. Legal terminology
8. Health information/record laws and regulations (such as retention, patient rights/advocacy, advanced directives, privacy)
9. Confidentiality, privacy, and security policies, procedures, and monitoring
10. Release of information policies and procedures
11. Professional and practice-related ethical issues

Table 10 Knowledge Cluster Content—RHIT (continued)

Domain 4: Information Technology and Systems
1. Computer concepts (such as hardware components, operating systems, languages, software packages)
2. Communication and Internet technologies (such as networks, intranet, standards) (3)
3. Common software applications (such as word processing, spreadsheet, database, graphics)
4. Health information systems (such as administrative, patient registration, ADT, EHR, personal health record (PHR), lab, radiology, pharmacy)
5. Voice recognition technology
6. Health information specialty systems (such as ROI, coding, registries)
7. Application of systems and policies to health information systems and functions and health care data requests
8. Document archival, retrieval, and imaging systems
9. Maintenance and monitoring of data storage systems
10. System architecture and design
11. System acquisition and evaluation
12. Screen design
13. Data retrieval and maintenance
14. Data security concepts
15. Data integrity concepts
16. Data integrity and security processes and monitoring
17. Data recovery and risk management
18. Work process design (such as ergonomics, equipment selection)
Domain 5: Organization and Management (continued)
1. Roles and functions of teams and committees
2. Teams/consensus building and committees
3. Communication and interpersonal skills
4. Team leadership concepts and techniques
5. Orientation and training (such as content, delivery, media)
6. Workflow and process monitors
7. Performance monitors
8. Revenue cycle monitors
9. Organizational plans and budgets (framework, levels, responsibilities, etc.)
10. Resource allocation monitors

ADDITIONAL INSIGHTS ABOUT PAST EXAMINATIONS

1. **Computerized exam.** The test is taken electronically in an approved testing center. You will be able to return to previously answered questions to check your answers before you close the exam file on the computer.

2. **Statistical formulas** needed to complete the questions on health statistics will be available in a drop-down table so that you can see it on the screen, thus eliminating the need to memorize all the formulas. However, it is critical that you know how to apply the formulas accurately. We recommend that you spend time working through as many statistical problems as possible.

3. **Math throughout.** Be aware that mathematical calculations may also be required in other types of questions (for instance, calculating FTE requirements, budget questions, etc.), so basic math skills are a must! Seek tutoring through your school or study partners to address any problems that you may have in this area. On the examination, you will need to use the calculator function on the computer. Become proficient in making mathematical calculations on the computer by practicing on the calculator provided in the accessories folder on your computer. If math is not a strong area for you, seek out assistance and practice, practice, practice.

4. **Informatics and information systems questions are interspersed throughout the other topics.** From the workplace setting you experienced during your professional practice experiences, you know that computers are involved in almost every aspect of HIM functions, e.g., coding, record tracking, incomplete charts, release of information, etc. Therefore, it stands to reason that questions related to information systems could show up in many other categories.

5. **Legal questions are at the national level.** In reference to questions in the category of health care legal aspects, keep in mind that this is a national examination. Therefore, any state-specific laws would not be applicable. Concentrate on federal legislation, statutes, and legal issues that would be appropriate nationally in all 50 states. You can count on federal questions that relate to the HIPAA standards for privacy and security.

6. **Questions on the examinations are scrambled** and change topics from question to question. Therefore, you may have a legal question, followed by a management question, followed by a coding question, followed by a quality assurance question, etc. Be prepared to shift gears quickly throughout the exam.

7. **Quality and performance improvement focus.** Because the implementation of QA/PI is at the forefront of the health care industry, give special attention to Quality Assessment and Performance Improvement issues. Become familiar with the various QA/PI tools. Several resources for this subject are listed at the end of the Quality Assessment and Performance Improvement chapter of this book.

8. **Be sure to spend some time reviewing organization and management** functions and techniques, especially those preparing for the RHIA examination. The RHIT examination focuses more on supervisory-level management issues. Both look at management more from a systems approach.

9. **You will not need to bring your ICD-9-CM or CPT-4 coding books to the test.** The questions are in a narrative form and any necessary codes and/or code narratives will be supplied on the computer screen for you to choose from. Study the Official ICD-9-CM Guidelines for Coding and Reporting. Don't forget to review reimbursement methodologies and compliance issues.

10. Application and analysis emphasis. The questions on both the RHIA and RHIT examinations have been increasingly skewed toward application and analysis, rather than recall level of question difficulty. Questions on the examination may combine several concepts into one question, increasing the level of difficulty of the question.

11. **The pass rates from January 1, 2008, and June 30, 2008:**

    Registered Health Information Administrator (RHIA)   69.12%

    Registered Health Information Technician (RHIT)   74.74%

THE DAY BEFORE AND THE MORNING OF THE EXAM

1. If necessary, spend the night before the examination in a hotel or motel near the exam test site.

2. Avoid studying the night before the exam. Last-minute studying tends to increase your anxiety level. However, you may want to spend a little time reviewing content you must memorize.

3. Organize in advance all the materials you need to take with you to the exam. Review the Candidate Handbook carefully and be sure to have all the items required, especially the admission card and appropriate proof of identity.

4. Get a good night's sleep and have a healthy meal before the exam.

5. Allow yourself plenty of time so that you arrive at the test site early.

6. Dress comfortably and plan for possible variations in room temperature. Dressing in layers may prove helpful.

TAKING THE EXAMINATION

You have stuck to your study schedule and have conditioned yourself to be in the best physical and mental shape possible. Now comes the moment of truth: the examination pops up on the screen before your eyes. Every paratrooper knows that, in addition to having a parachute, one must know how to open it. You have mastered the major topics; you have the parachute. Now you need to utilize good test-taking techniques to apply the knowledge you have gained; open the parachute!

1. Prior to starting the exam, you will be given a chance to practice taking an examination on the computer. Ten minutes will be allotted for this practice test; however, you may quit the practice test and begin the actual exam when you are comfortable with the computerized testing process.

2. Read all directions and questions carefully. Try to avoid reading too much into the questions. Be sensible and practical in your interpretation. Read ALL of the possible answers, because the first one that looks good may not be the best one.

3. Scan the computer screen quickly for the general format of the questions. Like the marathon runner, pace yourself for the distance. A good rule of thumb is 1 to 1.5 minutes per question. You may wish to keep the timer displayed on the computer to check your schedule throughout the exam. For example, at question 31, about one half hour will have elapsed, etc.

4. Some people answer all questions that they are certain of first, and then go back through the exam a second time to answer any questions they were uncertain about. Others prefer not to skip questions but make their best choice on encountering each question and go on. Both can be good approaches; choose the one that works best for you. You can "mark" questions that you have left unanswered and/or those questions you may want to review. Before you sign off of the exam or run out of time, you have the ability to go back to those questions for a final review.

5. Answer all the questions. There are no penalties for guessing, but putting no answer is definitely a wrong answer.

6. Use deductive reasoning and the process of elimination to arrive at the most correct answer. Some questions will have more than one correct answer. You will be asked to select the "best" possible answer based on the information presented.

7. If the question is written in a scenario format, first identify the question being asked and then review the entire question for the information needed to determine the correct answer.

8. Use all the time available to recheck your answers. However, avoid changing your answers unless you are absolutely certain it is necessary. Second-guessing yourself often results in a wrong answer.

9. A huge advantage to taking the computerized exam is that before you leave the testing center, you will be able to get your final test score instead of having to wait up to 6 weeks to receive it by mail.

AFTER THE EXAM

Our advice is to reclaim your life and focus on your career. One good way to start is to plan a special reward for yourself at some point immediately following or shortly after the exam. Schedule a family vacation or a relaxing weekend get-away. Just find some way of being good to yourself. You certainly deserve it! You have worked hard, so relish your success.

I. Examination Study Strategies and Resources

Patricia J. Schnering, RHIA, CCS

FORMAT OF THE EXAMINATION

The questions developed for the examinations are based on specifications currently referred to as domains and subdomains. A complete copy of these entry-level specifications will be provided in the RHIA/RHIT Candidate Handbook provided by AHIMA.

The general format of the exams is primarily designed to engage your problem-solving and critical-thinking skills. These types of questions require that you translate what you have learned and apply it to a situation. To get a preview, you can access sample questions on AHIMA's Web site: www.ahima.org.

EXAMINATION STRATEGIES

Preparing for a major exam is similar to preparing for a marathon athletic event. The time allotted for the RHIA examination is 4 hours. The time allotted for the RHIT examination is 3-1/2 hours. One suggestion is to use your study process to slowly build up your concentration time until you can focus your energy for the appropriate period of time. This is like the runner who begins jogging for 30 minutes and builds up to one hour, then one and a half hours, etc., and gradually increases the endurance time to meet the demands of the race. Try this strategy; it could work for you!

Everyone has his or her own particular study style. Some people prefer to study alone and others work best in a group. Regardless of your preference, we strongly recommend that you take advantage of group study at least some of the time. Studying with others can prove very helpful when working through your weakest areas. Each member of the study team will bring strengths and weaknesses to the table, and all can benefit from the collaboration. So, even if you are a solitary learner, you may occasionally want to work with a group for those topics you find more challenging.

Theoretically, material known thoroughly after one learning will fade predictably with time. After one day, the average person retains only 80% of what was learned; ultimately he or she will remember about 30% of it. That is why you are now relearning information you acquired over a period of years. Your aim is to achieve maximum recall through effective review.

Make your study process systematic. To facilitate this effort, we recommend that you design a 10-week study program. You should plan on spending an average of 10 to 12 hours per week studying. The idea is to study smart, not to bulldoze through tons of material in a haphazard way.

DEVELOPING YOUR STUDY HABITS

First, you must get organized. You have to be deliberate about making sure that you develop and stick to a regular study routine. Find a place where you can study, either at home or at the library.

How you schedule your study time during the week is an individual decision. However, we recommend that you avoid all-nighters and other unreasonably long study sessions. The last thing you want to do is burn yourself out by working too long and too hard at one time. Try to do a little bit at a time and maintain a steady pace that is manageable for you.

Develop your individual study program. Write the topics and subjects in a list. Outline the chapters in your HIM text (or use the outlines in the *Preparation Guide for the RHIA and RHIT Examinations, 2nd Edition,* by Ruth Leroy). Pause at each chapter outline and recall basic points. Do you draw a blank, recall them more or less, or do you feel comfortable with your recall? Pinpoint your weakest subjects. By using this approach, you can see where you stand.

Weigh the importance of each subject. How were the topics emphasized in textbooks, in your class notes, and on previous exams (review the examination content information in the introduction of this book)? Try to pick out concepts that would make good exam questions.

Avoid trying to make a head-on attack by giving equal time and attention to all topics. Use the outlines to identify your weakest topics. Determine which topics will require a significant amount of study time and which will only require a brief review. Make a list of the topics in the order that you plan to study them.

Your list will give you a clear mental picture of what you need to do and will keep you on track. There are three additional advantages to a list: (1) It builds your morale as you steadily cross off items that you have completed, and you can monitor your progress. (2) Glancing back at the list from time to time serves to reassure you that you are on target. (3) You can readily see that you are applying your time and effort where they are most needed.

Keep the list conspicuously in view. Carefully plan your pre-exam study time and stick to your plan. Go to the exam like a trained and disciplined runner going to a marathon event!

A SUMMARY OF TIPS FOR ORGANIZING YOUR TIME AND MATERIALS

1. **Assess your strengths and weaknesses.** Review the major topic categories and determine what your areas of strength are and what areas are in need of improvement.
2. **Set up a realistic study schedule.** Refer to the sample schedule provided in this book and customize it to meet your needs.
3. **Focus on your weaknesses.** Spend more time and energy studying your areas of weakness, especially if these categories had a significant number of questions associated with them on past exams. Remember, every question counts toward that passing score!
4. **Organize and review all of the following items:**
   a. Course syllabi and outlines
   b. Class notes
   c. Tests and examinations
   d. Textbooks
5. **One of the best ways to study for a test is to take tests.** Practice answering questions and working problems as much as possible. Work with your watch in front of you. Time yourself so that you become accustomed to taking only 1 to 1-1/2 minutes per question. Practice using the calculator on your computer to make mathematical calculations.
6. **Carefully read the AHIMA Candidate Handbook for the RHIA and RHIT Examinations.** If anything in the Candidate Handbook is unclear, seek assistance from your program director or call AHIMA. You are held accountable for the important information, deadlines, and instructions addressed in this material.

SAMPLE STUDY SCHEDULE

Week 1   Health Data Contents and Standards, and Information Retention and Access

Week 2   Legal and Ethical Aspects, Health Information Privacy and Security

Week 3   Informatics and Information Systems

Week 4   Organization and Management and Personnel Administration

Week 5   Classification Systems and Secondary Data Sources

Week 6   Billing and Reimbursement and Medical Science

Week 7   CPT Coding

Week 8   ICD-9-CM Coding

Week 9   Quality and Performance Improvement

Week 10   Health Statistics and Research

STUDY RESOURCES

There are three basic sources of information: books, people, and your educational program or college. If your studies become stagnant, do not sit and grind yourself down. If your text is not making the subject clear for you, don't spend time trying to memorize something you do not understand. The main issue is to understand the material so you can use the knowledge in a practical way. So search for additional information that will help make the subject clear to you.

Books and other written resources may use another style of presentation that you are more receptive to. A different textbook may be all you need to gain better insight into the subject. It can offer a fresh point of view, provide relief from boredom, and encourage critical thinking in the process of comparing the texts.

Periodical literature in the health field provides well-written articles that may open up the subject to you and turn study into an adventure in learning. AHIMA publishes authoritative and insightful information on every aspect of HIM. Sometimes an article can help put the text material into practical perspective and pull it together so that you gain a deeper understanding. With the rapidly changing health care world, HIM journals and magazines have the most current information and are frequently used as references for test questions.

Take advantage of the college library by using reserved materials set aside for your study purposes.

Professional contacts in your HIM community can also be helpful in your study effort. Most people in our field are eager to share their knowledge and are flattered by appeals for information.

Collaborating with classmates may reveal fresh viewpoints, stimulate thought by disagreement, or at least let you see that you are not alone in your quest. Organize study groups and set aside specific times to work together. This interaction can be truly beneficial in keeping you motivated and on task.

Classes, workshops, and seminars present opportunities to learn and review the subject matter in a new light. Take advantage of any examination review sessions available in your area. Talking to graduates who have recently taken the exam can also be of great assistance.

Don't overlook the power of AHIMA's Web site. In this dynamic, changing environment, the most up-to-date materials may not be available in a book. The AHIMA resources online are extensive and quite easy to access at www.ahima.org. In addition, the Communities of Practice (CoPs) are a phenomenal source of contact with HIM professionals and other students on a myriad of subjects.

In summary, some of the study resources available to you include:

1. HIM textbooks: There is a large variety of textbooks for the HIM student. For example, see the partial listing of books available through Delmar Cengage Learning.

2. Review books written for the RHIA and RHIT examinations.

3. Mock exam questions on CD-ROM for practicing taking computerized tests.

4. Class notes as well as the class tests and exams.

5. Class textbooks as well as looking over the great variety of HIM and coding books available on the market. AHIMA also has a variety of HIM books to choose from online at ahima.org.

6. Examination review sessions.

7. On-the-job experience (be cautious because the exam tests theory and not each particular practice)

8. Study groups or partners

9. Various Internet sites such as www.ahima.org and www.cms.gov for the latest information on the health care industry

Delmar Cengage Learning has a multitude of HIM products. Just a few of them are listed here.

Essentials of Health Information Management Principles and Practices
    Green, M. A., and Bowie, M. J.
    Published by Delmar Cengage Learning

Today's Health Information Management: An Integrated Approach
    McWay, D. C.
    Published by Delmar Cengage Learning

Basic Allied Health Statistics and Analysis
    Koch, G.
    Published by Delmar Cengage Learning

Health Services Research Methods
    Shi, L.
    Published by Delmar Cengage Learning

3-2-1 Code It!
    Green, M. A.
    Published by Delmar Cengage Learning

Understanding ICD-9-CM: A Worktest
    Bowie, M. J., and Schaffer, R.
    Published by Delmar Cengage Learning

Understanding Medical Coding: A Comprehensive Guide (2nd ed.)
    Johnson, S. L., and McHugh, C. S.
    Published by Delmar Cengage Learning

Applying Coding Concepts: Encoder Workbook
    Eid, D.
    Published by: Delmar Cengage Learning

PAT'S EXAM EXPERIENCE

The national examination was the moment of truth for me. Some people asked me what I was going to do if I failed the examination. Now there is something to give you nightmares — to co-author an exam review book and then FLUNK the exam! That was when I decided to borrow a line from the movie *True Lies*, "fear is not an option," and adapted it for my own motto — "failure is not an option."

There were many days and nights when I doubted that I had what it takes. When I felt really fearful and uncomfortable, I made myself look back over the years of going to classes. I had completed all the courses required. I had studied hard and long in each one of them. I had made good grades. In fact, I graduated with honors. I was studying virtually every day to prepare for the exam. What more could I do? ABSOLUTELY NOTHING!!! Therefore, if I had done the best I could and I was doing the best I could, then the worry was just taking up space in my head.

I told myself there was no way I could fail the exam. This was a routine that I had to repeat, sometimes several times a day when the doubt would creep in. Positive attitudes can and will make the pre-test jitters disappear. If you feel you can't do this, tell yourself that you have done it and that this is just one more test! I had prepared myself — I had done the homework and class work and taken many, many, many tests successfully before. This one is JUST ONE MORE!

The night before the test, I tried to study just a little, but I just could not concentrate. I gave up trying to cram more information into my head and went to bed.

The next morning my friend Lynn, a fellow graduate, drove over to the exam site with me. We had doughnuts and coffee while we waited for the room to be prepared. One of the students milling around commented that she hoped that the school had prepared us for the test. Another answered, "They did their part. The question is, did we do ours?" There were a lot of very nervous people there.

Lynn, my study buddy and friend, was being *The Little Engine That Could* by repeating, "I think I can. I think I can." My grandchildren had been watching Disney's *Cinderella*, and all I could think of was the animals singing "We can do it. We can do it. There is really nothing to it." We began saying these things to each other and started to laugh. Some of the students around us looked at us strangely, but it DID help calm us down.

After waiting what seemed like forever to start the exam, we were finally told to begin. I panicked at the first question. I could not understand what it asked. I had to stop, take a deep breath and relax. I went to the next question, and was able to answer it quickly. I went back to the first question and it looked simple! I found myself going down the page breezing along and answering the questions. Then, I gasped as I thought, "What if I am not going fast enough?" I stopped, looked at the question number, checked the time and figured that I was answering them in about one and one half minutes each. Right on schedule. So, I calmed myself down and got back to business.

When I took the examination, it was still paper and pencil with fill-in-the-answer bubbles. About halfway through the exam, I had another thought: "What if I am putting the answers in the wrong answer bubble?" After catching my breath, I looked at the question number and checked the answer bubble. Both were the same. I told myself to just relax and do the work at hand. Before I knew it, I had answered all the questions. I even had enough time to go back and review the ones I was not sure about.

One of the most difficult parts of the exam is the length of time sitting. I did take one break in the middle of the exam to use the restroom and walk around for a minute to clear my head. When the exam was over, I was relieved, to say the least. For months it had been hanging over my head and now IT WAS OVER! No matter what the results were, I had done the best I could and I was still a winner! Do the best you can and you will past the exam too. YOU CAN DO IT!

Affirmation: "I can handle anything on the exam — one question at a time." ~ Kathy DeAngelo, 1995

II. Test-Taking Skills

Patricia J. Schnering, RHIA, CCS

Debora J. Butts, EdD, RHIA

This section of the review book is designed to provide students with techniques that will help maximize their chances for success on the RHIA and RHIT national certification examinations. Five major areas will be explored in this section:

1. Becoming "test wise"
2. The "truth" about test taking
3. Characteristics of successful test takers
4. Multiple-choice test question construction
5. Practical advice for exam preparation

Health Information Administration/Technology (HIA/HIT) students may view the test-taking experience as one that causes great anxiety and concern. Test taking does not have to be a negative experience. Students can equip themselves with an array of techniques and practical strategies to master the test-taking situation. After all, the ultimate goal of taking the exam is to pass it and move forward with one's career aspirations.

BECOMING "TEST WISE"

This section will assist the student in becoming "test wise." Becoming test wise involves a set of skills that is acquired through practice and instruction. Being test wise does not mean that one will always achieve a very high score on the exam. What it does mean is that one will learn to overcome such factors as test anxiety which often prevent students from passing examinations. The ultimate key to being test wise is knowledge of the subject matter that will be covered on the certification examination. No amount of tips or techniques can replace adequate preparation. A colleague I know in academia often states, "Adequate preparation prevents poor performance." If one does not have thorough knowledge of the subject, no amount of test-taking knowledge or skills will improve your test performance. Now, let's turn our discussion to the first topic—the "truth" about test taking.

THE "TRUTH" ABOUT TEST TAKING

It is important to be realistic about what a test really is and what it is not. The exam is not a measure of your intelligence. It is not directly a measure of your knowledge of the course material. It is not a complete picture of what you know. It is certainly not a measure of your worth as a human being. Most importantly, failing to pass the certification examination does not imply that you are in the wrong profession. Many lawyers and certified public accountants require several attempts to obtain their credentials.

Now let's look at what a test is really all about. What does it measure? A test may measure your performance on a given day. It tells you how much you know about the questions you were asked, which represent a small sampling of the material you actually covered while studying to become a health information management professional. To some degree, a test measures your skills as a test taker, such as your ability to apply reasoning and logic, as well as your critical-thinking and problem-solving skills. The test will also measure your ability to recall "correct answers."

It is important as you prepare for the certification examination that you maintain a realistic perspective. The certification examination is a professionally designed test that has been developed by educators and practitioners in health information management. It will measure your ability to answer questions in the major domains.

Knowing what is expected of you in order to pass the examination and improving your test-taking skills will provide you with valuable tools to apply in your study process. If you keep the examination in the proper perspective and prepare well, you will obtain the credentials that you so rightly deserve.

Learning how to take tests will usually help you overcome inappropriate test-taking habits and allow you to demonstrate what you know to the fullest degree in the testing situation. Here are 10 truths that you should know before attempting the certification examination:

10 TRUTHS

TRUTH 1: Test-taking skills can be learned.
Good test-taking skills make the most of what you know. That's just what this chapter is focused on.

TRUTH 2: Test-taking skills make a difference.
Two people can get scores that differ greatly on the test because one person has better test-taking skills.

TRUTH 3: Good preparation reduces anxiety.
Reducing anxiety by proper preparation improves test performance.

TRUTH 4: Attitude does make a difference.
A significant percentage of success on the test will depend on your attitude toward test taking and your general attitude about yourself. Students should strive to feel good about the test-taking experience, knowing that they have done everything possible to prepare in advance for the examination.

TRUTH 5: Always answer the easy questions first.
Avoid attempting to answer the most difficult questions first, because they will interfere with your positive attitude and confidence. Agonizing over difficult questions will result in lost time and points.

TRUTH 6: Failure to plan to pass the exam ensures planning to fail the exam.
This might sound a bit harsh and bitter to swallow, but it is indeed the truth. Do not let poor planning and a lack of preparation hinder you from peak performance on the examination. As the saying goes, "Plan your work and work your plan."

TRUTH 7: Usually your first hunch is your best.
Changing answers after you have selected what you believe or know to be the correct answer is not recommended. Usually your first hunch is your best, unless of course you discover or uncover information in the examination that disqualifies or nullifies your first choice.

TRUTH 8: Educated guessing is better than guessing randomly.
It is appropriate to guess after you have narrowed down the four options to two possible answers.

TRUTH 9: The only thing that stands between you and passing the exam is ...
You guessed it: "YOU." If passing the exam is your number one goal at this point in your life, then your priorities should reflect this goal. Priority number one should be to find the time to plan to be successful on the exam.

TRUTH 10: No amount of "tips and tricks" replaces content knowledge.
As mentioned previously, strong content knowledge is essential. The suggestions in this chapter are meant to make the most of what you know, not to take the place of content preparation.

CHARACTERISTICS OF SUCCESSFUL TEST TAKERS

Have you ever wondered why it seems that some people pass the exam and others do not? What are the characteristics of successful test takers? If one looks at successful people in general, you will probably find that they demonstrate these traits and habits in different aspects of their personal and professional lives. Here are some of the characteristics of successful test takers in general.

1. **Good time management.** Time is looked upon by the successful test taker as something not to be feared, but rather a medium that must be mastered and controlled in order to complete the exam with confidence. Completion of the exam with confidence means that one will be able to manage his or her time effectively and have sufficient time to attempt to answer every question without heavily depending upon guessing, whether educated guessing or guessing randomly. Ultimately, if your time is not managed well, the minutes will pass whether you have completed the exam or not. Remember to avoid spending excessive time on any one question.

2. **Read questions carefully.** Read the question twice, if necessary, to fully understand the directions or to fully comprehend what exactly is being asked. In lengthy scenario questions, it may be helpful to read the question portion of the statement first. Also, have a good understanding of key terms or phrases often used in health information management, such as "confidentiality" or "skilled nursing facility." Remember, there is no substitute for knowing the facts.

3. **Take the question at face value.** In other words, avoid reading something into the question that was not intended or explicitly stated. For example, consider the following question.

> In progressive counseling, the first step in disciplining for a first offense is
> A. termination.
> B. suspension.
> C. oral reprimand.
> D. written warning.

The student who reads into the question may decide that in order to answer this question, he or she must know more about the specific offense. However, such details are not necessary. This question assumes that the offense is one that would not require immediate termination for the first offense. Therefore, in the process of applying progressive disciplinary action, an oral reprimand (answer C) is the correct answer.

4. **Read and consider all four options carefully.** One approach in answering multiple choice questions is to read the answers first. In using this method, you will evaluate each answer separately and equally. Look for an answer that not only seems right on its own, but completes the question statement smoothly. Statistically, the least likely correct answer on a multiple-choice question is the first option.

If you have narrowed the options down to two that seem correct, then you must study the options and compare them with each other to see what makes them different. Using deductive reasoning and the process of elimination, you should be able to arrive at the best answer.

5. **Approach questions systematically.** Break down each question into manageable parts and proceed systematically. Consider the following question:

> For a 2-week period, the HIM department had 1,200 worked hours and 1,280 total (or paid) hours on its payroll. During this same 2 weeks, there were 375 discharges. The department's standard is 3.3 worked hours per discharge. The number of worked hours per discharge for this 2-week period was
> A. 3.0.
> B. 3.2.
> C. 3.4.
> D. 3.8.

Following the above principle of breaking down the question into component parts, what would you do to make this question more manageable? There are often several ways to arrive at the same answer. Some students may answer, "I would first pull out the number of discharges," or some may answer "I would pull out the total hours worked." Whatever works for you to manage answering the question correctly is the right approach for you. The calculation for this question is 1,200 hours worked divided by 375 discharges equals 3.2 (answer B).

6. **Read carefully.** Reading directions thoroughly and identifying key words and phrases in the question are essential to test-taking success. For example, consider the following question:

> The health information manager exercises staff authority in the hospital when he or she
> A. abstracts a medical record.
> B. advises on a file system for the radiology department.
> C. teaches a file clerk a new procedure.
> D. writes a procedure for the correct filing of records.

The stem states "exercises staff authority." If the student did not read the question carefully, he or she may have missed these key terms, which are critical to selecting the correct answer, which is B.

7. **Avoid applying preset solutions.** The successful test taker does not try to remember solutions to similar problems; rather, he or she solves each new problem independently.

WHEN AND HOW TO GUESS

There will be questions on the exam that will be totally unfamiliar to you. Choosing the correct answer may lie in the concept of "informed guessing." In applying this technique, the test taker eliminates the absurd options and guesses on the basis of familiarity.

It is helpful to relate possible answers to the question being asked. Read all the options before selecting the correct one. Usually you can narrow the possible answers down to two by asking yourself:

- What is the question really asking?
- What is the main idea or point of this question?
- What answer would make the most sense?
- How can I rephrase or break down the question?

Sometimes the test taker can gain information about the correct answers from cues and information from other questions. Remember, however, this is when you are in the "informed guessing" mode. There will be information in a question that is irrelevant, and it is important for you to get to the heart of the question. Don't get too preoccupied with the content or meaning of a scenario before you know what the question is asking. Use logic and common sense whenever possible.

MULTIPLE-CHOICE TEST QUESTION CONSTRUCTION

The entire multiple-choice question is called an item. Each item consists of two main parts.

- **Stem:** The first part is known as the stem. The purpose of the stem is to present a problem in a clear and concise manner. The stem should contain all the details necessary to answer the question. The stem of an item can be a complete sentence that asks a question. It can also be presented as an incomplete sentence that becomes a complete sentence when it is combined with one of the options in the item.

- **Answer options:** The second part of the item is comprised of the options or possible answers. One of the options will answer the question posed in the stem correctly. The remaining options are called *distracters*. They are referred to as distracters because they are designed to distract you from the correct answer. Consider the following sample item.

	ITEM	
Stem	In quantitative research, the formulation of the hypothesis is an activity usually associated with	
Distracter	A.	data collection.
Correct	B.	identification of the problem.
Distracter	C.	analysis.
Distracter	D.	assembling the results.

COGNITIVE LEVELS: The examination is designed to test knowledge of subject matter at the highest cognitive levels when possible. To explain, let's look at examples of the three levels.

Recall: This question is testing the student at the "recall level." We simply want the student to be able to recall pertinent facts.

The medical record is the property of the
  A. patient.
  B. medical facility.
  C. Health Information Management Department.
  D. attending physician.

The answer is, of course, B. This question relied upon your memory of this fact.

Application: Now let's look at the second highest cognitive level, an application level question, which tests the student's ability to apply information.

The medical record is the property of the medical facility and can be removed in which of the following situations?
  A. The patient is suing the hospital and wants the original record mailed to the attorney representing his case.
  B. The attending physician wants to take the patient's original record to a professional conference for presentation.
  C. The court issues a subpoena and needs the original record in court within 24 hours.
  D. The attending physician is being sued and he wants to take the original patient record to court with him.

The correct answer in this case is C. The only instance when the original record should be removed from the hospital is in the case of the issuance of a subpoena duces tecum. This question required the student to apply information about when a record can be removed from the health care facility. The application level goes beyond the student recalling the rule about who has legal ownership of the record.

Analysis (problem solving): The third and highest cognitive level utilized by test developers is the analysis level. At this level the student will demonstrate the ability to analyze familiar information in new and different situations. This is sometimes referred to as a problem-solving or critical-thinking question.

The information below is from a transcription service in your department.
  Total average lines transcribed/month: 270,000
  Standard per person: 1,200 lines in one day
  21 work days in a month 15% adjustment factor
The number of transcriptionists needed by this facility is
  A. 10.7.
  B. 11.7.
  C. 12.3.
  D. 16.0.

The correct answer for this question is C.

The mathematical calculation to achieve the answer is
  270,000 x 0.15 adjustment factor = 40,500
  270,000 + 40,500 = 310,500 potential lines of transcription per month
  1,200 lines x 21 days = 25,200 lines one employee can produce in one month
  310,500/25,200 = 12.3 transcriptionists

COGNITIVE LEVELS FOR THE RHIA EXAMINATION QUESTIONS BY DOMAIN

Domain	R	App	An	Total
1. Health Data Management	8	20	12	40
2. Health Statistics, Biomedical Research, and Quality Management	0	8	8	16
3. Health Services Organization and Delivery	6	16	10	32
4. Information Technology and Systems	9	15	8	32
5. Organization and Management	10	19	11	40
Total questions by cognitive level	33	78	49	160
Percentage by cognitive level	20%	49%	31%	100%

For cognitive levels: R = recall, App = application, and An =Analysis.

COGNITIVE LEVELS FOR THE RHIT EXAMINATION QUESTIONS BY DOMAIN

Domain	R	APP	An	Total
1. Health Data Management	8	22	9	39
2. Health Statistics, Biomedical Research, and Quality Management	2	8	6	16
3. Health Services Organization and Delivery	5	12	5	22
4. Information Technology and Systems	12	15	6	33
5. Organizational Resources	4	8	8	20
Total questions by cognitive level	31	65	34	130
Percentage by cognitive level	24%	50%	26%	100%

For cognitive levels: R = recall, App = application, and An =Analysis.

After reviewing the cognitive level ranges, it is clear that for both the RHIA and RHIT examinations the student must be prepared to answer questions from the lowest cognitive level (recall) to the highest cognitive level (analysis). Testing at all three levels will help ensure that students can apply their newly acquired knowledge and skills on the job.

Refer to the current copy of the AHIMA Candidate Handbook for a complete listing of the domains, subdomains, and task competencies. There are separate competencies for the RHIA examination and the RHIT examination.

PRACTICAL ADVICE FOR EXAM PREPARATION

As you become more proficient at applying effective test-taking techniques, you will truly understand the phrase that "knowledge is power." This is exactly what this information hopes to do, and that is to provide you with the knowledge and skills to empower you to achieve your ultimate goal—certification.

Research demonstrates that the test taker that approaches a test with physical, mental, and emotional authority is in a better position to master the testing situation and the outcome. Remember, failing to plan means planning to fail. Here are some recommendations for you to incorporate as part of your "success plan."

Recommendation 1: Follow your regular routine.

Follow your regular nightly routine the evening before and morning of the exam. Abruptly changing your schedule and habits for this testing event could throw your system off balance and negatively affect your performance.

Recommendation 2: Arrive early for the examination.

It is always better to have 15 to 30 minutes of extra time prior to the start of a major examination. By arriving early on test day, you will be able to visit the restroom, survey the situation, and collect your thoughts. Decide where you want to sit in the test area, if the seats are not assigned. By collecting your thoughts prior to the start of the exam, you can improve your mental attitude by knowing you are truly prepared for this time, this situation, and this test-taking process. Remember, you want to be in control of the test anxiety that is normal, despite all of your preparation. If you are unfamiliar with the test site, it is usually a good practice to travel to the test site in advance of the exam date. Becoming familiar with the test site will prevent you from getting lost on exam day.

Recommendation 3: Maintain a positive mental attitude.

Perhaps you are sometimes plagued by a negative inner voice that says something like: "Well look at you... trying to pass the certification examination. Why don't you stop kidding yourself? You know you are not as smart as your classmates. They will probably all pass and you will probably fail!" Almost all of us have critical voices inside our heads. Sometimes the voice may tell us that we don't measure up to others in the class. At other times it tries to blame our performance on the test, the teacher, or some other convenient scapegoat. You can learn to replace your negative inner dialogue with positive self-talk.

Start by programming your inner voice to remind you of how long and hard you have prepared for this examination. Remind yourself that you deserve to pass because of the time and energy you have spent in school preparing for this examination. Repeat positive affirmation statements to yourself, such as "I am a wonderful, worthy person who is capable of achieving my goal of becoming an RHIA/RHIT."

Recommendation 4: Answer the questions you know first.

It is a good idea to begin the test by answering questions that build your confidence. Getting off to a good start allows you to establish a positive momentum, which will assist you when you encounter more difficult questions. Because time is critical, answering the easier questions first will assure you of getting credit for what you know.

Recommendation 5: Check your answers before exiting the computerized exam.

Make sure you have answered every question. Be careful about changing your answers. You may need to revisit any items in which you have made an educated guess or items you discovered answers to as you progressed through the questions. Submit your test knowing that you did your very best.

CONCLUSION

As you study for the exam, take a moment now and then to review the test-taking skills addressed in this section. Using these techniques will help you develop the characteristics of a successful test taker. Working through questions will help you become more and more comfortable with multiple-choice testing.

Knowing how questions are constructed and what to look for should greatly improve your correct answer ratio. A sense of the scheme of the test structure and cognitive levels will become second nature with practice.

During your exam preparation, you will find that you actually enjoy taking multiple-choice examinations as a study aid. Be sure to obtain any mock computerized test exams available on your CD-ROM or online to gain experience taking the test on the computer.

This comfort zone will free you to apply your knowledge and skills effectively during the examination process. The real bonus is that you will be more focused on demonstrating your knowledge through the medium of testing than on the exam process itself.

III. Health Data Content and Standards

Debra W. Cook, MAEd, RHIA

1. In preparation for an EHR, you are conducting a total facility inventory of all forms currently used. You must name each form for bar coding and indexing into a document management system. The unnamed document in front of you includes a microscopic description of tissue excised during surgery. The document type you are most likely to give to this form is

A. recovery room record.

B. pathology report.

C. operative report.

D. discharge summary.

REFERENCE: Abdelhak, p 110
Green and Bowie, p 156
Johns, p 66
LaTour and Eichenwald-Maki, p 182

2. Patient data collection requirements vary according to health care setting. A data element you would expect to be collected in the MDS, but NOT in the UHDDS would be

A. personal identification.

B. cognitive patterns.

C. procedures and dates.

D. principal diagnosis.

REFERENCE: Abdelhak, p 134-135
Green and Bowie, p 114, 243
Johns, p 164-168
LaTour and Eichenwald-Maki, p 152

3. A good first step toward protecting the security of data contained in a health information computer system would be to

A. establish a good record tracking system.

B. define levels of security for different types of information, depending on sensitivity.

C. provide remote terminals for improved access to the record.

D. provide internet access to facility records.

REFERENCE: Abdelhak, p 294
Johns, p 338
LaTour and Eichenwald-Maki, p 280-281

4. In the number "99–0001" listed in a tumor registry accession register, what does the prefix "99" represent?

A. the number of primary cancers reported for that patient

B. the year the case was entered into the database of the registry

C. the sequence number of the case

D. the stage of the tumor based upon the TNM system of staging

REFERENCE: Johns, p 400-403
LaTour and Eichenwald-Maki, p 290

5. A risk manager needs to locate a full report of a patient's fall from his bed, including witness reports and probable reasons for the fall. She would most likely find this information in the
   A. doctors' progress notes.
   C. incident report.
   B. integrated progress notes.
   D. nurses' notes.

REFERENCE: Abdelhak, p 456
            Green and Bowie, p 88
            Johns, p 528
            LaTour and Eichenwald-Maki, p 266, 512
            McWay (2003), p 109-110
            McWay, 110

6. For continuity of care, ambulatory care providers are more likely than providers of acute care services to rely on the documentation found in the
   A. interdisciplinary patient care plan.
   C. transfer record.
   B. discharge summary.
   D. problem list.

REFERENCE: Abdelhak, p 133
            Green and Bowie, p 79
            Johns, p 79
            LaTour and Eichenwald-Maki, p 184

7. Joint Commission does not approve of auto authentication of entries in a health record. The primary objection to this practice is that
   A. it is too easy to delegate use of computer passwords.
   B. evidence cannot be provided that the physician actually reviewed and approved each report.
   C. electronic signatures are not acceptable in every state.
   D. tampering too often occurs with this method of authentication.

REFERENCE: Green and Bowie, p 80
            LaTour and Eichenwald-Maki, p 197

8. As part of a quality improvement study you have been asked to provide information on the menstrual history, number of pregnancies, and number of living children on each OB patient from a stack of old obstetrical records. The best place in the record to locate this information is the
   A. prenatal record.
   C. postpartum record.
   B. labor and delivery record.
   D. discharge summary.

REFERENCE: Abdelhak, p 110-111
            Green and Bowie, p 172
            LaTour and Eichenwald-Maki, p 183

9. As a concurrent record reviewer for an acute care facility, you have asked Dr. Crossman to provide an updated history and physical for one of her recent admissions. Dr. Crossman pages through the medical record to a copy of an H&P performed in her office a week before admission. You tell Dr. Crossman
   A. a new H&P is required for every inpatient admission.
   B. that you apologize for not noticing the H&P she provided.
   C. the H&P copy is acceptable as long as she documents any interval changes.
   D. Joint Commission standards do not allow copies of any kind in the original record.

REFERENCE: Abdelhak, p 105
            Green and Bowie, p 136
            LaTour and Eichenwald-Maki, p 177-178

10. As a new CTR, you are interested in identifying every reportable case of cancer from the previous year. A key resource will be the facility's
   A. disease index.
   B. number control index.
   C. physicians' index.
   D. patient index.

REFERENCE: Abdelhak, p 267
               Johns, p 401
               LaTour and Eichenwald-Maki, p 290
               McWay, p 116

11. Joint Commission requires the attending physician to countersign health record documentation that is entered by
   A. interns or medical students.
   B. midwives.
   C. consulting physicians.
   D. physician partners.

REFERENCE: Green and Bowie, p 81

12. The minimum length of time for retaining original medical records is primarily governed by
   A. Joint Commission.
   B. medical staff.
   C. state law.
   D. readmission rates.

REFERENCE: Abdelhak, p 240-241
               Green and Bowie, p 96
               Johns, p 684, 696
               LaTour and Eichenwald-Maki, p 206

13. The use of personal signature stamps for authentication of entries in a paper-based record requires special measures to guard against delegated use of the stamp. In a completely computerized patient record system, similar measures might be utilized to govern the use of
   A. fingerprint signatures.
   B. voice recognition systems.
   C. expert systems.
   D. electronic signatures.

REFERENCE: Abdelhak, p 114, 514
               Green and Bowie, p 81-83
               LaTour and Eichenwald-Maki, p 196-197

14. Discharge summary documentation must include
   A. a detailed history of the patient.
   B. a note from social services or discharge planning.
   C. significant findings during hospitalization.
   D. correct codes for significant procedures.

REFERENCE: Abdelhak, p 109
               Green and Bowie, p 134-135
               Johns, p 68-72
               LaTour and Eichenwald-Maki, p 182

15. The performance of ongoing record reviews is an important tool in ensuring data quality through accurate health records. These reviews evaluate
    A. quality of care through the use of pre-established criteria.
    B. adverse effects and contraindications of drugs utilized during hospitalization.
    C. potentially compensable events.
    D. completeness, adequacy, and quality of documentation.

REFERENCE: Abdelhak, p 124
               Johns, p 851
               LaTour and Eichenwald-Maki, p 104-107

16. Ultimate responsibility for the quality and completion of entries in patient health records belongs to the
    A. chief of staff.   C. HIM director.
    B. attending physician.   D. risk manager.

REFERENCE: Abdelhak, p 113
               LaTour and Eichenwald-Maki, p 195

17. Quantitative and qualitative reviews performed on patient records by medical record personnel in either a skilled nursing facility or inpatient psychiatric facility are generally in the form of
    A. retrospective deficiency analysis.   C. concurrent chart review.
    B. special study audits.   D. occurrence screening.

REFERENCE: Abdelhak, p 124-126, 134
               LaTour and Eichenwald-Maki, p 185
               Peden, p 338-340

18. The foundation for communicating all patient care goals in long-term care settings is the
    A. legal assessment.   C. interdisciplinary patient care plan.
    B. medical history.   D. Uniform Hospital Discharge Data Set.

REFERENCE: Abdelhak, p 138, 142
               Johns, p 83-84
               LaTour and Eichenwald-Maki, p 185

19. Which interdisciplinary committee is most likely to be charged with the responsibility for monitoring trends in delinquent health record percentages?
    A. Health Record Committee   C. Risk Management Committee
    B. Utilization Review Committee   D. Joint Conference Committee

REFERENCE: Green and Bowie, p, 88-89

20. A health record analyst needs to quickly compare all lab values during one hospitalization. The paper-based health record format best suited for this purpose is
    A. problem-oriented.   C. reverse chronological.
    B. source-oriented.   D. integrated.

REFERENCE: Abdelhak, p 114
               Johns, p 41
               LaTour and Eichenwald-Maki, p 186

21. In preparing your facility for initial accreditation by Joint Commission, you are trying to improve the process of ongoing record review. All health record reviews are presently performed by a team of HIM department personnel. The committee meets quarterly and reports to a Quality Management Committee. In reviewing Joint Commission standards, your first recommended change is to
    A. have more frequent committee meetings.
    B. have the committee report to the Executive Committee.
    C. have a physician perform all the reviews.
    D. provide for record reviews to be performed by an interdisciplinary team of care providers.

REFERENCE: Abdelhak, p 124-127

22. As the privacy officer of your facility, you have been charged with developing policies and procedures for protecting the confidentiality and security of the clinical data collected in your computerized system. One of the first steps you will take is to judge the value of information processed by your system and classify it. Another step you will need to take is to
    A. authorize access to information collected based on level of data sensitivity.
    B. prevent all nonclinicians' access to any confidential information in the system.
    C. establish firewalls to protect aggregate data collected within your facility.
    D. establish passwords for all customers, both internal and external, who request access to the information in your system.

REFERENCE: Green and Bowie, p 136
                Johns, p 820
                LaTour and Eichenwald-Maki, p 280, 307

23. A qualitative review of a health record reveals that the history and physical for a patient admitted on June 26 was performed on June 30 and transcribed on July 1. Which of the following statements regarding the history and physical is true in this situation? Completion and charting of the H&P indicates
    A. noncompliance with Joint Commission standards.
    B. compliance with Joint Commission standards.
    C. compliance with Medicare regulations.
    D. compliance with Joint Commission standards for nonsurgical patients.

REFERENCE: Abdelhak, p 105
                Johns, p 684
                LaTour and Eichenwald-Maki, p 177-178

24. As your acute care facility moves toward the adoption of an EHR, your planning committee is trying to prioritize systems that will contribute to patient safety. Your physicians have indicated readiness to enter data directly into the EHR, and they acknowledge the need for decision support regarding drug dosages and contraindications. You think they are ready for a
    A. computer-output-to-laser-disk system.
    B. electronic medication administration record system.
    C. electronic document management system.
    D. computerized provider order-entry system.

REFERENCE: Abdelhak, p 285-286
                Green and Bowie, p 230
                LaTour and Eichenwald-Maki, p 122

25. You have been asked by a peer review committee to print a list of the medical record numbers of all patients who had CABGs performed in the past year at your acute care hospital. Which secondary data source could be used to quickly gather this information?
    A. disease index
    B. physician index
    C. master patient index
    D. operation index

REFERENCE: Johns, p 376-377
               LaTour and Eichenwald-Maki, p 289

26. The best example of point-of-care service and documentation is
    A. using an automated tracking system to locate a record.
    B. using occurrence screens to identify adverse events.
    C. doctors using voice recognition systems to dictate radiology reports.
    D. nurses using bedside terminals to record vital signs.

REFERENCE: Abdelhak, p 38
               LaTour and Eichenwald-Maki, p 64-65

27. Many of the principles of forms design apply to both paper-based and computer-based systems. For example, the physical layout of the form and/or screen should be organized to match the way the information is requested. Facilities that are scanning and imaging paper records as part of a computer-based system must give careful consideration to
    A. placement of hospital logo.
    B. signature line for authentication.
    C. use of box design.
    D. bar code placement.

REFERENCE: Abdelhak, p 256
               LaTour and Eichenwald-Maki, p 197-199

28. Which of the following is a form or view that is typically seen in the health record of a long-term care patient, but is rarely seen in records of acute care patients?
    A. pharmacy consultation
    B. medical consultation
    C. physical exam
    D. emergency record

REFERENCE: Abdelhak, p 118
               Green and Bowie, p 93

29. One distinct advantage of the EHR over paper-based health records is the
    A. ease of developing screen designs over form designs.
    B. accessibility of the record by multiple data users.
    C. standardized format.
    D. ease of data collection.

REFERENCE: Johns, p 116
               LaTour and Eichenwald-Maki, p 229

30. The first cancer patient seen in your facility on January 1, 2008, was diagnosed with colon cancer, with no known history of previous malignancies. The accession number assigned to this patient is
    A. 2008-0000/00.
    B. 2008-0000/01.
    C. 2008-0001/00.
    D. 2008-0001/01.

REFERENCE: Johns, p 400
               LaTour and Eichenwald-Maki, p 290

31. As the Data Security Officer for your institution, you plan to implement a log-on process for electronic signing that is LEAST susceptible to improper delegation of use. The method you will recommend is
    A. password assigned by system administrator.
    B. password assigned by user.
    C. biometrics-based identifier.
    D. encryption.

REFERENCE: Green and Bowie, p 26

32. In determining your acute care facility's degree of compliance with prospective payment requirements for Medicare, the best resource to reference for recent certification standards is the
    A. CARF manual.   C. Joint Commission accreditation manual.
    B. hospital bylaws.   D. Federal Register.

REFERENCE: Abdelhak, p 438
               Green and Bowie, p 29
               LaTour and Eichenwald-Maki, p 365

33. In an acute care hospital, a complete history and physical may not be dictated for a new admission when
    A. the patient is readmitted for a similar problem within 1 year.
    B. the patient's stay is less than 24 hours.
    C. the patient has an uneventful course in the hospital.
    D. a legible copy of a recent H&P performed in the attending physician's office is available.

REFERENCE: Abdelhak, p 105
               Green and Bowie, p 136
               LaTour and Eichenwald-Maki, p 177-178

34. You are developing a complete data dictionary for your facility. Which of the following resources will be most helpful in providing standard definitions for data commonly collected in acute care hospitals?
    A. Minimum Data Set
    B. Uniform Hospital Discharge Data Set
    C. Conditions of Participation
    D. Federal Register

REFERENCE: Abdelhak, p 99
               Green and Bowie, p 114
               Johns, p 162-163
               LaTour and Eichenwald-Maki, p 150

35. Sarasota Community Health Center has an approved cancer registry. A patient is readmitted for further treatment of a previously diagnosed cancer. The CTR should
    A. complete a new cancer abstract.   C. update the follow-up file.
    B. assign a new accession number.   D. complete a new master index file.

REFERENCE: Johns, p 400-403
               LaTour and Eichenwald-Maki, p 290-291

36. When developing a data collection system, the most effective approach first considers
    A. the end user's needs.
    B. applicable accreditation standards.
    C. hardware requirements.
    D. facility preference.

REFERENCE: Johns, p 144-145
               LaTour and Eichenwald-Maki, p 466-468

37. A key data item you would expect to find recorded on an ER record, but would probably NOT see in an acute care record is the
    A. physical findings.
    B. lab and diagnostic test results.
    C. time and means of arrival.
    D. instructions for follow-up care.

REFERENCE: Abdelhak, p 111
               Peden, p 31
               Johns, p 78
               LaTour and Eichenwald-Maki, p 184

38. A data item to include on a qualitative review checklist of infant and children inpatient health records which need not be included on adult records would be
    A. chief complaint.
    B. condition on discharge.
    C. time and means of arrival.
    D. growth and development record.

REFERENCE: Johns, p 82
               Peden, p 72

39. For each report of care rendered to a patient, the health record entry should include the date plus the provider's name and
    A. department.
    B. discipline.
    C. initials.
    D. supervising physician.

REFERENCE: Green and Bowie, p 111
               Johns, p 92
               LaTour and Eichenwald-Maki, p 194

40. In creating a new form or computer view, the designer should be most driven by
    A. QIO standards.
    B. medical staff bylaws.
    C. needs of the users.
    D. flow of data on the page or screen.

REFERENCE: Abdelhak, p 116
               Green and Bowie, p 184
               Johns, p 368-369
               LaTour and Eichenwald-Maki, p 197-199

41. Under which of the following conditions can an original patient health record be physically removed from the hospital?
    A. when the patient is brought to the hospital emergency department following a motor vehicle accident and, after assessment, is transferred with his health record to a trauma designated emergency department at another hospital
    B. when the director of health records is acting in response to a subpoena duces tecum and takes the health record to court
    C. when the patient is discharged by the physician and at the time of discharge is transported to a long-term care facility with his health record
    D. when the record is taken to a physician's private office for a follow-up patient visit postdischarge

REFERENCE: Abdelhak, p 527
                   Johns, p 685
                   McWay (2003), p 139

42. According to the following table, the most serious record delinquency problem occurred in which of the following months?

	April	May	June
Percentage incomplete records	70%	88%	79%
Percentage delinquent records	51%	43%	61%
Percentage delinquent due to missing H&P	3%	1.4%	0.5%

    A. April
    B. May
    C. June
    D. cannot determine from this data

REFERENCE: Abdelhak, p 105
                   Green and Bowie, p 83-84, 136

43. Using the SOAP style of documenting progress notes, choose the "subjective" statement from the following.
    A. sciatica unimproved with hot pack therapy
    B. patient moving about very cautiously, appears to be in pain
    C. adjust pain medication; begin physical therapy tomorrow
    D. patient states low back pain is as severe as it was on admission

REFERENCE: Abdelhak, p 115
                   Green and Bowie, p 92
                   LaTour and Eichenwald-Maki, p 186

44. In 1987, OBRA helped shift the focus in long-term care to patient outcomes. As a result, core assessment data elements are collected on each resident as defined in the
    A. UHDDS.
    B. MDS.
    C. Uniform Clinical Data Set.
    D. Uniform Ambulatory Core Data.

REFERENCE: Abdelhak, p 134
                   Green and Bowie, p 243
                   Johns, p 83
                   LaTour and Eichenwald-Maki, p 366
                   Peden, p 337

45. As the chair of a Forms Review Committee, you need to track the origin of data in a particular field and the security levels applicable to that field. Your best source for this information would be the

A. facility's data dictionary.
B. MDS.
C. Glossary of Health Care Terms.
D. UHDDS.

REFERENCE: Abdelhak, p 496
Johns, p 762-765
LaTour and Eichenwald-Maki, p 115

46. You notice on the admission H&P that Mr. McKahan, a Medicare patient, was admitted for disc surgery, but the progress notes indicate that due to some heart irregularities, he may not be a good surgical risk. Because of your knowledge of COP regulations, you expect that a(n) _____ will be added to his health record

A. interval summary
B. consultation report
C. advance directive
D. interdisciplinary care plan

REFERENCE: Abdelhak, p 109
Green and Bowie, p 142

47. An example of objective entry in the health record supplied by a health care practitioner is the

A. past medical history.
B. physical assessment.
C. chief complaint.
D. review of systems.

REFERENCE: Abdelhak, p 107
Green and Bowie, p 138-139
Johns, p 54-55
LaTour and Eichenwald-Maki, p 177

48. You have been appointed as chair of the Health Record Committee at a new hospital. Your committee has been asked to recommend time-limited documentation standards for inclusion in the Medical Staff Bylaws, Rules and Regulations. The committee documentation standards must meet the standards of both the Joint Commission and the Medicare Conditions of Participation. The standards for the history and physical exam documentation are discussed first. You advise them that the time period for completion of this report be should be set at

A. 12 hours after admission.
B. 24 hours after admission.
C. 12 hours after admission or prior to surgery.
D. 24 hours after admission or prior to surgery.

REFERENCE: Abdelhak, p 105
Green and Bowie, p 136
LaTour and Eichenwald-Maki, p 177-178

49. A pathologist on the Health Record Committee asks about the time requirement for reporting a provisional diagnosis when an autopsy is performed. You respond confidently that this information must be on the health record within

A. 24 hours.
B. 3 days.
C. 15 days.
D. 60 days.

REFERENCE: Abdelhak, p 110
Green and Bowie, p 170

50. A surgeon on the Health Record Committee voices a concern that, although he has been told that the operative report is to be dictated immediately after surgery, he has often had to deal with the problem of transcription backlog which prevented the report from getting on the health record in a timely manner. Your advice to this doctor is that when a known backlog exists, he should
    A. provide the dictated tape to his staff.
    B. request a "stat" report.
    C. write a detailed operative note in the record.
    D. request that administration hire more transcriptionists.

REFERENCE: Abdelhak, p 110
               Green and Bowie, p 153
               LaTour and Eichenwald-Maki, p 182

51. Joint Commission standards require that a complete history and physical be documented on the health records of operative patients. Does this report carry a time requirement?
    A. yes, within 8 hours post-surgery   C. yes, prior to surgery
    B. no, as long as it is dictated before surgery   D. yes, within 24 hours post-surgery

REFERENCE: Abdelhak, p 110
               Green and Bowie, p 153
               LaTour and Eichenwald-Maki, p 182

52. The old practices of flagging records for deficiencies and requiring retrospective documentation add little or no value to patient care. You try to convince the entire health care team to consistently enter data into the patient's record at the time and location of service instead of waiting for retrospective analysis to alert them to complete the record. You are proposing
    A. quantitative record review.   C. concurrent record analysis.
    B. clinical pertinence review.   D. point-of-care documentation.

REFERENCE: Abdelhak, p 287
               LaTour and Eichenwald-Maki, p 193-196

53. An example of a primary data source for health care statistics other than the patient health record is the
    A. disease index.   C. MPI.
    B. accession register.   D. hospital census.

REFERENCE: Abdelhak, p 382, 474
               Horton, p 3
               Koch, p 65

54. In the computerization of forms, good screen view design, along with the options of alerts and alarms, makes it easier to ensure that all essential data items have been captured. One essential item to be captured on the physical exam is the
    A. objective survey of body systems.   C. family history.
    B. chief complaint.   D. subjective review of systems.

REFERENCE: Abdelhak, p 107
               Green and Bowie, p 139-141
               Johns, p 55
               LaTour and Eichenwald-Maki, p 177-179

55. During a retrospective review of Rose Hunter's inpatient health record, the health information clerk notes that on day four of hospitalization there was one missed dose of insulin. What type of review is this clerk performing?
    A. utilization review
    B. quantitative review
    C. legal review
    D. qualitative review

REFERENCE: Abdelhak, p 127
               Green and Bowie, p 102
               LaTour and Eichenwald-Maki, p 194-195

56. Which of the following is least likely to be identified by the deficiency analysis clerk?
    A. missing discharge summary
    B. need for physician authentication of two verbal orders
    C. discrepancy between post-op diagnosis by the surgeon and pathology diagnosis by the pathologist
    D. x-ray report charted on the wrong record

REFERENCE: Abdelhak, p 127-127
               Green and Bowie, p 102
               Johns, p 351-353

57. The Conditions of Participation requires that the medical staff bylaws, rules, and regulations address the status of consultants. Which of the following reports would normally be considered a consultation?
    A. tissue examination done by the pathologist
    B. impressions of a cardiologist asked to determine whether patient is a good surgical risk
    C. interpretation of a radiologic study
    D. technical interpretation of electrocardiogram

REFERENCE: Abdelhak, p 109
               Green and Bowie, p 142

58. The health care providers at your hospital do a very thorough job of periodic open record review to ensure the completeness of record documentation. A qualitative review of surgical records would likely include checking for documentation regarding
    A. the presence or absence of such items as preoperative and postoperative diagnosis, description of findings, and specimens removed.
    B. whether a postoperative infection occurred and how it was treated.
    C. the quality of follow-up care.
    D. whether the severity of illness and/or intensity of service warranted acute level care.

REFERENCE: Abdelhak, p 110
               Green and Bowie, p 153
               Johns, p 62
               LaTour and Eichenwald-Maki, p 182, 195

59. In your facility it has become critical that information regarding patients who are transferred to the oncology unit be sent to an outpatient scheduling system to facilitate outpatient appointments. This information can be obtained most efficiently from

A. generic screens used by record abstractors.
B. disease index.
C. R-ADT system.
D. indicator monitoring program.

REFERENCE: Abdelhak, p 163
               Johns, p 68
               LaTour and Eichenwald-Maki, p 214

60. In your facility, the health care providers from every discipline document progress notes sequentially on the same form. Your facility is utilizing

A. integrated progress notes.   C. source-oriented records.
B. interdisciplinary treatment plans.   D. SOAP notes.

REFERENCE: Abdelhak, p 109
               Green and Bowie, p 146
               Johns, p 54

61. Which of the following services is LEAST likely to be provided by a facility accredited by CARF?

A. chronic pain management   C. brain injury management
B. palliative care   D. vocational evaluation

REFERENCE: Abdelhak, p 26-29
               Green and Bowie, p 30
               Johns, p 85-88
               Peden, p 375-377, 448

62. Which method of identification of authorship or authentication of entries would be inappropriate to use in a patient's health record?

A. written signature of the provider of care
B. identifiable initials of a nurse writing a nursing note
C. a unique identification code entered by the person making the report
D. delegated use of computer key by radiology secretary

REFERENCE: Abdelhak, p 114
               Green and Bowie, p 80-82
               LaTour and Eichenwald-Maki, p 196-197

63. Though you work in an integrated delivery network, not all systems in your network communicate with one another. As you meet with your partner organizations, you begin to sell them on the concept of an important development intended to support the exchange of health information across the continuum within a geographical community. You are promoting that your organization join a

A. data warehouse.
B. regional health information organization.
C. continuum of care.
D. data retrieval portal group.

REFERENCE: Abdelhak, p 82-83
               LaTour and Eichenwald-Maki, p 217-218
               McWay, p 181

64. As a trauma registrar working in an emergency department, you want to begin comparing your trauma care services to other hospital-based emergency departments. To ensure that your facility is collecting the same data as other facilities, you review elements from which data set?
   A. DEEDS
   B. UHDDS
   C. MDS
   D. ORYX

REFERENCE: Green and Bowie, p 243
              LaTour and Eichenwald-Maki, p 154

65. As a new HIM manager of an acute care facility, you have been asked to update the facility's policy for a physician's verbal orders in accordance with Joint Commission standards and state law. Your first area of concern is the qualifications of those individuals in your facility who have been authorized to record verbal orders. For this information, you will consult
   A. Consolidated Manual for Hospitals
   B. Federal Register
   C. Policy and Procedure Manual
   D. Hospital Bylaws, Rules, and Regulations

REFERENCE   Green and Bowie, p 144
             Johns, p 54

66. Reviewing a medical record to ensure that all diagnoses are justified by documentation throughout the chart is an example of
   A. peer review.
   B. quantitative review.
   C. qualitative review.
   D. legal analysis.

REFERENCE:
              Abdelhak, p 127
              Green and Bowie, p 102
              LaTour and Eichenwald-Maki, p 194-195
              McWay, p 104

67. Accreditation by Joint Commission is a voluntary activity for a facility and it is
   A. considered unnecessary by most health care facilities.
   B. required for state licensure in all states.
   C. conducted in each facility annually.
   D. required for reimbursement of certain patient groups..

REFERENCE: Abdelhak, p 15

68. Which of the following indices might be protected from unauthorized access through the use of unique identifier codes assigned to members of the medical staff?
   A. disease index
   B. procedure index
   C. master patient index
   D. physician index

REFERENCE: Green and Bowie, p 230
              Johns, p 377
              LaTour and Eichenwald-Maki, p 289

69. Which of the four distinct components of the problem-oriented record serves to help index documentation throughout the record?
   A. database
   B. problem list
   C. initial plan
   D. progress notes

REFERENCE: Abdelhak, p 114-115
               Green and Bowie, p 89-90
               Johns, p 91-99

70. As supervisor of the cancer registry, you report the registry's annual caseload to administration. The most efficient way to retrieve this information would be to use
   A. patient abstracts.
   B. patient index.
   C. accession register.
   D. follow-up files.

REFERENCE: Johns, p 401-402
               LaTour and Eichenwald-Maki, p 290-291

71. An important element of data quality is security in preventing unauthorized access, corruption, misuse, and loss of data. Both technical and procedural methods will be used with the CPR to control and manage confidential information. An example of a procedural method for protecting data is
   A. confidentiality statements signed by all staff.
   B. limiting access of certain screens based on the staff's need to know.
   C. auditing capability of system to track data access.
   D. computer backup systems.

REFERENCE: Green and Bowie, p 271
               Johns, p 850

72. Select the appropriate situation for which a final progress note may legitimately be substituted for a discharge summary in an inpatient medical record.
   A. patient admitted with COPD 1/4/2008 and discharged 1/7/2008
   B. Baby Boy Hiltz, born 1/5/2008, maintained normal status, discharged 1/7/2008
   C. Baby Boy Hiltz's mother admitted 1/5/2008, C-section delivery, discharged 1/7/2008
   D. Baby Boy Doe admitted 1/3/2008, died 1/4/2008

REFERENCE: Abdelhak, p 109
               Green and Bowie, p 133-134
               LaTour and Eichenwald-Maki, p 183

73. Which of the following is a type of laser technology that is ideal for health records because it stores data in a permanent capacity, prohibiting users from altering, misfiling, or erasing data?
   A. EDI
   B. OCR
   C. WORM
   D. COM

REFERENCE: Abdelhak, p 257
               Green and Bowie, p 94
               LaTour and Eichenwald-Maki, p 205

74. As information security officer, you are revising the policies at your rehabilitation facility for handling all patient clinical information. Your best resource for checking out specific accreditation standards and guidelines is the
    A. Conditions of Participation for Rehabilitation Facilities
    B. Medical Staff Bylaws, Rules, and Regulations
    C. Joint Commission manual
    D. CARF manual

REFERENCE: Green and Bowie, p 30
               Johns, p 87-88
               LaTour and Eichenwald-Maki, p 496

75. Which of the four distinct components of the problem-oriented record contains the medical and social history of the patient?
    A. database   C. initial plan
    B. problem list   D. progress notes

REFERENCE: Abdelhak, p 114-115
               Green and Bowie, p 89
               Johns, p 97-98

76. Which of the following is a secondary data source that would be used to quickly gather the health records of all juvenile patients treated for diabetes within the past 6 months?
    A. disease index   C. pediatric census sheet
    B. patient register   D. procedure index

REFERENCE: Green and Bowie, p 230
               Johns, p 376-377
               LaTour and Eichenwald-Maki, p 289

77. In a manual record tracking system, outguides replace a file that has been checked out of the system. A secondary function of outguides is to
    A. serve as a visual check for misfiled records.
    B. expedite correct placement of refiled records.
    C. enhance the use of file guides.
    D. cross-reference a file that has been moved forward to a new number.

REFERENCE:
               Abdelhak, p 237
               Green and Bowie, p 214
               Johns, p 349

78. Key reports in a health record, such as history and physicals, discharge summaries, and operative reports, are generally dictated and transcribed. This recommended standard contributes most to data
    A. timeliness.   C. legibility.
    B. accuracy.   D. security.

REFERENCE: Abdelhak, p 177
               Green and Bowie, p 83

79. In preparation for an upcoming site visit by Joint Commission, you discover that the number of delinquent records for the preceding month exceeded 50% of discharged patients. Even more alarming was the pattern you noticed in the type of delinquencies. Which of the following represents the most serious pattern of delinquencies? Fifteen percent of delinquent records show
    A. missing signatures on progress notes
    B. missing discharge summaries
    C. absence of SOAP format in progress notes
    D. missing operative reports

REFERENCE: Abdelhak, p 110
                Green and Bowie, p 153
                LaTour and Eichenwald-Maki, p 182, 196

80. A primary focus of screen format design in a health record computer application should be to ensure that
    A. programmers develop standard screen formats for all hospitals.
    B. the user is capturing essential data elements.
    C. paper forms are easily converted to computer forms.
    D. data fields can be randomly accessed.

REFERENCE: Abdelhak, p 116
                Johns, p 370
                LaTour and Eichenwald-Maki, p 197-198

81. A quality improvement team is focusing on the unacceptable number of unsigned doctors' orders in your facility. The most effective method for increasing the timeliness of signatures on orders and positively impacting the patient care process would be
    A. performing a retrospective review where all orders can be flagged at one time.
    B. holding a printed order sheet on the medical care unit at least 24 hours postdischarge to give the physician time to sign.
    C. developing an open-record review process.
    D. devising a signature sheet for the attending physician to sign prospectively that will apply to all orders given during the current episode of his patient's care.

REFERENCE: Johns, p 351
                LaTour and Eichenwald-Maki, p 180

82. Before making recommendations to the Executive Committee regarding new physicians who have applied for active membership, the Credentials Committee must query the
    A. peer review organization.
    B. National Practitioner Data Bank.
    C. risk manager.
    D. Health Plan Employer Data and Information Set.

REFERENCE: Abdelhak, p 468
                Green and Bowie, p 16
                Johns, p 412
                LaTour and Eichenwald-Maki, p 16-17

83. A qualitative analysis of OB records reveals a pattern of inconsistent data entries when comparing documentation of the same data elements captured on both the prenatal form and labor and delivery form. The characteristic of data quality that is being compromised in this case is data
    A. reliability.
    B. accessibility.
    C. legibility.
    D. completeness.

REFERENCE: Green and Bowie, p 247
                Johns, p 421
                LaTour and Eichenwald-Maki, p 944

84. Medicare rules state that the use of verbal orders should be infrequent and used only when the orders cannot be written or given electronically. In addition, verbal orders must be
    A. written within 24 hours of the patient's admission.
    B. accepted by a charge nurses only.
    C. co-signed by the attending physician within 12 hours of giving the order.
    D. accepted by persons authorized by hospital regulations and procedures.

REFERENCES: Green and Bowie, p 144
                Johns, p 537
                LaTour and Eichenwald-Maki, p 180

85. The lack of a discharge order may indicate that the patient left against medical advice. If this situation occurs, you would expect to see the circumstances of the leave
    A. documented in an incident report and filed in the patient's health record.
    B. reported as a potentially compensable event.
    C. reported to the Executive Committee.
    D. documented in both the progress notes and the discharge summary

REFERENCE: Abdelhak, p 109
                LaTour and Eichenwald-Maki, p 180

86. Your committee is charged with developing procedures for the Health Information Services staff of a new home health agency. You recommend that the staff routinely check to verify that a summary on each patient is provided to the attending physician so that he or she can review, update, and recertify the patient as appropriate. The time frame for requiring this summary is at least every
    A. week.
    B. month.
    C. 60 days.
    D. 90 days.

REFERENCE: Abdelhak, p 138
                Johns, p 85
                Peden, p 425

87. You want to review the one document in your facility that will spell out the documentation requirements for patient records; designate the time frame for completion by the active medical staff; and indicate the penalties for failure to comply with these record standards. Your best resource will be
    A. medical staff bylaws.
    B. quality management plan.
    C. Joint Commission accreditation manual.
    D. medical staff rules and regulations.

REFERENCE: Green and Bowie, p 16
               Johns, p 620
               LaTour and Eichenwald-Maki, p 504-505

88. A quarterly review reveals the following data for Springfield Hospital:

Springfield Hospital Quarterly Statistics	
Average monthly discharges	1,820
Average monthly operative procedures	458
Number incomplete records	1,002
Number delinquent records	590
Number records delinquent due to missing H&P	30
Number records delinquent due to missing operative report	10

What is the percentage of incomplete records during this quarter?
A. 55%   C. 33%
B. 54%   D. 32%

REFERENCE: Horton, p 17-18, 106
               Koch, p 48

89. Referring to the data in the previous question, determine the delinquent record rate for Springfield Hospital.
    A. 55%   C. 33%
    B. 32%   D. 54%

REFERENCE: Green and Bowie, p 83-84
               Horton, p 17-18, 106
               Koch, p 48

90. Still referring to the information in the table in question number 88, which area represents the greatest area of concern for Springfield Hospital's compliance with Joint Commission standards?
    A. incomplete records   C. delinquent H&P
    B. delinquent records   D. delinquent operative reports

REFERENCE: Abdelhak, p 110
               Green and Bowie, p 83-84
               Horton, p 17-18, 106

91. In an acute care facility, the responsibility for educating physicians and other health care providers regarding proper documentation policies belongs to the
    A. information security manager.
    C. health information manager.
    B. clinical data specialist.
    D. risk manager.

REFERENCE: Green and Bowie, p 101-102
                Johns, p 652
                LaTour and Eichenwald-Maki, p 195

92. For inpatients, the first data item collected of a clinical nature is usually
    A. principal diagnosis.
    C. admitting diagnosis.
    B. expected payer.
    D. review of systems.

REFERENCE: Johns, p 51
                Green and Bowie, p 130

93. Documentation found in acute care health records should include core measure quality indicators required for compliance with Medicare's Health Care Quality Improvement Program (HCQIP). A typical indicator for pneumonia patients is
    A. beta blocker at discharge.
    B. blood culture before first antibiotic received.
    C. early administration of aspirin.
    D. discharged on antithrombotic.

REFERENCE: Johns, p 513

94. One record documentation requirement shared by BOTH acute care and emergency departments is
    A. patient's condition on discharge.
    C. advance directive.
    B. time and means of arrival.
    D. problem list.

REFERENCE: Abdelhak, p 109, 133
                Green and Bowie, p 130
                Johns, p 68, 78-79

95. In addition to diagnostic and therapeutic orders from the attending physician, you would expect every completed inpatient health record to contain
    A. standing orders.
    C. stop orders.
    B. telephone orders.
    D. discharge order.

REFERENCE: Abdelhak, p 108
                Green and Bowie, p 144
                Johns, p 54

96. As the Chair of the Forms Committee at your hospital, you are helping to design a template for house staff members to use while collecting information for the history and physical. When asked to explain how "review of systems" differs from "physical exam," you explain that the review of systems is used to document
    A. objective symptoms observed by the physician.
    B. past and current activities, such as smoking and drinking habits.
    C. a chronological description of patient's present condition from time of onset to present.
    D. subjective symptoms that the patient may have forgotten to mention or that may have seemed unimportant.

REFERENCE: Green and Bowie, p 138

97. Skilled nursing facilities may choose to submit MDS data using RAVEN software, or software purchased commercially through a vendor, provided that the software meets
    A. Joint Commission standards.
    B. NHIN standards.
    C. HL-7 standards.
    D. CMS standards.

REFERENCE: Peden, p 353

Answer Key for Health Data Content and Standards

ANSWER   EXPLANATION

1. B   (C and D) Although a gross description of tissue removed may be mentioned on the operative note or discharge summary, only the pathology report will contain a microscopic description.

2. B   Answers A, C, and D represent items collected on Medicare inpatients according to UHDDS requirements. Only B represents a data item collected more typically in long-term care settings and required in the MDS.

3. B   Information of a higher sensitivity (e.g., substance abuse, psychiatric treatment, etc.) should be defined in release of information policies and special measures taken to protect against unauthorized access to this information. In computer-based systems, control is often achieved by limiting access to authorized personnel via ID or passwords.

4. B   Every case entered into the registry is assigned a unique accession number preceded by the accession year, or the year the case is entered into the database.

5. C   Factual summaries investigating unexpected facility events should not be treated as part of the patient's health information and therefore would not be recorded in the health record.

6. D   (A, B, and C) Patient care plans, pharmacy consultations, and transfer summaries are likely to be found on the records of long-term care patients.

7. B   Auto authentication is a policy adopted by some facilities that allows physicians to state in advance that transcribed reports should automatically be considered approved and signed (or authenticated) when the physician fails to make corrections within a pre-established time frame (e.g., "Consider it signed if I do not make changes within 7 days."). Another version of this practice is when physicians authorize the HIM department to send weekly lists of unsigned documents. The physician then signs the list in lieu of signing each individual report. Neither practice ensures that the physician has reviewed and approved each report individually.

8. A   The antepartum record should include a comprehensive history and physical exam on each OB patient visit, with particular attention to menstrual and reproductive history.

9. C   Joint Commission and COP allow a legible copy of a recent H&P done in a doctor's office in lieu of an admission H&P as long as interval changes are documented in the record upon admission. In addition, when the patient is readmitted within 30 days for the same or a related problem, an interval history and physical exam may be completed if the original H&P is readily available.

10. A   The major sources of case findings for cancer registry programs are the pathology department, the disease index, and the logs of patients treated in radiology and other outpatient departments. B. The number index identifies new health record numbers and the patients to whom they were assigned. C. The physicians' index identifies all patients treated by each doctor. D. The patient index links each patient treated in a facility with the health number under which the clinical information can be located.

11. A   Those who make entries in the medical record are given that privilege by the medical staff. Only house staff members who are under the supervision of active staff members require countersignatures once the privilege has been granted.

12. C   The statute of limitations for each state is information that is crucial in determining record retention schedules.

13. D   Authentication by signature stamps requires a written agreement with the facility not to delegate the use of the stamps. Similarly, in a computer-based system, it is important to ensure that personal identification codes used to authenticate entries are used only by the persons to whom they are assigned. A. Fingerprint signatures are individualized automatically.

Answer Key for Health Data Content and Standards

ANSWER   EXPLANATION

14. C A. Some reference to the patient's history may be found in the discharge summary, but not a detailed history. B. The attending physician records the discharge summary. D. Codes are usually recorded on a different form in the record.

15. D A and B deal with issues directly linked to quality of care reviews. C deals with risk management. Only D points to a review aimed at evaluating the quality of documentation in the health record.

16. B Although the nursing staff, hospital administration, and the health information management professional play a role in ensuring an accurate and complete record, the major responsibility lies with the attending physician.

17. C Periodic, concurrent chart review contributes to the timeliness and accuracy of documentation in a way that retrospective review and audits cannot. D. Occurrence screening is designed to identify documentation of adverse events for which the hospital would be liable.

18. C Unlike the acute care hospital, where most health care practitioners document separately, the patient care plan is the foundation around which patient care is organized in long-term care facilities because it contains the unique perspective of each discipline involved.

19. A B. Utilization review committees deal with the issues of the medical necessity of admissions and efficient utilization of facility resources. C. Risk management committees consider methods for reducing injury and financial loss. D. Joint conference committees act as a liaison between the governing body and the medical staff.

20. B Because the source-oriented record is organized into sections according to the practitioners who are the source of treatment, all lab treatments would be arranged in chronological order within a lab section, making it easy to compare all values.

21. D Joint Commission suggests that HIM department, nursing, medical staff, administrative personnel, and other services participate in the record reviews.

22. A Highly sensitive information (e.g., psychiatric records) should be defined as sensitive and special measures should be taken to protect against unauthorized access. In computer-based information systems, control is often achieved by limit of access to authorized personnel through the designated use of ID/passwords or access denial of certain information types.

23. A Joint Commission specifies that H&Ps must be completed within 24 hours.

24. D CPOE systems allow physicians to enter orders, including medication orders, and receive clinical advice about contraindications and dosages of various drugs. These systems also enhance the legibility of medication orders—a key issue in patient safety.

25. D A. The disease index is a listing in diagnostic code number order. B. The physician index is a listing of cases in order by physician name or number. C. The MPI cross-references the patient name and medical record number.

26. D A, B, and C all refer to a computer application of managing health information, but only answer D deals with the clinical application of data entry into the patient's record at the time and location of service.

27. D Most facilities use bar-coded patient identification to ensure proper indexing into the imaging system.

28. A Pharmacy consults are required for elderly patients who typically take multiple medications. These consults review for potential drug interactions and/or discrepancies in medications given and those ordered.

29. B The average health record is viewed by approximately 150 end users, yet the paper-based health record can be viewed by only one at a time. In contrast, the EHR can be accessed by multiple users simultaneously in remote locations.

Answer Key for Health Data Content and Standards

ANSWER   EXPLANATION

30. C   In accession number 2008–0001/00, "2008" represents the year that the patient first entered the database; "0001" indicates that this was the first case entered that year; "00" indicates that this patient has only one known neoplasm.

31. C   Biometrics is a type of identifier that measures a borrower's unique physical characteristics, such as fingerprints or a retinal scan, and compares them to a stored digital template to identify the borrower.

32. D   CMS (HCFA) publishes both proposed and final rules for the Conditions of Participation for hospitals in the daily Federal Register.

33. D   A. An interval H&P can be used when a patient is readmitted for the same or related problem within 30 days. B and C. No matter how long the patient stays or how minor the condition, an H&P is required.

34 B   A. The MDS is designed for use in long-term care facilities. C. The COP is the set of regulations that health care institutions must follow to receive Medicare reimbursement. D. The *Federal Register* is a daily government newspaper for publishing proposed and final rules of federal agencies.

35. C   Readmission to the hospital requires documentation in the follow-up file. B and D. Only one accession number and one master index card are assigned for each patient entered into the registry. A. An abstract is prepared when the case is entered into the database.

36. A   The needs of the end user are always the primary concern when designing systems.

37. C   Answers A, B, and D are required items in BOTH acute and ER records.

38. D   Answers A and B are items that should be documented on any inpatient record. Answer C reflects a data item you would expect to find on ER records only.

39. B   All health record signatures should be identified by a minimum of name and discipline, e.g., "J. Smith, P.T." Other types of authentication other than signature (such as written initials or computer entry) must be uniquely identifiable.

40. C   The needs of the user are the primary concern in forms design.

41. B   A and C. In these situations a transfer summary or pertinent copies from the inpatient health record may accompany the patient, but the original record stays on the premises.

42. A   A recommendation for improvement from Joint Commission is indicated if the number of delinquent records is greater than 50% or if the percentage of records with delinquent records due to missing H&Ps exceeds 2% of the average monthly discharges. In the month of April, both of these delinquency problems are reflected. The percentage of incomplete records is not relevant.

43. D   A represents the assessment statement, B the objective, and C the plan.

44. B   OBRA mandates comprehensive functional assessments of long-term care residents using the Minimum Data Set for Long-Term Care.

45. A   Answers B and D are types of data sets for collecting data in long-term (MDS) and acute care (UHDDS) facilities. A data dictionary should include security levels for each field as well as definitions for all entities.

46. B   COP requires a consultation report on patients who are not a good surgical risk, as well as those with obscure diagnoses, patients whose physicians have doubts as to the best therapeutic measure to be taken, and patients for whom there is a question of criminal activity.

47. B   The medical history, including a review of systems and chief complaint, is information supplied by the patient. A physical assessment adds objective data to the subjective data provided by the patient in the history.

Answer Key for Health Data Content and Standards

ANSWER   EXPLANATION

48. D This meets both Joint Commission and COP standards.
49. B An autopsy is a lengthy procedure with outside lab results sometimes required. As many as 60 days may pass before reports are completed. A provisional autopsy diagnosis should be recorded within 3 days.
50. C Joint Commission requires that a detailed OP note be written in the health record when expeditious transcription of the dictated report is impossible to maintain continuity of care.
51. C Joint Commission standards require the surgeon to document the history and physical examination prior to surgery.
52. D AHIMA's Position Statement supports that point-of-care documentation raises documentation standards and improves patient care. It is defined as data entry that occurs at the point and location of service.
53. D Answers A, B, and C are examples of secondary data sources.
54. A The medical history (including chief complaint, history of present illness, past medical history, personal history, family history, and a review of systems) is provided by the patient or the most knowledgeable available source. The physical examination adds objective data to the subjective data provided by the patient. The exam includes all body systems.
55. D Quantitative analysis involves checking for the presence or absence of necessary reports and/or signatures, while qualitative analysis may involve checking documentation consistency, such as comparing a patient's pharmacy drug profile with the medication administration record.
56. C A, B, and D all represent common checks performed by a quantitative analysis clerk: missing reports, signatures, or patient identification. Answer C represents a more in-depth review dealing with the quality of the data documented.
57. B A, C, and D represent routine interpretations that are not normally considered to be consultations.
58. A B represents an appropriate job for the infection control officer. Answer C represents the clinical care evaluation process, rather than the review of quality documentation. Answer D is a function of the utilization review program.
59. C For tracking in-house patients who have been transferred to a specialty unit, the best source of information is the registration-admission, discharge, and transfer system.
60. A Progress notes may be integrated or they may be separated, with nurses, physicians, and other health care providers writing on designated forms for each discipline.
61. B The Commission on Accreditation of Rehabilitation Facilities is an independent accrediting agency for rehabilitation facilities. Palliative care (answer B) is most likely to be provided at a hospice.
62. D Written signatures, identifiable initials, unique computer codes, and rubber stamp signatures may all be allowed as legitimate means of authenticating an entry. However, the use of codes and stamped signatures MUST be confined to the owners and they are never to be used by anyone else.
63. B Regional health information organizations are intended to support health information exchange within a geographic region.
64. A A. Data Elements for Emergency Departments—recommended data set for hospital-based emergency departments; B. Uniform Hospital Data Set—required data set for acute care hospitals; C. Minimum Data Set—required data set for long-term care facilities; D. ORYX—an initiative of Joint Commission whereby five core measures are implemented to improve safety and quality of health care.

Answer Key for Health Data Content and Standards

    ANSWER   EXPLANATION

65. D   Although Joint Commission, CMS, and state laws may include standards for verbal orders, the specific information regarding which employees have been given authority to transcribe verbal orders in your facility should be located in your hospital's bylaws, rules, and regulations.

66. C   A. Peer review typically involves quality of care issues rather than quality of documentation issues. D. Legal analysis ensures that the record entries would be acceptable in a court of law.

67. D   A. Advantages of accreditation are numerous and include financial and legal incentives. B. State licensure is required for accreditation, but not the reverse. C. Joint Commission conducts unannounced on-site surveys approximately every 3 years.

68. D   Because information contained in the physicians' index is considered confidential, identification codes are often used rather than the physicians' names.

69. B   In a POMR, the database contains the history and physical; the problem list includes titles, numbers, and dates of problems and serves as a table of contents of the record; the initial plan describes diagnostic, therapeutic, and patient education plans; and the progress notes document the progress of the patient throughout the episode of care, summarized in a discharge summary or transfer note at the end of the stay.

70. C   The accession register is a permanent log of all the cases entered into the database. Each number assigned is preceded by the accession year, making it easy to assess annual workloads.

71. A   Answers B, C, and D all represent technical methods of protecting computerized data. Additional procedural techniques include developing policies, procedures, and educational training, which address confidentiality.

72. B   A final progress note may substitute for a discharge summary in the following cases: patients who are hospitalized less than 48 hours with problems of a minor nature, normal newborns, and uncomplicated obstetrical deliveries. Answer A does not qualify because of the nature of the problem and the length of stay. Answer C describes a complicated delivery, and answer D cites a severely ill patient rather than one with a minor problem.

73. C   In answer A, EDI stands for "electronic data interchange." In answer B, OCR stands for "optical character recognition." In answer D, COM stands for "computer output microfiche." WORM stands for "write once, read many" and refers to the laser technology that stores data permanently and allows users to read, but not alter, the data.

74. D   The manual published by the Commission on Accreditation of Rehabilitation Facilities will have the most specific and comprehensive standards for a rehabilitation facility.

75. A   In a POMR, the database contains the history and physical; the problem list includes titles, numbers, and dates of problems, and serves as a table of contents of the record; the initial plan describes diagnostic, therapeutic, and patient education plans; and the progress notes document the progress of a patient throughout the episode of care, summarized in a discharge summary or transfer note at the end of the stay.

76. A   The disease index is compiled as a result of abstracting patient code numbers into a computer database, allowing a variety of reports to be generated.

77. B   An outguide is a plastic folder used in place of the record when the record has been removed from the files. When refiling the record, the outguide often speeds up the process of visually identifying the empty place in the file.

Answer Key for Health Data Content and Standards

ANSWER   EXPLANATION

78. C   Answers A and B. The processes of dictation and transcribing reports may actually delay its appearance on the chart, and transcription errors may be more frequent than errors in handwritten reports. D. These processes should not affect record security.

79. D   Answers A and B. Both signature omissions and discharge summary reports can be captured after discharge, but history and physicals should be on the chart within 24 hours of the patient's admission. Answer C. the SOAP format is not a requirement of Joint Commission. Answer D. Institutions are given a Type I recommendation when 2% of delinquent records are due to missing history and physicals or operative reports.

80. B   Both paper-based and computer-based records share similar forms and view design considerations. Among these are the selection and sequencing of essential data items.

81. C   A and B. Signing orders after discharge does not affect the patient's care process. D. Although this process would speed up the signature process, it is not a legally sound method of obtaining signatures on orders.

82. B   With the passage of the Health Care Quality Improvement Act of 1986, the NPDB was established. Hospitals are required to query the data bank before granting clinical privileges to physicians.

83. A   Data reliability implies that data are consistent, no matter how many times the same data are collected and entered into the system. Accessibility implies that data are available to authorized people when and where needed. Legibility implies data that are readable. Completeness implies that all required data are present in the information system.

84. D   Only persons designated by hospital policies and procedures and state and federal law are to accept verbal orders.

85. D   A. Incident reports are written accounts of unusual events that have an adverse effect on a patient, employee, or facility visitor and should never be filed with the patient's record. B. PCEs are occurrences that could result in financial liability at some future time. A patient leaving AMA does not in itself suggest a PCE. C. It is not typical to report AMAs to the Executive Committee. D. Documenting the event is crucial in protecting the legal interests of the health care team and facility.

86. C   This 60-day time frame is often referred to as the patient's certification period. Recertification can continue every 62 days until the patient is discharged from home health services.

87. D   Although the medical staff bylaws reflect general principles and policies of the medical staff, the rules and regulations outline the details for implementing these principles, including the process and time frames for completing records, and the penalties for failure to comply.

88. A   Using the basic rate formula, calculate as follows:
Incomplete records × 100 divided by average monthly discharges, or
$$\frac{1{,}002 \times 100}{1820} = 55.1\%$$

89. B   Using the basic rate formula, calculate as follows:
Delinquent records × 100 divided by average monthly discharges, or
$$\frac{590 \times 100}{1820} = 32.4\%$$

Answer Key for Health Data Content and Standards

ANSWER   EXPLANATION

90. D   Using the basic rate formula, the incomplete record rate is 55%, but records that are incomplete have not yet met the criteria for delinquent records. The delinquent record rate is 32%; the delinquent H&P rate is 1.6%; and the delinquent operative record rate is 2.2% (delinquent records × 100 divided by average monthly procedures). Even though the delinquent record rate is 32%, this does not exceed the Joint Commission requirement to keep this statistic below 50%. The percentage of delinquent operative reports is a more serious deficiency (should be kept below 2%), because operative reports should be completed immediately after surgery, not postdischarge.

91. C   Although all of the positions listed have an interest in proper documentation in an acute care facility, the health information manager is in the best position to keep abreast of documentation standards and advocate change where poor documentation patterns exist.

92. C   Clinical data include all health care information collected during a patient's episode of care. During the registration or intake process, the admitting diagnosis, provided by the attending physician, is entered on the face sheet. If the patient is admitted through the ED, the chief complaint listed on the ED record is usually the first clinical data collected. A. The principal diagnosis is often not known until after diagnostic tests are conducted. B. Demographic data are not clinical in nature. D. The review of systems is collected during the history and physical, which is typically done after admission to the hospital.

93 B   Answers A and C represent quality indicators for patients with acute myocardial infarction; answer D represents a quality indicator for stroke patients.

94. A   B. Time and means of arrival is required on ED records only. C. Evidence of known advance directive is required on inpatient records only. D. Problem list is required on ambulatory records by the third visit.

95. D   Although many patient health records may feasibly contain all of the orders listed, only the discharge order is required to document the formal release of a patient from the facility. Absence of a discharge order would indicate that the patient left against medical advice and this event should be thoroughly documented as well.

96. D   Answer A refers to the Physical Exam. Answer B refers to the Social History. Answer C refers to the History of Present Illness.

97. D   MDS data is reported directly to Centers for Medicare and Medicaid Services and must conform to agency standards.

REFERENCES

Abdelhak, M., Grostick, S., Hanken, M.A., & Jacobs, E. (Eds.). (2007). *Health information: Management of a strategic resource* (3rd ed.). Philadelphia: W. B. Saunders.

Green, M. A., & Bowie, J. (2006). *Essentials of health information management: Principles and practices.* Clifton Park, NY: Thomson Delmar Learning.

Horton, L. (2006) *Calculating and reporting health care statistics* (2nd ed.) Chicago: American Health Information Management Association (AHIMA).

Johns, M. L. (2006). *Health information management technology: An applied approach* (2nd ed.). Chicago: American Health Information Management Association (AHIMA).

Koch, G. (2008). *Basic allied health statistics and analysis* (3rd ed.). Clifton Park, NY: Thompson Delmar Learning.

LaTour, K., & Eichenwald-Maki, S. (2006). *Health information management: Concepts, principles and practice* (2nd ed.). Chicago: American Health Information Management Association (AHIMA).

McWay, D. C. (2003). *Legal aspects of health information management.* Clifton Park, NY: Thompson Delmar Learning.

McWay, D. C. (2008). *Today's health information management, an integrated approach.* Clifton Park, NY: Thompson Delmar Learning.

Peden, A. H. (2005). *Comparative health information management* (2nd ed.). Clifton Park, NY: Thompson Delmar Learning.

IV. Information Retention and Access

Marjorie H. McNeill, PhD, RHIA, CCS

1. Stewardship guidelines that lead to responsible handling of patient health information include all but which one of the following actions?
   A. Educate consumers about their rights and responsibilities regarding the use of their personal health information.
   B. Extend privacy and security principles into all aspects of the data use, access, and control program adopted in the organization.
   C. Honor the patient-centric direction of the national agenda.
   D. Take a compromising position toward optimal interpretation of nonspecific regulations and laws.

REFERENCE: Burrington-Brown, Hjort, and Washington, p 63-66

2. If there is more than one patient with the identical last name, first name, and middle initial, the master patient index entries are then arranged according to
   A. date of birth.   C. social security number.
   B. date of admission.   D. mother's maiden name.

REFERENCE: Abdelhak, p 224
               Green and Bowie, p 199
               Johns, p 783

3. Which one of the following is NOT a step in developing a record retention program?
   A. conducting an inventory of the facility's records
   B. determining the format and location of storage
   C. assigning all records the same retention period
   D. destroying records that are no longer needed

REFERENCE: Green and Bowie, p 96-97
               LaTour and Eichenwald-Maki, p 202-206
               McWay, p 112-113

4. What type of filing system is being used if records are filed in the following order: 12-23-75, 12-34-29, 12-35-71, 13-42-14, 14-32-79?
   A. terminal digit   C. social security number
   B. straight numeric   D. middle digit

REFERENCE: Abdelhak, p 224-225
               Green and Bowie, p 200-203
               Johns, p 340-343

5. If there are 150,000 records and the HIM Department receives 3,545 requests for records within a given period of time, what is the request rate?
   A. 2.4%   C. 4.6%
   B. 3.5%   D. 5.1%

REFERENCE: Johns, p 372-373
               LaTour and Eichenwald-Maki, p 201-202
               McWay, p 193-197

6. Advantages of a centralized filing system include all but which one of the following?
   A. There is less transportation time and effort when a facility operates from several sites.
   B. There is less duplication of effort to create, maintain, and store records.
   C. Record control and security are easier to maintain.
   D. There is decreased cost in space and equipment.

REFERENCE: Abdelhak, p 223
                 Green and Bowie, p 203-205
                 McWay, p 111-113

7. In a terminal digit filing system, what would be the record number immediately in front of record number 01-06-26?
   A. 00-06-26   C. 03-06-26
   B. 02-06-26   D. 99-99-25

REFERENCE: Abdelhak, p 225
                 Green and Bowie, p 201-202
                 LaTour and Eichenwald-Maki, p 200-201
                 Johns, p 342

8. The HIM Department at General Hospital has been experiencing an average 30-minute delay in the retrieval of records requested by the Emergency Department. Which one of the following corrective actions would be most effective in reducing the delay in retrieval of requested records?
   A. offer a prize to the employee who locates the requested records first
   B. review and possibly re-engineer the retrieval process to decrease retrieval time
   C. allow the requesters to retrieve the record themselves
   D. increase file area staff to include one additional file clerk devoted to pulling records for the emergency room

REFERENCE: Abdelhak, p 237-238, 636
                 McWay, p 261-262

9. Which one of the following is NOT an advantage of a computerized master patient index?
   A. It allows access to data alphabetically, phonetically, or by date of birth, social security number, medical record, or billing number.
   B. It solves most space and retrieval problems.
   C. It provides other departments with immediate access to the information maintained in the master patient index.
   D. Duplication of patient registration can never occur.

REFERENCE: Abdelhak, p 226-233
                 Green and Bowie, p 230
                 Johns, p 375-376
                 McWay, p 115-116

10. Color coding of record folders is used to assist in the control of
    A. record tracking.   C. record completion.
    B. loose reports.   D. misfiles.

REFERENCE: Abdelhak, p 234
                 Green and Bowie, p 208-209
                 Johns, p 347
                 LaTour and Eichenwald-Maki, p 201

11. Which of the following would NOT be considered secondary data?
    A. disease index
    B. implant registry
    C. X-ray
    D. incident report

REFERENCE: Green and Bowie, p 226
              McWay, p 115

12. Under the Patient Self-Determination Act of 1990, advance directives
    A. are required to be included in the patient chart.
    B. are not required to be included in the patient chart.
    C. require a doctor's approval.
    D. must be prepared by an attorney.

REFERENCE: Abdelhak, p 105
              Green and Bowie, p 119-122
              Johns, p 75
              McWay, p 65, 85

13. A new Health Information Department has purchased 200 units of 6-shelf files and plans to implement a terminal digit filing system. How many shelves should be allocated to each primary number?
    A. 6
    B. 8
    C. 10
    D. 12

REFERENCE: Abdelhak, p 226

14. A 200-bed acute care hospital currently has 15 years of records in hard copy and filing space is limited. What action should be taken?
    A. Return inactive records to each individual patient.
    B. Destroy records of all deceased patients.
    C. Destroy inactive records that exceed the statute of limitations.
    D. Maintain the records indefinitely in hard copy.

REFERENCE: Abdelhak, p 241
              Green and Bowie, p 96-97
              LaTour and Eichenwald-Maki, p 203-206
              McWay, p 110-113

15. Which filing system would provide the most convenient method for the record retrieval of 200 patients consecutively admitted to the hospital?
    A. terminal digit
    B. unit
    C. straight numeric
    D. serial unit

REFERENCE: Abdelhak, p 224-225
              Green and Bowie, p 201
              Johns, p 340-343
              McWay, p 11

16. What is the chief criterion for determining record inactivity?
    A. Medicare's definition of inactivity
    B. amount of space available for storage of newer records
    C. efficiency of microfilming
    D. preference of the medical staff

REFERENCE: Abdelhak, p 234-235
                    Green and Bowie, p 97
                    LaTour and Eichenwald-Maki, p 204

17. Out of 2,543 records requested from the HIM Department, 2,375 were located. What is the filing accuracy ratio?
    A. 6.61%
    B. 75.33%
    C. 89.01%
    D. 93.39%

REFERENCE: LaTour and Eichenwald-Maki, p 201-202
                    McWay, p 193-194

18. Which set of records filed consecutively on a shelf displays terminal digit filing order?
    A. 00-79-99, 00-79-01, 99-78-99
    B. 57-78-00, 57-78-01, 56-78-99
    C. 99-05-26, 01-06-26, 49-04-02
    D. 55-55-55, 33-33-33, 44-44-44

REFERENCE: Abdelhak, p 225
                    Green and Bowie, p 201-203
                    LaTour and Eichenwald-Maki, p 200
                    Johns, p 342-343

19. In the master patient index, which is filed by last name, Jill Thomas-Jones would be
    A. J-I-L-L-T-H-O-M-A-S-J-O-N-E-S
    B. T-H-O-M-A-S, J-I-L-L-J-O-N-E-S
    C. T-H-O-M-A-S-J-O-N-E-S, J-I-L-L
    D. J-O-N-E-S, J-I-L-L-T-H-O-M-A-S

REFERENCE: Abdelhak, p 224
                    Green and Bowie, p 198-200
                    Johns, p 341
                    McWay, p 111

20. According to terminal digit filing, what would be the number of the record immediately after record number 99-99-30?
    A. 99-98-30
    B. 00-00-31
    C. 01-00-31
    D. 99-99-31

REFERENCE: Abdelhak, p 225
                    Green and Bowie, p 201-202
                    LaTour and Eichenwald-Maki, p 200
                    Johns, p 342-343

21. Medicare's Conditions of Participation for Hospitals requires that patient health records be retained for at least _____ years unless a longer period is required by state or local laws.
    A. 3
    B. 5
    C. 7
    D. 10

REFERENCE: Green and Bowie, p 96
                    LaTour and Eichenwald-Maki, p 203

22. Your state regulations require records to be kept for a statute of limitations period of 7 years. Federal law requires records to be retained for 5 years. The minimum retention period for health records in your facility should be
   A. 5 years.
   B. 7 years.
   C. 10 years.
   D. either 5 or 7 years, as determined by

REFERENCE: Abdelhak, p 240-241
               Green and Bowie, p 96-97
               LaTour and Eichenwald-Maki, p 202-206, 251
               Johns, p 695-699

               McWay, p 112-113

23. Which of the following technologies works well with automated record-tracking systems to speed the data entry process?
   A. discharge lists
   B. bar codes
   C. compressible filing units
   D. computerized chart-out slips

REFERENCE: Abdelhak, p 238-239
               Green and Bowie, p 209-211
               LaTour and Eichenwald-Maki, p 51
               Johns, p 349-350

24. A HIM Department, currently using 2,540 linear filing inches to store records, plans to purchase new open-shelf filing units. Each of the shelves in a new 6-shelf unit measures 36 linear filing inches. It is estimated that an additional 400 filing inches should be planned for to allow for 5-year expansion needs. How many new file shelving units should be purchased?
   A. 11
   B. 12
   C. 13
   D. 14

REFERENCE: Green and Bowie, p 205-208
               LaTour and Eichenwald-Maki, p 202
               Johns, p 343-347

               McWay, p 110-112

25. Microfilmed records are considered
   A. inadmissible evidence.
   B. never admissible as hearsay evidence.
   C. acceptable as courtroom evidence.
   D. not admissible as secondary evidence.

REFERENCE: Abdelhak, p 250
               Johns, p 348

26. A research request has been received by the HIM Department from the Quality Improvement Committee. The Committee plans to review the records of all patients who were admitted with CHF in the month of January 2008. Which of the following indices would be the best source in locating the needed records?
    A. master patient index
    B. physicians' index
    C. disease index
    D. operation index

REFERENCE: Green and Bowie, p 230
               Johns, p 375-377
               LaTour and Eichenwald-Maki, p 289
               McWay, p 116-117

27. When using stationary open-shelf files, _____ inches are recommended for aisles between file units.
    A. 24
    B. 36
    C. 60
    D. 72

REFERENCE: Abdelhak, p 222
               LaTour and Eichenwald-Maki, p 202

28. In a manual record-tracking system, no record should be removed from the file without being replaced by a(n)
    A. 8 1/2 × 11-inch charge-out slip.
    B. empty file folder.
    C. paddle.
    D. outguide.

REFERENCE: Abdelhak, p 237
               Green and Bowie, p 213-214
               Johns, p 349-350

29. Documentation of record destruction should include all but which one of the following?
    A. statement that records were destroyed in the normal course of business
    B. method of destruction
    C. signature of the individuals supervising and witnessing the destruction
    D. dates not covered in destruction

REFERENCE: AHIMA Practice Brief "Destruction of Patient Health Information"
               Green and Bowie, p 98-99
               LaTour and Eichenwald-Maki, p 202-203, 206
               McWay, p 112-113

30. If the HIM Department has purchased 100 units of 8-shelf files and plans to use the terminal digit filing system, how many shelves should be allocated to each primary number?
    A. 8
    B. 10
    C. 12
    D. 100

REFERENCE: Abdelhak, p 225-226
               McWay, p 112-113

31. In the event of water damage to a large volume of records, what action should be taken immediately to assist in disaster recovery?
   A. Turn on the heat to help retard mold or mildew from forming.
   B. Turn off the air conditioning to reduce temperature and humidity.
   C. Turn off the fans to prevent circulation of air.
   D. Freeze the records to prevent mold or mildew from forming.

REFERENCE: Abdelhak, p 242
               LaTour and Eichenwald-Maki, p 201

32. Which of the following lists is in correct alphabetical order?
   A. Ferlazzo, Joshua; Ferlazzo, Joshua P.; Ferlazzo, Joshua Philip; Ferlazzo, J.
   B. Ferlazzo, J.; Ferlazzo, Joshua; Ferlazzo, Joshua P.; Ferlazzo, Joshua Philip
   C. Ferlazzo, Joshua; Ferlazzo, Joshua P.; Ferlazzo, J.; Ferlazzo, Joshua Philip
   D. Ferlazzo, Joshua A.; Ferlazzo, B.; Ferlazzo, Joshua; Ferlazzo, Joshua Phillip

REFERENCE: Abdelhak, p 224
               Green and Bowie, p 198-199
               Johns, p 341
               McWay, p 111-112

33. Mary Schnering was admitted to Community Hospital on 1/3/08 and assigned a record number of 54-47-53. The patient was later admitted on 2/14/08 and assigned the number 54-88-42. Both records were eventually filed under 54-88-42. What type of numbering/filing system is being used at Community Hospital?
   A. serial-unit   C. unit
   B. serial   D. terminal digit

REFERENCE: Abdelhak, p 221
               Green and Bowie, p 197
               Johns, p 338-343
               LaTour and Eichenwald-Maki, p 199
               McWay, p 111

34. What type of filing system would store records in the following order: 00-76-05, 01-76-04, 01-77-04, 02-76-05?
   A. terminal digit   C. serial unit
   B. middle digit   D. straight numeric

REFERENCE: Abdelhak, p 224-225
               Green and Bowie, p 201
               Johns, p 388-341
               LaTour and Eichenwald-Maki, p 198-199

35. What microform should the HIM practitioner select if the records must be unitized and color-coded for filing purposes?
   A. roll microfilm   C. jacket microfilm
   B. cartridge   D. cassette

REFERENCE: Abdelhak, p 247-249
               LaTour and Eichenwald-Maki, p 204
               Johns, p 347-349

36. In retrieval of optical image files, cache memory
    A. decreases access time for all users on the system.
    B. increases exchange time on the jukebox.
    C. is resident on the jukebox.
    D. is a way of defragmenting a WORM platter.

REFERENCE: Abdelhak, p 257
               Green and Bowie, p 94

37. At Community Hospital the average admission will create a file that will take up 0.25 inch of file space. Each new ER record requires 0.125 inch of file space. Approximately 25,000 new patients are admitted per year and 15,000 ER patients are treated per year. The shelving cost is $1.05 per filing inch. How much money should be allocated for storage space in next year's budget?
    A. $8,531.25   C. $853.25
    B. $8,125.00   D. $1,875.00

REFERENCE: Green and Bowie, p 205-208
               LaTour and Eichenwald, p 202
               Johns, p 345-346
               McWay, p 111-112

38. On his 5/23/08 admission to Metropolitan Hospital, David Robinson was assigned the medical record number 07-23-38. The previous record number assigned to Mr. Robinson during a 4/1/07 admission was 07-10-47. In a serial numbering/filing system, how would these records be filed?
    A. Both records are combined under 07-10-47.
    B. Both records are combined under 07-23-38.
    C. Each admission is filed under its own number.
    D. Previous records are brought forward and filed under the latest number issued.

REFERENCE: Abdelhak, p 221
               Green and Bowie, p 197
               LaTour and Eichenwald-Maki, p 199
               Johns, p 338-341
               McWay, p 111

39. The same patient was admitted on three different occasions and assigned a new medical record number each time. In order to correct this situation in a unit numbering system, which medical record number should be used given the following information?

Admitted 5/04/07	Patty Miller	23-33-56
Admitted 6/05/07	P. J. Miller	25-56-88
Admitted 9/27/07	Patricia Miller	27-12-12

    A. Void the first and last numbers and file all admissions under 25-56-88.
    B. Delete all previous numbers and assign a completely new number.
    C. Void the first two numbers and file all admissions under 27-12-12.
    D. Void the last two numbers and file all admissions under 23-33-56.

REFERENCE: Abdelhak, p 221
               Green and Bowie, p 195-196
               LaTour and Eichenwald-Maki, p 199
               Johns, p 338-341
               McWay, p 111

40. The health care providers in a large teaching hospital require access to health records 24 hours a day, 7 days a week. To secure the area and continue to maintain accessibility, the Director of the HIM Department should
    A. staff the department with personnel 24 hours a day.
    B. be on call every evening and weekends for emergency requests.
    C. train security guards to retrieve records after the department closes.
    D. arrange for records to be retrieved at 7:00 AM every morning.

REFERENCE: Abdelhak, p 573-574

41. As a prerequisite to phasing in a new imaging system, what process would facilitate automatic indexing?
    A. redesigning forms to include bar codes
    B. removing portions of the patient record that will not be scanned
    C. converting all microfilm to optical disk format
    D. scanning only emergency room records initially

REFERENCE: Abdelhak, p 262
               Green and Bowie, p 209, 211
               LaTour and Eichenwald-Maki, p 205

42. Which of the following is NOT a safety hazard in the file area of the HIM Department?
    A. tightly packed open-shelf files
    B. heavy objects placed on top file drawers
    C. stepladders which are fully open and locked in place
    D. plastic wastebasket for trash

REFERENCE: Abdelhak, p 640-641

43. A HIM Department wants to buy new open-shelf filing units for its file expansion. Each of the shelves in a new 6-shelf unit measures 33 linear filing inches. There will be an estimated 1,000 records to file. The average record is 1 inch thick. How many filing units should be purchased?
    A. 2   C. 6
    B. 4   D. 8

REFERENCE: Green and Bowie, p 205-208
               LaTour and Eichenwald-Maki, p 202
               Johns, p 343-347
               McWay, p 111-112

44. Which of the following microform types is the least expensive to prepare and results in the greatest storage density?
    A. microfilm jackets   C. microfiche
    B. roll microfilm   D. ultrafiche

REFERENCE: Abdelhak, p 247-249

45. Brian Hiltz was discharged from the hospital after a 3-day hospitalization and instructed to return to the outpatient department for follow-up care. On his first visit as an outpatient, a new record was created and he was assigned a new record number. Following completion of the outpatient appointment, his outpatient record is filed permanently in the outpatient department. What is the filing system used in this situation?

    A. decentralized   C. centralized
    B. unit record   D. terminal digit

REFERENCE: Abdelhak, p 223
                          Green and Bowie, p 203-204
                          Johns, p 343
                          McWay, p 111

46. The master patient index must, at a minimum, include sufficient information to
    A. summarize the patient's medical history.
    B. list all physicians who have ever treated the patient.
    C. uniquely identify the patient.
    D. justify the patient's hospital bill.

REFERENCE: Abdelhak, p 226
                          Green and Bowie, p 227-230
                          LaTour and Eichenwald-Maki, p 206-207
                          Johns, p 375-376
                          McWay, p 115-116

47. Using terminal digit filing, the record number on the folders immediately in front of and behind the number 24-31-83 would be
    A. 23-31-83 and 25-31-83.   C. 25-31-83 and 23-41-83.
    B. 24-31-82 and 23-31-83.   D. 24-32-83 and 24-33-83.

REFERENCE: Abdelhak, p 225
                          Green and Bowie, p 201-203
                          LaTour and Eichenwald-Maki, p 200
                          Johns, p 342-343

48. The Joint Commission suggests that hospitals use which type of patient information system?
    A. unit record
    B. computer-based patient record
    C. protocol for requesting information, whereby the request is provided to the practitioner in a timely manner
    D. any one of the above

REFERENCE: Joint Commission

49. A health information manager develops a formal plan or record retention schedule for the automatic transfer of records to inactive storage and potential destruction based on all but which one of the following factors?
    A. statute of limitations   C. readmission rate
    B. volume of research   D. file area staffing

REFERENCE: Abdelhak, p 240-241
                          Green and Bowie, p 97-100
                          LaTour and Eichenwald-Maki, p 202-203, 251
                          McWay, p 112-114

50. Which of the following is NOT a benefit of the electronic document management system in the HIM Department?
    A. on-line availability of information
    B. multiuser simultaneous access
    C. decreased use of computer technology
    D. system security and confidentiality

REFERENCE: Abdelhak, p 258-260
             McWay, p 104

51. Which one of the following is an advantage of straight numeric filing over terminal digit filing?

    A. All sections of the file expand uniformly.
    B. The training period is short.
    C. Work can be evenly distributed, causing accountability for accuracy in each of the 100 sections.
    D. Inactive records can be purged evenly.

REFERENCE: Abdelhak, p 226
             Green and Bowie, p 201-203
             LaTour and Eichenwald-Maki, p 199-201
             Johns, p 339-343

52. Which one of the following is NOT an electronic document management system component?
    A. scanner   C. jukebox
    B. optical disk platter   D. reader-printer

REFERENCE: Abdelhak, p 255-258
             Green and Bowie, p 94

53. When purchasing file guides, the Health Information Manager should be primarily concerned with which of the following?
    A. cost and color   C. cost and visibility
    B. durability and visibility D. color and durability

REFERENCE: Abdelhak, p 224-226
             Green and Bowie, p 213-214
             Johns, p 347

54. General Hospital has been in operation for 13 years. It has 6,000 admissions per year. The facility has expanded and will allow for 200 more admissions per year from now on. There are 2,500 linear feet of filing space available and half is being used. The facility expects a 30% readmission rate. If a unit numbering/filing system is used, how many file folders will be needed for the next year?
    A. 1,800   C. 4,340
    B. 1,860   D. 6,200

REFERENCE: Green and Bowie, p 205-208
             LaTour and Eichenwald-Maki, p 202
             Johns, p 346-347
             McWay, p 111-112

55. As Director of the HIM Department you have become aware of instances of unauthorized access to the record file area. After considering several options to limit or restrict access to the area, you decide to
    A. install a computerized access panel.
    B. hire a security guard to monitor entrance to the file area.
    C. convert from a terminal digit filing system to serial unit filing.
    D. utilize a sign-in and sign-out log for admittance to the file area.

REFERENCE: Abdelhak, p 234

56. In planning for a file system conversion to a new physical location, it is wise to schedule the actual conversion process to occur
    A. during a Joint Commission survey.
    B. during a 2-week period when the department is closed.
    C. at an off-peak time for the department such as a weekend (Friday to Monday).
    D. before purging inactive records.

REFERENCE: Abdelhak, p 235-236

57. The President of the Medical Staff requests a report on the number of coronary artery bypass grafts performed by a particular physician in April of the previous year. Where would the health information manager look for this information?
    A. patient register   C. operation index
    B. disease index   D. birth defects register

REFERENCE: Green and Bowie, p 230-234
               LaTour and Eichenwald-Maki, p 289
               Johns, p 375-377, 399-400
               McWay, p 115-116

58. A major consideration in a hospital or facility closure is to
    A. notify all patients to pick up their original records by the date of closure.
    B. seek approval for destruction of all records with a last date of treatment over 3 years ago.
    C. ensure that authorized parties have access to the information as provided by law.
    D. arrange for donating the records to an HIA/HIT education program for student use.

REFERENCE: Abdelhak, p 241-242
               Green and Bowie, p 100-101
               LaTour and Eichenwald-Maki, p 203
               McWay, p 113

59. The American College of Surgeons mandates a successful follow-up rate for all cancer cases of at least _____ to meet approval requirements as a cancer program.
    A. 70%   C. 90%
    B. 80%   D. 100%

REFERENCE: Abdelhak, p 475
               American College of Surgeons' Cancer Program Manual

60. In negotiating a contract with a commercial storage company for storage of inactive records, what would be the most important issue to clarify in writing?
    A. who completes the list of what records are to be stored
    B. what are the billing terms
    C. who will purge inactive files for transfer
    D. confidentiality policies and liability concerns

REFERENCE: Abdelhak, p 235
               Green and Bowie, p 97
               LaTour and Eichenwald-Maki, p 206

61. Which one of the following master patient index core data elements is OPTIONAL, NOT RECOMMENDED, by AHIMA?
    A. internal patient identification   C. marital status
    B. discharge date   D. ethnicity

REFERENCE: AHIMA Practice Brief "Master Patient (Person) Index (MPI)—Recommended Core Data Elements"
               Green and Bowie, p 227-230

62. Unless state or federal laws require longer time periods, AHIMA recommends that patient health information for minors be retained for at least how long?
    A. age of majority plus statute of limitation
    B. 10 years after the most recent encounter
    C. 10 years after the age of majority
    D. permanently

REFERENCE: AHIMA Practice Brief "Retention of Health Information"
               Green and Bowie, p 96
               Johns, p 696-697
               McWay, p 112-113

63. When a health care facility makes a decision to destroy computerized data, AHIMA recommends all but which one of the following as methods of destruction?
    A. overwriting data with a series of characters
    B. reformatting the disk
    C. deleting the file on the disk
    D. overwriting the backup tapes

REFERENCE: AHIMA Practice Brief "Destruction of Patient Health Information"
               Green and Bowie, p 98-99
               McWay, p 113

64. Which of the following statements would be found in the laboratory report section of the health record?
    A. BUN reported as 20 mg
    B. morphine sulfate gr. 1/4 q.4h. for pain
    C. IV sodium Pentothal 1% started at 9:05 AM
    D. TPR recorded q.h. for 12 hr.

REFERENCE: Abdelhak, p 112
               Green and Bowie, p 158-159
               LaTour and Eichenwald-Maki, p 181

65. Which of the following is a DISADVANTAGE of terminal digit filing as compared to straight numeric filing?
    A. File personnel are crowded in the highest numbers.
    B. Inactive records are pulled from one common area.
    C. The training period is slightly longer.
    D. Files expand at the end of the number series, requiring backshifting.

REFERENCE: Abdelhak, p 226
               Green and Bowie, p 201-202

66. The main advantage of phonetic filing is
    A. typographical errors are eliminated.
    B. spelling accuracy is encouraged.
    C. emphasis is placed on a foreign language.
    D. names that sound alike are filed together.

REFERENCE: Green and Bowie, p 199

67. Technologies that can make data capture easier include all but which one of the following?
    A. digital dictation
    B. direct data capture from a medical device attached to the HIM employee
    C. handheld wireless devices
    D. speech recognition

REFERENCE: LaTour and Eichenwald-Maki, p 222-223

68. If the file clerks are having trouble locating the terminal digit sections quickly, the filing supervisor could add more
    A. outguides.   C. requisitions.
    B. file guides.   D. file maintenance staff.

REFERENCE: Abdelhak, p 225-226

69. The HIM Department receives a request for a certified copy of a birth certificate on a patient born in the hospital 30 years ago. The Department should
    A. issue a copy of the birth certificate from the patient's record.
    B. direct the request to the state's office of vital records.
    C. direct the request to the attending physician.
    D. issue a copy of the newborn's record.

REFERENCE: Abdelhak, p 372-373
               Green and Bowie, p 125

70. A surgeon requests the name of a patient he admitted on January 4, 2009. Which of the following would be used to retrieve this information?
    A. master patient index   C. admission register
    B. number index   D. operation index

REFERENCE: Green and Bowie, p 234
               Johns, p 375-377, 398-400
               LaTour and Eichenwald-Maki, p 205, 288-289
               McWay, p 117

71. Which of the following is NOT a consideration in the file folder size and design?
  A. reinforced top and side panels
  B. scoring on folder bottoms
  C. vendor location
  D. weight of folder

REFERENCE: Abdelhak, p 234
               Green and Bowie, p 208-213
               Johns, p 347

72. Where in the health record would the following statement be located: "Microscopic Diagnosis: Liver (needle biopsy), metastatic adenocarcinoma"?
  A. operative report
  B. pathology report
  C. anesthesia report
  D. radiology report

REFERENCE: Abdelhak, p 110
               Green and Bowie, p 153, 155-156
               LaTour and Eichenwald-Maki, p 182
               Johns, p 66

73. The HIM Department is located in a teaching hospital and provides record access 24 hours a day, 7 days a week. To secure the file area and continue to maintain accessibility, the department director should
  A. be on call during the evening hours.
  B. staff the file area with file clerks on all three shifts.
  C. instruct medical staff in record retrieval.
  D. instruct nurse supervisors in record retrieval.

REFERENCE: Green and Bowie, p 219

74. A file area has limited space, medium file activity, and two file clerks. The HIM department would benefit from choosing which type of storage equipment?
  A. compressible filing units
  B. lateral filing cabinets
  C. open shelf files
  D. motorized revolving units

REFERENCE: Abdelhak, p 222-223
               Johns, p 343-345
               LaTour and Eichenwald-Maki, p 202

75. When evaluating a microfilm service bureau, all but which of the following are important factors to rate?
  A. cost
  B. emergency returns
  C. storage after filming
  D. cache memory

REFERENCE: Abdelhak, p 252-253
               LaTour and Eichenwald-Maki, p 205

76. When merging or overwriting demographic information for duplicate and overlap master patient index entries, AHIMA recommends converting all but which one of the following minimum data elements?
  A. encounter type
  B. alias/previous name
  C. attending physician
  D. facility identification

REFERENCE: AHIMA Practice Brief "Merging Master Patient (Person) Indexes"

77. Which of the following steps would NOT be taken when bringing all patient health information together in a complete record, regardless of media output form?
    A. Look at the past composition of records in the facility.
    B. Determine storage requirements for information currently not filed in the medical record.
    C. Decide if all patient health information is being collected and managed uniformly.
    D. Evaluate what patient data, if any, is not incorporated in the medical record.

REFERENCE: AHIMA Practice Brief "Managing Multimedia Medical Records: A Health Information Manager's Role"
McWay, p 110

78. When operating under the Health Insurance Portability and Accountability Act of 1996, what is a basic tenet in information security for health care professionals to follow?
    A. Security training is provided to all levels of staff.
    B. Patients are not educated about their right to confidentiality of health information.
    C. The information system encourages mass copying, printing, and downloading of patient records.
    D. When paper-based records are no longer needed, they are bundled and sent to a recycling center.

REFERENCE: AHIMA Practice Brief "Information Security: A Checklist for Health care Professionals"
Green and Bowie, p 269
McWay, p 322-323

79. When designing a computer view for information capture, all of the following should be considered except for which one?
    A. external standards such as those developed by HL7 and NCVHS
    B. standardized vocabularies
    C. size of the document
    D. forms committee membership

REFERENCE: AHIMA Practice Brief "Developing Information Capture Tools"
McWay, p 109-112

80. When health care facilities close or medical practices dissolve, procedures for disposition of patient records should take into consideration all of the following EXCEPT for
    A. state laws and licensing standards.
    B. Communities of Practice requirements.
    C. needs and wishes of patients.
    D. Medicare requirements.

REFERENCE: AHIMA Practice Brief "Protecting Patient Information After A Facility Closure"
Green and Bowie, p 100-101
McWay, p 113-114

81. Case finding methods for patients with diabetes includes a review of all but which one of the following?
   A. health plans
   B. CPT diagnostic codes
   C. billing data
   D. medication lists

REFERENCE: LaTour and Eichenwald-Maki, p 293
               Johns, p 407

82. To protect health information from catastrophes such as fire, flooding, bomb threats, and theft, Joint Commission-accredited facilities are required to maintain a _____ plan.
   A. budget
   B. disaster
   C. case management
   D. patient care

REFERENCE: AHIMA Practice Brief "Disaster Planning for Health Information (Updated)"
               McWay, p 112

83. Which of the following is NOT an alternative storage method for paper records?
   A. microfilm
   B. optical imaging
   C. computer
   D. outguide

REFERENCE: Green and Bowie, p 97-99
               LaTour and Eichenwald-Maki, p 204-205
               Johns, p 343-349

84. Which of the following issues would be of LEAST concern when storing health records in off-site storage?
   A. operating hours of the storage facility
   B. safety and confidentiality procedures
   C. filing order of the records
   D. procedure for request of a record in an emergency

REFERENCE: Green and Bowie, p 97

85. The HIM Department maintains 500,000 records and responds to 5,000 requests for records in a given period of time. What is the record usage rate?
   A. 0.01%
   B. 1%
   C. 5%
   D. 10%

REFERENCE: LaTour and Eichenwald-Maki, p 201-202
               McWay, p 193-194

86. Which one of the following is NOT a data retrieval technology?
   A. color
   B. sound
   C. point and click fields
   D. icons

REFERENCE: LaTour and Eichenwald-Maki, p 221-222

87. When engaging the services of a microfilm vendor, all but which one of the following factors should be included in the contract?
   A. cost
   B. provision for destruction of original records
   C. type of reader or printer needed to view the microfilm
   D. confidentiality of information being filmed

REFERENCE: Abdelhak, p 252-253
               LaTour and Eichenwald-Maki, p 204-206

88. What would be the most cost-effective and prudent course of action for the storage or disposition of 250,000 records at a large teaching and research hospital?
    A. storing the records off-site at a cost of $25,000 per year
    B. microfilming all 250,000 records for the cost of $195,000
    C. purging all death records and storing them off-site
    D. destroying all records older than the time frame required by the statute of limitations

REFERENCE: Abdelhak, p 240-241
               McWay, p 112

89. The total number of records filed during the month is 2,500 and, upon completion of a filing accuracy study, 90 records were not found. What is the accuracy of filing?
    A. 1%   C. 28%
    B. 4%   D. 96%

REFERENCE: Johns, p 354, 372-374
               LaTour and Eichenwald-Maki, p 201-202
               McWay, p 192-194

90. A quality control measure that should be established for the filing, storage, and retrieval of health records includes criteria for the
    A. accuracy of analyzing records.   C. filing of loose materials.
    B. number of incomplete records.   D. tracking of release of information requests.

REFERENCE: Johns, p 354, 372-374
               LaTour and Eichenwald-Maki, p 201-202

91. According to AHIMA's recommended retention standards, which one of the following types of health information does NOT need to be retained permanently?
    A. physician index   C. register of surgical procedures
    B. register of births   D. register of deaths

REFERENCE: AHIMA Practice Brief "Retention of Health Information"
               McWay, p 112

92. For a health care facility to meet its document destruction needs, the certificate of destruction should include all but which one of the following elements?
    A. unique and serialized transaction number
    B. location of destruction
    C. patient notification
    D. acceptance of fiduciary responsibility

REFERENCE: Johnson, p 54-55, 59
               LaTour and Eichenwald-Maki, p 203, 206
               McWay, p 112

93. The steps in developing a record retention program include all but which one of the following?
    A. determining the format and location of storage
    B. notifying the courts of the destruction
    C. assigning each record a retention period
    D. destroying records that are no longer needed

REFERENCE: LaTour and Eichenwald-Maki, p 203, 206
               McWay, p 112-114

94. A health care facility has received a request to participate in a statewide study on cleft lip and cleft palate. This study would include data from the past year and subsequent years. Given that each of the data sources cited below contains the necessary information, the initial data would be most easily collected from the
    A. newborn records.
    C. maternal records.
    B. state bureau of vital statistics.
    D. birth defects registry.

REFERENCE: LaTour and Eichenwald-Maki, p 292
                     Abdelhak, p 479-481
                     Johns, p 405

95. An example of a primary data source is the
    A. physician index.
    C. cancer registry.
    B. health record.
    D. hospital statistical report.

REFERENCE: LaTour and Eichenwald-Maki, p 288
                     Abdelhak, p 474
                     Johns, p 398
                     McWay, p 115

96. Which one of the following is NOT considered a challenge in the adoption of an electronic health record system?
    A. executive commitment and support
    B. physician willingness to adopt
    C. contribution to the quality of patient care
    D. individual state legal and regulatory issues

REFERENCE: LaTour and Eichenwald-Maki, p 229-232

97. Fetal monitoring strips are part of the _____ record and should be maintained_____.
    A. newborn's; 10 years past the age of majority
    B. mother's; according to the length of time required for a minor's records
    C. newborn's; according to the time period specified in the state's statute of limitations
    D. mother's; 10 years

REFERENCE: LaTour and Eichenwald-Maki, p 203

98. Which one of the following is NOT a strategy when purchasing an electronic health record system?
    A. Identify stakeholders from different organizational levels and engage them appropriately.
    B. Identify return on investment or cost-benefit analysis.
    C. Identify system requirements.
    D. Broaden the vendor field and select several vendors of choice.

REFERENCE: AHIMA Practice Brief "Purchasing Strategies for EHR Systems"

99. Which one of the following describes the electronic health record's impact on the record retrieval function?
    A. This function will be eliminated except for historical files maintained in paper or on microform.
    B. There will be more online management through computer-generated reports using logic rules.
    C. This function will remain the same as the paper record function.
    D. There will be increased record pulling as records are scanned or online documents become available.

REFERENCE: AHIMA Practice Brief "The EHR's Impact on HIM Functions"

100. What data cannot be retrieved from the MEDPAR?
    A. ICD-9-CM diagnosis and procedure codes
    B. charges broken down by specific types of services
    C. non-Medicare patient data
    D. data on the provider

REFERENCE: LaTour and Eichenwald-Maki, p 296

Answer Key for Information Retention and Access

NOTE: *Explanations are provided for those questions that require mathematical calculations and questions that are not clearly explained in the references that are cited.*

ANSWER   EXPLANATION

1. D

2. A

3. C

4. B

5. A $\dfrac{3{,}545 \times 100}{150{,}000} = 2.36\% = 2.4\%$

6. A

7. A

8. B

9. D

10. D

11. C

12. B

13. D   200 units × 6 shelves/unit   = 1200 shelves total

           $\dfrac{1200 \text{ shelves}}{100 \text{ primary numbers (00-99)}}$ = 12 shelves/primary number

14. C

15. C

16. B

17. D $\dfrac{2{,}375 \text{ records retrieved from proper locations} \times 100}{2{,}543 \text{ records requested}} = 93.39\%$ filing accuracy

18. B

19. C

20. B

21. B

22. B

23. B

24. D $\dfrac{2540 + 400}{36 \times 6}$ $\dfrac{2940 \text{ inches needed}}{216 \text{ inches per unit}} = 13.61$ shelves

      Because you cannot purchase a 0.14 filing shelf, you must buy 14 units.

25. C

26. C

27. B

28. D

29. D

30. A   8 shelves/unit × 100 units   = 800 total shelves

           $\dfrac{800 \text{ shelves}}{100 \text{ primary digits}}$ = 8 shelves/primary digit

31. D

32. B

33. A

34. D

35. C

Answer Key for Information Retention and Access

ANSWER   EXPLANATION

36. A

37. A   25,000 inpatients × 0.25 inches/record = 6,250 inches

15,000 ER patients × 0.125 inches/record = 1,875 inches

6,250 inches + 1,875 inches = 8,125 total inches of filing space/year

8,125 total inches × $1.05/filing inch = $8,531.25 budget allocation for storage space

38. C

39. D

40. A

41. A

42. C

43. C   33 inches/shelf × 6 shelves/unit = 198 linear filing inches/unit

1,000 records × 1 inch/record = 1,000 inches of records to be filed

$$\frac{1,000 \text{ inches of records}}{198 \text{ inches/unit}} = 5.05 \text{ filing units}$$

In order to provide for the total expansion, 6 filing units need to be purchased.

44. B

45. A

46. C

47. A

48. D

49. D

50. C

51. B

52. D

53. B

54. C   6,000 admissions/year currently

+ 200 additional admissions/year

6,200 total admissions next year

6,200 total admissions

× 30% readmission rate

1,860 readmissions next year

6,200 total admissions

-1,860 readmissions

4,340 new file folders needed for next year

55. A

56. C

57. C

58. C

59. C

60. D

61. C

62. A

63. C

64. A

65. C

Answer Key for Information Retention and Access

	ANSWER	EXPLANATION
66.	D	
67.	B	
68.	B	
69.	B	
70.	C	
71.	C	
72.	B	
73.	B	In a teaching hospital where records are routinely requested 24 hours a day, it would be beneficial to have 24-hour staffing. If it were a small facility with few requests in the evenings, it could be more appropriate to have a nurse supervisor assigned responsibility for record retrieval.
74.	A	
75	D	
76	C	
77.	A	The current, not the past, composition of records is studied.
78.	A	
79.	D	
80.	B	
81.	B	
82.	B	
83.	D	
84.	C	
85.	B	(5,000 × 100) divided by 500,000 = 1%
86.	C	
87.	C	
88.	B	
89.	D	2500 - 90 = 2410 (2410 × 100) divided by 2,500 = 96.4% filing accuracy
90.	C	
91.	A	
92.	C	
93.	B	
94.	D	
95.	B	
96.	C	
97.	B	
98.	D	
99.	A	
100.	C	

REFERENCES

Abdelhak, M., Grostick, S., Hanken, M.A., & Jacobs, E. (Eds.). (2007). *Health information: Management of a strategic resource* (3rd ed.). St. Louis: Saunders Elsevier.

AHIMA Practice Briefs. All are published by the American Health Information Management Association, Chicago.

    AHIMA Practice Brief: "Managing Multimedia Medical Records: A Health Information Manager's Role"

    AHIMA Practice Brief: "Information Security: A Checklist for Health care Professionals"

    AHIMA Practice Brief: "Developing Information Capture Tools"

    AHIMA Practice Brief: "Protecting Patient Information After A Facility Closure"

    AHIMA Practice Brief: "Disaster Planning for Health Information (Updated)"

    AHIMA Practice Brief: "Master Patient (Person) Index (MPI) – Recommended Core Data Elements"

    AHIMA Practice Brief: "Retention of Health Information"

    AHIMA Practice Brief: "Destruction of Patient Health Information"

    AHIMA Practice Brief: "Merging Master Patient (Person) Indexes"

    AHIMA Practice Brief: "Purchasing Strategies for EHR Systems"

    AHIMA Practice Brief: "HR's Impact on HIM Functions"

American College of Surgeons. (2006). *Cancer program standards 2004 Revised Edition*. American College of Surgeons Commission on Cancer.

Burrington-Brown, Jill, Hjort, Beth, & Washington, Lydia. "Health Data Access, Use, and Control." *Journal of AHIMA* 78, no.5 (May 2007): 63-66.

Green, M.A., & Bowie, M.J. (2004). *Essentials of health information management*. Clifton Park, NY: Thomson Delmar Learning.

Johns, M.L. (2006). *Health information management technology: An applied approach* (2nd ed.). Chicago: American Health Information Management Association.

Johnson, Robert. "The Certificate of Destruction: What It Is, What It's Not." *Journal of AHIMA* 76, no. 6 (June 2005): 54-55, 59.

Joint Commission. (2008) *Comprehensive accreditation manual for hospitals: The official handbook*. Oak Brook Terrace, IL: Joint Commission.

LaTour, K., & Eichenwald-Maki, S. (2006). *Health information management: Concepts, principles and practice* (2nd ed.). Chicago: American Health Information Management Association.

Mc Way, D. C. (2008). *Today's health information management: An integrated approach*. Clifton Park, NY: Thomson Delmar Learning.

V. Classification Systems and Secondary Data Sources

Lisa Delhomme, MHA, RHIA

1. Robert Thompson was seen in the outpatient department with a chronic cough and the record
    states "rule out lung cancer." What should be coded as the patient's diagnosis?
    A. chronic cough
    B. observation and evaluation without need for further medical care
    C. diagnosis of unknown etiology
    D. lung cancer

REFERENCE: Frisch, p 134
               Green, p 209
               Hazelwood and Venable, p 4-5
               Johnson and McHugh, p 31, 574
               Schraffenberger (2009), p 520

2. Which of the following is a valid ICD-9-CM principal diagnosis code?
    A. V27.2   Outcome of delivery, twins, both live born
    B. V30.00   Single live born, born in hospital
    C. E867   Accidental poisoning by gas distributed by pipeline
    D. M9010/0   Fibroadenoma, NOS

REFERENCE: Frisch, p 150-151
               Green, p 168
               Johnson and McHugh, 16, 45, 60
               Brown, p 222, 260, 313-314, 336-337

3. A physician performed an outpatient surgical procedure on the eye orbit of a Medicare patient.
    Upon searching the CPT codes and consulting with the physician, the coder is unable to find a
    code for the procedure. The coder should assign
    A. an unlisted Evaluation and Management code from the E/M section.
    B. an unlisted procedure code located in the eye and ocular adnexa section.
    C. a HCPCS Level Two (alphanumeric) code.
    D. an ophthalmologic treatment service code.

REFERENCE: AMA (2009), p 49-50
               Green, p 331, 471-472
               Frisch, 7
               Smith, p 23

4. A system of preferred terminology for naming disease processes is known as a
    A. set of categories.   C. medical nomenclature.
    B. classification system.   D. diagnosis listing.

REFERENCE: Green, 8
               Green and Bowie, p 294
               McWay, p 125-128
               Abdelhak, p 201
               Johns, p 194
               LaTour and Eichenwald-Maki, p 306, 936

5. A patient who is taking the drug Antivert may have a diagnosis of
    A. dizziness.   C. arthritis.
    B. urinary tract infection.   D. congestive heart failure.

REFERENCE: Nobles, p 543

6. Which of the following is NOT included as a part of the minimum data maintained in the MPI?
   A. principal diagnosis
   B. patient medical record number
   C. full name (last, first, and middle)
   D. date of birth

REFERENCE: McWay, p 115-116
              Green & Bowie, p 227-230
              Abdelhak, p 226
              Johns, p 399
              LaTour and Eichenwald-Maki, p 207, 289

7. The Health Information Department receives research requests from various committees in the hospital. The Medicine Committee wishes to review all patients having a diagnosis of anterolateral myocardial infarction within the past 6 months. Which of the following would be the best source to identify the necessary charts?
   A. operation index
   B. consultation index
   C. disease index
   D. physician's index

REFERENCE: Green and Bowie, p 230
              McWay, p 116-117
              Green, 103
              Johnson and McHugh, p 38-39
              Johns, p 400
              LaTour and Eichenwald-Maki, p 289

8. One of the major functions of the cancer registry is to ensure that patients receive regular and continued observation and management. How long should patient follow-up be continued?
   A. until remission occurs
   B. 10 years
   C. for the life of the patient
   D. 1 year

REFERENCE: Green, p 134-138
              McWay, p 117
              Abdelhak, p 475
              Johns, p 402-403
              LaTour and Eichenwald-Maki, p 291

9. In reviewing the medical record of a patient admitted for a left herniorrhaphy, the coder discovers an extremely low potassium level on the laboratory report. In examining the physician's orders, the coder notices that intravenous potassium was ordered. The physician has not listed any indication of an abnormal potassium level or any related condition on the discharge summary. The best course of action for the coder to take is to
   A. confer with the physician and ask him or her to list the condition as a final diagnosis if he or she considers the abnormal potassium level to be clinically significant.
   B. code the record as is.
   C. code the condition as an abnormal blood chemistry.
   D. code the abnormal potassium level as a complication following surgery.

REFERENCE: Bowie and Shaffer (2006), p 62
              Green, p 211
              Johnson and McHugh, p 31, 579
              Brown, p 27
              Green, p 211

10. DSM-IV-TR is used most frequently in what type of healthcare setting?
    A. behavioral health centers   C. home health agencies
    B. ambulatory surgery centers   D. nursing homes

REFERENCE: Green, p 297
                McWay, p 134
                LaTour and Eichenwald-Maki, p 311-312
                Johns, p 214-215

11. A coder notes that a patient is taking prescription Pilocarpine. The final diagnoses on the discharge summary are congestive heart failure and diabetes mellitus. The coder should query the physician about adding a diagnosis of
    A. arthritis.   C. bronchitis.
    B. glaucoma.   D. laryngitis.

REFERENCE: Green, p 13-14
                Johnson and McHugh, p 76
                Nobles, p 689

12. The patient is diagnosed with congestive heart failure. A drug of choice is
    A. ibuprofen.   C. haloperidol.
    B. oxytocin.   D. digoxin.

REFERENCE: Nobles, p 329

13. ICD-10-CM has two categories for myocardial infarction:

                I21, Acute myocardial infarction

                I22, Subsequent acute myocardial infarction.

    According to the guidelines, a code from I21 is to be used from onset of the acute MI until _____ following onset.

    A. 10 weeks

    B. 8 weeks

    C. 6 weeks

    D. 4 weeks

REFERENCE: Draft ICD-10-CM Official Guidelines

14. The local safety council requests statistics on the number of head injuries occurring as a result of skateboarding accidents during the last year. To retrieve this data, you will need to have the correct
    A. CPT code.
    B. Standard Nomenclature of Injuries codes.
    C. E-codes and ICD-9-CM codes.
    D. HCPCS Level II codes.

REFERENCE: Bowie and Shaffer (2006), p 293-298
                Frisch, p 150-151
                Green, p 178
                Johnson and McHugh, p 16, 60-63
                McWay, p 130
                Brown, p 336
                Schraffenberger (2009), p 296

15. A patient was admitted with severe abdominal pain, elevated temperature, and nausea. The physical examination indicated possible cholecystitis. Acute and chronic pancreatitis secondary to alcoholism was recorded on the face sheet as the final diagnosis. The principal diagnosis is
    A. alcoholism.
    B. abdominal pain.
    C. cholecystitis.
    D. acute pancreatitis.

REFERENCE: AHA, Coding Clinic, 2nd quarter, 1990, p 4
               Brown, p 47
               Green, p 204-205
               Green and Bowie, p 118-119
               Johnson and McHugh, p 74-75

16. The use of radioactive sources placed into a tumor-bearing area to generate high intensity radiation is termed
    A. stereotactic radiation treatment.
    B. proton beam treatment.
    C. brachytherapy.
    D. external beam radiation.

REFERENCE: Bowie and Shaffer (2008), p 328
               Johnson and McHugh, p 392-393
               Smith, p 167

17. In general, all three key components (history, physical examination, and medical decision making) for the E/M codes in CPT should be met or exceeded when
    A. the patient is established.
    B. a new patient is seen in the office.
    C. the patient is given subsequent care in the hospital.
    D. the patient is seen for a follow-up inpatient consultation.

REFERENCE: AMA (2009), p 7-8
               Bowie and Shaffer (2008), p 36-50
               Frisch, p 11-12
               Green, p 375-376
               Johnson and McHugh, p 126-127

18. A direction to "code first underlying disease" should be considered
    A. only when coding inpatient records.
    B. a mandatory instruction.
    C. mandatory dependent upon the code selection.
    D. a suggestion only.

REFERENCE: Bowie and Shaffer (2006), p 44
               Frisch, p 130
               Green, p 83, 105, 130
               Brown, p 14-15
               Schraffenberger, (2009), p 23
               Hazelwood and Venable, p 22

19. Which classification system was developed to standardize terminology and codes for use in clinical laboratories?
   A. Systematized Nomenclature of Human and Veterinary Medicine International (SNOMED)
   B. Systematized Nomenclature of Pathology (SNOP)
   C. Read Codes
   D. Logical Observation Identifiers, Names and Codes (LOINC)

REFERENCE: McWay, p 127
               Abdelhak, p 205-207
               LaTour and Eichenwald-Maki, p 325-326

20. Which classification system is used to classify neoplasms according to site, morphology, and behavior?
   A. International Classification of Diseases for Oncology (ICD-O)
   B. Systematized Nomenclature of Human and Veterinary Medicine International (SNOMED)
   C. Diagnostic and Statistical Manual of Mental Disorders (DSM)
   D. Current Procedural Terminology (CPT)

REFERENCE: Green, p 298
               McWay, p 127, 135
               Abdelhak, p 203
               Johns, p 206-207
               LaTour and Eichenwald-Maki, p 310

21. According to the UHDDS, a procedure that is surgical in nature, carries a procedural or anesthetic risk, or requires special training is defined as a
   A. principal procedure.   C. operating room procedure.
   B. significant procedure.   D. therapeutic procedure.

REFERENCE: Brown, p 53
               Green, p 113
               Johnson and McHugh, p 873
               Schraffenberger (2009), p 43-44, 49

22. The "cooperating party" responsible for maintaining the ICD-9-CM disease classification is the
   A. Centers for Medicare and Medicaid Services (CMS).
   B. National Center for Health Statistics (NCHS).
   C. American Hospital Association (AHA).
   D. American Health Information Management Association (AHIMA).

REFERENCE: Green, p 30
               Johns, p 197
               Johnson and McHugh, p 12
               LaTour and Eichenwald-Maki, p 307

23. An encoder that prompts the coder to answer a series of questions and choices based on the documentation in the medical record is called a(n)
   A. logic-based encoder.   C. grouper.
   B. automated codebook.   D. automatic code assignment.

REFERENCE: LaTour and Eichenwald-Maki, p 318-319
               McWay, p 132

24. A disadvantage of adopting SNOMED for diagnosis coding is that it
    A. is too difficult to use as a reimbursement system.
    B. is not compatible with computer technology.
    C. would hinder communication among diverse computer systems.
    D. is not possible to conduct outcomes research with SNOMED.

REFERENCE: Abdelhak, p 204-205
               LaTour and Eichenwald-Maki, p 324-325
               McWay, p 126-127
               Schraffenberger (2007), p 123-124

25. The Unified Medical Language System (UMLS) is a project sponsored by the
    A. National Library of Medicine.   C. World Health Organization.
    B. CMS.   D. Office of Inspector General.

REFERENCE: Green, p 296
               Johns, p 228-229
               LaTour and Eichenwald-Maki, p 332-333
               McWay, p 127

26. A patient is admitted with shortness of breath and hemoptysis. A chest x-ray revealed patchy infiltrates in the left lung and possible pneumonia. On the third day of hospitalization a bronchoscopy with biopsy was done which revealed a small cell carcinoma of the left upper lobe of the lung. A metastatic lesion in the brain was detected. The principal diagnosis is the
    A. metastatic brain carcinoma.   C. hemoptysis.
    B. small cell lung carcinoma.   D. pneumonia.

REFERENCE: Bowie and Shaffer (2006), p 59, 502
               Brown, p 21-22
               Frisch, p 132-133
               Green, p 118
               Johnson and McHugh, p 570-571
               Schraffenberger, (2009), p 51-52

27. Jane Moore was admitted to the ambulatory care unit of the hospital for a planned cholecystectomy for cholelithiasis. Shortly before surgery, Jane developed tachycardia, and the surgery was canceled. After a thorough workup for the tachycardia, Jane was discharged. This outpatient admission should be coded in the following sequence:
    A. V code for canceled surgery, tachycardia, cholelithiasis.
    B. tachycardia, V code for canceled surgery, cholelithiasis.
    C. cholelithiasis, V code for canceled surgery.
    D. cholelithiasis, V code for canceled surgery, tachycardia.

REFERENCE: Bowie and Shaffer (2006), p 307
               Brown, p 60-61
               Green, p 110-112
               Schraffenberger (2009), p 40-41

28. A patient has a total abdominal hysterectomy with bilateral salpingectomy. The coder selected the following codes:

> 58150 Total abdominal hysterectomy (corpus and cervix), with or without removal of tube(s) with or without removal of ovary(s)
>
> 58700 Salpingectomy, complete or partial unilateral or bilateral (separate procedure)

This type of coding is referred to as
A. upcoding.
B. unbundling.
C. maximizing.
D. optimization.

REFERENCE: Bowie and Schaffer (2008), p 92-93
                  Frisch, p 235-240, 341
                  Green, p 11
                  Johnson and McHugh, p 559
                  McWay, p 67, 356
                  Smith, p 52-53

29. A 75-year-old female was admitted for repair of a hiatal hernia which was performed on the first day of admission. While recovering, the patient fell out of her bed and sustained a fractured femur which was surgically reduced. Further complications included severe angina for which a cardiac catheterization and PTCA were performed. The principal procedure is
A. femur reduction.
B. herniorrhaphy.
C. catheterization.
D. PTCA.

REFERENCE: Bowie and Schaffer (2006), p 307
                  Brown, p 54
                  Green, p 113, 211
                  Johnson and McHugh, p 873
                  Schraffenberger (2009), p 44

30. Code 402, Hypertensive Heart Disease, would appropriately be used in which of the following situations?
A. left heart failure with benign hypertension
B. congestive heart failure; hypertension
C. hypertensive cardiovascular disease with congestive heart failure
D. cardiomegaly with hypertension

REFERENCE: Bowie and Schaffer (2006), p 165-166
                  Brown, p 289
                  Frisch, p 146-147
                  Green, p 140
                  Hazelwood and Venable, p 143-144
                  Johnson and McHugh, p 34-35, 279-280
                  Schraffenberger (2009), p 137-138

31. A patient is admitted to your hospital 6 weeks post myocardial infarction with severe chest pains. Which is the correct code?
    A. 414.8   chronic MI
    B. 410.1x   acute MI
    C. 412   old MI
    D. 413.0   angina

REFERENCE: Bowie and Schaffer (2006), p 168
                    Brown, p 275-276
                    Green, p 103
                    Green and Bowie, p 230
                    Hazelwood and Venable, p 146-148
                    Johnson and McHugh, p 38-39
                    McWay, p 116-117
                    Schraffenberger (2009), p 141-144

32. Which of the following is classified as a poisoning in ICD-9-CM?
    A. syncope due to Contac pills and a three martini lunch
    B. digitalis intoxication
    C. reaction to dye administered for pyelogram
    D. idiosyncratic reaction between various drugs

REFERENCE: Bowie and Schaffer (2006), p 273-274, 293-295, 493
                    Brown, p 365-367
                    Frisch, p 149-150
                    Hazelwood and Venable, p 263-264
                    Green, p 160-162
                    Johnson and McHugh, p 68-69
                    Schraffenberger, (2009), p 283-284

33. Susan Dawn is status post mastectomy (6 weeks) due to carcinoma of the breast. She is admitted to the outpatient clinic for chemotherapy. What is the correct sequencing of the codes?
    A. V58.11   chemotherapy; 174.9 malignant neoplasm of breast
    B. V58.11   chemotherapy; V10.3 personal history of neoplasm of the breast
    C. V67.00   follow-up exam after surgery; V58.11 chemotherapy
    D. V10.3   personal history of neoplasm of the breast; V58.11 chemotherapy

REFERENCE: Bowie and Schaffer (2006), p 106-108
                    Brown, p 326
                    Frisch, p 153
                    Green, p 132
                    Hazelwood and Venable, p 86-87
                    Johnson and McHugh, p 56-57
                    Schraffenberger (2009), p 79-80

34. Which of the following is coded as an adverse effect in ICD-9-CM?
    A. mental retardation due to intracranial abscess
    B. rejection of transplanted kidney
    C. tinnitus due to allergic reaction after administration of eardrops
    D. nonfunctioning pacemaker due to defective soldering

REFERENCE: Bowie and Schaffer (2006), p 273-274, 293-295, 493
               Brown, p 365
               Frisch, p 149-150
               Green, p 160-162
               Hazelwood and Venable, p 259-261
               Johnson and McHugh, p 68-69
               Schraffenberger (2009), p 278-280

35. A service provided by a physician whose opinion or advice regarding evaluation and/or management of a specific problem is requested by another physician is referred to as
    A. a referral.   C. risk factor intervention.
    B. a consultation.   D. concurrent care.

REFERENCE: AMA (2009), p 14
               Bowie and Shaffer (2008), p 56-57
               Frisch, p 77
               Green, p 387
               Johnson and McHugh, p 165-168, 595
               Smith, p 199

36. A patient with leukemia is admitted for chemotherapy 5 weeks after experiencing an acute myocardial infarction. How will the MI be coded?
    A. acute MI with 5th digit 1—initial episode of care
    B. acute MI with 5th digit 2—subsequent episode of care
    C. history of MI
    D. chronic MI

REFERENCE: Bowie and Schaffer (2006), p 168
               Brown, p 275-276
               Green, 103
               Green and Bowie, p 230
               Hazelwood and Venable, p 146-148
               Johnson and McHugh, p 38-39
               McWay, p 116-117
               Schraffenberger (2009), p 141-144

37. In ICD-9-CM, when an exploratory laparotomy is performed followed by a therapeutic procedure, the coder lists
    A. therapeutic procedure first, exploratory laparotomy second.
    B. exploratory laparotomy, therapeutic procedure, closure of wound.
    C. therapeutic procedure only.
    D. exploratory laparotomy first, therapeutic procedure second.

REFERENCE: Bowie and Schaffer (2006), p 306-307
               Brown, p 56
               Green, p 59
               Schraffenberger (2009), p 37-38

38. The most widely discussed and debated unique patient identifier is the
    A. patient's date of birth.
    B. patient's first and last names.
    C. patient's Social Security number.
    D. Unique Physician Identification Number (UPIN).

REFERENCE: LaTour and Eichenwald-Maki, p 163

39. The Central Office on ICD-9-CM, which publishes *Coding Clinic,* is maintained by the
    A. National Center for Health Statistics.
    B. Centers for Medicare and Medicaid Services.
    C. American Hospital Association.
    D. American Health Information Management Association.

REFERENCE: Johnson and McHugh, p 12
               Schraffenberger (2007), p 13

40. A nomenclature of codes and medical terms that provides standard terminology for reporting physicians' services for third-party reimbursement is
    A. Current Medical Information and Terminology (CMIT).
    B. Current Procedural Terminology (CPT).
    C. Systematized Nomenclature of Pathology (SNOP).
    D. Diagnostic and Statistical Manual of Mental Disorders (DSM).

REFERENCE: Bowie and Schaffer (2008), 1-2, 6-7
               Frisch, p 5
               Green, p 9
               Johnson and McHugh, p 103
               Schraffenberger (2007), p 8-9

41. A cancer program is surveyed for approval by the
    A. American Cancer Society.
    B. Commission on Cancer of the American College of Surgeons.
    C. State Department of Health.
    D. Joint Commission on Accreditation of Health care Organizations.

REFERENCE: Abdelhak, p 475-476
               Johns, p 403
               LaTour and Eichenwald-Maki, p 291

42. The nursing staff would most likely use which of the following to facilitate aggregation of data for comparison at local, regional, national, and international levels?
    A. READ codes   C. SPECIALIST Lexicon
    B. ABC codes   D. LOINC

REFERENCE: Green and Bowie, p 299
               LaTour and Eichenwald-Maki, p 315
               McWay, p 135

43. The Level II (national) codes of the HCPCS coding system are maintained by the
    A. American Medical Association.
    B. CPT Editorial Panel.
    C. local fiscal intermediary.
    D. Centers for Medicare and Medicaid Services.

REFERENCE: Bowie and Schaffer (2008), p 6-7
               Frisch, p 8
               Green and Bowie, p 24
               Johnson and McHugh, p 85-86

44. A patient is admitted in alcohol withdrawal suffering from delirium tremens. The patient is a chronic alcoholic and cocaine addict. Which of the following is the principal diagnosis?
    A. alcoholic withdrawal   C. cocaine dependence
    B. chronic alcoholism   D. delirium tremens

REFERENCE: Bowie and Schaffer (2006), p 137-140
               Brown, p 119
               Frisch, p 132
               Schraffenberger (2009), p 116-117

45. A patient is admitted with pneumonia. Cultures are requested to determine the infecting organism. Which of the following, if present, would alert the coder to ask the physician whether or not this should be coded as gram-negative pneumonia?
    A. Pseudomonas   C. Staphylococcus
    B. Clostridium   D. Listeria

REFERENCE: Brown, p 94
               Green, p 12-14

46. The Level I (CPT) codes of the HCPCS coding system are maintained by the
    A. American Medical Association.
    B. American Hospital Association.
    C. local fiscal intermediary.
    D. Centers for Medicare and Medicaid Services.

REFERENCE: Bowie and Schaffer (2008), 1-2, 6
               Frisch, p 5
               Green, p 9
               Green and Bowie, p 24, 297-298
               Johnson and McHugh, p 103-104
               McWay, p 127-130

47. A physician excises a 3.1-cm malignant lesion of the scalp that requires full-thickness graft from the thigh to the scalp. In CPT, which of the following procedures should be coded?
    A. full-thickness skin graft to scalp only
    B. excision of lesion; full-thickness skin graft to scalp
    C. excision of lesion; full-thickness skin graft to scalp; excision of skin from thigh
    D. code 15000 for surgical preparation of recipient site; full-thickness skin graft to scalp

REFERENCE: AMA, CPT Assistant, vol. 7, no. 9, Sept. 1997, p 1-3
                Green, p 447-449, 482-484
                Johnson and McHugh, p 224, 229-230
                Smith, p 64-65

48. A patient is seen by a surgeon who determines that an emergency procedure is necessary. Identify the modifier that may be reported to indicate that the decision to do surgery was made on this office visit.
    A. -25   B. -55   C. -57   D. -58
REFERENCE: AMA (2009), p 478
                Bowie and Schaffer, p 18
                Frisch, p 18
                Green, p 337-338
                Smith, p 196

49. A patient develops difficulty during surgery and the physician discontinues the procedure. Identify the modifier that may be reported by the physician to indicate that the procedure was discontinued.
    A. -52   B. -53   C. -73   D. -74
REFERENCE: AMA (2009), p 477
                Bowie and Schaffer (2008), p 16-17
                Frisch, p 18
                Green, p 337-338
                Johnson and McHugh, p 117
                Smith, p 42

50. A patient has major surgery and sees the surgeon 10 days later for an unrelated E/M service. Indicate the modifier that should be attached to the E/M code for the service provided.
    A. -24   B. -25   C. -59   D. -79

REFERENCE: AMA (2009), p 477
                Bowie and Schaffer (2008), p 14
                Frisch, p 15, 30
                Green, p 336, 338
                Johnson and McHugh, p 115
                Smith, p 194-195

51. A barrier to widespread use of automated code assignment is
    A. inadequate technology.   C. resistance by physicians.
    B. poor quality of documentation.   D. resistance by HIM professionals.

REFERENCE: Green and Bowie, p 75, 80
                LaTour and Eichenwald-Maki, p 319
                McWay, p 136

52. In assigning E/M codes, three key components are used. These are
    A. history, examination, counseling.
    B. history, examination, time.
    C. history, nature of presenting problem, time.
    D. history, examination, medical-decision making.

REFERENCE: AMA (2009), p 3
                Bowie and Schaffer (2008), p 36-37
                Frisch, p12
                Green, p 369
                Johnson and McHugh, p 127-142
                Smith, p 181

53. Mrs. Jones had an appendectomy on November 1. She was taken back to surgery on November 2
    for evacuation of a hematoma of the wound site. Identify the modifier that may be reported for
    the November 2 visit.
    A. -58   B. -76   C.   -78   D. -79

REFERENCE: AMA (2009), p 478-479
                Bowie and Schaffer (2008), p 20
                Frisch, p 22, 240
                Green, p 337, 343
                Johnson and McHugh, p 119
                Smith, p 44

54. The primary goal of a hospital-based cancer registry is to
    A. improve patient care.
    B. allocate hospital resources appropriately.
    C. determine the need for professional and public education programs.
    D. monitor cancer incidence.

REFERENCE: Abdelhak, p 476
                Green, p 238
                McWay, p 117

55. A pregnant patient was admitted to the hospital with uncontrolled diabetes mellitus. She is a type
    I diabetic and was brought under control and subsequently discharged. The following code was
    assigned:

> 648.03 Other current condition in the mother classifiable elsewhere but complicating
> pregnancy, childbirth of the puerperium, diabetes mellitus

    Which of the following describe why the coding is in error?
    A. The incorrect fifth digit was used.
    B. The condition should have been coded as gestational diabetes because she is pregnant.
    C. An additional code describing the diabetes mellitus should be used.
    D. Only the code for the diabetes mellitus should have been used.

REFERENCE: Bowie and Schaffer (2006), p 119-118
                Brown, p 228-229
                Frisch, p 130
                Green, p 134-135
                Johnson and McHugh, p 43-44, 339-340
                Schraffenberger (2009), p 209-210

56. A secondary data source that houses and aggregates extensive data about patients with a certain diagnosis is a
    A. disease index.
    B. master patient index.
    C. disease registry.
    D. admissions register.

REFERENCE: Green, p 230, 232-233
               LaTour and Eichenwald-Maki, p 289
               McWay, p 116-117

57. After reviewing the following excerpt from CPT, code 27646 would be interpreted as

27645	Radical resection of tumor, bone; tibia
27646	fibula
27647	talus or calcaneus

    A. 27646   radical resection of tumor, bone; tibia and fibula.
    B. 27646   radical resection of tumor, bone; fibula.
    C. 27646   radical resection of tumor, bone; fibula or tibia.
    D. 27646   radical resection of tumor, bone; fibula, talus or calcaneus.

REFERENCE: Bowie and Schaffer (2008), p 3-5
               Green, p 327
               Smith, p 18-19

58. A patient was admitted to the hospital with hemiplegia and aphasia. The hemiplegia and aphasia were resolved before discharge and the patient was diagnosed with cerebral thrombosis. What is the correct coding and sequencing?
    A. hemiplegia; aphasia
    B. cerebral thrombosis
    C. cerebral thrombosis; hemiplegia; aphasia
    D. hemiplegia; cerebral thrombosis; aphasia

REFERENCE: Brown, p 286
               Hazelwood and Venable, p 153
               Schraffenberger, (2009), p 152

59. A 36-year-old woman was admitted to the hospital for an obstetrical delivery of her third child. During the admission, a sterilization procedure was performed for contraceptive purposes. The V25.2 code for sterilization would be
    A. assigned as a principal diagnosis.
    B. assigned as a secondary diagnosis.
    C. not assigned because this was the patient's third child.
    D. not assigned because it is the same admission as the delivery.

REFERENCE: Brown, p 236
               Schraffenberger, (2009), p 319

60. According to ICD-9-CM, which one of the following is NOT a mechanical complication of an internal implant?
    A. erosion of skin by pacemaker electrodes
    B. inflammation of urethra due to indwelling catheter
    C. leakage of breast prosthesis
    D. IUD embedded in uterine wall

REFERENCE: Brown, p 377-378
                    Hazelwood and Venable, p 276-278
                    Johnson and McHugh, p 71-72
                    Schraffenberger (2009), p 287

61. A population-based cancer registry that is designed to determine rates and trends in a defined population is a (an)
    A. incidence-only population-based registry.
    B. cancer control population-based registry.
    C. research-oriented population-based registry.
    D. patient care population-based registry.

REFERENCE: Abdelhak, p 476
                    Johns, p 401
                    LaTour and Eichenwald-Maki, p 290

62. Given the diagnosis "carcinoma of axillary lymph nodes and lungs, metastatic from breast," what is the primary cancer site(s)?
    A. axillary lymph nodes   C. breast
    B. lungs   D. both A & B

REFERENCE: Bowie and Schaffer (2006), p 98-100, 102-204
                    Brown, p 318
                    Frisch, p 142-144
                    Green, p 128-133
                    Hazelwood and Venable, p 93
                    Johnson and McHugh, p 55-58
                    Schraffenberger (2009), p 88

63. In the diagnosis "first-, second-, and third-degree burns of the chest wall," a code is required for
    A. the first-degree burn only.
    B. the second-degree burn only.
    C. the third-degree burn only.
    D. each first-, second-, and third-degree burn.

REFERENCE: Bowie and Schaffer (2006), p 273-275
                    Brown, p 360
                    Frisch, p 140-141
                    Hazelwood and Venable, p 250
                    Johnson and McHugh, p 65-67, 214-215, 236-237
                    Schraffenberger, (2009), p 269-270

64. When is it appropriate to use category V10, history of malignant neoplasm?
    A. primary malignancy recurred at original site and adjunct chemotherapy is directed at the site
    B. primary malignancy has been eradicated and no adjunct treatment is being given at this time
    C. primary malignancy eradicated and the patient is admitted for adjunct chemotherapy to primary site
    D. primary malignancy is eradicated; adjunct treatment is refused by patient even though there is some remaining malignancy

REFERENCE: Bowie and Schaffer (2006), p 101-102
                Frisch, p 142-144
                Green, p 131-133
                Johnson and McHugh, p 55-58
                Schraffenberger (2009), p 79-80, 316-317

65. According to CPT, in which of the following cases would an established E/M code be used?
    A. A home visit with a 45-year-old male with a long history of drug abuse and alcoholism. The man is seen at the request of Adult Protective Services for an assessment of his mental capabilities.
    B. John and his family have just moved to town. John has asthma and requires medication to control the problem. He has an appointment with Dr. You and will bring his records from his previous physician.
    C. Tom is seen by Dr. X for a sore throat. Dr. X is on-call for Tom's regular physician, Dr. Y. The last time that Tom saw Dr. Y was a couple of years ago.
    D. A 78-year-old female with weight loss and progressive agitation over the past 2 months is seen by her primary care physician for drug therapy. She has not seen her primary care physician in 4 years.

REFERENCE: AMA (2009), p 1
                AMA, CPT Assistant, Vol. 8, No. 10, Oct 1998
                Bowie and Schaffer (2008), p 32-33
                Frisch, p 49-50
                Green, p 355-356
                Smith, p 180

66. In order to use the inpatient CPT consultation codes, the consulting physician must
    A. order diagnostic tests.
    B. document his findings in the patient's medical record.
    C. communicate orally his opinion to the attending physician.
    D. use the term "referral" in his report.

REFERENCE: AMA (2009), p 14-15
                Bowie & Schaffer (2008), 56-57
                Frisch, 85-86
                Green, p 387-389
                Smith, p 199

67. The attending physician requests a consultation from a cardiologist. The cardiologist takes a detailed history, performs a detailed examination, and utilizes moderate medical decision making. The cardiologist orders diagnostic tests and prescribes medication. He documents his findings in the patient's medical record and communicates in writing with the attending physician. The following day the consultant visits the patient to evaluate the patient's response to the medication, to review results from the diagnostic tests, and to discuss treatment options. What codes should the consultant report for the two visits?
   A. an initial inpatient consult and a follow-up consult
   B. an initial inpatient consult for both visits
   C. an initial inpatient consult and a subsequent hospital visit
   D. an initial inpatient consult and initial hospital care

REFERENCE: Bowie and Schaffer (2008), p 56-57
               Frisch, 85-86
               Green, p 388-389
               Smith, p 199

68. According to the American Medical Association, medical decision making is measured by all of the following except
   A. number of diagnoses or management options.
   B. amount and complexity of data reviewed.
   C. risk of complications.
   D. specialty of the treating physician.

REFERENCE: AMA (2009), p 7
               Bowie and Schaffer (2008), p 47-50
               Frisch, p 322
               Green, p 373-374
               Johnson, p 133
               Smith, p 188-189

69. CPT provides Level I modifiers to explain all of the following situations EXCEPT
   A. when a service or procedure is partially reduced or eliminated at the physician's discretion.
   B. when one surgeon provides only postoperative services.
   C. when a patient sees a surgeon for follow-up care after surgery.
   D. when the same laboratory test is repeated multiple times on the same day.

REFERENCE: AMA (2009), p 477-481
               Bowie and Schaffer (2008), p 13-22
               Frisch, p 13-23
               Green, p 334-349
               Johnson and McHugh, p 113-120

70. The best place to ascertain the size of an excised lesion for accurate CPT coding is the
   A. discharge summary.   C. operative report.
   B. pathology report.   D. anesthesia record.

REFERENCE: Green, p 477-479
               Johnson and McHugh, p 221
               Smith, p 55-56

71. Which of the following is expected to enable hospitals to collect more specific information for use in patient care, benchmarking, quality assessment, research, public health reporting, strategic planning, and reimbursement?
    A. LOINC
    B. ICD-10-CM
    C. NDC
    D. NANDA

REFERENCE: Abdelhak, p 202
               Green, p 920
               Johnson and McHugh, p 78

72. Which of the following contains a list of coding edits developed by CMS in an effort to promote correct coding nationwide and to prevent the inappropriate unbundling of related services?
    A. National Coverage Determination (NCD)
    B. National Correct Coding Initiative (NCCI)
    C. CPT Assistant
    D, Health care Common Procedure Coding System (HCPCS)

REFERENCE: Bowie and Schaffer (2008), p 91-93
               Frisch, p 235-240
               Green, p 350-351
               Johnson and McHugh, p 556
               Smith, p 53

73. Case definition is important for all types of registries. Age will certainly be an important criterion for accessing a case in a(n) _____ registry.
    A. implant   C. HIV/AIDS
    B. trauma   D. birth defects

REFERENCE: LaTour and Eichenwald-Maki, p 292

74. To gather statistics for surgical services provided on an outpatient basis, which of the following codes are needed?
    A. ICD-9-CM codes
    B. Evaluation and Management Codes
    C. HCPCS Level II Codes
    D. CPT codes

REFERENCE: Green and Bowie, p 230
               McWay, p 116
               Schraffenberger (2007), p 8-9

75. The Cancer Committee at your hospital requests a list of all patients entered into your cancer registry in the last year. This information would be obtained by checking the
    A. disease index.   C. accession register.
    B. tickler file.   D. suspense file.

REFERENCE: Johns, p 401-402
               LaTour and Eichenwald-Maki, p 290

76. The reference date for a cancer registry is
    A. January 1 of the year in which the registry was established.
    B. the date when data collection began.
    C. the date that the Cancer Committee is established.
    D. the date that the cancer program applies for approval by the American College of Surgeons.

REFERENCE: Abdelhak, p 476

77. The abstract completed on the patients in your hospital contains the following items: patient demographics; pre-hospital interventions; vital signs on admission; procedures and treatment prior to hospitalization; transport modality; and injury severity score. The hospital uses this data for its
    A. AIDS registry.   C. implant registry.
    B. diabetes registry.   D. trauma registry.

REFERENCE: Abdelhak, p 484
                Johns, p 403-404
                LaTour and Eichenwald-Maki, p 292

78. In relation to birth defects registries, active surveillance systems
    A. use trained staff to identify cases in all hospitals, clinics, and other facilities through review of patient records, indexes, vital records, and hospital logs.
    B. are commonly used in all 50 states.
    C. miss 10% to 30% of all cases.
    D. rely on reports submitted by hospitals, clinics, or other sources.

REFERENCE: Abdelhak, p 479

79. In regard to quality of coding, the degree to which the same results (same codes) are obtained by different coders or on multiple attempts by the same coder refers to
    A. reliability.   C. completeness.
    B. validity.   D. timeliness.

REFERENCE: LaTour and Eichenwald-Maki, p 317

80. The Health care Cost and Utilization Project (HCUP) consists of a set of databases that include data on inpatients whose care is paid for by third-party payers. HCUP is an initiative of the
    A. Agency for Health care Research and Quality.
    B. Centers for Medicare and Medicaid Services.
    C. National Library of Medicine.
    D. World Health Organization.

REFERENCE: LaTour and Eichenwald-Maki, p 299
                McWay, p 145

81. In regards to quality of coding, the degree to which the codes selected accurately reflect the diagnoses and procedures refers to
    A. reliability.   C. completeness.
    B. validity.   D. timeliness.

REFERENCE: Green and Bowie, p 247-248
                LaTour and Eichenwald-Maki, p 317

82. The coding supervisor notices that the coders are routinely failing to code all possible diagnoses and procedures for a patient encounter. This indicates to the supervisor that there is a problem with
    A. reliability.
    B. validity.
    C. completeness.
    D. timeliness.

REFERENCE: LaTour and Eichenwald-Maki, p 317

83. When coding free skin grafts, which of the following is NOT an essential item of data needed for accurate coding?
    A. recipient site
    B. donor site
    C. size of defect
    D. type of repair

REFERENCE: Bowie and Schaffer (2008), p 103-104
               Green, p 485-487
               Johnson and McHugh, p 231, 233-234
               Smith, p 66-67

84. In CPT, Category III codes include codes
    A. to describe emerging technologies.
    B. to measure performance.
    C. for use by nonphysician practitioners.
    D. for supplies, drugs, and durable medical equipment.

REFERENCE: AMA (2009), p 467
               Bowie and Schaffer (2008), p 7
               Green, p 321
               Johnson and McHugh, p 103, 112, 327-328
               Smith, p 3

85. The information collected for your registry includes patient demographic information, diagnosis codes, functional status, and histocompatibility information. This type of registry is a
    A. birth defects registry.
    B. diabetes registry.
    C. transplant registry.
    D. trauma registry.

REFERENCE: LaTour and Eichenwald-Maki, p 294

86. In the ICD-9-CM classification system, shooting pain in the right eye due to the presence of an intact, correctly positioned permanent contact lens would be coded as a(n)
    A. current injury.
    B. late effect.
    C. mechanical complication of an internal prosthetic device.
    D. abnormal reaction of the body to the presence of an internal prosthetic device.

REFERENCE: Brown, p 377-378
               Hazelwood and Venable, p 276-277
               Schraffenberger, (2009), p 287-288

87. In the ICD-9-CM classification system, severe shock due to third-degree burns sustained in an industrial accident would be coded as a(n)
   A. current injury.
   B. late effect.
   C. mechanical complication of an internal prosthetic device.
   D. abnormal reaction of the body to the presence of an internal prosthetic device.

REFERENCE: Bowie and Schaffer (2006), 59-60
               Brown, p 362
               Frisch, p 131-132
               Johnson and McHugh, p 74-75

88. In the ICD-9-CM classification system, a nonfunctioning pacemaker due to the disintegration of the electrodes (leads) would be coded as a(n)
   A. current injury.
   B. late effect.
   C. mechanical complication of an internal prosthetic device.
   D. abnormal reaction of the body to the presence of an internal prosthetic device.

REFERENCE: Brown, p 377-378
               Hazelwood and Venable, p 276-277
               Johnson and McHugh, p 71
               Schraffenberger (2009), p 287-288

89. In the ICD-9-CM classification system, an esophageal stricture due to a burn received in a house fire several years ago would be coded as a(n)
   A. current injury.
   B. late effect.
   C. mechanical complication of an internal prosthetic device.
   D. abnormal reaction of the body to the presence of an internal prosthetic device.

REFERENCE: Bowie and Schaffer (2006), 57-58
               Brown, p 354
               Hazelwood and Venable, p 50-51
               Schraffenberger, (2009), p 305-306

90. Dizziness and blurred vision following ingestion of prescribed Allegra and a glass of wine at dinner would be reported as a(n)
   A. poisoning.
   B. adverse reaction to a drug.
   C. late effect of a poisoning.
   D. late effect of an adverse reaction.

REFERENCE: Bowie and Schaffer (2006), p 273-274, 293-295, 493
               Brown, p 366
               Frisch, p 149-150
               Green, p 160-162
               Hazelwood and Venable, p 263
               Johnson and McHugh, p 68-69
               Schraffenberger (2009), p 283

91. Tachycardia after taking a correct dosage of prescribed Lortab would be reported as a(n)
    A. poisoning.
    B. adverse reaction to a drug.
    C. late effect of a poisoning.
    D. late effect of an adverse reaction.

REFERENCE: Bowie and Schaffer (2006), p 273-274, 293-295, 493
                    Brown, p 365
                    Frisch, p 149-150
                    Green, p 160-162
                    Hazelwood and Venable, p 259-260
                    Johnson and McHugh, p 68-69
                    Schraffenberger (2009), p 278-279

92. Blindness due to an allergic reaction to ampicillin administered 6 years ago would be reported as a(n)
    A. poisoning.
    B. adverse reaction to a drug.
    C. late effect of a poisoning.
    D. late effect of an adverse reaction.

REFERENCE: Bowie and Schaffer (2006), p 273-274, 293-295, 493
                    Brown, p 372-373
                    Frisch, p 149-150
                    Green, p 160-162
                    Hazelwood and Venable, p 261-262
                    Johnson and McHugh, p 68-69
                    Schraffenberger (2009), p 282

93. The patient underwent bypass surgery for life-threatening coronary artery disease. With the aid of extracorporeal circulation, the right internal mammary artery was taken down to the left anterior descending artery and saphenous vein grafts were brought from the aorta to the diagonal, the right coronary artery, and the posterior descending artery. What is the correct ICD-9-CM coding for this procedure?
    A. single internal mammary artery bypass; aortocoronary artery bypass of three vessels
    B. aortocoronary bypass of three coronary arteries
    C. aortocoronary bypass of four coronary arteries
    D. single internal mammary artery bypass; aortocoronary bypass of three vessels, extracorporeal circulation

REFERENCE: Brown, p 301-303
                    Schraffenberger, (2009), p 157-158

94. Patient Jamey Smith has been seen at Oceanside Hospital three times prior to this current encounter. Unfortunately, because of clerical errors, Jamey's information was entered into the MPI incorrectly on the three previous admissions and consequently has three different medical record numbers. The unit numbering system is used at Oceanside Hospital. Jamey's previous entries into the MPI are as follows:

09/03/04	Jamey Smith	MR# 10361
03/10/05	Jamey Smith Doe	MR# 33998
07/23/06	Jamie Smith Doe	MR# 36723

The next available number to be assigned at Oceanside Hospital is 41369. Duplicate entries in the MPI should be scrubbed and all of Jamey's medical records should be filed under medical record number

A. 10361.
B. 33998.
C. 36723.
D. 41369.

REFERENCE: Green and Bowie, p 195-197
                        McWay, p 111

95. The method of calculating errors in a coding audit that allows for benchmarking with other hospitals, and permits the reviewer to track errors by case type, is the

A. record method.
B. benchmarking method.
C. code method.
D. focused review method.

REFERENCE: Schraffenberger (2007), p 237

96. The most common type of registry located in hospitals of all sizes and in every region of the country is the

A. trauma registry.
B. cancer registry.
C. AIDS registry.
D. birth defects registry.

REFERENCE: Green, p 24, 238
                        McWay, p 117

97. Which code represents an HCPCS Level II National Code?

A. W0166
B. 99281
C. D0417
D. 66690

REFERENCE: Frisch, p 8
                        Green, p 285
                        Green and Bowie, p 24
                        Johns, p 208-209
                        Johnson and McHugh, p 85-87
                        Smith, p 4

98. A radiologist is asked to review a patient's CT scan that was taken at another facility. The modifier -26 attached to the code indicates that the physician is billing for what component of the procedure?

A. professional
B. technical
C. global
D. confirmatory

REFERENCE: Bowie and Schaffer, p 15
                        Frisch, p 14, 16
                        Green, p 336, 347, 714
                        Johnson and McHugh, p 116

99. When coding neoplasms, topography means
   A. cell structure and form.
   B. site.
   C. variation from normal tissue.
   D. extent of the spread of the disease.

REFERENCE: Abdelhak, p 477

100. According to CPT, antepartum care includes all of the following EXCEPT
   A. initial and subsequent history.
   B. physical examination.
   C. monthly visits up to 36 weeks.
   D. routine chemical urinalysis.

REFERENCE: Bowie and Schaffer (2008), p 267-268
               Green, p 664
               Johnson and McHugh, p343, 351
               Smith, p 136

101. The Cancer Committee at Wharton General Hospital wants to compare long-term survival rates for pancreatic cancer by evaluating medical versus surgical treatment of the cancer. The best source of this data is the
   A. disease index.
   B. operation index.
   C. master patient index.
   D. cancer registry abstracts.

REFERENCE: Abdelhak, p 477-478
               Green, p 134-138
               LaTour and Eichenwald-Maki, p 290-291
               McWay, p 117

102. A list or collection of clinical words or phrases with their meanings is a
   A. data dictionary.
   B. language.
   C. medical nomenclature.
   D. clinical vocabulary.

REFERENCE: Green, 8
               Green and Bowie, p 294
               McWay, p 125-128

103. The main difference between concurrent and retrospective coding is
   A. when the coding is done.
   B. what classification system is used.
   C. the credentials of the coder.
   D. the involvement of the physician.

REFERENCE: Schraffenberger (2007), p 27

104. A patient was discharged from the acute care hospital with a final diagnosis of bronchial asthma. As the coder reviews the record, she notes that the patient was described as having prolonged and intractable wheezing, airway obstruction that was not relieved by bronchodilators and the lab values showed decreased respiratory function. The coder queried the physician to determine whether the code for _____ is appropriate to be added to the final diagnoses.
   A. acute and chronic bronchitis
   B. chronic obstructive pulmonary disease
   C. respiratory failure
   D. status asthmaticus

REFERENCE: Bowie and Schaffer (2006), p 181
               Brown, p 154-155
               Frisch, p 139
               Green, 143
               Hazelwood and Venable, p 166
               Schraffenberger (2009), p 166-167

105. A patient is undergoing hemodialysis for end-stage renal disease in the outpatient department of an acute care hospital. The patient develops what is believed to be severe heartburn, but is sent to observation for several hours, at which time the patient is admitted to inpatient care for further workup. The cardiologist diagnoses the patient's problem as unstable angina. What is the principal diagnosis for the acute hospital stay?
   A. complications of hemodialysis   C. unstable angina
   B. heartburn   D. renal disease

REFERENCE: Bowie and Schaffer (2006), 59
               Green, p 204-205
               Johnson and McHugh, p 570-571
               Schraffenberger (2009), p 516-517

106. A patient is seen in the emergency room of an acute care hospital with tachycardia and hypotension. The patient had received an injection of tetanus toxoid (correct dosage) earlier at his primary care physician's office. Which of the following is the appropriate sequencing for this encounter?
   A. hypotension; tachycardia; accidental poisoning E code (tetanus toxoid)
   B. unspecified adverse reaction to tetanus toxoid; undetermined cause E code (tetanus toxoid)
   C. hypotension; tachycardia; therapeutic use E code (tetanus toxoid)
   D. poisoning code (tetanus toxoid); hypotension; tachycardia; accidental poisoning E code (tetanus toxoid)

REFERENCE: Bowie and Schaffer (2006), p 273-274, 293-295, 493
               Brown, p 365-368
               Frisch, p 149-150
               Green, p 160-162
               Hazelwood and Venable, p 259-261
               Johnson and McHugh, p 68-69
               Schraffenberger, (2009), p 278-279

107. A rare malignant tumor often associated with AIDS is
    A. Kaposi's sarcoma.
    C. pheochromocytoma.
    B. glioblastoma multiforme.
    D. melanoma.

REFERENCE: Hazelwood and Venable, p 77-78
                Schraffenberger (2009), p 71-73

108. A PEG procedure would most likely be done to facilitate
    A. breathing.
    C. urination.
    B. eating.
    D. none of the above

REFERENCE: Johnson and McHugh, p 194
                Schraffenberger (2009), p 183

109. What ICD-9-CM coding scheme is used to show that a therapeutic abortion resulted in a live
     fetus?

    A. spontaneous abortion; V30 code to show a newborn birth
    B. code 644.21, early onset of delivery; V27 code (outcome of delivery)
    C. abortion by type; V27 code (outcome of delivery)
    D. therapeutic abortion

REFERENCE: Bowieand Schaffer (2006), p 213
                Brown, p 247
                Green, p 147, 151
                Hazelwood and Venable, p 203
                Johnson and McHugh, p 340
                Schraffenberger (2009), p 201

110. Prolonged pregnancy is a pregnancy that has advanced beyond _____ completed weeks of
     gestation.
    A. 39
    C. 41
    B. 40
    D. 42

REFERENCE: Hazelwood and Venable, p 204
                Schraffenberger (2009), p 203

Answer Key for Classification Systems and Secondary Data Sources

NOTE: Explanations are provided for those questions that require mathematical calculations and questions that are not clearly explained in the references that are cited.

	ANSWER	EXPLANATION
1.	A	
2.	B	M codes and E codes are never principal diagnosis codes and, in fact, are optional for coding. V codes to describe the outcome of delivery are always secondary codes on the mother's chart.
3.	B	
4.	C	
5.	A	Antivert is used for the management of nausea and dizziness associated with motion sickness and in vertigo associated with diseases affecting the vestibular system.
6.	A	
7.	C	
8.	C	
9.	A	A coder should never assign a code on the basis of laboratory results alone. If findings are clearly outside the normal range and the physician has ordered additional testing or treatment, it is appropriate to consult with the physician as to whether a diagnosis should be added or whether the abnormal finding should be listed.
10.	A	
11.	B	Pilocarpine is used to treat open-angle and angle-closure glaucoma to reduce intraocular pressure.
12.	D	Digoxin is used for maintenance therapy in congestive heart failure, atrial fibrillation, atrial flutter, and paroxysmal atrial tachycardia. Ibuprofen is an anti-inflammatory drug. Oxytocin is used to initiate or improve uterine contractions at term, and haloperidol is used to manage psychotic disorders.
13.	D	
14.	C	HCPCS codes (Levels I and II) would only give the code for any procedures that were performed and would not identify the diagnosis code or cause of the accident. The correct name of the nomenclature for athletic injuries is the Standard Nomenclature of Athletic Injuries and is used to identify sports injuries. It has not been revised since 1976.
15.	D	
16.	C	
17.	B	All three key components (history, physical examination, and medical decision making) are required for new patients and initial visits. At least two of the three key components are required for established patients, and subsequent visits.
18.	B	
19.	D	
20.	A	
21.	B	
22.	B	
23.	A	
24.	A	
25.	A	
26.	B	

Answer Key for Classification Systems and Secondary Data Sources

	ANSWER	EXPLANATION

27.   D   There are V codes that indicate various reasons for canceled surgery. Review codes V64.0x, V64.1, V64.2, and V64.3. As usual, the principal diagnosis is always the reason for admission, in this case, the cholelithiasis. The contraindication (the tachycardia) should also be coded.

28.   B

29.   B   The principal procedure is defined as the procedure performed for definitive treatment (rather than for diagnostic purposes) or one that was necessary to take care of the complication. If two or more procedures meet this definition, the one most related to the principal diagnosis is designated as the principal procedure.

30.   C   In order to use category 402 there must be a cause-and-effect relationship shown between the hypertension and the heart condition. "With" does not show this relationship, nor does the fact that both conditions are listed on the same chart. The term "hypertensive" indicates a cause and effect relationship.

31.   B   An acute MI is considered to be anything under 8 weeks' duration from the time of initial onset. A chronic MI is considered anything over 8 weeks with symptoms. An old MI is considered anything over 8 weeks with NO symptoms.

32.   A   A reaction due to mixing drugs and alcohol is coded as a poisoning.

33.   A   The patient is admitted for chemotherapy (V58.11) and, because the breast cancer is still actively being treated, it is still coded as current.

34.   C   Mental retardation is a late effect, rejection of the kidney is a complication, and a nonfunctioning pacemaker is a mechanical complication.

35.   B
36.   B
37.   C
38.   C
39.   C
40.   B
41.   B
42.   B
43.   D
44.   D
45.   A
46.   A
47.   B
48.   C
49.   B
50.   A
51.   B
52.   D
53.   C
54.   A
55.   C
56.   C

Answer Key for Classification Systems and Secondary Data Sources

	ANSWER	EXPLANATION
57.	B	
58.	B	
59.	B	
60.	B	
61.	A	
62.	C	
63.	C	
64.	B	
65.	C	
66.	B	
67.	C	The first visit would be an inpatient consult. Because the physician continued to treat the patient and participate in his care, all subsequent visits are considered as subsequent hospital care and are no longer consults.
68.	D	
69.	C	Modifier -52 can be used if a physician elects to partially reduce or eliminate a service or procedure. Modifier -55 is used by a physician who only provides postoperative services. Modifier -91 is used when a laboratory test is repeated multiple times on the same day. CPT code 99024 is used to report a follow-up visit after surgery.
70.	C	
71.	B	
72.	B	
73.	D	
74	D	
75.	C	
76.	B	
77.	D	
78.	A	
79.	A	
80.	A	
81.	B	
82.	C	
83.	B	
84.	A	
85.	C	
86.	D	
87.	A	
88.	C	
89.	B	
90.	A	
91.	B	
92.	D	

Answer Key for Classification Systems and Secondary Data Sources

	ANSWER	EXPLANATION

93.   D   The procedure described includes one internal mammary artery, which is not considered an aortocoronary bypass. There were 3 aortocoronary bypasses: aorta to diagonal, aorta to right coronary artery, and aorta to the posterior descending artery. The description states that extracorporeal circulation was used.

94.   A

95.   A

96.   B

97.   C   HCPCS Level I codes are five-digit (numeric) codes found in the CPT book. HCPCS Level II National Codes are alphanumeric starting with letters A-V. HCPCS Level III Local Codes are alphanumeric starting with a letter W-Z. Level III codes were eliminated as of December 31, 2003.

98.   A   With CPT radiology codes, there are three components that have to be considered: the professional, technical, and global components. The professional component describes the services of a physician who supervises the taking of an x-ray film and the interpretation with report of the results. The technical component describes the services of the person who uses the equipment, the film, and other supplies. The global component describes the combination of both professional and technical components. If the billing radiologist's services include only the supervision and interpretation component, the radiologist bills the procedure code and adds the modifier -26 to indicate that he or she did only the professional component of the procedure.

99.   B

100.   C

101.   D

102.   D

103.   A

104.   D

105.   C

106.   C

107.   A

108.   B

109.   B

110.   D

REFERENCES

Abdelhak, M., Grostick, S., Hanken, M.A., & Jacobs, E. (Eds.). (2007). *Health information: Management of a strategic resource* (3rd ed.). St. Louis: Saunders Elsevier.

American Hospital Association. *Coding clinic.* Chicago: American Hospital Association (AHA).

American Medical Association. *CPT assistant.* Chicago: American Medical Association (AMA).

American Medical Association. (2009). *Physicians' current procedural terminology (CPT) 2009, professional edition.* Chicago: American Medical Association (AMA).

Bowie, M. J. & Schaffer, R. (2006). *Understanding ICD-9-CM: A worktext.* Clifton Park, New York: Delmar Cengage Learning.

Bowie, M. J. & Schaffer, R. (2008). *Understanding procedural coding: A worktext.* Clifton Park, New York: Delmar Cengage Learning.

Brown, F. (2009). *ICD-9-CM coding handbook 2009 with answers.* Chicago: American Hospital Association (AHA).

Centers for Disease Control and Prevention. *Draft ICD-10-CM Official guidelines for coding and reporting for acute short-term and long-term hospital inpatient and physician office and other outpatient encounters.* http://www.cdc.gov. Accessed 11/10/2008 at http://www.cdc.gov/nchs/about/otheract/icd9/icd10cm.htm.

Frisch, B. (2007). *Correct coding for medicare, compliance, and reimbursement.* New York: Thompson Delmar Learning.

Green, M. (2007). *3-2-1 code it.* New York: Thompson Delmar Learning.

Green, M. A. & Bowie, M. J. (2005). *Essentials of health information management: Principles and practices.* New York: Thompson Delmar Learning.

Hazelwood, A. C., & Venable, C. A. (2009). *ICD-9-CM diagnostic coding and reimbursement for physician services.* Chicago: American Health Information Management Association (AHIMA).

ICD-9-CM. *Code book professional edition 2009.* Salt Lake City: INGINEX.

Johns, M. (2007). *Health information management technology: An applied approach* (2nd ed.). Chicago: American Health Information Management Association (AHIMA).

Johnson, S. L. & McHugh, C. S. (2006). *Understanding medical coding: a comprehensive guide* (2nd ed.) New York: Thompson Delmar Learning.

LaTour, K., & Eichenwald-Maki, S. (2006). *Health information management: concepts, principles and practice* (2nd ed.). Chicago: American Health Information Management Association (AHIMA).

McWay, D. C. (2008). *Today's health information management: An integrated approach.* New York: Thompson Delmar Learning.

Nobles, S. (2002). *Delmar's drug reference for health care professionals.* New York: Delmar.

Schraffenberger, L. A., & Kuehn, L. (2007). *Effective management of coding services* (3rd ed.). Chicago: American Health Information Management Association (AHIMA).

Schraffenberger, L.A. (2009). *Basic ICD-9-CM coding.* Chicago: American Health Information Management Association (AHIMA).

Smith, G. (2008). *Basic CPT/HCPCS coding 2008.* Chicago: American Health Information Management Association (AHIMA).

VI. Medical Billing and Reimbursement Systems

Toni Cade, MBA, RHIA, CCS, FAHIMA

1. The case-mix management system that utilizes information from the minimum data set (MDS) in long-term care settings is called
   A. Medicare severity diagnosis related groups (MS-DRGs).
   B. resource based relative value system (RBRVS).
   C. resource utilization groups (RUGs).
   D. ambulatory patient classifications (APCs).

REFERENCE: Green and Rowell, p 284-285
               Schraffenberger and Kuehn, p 145
               Frisch, p 185-186, 235

2. The prospective payment system used to reimburse home health agencies for Medicare patients utilizes data from
   A. MDS (Minimum Data Set).
   B. OASIS (Outcome and Assessment Information Set).
   C. UHDDS (Uniform Hospital Discharge Data Set).
   D. UACDS (Uniform Ambulatory Core Data Set).

REFERENCE: Green and Rowell, p 23, 281
               Schraffenberger and Kuehn, p 147
               Frisch, p 37

3. _____ indicates that the claim has been released as complete for submission to the insurer for payment.
   A. bill drop
   B. accounts receivables
   C. bill hold
   D. concurrent review

REFERENCE: Schraffenberger and Kuehn, p 282

4. All of the following items are packaged under the Medicare outpatient prospective payment system, EXCEPT for
   A. recovery room.
   B. supplies.
   C. anesthesia.
   D. medical visits.

REFERENCE: Johns, p 283
               LaTour and Eichenwald-Maki, p 367

5. Under the RBRVS, each HCPCS/CPT code contains 3 components, each having assigned relative value units. These 3 components are
   A. geographic index, wage index, and cost of living index.
   B. fee-for-service, per diem payment, and capitation.
   C. conversion factor, CMS weight, and hospital-specific rate.
   D. physician work, practice expense, and malpractice insurance expense.

REFERENCE: Frisch, p 185-186, 235

6. The prospective payment system to hospitals for Medicare hospital outpatients is called _____ and became effective on _____
   A. APGs, October 1, 2000
   B. RBRVS, January 1, 2000
   C. APCs, August 1, 2000
   D. DRGs, October 1, 1983

REFERENCE: Schraffenberger and Kuehn, p 140-141
               Green and Rowell, p 23-24, 286-287

7. A patient was seen by Dr. Zachary. The charge for the office visit was $125. The Medicare beneficiary had already met his deductible. The Medicare fee schedule amount is $100. Dr. Zachary does not accept assignment. The office manager will apply a practice termed as "balance billing," which means that the patient is
   A. financially liable for the Medicare fee schedule amount.
   B. financially liable for charges in excess of the Medicare fee schedule.
   C. not financially liable for any amount.
   D. is financially liable for the entire charge for the office visit.

REFERENCE: Johns, p 308
                LaTour and Eichenwald-Maki, p 383-384
                Green and Rowell, p 52, 294, 366-367, 437

8. The prospective payment system based upon resource utilization groups (RUGs) is used for reimbursement to _____ for Medicare patients.
   A. freestanding ambulatory surgery centers
   B. hospital-based outpatients
   C. intermediate care facilities
   D. skilled nursing facilities

REFERENCE: Schraffenberger and Kuehn, p 145
                Green and Bowie, p 23
                Green, p 202-203

9. The _____ is a statement sent to the provider to explain payments made by third party payers.
   A. remittance advice   C. attestation statement
   B. advance beneficiary notice D. acknowledgment notice

REFERENCE: Frisch, p 188-192
                Green and Rowell, p 6, 69-71, 73
                Rimmer, p 95

10. How many major diagnostic categories are there in the MS-DRG system?
    A. 29   C. 19
    B. 20   D. 25

REFERENCE: Green and Rowell, p 284

11. The MS-DRG (Medicare Severity—Diagnosis-Related Group) system was designed to pay
    A. multiple groups of reimbursement based on each diagnosis.
    B. only one amount (group) of reimbursement per hospitalization.
    C. multiple groups of reimbursement based on the per diem rates.
    D. multiple groups of reimbursement based on the principal diagnosis and the most substantial comorbidity.

REFERENCE: Scott, p 47
                Green and Rowell, p 284-285

12. A computer software program that assigns appropriate MS-DRGs according to the information provided for each episode of care is called a(n)
    A. encoder.
    B. case-mix analyzer.
    C. grouper.
    D. DRG creeper.

REFERENCE: Castro and Layman, p 106

13. The standard claim form used by hospitals to request reimbursement for inpatient and outpatient procedures performed or services provided is called the
    A. UB-04.
    B. CMS-1500.
    C. CMS-1491.
    D. CMS-1600.

REFERENCE: Green, p 834, 838
                   Green and Rowell, p 302-318

14. Under ASCs, when multiple procedures are performed during the same surgical session, a payment reduction is applied. The procedure in the highest level group is reimbursed at _____ (percent) and all remaining procedures are reimbursed at _____ (percent).
    A. 50%, 25%
    B. 100%, 50%
    C. 100%, 25%
    D. 100%, 75%

REFERENCE: Casto and Layman, p 191

15. The _____ refers to a statement sent to the patient to clarify which services were provided, amount billed, and amount of payments made by the health plan.
    A. Medicare summary notice
    B. remittance advice
    C. health care claims transaction
    D. coordination of benefits

REFERENCE: Green and Rowell, p 294-295, 447-448
                   Johns, p 294
                   LaTour and Eichenwald-Maki, p 372

16. Currently, payment to the physician for outpatient surgery performed on a Medicare patient is based upon which prospective payment system?
    A. MS-DRGs
    B. APGs
    C. RBRVS
    D. ASCs

REFERENCE: Schraffenberger and Kuehn, p 144

17. Which of the following best describes the situation of a provider who agrees to accept assignment for Medicare Part B services?
    A. The provider is reimbursed at 15% above the allowed charge.
    B. The provider is paid according to the Medicare physician fee schedule (MPFS) plus 10%.
    C. The provider cannot bill the patients for the balance between the MPFS amount and the total charges.
    D. The provider is a nonparticipating provider.

REFERENCE: Green and Rowell, p 52

18. According to the Federal Register, the definition of a "new" patient when assigning a CPT Evaluation and Management (medical visit) code to a Medicare hospital outpatient under the prospective payment system is a patient that has
   A. not seen the physician within the last 3 years.
   B. not seen the physician within the last 5 years.
   C. not already been assigned a medical record number.
   D. never seen the physician before.

REFERENCE: Federal Register, April 7, 2000, p 18451

19. Under ASCs, bilateral procedures are reimbursed at _____ of the payment rate for their group
   A. 50%   C. 200%
   B. 100%   D. 150%

REFERENCE: Casto and Layman, p 191

Use the following table to answer questions # 20 - # 23.

Plantation Hospital's TOP 10 MS-DRGs (Based on FY 2006 data)

MS-DRG	Description	Number of Patients	CMS Relative Weight	Total CMS Relative Weight
470	Major joint replacement or reattachment of lower extremity w/o MCC	2750	1.9871	
392	Esophagitis, gatroent & misc digest disorders w/o MCC	2200	071.21	
194	Simple pneumonia & pleurisy w CC	1150	1.0235	
247	Perc cardiovasc proc 2 drug-eluting stent w/o MCC	900	2.1255	
293	Heart failure & shock w/o CC/MCC	850	0.8765	
313	Chest pain	650	0.5489	
292	Heart failure & shock w CC	550	1.0134	
690	Kidney & urinary tract infections w/o MCC	400	0.8000	
192	Chronic obstructive pulmonary disease w/o CC/MCC	300	0.8145	
871	Septicemia w/o MV 96+ hours w MCC	250	1.7484	

20. The case-mix index (CMI) for the top 10 MS-DRGs above is
   A. 1.164.   C. .7823.
   B. 1.278.   D. 1.097.

REFERENCE: Casto and Layman, p 105
               Johns, p 278

21. Which of the listed MS-DRGs has the highest CMS relative weight?
   A. 247   C. 871
   B. 470   D. 293

REFERENCE: Casto and Layman, p 105
               Johns, p 278

22. Based on this patient volume, the MS-DRG which brings in the highest total reimbursement to the hospital is
    A. 470.   C. 392.
    B. 247.   D. 871.

REFERENCE: Casto and Layman, p 105
                Johns, p 278

23. Based on this patient volume, the MS-DRG which brings in the highest total profit to the hospital is
    A. 470.   C. 392.
    B. 247.   D. It cannot be determined from this information.

REFERENCE: Casto and Layman, p 105
                Johns, p 278

24. All of the following elements are found in the charge description master, EXCEPT for
    A. ICD-9-CM code.   C. HCPCS/CPT code.
    B. charge.   D. narrative description.

REFERENCE: Green and Rowell, p 298-299
                Johns, p 312

25. Home health agencies are reimbursed on a prospective payment system (PPS) for Medicare patients. This PPS is called
    A. home health resource groups (HHRGs).
    B. case-mix groups (CMGs).
    C. diagnosis-related groups (DRGs).
    D. resource utilization groups (RUGs).

REFERENCE: Green and Rowell, p 281
                Johns, p 285

26. These are assigned to every HCPCS/CPT code under the Medicare hospital outpatient prospective payment system to identify how the service or procedure described by the code would be paid.
    A. geographic practice cost indices   C. minimum data set
    B. major diagnostic categories   D. payment status indicator

REFERENCE: Green and Rowell, p 286-287
                Casto and Layman, p 175-176

27. This means that the service or procedure is reasonable and necessary for the diagnosis or treatment of illness or injury consistent with generally accepted standards of care.
    A. peer review   C. benchmarking
    B. optimization   D. medical necessity

REFERENCE: Green and Rowell, p 3, 97, 125
                Valerius, Bayes, Newby, and Seggern, p 37

Answer questions #28 - #31 by indicating, in proper sequence, the MS-DRG logic that is used to assign a case to a particular MS-DRG. You must select from the options presented in the question.

28. The first step is

   ✗ A. cases are differentiated based on the presence or absence of complications/ comorbidities (CCs) or major complications/comorbidities (MCCs).

       B. cases are divided into either a surgical partition or a medical partition.

       C. the principal diagnosis determines the MDC assignment.

       D. diagnoses and procedures are coded using ICD-9-CM.

REFERENCE: Casto and Layman, p 104
                      Johns, p 276-278

29. The second step is

       A. cases are differentiated based on the presence or absence of complications/ comorbidities (CCs) or major complications/comorbidities (MCCs).

       B. cases are divided into either a surgical partition or a medical partition.

       C. the principal diagnosis determines the MDC assignment.

       D. diagnoses and procedures are coded using ICD-9-CM.

REFERENCE: Casto and Layman, p 104
                      Johns, p 276-278

30. The third step is

       A. cases are differentiated based on the presence or absence of complications/comorbidities (CCs) or major complications/comorbidities (MCCs).

       B. cases are divided into either a surgical partition or a medical partition.

       C. the principal diagnosis determines the MDC assignment.

       D. diagnoses and procedures are coded using ICD-9-CM.

REFERENCE: Casto and Layman, p 104
                      Johns, p 276-278

31. The fourth step is

       A. cases are differentiated based on the presence or absence of complications/comorbidities (CCs) or major complications/comorbidities (MCCs).

       B. cases are divided into either a surgical partition or a medical partition.

       C. the principal diagnosis determines the MDC assignment.

       D. diagnoses and procedures are coded using ICD-9-CM.

REFERENCE: Casto and Layman, p 104-106
                      Johns, p 276-278

32. If the Medicare nonPAR approved payment amount is $128.00 for a proctoscopy, what is the total Medicare approved payment amount for a doctor who does not accept assignment, applying the limiting charge for this procedure?

       A. $ 140.80   C. $ 192.00

       B. $ 143.00   D. $ 147.20

REFERENCE: Green and Rowell, p 292-294, 437-439

33. Under the inpatient prospective payment system (IPPS), there is a three-day payment window (formerly referred to as the 72-hour rule). This rule requires that outpatient preadmission services that are provided by a hospital up to three calendar days prior to a patient's inpatient admission be covered by the IPPS MS-DRG payment for
    A. diagnostic services.
    B. therapeutic (or non-diagnostic) services whereby the inpatient principal diagnosis code (ICD-9-CM) exactly matches the code used for pre-admission services.
    C. therapeutic (or non-diagnostic) services whereby the inpatient principal diagnosis code (ICD-9-CM) does not match the code used for pre-admission services.
    D. both A and B.

REFERENCE: Green, p 199-200
               Green and Rowell, p 285-286

34. Under the outpatient prospective payment system (OPPS), status indicator "____" is a payment indicator that refers to "significant procedures for which the multiple procedure reduction applies." This means that the reported CPT and/or HCPCS Level II code will be paid a discounted APC reimbursement rate when reported with other procedures on the same claim.
    A. "T"   C. "S"
    B. "X"   D. "A"

REFERENCE: Green and Rowell, p 286
               Green, p 847

35. A discharge in which the patient was discharged from the inpatient rehabilitation facility and returned within 3 calendar days is called a(n)
    A. interrupted stay.   C. per diem.
    B. transfer.   D. qualified discharge.

REFERENCE: Casto and Layman, p 142

36. In a global payment methodology which is sometimes applied to radiological and similar types of procedures that involve professional and technical components, all of the following are part of the "technical" components EXCEPT
    A. radiological equipment.   C. radiological supplies.
    B. physician services.   D. support services.

REFERENCE: Johns, p 272
               LaTour and Eichenwald-Maki, p 361
               Green, p 714

37. Changes in case mix index (CMI) may be attributed to all of the following factors EXCEPT
    A. changes in medical staff composition
    B. changes in coding rules
    C. changes in services offered
    D. changes in coding productivity

REFERENCE: Green, p 198, 851-852
               Schraffenberger and Kuehn, p 277

38. This prospective payment system replaced the Medicare physician payment system of "customary, prevailing, and reasonable (CPR)" charges whereby physicians were reimbursed according to historical record of the charge for the provision of each service.
    A. Medicare Physician Fee Schedule (MPFS)
    B. Medicare Severity Diagnosis Related Groups (MS-DRGs)
    C. Medicare Case Mix Index
    D. MEDISGRPS

REFERENCE: Green, p 849-850
              Green and Rowell, p 292-298
              Frisch, p 185-189

39. A Medicare patient has arthroscopic lysis of adhesions and shaving of the articular cartilage of the right knee. The codes are:

29884-RT   Arthroscopy, knee, surgical, with lysis of adhesions (separate procedure), right
29877-RT   Arthroscopy, knee, surgical, debridement/shaving of articular cartilage, right

Comprehensive Codes	Component Codes
29877	20610, 27570, 29870, 29871, 29874, 29875, 29884

The Medicare CCI (Correct Coding Initiative) edits indicate that code 29877 is not a component code for 29884, but code 29884 is a component code for 29877. The correct code(s) to be reported on this claim is (are)
    A. 29884-RT and 29877-RT.   C. 29877-RT.
    B. 29884-RT.   D. neither code.

REFERENCE: Jones (2001), p 28, 51, 235
              Green and Rowell, p 105-109, 251-253
              Frisch, p 236-237

40. The hospital outpatient prospective payment system for Medicare applies to all of the following, EXCEPT
    A. professional services, such as physician fees.
    B. facility reimbursement for outpatient hospital clinic visits.
    C. facility reimbursement for emergency department visits.
    D. facility reimbursement for hospital-based ambulatory surgery.

REFERENCE: Casto and Layman, p 171
              Green and Rowell, p 286-287
              Green, p 847-848

41. The Correct Coding Initiative (CCI) edits contain a listing of codes under two columns titled, "comprehensive codes" and "component codes." According to the CCI edits, when a provider bills Medicare for a procedure that appears in both columns for the same beneficiary on the same date of service
    A. code only the component code.
    B. do not code either one.
    C. code only the comprehensive code.
    D. code both the comprehensive code and the component code.

REFERENCE: Frisch, p, 236-237
              Green, p 350-353, 861-862
              Green and Rowell, p 105-109, 251-253

42. The following type of hospital is considered excluded, which means that it does not participate in any type of prospective payment system (PPS).
    A. rehabilitation hospital
    B. long-term care hospital
    C. psychiatric hospital
    D. cancer hospital

REFERENCE: Green, p 845

43. These are financial protections to ensure that certain types of facilities (e.g., children's hospitals) recoup all of their losses due to the differences in their APC payments and the pre-APC payments.
    A. limiting charge   C. hold harmless
    B. indemnity insurance   D. pass through

REFERENCE: Casto and Layman, p 174

44. LCDs and NCDs are review policies that describe the circumstances of coverage for various types of medical treatment. They advise physicians which services Medicare considers reasonable and necessary and may indicate the need for an advance beneficiary notice. They are developed by the Centers for Medicare and Medicaid Services (CMS), Medicare carriers, or fiscal intermediaries. LCD and NCD are acronyms that stand for
    A. local covered determinations and non-covered determinations.
    B. local coverage determinations and national coverage determinations.
    C. list of covered decisions and non-covered decisions.
    D. local contractor's decisions and national contractor's decisions.

REFERENCE: Frisch, p 167
               Green and Rowell, p 330
               Green, p 307

45. This information is printed on the UB-04 claim form to represent the cost center (e.g., lab, radiology, cardiology, respiratory, etc.) for the department in which the item is provided. It is used for Medicare billing.
    A. modifier   C. charge code
    B. revenue code   D. general ledger key

REFERENCE: Green, p 853
               Green and Rowell, p 298-300
               Schraffenberger and Kuehn, p 158-160, 163
               Valerius, Bayes, Newby, and Seggern, p 533

46. This information is used because it provides a uniform system of identifying procedures, services, or supplies. Multiple columns can be available for various financial classes.
    A. HCPCS code   C. general ledger key
    B. revenue code   D. charge code

REFERENCE: Green, p 853
               Green and Rowell, p 298-300
               Schraffenberger and Kuehn, p 160

Use the following table to answer questions #47 - #50.

EXAMPLE OF A CHARGE DESCRIPTION MASTER (CDM) FILE LAYOUT

Charge Code	Item Description	General Ledger Key	HCPCS Code		Charges	Revenue Code	Activity Date
			Medicare	Medicaid			
49683105	CT scan; head; w/out contrast	3	70450	70450	500.00	0351	1/1/08
49683106	CT scan; head; with contrast	3	70460	70460	675.00	0351	1/1/08

47. This information provides a narrative name of the services provided. This information should be presented in a clear and concise manner. When possible, the narratives from the HCPCS/CPT book should be utilized.
   A. general ledger key
   B. charge code
   C. item description
   D. revenue code

REFERENCE: Green, p 853
               Green and Rowell, p 298-300
               Schraffenberger and Kuehn, p 158

48. This information is the numerical identification of the service or supply. Each item has a unique number with a prefix that indicates the department number (the number assigned to a specific ancillary department) and an item number (the number assigned by the accounting department or the business office) for a specific procedure or service represented on the chargemaster.
   A. charge code
   B. HCPCS code
   C. revenue code
   D. general ledger key

REFERENCE: Green, p 853
               Green and Rowell, p 298-300
               Schraffenberger and Kuehn, p 158

49. This information is used to assign each item to a particular section of the general ledger in a particular facility's accounting section. Reports can be generated from this information to include statistics related to volume in terms of numbers, dollars, and payer types.
   A. general ledger key
   B. charge code
   C. revenue code
   D. HCPCS code

REFERENCE: Schraffenberger and Kuehn, p 158

50. This information indicates the most recent activity of an item.
   A. general ledger key
   B. charge code
   C. activity date
   D. activity code

REFERENCE: Schraffenberger and Kuehn, p 159-160

51. A company that contracts with the Centers for Medicare and Medicaid Services (CMS) to pay Medicaid claims is called a
    A. carrier.
    B. fiscal intermediary.
    C. fiscal agent.
    D. preferred provider.

REFERENCE: Rimmer, p 11

52. The DNFB report includes all patients who have been discharged from the facility but for whom, for one reason or another, the billing process is not complete.
    A. diagnosis not finally balanced   C. dollars not fully billed
    B. days not fiscally balanced   D. discharged not final billed

REFERENCE: Schraffenberger and Kuehn, p 410

53. The limiting charge is a percentage limit on fees specified by legislation that the nonparticipating physician may bill Medicare beneficiaries above the nonPAR fee schedule amount. The limiting charge is
    A. 10%.   C. 20%.
    B. 15%.   D. 50%.

REFERENCE: Green and Rowell, p 292-294, 437-439

Use the following case scenario to answer questions #54 – #58.

> A Medicare patient is seen in the physician's office.
> The total charge for this office visit is $250.00.
> The patient has previously paid his deductible under Medicare Part B.
> The Par Medicare fee schedule amount for this service is $200.00.
> The nonPAR Medicare fee schedule amount for this service is $190.00.

54. The patient is financially liable for the coinsurance amount which is
    A. 80%.   C. 20%.
    B. 100%.   D. 15%.

REFERENCE: Green and Rowell, p 291-294, 436-439
              Rizzo, p 187
              Valerius, Bayes, Newby, and Seggern, p 226-227

55. If this physician is a participating physician who accepts assignment for this claim, the total amount he will receive is
    A. $200.00.   C. $218.50.
    B. $250.00.   D. $190.00.

REFERENCE: Green and Rowell, p 291-294, 436-439
              Rizzo, p 187
              Valerius, Bayes, Newby, and Seggern, p 226-227

56. If this physician is a nonparticipating physician who does NOT accept assignment for this claim, the total amount he will receive is
    A. $250.00.   C. $218.50.
    B. $200.00.   D. $190.00.

REFERENCE: Green and Rowell, p 291-294, 436-439
                  Rizzo, p 187
                  Valerius, Bayes, Newby, and Seggern, p 226-227

57. If this physician is a participating physician who accepts assignment for this claim, the total amount of the patient's financial liability (out-of-pocket expense) is
    A. $200.00.   C. $160.00.
    B. $40.00.   D. $30.00.

REFERENCE: Green & Rowell, p 291-294, 436-439
                  Rizzo, p 187
                  Valerius, Bayes, Newby, and Seggern, p 226-227

58. If this physician is a nonparticipating physician who does not accept assignment for this claim, the total amount of the patient's financial liability (out-of-pocket expense) is
    A. $66.50.   C. $190.00.
    B. $38.00.   D. $152.00.

REFERENCE: Green and Rowell, p 291-294, 436-439
                  Rizzo, p 187
                  Valerius, Bayes, Newby, and Seggern, p 226-227

59. A fiscal year is a yearly accounting period. It is the 12-month period on which a budget is planned. The federal fiscal year is
    A. October 1st through September 30th of the next year.
    B. January 1st through December 31st.
    C. July 1st through the June 30th of the next year.
    D. April 1st through March 31st of the next year.

REFERENCE: Casto and Layman, p 243

60. There are times when documentation is incomplete or insufficient to support the diagnoses found in the chart. The most common way of communicating with the physician for answers is by
    A. emailing physicians.   C. calling the physician's office.
    B. using physician query forms.   D. leaving notes in the chart.

REFERENCE: Green, p 13-14
                  Scott, p 78

61. Under APCs, payment status indicator "X" means
    A. ancillary services.
    B. medical visits.
    C. multiple procedure reduction applies.
    D. multiple procedure reduction does not apply.

REFERENCE: Casto and Layman, p 176

62. Under APCs, payment status indicator "V" means
    A. ancillary services.
    B. medical visits.
    C. inpatient procedure.
    D. multiple procedure reduction does not apply.

REFERENCE: Casto and Layman, p 176

63. Under APCs, payment status indicator "S" means
    A. ancillary services.
    B. medical visits.
    C. multiple procedure reduction applies.
    D. multiple procedure reduction does not apply.

REFERENCE: Green and Rowell, p 286
               Casto and Layman, p 176
               Green, p 847

64. Under APCs, payment status indicator "T" means
    A. ancillary services.
    B. medical visits.
    C. multiple procedure reduction applies.
    D. multiple procedure reduction does not apply.

REFERENCE: Green and Rowell, p 286
               Green, p 847
               Casto and Layman, p 176

65. Under APCs, payment status indicator "C" means
    A. ancillary services.
    B. inpatient only services.
    C. multiple procedure reduction applies.
    D. multiple procedure reduction does not apply.

REFERENCE: Casto and Layman, p 176

66. This is a ten digit, intelligence-free, numeric identifier designed to replace all previous provider legacy numbers. This number identifies the physician universally to all payers. This number is issued to all HIPAA-covered entities. It is mandatory on the CMS-1500 and UB-04 claim forms.
    A. National Practitioner Databank (NPD)
    B. Universal Physician Number (UPN)
    C. Master Patient Index (MPI)
    D. National Provider Identifier (NPI)

REFERENCE: Frisch, p 198
               Rimmer, p 45-46
               Green, p 866
               Green and Rowell, p 365-366

67. In the managed care industry, there are specific reimbursement concepts, such as "capitation." All of the following statements are true in regard to the concept of "capitation," EXCEPT
    A. each service is paid based upon the actual charges.
    B. the volume of services and their expense does not affect reimbursement.
    C. capitation means paying a fixed amount per member per month.
    D. capitation involves a group of physicians or an individual physician.

REFERENCE: Casto and Layman, p 87
               Green and Rowell, p 334

68. When billing for the admitting physician for a patient that is admitted to the hospital as an inpatient, one must use a CPT Evaluation and Management code based upon the level of care provided. These are the codes to be selected from for initial hospital care.
        99221 Initial hospital care, per day, for the evaluation and management of a patient, which requires these 3 key components:
             - a detailed or comprehensive history
             - a detailed or comprehensive examination and
             - medical decision making that is straightforward or of low complexity
        99222 Initial hospital care, per day, for the evaluation and management of a patient, which requires these 3 key components:
             - a comprehensive history
             - a comprehensive examination and
             - medical decision making of moderate complexity
        99223 Initial hospital care, per day, for the evaluation and management of a patient, which requires these 3 key components:
             - a comprehensive history
             - a comprehensive examination and
             - medical decision making of high complexity
    The following statement is true.
    A. This code can be used only once per hospitalization.
    B. This code can be used by the admitting physician or consulting physician.
    C. This code can be used for patients admitted to observation status.
    D. This code can be used by the hospital to bill for facility services.

REFERENCE: Frisch, p 60
               Rimmer, p 73-74

69. This document is published by the Office of Inspector General (OIG) every year. It details the OIG's focus for Medicare fraud and abuse for that year. It gives health care providers an indication of general and specific areas that are targeted for review. It can be found on the Internet on CMS' Web site.
    A. The OIG's Evaluation and Management Documentation Guidelines
    B. The OIG's Model Compliance Plan
    C. The Federal Register
    D. The OIG's Workplan

REFERENCE: Frisch, p 341

70. Accounts Receivable (A/R) refers to
    A. cases that have not yet been paid.
    B. the amount the hospital was paid.
    C. cases that have been paid.
    D. denials that have been returned to the hospital.

REFERENCE: Green and Bowie, p 76
               Schraffenberger and Kuehn, p 355
               Rimmer, p 118

71. The following coding system(s) is/are utilized in the MS-DRG prospective payment methodology
    for assignment and proper reimbursement.
    A. HCPCS/CPT codes
    B. ICD-9-CM codes
    C. both HCPCS/CPT codes and ICD-9-CM codes
    D. none of the above

REFERENCE: Green and Bowie, p 285
               Green, p 191-194
               Johns, p 276

72. The following coding system(s) is/are utilized in the Inpatient Psychiatric Facilities (IPFs)
    prospective payment methodology for assignment and proper reimbursement.
    A. HCPCS/CPT codes
    B. ICD-9-CM codes
    C. both HCPCS/CPT codes and ICD-9-CM codes
    D. none of the above

REFERENCE: Green, p 195
               Johns, p 290-291

73. In employer-sponsored health plans, employees may select their health plan
    A. during the contract period.
    B. at the beginning of each fiscal year.
    C. during the open enrollment period.
    D. on the first day of any month.

REFERENCE: Valerius, Bayes, Newby, and Seggern, p 288

74. Which modifier indicates that a signed ABN is on file?
    A. AB   C. GY
    B. GA   D. GZ

REFERENCE: Valerius, Bayes, Newby, and Seggern, p 342-343
               Frisch, p 175

75. Under Medicare Part B, all of the following statements are true and are applicable to
    nonparticipating physician providers, EXCEPT
    A. providers must file all Medicare claims.
    B. nonparticipating providers have a higher fee schedule than that for participating providers.
    C. fees are restricted to charging no more than the "limiting charge" on nonassigned claims.
    D. collections are restricted to only the deductible and coinsurance due at the time of service on
       an assigned claim.

REFERENCE: Green and Rowell, p 292-295

76. Under Medicare, a beneficiary has lifetime reserve days. All of the following statements are true, EXCEPT
    A. the patient has a total of 60 lifetime reserve days.
    B. lifetime reserve days are usually reserved for use during the patient's final terminal hospital stay.
    C. lifetime reserve days are paid under Medicare Part B.
    D. lifetime reserve days are not renewable, meaning once a patient uses all of their lifetime reserve days, the patient is responsible for the total charges.

REFERENCE: Green and Rowell, p 431-432

77. The term used to describe a diagram depicting grouper logic in assigning MS-DRGs is
    A. blended chart.   C. decision tree.
    B. case-mix index.   D. grouper hierarchy.

REFERENCE: Green and Bowie, p 281, 283-285
                Green, p 199-200
                Casto and Layman, p 107
                Schraffenberger and Kuehn, p 136-137

78. Once all data are posted to a patient's account, the claim can be reviewed for accuracy and completeness. Many facilities have internal auditing systems. The auditing systems run each claim through a set of edits specifically designed for the various third-party payers. The auditing system identifies data that have failed edits and flags the claim for correction. These "internal" auditing systems are called
    A. scrubbers.   C. groupers.
    B. outliers.   D. encoders.

REFERENCE: Casto and Layman, p 210

79. To compute the reimbursement to a particular hospital for a particular MS-DRG, multiply the hospital's base payment rate by the
    A. conversion factor.   C. geographic price index.
    B. case-mix index.   D. relative weight for the MS-DRG.

REFERENCE: Green and Rowell, p 281-285
                Green, p 199
                Casto and Layman, p 111-112

80. Under the APC methodology, discounted payments occur when
    A. there are two or more (multiple) procedures that are assigned to status indicator "T."
    B. there are two or more (multiple) procedures that are assigned to status indicator "S."
    C. modifier -73 is used to indicate a procedure is terminated after the patient is prepared, but before anesthesia is started.
    D. both A and C

REFERENCE: Green and Bowie, p 286
                Schraffenberger and Kuehn, p 142-143

81. This prospective payment system is for _____ and utilizes a patient assessment instrument (PAI) to classify patients into case-mix groups (CMGs).
    A. skilled nursing facilities
    B. inpatient rehabilitation facilities
    C. home health agencies
    D. long-term acute care hospitals

REFERENCE: Green and Bowie, p 288
              Schraffenberger and Kuehn, p 147-149

82. Home health agencies (HHAs) utilize a data entry software system developed by the Centers for Medicare and Medicaid Services (CMS). This software is available to HHAs at no cost through the CMS Web site or on a CD-ROM.
    A. PACE (Patient Assessment and Comprehensive Evaluation)
    B. HAVEN (Home Assessment Validation and Entry)
    C. HHASS (Home Health Agency Software System)
    D. PEPP (Payment Error Prevention Program)

REFERENCE: Green and Bowie, p 281
              Johns, p 285
              LaTour and Eichenwald-Maki, p 368

83. This information is published by the Medicare contractors to describe when and under what circumstances Medicare will cover a service. The ICD-9-CM and CPT/HCPCS codes are listed in the memoranda.
    A. LCD (Local Coverage Determinations)
    B. CCI (Correct Coding Initiatives)
    C. OSHA (Occupational Safety and Health Administration)
    D. PEPP (Payment Error Prevention Program)

REFERENCE: Green and Bowie, p 330
              Schraffenberger and Kuehn, p 170

84. The term "hard coding" refers to
    A. HCPCS/CPT codes that are coded by the coders.
    B. HPCS/CPT codes that appear in the hospital's chargemaster and will be included automatically on the patient's bill.
    C. ICD-9-CM codes that are coded by the coders.
    D. ICD-9-CM codes that appear in the hospital's chargemaster.

REFERENCE: Schraffenberger and Kuehn, p 156-157

85. This is the amount collected by the facility for the services it bills.
    A. costs
    B. charges
    C. reimbursement
    D. contractual allowance

REFERENCE: Green, p 17-23
              Schraffenberger and Kuehn, p 335

86. Assume the patient has already met his or her deductible and that the physician is a Medicare participating (PAR) provider. The physician's standard fee for the services provided is $120.00. Medicare's PAR fee is $60.00. How much reimbursement will the physician receive from Medicare?
    A. $120.00
    B. $ 60.00
    C. $ 48.00
    D. $ 96.00

REFERENCE: Green and Rowell, p 292, 294, 437-439

87. This accounting method attributes a dollar figure to every input required to provide a service.
    A. cost accounting
    B. charge accounting
    C. reimbursement
    D. contractual allowance

REFERENCE: Schraffenberger and Kuehn, p 334

88. This is the amount the facility actually bills for the services it provides.
    A. costs
    B. charges
    C. reimbursement
    D. contractual allowance

REFERENCE: Green and Rowell, p 58-59
               Schraffenberger and Kuehn, p 334

89. This is the difference between what is charged and what is paid.
    A. costs
    B. charges
    C. reimbursement
    D. contractual allowance

REFERENCE: Schraffenberger and Kuehn, p 334

90. When appropriate, under the outpatient PPS, a hospital can use this CPT code in place of, but not in addition to, a code for a medical visit or emergency department service.
    A. CPT Code 99291 (critical care)
    B. CPT Code 99358 (prolonged evaluation and management service)
    C. CPT Code 35001 (direct repair of aneurysm)
    D. CPT Code 50300 (donor nephrectomy)

REFERENCE: Green, p 392
               Jones, p 34-35

91. To monitor timely claims processing in a hospital, a summary report of "patient receivables" is generated frequently. Aged receivables can negatively affect a facility's cash flow; therefore, to maintain the facility's fiscal integrity, the HIM manager must routinely analyze this report.
    A. remittance advice
    B. periodic interim payments
    C. DNFB (discharged, no final bill)
    D. chargemaster

REFERENCE: LaTour and Eichenwald-Maki, p 754

92. Assume the patient has already met his or her deductible and that the physician is a nonparticipating Medicare provider, but does accept assignment. The standard fee for the services provided is $120.00. Medicare's PAR fee is $60.00 and Medicare's nonPAR fee is $57.00. How much reimbursement will the physician receive from Medicare?
    A. $120.00
    B. $60.00
    C. $57.00
    D. $45.60

REFERENCE: Green and Rowell, p 292, 294, 437-439

93. The occurrence of an OCE (outpatient code editor) edit can result in one of _____ different dispositions, which help to ensure that the fiscal intermediaries in all parts of the country are following similar claims processing procedures. An example of one of these dispositions is "claim rejection."

    A. 100
    B. 50
    C. 3
    D. 6

REFERENCE: Green and Rowell, p 251
               Jones, p 61-62

94. All of the following statements are true of MS-DRGs, EXCEPT
    A. A patient claim may have multiple MS-DRGs.
    B. The MS-DRG payment received by the hospital may be lower than the actual cost of providing the services.
    C. Special circumstances can result in an outlier payment to the hospital.
    D. There are several types of hospitals that are excluded from the Medicare inpatient PPS.

REFERENCE: Green and Rowell, p 281-286
               Green, p 199
               Johns, p 275-278
               LaTour and Eichenwald-Maki, p 363-365

95. This program, formerly called CHAMPUS (Civilian Health and Medical Program-Uniformed Services), is a health care program for active members of the military and other qualified family members.

    A. TRICARE
    B. CHAMPVA
    C. Indian Health Service
    D. workers' compensation

REFERENCE: Green, p 839
               Green and Rowell, p 502-505
               Johns, p 258-259

96. Under Medicare Part B, Medicare participating providers
    A. will be able to collect his or her total charges.
    B. agrees to charge no more than 15% (limiting charge) over the allowed charge from the nonPAR fee schedule.
    C. accepts, as payment in full, the allowed charge from the nonPAR fee schedule.
    D. agrees to charge no more than 10% (limiting charge) over the allowed charge from the nonPAR fee schedule.

REFERENCE: Green and Rowell, p 292, 294, 437-439
               Valerius, Bayes, Newby, and Seggern, p 226

97. If the physician's standard fee for a service is $210.00 and the Medicare PAR fee is $115.00, what is the limiting charge for a nonparticipating (nonPAR) provider?

    A. $241.50
    B. $109.25
    C. $132.25
    D. $125.63

REFERENCE: Green and Rowell, p 292, 294, 437-439

98. CMS adjusts the Medicare Severity DRGs and the reimbursement rates every
   A. calendar year beginning January 1.
   B. quarter.
   C. month.
   D. fiscal year beginning October 1.

REFERENCE: Johns, p 278

99. In calculating the fee for a physician's reimbursement, the three relative value units are each multiplied by
   A. geographic practice cost indices.
   B. national conversion factor.
   C. usual and customary fees for the service.
   D. the cost of living index for the particular region.

REFERENCE: Green, p 849
               Frisch, p 186
               Green and Rowell, p 23

100. If a participating provider's usual fee for a service is $700.00 and Medicare's allowed amount is $450.00, what amount is written off by the physician?
   A. none of it is written off   C. $340.00
   B. $250.00   D. $391.00

REFERENCE: Green and Rowell, p 292, 294, 437-439
               Valerius, Bayes, Newby, and Seggern, p 226

101. Health plans that use _____ reimbursement methods issue lump-sum payments to providers to compensate them for all the health care services delivered to a patient for a specific illness and/or over a specific period of time.
   A. episode-of-care (EOC)   C. fee-for-service
   B. capitation   D. bundled

REFERENCE: Johns, p 270

102. Fee schedules are updated by third party payers
   A. monthly   C. annually
   B. weekly   D. semiannually

REFERENCE: Johns, p 308

103. Commercial insurance plans usually reimburse health care providers under some type of _____ payment system, whereas the federal Medicare program uses some type of _____ payment system.
   A. prospective, retrospective   C. retrospective, prospective
   B. retrospective, concurrent   D. prospective, concurrent

REFERENCE: Green and Rowell, p 275-276, 281
               Green, p 843-45
               Johns, p 268

104. The difference between a rejected claim and a denied claim is that
    A. a rejected claim is sent back to the provider; errors may be corrected and the claim resubmitted.
    B. a denied claim is sent back to the provider; errors may be corrected and the claim resubmitted.
    C. a rejected claim may be appealed, but a denied claim may not be appealed.
    D. if a procedure or service is unauthorized, the claim will be rejected, not denied.

REFERENCE: Rimmer, p 105-109
               Green and Rowell, p 73-76, 78-79

105. These services are those performed by a nonphysician practitioner (such as a Physician Assistant) that are an integral yet incidental component of a physician's treatment for illness or injury. A physician must have personally performed an initial visit and must remain actively involved in the continuing care to the patient. Medicare requires direct supervision for these services to be billed
    A. "technical component" billing.
    B. "assignment" billing.
    C. "incident to" billing.
    D. "assistant" billing.

REFERENCE: Frisch, p 114
              Green and Bowie, p 297-298

106. The Quality Improvement Organizations (QIO) are given hospital-specific data from the Hospital Payment Monitoring Program (HPMP). Hospital data is provided to the QIOs for fourteen target areas on a quarterly basis. This report is called the

    A. Program for Evaluation Payment Patterns Electronic Report (PEPPER).
    B. Payment Error Prevention program (PEP).
    C. Office of Inspector General (OIG) Workplan.
    D. National Correct Coding Initiative (NCCI).

REFERENCE: Green and Rowell, p 96
              Casto and Layman, p 34

107. Targeted states (California, Florida, and New York) with a large Medicare population were included in a Medicare payment recovery demonstration project. This project's purpose was to determine if the use of _____ is a cost-effective means of ensuring correct payments are provided under Medicare. These are charged with identifying underpayments and overpayments for claims filed under Medicare Part A and Part B. They recoup overpayments from the providers.
    A. clinical data abstraction centers (CDAC)
    B. quality improvement organizations (QIO)
    C. recovery audit contractors (RAC)
    D. peer review organizations (PRO)

REFERENCE: Casto and Layman, p 33-34, 36

108. A HIPPS (Health Insurance Prospective Payment System) code is a five-character alphanumeric code. A HIPPS code is used by
    A. ambulatory surgery centers (ASCs).
    B. home health agencies (HHAs).
    C. inpatient rehabilitation facilities (IRFs).
    D. both B & C.

REFERENCE: Green and Bowie, p 281
                       Casto and Layman, p 139, 197

109. The Centers for Medicare and Medicaid Services (CMS) will make an adjustment to the MS-DRG payment for certain conditions that were not present on hospital admission, but were acquired during the hospital stay. Therefore hospitals are required to report an _____ indicator for each diagnosis.
    A. sentinel event
    B. payment status
    C. hospital acquired
    D. present on admission

REFERENCE: Casto and Layman, p 230-231

The following are the reporting options and definitions for the Present on Admission (POA) indicators preceded by answers to be used to answer questions # 110-113.

    A. Y = Present at the time of inpatient admission
    B. N = Not present at the time of inpatient admission
    C. U = Documentation is insufficient to determine whether condition is POA
    D. W = Provider is unable to clinically determine whether condition is POA

110. A patient is admitted for a diagnostic workup for cachexia. The final diagnosis is malignant neoplasm of lung with metastasis.
    A. Y
    B. N
    C. U
    D. W

REFERENCE: Garrett, p 24-26

111. A patient undergoes outpatient surgery. During the recovery period, the patient develops atrial fibrillation and is subsequently admitted to the hospital as an inpatient.
    A. Y
    B. N
    C. U
    D. W

REFERENCE: Garrett, p 24-26

112. A patient is admitted to the hospital for a coronary artery bypass surgery. Postoperatively, he develops a pulmonary embolism.
    A. Y
    B. N
    C. U
    D. W

REFERENCE: Garrett, p 24-26

113. The nursing initial assessment upon admission documents the presence of a decubitus ulcer. There is no mention of the decubitus ulcer in the physician documentation until several days after admission.
    A. Y
    B. N
    C. U
    D. W

REFERENCE: Garrett, p 24-26

Answer Key for Medical Billing and Reimbursement Systems

ANSWER   EXPLANATION

1.   C
2.   B
3.   A
4.   D
5.   D
6.   C   The effective date in the Federal Register was July 1, 2000, but it was delayed until August 1, 2000.
7.   B
8.   D
9.   A
10.   D
11.   B
12.   C
13.   A   The UB-04 is used by hospitals. The CMS-1500 is used by physicians and other non-institutional providers and suppliers. The CMS-1491 is used by ambulance services.
14.   B
15.   A
16.   C
17.   C   The Medicare Physician Fee Schedule (MPFS) amounts are 5% higher for participating (PAR) providers than for nonparticipating (nonPAR) providers. Only nonPAR physicians are subject to the "limiting" charge.
18.   C   The definition of "new patient" in the CPT Code Book is "one who has not received any professional services from the physician or another physician of the same specialty who belongs to the same group practice within the past three years". This definition is used by physicians. In the April 7, 2000, Federal Register (page 18451), CMS defined "new patient" as "one who does not already have a medical record number." This definition is used by hospitals under the outpatient prospective payment system (APCs).
19.   D
20.   B   12781.75/10,000 = 1.278
21.   A
22.   A
23.   D   Total profit cannot be determined from this information alone. A comparison of the total charges on the bills and the PPS amount (reimbursement amount) that the hospital would receive for each MS-DRG could identify the total profit.
24.   A
25.   A
26.   D
27.   D
28.   D
29.   C
30.   B
31.   A
32.   D   The limiting charge is 15% above Medicare's approved payment amount for doctors who do NOT accept assignment ($128.00 X 1.15 = $147.20).

Answer Key for Medical Billing and Reimbursement Systems

ANSWER   EXPLANATION

33.   D

34.   C

35.   A

36.   B

37.   D

38.   A   The Medicare Physician Fee Schedule (MPFS) reimburses providers according to predetermined rates assigned to services.

39.   C   CPT code 29884 is an integral component of code 29877; therefore code 29884 cannot be reported with code 29877 for this patient. Only code 29877 is reported with the modifier –RT. The fact that code 29884 also specifies that it is a "separate procedure" indicates that this procedure code is commonly carried out as an integral component of a total service or procedure and therefore the codes designated as "separate procedure" should not be reported in addition to the code for the total procedure or service for which it is considered an integral component.

40.   A

41.   C

42.   D   Cancer hospitals can apply for and receive waivers from the Centers for Medicare and Medicaid Services (CMS) and are therefore excluded from the inpatient prospective payment system (MS-DRGs). Rehabilitation hospitals are reimbursed under the Inpatient Rehabilitation Prospective Payment System (IRF PPS). Long-term care hospitals are reimbursed under the Long Term Care Hospital Prospective Payment System (LTCH PPS). Skilled nursing facilities are reimbursed under the Skilled Nursing Facility Prospective Payment System (SNF PPS).

43.   C

44.   B

45.   B

46.   A

47.   C

48.   A

49.   A

50.   C

51.   C

52.   D

53.   B

54.   C

55.   A   If a physician is a participating physician who accepts assignment, he will receive the lesser of "the total charges" or "the PAR Medicare fee schedule amount." In this case, the Medicare fee schedule amount is less; therefore, the total received by the physician is $200.00.

56.   C   If a physician is a nonparticipating physician who does not accept assignment, he can collect a maximum of 15% (the limiting charge) over the nonPAR Medicare fee schedule amount. In this case, the nonPAR Medicare fee schedule amount is $190.00 and 15% over this amount is $28.50; therefore, the total that he can collect is $218.50.

Answer Key for Medical Billing and Reimbursement Systems

ANSWER   EXPLANATION

57.   B   The PAR Medicare fee schedule amount is $200.00. The patient has already met the deductible. Of the $200.00, the patient is responsible for 20% ($40.00). Medicare will pay 80% ($160.00). Therefore, the total financial liability for the patient is $40.00.

58.   A   If a physician is a nonparticipating physician who does not accept assignment, he may collect a maximum of 15% (the limiting charge) over the nonPAR Medicare fee schedule amount.

$190.00 = nonPAR Medicare schedule amount.

$190.00 × .20 = $38.00 = patient liable for 20% coinsurance

$190.00 − $38.00 = $152.00 = Medicare pays 80%

$190.00 × .15 = $28.50 = 15% (limiting charge) over nonPAR Medicare fee schedule amount

Physician can balance bill and collect from the patient the difference between the nonPAR Medicare fee schedule amount and the total charge amount. Therefore, the patient's financial liability is $38.00 + 28.50 = $66.50.

59.   A

60.   B

61.   A   Under the APC system, there exists a list of status indicators (also called service indicators, payment status indicators, or payment indicators). This indicator is provided for every HCPCS/ CPT code and identifies how the service or procedure would be paid (if covered) by Medicare for hospital outpatient visits.

62.   B   Under the APC system, there exists a list of status indicators (also called service indicators, payment status indicators, or payment indicators). This indicator is provided for every HCPCS/ CPT code and identifies how the service or procedure would be paid (if covered) by Medicare for hospital outpatient visits.

63.   D   Under the APC system, there exists a list of status indicators (also called service indicators, payment status indicators, or payment indicators). This indicator is provided for every HCPCS/ CPT code and identifies how the service or procedure would be paid (if covered) by Medicare for hospital outpatient visits.

64.   C   Under the APC system, there exists a list of status indicators (also called service indicators, payment status indicators, or payment indicators). This indicator is provided for every HCPCS/ CPT code and identifies how the service or procedure would be paid (if covered) by Medicare for hospital outpatient visits.

65.   B   Under the APC system, there exists a list of status indicators (also called service indicators, payment status indicators, or payment indicators). This indicator is provided for every HCPCS/ CPT code and identifies how the service or procedure would be paid (if covered) by Medicare for hospital outpatient visits.

66.   D

67.   A

68.   A

69.   D

70.   A

71.   B

72.   B

73.   C

Answer Key for Medical Billing and Reimbursement Systems

ANSWER   EXPLANATION

74.   B   GA indicates that a waiver of liability statement is on file. GZ indicates that an item or service is expected to be denied as not reasonable and necessary, but the physician's office does not have a signed ABN. GY indicates that an item or service is statutorily excluded or does not meet the definition of a Medicare benefit.

75.   B   Under Medicare Part B, Congress has mandated special incentives to increase the number of health care providers signing PAR (participating) agreements with Medicare. One of those incentives includes a 5% higher fee schedule for PAR providers than for nonPAR (nonparticipating) providers.

76.   C   Lifetime reserve days are applicable for hospital inpatient stays that are payable under Medicare Part A.

77.   C

78.   A

79.   D   Each hospital's PPS rate is a dollar amount based on that hospital's costs of operating as determined by several blended factors. This blended rate is multiplied by the MS-DRG (relative) weight to calculate that hospital's reimbursement for a given MS-DRG. The (relative) weight is a number assigned to each MS-DRG published in the Federal Register, and it is used as a multiplier to determine reimbursement.

80.   D   Discounts are applied to those multiple procedures identified by CPT codes with status indicator "T" and also those CPT codes assigned with the modifier -73.

81.   B

82.   B

83.   A   Local coverage determinations (LCDs) were formerly called local medical review policies (LMRPs).

84.   B

85.   C

86.   C   The physician receives 80% of the MPFS amount ($48.00) from Medicare. (The remaining 20% ($12.00) is paid by the patient to the physician. The total amount paid is $60.00.)

87.   A

88.   B

89.   D

90.   A   When a patient meets the definition of critical care, the hospital must use CPT Code 99291 to bill for outpatient encounters in which critical care services are furnished. This code is used instead of another E&M code.

91.   C

92.   D   The Medicare nonPAR fee is 5% less than the Medicare PAR fee, which is $57.00 ($60.00 × .95 = $57.00).
The physician then receives 80% ($57.00 × .80) of the nonPAR fee, which is $45.60 from Medicare. He will also collect 20% from the patient, which is $11.40.

93.   D   The six dispositions are: claim rejection, claim denial, claim return to provider, claim suspension, line item rejection, and line item denial.

94.   A

Answer Key for Medical Billing and Reimbursement Systems

	ANSWER	EXPLANATION
95.	A	
96.	C	

97. D

Physician's standard fee	$210.00	
Medicare fee	$115.00	
Medicare PAR fee	$109.25	$(115.00 \times .95)$
Limiting charge	$125.63	(109.25×1.15)

98.	D	
99.	A	

100. B The participating physician agrees to accept Medicare's fee as payment in full; therefore, the physician would collect $450.00. The remainder ($700.00 – $450.00 = $250.00) is written off.

101.	A	
102.	C	
103.	C	
104.	A	
105.	C	
106.	A	
107.	C	

108. D Inpatient Rehabilitation Facilities (IRF) reports the HIPPS (Health Insurance Prospective Payment System) code on the claim. The HIPPS code is a five-character alphanumeric code. The first character is the letter designation of the comorbidity tier (A to D). The last four characters are the four-digit CMG (Case Mix Group). Therefore, the HIPPS code for a patient with a tier 1 comorbidity and a CMG of 0109 is B0109.

Home Health Agencies (HHA) report the HIPPS (Health Insurance Prospective Payment System) code on the claim. The HIPPS code is a five-character alphanumeric code. The first character is the letter "H." The second, third, and fourth characters represent the HHRG (Home Health   Resource Group). The fifth character represents what elements are computed or derived. Therefore, the HIPPS code for the HHRG C0F0S0 would be HAEJ1.

109. D

110. A The malignant neoplasm was clearly present on admission, although it was not diagnosed until after the admission occurred.

111. A The atrial fibrillation developed prior to a written order for inpatient admission.

112. B The pulmonary embolism is an acute condition that was not present on admission because it developed after the patient was admitted and after the patient had surgery.

113. C Query the physician as to whether the decubitus was present on admission or developed after admission.

REFERENCES

Casto, A. B., & Layman, E. (2009). *Principles of health care reimbursement* (2nd ed.). Chicago: American Health Information Management Association (AHIMA).

CMS Web site: http://www.cms.hhs.gov/home/Medicare.asp (This Web site provides links to pages containing official informational materials on all of the Medicare Fee-For-Service Payment Systems.)

Federal Register, Department of Health and Human Services-Center for Medicare and Medicaid Services, Vol. 65 No. 68. Medicare Program, *"Prospective Payment System for Hospital Outpatient Services; Final Rule."* Friday, April 7, 2000.

Frisch, Belinda. (2007). *Correct coding for Medicare, compliance, and reimbursement.* Clifton Park, NY: Thomson Delmar Learning.

Green, M. A., & Rowell, J.C. (2008). *Understanding health insurance: A guide to billing and reimbursement* (9th edition). Clifton Park: Thomson Delmar Learning.

Green, Michelle A. (2007). *3-2-1- code it!* Clifton Park, NY: Thomson Delmar Learning.

Johns, M.L. (2007). *Health information management technology: An applied approach* (2nd ed.). Chicago: American Health Information Management Association (AHIMA).

Jones, L. (2005). *Coding and reimbursement for hospital outpatient services.* Chicago: American Health Information Management Association (AHIMA).

LaTour, K., & Eichenwald-Maki, S. (2006). *Health information management: Concepts, principles, and practice* (2nd ed.). Chicago: American Health Information Management Association (AHIMA).

Rimmer, M. (2009). *Medical billing 101.* Clifton Park, NY: Thomson Delmar Learning.

Rizzo, Christina (2000). *Uniform billing: A guide to claims processing.* Albany, NY: Delmar Thomson Learning.

Schraffenberger, L. A. (2007). *Effective management of coding services* (3rd ed.). Chicago: American Health Information Management Association (AHIMA).

Scott, K. (2009). *Coding and reimbursement for hospital inpatient services* (2nd ed.). Chicago: American Health Information Management Association (AHIMA).

Valerius, J., Bayes, N., Newby, C., and Seggern, J. (2008). *Medical insurance: An integrated claims process approach* (3rd ed.). Columbus: McGraw-Hill Companies.

VII. Medical Science

Irene L. E. Mueller, EdD, RHIA

According to the breakdown of content for both the RHIA and RHIT exams, medical science type questions have been included in domain I, Health Care Data. In many instances medical science knowledge is virtually a prerequisite in order to be able to work with clinical classification systems such as ICD-9-CM and CPT.

1. The cause of aplastic anemia is
   A. acute blood loss.
   B. bone marrow failure.
   C. chronic blood loss.
   D. inadequate iron intake.

   REFERENCE: Jones, p 311
                           Neighbors and Tannehill-Jones, p 117
                           Scott and Fong, p 250

2. The most common cause of dementia in the United States is
   A. autism.
   B. Alzheimer's disease.
   C. alcohol abuse.
   D. anxiety disorder.

   REFERENCE: Jones, p 946
                           Neighbors and Tannehill-Jones, p 273

3. Dr. Zambrano ordered a CEA test for Mr. Logan. Dr. Zambrano may be considering a diagnosis of
   A. cancer.
   B. carpal tunnel syndrome.
   C. cardiomyopathy.
   D. congestive heart failure.

   REFERENCE: Moisio, p 219-220

4. The prevention of illness through vaccination occurs due to the formation of
   A. helper B cells.
   B. immunosurveillance.
   C. mast cells.
   D. memory cells.

   REFERENCE: Jones, p 329
                           Scott and Fong, p 338

5. A bee stung little Bobby. He experiences itching, erythema, and respiratory distress caused by laryngeal edema and vascular collapse. In the emergency department, Bobby is diagnosed with
   A. allergic rhinitis.
   B. allergic sinusitis.
   C. anaphylactic shock.
   D. asthma.

   REFERENCE: Jones, p 329-330
                           Neighbors and Tannehill-Jones, p 69

6. Genital warts are caused by
   A. HAV.
   B. HIV.
   C. HPV.
   D. VZV.

   REFERENCE: Jones, p 663
                           Scott and Fong, p 468,

7. A patient's history includes the following documentation:
    *   Small ulcers (chancres) appeared on the genitalia and disappeared after 4 to 6 weeks
    *   Elevated temperature, skin rash, and enlarged lymph nodes
    Which of the following procedures will be used to initially diagnose the patient?
    A. bone marrow test   C. serology test
    B. chest x-ray   D. thyroid scan

REFERENCE: Jones, p 668
                Moissio, p 114-115
                Neighbors and Tannehill-Jones, p 329

8. What cells produce histamine in a type I hypersensitivity reaction?
    A. lymphocyte   C. mast cells
    B. macrophages   D. neutrophils

REFERENCE: Jones, p 100
                Neighbors and Tannehill-Jones, p 47
                Rizzo, p 104

9. Which one of the following cells produces antibodies?
    A. A cells   C. helper T cells
    B. cytotoxic T cells   D. plasma cells

REFERENCE: Neighbors and Tannehill-Jones, p 64
                Rizzo, p 349, 350, 352
                Scott and Fong, p 338

10. Which of the following conditions is NOT a predisposing risk associated with essential hypertension?
    A. age   C. low dietary sodium intake
    B. cigarette smoking   D. obesity

REFERENCE: Jones, p 374-375
                Neighbors and Tannehill-Jones, p 134
                Scott and Fong, p 300-301

11. A patient, who is HIV positive, has raised lesions, red or purple in color, appearing on the skin, in the mouth, or anywhere on the body. What is the stage of his disease process in today's medical terminology?
    A. ARC   C. AZT
    B. AIDS   D. HIV positive

REFERENCE: Jones, p 660-661
                Neighbors and Tannehill-Jones, p. 78

12. Each of the following pertains to COPD EXCEPT
    A. chronic bronchitis.   C. pneumonia.
    B. emphysema.   D. smoking.

REFERENCE: Neighbors and Tannehill-Jones, p 160-161
                Rizzo, p 407
                Scott and Fong, p 368

13. Which of the following is a lethal arrhythmia?
    A. atrial fibrillation
    B. atrial tachycardia
    C. bradycardia
    D. ventricular fibrillation

REFERENCE: Jones, p382
               Neighbors and Tannehill-Jones, p 144

14. The drug commonly used to treat bipolar mood swings is
    A. Lanoxin.
    B. Lasix.
    C. lithium carbonate.
    D. lorazepam.

REFERENCE: Neighbors and Tannehill-Jones, p 417
               Nobles, p 526
               Woodrow, p 357-358

15. A vision-related pathology that is caused by diabetes is
    A. retinal detachment.
    B. retinoblastoma.
    C. retinopathy.
    D. rhabdomyosarcoma.

REFERENCE: Jones, p 525, 560, 1009
               Neighbors and Tannehill-Jones, p 254-255, 289, 294-295, 300
               Scott and Fong, p 195, 231-232

16. Penicillin is effective in the treatment of all the following diseases EXCEPT
    A. lordosis.
    B. Lyme disease.
    C. strep throat.
    D. syphilis.

REFERENCE: Jones, 167, 213-214, 418, 664
               Neighbors and Tannehill-Jones, p 89-90, 190, 345, 325
               Rizzo, 459

17. Impetigo can

    A. spread through autoinoculation.
    B. be caused by *Streptococcus.*
    C. be caused by *Staphlococcus aureus.*
    D. all of the above.

REFERENCE: Jones, p 115, 800, 1069
               Neighbors and Tannehill-Jones, p 344, 393
               Scott and Fong, p 78-79

18. Diagnostic testing for meningitis usually involves
    A. blood cultures.
    B. cerebrospinal fluid analysis.
    C. stool CandS.
    D. testing urine.

REFERENCE: Jones, p 264
               Neighbors and Tannehill-Jones, p 266

19. Which disease is a malignancy of the lymphatic system?
    A. cystic fibrosis
    B. Hodgkin's disease
    C. neutropenia
    D. von Willebrand's disease

REFERENCE: Jones, p 333
               Neighbors and Tannehill-Jones, p 114, 119,121, 380
               Rizzo, p 354
               Scott and Fong, p 312

20. Which of the following is a hereditary disease of the cerebral cortex?
    A. Huntington chorea
    B. Lou Gehrig disease
    C. Bell's palsy
    D. Guillain-Barre syndrome

REFERENCE: Jones, p 390
                Neighbors and Tannehill-Jones, p 280
                Scott and Fong, p 481

21. Which of the following autoimmune diseases affects tissues of the nervous system?
    A. Goodpasture's syndrome
    B. Hashimoto's disease
    C. myasthenia gravis
    D. rheumatoid arthritis

REFERENCE: Jones, p 265-266, 333-334
                Neighbors and Tannehill-Jones, p 72, 107
                Scott and Fong, p 139

22. Pain is a symptom of which of the following conditions?
    A. first-degree burn (superficial)
    B. second-degree burn (partial thickness)
    C. third-degree burn (full thickness)
    D. A and B

REFERENCE: Jones, p 110-111
                Neighbors and Tannehill-Jones, p 356
                Scott and Fong, p 81-82

23. A 75-year-old patient has a sore tongue with tingling and numbness of the hands and feet. She has headaches and is fatigued. Following diagnostic workup, the doctor orders monthly injections of vitamin B12. This patient mostly likely has which of the following conditions?
    A. aplastic anemia
    B. autoimmune hemolytic anemia
    C. pernicious anemia
    D. sickle cell anemia

REFERENCE: Jones, p 312
                Neighbors and Tannehill-Jones, p 116
                Scott and Fong, p 250

24. Which one of the following is NOT a pathophysiological factor in anemia?
    A. excessive RBC breakdown
    B. lack of RBC maturation
    C. loss of bone marrow function
    D. loss of spleen function

REFERENCE: Jones, p 310-312
                Neighbors and Tannehill-Jones, p 116
                Rizzo, p 308
                Scott and Fong, p 250-251

25. Many bacterial diseases are transmitted directly from person to person. Which of the diseases listed below is a bacterial disease that is transmitted by way of a tick vector?
    A. Legionnaires' disease
    B. Lyme disease
    C. tetanus
    D. tuberculosis

REFERENCE: Jones, p 213-214
                Neighbors and Tannehill-Jones, p 345
                Scott and Fong, p 335

26. Necrosis extending down to the underlying fascia is characteristic of a decubitus ulcer in stage
   A. one.   C. three.
   B. two.   D. four.

REFERENCE: Scott and Fong, p 83

27. Scabies, a highly contagious condition that produces intense pruritus and rash, is caused by
   A. head lice.   C. jock itch.
   B. itch mites.   D. ringworm.

REFERENCE: Jones, p 119
                  Neighbors and Tannehill-Jones, p 347
                  Erlich and Schroeder

28. A physician prescribes a diuretic for his patient. He could be treating any of the following disorders EXCEPT
   A. congestive heart failure.   C. pneumonia.
   B. mitral stenosis.   D. pulmonary edema.

REFERENCE: Neighbors and Tannehill-Jones, p 162
                  Scott and Fong, p 274, 366

29. All of the following are examples of direct transmission of a disease EXCEPT
   A. contaminated foods.   C. droplet spread.
   B. coughing or sneezing.   D. physical contact.

REFERENCE: Neighbors and Tannehill-Jones, p 5-6
                  Scott and Fong, p 332-336

30. _____ is the most common type of skin cancer and _____ is the most deadly type of skin cancer?
   A. malignant melanoma, basal cell carcinoma
   B. basal cell carcinoma, malignant melanoma
   C. oat cell carcinoma, squamous cell carcinoma
   D. squamous cell carcinoma, oat cell carcinoma

REFERENCE: Jones, p 111, 872, 988
                  Neighbors and Tannehill-Jones, p 351
                  Rizzo, p 132
                  Scott and Fong, p 81
                  Sormunen, p 262

31. John Palmer was in a car accident and sustained severe chest trauma resulting in a tension pneumothorax. Manifestations of this disorder include all of the following EXCEPT
   A. severe chest pain.   C. shock.
   B. dyspnea.   D. clubbing.

REFERENCE: Jones, p 422
           Neighbors and Tannehill-Jones, p166

32. Cancer derived from epithelial tissue is classified as a(n)
   A. adenoma.   C. lipoma.
   B. carcinoma.   D. sarcoma.

REFERENCE: Jones, p 870
                  Neighbors and Tannehill-Jones, p 26
                  Rizzo, p 90
                  Sormunen, p 262

33. Sex-linked genetic diseases
    A. are transmitted during sexual activity.
    B. involve a defect on a chromosome.
    C. occur equally between males and females.
    D. occur only in males.

REFERENCE: Neighbors and Tannehill-Jones, p 14
              Rizzo, p 457
              Scott and Fong, p 480-485

34. A stapedectomy is a common treatment for
    A. atherosclerosis.   C. otosclerosis.
    B. multiple sclerosis.   D. scoliosis.

REFERENCE: Jones, p 584
              Neighbors and Tannehill-Jones, p 298
              Scott and Fong, p 201

35. In systemic circulation which of the following veins carry oxygenated blood?
    A. right vena cava
    B. renal veins
    C. varicose veins
    D. pulmonary veins

REFERENCE: Jones, p 353
              Neighbors and Tannehill-Jones, p 128
              Rizzo, p 322, 335
              Scott and Fong, p 286-287, 295
              Sormunen, p 188

36. Which of the following sequences correctly depicts the flow of blood through the heart to the lungs?
    A. right atrium, right ventricle, lungs, pulmonary artery
    B. right atrium, right ventricle, pulmonary artery, lungs
    C. right ventricle, right atrium, lungs, pulmonary artery
    D. right ventricle, right atrium, pulmonary artery, lungs

REFERENCE: Jones, p 353-354
              Neighbors and Tannehill-Jones, p 128
              Rizzo, p 322, 325
              Scott and Fong, p 286-288, 295
              Sormunen, p 188

37. Diastole occurs when
    A. cardiac insufficiency is present.   C. the ventricles contract.
    B. the atria contracts.   D. the ventricles fill.

REFERENCE: Jones, p 357
              Neighbors and Tannehill-Jones, p 130
              Rizzo, p 333
              Scott and Fong, p 295
              Sormunen, p 189

38. The most fatal type of lung cancer is
    A. adenocarcinoma.
    B. large cell cancer.
    C. small cell cancer.
    D. squamous cell cancer.

REFERENCE: Scott and Fong, p 368-369

39. Gas exchange in the lungs takes place at the
    A. alveoli.
    B. bronchi.
    C. bronchioles.
    D. trachea.

REFERENCE: Neighbors and Tannehill-Jones, p 154
               Rizzo, 402-404
               Scott and Fong, p 358
               Sormunen, p 314

40. Oxygen is carried in the blood
    A. bound to hemoglobin.
    B. in the form of carbonic acid.
    C. plasma.
    D. serum.

REFERENCE: Neighbors and Tannehill-Jones, p 112
               Rizzo, p 408, 413
               Sormunen, p 223, 230

41. Which of the following anatomical parts is involved in both the respiratory and digestive systems?
    A. larynx
    B. nasal cavity
    C. pharynx
    D. trachea

REFERENCE: Rizzo, p 371
               Scott and Fong, p 355-356
               Sormunen, p 313

42. A disease of the ear that causes vertigo is
    A. labyrinthitis.
    B. mastoiditis.
    C. Meniere's disease.
    D. A and C

REFERENCE: Neighbors and Tannehill-Jones, p 300-301
               Scott and Fong, p 201

43. _____ causes of softening of the bone in children.
    A. Raynaud's disease.
    B. Reye's syndrome.
    C. Rickets.
    D. Rubella.

REFERENCE: Neighbors and Tannehill-Jones, p 92
               Scott and Fong, p 112
               Rizzo, p 147

44. A pathological diagnosis of transitional cell carcinoma is made. The examined tissue was removed from the
    A. bladder.
    B. esophagus.
    C. oral cavity.
    D. pleura.

REFERENCE: Rizzo, p 102-103
               Neighbors and Tannehill-Jones, p 235

45. Most carbon dioxide is carried in the
    A. blood as CO_2 gas.
    B. blood bound to hemoglobin.
    C. blood plasma in the form of carbonic acid.
    D. red blood cells.

REFERENCE: Scott and Fong, p 243
                 Rizzo, p 408, 413
                 Sormunen, p 223

46. The key diagnostic finding for typical pneumonia is
    A. abnormal blood electrolytes.
    B. elevated WBC.
    C. lung consolidation x-ray.
    D. positive sputum culture.

REFERENCE: Neighbors and Tannehill-Jones, p 162

47. The presence of fluid in the alveoli of the lungs is characteristic of
    A. COPD.
    B. Crohn's disease.
    C. pneumonia.
    D. tuberculosis.

REFERENCE: Neighbors and Tannehill-Jones, p 163
                 Rizzo, p 407

48. Full-blown AIDS sets in as
    A. CD4 receptors increase.
    B. helper T-cell concentration decreases.
    C. HIV virus concentration decreases.
    D. immunity to HIV increases.

REFERENCE: Scott and Fong, p 321-324
                 Sormunen, p 239

49. Which of the following BEST describes tuberculosis?
    A. a chronic, systemic disease whose initial infection is in the lungs
    B. an acute bacterial infection of the lung
    C. an ordinary lung infection
    D. a viral infection of the lungs

REFERENCE: Neighbors and Tannehill-Jones, p 49, 392-393
                 Scott and Fong, p 366
                 Sormunen, p 240, 323

50.   Treatments for sensorineural hearing loss include
    A. cochlear implants.
    B. myringotomy.
    C. removal of impacted cerumen.
    D. stapedectomy.

REFERENCE: Jones, p 580
                 Scott and Fong, p 202

51. Mary Mulholland has diabetes. Her physician has told her about some factors that put her more at risk for infections. Which of the following factors would probably NOT be applicable?
    A. hypoxia
    B. increased glucose in body fluids
    C. increased blood supply
    D. A and C

REFERENCE: Neighbors and Tannehill-Jones, p 253-257

52. Most of the digestion of food and absorption of nutrients occurs in the
    A. ascending colon.
    B. esophagus.
    C. small intestine.
    D. stomach.

REFERENCE: Neighbors and Tannehill-Jones, p 185
               Rizzo, p 377-378
               Scott and Fong, p 385-386
               Sormunen, p 339, 341

53. The Phalen's wrist flexor test is a noninvasive method for diagnosing
    A. carpal tunnel syndrome.
    B. Down syndrome.
    C. severe acute respiratory syndrome.
    D. Tourette's syndrome.

REFERENCE: NLM

54. Ulcerations of the small intestine are characteristic of
    A. appendicitis.
    B. Crohn's disease.
    C. diverticulitis.
    D. Graves' disease.

REFERENCE: Neighbors and Tannehill-Jones, p 193, 198
               Rizzo, p 381
               Sormunen, p 351

55. The patient's pathology report revealed the presence of Reed-Sternberg cells. This is indicative of
    A. Hodgkin's disease.
    B. leukemia.
    C. non-Hodgkin's lymphoma.
    D. sarcoma.

REFERENCE: Neighbors and Tannehill-Jones, p 119

56. The most common rickettsial disease in the United States is
    A. Hantavirus.
    B. Lyme disease.
    C. Rocky Mountain spotted fever.
    D. syphilis.

REFERENCE: Neighbors and Tannehill-Jones, p 57
               Scott and Fung, 331-332

57. Which of the following is NOT a diagnostic or screening test for colorectal cancer?
    A. double contrast barium enema
    B. sigmoidoscopy
    C. stool occult blood
    D. upper GI x-ray

REFERENCE: ACS (1)
               Neighbors and Tannehill-Jones, p 200
               Scott and Fong, p 399

58. Which of the following is NOT an identified risk factor for colorectal cancer?
    A. alcohol use
    B. physical inactivity
    C. high-fiber diet
    D. obesity

REFERENCE: ACS (2)

59. In general, excessive RBC breakdown could result in
    A. Crohn's disease.
    B. elevated BUN.
    C. high bilirubin levels.
    D. peptic ulcers.

REFERENCE: Neighbors and Tannehill-Jones, p 209
               NLM (2)
               Labtestsonline (1)

60. The most common bloodborne infection in the United States is
    A. *Helicobacter pylori.*   C. hepatitis C.
    B. hepatitis A.   D. hemophilia.

REFERENCE: Scott and Fong, p 397

61. The first stage of alcoholic liver disease is
    A. alcoholic hepatitis.   C. fatty liver.
    B. cirrhosis.   D. jaundice.

REFERENCE: Neighbors and Tannehill-Jones, p 211

62. Portal hypertension can contribute to all of the following EXCEPT
    A. ascites.
    B. dilation of blood vessels lining the intestinal tract.
    C. esophageal varices.
    D. kidney failure.

REFERENCE: Mayo Clinic (1)
                 Neighbors and Tannehill-Jones, p 211-214

63. Which of the following is a liver function test?
    A. AST (SGOT)   C. ECG
    B. BUN   D. TSH

REFERENCE: Neighbors and Tannehill-Jones, p 211-214
                 Sormunen, p 348-349

64. Which of the following is a risk factor involved in the etiology of gallstones?
    A. being overweight   C. low-fat diets
    B. being an adolescent   D. presence of peptic ulcer

REFERENCE: Rizzo, p 215

65. A serum potassium level of 2.8 would indicate
    A. Addison disease.   C. diabetic ketoacidosis.
    B. anemia.   D. hyperkalemia.

REFERENCE: Mayo Clinic (2)

66. A procedure performed with an instrument that freezes and destroys abnormal tissues (including
    seborrheic keratoses, basal cell carcinomas, and squamous cell carcinomas) is
    A. cryosurgery.   C. phacoemulsification.
    B. electrodesiccation.   D. photocautery.

REFERENCE: Rizzo, p 81, 469

67. Which of the organs listed below has endocrine and exocrine functions?
    A. kidney   C. lung
    B. liver   D. pancreas

REFERENCE: Neighbors and Tannehill-Jones, p 252
                 Rizzo, p 282-283, 274
                 Scott and Fong, p 386

68. Which of the following is an effect of insulin?
    A. decreases glycogen concentration in liver
    B. increases blood glucose
    C. increases the breakdown of fats
    D. increases glucose metabolism

REFERENCE: Neighbors and Tannehill-Jones, p 244, 252-256
                Rizzo, p 274-276, 282, 284-285
                Scott and Fong, p 225-226, 233, 504
                Sormunen, p 499

69. The causative organism for severe acute respiratory syndrome (SARS) is a
    A. bacterium.   C. fungus.
    B. coronavirus.   D. retrovirus.

REFERENCE: Neighbors and Tannehill-Jones, p 165
                Scott and Fong, p 366

70. Before leaving the hospital, all newborns are screened for an autosomal recessive genetic disorder
    of defective enzymatic conversion in protein metabolism. With early detection and a protein-
    restricted diet, brain damage is prevented. This disease is
    A. cystic fibrosis.   C. phenylketonuria.
    B. hereditary hemochromatosis.   D. Tay-Sachs disease.

REFERENCE: Neighbors and Tannehill-Jones, p 378
                Scott and Fong, p 481

71. Diabetic microvascular disease occurs
    A. as a direct result of elevated serum glucose.
    B. as a result of elevated fat in blood.
    C. due to damage to nerve cells.
    D. only in type 1 diabetics.

REFERENCE: Neighbors and Tannehill-Jones, p 254-255
                Rizzo, p 284-285
                Scott and Fong, p 231-232

72. Older age, obesity, and family history of diabetes are all characteristics of
    A. type I diabetes.   C. type III diabetes.
    B. type II diabetes.   D. type IV diabetes.

REFERENCE: Rizzo, p 284-285
                Scott and Fong, p 232

73. An elevated serum amylase would be characteristic of
    A. acute pancreatitis.   C. post-renal failure.
    B. gallbladder disease.   D. pre-renal failure.

REFERENCE: Neighbors and Tannehill-Jones, p 219

74. Clinical manifestations of this disease include polydipsia, polyuria, weight loss, and
    hyperglycemia. Which of the following tests would be ordered to confirm the disease?
    A. fasting blood sugar   C. glucose tolerance test
    B. glucagon   D. postprandial blood sugar

REFERENCE: Neighbors and Tannehill-Jones, p 253-254
                Rizzo, p 84-85
                Scott and Fong, p 231, 235

75. Common kidney stone treatments that allow small particles to be flushed out of the body through the urinary system include all of the following EXCEPT
    A. extracorporeal shock wave lithotripsy.
    B. fluid hydration.
    C. ureteroscopy and stone basketing.
    D. using medication to dissolve the stone(s).

REFERENCE: Neighbors and Tannehill-Jones, p 229

76. When a decubitus ulcer has progressed to a stage in which osteomyelitis is present, the ulcer has extended to the
    A. bone.   C. muscle.
    B. fascia.   D. subcutaneous tissue.

REFERENCE: Neighbors and Tannehill-Jones, p 92-93
                Scott and Fong, p 83-84

77. The patient has no visible bleeding, but remains anemic. Her physician is concerned about possible gastrointestinal bleeding. Which of the following tests might be ordered?
    A. DEXA scan   C. Pap smear test
    B. guaiac smear test   D. prostatic-specific antigen test

REFERENCE: Estridge and Reynolds, p 694-695
                Sormunen, p 37

78. Which of the following tests is NOT part of a liver panel?
    A. albumin   C. bilirubin
    B. alkaline phosphatase   D. creatinine

REFERENCE: Estridge and Reynolds, p 519-520

79. Maria Giovanni is in the hospital recovering from surgery. Based on her symptoms, her doctors are concerned about the possibility that she has developed a pulmonary embolism. Which of the following procedures will provide the definitive diagnosis?
    A. chest x-ray   C. pulmonary angiography
    B. lung scan   D. none of the above

REFERENCE: Neighbors and Tannehill-Jones, p 168
                Scott and Fong, p 369

80. A condition that involves the fifth cranial nerve, also known as "tic douloureux," causes intense pain in either the eye and forehead; lower lip, the section of the cheek closest to the ear and the outer segment of the tongue; or the upper lip, nose and cheek.
    A. Bell palsy   C. trigeminal neuralgia
    B. thrush   D. Tourette disorder

REFERENCE: Jones, p 272
                Scott and Fong, p 182

81. Which of the following is a congenital condition that is the most severe neural tube defect?
    A. meningocele   C. severe combined immunodeficiency
    B. myelomeningocele   D. spina bifida occulta

REFERENCE: Neighbors and Tannehill-Jones, p 374

82. Which of the following tubes conveys sperm from the seminal vesicle to the urethra?
    A. ejaculatory duct
    B. epididymis
    C. oviduct
    D. vas deferens

REFERENCE: Neighbors and Tannehill-Jones, p 481
               Rizzo, p 444

83. The most common type of vaginitis is
    A. yeast.
    B. protozoan.
    C. viral.
    D. A and B.

REFERENCE: Neighbors and Tannehill-Jones, p 315

84. The childhood viral disease that unvaccinated pregnant women should avoid because it may be passed to the fetus, causing congenital anomalies such as mental retardation, blindness, and deafness, is
    A. rickets.
    B. rubeola.
    C. rubella.
    A. tetanus.

REFERENCE: Neighbors and Tannehill-Jones, p 389

85. In _____ anemia the red blood cells become shaped like elongated crescents in the presence of low oxygen concentration.
    A. aplastic
    B. folic acid
    C. sickle cell
    D. vitamin B_{12}

REFERENCE: Jones, p 312
               Rizzo, p 308
               Scott and Fong, p 250-251

86. _____ is usually the first symptom of benign prostate hyperplasia.
    A. Abdominal pain
    B. Burning pain during urination
    C. Difficulty in urinating
    D. Pelvic pain

REFERENCE: Neighbors and Tannehill-Jones, p 322-324
               Rizzo, 444
               Scott and Fong, p 467-468

87. The hypothalamus, thalamus, and pituitary gland are all parts of the
    A. brainstem.
    B. cerebellum.
    C. exocrine system.
    D. limbic system.

REFERENCE: Rizzo, p 157-158

88. Which of the following BEST summarizes the current treatment of cervical cancer?
    A. A new three-shot vaccination series protects against the types of HPV that cause most cervical cancer cases.
    B. All stages have extremely high cure rates.
    C. Early detection and treatment of cervical cancer does not improve patient survival rates.
    D. Over 99 percent of cases are linked to long-term HPV infections.

REFERENCE: CDC (2)

89. Children at higher risk for sudden infant death syndrome (SIDS) include those
   A. with sleep apnea.
   B. with respiratory problems.
   C. who are premature infants.
   D. all of the above.

REFERENCE: Jones, p 423, 809
               Neighbors and Tannehill-Jones, p 395
               Scott and Fong, p 369

90. Decrease in blood pressure, salivation, and heart rate are examples of
   A. automatic nervous system responses.
   B. higher brain function.
   C. parasympathetic nervous system responses.
   D. sympathetic nervous system responses.

REFERENCE: Jones, p 235, 247
               Rizzo, p 227, 251
               Scott and Fong, p 177-179
               Sormunen, p 530

91. Photophobia or visual aura preceding a headache is characteristic of
   A. malnutrition.
   B. mastitis.
   C. migraines.
   D. myasthenia gravis.

REFERENCE: Jones, p 259-260
               Neighbors and Tannehill-Jones, 271
               Scott and Fong, p 163

92. Graves' disease
   A. is an autoimmune disease.
   B. most commonly affects males.
   C. usually cannot be treated.
   D. usually affects the elderly.

REFERENCE: Jones, p 517-518
               Neighbors and Tannehill-Jones, p 248
               Rizzo, p 280, 285
               Scott and Fong, p 228

93. "Pill-rolling" tremor is a characteristic symptom of
   A. epilepsy.
   B. Guillain-Barre syndrome.
   C. myasthenia gravis.
   D. Parkinson disease.

REFERENCE: Jones, p 267
               Neighbors and Tannehill-Jones, p 281
               Scott and Fong, p 162-164

94. Rheumatoid arthritis typically affects the
   A. intervertebral disks.
   B. hips and shoulders.
   C. knees and small joints of the hands and feet.
   D. large, weight-bearing joints.

REFERENCE: Jones, p 215
               Neighbors and Tannehill-Jones, p 71-72, 94-95
               Rizzo, p 183
               Scott and Fong, p 110-111

95. Henry experienced sudden sharp chest pain that he described as heavy and crushing. His pain and past medical history caused Dr. James to suspect that Henry was having a myocardial infarction. Which of the following tests is a more specific marker for a MI?
   A. AST
   B. CK-MB
   C. LDH1
   D. troponin I

REFERENCE: Lab Tests Online (2)

96. Bone mineral density (BMD) is a useful diagnostic test for
   A. osteoarthritis.
   B. osteomyelitis.
   C. osteoporosis.
   D. rheumatoid arthritis.

REFERENCE: Jones, p 173
              Neighbors and Tannehill-Jones, p 90-92
              Scott and Fong, p 113

97. A patient is on Coumadin therapy. Which of the following tests is commonly ordered to monitor the patient's Coumadin levels?
   A. bleeding time
   B. blood smear
   C. partial thromboplastin time
   D. prothrombin time

REFERENCE: Jones, p 318
              Labtestsonline (3)
              Neighbors and Tannehill-Jones, p 235

98. A toxic goiter has what distinguishing characteristic?
   A. iodine deficiency
   B. parathyroid involvement
   C. presence of muscle spasm
   D. thyroid hyperfunction

REFERENCE: Neighbors and Tannehill-Jones, p 247-248
              Rizzo, p 280
              Sormunen, p 511

99. How can Graves' disease be treated?
   A. antithyroid drugs
   B. radioactive iodine therapy
   C. surgery
   D. all of the above

REFERENCE: Jones, p 517
              Neighbors and Tannehill-Jones, p 247-248
              Rizzo, p 285
              Sormunen, p 511

100. Fractures occur in patients with osteoporosis due to
   A. falling from loss of balance.
   B. fibrous joint adhesions tearing apart small bones.
   C. loss of bone mass.
   D. tendency to fall from lack of joint mobility.

REFERENCE: Jones, p 163
              Neighbors and Tannehill-Jones, p 90-92
              Scott and Fong, p 113

101. United States healthcare providers are concerned about a possible pandemic of avian flu because
   A. there is no vaccine currently available.
   B. it is caused by a group of viruses that mutate very easily.
   C. the causative virus is being spread around the world by migratory birds.
   D. all of the above.

REFERENCE: CDC (2)

102. A sweat test was done on a patient with the following symptoms: frequent respiratory infections, chronic cough, and foul-smelling bloody stools. Which of the following diseases is probably suspected?
    A. cystic breast disease
    B. cystic fibrosis
    C. cystic lung disease
    D. cystic pancreas

REFERENCE: Neighbors and Tannehill-Jones, p 380

103. Margaret Vargas needs to have her mitral valve replaced. Her surgeon will discuss which of the following issues with her before the surgery?
    A. a mechanical valve will require that she take a "blood thinner" for the rest of her life
    B. a biological valve (usually porcine) will last 10 to 15 years
    C. a mechanical valve increases the risk of blood clots that can cause stroke
    D. all of the above

REFERENCE: NHLBI

104. Cervical cerclage is a procedure used to help prevent
    A. breathing restrictions.
    B. miscarriage.
    C. torsion.
    D. torticollis.

REFERENCE: Jones, p 746

105. Sam Spade has been injured in a MVA. The organ in his body, situated at the upper left of his abdominal cavity, under the ribs, that is part of his lymphatic system has been ruptured and he is bleeding internally. Sam needs a surgical procedure known as a
    A. sequestrectomy.
    B. sialoadenectomy.
    C. sigmoidoscopy.
    D. splenectomy.

REFERENCE: Jones, p 324
                Rizzo, p 346
                Sormunen, p 229, 242

106. Henrietta Dawson presents with a chief complaint of pain and weakness in her arms and neck. After an H&P and review of diagnostic tests that include a myelogram, her doctor diagnoses a herniated nucleus pulposus at the _____ level of her spine.
    A. cervical
    B. lumbar
    C. sacral
    D. thoracic

REFERENCE: Jones, p 64, 149, 213, 261,
                Neighbors and Tannehill-Jones, p 103
                Rizzo, p157, 170
                Scott and Fong, p 99, 112
                Sormunen, p 119, 120, 135

107. Ingrid Anderson presents with a skin infection that began as a raised itchy bump, resembling an insect bite. Within 1 to 2 days it developed into a vesicle. Now it is a painless ulcer, about 2 cm in diameter, with a black necrotic area in the center. During the history, her doctor learns that she has recently returned from an overseas vacation and becomes concerned that she may have become infected with anthrax. He will prescribe an
    A. antibiotic.
    B. antineoplastic.
    C. antiparasitic.
    D. antiviral.

REFERENCE: Scott and Fong, p 342, 366-367

108. Etiologies of dementia include
A. brain tumors.
B. ischemia.
C. trauma.
D. all of the above.

REFERENCE:　　　　　Neighbors and Tannehill-Jones, p 414
Rizzo, p 937, 946
Scott and Fong, p 164
Sormunen, p 539

109. Carpal tunnel syndrome is caused by entrapment of the
A. medial nerve.
B. radial nerve.
C. tibial nerve.
D. ulnar nerve.

REFERENCE:　　　　　Jones, 254,
Neighbors and Tannehill-Jones, p 104
Rizzo, p 182
Sormunen, p 134

110. The organism transmitted by a mosquito bite that causes malaria is a
A. bacteria.
B. prion.
C. protozoa.
D. virus.

REFERENCE:　　　　　Neighbors and Tannehill-Jones, p 54-55, 57
Rizzo, p 309
Scott and Fong, p 309

111. Contributing factors of mental disorders include
A. heredity.
B. stress.
C. trauma.
D. all of the above.

REFERENCE:　　　　　Jones, p 933
Neighbors and Tannehill-Jones, p 408

Answer Key for Medical Science

1.	B	49.	A	97.	D
2.	B	50.	A	98.	D
3.	A	51.	C	99.	D
4.	D	52.	C	100.	C
5.	C	53.	A	101.	D
6.	C	54.	B	102.	B
7.	C	55.	A	103.	D
8.	C	56.	C	104.	B
9.	D	57.	D	105.	D
10.	C	58.	C	106.	A
11.	B	59.	C	107.	A
12.	C	60.	C	108.	D
13.	D	61.	C	109.	A
14.	C	62.	D	110.	C
15.	C	63.	A	111.	D
16.	A	64.	A		
17.	B	65.	C		
18.	B	66.	A		
19.	B	67.	D		
20.	B	68.	D		
21.	C	69.	B		
22.	D	70.	C		
23.	C	71.	A		
24.	D	72.	B		
25.	B	73.	A		
26.	C	74.	C		
27.	B	75.	C		
28.	C	76.	A		
29.	A	77.	B		
30.	B	78.	D		
31.	D	79.	C		
32.	B	80.	C		
33.	B	81.	B		
34.	C	82.	A		
35.	D	83.	D	Candida	
36.	B	84.	C		
37.	D	85.	C		
38.	C	86.	C		
39.	A	87.	D		
40.	A	88.	A		
41.	C	89.	D		
42.	D	90.	C		
43.	C	91.	C		
44.	A	92.	A		
45.	D	93.	D		
46.	C	94.	C		
47.	C	95.	D		
48.	B	96.	C		

REFERENCES

American Cancer Society (ACS), http://www.cancer.org (accessed 11/12/08)

ACS (1)

http://www.cancer.org/docroot/CRI/content/CRI_2_4_3X_Can_colon_and_rectum_cancer_be_found_early.asp

ACS (2)

http://www.cancer.org/docroot/CRI/content/CRI_2_4_2X_What_are_the_risk_factors_for_colon_and_rectum_cancer.asp?rnav=cri (accessed 11/12/08)

American Medical Association. (2003) *Complete medical encyclopedia.* Chicago: American Medical Association (AHIMA).

Centers for Disease Control and Prevention (CDC), http://www.cdc.gov/index.htm

CDC (1)

http://www.cdc.gov/std/hpv/STDFact-HPV-vaccine.htm

CDC (2)

http://www.cdc.gov/flu/avian/gen-info/pdf/avian_facts.pdf

Damjanov, I. (2005). *Pathology for the health professions* (3rd ed.). Philadelphia: W. B. Saunders.

Erlich, A., & Schroeder, C. L. (2005). *Medical terminology for health professions* (5th ed.)

Jones, B. D. (2008). *Comprehensive medical terminology* (3rd ed.). Clifton Park, NY: Delmar Cengage Learning.

Labtestsonline, http://www.labtestsonline.org

Labtestsonline (1)

http://www.labtestsonline.org/understanding/analytes/bilirubin/glance.html

Labtestsonline (2)

http://www.labtestsonline.org/understanding/analytes/troponin/related.html (Accessed 11/20/08)

Labtestsonline (3)

http://www.labtestsonline.org/understanding/analytes/pt/test.html

Mayo Clinic, http://www.mayoclinic.com

Mayo Clinic (1)

http://www.mayoclinic.com/print/esophageal- varices/DS00820/DSECTION

Mayo Clinic (2)

http://www.mayoclinic.com/print/diabetic-ketoacidosis/DS00674/DSECTION=allandMETHOD=print (accessed 11/10/08)

The Merck manual of diagnosis and therapy (18th ed.). (2007). Rahway, NJ: Merck.

Mosby's medical, nursing, and allied health dictionary (5th ed.). (1998). St. Louis, MO: Mosby.

National Heart Lung and Blood Institute (NHLBI), http://www.nhlbi.nih.gov

NHLBI http://www.nhlbi.nih.gov/health/dci/Diseases/hvd/hvd_treatments.html

National Institute of Neurological Disorders and Stroke (NINDS),

http://www.ninds.nih.gov/disorders/carpal_tunnel/detail_carpal_tunnel.htm (accessed 11/12/08)

National Library of Medicine. http://www.nlm.nih.gov/medlineplus/

NLM (1)

http://www.nlm.nih.gov/medlineplus/ency/article/000433.htm

NLM (2)

http://www.nlm.nih.gov/medlineplus/ency/article/003479.htm (accessed 11/12/08)

NLM (3)

http://www.labtestsonline.org/understanding/analytes/pt/test.html

Neighbors, M. and Tannehill-Jones, R. (2006). *Human diseases (2nd ed.).* Clifton Park, NY. Delmar Cengage Learning.

Nobles, S. *Delmar's drug reference for health care professionals.* Clifton Park, NY: Delmar Cengage Learning.

Scott, A. S., & Fong, P. E. (2009). *Body structures and functions* (11th ed.) Clifton Park, NY: Delmar Cengage Learning.

Sormunen, C. (2006). *Terminology for allied health professionals* (5th ed.) Clifton Park, NY: Delmar Cengage Learning.

Woodrow, R. (2007). *Essentials of pharmacology for health occupations* (5th ed.). Clifton Park, NY: Delmar Cengage Learning.

VIII. ICD-9-CM Coding

Toni Cade, MBA, RHIA, CCS, FAHIMA

Infectious and Parasitic Diseases

1. Patient is admitted with a left ankle fracture. Patient also has AIDS with Kaposi's sarcoma of the skin. Patient received a closed reduction with internal fixation of the ankle fracture.
   A. 042, 176.0, 824.8, 79.16
   B. 824.8, 176.0, V08, 79.16
   C. 176.1, 824.8, V08, 79.16
   D. 824.8, 042, 176.0, 79.16

REFERENCE: Brown, p 97-98, 343-344, 346-347
                Schraffenberger, p 71-72

2. Septicemia due to methicillin-resistant Staphylococcus aureus. Patient also was admitted with septic shock and decubitus ulcer of the sacrum. Patient had a central line inserted and infusion of drotrecogin alfa.
   A. 038.19, 785.59, 707.02, 38.91
   B. 038.11, V09.0, 707.03, 995.92, 785.52, 38.93, 00.11
   C. 707.00, 038.11, 785.59, 38.93, 00.11
   D. 038.11, 755.59, 995.92, 38.93

REFERENCE: Bowie and Shaffer, p 84-85
                Brown, p 91-95, 200-201
                Lovaasen and Schwerdtfeger, p 165-166
                Schraffenberger, p 68-69

3. Nephropathy due to tuberculosis (confirmed histologically) of the kidney. Patient has a right nephrectomy performed.
   A. 016.05, 583.81, 55.51
   B. 583.81, 016.0, 55.52
   C. 016.02, 583.81, 55.51
   D. 016.02, 583.81, 55.52

REFERENCE: Brown, p 90-91, 184-186
                Eid, p 217
                Lovaasen and Schwerdtfeger, p 163-164
                Schraffenberger, p 67

4. A patient is admitted with fever and severe headache. Diagnostic workup revealed viral meningitis. Patient also has asthma with acute exacerbation and hypertension, both of which are treated.
   A. 047.9, 780.60, 784.0, 493.90, 401.9
   B. 047.8, 493.92, 401.1
   C. 047.9, 493.92, 401.9
   D. 780.60, 784.0, 047.9, 493.90, 401.9

REFERENCE: Brown, p 89, 133, 154-155, 288-290
                Schraffenberger, p 65-66, 136-138, 166-168

5. Nurse Jones suffers a needlestick and presents for HIV testing. She sees her physician for the test results and counseling.
   A. V72.6, 795.71
   B. 795.71, V65.8
   C. V08, V72.6, V65.44
   D. V73.89, V65.44, V01.79

REFERENCE: Brown, p 97-98
                Lovaasen and Schwerdtfeger, 158
                Schraffenberger, p 73

6. Right arm paralysis due to poliomyelitis that patient suffered as a child.
   A. 045.11, 342.81
   B. 138, 344.41
   C. 344.40, 138
   D. 138, 344.41

   REFERENCE: Brown, p 90-91

Neoplasms

7. Patient is admitted for chemotherapy for treatment of breast cancer with liver metastasis. Patient had a mastectomy 4 months ago. Chemotherapy is given.
   A. 197.7, V10.3, 99.25
   B. 174.9, 197.7, 99.25
   C. V58.11, V10.3, 197.7, 99.25
   D. V58.11, 174.9, V45.71, 197.7, 99.25

   REFERENCE: Bowie and Schaffer, p 107
                   Brown, p 314-315, 317-319, 324-328
                   Schraffenberger, p 79-80

8. Patient with a history of malignant neoplasm of the lung is admitted with seizures. Workup revealed metastasis of the lung cancer to the brain.
   A. 780.39, V10.11, 198.3
   B. 162.9, V10.11, 198.3, 780.39
   C. 198.3, 780.39, V10.11
   D. 198.3, 780.39, 162.9

   REFERENCE: Bowie and Schaffer, p 102-103
                   Brown, p 314-315, 317-319
                   Schraffenberger, p 89

9. Patient is admitted to the hospital for treatment of dehydration following chemotherapy as treatment for ovarian cancer.
   A. 276.51, 183.0
   B. 183.0, 276.51, 99.25
   C. 276.50, 183.0, 99.25
   D. 183.0, 276.51

   REFERENCE: Bowie and Schaffer, p 105
                   Brown, p 324-328

10. Malignant melanoma, skin of back. Patient undergoes a radical excision of the melanoma with full-thickness skin graft.

    A. 173.5, 86.4, 86.63
    B. 172.5, 86.4, 86.63
    C. 173.5, 86.3, 86.63
    D. 172.5, 86.3, 86.63

    REFERENCE: Brown, p 311
                    Schraffenberger, p 85

11. Patient is admitted with abdominal pain. Needle biopsy of the liver reveals secondary malignancy of the liver. Patient has an exploratory laparotomy to determine primary site. Primary site is unknown at time of discharge.
    A. 197.7, 199.1, 54.11, 50.12
    B. 197.7, 789.00, 54.11, 50.11
    C. 197.7, 199.1, 54.11, 50.11
    D. 197.7, 199.1, 789.00, 54.11, 50.12

    REFERENCE: Brown, p 317-319

12. Patient with a history of cancer of the colon and status post-colostomy is admitted for closure of the colostomy. Patient is also being treated for chronic obstructive pulmonary disease and diastolic heart failure. Patient has a takedown of the colostomy.
   A. 153.2, 496, 428.30, 46.52
   B. V55.3, 496, V10.05, 428.30, 46.52
   C. V55.3, 496, V10.05, 428.0, 46.52, 45.79
   D. V10.05, 492.8, 428.30, 46.52

REFERENCE: Brown, p 154, 281-282, 329
                Schraffenberger, p 87, 326

Endocrine, Nutritional, and Metabolic Disorders and Immunity Disorders

13. Female, 68 years old, was admitted with type II diabetes mellitus with a diabetic ulcer of the left heel. Patient was taken to the operating room for excisional debridement of the ulcer.
   A. 250.80, 707.14, 86.22   C. 250.81, 707.13, 86.22
   B. 707.14, 250.80, 86.22   D. 250.82, 707.14, 86.28

REFERENCE: Brown, p 101-105, 203-204
                Lovaasen and Schwerdtfeger, p 238-242
                Schraffenberger, p 96-98, 222

14. Sixty-seven-year-old is admitted with acute dehydration secondary to nausea and vomiting that is due to acute gastroenteritis. Patient is treated for dehydration. Esophagogastroduodenoscopy is performed.
   A. 558.9, 787.01, 276.51, 45.13   C. 276.51, 787.01, 558.9, 45.13
   B. 558.9, 787.01, 276.51, 45.16   D. 276.51, 558.9, 45.13

REFERENCE: Schraffenberger, p 100, 178

15. Patient was found at home in a hypoglycemic coma. This patient had never been diagnosed as being diabetic.
   A. 250.30   C. 251.1
   B. 251.0   D. 251.2

REFERENCE: Brown, p 107

16. Aplastic anemia secondary to chemotherapy administered for multiple myeloma.
   A. 284.89, 203.00, E933.1   C. 284.9, 203.00, E933.1
   B. 203.00, 284.81, E933.1   D. 203.01, 284.89, E933.1

REFERENCE: Bowie and Schaffer, p 127
                Brown, p 127-128, 367-368

17. Male patient admitted with gastrointestinal hemorrhage resulting in acute blood loss anemia. Colonoscopy and Esophagogastroduodenoscopy fail to reveal source of bleed.
   A. 285.9, 578.1, 45.13, 45.23   C. 578.9, 285.1, 45.13, 45.23
   B. 578.1, 285.1, 45.13, 45.23   D. 578.9, 280.0, 45.13, 45.23

REFERENCE: Brown, p 126-127, 167-168

18. Severe malnutrition, percutaneous endoscopic gastrostomy
    A. 263.9, 43.11   C. 261, 43.19
    B. 261, 43.11   D. 263.8, 43.11

REFERENCE: Brown, p 108
               Lovaasen and Schwerdtfeger, p 248

Diseases of the Blood and Blood-Forming Organs

19. Thrombocytopenia, purpura; splenectomy
    A. 287.4, 41.5   C. 287.9, 41.42
    B. 287.8, 41.5   D. 287.30, 41.5

REFERENCE: Lovaasen and Schwerdtfeger, p 191
               Schraffenberger, p 106

20. Sickle cell anemia with crisis
    A. 282.61   C. 282.63
    B. 282.62   D. 282.69
REFERENCE: Brown, p 128
               Lovaasen and Schwerdtfeger, p 186-187
               Schraffenberger, p 104

21. Sickle cell pain crisis
    A. 282.62   C. 282.5
    B. 282.60   D. 282.42

REFERENCE: Bowie and Schaffer, p 126-127
               Brown, p 128
               Eid, p 223
               Schraffenberger, p, 104

22. Cooley's anemia
    A. 282.41   C. 282.49
    B. 282.0   D. 282.42

REFERENCE: Brown, p 125
               Schraffenberger, p 104

23. Anemia due to end-stage renal disease, patient treated for anemia
    A. 285.8   C. 285.22, 585.6
    B. 285.21, 585.6   D. 285.9

REFERENCE: Brown, p 125
               Schraffenberger, p 105

24. Pernicious anemia
    A. 280.9   C. 281.1
    B. 280.8   D. 281.0

REFERENCE: Brown, p 125
               Schraffenberger, p 104

Mental Disorders

25. Mild mental retardation due to old viral encephalitis
    A. 319, 049.8
    B. 317, 326
    C. 317, 047.8
    D. 317, 139.0

REFERENCE: Brown, p 90

26. Anxiety with depression
    A. 300.11, 311
    B. 300.4
    C. 309.28
    D. 300.00, 311

REFERENCE: Brown, p 115
               Lovaasen and Schwerdtfeger, p 540-541

27. Delirium tremens with alcohol dependence
    A. 291.0, 303.90
    B. 303.91, 291.0
    C. 291.3, 303.90
    D. 291.0, 303.00

REFERENCE: Brown, p 117-118
               Schraffenberger, p 116-117

28. Latent schizophrenia, chronic with acute exacerbation
    A. 295.52
    B. 295.55
    C. 295.54
    D. 295.53

REFERENCE: Bowie and Schaffer, p 137-138
               Brown, p 113

29. Chronic paranoia due to continuous cocaine dependence. Drug rehabilitation provided.
    A. 301.0, 305.61, 94.63
    B. 297.1, 304.21, 94.64
    C. 297.1, 305.61, 96.64
    D. 297.1, 304.21, 96.63

REFERENCE: Brown, p 118
               Schraffenberger, p 117

30. Psychogenic paroxysmal tachycardia
    A. 427.2, 316
    B. 306.2, 427.1
    C. 427.1, 306.2
    D. 316, 427.2

REFERENCE: Brown, p 115

Diseases of the Nervous System and Sense Organs

31. A 5-year-old female is admitted to ambulatory surgery with chronic otitis media. Patient has bilateral myringotomy with insertion of tubes.
    A. 381.20, 20.01
    B. 381.3, 20.01
    C. 382.9, 20.01, 20.01
    D. 381.89, 20.01

REFERENCE: Schraffenberger, p 128-129

32. Patient is a type II diabetic with a diabetic cataract. Patient has phacoemulsification of the cataract with synchronous insertion of lens.
   A. 250.51, 366.42, 13.59, 13.71
   B. 250.50, 366.41, 13.41, 13.71
   C. 250.52, 366.41, 13.41, 13.71
   D. 366.41, 250.50, 13.41, 13.71

REFERENCE: Brown, p 104, 142
               Schraffenberger, p 128

33. Epilepsy and paraplegia as residuals of a head injury suffered 5 years ago
   A. 345.90, 344.1, 907.0
   B. 345.91, 344.1, 907.0
   C. 959.01, 345.90, 344.1
   D. 345.81, 344.2, 907.0

REFERENCE: Brown, p 136
               Lovaasen and Schwerdtfeger, p 564-565
               Schraffenberger, p 125-126

34. Alzheimer's disease with dementia
   A. 331.0, 294.8
   B. 294.8
   C. 331.0, 294.10
   D. 331.0

REFERENCE: Brown, p 112

35. Meningitis sarcoidosis
   A. 321.2, 136.1
   B. 135, 321.4
   C. 136.1, 321.2
   D. 321.4, 135

REFERENCE: Brown, p 133

36. Carpal tunnel syndrome; arthroscopic release of carpal tunnel
   A. 354.0, 04.43
   B. 354.1, 80.23
   C. 354.1, 04.43, 80.23
   D. 354.0, 04.43, 80.23

REFERENCE: Brown, p 138

Diseases of the Circulatory System

37. Patient admitted with carotid artery disease and acute cerebral infarction with left hemiparesis, dysphagia, and aphasia. Dysphagia and aphasia have resolved by discharge, but residual hemiparesis remains.
   A. 433.11, 342.90
   B. 433.11, 434.91, 342.90, 784.3, 787.20
   C. 436, 342.90, 784.3, 787.20
   D. 433.11, 342.90, 784.3, 787.20

REFERENCE: Brown, p 284-286
               Schraffenberger, p 152

38. Hypertensive kidney disease, congestive heart failure, and acute systolic heart failure
    A. 593.9, 401.9, 482.0, 428.21
    B. 404.11, 428.0, 428.21
    C. 403.90, 428.0, 428.21
    D. 404.91

REFERENCE: Brown, p 289-290
                Schraffenberger, p 138-139

39. Acute inferior wall myocardial infarction with unstable angina. Patient also has coronary artery disease and atrial fibrillation.
    A. 410.41, 411.1, 414.01, 427.31   C. 410.40, 414.00, 427.31
    B. 410.41, 414.00, 411.1, 427.31   D. 410.41, 414.01, 427.31

REFERENCE: Bowie and Schaffer, p 168
                Brown, p 275-281
                Eid, p 226
                Schraffenberger, p 141-144, 149

40. Patient with a diagnosis of aortic valve stenosis and mitral valve regurgitation is admitted for aortic valve replacement. Patient is also under treatment for congestive heart failure. Patient undergoes placement of aortic valve prosthesis with cardiopulmonary bypass.
    A. 396.2, 398.91, 35.22, 39.61   C. 396.2, 428.0, 35.22, 39.61
    B. 424.1, 424.0, 428.0, 35.22   D. 424.1, 424.0, 428.0, 35.21, 39.61

REFERENCE: Brown, p 273-274
                Lovaasen and Schwerdtfeger, p 297
                Schraffenberger, p 135

41. Atherosclerotic peripheral vascular disease of the lower leg with claudication. Angioplasty of the lower leg artery performed.
    A. 440.20, 39.50   C. 444.22, 38.08
    B. 440.21, 39.50   D. 443.9, 39.50

REFERENCE: Brown, p 292-293

Diseases of the Respiratory System

42. Patient presents to the outpatient department for a chest x-ray. Physician order lists the following reasons for the chest x-ray: fever and cough, rule out pneumonia. Radiologist reports the chest x-ray is positive for pneumonia.
    A. 486   C. 780.61, 786.2
    B. 486, 780.61, 786.2, V72.5   D. V72.5, 780.60, 786.2

REFERENCE: Brown, p 149-152
                Schraffenberger, p 165

43. Aspiration pneumonia with pneumonia due to *Staphylococcus aureus*. Patient also has emphysema.
    A. 507.0, 482.9, 496   C. 507.0, 491.21
    B. 507.0, 482.41, 496   D. 507.0, 482.41, 492.8

REFERENCE: Brown, p 149-151
                Schraffenberger, p 166

44. Acute respiratory failure due to congestive heart failure. Patient is placed on the ventilator for 3 days following insertion of endotracheal tube.
    A. 518.81, 428.0, 96.71, 96.04
    B. 518.81, 428.0, 96.72, 96.04
    C. 428.0, 518.81, 96.71, 96.04
    D. 428.0, 518.83, 96.72, 96.04

REFERENCE: Brown, p 157-159, 281-282
                Lovaasen and Schwerdtfeger, p 263-264
                Schraffenberger, p 169-171

45. Hypertrophic tonsillitis; bilateral tonsillectomy and adenoidectomy
    A. 463, 28.3, 28.3
    B. 474.00, 28.3
    C. 474.02, 28.3, 28.3
    D. 463, 28.3

REFERENCE: Schraffenberger, p 163

46. Chronic obstructive pulmonary disease with an exacerbation of acute bronchitis
    A. 491.22
    B. 496, 466.0
    C. 466.0, 496
    D. 491.22, 466.0

REFERENCE: Brown, p 154-155
                Schraffenberger, p 168

47. Extrinsic asthma with status asthmaticus
    A. 493.11
    B. 493.90
    C. 493.91
    D. 493.81

REFERENCE: Brown, p 154-156
                Schraffenberger, p 167-168
                Lovaasen and Schwerdtfeger, p 270-271

48. Exacerbation of myasthenia gravis resulting in acute respiratory failure. Patient required mechanical ventilation for 10 hours, following endotracheal intubation.
    A. 358.00, 518.81, 96.71, 96.04
    B. 518.81, 358.01, 96.71, 96.04
    C. 358.00, 581.89, 96.71, 96.05
    D. 518.82, 358.00, 96.72, 96.04

REFERENCE: Brown, p 157-159, 162-163
                Schraffenberger, p 169-170

Disease of the Digestive System

49. Patient admitted to the hospital for repair of ventral hernia. Surgery is canceled after chest x-ray revealed lower lobe pneumonia. Patient is placed on antibiotics to treat the pneumonia.
    A. 553.20, 486, V64.1
    B. 486, 553.20, V64.3
    C. 486, 553.20
    D. 553.20, 486

REFERENCE: Brown, p 60-61, 149, 174-175
                Schraffenberger, p 165, 177

50. Gastric ulcer with hemorrhage resulting in acute blood-loss anemia. Esophagogastroduodenoscopy performed.
    A. 531.20, 285.1, 45.13
    B. 285.1, 531.20, 45.13
    C. 531.40, 280.0, 45.14
    D. 531.40, 285.1, 45.13

REFERENCE: Bowie and Schaffer, p 188-189
                Brown, p 98-99, 169
                Schraffenberger, p 105, 176

51. Diverticulitis large bowel with abscess; right hemicolectomy with colostomy performed
    A. 562.10, 45.74, 46.03
    B. 562.11, 45.73, 46.10
    C. 562.11, 569.5, 45.73, 46.10
    D. 562.11, 569.5, 45.74, 46.11

REFERENCE: Brown, p 170-171

52. Acute and chronic cholecystitis with cholelithiasis. Laparoscopic cholecystectomy attempted and converted to open.
    A. 574.00, 574.10, V64.41, 51.22
    B. 574.00, 574.10, 51.22, 51.23
    C. 574.00, 51.22, 51.23
    D. 574.00, V64.41, 51.22

REFERENCE: Brown, p 172, 173
               Eid, p 230
               Lovaasen and Schwerdtfeger, p 523
               Schraffenberger, p 179

53. Bleeding esophageal varices with alcoholic liver cirrhosis and portal hypertension. Patient is alcohol dependent. Esophagogastroduodenoscopy for control of hemorrhage.
    A. 456.20, 571.2, 303.90, 42.33
    B. 571.2, 456.20, 303.90, 280.0, 42.33
    C. 572.3, 571.2, 303.90, 456.20, 42.33
    D. 303.90, 456.20, 303.90, 42.33

REFERENCE: Brown, p 117-120, 168

54. Patient is admitted for workup for melena. Laboratory results reveal chronic blood loss anemia. Colonoscopy with biopsy reveals Crohn's disease of the descending colon.
    A. 578.1, 555.1, 45.25, 45.43
    B. 555.1, 45.25
    C. 555.1, 578.1, 45.25
    D. 555.1, 578.1, 45.25, 45.23

REFERENCE: Brown, p 125
               Schraffenberger, p 178

Diseases of the Genitourinary System

55. Acute urinary tract infection due to E. coli
    A. 599.0, 041.4
    B. 599.0
    C. 041.4, 599.0
    D. 590.2, 041.4

REFERENCE: Brown, p 94
               Schraffenberger, p 188-189

56. Patient presents with complaint of gross hematuria. Diagnosis of benign prostatic hypertrophy is made and patient undergoes transurethral prostatectomy.
    A. 600.01, 60.21
    B. 600.00, 60.29
    C. 600.00, 599.71, 60.29
    D. 600.00, 599.71, 60.21

REFERENCE: Brown, p 189-190
               Lovaasen and Schwerdtfeger, p 206-207

57. Male patient presents to the ER in acute renal failure; he is also being treated for hypertension
    A. 410.00, 586
    B. 401.9, 584.9
    C. 585.9, 401.1
    D. 584.9, 401.9

REFERENCE: Brown, p 183-185

58. Hemorrhagic cystitis; cystoscopy with biopsy of bladder
   A. 595.9, 57.33
   B. 595.9, 041.4, 57.32
   C. 595.82, 57.33
   D. 596.7, 57.33

REFERENCE: Brown, p 181
               Schraffenberger, p 189

59. Chronic kidney disease due to hypertension and type I diabetes mellitus
   A. 250.41, 403.90, 585.9
   B. 250.40, 403.10, 585.1
   C. 403.90, 250.41, 585.9
   D. 403.10, 250.41, 585.2

REFERENCE: Brown, p 184

60. End-stage kidney disease which resulted from malignant hypertension
   A. 403.01, 585.6
   B. 585.9, 401.0
   C. 403.00
   D. 401.0, 585.9

REFERENCE: Brown, p 183-184
               Schraffenberger, p 138, 188

Obstetrics

61. Vaginal delivery of a full-term liveborn infant. Patient undergoes episiotomy with repair and post delivery elective tubal ligation.
   A. 650, V25.2, V27.0, 73.6, 66.32
   B. 648.91, V27.0, 73.6, 66.32
   C. 650, V27.0, 66.32
   D. 650, V27.0

REFERENCE: Bowie and Schaffer, p 216
               Brown, p 221-223, 234-235
               Schraffenberger, p 206-207

62. Incomplete spontaneous abortion complicated by excessive hemorrhage; dilation and curettage performed.
   A. 634.12, 69.09
   B. 634.12, 285.1, 69.09
   C. 634.11, 69.02
   D. 634.91, 69.02

REFERENCE: Brown, p 243-245
               Lovaasen and Schwerdtfeger, p 386-387
               Schraffenberger, p 198-199

63. Obstructed labor due to breech presentation; single liveborn delivered via Cesarean section
   A. 660.81, 74.1
   B. 660.01, 652.21, V27.0, 74.99
   C. 660.01, V27.0, 74.1
   D. 660.81, 652.21, 74.99

REFERENCE: Brown, p 221-223, 235

64. Delivery of a single newborn at 43 weeks' gestation; manually assisted delivery
   A. 650, V27.0, 73.59
   B. 645.20, V27.0, 73.59
   C. 644.21, V27.0, 73.59
   D. 645.21, V27.0, 73.59

REFERENCE: Brown, p 231-235
           Schraffenberger, p 206-207

65. Female, 26 weeks' pregnancy is treated for a fractured distal radius and ulna; closed reduction of fracture performed
    A. 813.44, 79.02
    B. 648.93, 813.44, 79.02
    C. 813.44, V22.2, 79.02
    D. V22.2, 813.44, 79.02

REFERENCE: Brown, p 221
                 Schraffenberger, p 209

66. Patient diagnosed with tubal pregnancy; unilateral salpingectomy for removal of tubal pregnancy performed.
    A. 633.20, 66.63
    B. 633.11, 66.62
    C. 633.00, 66.61
    D. 633.10, 66.62

REFERENCE: Brown, p 248-249
                 Schraffenberger, p 204-205

Diseases of the Skin and Subcutaneous Tissue

67. Abscess with cellulitis of the abdominal wall. Culture is positive for Staph aureus.
    A. 682.8, 041.11
    B. 682.2, 041.11
    C. 682.2, 707.8
    D. 682.2

REFERENCE: Brown, p 200-201
                 Schraffenberger, p 220

68. Patient had a cholecystectomy 6 days ago and is now coming back with evidence of staphylococcal cellulitis at the site of operative incision.
    A. 958.3, 682.2, 041.19
    B. 998.51, 682.8, 041.11
    C. 958.3, 682.8, 041.11
    D. 998.59, 682.2, 041.10

REFERENCE: Brown, p 202
                 Eid, p 233

69. Chronic ulcers of the calf and back. Both ulcers are excisionally debrided and the ulcer on the back has a split-thickness skin graft.
    A. 707.12, 707.8, 86.22, 86.22, 86.69
    B. 707.12, 707.8, 86.22
    C. 707.8, 86.22, 86.69
    D. 707.8, 86.22, 86.22, 86.69

REFERENCE: Brown, p 200-204
                 Lovaasen and Schwerdtfeger, p 583-584
                 Schraffenberger, p 221-222

70. Dermatitis due to prescription topical antibiotic cream used as directed by physician
    A. 692.4
    B. 692.3, E930.9
    C. 692.3
    D. 692.3, E930.1

REFERENCE: Brown, p 199-200
                 Lovaasen and Schwerdtfeger, p 582
                 Schraffenberger, p 220

71. Boil, left face; incision and drainage
    A. 680.0, 86.04
    B. 680.0, 86.09
    C. 680.8, 86.11
    D. 680.0, 86.04, 86.11

REFERENCE: Brown, p 199

72. Abscessed pilonidal cyst; excision of cyst
    A. 685.1, 86.04
    B. 686.09, 86.04
    C. 685.0, 86.21
    D. 686.01, 86.22

REFERENCE: Brown, p 199

Diseases of the Musculoskeletal System and Connective Tissue

73. Pathological fracture of the femur due to metastatic bone cancer. Patient has a history of lung cancer.
    A. 198.5, 733.14, V10.11
    B. 733.14, 198.5, V10.11
    C. 733.19, 198.5, V10.11
    D. 821.00, 162.9

REFERENCE: Brown, p 210-211
               Lovaasen and Schwerdtfeger, p 428-429
               Schraffenberger, p 89, 229

74. Herniated lumbar intervertebral disc with paresthesia; lumbar laminectomy with diskectomy performed.
    A. 722.11, 80.51, 03.09
    B. 839.20, 80.51
    C. 722.10, 80.59, 03.09
    D. 722.10, 80.51

REFERENCE: Brown, p 207-208
               Schraffenberger, p 228

75. Pyogenic arthritis of the hip due to Group A Streptococcus; arthrocentesis done
    A. 716.95, 041.01, 81.91
    B. 715.95, 041.01, 81.92
    C. 711.05, 041.01, 81.91
    D. 711.05, 81.91

REFERENCE: Brown, p 208-209
               Schraffenberger, p 228

76. Bunion left foot and hammertoe right foot; Keller procedure and hammer toe repair performed.
    A. 727.1, 735.4, 77.59, 77.56
    B. 727.1, 735.8, 77.52, 77.59
    C. 727.2, 735.4, 77.52, 77.58
    D. 727.1, 735.3, 77.56, 77.59

REFERENCE: Schraffenberger, p 228-229

77. Malunion of humeral fracture (original injury occurred 1 year ago). Open reduction with internal fixation performed.
    A. 812.20, 79.39
    B. 733.82, 905.2, 79.31
    C. 733.81, 905.2, 79.31
    D. 733.94, 905.2, 79.32

REFERENCE: Schraffenberger, p 229-230

78. Recurrent internal derangement of the left knee; diagnostic arthroscopy of the knee.
    A. 715.96, 80.26
    B. 718.36, 80.26
    C. 836.2, 80.26
    D. 718.36, 80.6

REFERENCE: Brown, p 210

Congenital Anomalies

79. Liveborn infant, born in hospital, cleft palate and lip
    A. 749.00, 749.10
    B. 749.20
    C. V30.00, 749.20
    D. V30.00, 749.00, 749.10

REFERENCE: Bowie and Schaffer, p 246
              Brown, p 255, 260
              Schraffenberger, p 238

80. Newborn, born in hospital with tetralogy of Fallot
    A. 745.8
    B. V30.01, 746.09
    C. 745.2
    D. V30.00, 745.2

REFERENCE: Brown, p 255, 260

81. Newborn infant transferred to Manasota Hospital for treatment of esophageal atresia. Code for Manasota Hospital.
    A. V30.00
    B. 750.3
    C. V30.00, 750.3
    D. 750.3, V30.00

REFERENCE: Brown, p 255

82. Cervical spina bifida with hydrocephalus
    A. 741.02
    B. 741.93
    C. 741.01
    D. 741.91

REFERENCE: Brown, p 255
              Eid, p 235
              Schraffenberger, p 236

83. Infant with clubfoot. Correction by Evans operation
    A. 754.70, 83.84
    B. 754.71, 83.84
    C. 736.71, 83.84
    D. 736.79, 83.84

REFERENCE: Brown, p 255
              Schraffenberger, p 239-240

84. Full-term infant, born in hospital. Diagnosed with polycystic kidneys.
    A. 753.12
    B. V30.00, 753.12
    C. V30.00
    D. 753.12, V30.00

REFERENCE: Brown, p 255, 260
              Schraffenberger, p 239

Certain Conditions Originating in the Perinatal Period

85. Full-term newborn, born in hospital. Mother is addicted to cocaine; however, infant tested negative.
    A. V30.00, 760.75
    B. 779.5 V29.8
    C. V30.00, 779.5
    D. V30.00, V29.8

REFERENCE: Brown, p 260, 264
              Schraffenberger, p 321-323

86. Preterm infant born via Cesarean section admitted to Children's Hospital for severe birth asphyxia
    A. V30.01, 765.10, 768.5
    B. 765.10, 768.5, V30.01
    C. 768.5, 765.10
    D. 768.5

REFERENCE: Brown, p 262

87. Neonatal jaundice in preterm infant born in hospital. Phototherapy done to treat jaundice.
    A. V30.00, 774.2, 99.83
    B. 774.2, 99.83
    C. V30.00, 99.83
    D. V30.00, 774.2

REFERENCE: Brown, p 260

88. One-week-old infant admitted to the hospital with diagnosis of urinary tract infection contracted prior to birth. Urine culture positive for E. coli.
    A. V30.00, 599.0
    B. 599.0, 041.4
    C. V30.00, 599.0, 041.4
    D. 771.82, 599.0, 041.4

REFERENCE: Brown, p 89, 264-265

89. Hypoglycemia in infant with diabetic mother
    A. 251.2
    B. 775.1
    C. 775.0
    D. 251.1

REFERENCE:
              Brown, p 259, 266

90. Full-term infant born in hospital. Birth complicated by cord compression which affected newborn.
    A. V30.00, 762.5
    B. V30.00
    C. 762.5
    D. 762.6, V30.00

REFERENCE: Bowie and Schaffer, p 254
              Brown, p 260, 265
              Schraffenberger, p 321-322

Symptoms, Signs, and Ill-Defined Conditions

91. Patient admitted with abdominal pain. Discharge diagnosis is listed as abdominal pain due to gastroenteritis or diverticulosis.
    A. 789.00
    B. 562.10, 558.9
    C. 789.00, 558.9, 562.10
    D. 558.9, 562.10, 789.00

REFERENCE: Bowie and Schaffer, p 261-262
              Brown, p 81-83
              Schraffenberger, p 252

92. Lung mass; diagnostic bronchoscopy.
    A. 518.89, 33.23
    B. 786.6, 33.23
    C. 793.1, 33.27
    D. 786.6, 33.27

REFERENCE: Brown, p 81-83

93. Pap smear with cervical high-risk human papillomavirus (HPV) DNA test positive
    A. 795.05   C. 795.04
    B. 795.09   D. 795.02

REFERENCE: Brown, p 81-83

94. Patient presents to the emergency room with ascites. Paracentesis done.
    A. 789.30, 54.91   C. 789.59, 54.91
    B. 789.51, 54.91   D. 782.3, 54.91

REFERENCE: Brown, p 81-83

95. Patient admitted with fever due to bacteremia.
    A. 780.61, 790.7   C. 780.61
    B. 038.9   D. 790.7, 780.61

REFERENCE: Brown, p 81-83
                Eid, p 236-237
                Lovaasen and Schwerdtfeger, p 131-132

96. Urinary retention requiring insertion of Foley catheter
    A. 788.21, 57.94   C. 788.20, 57.94
    B. 788.20, 57.93   D. 788.29, 57.93

REFERENCE: Brown, p 81-83

Injury and Poisoning

97. Fracture of the medial malleolus due to fall down steps. Fracture treated with closed reduction.
    A. 824.1, E880.9, 79.05   C. 824.0, 79.09
    B. 824.0, E880.9, 79.06   D. 824.1, E880.1, 79.05

REFERENCE: Bowie and Schaffer, p 268-269
                Brown, p 343-344, 346
                Schraffenberger, p 259-261

98. Closed head injury, patient was a passenger in a motor vehicle involved in a head-on collision with another motor vehicle.
    A. 959.01, E812.1   C. 959.01, E813.1
    B. 959.09, E812.2   D. 959.09, E813.1

REFERENCE: Brown, p 335-337
                Schraffenberger, p 273-274

99. Gunshot wound to abdomen with moderate laceration of liver. Patient was assaulted with a pistol.
    A. 864.00, E965.1   C. 864.13, E965.1
    B. 864.10, E965.0   D. 864.13, E965.0

REFERENCE: Brown, p 335-338
                Schraffenberger, p 265

100. Patient was admitted with third-degree burn of upper back which involved 20% of his body surface. There was an explosion and fire at his home.

    A. 942.25, 948.02, E890.2   C. 942.34, 948.22, E890.3
    B. 942.44, 948.21, E895   D. 942.24, 949.3, E897

REFERENCE: Brown, p 359-362
                    Schraffenberger, p 269-271

101. Third-degree burn to thigh and second-degree burn to foot. Patient was burned by hot liquid.

    A. 945.36, 945.22, E924.0   C. 945.22, E924.00
    B. 945.22, 945.36, E924.0   D. 945.29, 945.39, E924.0

REFERENCE: Brown, p 359-362
                    Lovaasen and Schwerdtfeger, p 479-480
                    Schraffenberger, p 269-271

102. Laceration of left wrist with injury to radial nerve as a result of an accident with embedded glass. Wrist laceration repaired with sutures.

    A. 881.02, 86.59   C. 955.3, E920.8, 86.59
    B. 881.12, E920.8, 86.59   D. 881.12, 955.3, E920.8, 86.59

REFERENCE: Brown, p 335-338, 350
                    Schraffenberger, p 266-267, 273

103. Female, 76 years old, admitted with tachycardia due to theophylline toxicity.

    A. 785.0, E942.1   C. 785.0, E944.1
    B. 995.20, E942.1   D. 995.20, E944.1

REFERENCE: Brown, p 365-368
                    Lovaasen and Schwerdtfeger, p 483-484
                    Schraffenberger, p 278-279

104. Patient suffered dizziness as a result of taking prescribed Phenobarbital. Patient took medication with beer.

    A. 780.4, 980.0, E860.0
    B. 967.0, 980.0, 780.4, E851, E860.0
    C. 967.0, 708.4, E851
    D. 780.4, E851, E860.0

REFERENCE: Brown, p 365-368
                    Eid, p 262-263
                    Schraffenberger, p 283-285

105. Pain in hip due to displaced hip prosthesis. Patient is admitted and undergoes revision of hip prosthesis.

    A. 996.49, 81.53   C. 719.45, 81.53
    B. 996.77, 81.53   D. 996.49, 719.45, 81.53

REFERENCE: Schraffenberger, p 285-268

106. Post-operative hemorrhage resulting in acute blood-loss anemia
    A. 997.72, 285.1   C. 998.11, 285.1
    B. 999.1, 285.1   D. 998.11

REFERENCE: Brown, p 126, 381
               Schraffenberger, p 285-286

V-Codes

107. Admission for colostomy takedown. Takedown performed.
    A. V44.3, 46.52   C. 997.4, 46.52
    B. 569.60, 46.52   D. V55.3, 46.52

REFERENCE: Brown, p 70-71
               Schraffenberger, p 326

108. The patent is being admitted for a preoperative EKG on an outpatient basis. He is scheduled to have an elective cholecystectomy tomorrow for chronic cholecystitis and cholelithiasis. EKG reveals atrial flutter.
    A. 574.10   C. V72.81, 574.10, 427.32
    B. V72.81, 51.23   D. 427.32

REFERENCE: Brown, p 74
               Schraffenberger, p 335-336

109. Screening examination for lung cancer
    A. V72.82   C. V72.5
    B. 162.9   D. V76.0

REFERENCE: Brown, p 75
               Eid, p 238
               Lovaasen and Schwerdtfeger, p 140
               Schraffenberger, p 337

110. Patient admitted for observation for head injury following a fall. Patient also suffered a minor laceration to the forehead. Head injury was ruled out.
    A. V71.4, 873.42, E888.9   C. 959.01, 873.42, E888.9
    B. 873.42, E888.9   D. V71.4, E888.9

REFERENCE: Brown, p 72-73
               Lovaasen and Schwerdtfeger, p 140-141
               Schraffenberger, p 266-268, 334-335

When the question has the ICD-9-CM codes and their respective narrative description, you should practice answering the question without using your coding book.

111. Elderly man was admitted through the emergency department for severe urinary retention. Upon study, it was determined that his hypertension was uncontrolled (215/108). Prior medical records show admission 8 weeks ago for the same problem. As per conditions on previous admission, his BPH is complicated by acute cystitis. He is noncompliant with medications. Medication for the hypertension was immediately started and his hypertension was quickly brought under control. Urinary retention was relieved by placement of a Foley catheter. Transurethral resection of the prostate was done.

600.00	Hypertrophy, (benign) of prostate without urinary obstruction and other lower urinary tract symptoms (LVTS)
600.01	Hypertrophy (benign) of prostate with urinary obstruction and other lower urinary tract symptoms (LVTS)
600.3	Cyst of prostate
595.0	Acute cystitis
595.9	Cystitis, unspecified
788.20	Retention of urine, unspecified
401.9	Essential hypertension, unspecified
401.0	Essential hypertension, malignant
V15.81	Non-compliance with medical treatment
57.94	Insertion of indwelling urinary catheter
57.92	Dilation of bladder neck
60.29	Other transurethral prostatectomy
60.61	Local excision of lesion of prostate

- A. 600.01, 595.0, 788.20, 401.9, V15.81, 57.94, 60.29
- B. 600.3, 595.0, 401.0, V15.81, 57.92, 60.61
- C. 600.00, 595.9, 788.20, 401.9, V15.81, 57.94, 60.61
- D. 600.3, 595.0, 788.20, 401.0, V15.81, 57.94, 60.61

REFERENCE: Brown, p 70, 81-82, 288-289
Schraffenberger, p 137, 189-190, 248-249, 316-318

112. A 32-year-old female known to be HIV positive was admitted with lesions of the anterior trunk. Excisional biopsies of the skin lesions were positive for Kaposi's sarcoma. Further examination revealed thrush.

042	Human Immunodeficiency Virus (HIV) Disease
795.71	Non-specific serological evidence of HIV
176.0	Kaposi's sarcoma of skin
686.00	Pyoderma, unspecified
112.0	Candidiasis of mouth
528.9	Other and unspecified diseases of the oral soft tissues
86.11	Biopsy of skin and subcutaneous tissue
86.22	Excisional debridement of wound, infection or burn

A. 042, 686.00, 112.0, 86.22   C. 795.71, 176.0, 528.9, 86.11
B. 042, 176.0, 112.0, 86.11   D. 795.71, 686.00, 528.9, 86.22

REFERENCE: Brown, p 97-99
                  Schraffenberger, p 66, 71-73, 84

113. A female patient was admitted with uncontrolled type II diabetes. Patient also had an abscessed diabetic ulcer of the foot that was treated with incision and drainage. Culture and sensitivity of abscess shows growth of Staphylococcus aureus, methicillin resistant. Patient was started on the appropriate antibiotic. Patient is on oral as well as injectional insulin for control of diabetes.

041.11	Bacterial infection in conditions classified elsewhere and of unspecified site, methicillin susceptible staphylococcus aureus
041.19	Bacterial infection in conditions classified elsewhere and of unspecified site, other staphylococcus
250.82	Diabetes mellitus with other specified manifestation, type II, or unspecified type uncontrolled
250.83	Diabetes mellitus with other specified manifestation, type I, (juvenile type) uncontrolled
682.7	Other cellulitis and abscess of foot, except toes
682.8	Other cellulitis and abscess of other specified sites
707.00	Chronic ulcer of skin, pressure ulcer, unspecified site
707.15	Ulcer of lower limbs, except pressure ulcer, of other part of foot (toes)
707.8	Chronic ulcer of other specified sites
V09.0	Infection with microorganisms resistant to penicillins
86.01	Aspiration of skin and subcutaneous tissue
86.04	Other incision with drainage of skin and subcutaneous tissue

A. 250.83, 682.8, V09.0, 86.04
B. 682.7, 682.7, 707.15, 041.19, 86.01
C. 682.8, 041.19, 250.82, 707.00, 86.04,
D. 250.82, 682.7, 707.15, 041.11, V09.0, 86.04

REFERENCE: Brown, p 94, 101-105, 199-201
                  Schraffenberger, p 67, 96-99, 220-222

114. Patient was admitted from the nursing home in acute respiratory failure that was due to congestive heart failure. Chest x-ray also showed pulmonary edema. Patient was intubated and placed on mechanical ventilation and expired the day after admission.

428.0	Congestive heart failure, unspecified
428.1	Left heart failure
428.20	Systolic heart failure, unspecified
518.4	Acute edema of lung, unspecified
518.81	Acute respiratory failure
518.84	Acute and chronic respiratory failure
96.71	Continuous invasive mechanical ventilation for less than 96 consecutive hours
96.04	Insertion of endotracheal tube

A. 428.1, 518.84, 518.4, 96.71, 96.04
B. 428.20, 428.0, 518.81, 518.4, 96.71, 96.04
C. 518.81, 428.0, 96.71, 96.04
D. 428.0, 518.4, 96.04, 96.71

REFERENCE: Brown, p 157-160, 162-163
               Lovaasen and Schwerdtfeger, p 307-308
               Schraffenberger, p 148-149, 168-171

115. The patient has hypertensive heart disease and nephrosclerosis with chronic kidney failure. The patient had placement of arteriovenous fistula in his left wrist to prepare for the hemodialysis. Dialysis was also performed on this admission.

404.92	Hypertensive heart and chronic kidney disease, unspecified as malignant or benign, without heart failure, and with chronic kidney disease Stage V or end stage renal disease
404.93	Hypertensive heart and chronic kidney disease unspecified as malignant or benign, with heart failure and chronic kidney disease Stage V or end stage renal disease
585.6	End stage renal disease
585.9	Chronic kidney disease, unspecified
V56.0	Extracorporeal dialysis
54.98	Peritoneal dialysis
38.95	Venous catheterization for renal dialysis
39.27	Arteriovenostomy for renal dialysis
39.95	Hemodialysis

A. 404.93, 585.9, 54.98, 39.27   C. 404.93, 585.6, 39.95, 39.27
B. 404.92, 585.6, 39.95, 39.27   D. 404.92, 585.9, 38.95, 39.27

REFERENCE: Brown, p 185-186
               Lovaasen and Schwerdtfeger, p 298-299

116. The patient has had abnormal heavy uterine bleeding and abdominal pain. There was bright red blood in the vagina and the right adnexa was enlarged. The woman was admitted. In surgery, a laparoscopy revealed a right follicular ovarian cyst. A laparoscopic ovarian cystectomy was performed. Following surgery she was transfused two units of packed red blood cells for acute blood-loss anemia.

620.0	Follicular cyst of ovary
280.0	Iron deficiency anemia secondary to blood loss (chronic)
285.1	Acute posthemorrhagic anemia
65.25	Other laparoscopic local excision or destruction of ovary
65.39	Other unilateral oophorectomy

A. 620.0, 285.1, 65.25
B. 620.0, 280.0, 65.39
C. 620.0, 285.1, 65.39
D. 620.0, 280.0, 65.25

REFERENCE: Brown, p 127
               Schraffenberger, p 105, 191

117. Jane Doe is 6 weeks post mastectomy for carcinoma of the breast. She is admitted for chemotherapy. What is the correct sequencing of the codes?
A. V58.11 (chemotherapy), 174.9 (malignant neoplasm of the breast), V45.71 (acquired absence of breast)
B. V58.11 (chemotherapy), V10.3 (personal history of malignant neoplasm of breast), V45.71 (acquired absence of breast)
C. V67.00 (follow-up exam after surgery), V58.11 (chemotherapy)
D. V10.3 (personal history of malignant neoplasm of breast)

REFERENCE: Brown, p 324-328
               Schraffenberger, p 324, 327-329

118. The patient was admitted due to increasingly severe pain in his right arm, shoulder, and neck for the past 6 weeks. MRI tests showed herniation of the C5-C6 disc. Patient underwent cervical laminotomy and diskectomy C5-C6 disc. The patient is currently being treated for COPD and CAD with a history of a PTCA.

722.0	Displacement of cervical intervertebral disc without myelopathy
722.11	Displacement of thoracic or lumbar intervertebral disc without myelopathy
492.8	Other emphysema
496	Chronic airway obstruction, not elsewhere classified
414.01	Coronary atherosclerosis of native coronary artery
414.00	Coronary atherosclerosis, unspecified type of vessel, native or graft
V45.82	Percutaneous transluminal coronary angioplasty status
80.51	Excision of intervertebral disc
03.09	Other exploration and decompression of spinal canal

A. 722.0, 492.8, 414.01, V45.82, 80.51
B. 722.11, 496, 414.01, V45.82, 03.09, 80.51
C. 722.11, 492.8, 414.00, 03.09, 80.51
D. 722.0, 496, 414.01, V45.82, 80.51

REFERENCE: Brown, p 154, 207-208, 279-280, 295
               Schraffenberger, p 145-147, 168, 228, 324

119. A 75-year-old man is admitted to your facility with acute cerebral embolism with infarction. He had hemiplegia and dysphagia. Physical therapy was given for the hemiplegia. Dysphagia was resolved at the time of discharge

434.11	Cerebral embolism with cerebral infarction
342.90	Hemiplegia, unspecified, affecting unspecified side
787.20	Dysphagia, unspecified
V57.1	Other physical therapy

A. 434.11, 342.90, V57.1   C. 434.11, 342.90
B. 434.11, 342.90, 787.20   D. 434.11, 342.90, 787.20, V57.1

REFERENCE: Bowie and Schaffer, p 169-170
                 Brown, p 284-285
                 Schraffenberger, p 125, 152

Infectious Diseases

120. Patient is admitted to St. Mary's Hospital with hyperthermia, tachycardia, hypoxemia, and altered mental status. Urinalysis is positive for E. coli and blood cultures are negative. Patient is immediately started on broad-spectrum IV antibiotics. Physician documents urosepsis as the final diagnosis. The coder should
    A. report 599.0 (UTI) and 041.4 (E. coli).
    B. report 038.42 (septicemia due to E. coli) and 995.91 (SIRS-sepsis).
    C. report 038.42 (septicemia due to E. coli), 599.0 (UTI) and 995.91 (SIRS-sepsis).
    D. confer with physician for reporting 038.9 (unspecified septicemia) based upon the clinical findings with 041.4 (E. coli) and 995.91 (SIRS-sepsis).

REFERENCE: Brown, p 91-92
                 Schraffenberger, p 68-69

121. Six-year-old Alex attended a birthday party where hot dogs and potato salad were served for lunch. Several hours after returning home, Alex began vomiting and having severe diarrhea. Alex was admitted to the hospital for treatment of his vomiting and diarrhea and was diagnosed with Salmonella food poisoning. Alex was given IV fluids for dehydration. Alex also has asthma, so he was given respiratory treatments while in the hospital.

003.9	Salmonella infection, unspecified
005.9	Food poisoning, unspecified
276.51	Dehydration
493.90	Asthma, unspecified
787.03	Vomiting alone
787.91	Diarrhea

A. 003.9, 276.51, 493.90   C. 005.9, 276.51, 493.90
B. 005.9, 003.9, 276.51, 493.90   D. 005.9, 003.9, 267.51, 787.03, 787.91, 493.90

REFERENCE: Schraffenberger, p 65-66, 99-100, 166-168

122. A patient is admitted to the hospital with listlessness, fever, and persistent cough. Work-up reveals HIV infection with HIV-related pneumonia. The patient is treated for pneumonia.

042	HIV disease
486	Pneumonia, organism unspecified
795.71	Nonspecific serologic evidence of HIV
V08	Asymptomatic HIV infection status

A. 486, 042
B. 042, 486

C. 486, 795.71
D. 486, V08

REFERENCE: Schraffenberger, p 70-72, 165
Brown, p 97

123. David was experiencing chronic fatigue and was experiencing flulike symptoms. Blood testing indicated that he had hepatitis C. A percutaneous liver biopsy was performed to determine the stage of the disease.

070.41	Acute hepatitis C with hepatic coma
070.51	Acute hepatitis C without mention of hepatic coma
487.1	Influenza with other respiratory manifestations
780.79	Other malaise and fatigue
50.11	Closed (percutaneous) (needle) biopsy of liver
50.12	Open biopsy of liver

A. 070.51, 487.1, 780.79, 50.12
B. 070.41, 50.11

C. 070.51, 487.1, 50.11
D. 070.51, 50.11

REFERENCE: Brown, p 58-59, 89
Schraffenberger, p 66

124. A 40-year-old female suddenly develops a painful rash. A visit to her physician reveals she has shingles. She is experiencing a great amount of anxiety and stress, so her physician prescribes medication for the shingles and for the anxiety that occurred as a reaction to the stress.

053.8	Herpes zoster with unspecified complication
053.9	Herpes zoster without mention of complication
300.00	Anxiety state, unspecified
308.0	Predominant disturbance of emotions
308.3	Other acute reactions to stress

A. 053.9, 308.0
B. 053.9, 308.3, 300.00

C. 053.8, 300.00
D. 053.8, 308.0

REFERENCE: Brown, p 89, 115
Schraffenberger, p 66, 111

Neoplasms

125. James is admitted to the hospital for severe anemia that is a result of the chemotherapy treatments he is receiving for metastatic prostate cancer to bone. James receives blood transfusions and is discharged home.

185	Malignant neoplasm of prostate
198.5	Secondary malignant neoplasm, bone and bone marrow
285.22	Anemia in neoplastic disease
E933.1	Adverse effect of antineoplastic and immunosuppressive drugs

A. 185, 198.5, 285.22, E933.1   C. 285.22, E933.1
B. E933.1, 285.22   D. 285.22, 185, 198.5, E933.1

REFERENCE: Brown, p 125, 127, 317-319
Schraffenberger, p 89, 105, 298

126. Mary had resection of the large bowel for carcinoma of the colon. She is admitted for further staging of her cancer and receives radiation therapy during this admission.

V10.05	Personal history of malignant neoplasm of large intestine
V58.0	Admission for radiotherapy
V67.09	Follow-up exam following other surgery
153.9	Malignant neoplasm of colon, unspecified
92.29	Other radiotherapeutic procedure

A. 153.9, 92.29   C. V67.09, V58.0
B. V58.0, V10.05   D. V10.05, V58.0

REFERENCE: Brown, p 316-317, 324-325

127. Jackie has developed a lesion on her right shoulder. A biopsy was obtained and was positive for malignant melanoma. She is now admitted for radical excision of the melanoma lesion and full-thickness skin graft.

172.6	Malignant melanoma of skin, upper limb, including shoulder
173.5	Other malignant neoplasm of skin of trunk, except scrotum
173.6	Other malignant neoplasm of skin of upper limb, including shoulder
86.3	Other local excision or destruction of lesion or tissue of skin and subcutaneous tissue
86.4	Radical excision of skin lesion
86.63	Full thickness skin graft to other sites

A. 172.6, 86.4, 86.63   C. 173.5, 86.3, 86.63
B. 172.5, 86.4, 86.63   D. 172.6, 86.3, 86.63

REFERENCE: Brown, p 203, 311-313
Schraffenberger, p 85

128. Richard is admitted for chemotherapy for leukemia. Chemotherapy is administered. Given this information,
    A. the leukemia code and a procedure code for the chemotherapy will be assigned.
    B. an admission for chemotherapy code and a chemotherapy procedure code will be assigned.
    C. an admission for chemotherapy code, a leukemia code, and a procedure code for the chemotherapy should be assigned and the principal diagnosis will be the admission for chemotherapy V code.
    D. an admission for chemotherapy code, a leukemia code, and a procedure code for the chemotherapy should be assigned and the principal diagnosis will be the leukemia code.

REFERENCE: Brown, p 316-319
               Lovaasen and Schwerdtfeger, p 355
               Schraffenberger, p 327-328

129. Sophia has been diagnosed with metastatic carcinoma of lung, primary site breast. Simple mastectomy performed 2 years ago. What is the principal diagnosis?
    A. metastatic carcinoma of lung
    B. carcinoma of breast
    C. history of carcinoma of breast
    D. status post mastectomy

REFERENCE: Brown, p 316-319
               Schraffenberger, p 87-91

130. Given the following diagnosis: "Carcinoma of axillary lymph nodes and lungs, metastatic from breast." What is the primary cancer site(s)?
    A. axillary lymph nodes   C. breast
    B. lungs   D. both A and B

REFERENCE: Brown, p 316-319, 321
               Schraffenberger, p 87-91

131. When is it appropriate to use category V10, history of malignant neoplasm?
    A. Primary malignancy recurred at original site and adjunct chemotherapy is directed at the site.
    B. Primary malignancy has been eradicated and no adjunct treatment is being given at this time.
    C. Primary malignancy eradicated and the patient is admitted for adjunct chemotherapy to primary site.
    D. Primary malignancy is eradicated; adjunct treatment is refused by patient even though there is some remaining malignancy.

REFERENCE: Brown, p 75-76
               Lovaasen and Schwerdtfeger, p 356
               Schraffenberger, p 316-318

Endocrine/Nutritional/Metabolic

132. Ralph is a 96-year-old nursing home resident who is admitted for malnutrition. Ralph has suffered a previous stroke that has left him with dysphagia. Ralph is treated for malnutrition with hyperalimentation. Ralph was also found to have hypokalemia that was treated with IV potassium replacement. On the day prior to discharge, Ralph underwent a PEG tube insertion.

263.9	Unspecified protein-calorie malnutrition
276.8	Hypokalemia/hypopotassemia
438.82	Dysphagia, late effect of cerebrovascular disease
787.20	Dysphagia, unspecified
43.11	Percutaneous endoscopic gastrostomy (PEG) insertion

A. 438.82, 263.9, 787.20, 43.11
B. 787.20, 276.8, 43.11
C. 263.9, 276.8, 438.82, 43.11
D. 263.9, 787.20, 276.8, 43.11

REFERENCE: Brown, p 108, 284-285
Schraffenberger, p 96, 99-100

133. Jessica has been diagnosed with hyperthyroidism due to toxic multinodular goiter with crisis. She also has hypertension and has a history of sick sinus syndrome with pacemaker insertion. Jessica has a partial thyroidectomy on this admission.

240.9	Goiter, unspecified
241.1	Non-toxic multinodular goiter
242.21	Toxic multinodular goiter with mention of thyrotoxic crisis or storm
401.0	Essential hypertension, malignant
401.9	Essential hypertension, unspecified
427.81	Sinoatrial node dysfunction
V45.01	Other postprocedural states, cardiac pacemaker
06.39	Other partial thyroidectomy
06.4	Complete thyroidectomy

A. 240.9, 401.0, 427.81, 06.4
B. 242.21, 401.9, 427.81, V45.01, 06.39
C. 240.9, 242.21, 401.9. V45.01, 06.4
D. 242.21, 401.9. V45.01, 06.39

REFERENCE: Brown, p 288
Lovaasen and Schwerdtfeger, p 236-237
Schraffenberger, p 96, 136-137, 324

134. Laura is 7 years old and has acute bronchitis and cystic fibrosis. She is admitted to ambulatory surgery for bronchoscopy.

277.00 Cystic fibrosis without mention of meconium ileus
277.01 Cystic fibrosis with mention of meconium ileus
466.0 Acute bronchitis
33.23 Other bronchoscopy
33.24 Closed endoscopic biopsy of bronchus
96.56 Other lavage of bronchus and trachea

 A. 466.0, 277.00, 33.23   C. 277.00, 96.56, 33.23
 B. 466.0, 277.01, 33.24   D. 277.00, 33.23, 33.24, 96.56

REFERENCE: Brown, p 108
       Schraffenberger, p 100

135. Estelle has had nausea and vomiting and is unable to eat. She develops dehydration and is subsequently admitted for rehydration with intravenous fluids.

276.51 Dehydration
787.01 Nausea with vomiting
787.02 Nausea alone
787.03 Vomiting alone

with dehydration do not code nausea & vomit —

 A. 276.51, 787.01   C. 276.51, 787.02
 B. 276.51   D. 276.51, 787.02, 787.03

REFERENCE: Schraffenberger, p 100

136. A patient is admitted for treatment of peripheral vascular disease, renal failure, and diabetes mellitus. The coder would
 A. assign codes for PVD, renal failure, and diabetes.
 B. assign codes for diabetes with peripheral vascular and renal manifestations.
 C. query physician for causal relationship between the PVD, renal failure, and diabetes.
 D. assign codes of diabetes with PVD and a code for renal failure.

REFERENCE: Brown, p 103-105

137. Lucy is admitted because of diabetic coma. She is a type II diabetic with nephritic syndrome and gangrene of her toes, all due to her diabetes.

250.30	Diabetes mellitus with other coma, type II or unspecified type, not stated as uncontrolled
250.31	Diabetes mellitus with other coma, type I (juvenile type), not stated as uncontrolled
250.40	Diabetes mellitus with renal manifestations, type II or unspecified type, not stated as uncontrolled
250.41	Diabetes mellitus with renal manifestations, type I (juvenile type), not stated as uncontrolled
250.70	Diabetes mellitus with peripheral circulatory disorders, type II or unspecified type, not stated as uncontrolled
581.81	Nephrotic syndrome in disease classified elsewhere
785.4	Gangrene

A. 250.30, 250.40, 581.81, 250.70, 785.4
B. 250.31, 581.81, 785.4
C. 250.30, 250.40, 581.81
D. 250.30 250.41, 785.4

REFERENCE: Brown, p.101-105
               Schraffenberger, p 96-99

138. George is a type II diabetic who is admitted in a coma with a blood glucose of 876. He is diagnosed with diabetic ketoacidosis. George also has a diabetic cataract.

250.10	Diabetes mellitus with ketoacidosis, type II or unspecified type, not stated as uncontrolled
250.11	Diabetes mellitus with ketoacidosis, type I (juvenile type), not stated as uncontrolled
250.30	Diabetes mellitus with other coma, type II or unspecified type, not stated as uncontrolled
250.31	Diabetes mellitus with other coma, type I (juvenile type), not stated as uncontrolled
250.50	Diabetes mellitus with ophthalmic manifestations, type II or unspecified type, not stated as uncontrolled
250.51	Diabetes mellitus with ophthalmic manifestations, type I (juvenile type), not stated as uncontrolled
366.41	Diabetic cataract
366.9	Unspecified cataract

A. 250.11, 250.31, 366.9   C. 250.30, 250.50, 366.41
B. 250.10, 250.30, 250.50, 366.9 D. 250.31, 250.51, 366.41

REFERENCE: Brown, p 101-105
               Lovaasen and Schwerdtfeger, p 238-242
               Schraffenberger, p 96-99

139. Spencer has hypercholesterolemia and is treated with medication.

> 272.0   Pure hypercholesterolemia
> 272.1   Pure hyperglyceridemia
> 272.3   Hyperchylomicronemia
> 272.8   Other disorders of lipoid metabolism

A. 272.0   C. 272.3
B. 272.1   D. 272.8

REFERENCE: Schraffenberger, p 96

140. Edward is diagnosed with syndrome of inappropriate antidiuretic hormone with resultant electrolyte imbalance.

> 253.6   Other disorders of neurophyophysis (syndrome of inappropriate secretion of antidiuretic hormone-ADH)
> 272.9   Unspecified disorder of lipoid metabolism
> 276.50   Volume depletion, unspecified
> 276.8   Hypopotassemia (hypokalemia)
> 276.9   Electrolyte and fluid disorders, not elsewhere classified

A. 276.50   C. 253.6, 276.9
B. 276.9, 272.9   D. 253.6. 276.8

REFERENCE: Schraffenberger, p 96

Blood and Blood-Forming Organs

141. Ruth is admitted for an axillary lymph node biopsy to determine the cause of her chronic lymphadenitis. She is on medication for gout and atrial fibrillation.

> 274.9   Gout, unspecified
> 289.1   Chronic lymphadenitis
> 289.2   Nonspecific mesenteric lymphadenitis
> 427.31   Atrial fibrillation
> 40.11   Biopsy of lymphatic structure
> 40.23   Excision of axillary lymph node
> 40.51   Radical excision of axillary lymph nodes

A. 289.1, 274.9, 427.31, 40.11   C. 289.1, 427.31, 40.23
B. 274.9, 289.2, 427.31, 40.11   D. 289.1, 427.31, 274.9, 40.51

REFERENCE: Brown, p 58-59
               Schraffenberger, p 96, 107, 149

142. Elizabeth has a history of von Willebrand's disease and frequently requires transfusions for chronic blood loss anemia associated with her condition. She presents to the outpatient department for routine blood transfusion.

280.0	Iron deficiency anemia secondary to blood loss (chronic)
280.1	Iron deficiency anemia secondary to inadequate dietary iron intake
285.1	Acute posthemorrhagic anemia
286.4	Von Willebrand's disease
286.7	Acquired coagulation factor deficiency

    A. 285.1, 286.4   C. 286.4, 280.1
    B. 286.7, 286.4   D. 280.0, 286.4

REFERENCE: Brown, p 125-128
                      Schraffenberger, p 104-106

143. Steven, a 7 year old, is seen in the emergency department with severe joint pain. Following work-up it is discovered that he is having a severe crisis due to sickle cell anemia.

282.61	Sickle-cell disease (Hb-SS disease without crisis)
282.62	Sickle-cell disease (Hb-S disease with crisis)
282.63	Sickle-cell /Hb-C disease without crisis
282.69	Other sickle-cell disease with crisis

    A. 282.61   C. 282.63
    B. 282.62   D. 282.69

REFERENCE: Bowieand Schaffer, p 126-127
                      Brown, p 128
                      Schraffenberger, p 104

144. Angela has just undergone orthopedic surgery. Documentation indicates that she lost 700 cc of blood during surgery. Her hemoglobin and hematocrit are monitored following surgery. Subsequently she is transfused. The physician documents anemia as a secondary diagnosis. The coder would

    A. query the physician to clarify the type of anemia as acute blood loss.
    B. assign a code for unspecified anemia.
    C. assign a code for acute blood loss anemia.
    D. not assign a code for anemia.

REFERENCE: Brown, p 126

145. Liza has been diagnosed with anemia. She is being admitted for a bone marrow aspiration to determine the specific type of anemia. The pathology report indicates that she has iron-deficiency anemia.

280.0	Iron deficiency anemia secondary to blood loss (chronic)
280.8	Other specified iron deficiency anemia
280.9	Iron deficiency anemia, unspecified
41.31	Biopsy of bone marrow
41.38	Other diagnostic procedures on bone marrow
41.91	Aspiration of bone marrow from donor for transplant

A. 280.0, 41.38 C. 280.9, 41.91
B. 280.9, 41.31 D. 280.8, 41.38

REFERENCE: Bowie and Schaffer, p 126
Brown, p 125

146. Peggy has thymic dysplasia with immunodeficiency.

254.0	Persistent hyperplasia of thymus
254.8	Other specified diseases of thymus gland
254.9	Unspecified disease of thymus gland
279.2	Combined immunity deficiency (thymic dysplasia with immunodeficiency)
279.3	Unspecified immunity deficiency

A. 279.3, 254.8 C. 279.2
B. 254.0 D. 279.2, 254.9

REFERENCE: Brown, p 109

147. Aaron has suffered a hypoglycemic reaction due to alcohol intoxication. Hypoglycemia is treated.

250.80	Diabetes mellitus with other specified manifestations, type II or unspecified type, not stated as uncontrolled
251.2	Hypoglycemia, unspecified
303.90	Other and unspecified alcohol dependence, unspecified
305.00	Alcohol abuse, unspecified
995.29	Unspecified adverse effect of other drug, medicinal and biological substance

A. 251.2, 305.00 C. 995.2, 303.90
B. 251.2, 303.90 D. 250.80, 305.00

REFERENCE: Brown, p 107, 117

Mental Disorders

148. Joe is being admitted for treatment of chronic alcoholism. As a result of Joe's drinking he also has chronic alcoholic gastritis for which he receives medication. Joe is scheduled to spend 30 days in the inpatient rehab unit of Sunshine Hospital.

303.01	Acute alcoholic intoxication, continuous
303.91	Other and unspecified alcohol dependence, continuous
535.00	Acute gastritis without mention of hemorrhage
535.30	Alcoholic gastritis without mention of hemorrhage
535.31	Alcoholic gastritis with mention of hemorrhage
94.61	Alcohol rehabilitation
94.62	Alcohol detoxification
94.63	Alcohol rehabilitation and detoxification

A. 303.01, 535.00, 94.63
B. 303.91, 535.00, 94.63
C. 303.91, 535.30, 94.61
D. 303.01, 303.91, 535.30, 94.63

REFERENCE: Brown, p 117, 167
Schraffenberger, p 115-117

149. Sheila has paranoid alcoholic psychosis with chronic alcoholism, continuous. She is admitted for treatment of her psychosis.

291.5	Alcohol induced psychotic disorder with delusions
303.91	Other and unspecified alcohol dependence, continuous
V57.89	Other specified rehabilitation procedure

A. 291.5, 303.91
B. 303.91, 291.5
C. V57.89, 303.91
D. 291.5, 303.91, V57.89

REFERENCE: Brown, p 111, 117
Lovaasen and Schwerdtfeger, p 537-538
Schraffenberger, p 102-104

150. Sybil has been admitted to Shady Acres Psychiatric facility for treatment of schizophrenia. Sybil is also manic depressive and has been noncompliant with her medications.

295.40	Schizophreniform disorder, unspecified
295.41	Schizophreniform disorder, subchronic
295.90	Unspecified schizophrenia
296.7	Bipolar I , disorder most recent episode (or current) unspecified
296.80	Bipolar disorder, unspecified
296.89	Other and unspecified bipolar disorders (manic-depressive psychosis, mixed type)
V15.81	Personal history of noncompliance with medical treatment

A. V15.81, 296.89, 295.40
B. 296.89, 295.41, V15.81
C. 296.7, 295.90
D. 295.90, 296.80, V15.81

REFERENCE: Brown, p 113

151. Allen is addicted to Vicodin. He has stopped taking the drug and is now having withdrawal symptoms. Allen has chronic back pain for which he has been prescribed the medication. Allen is admitted for treatment of his withdrawal symptoms.

292.0	Drug withdrawal
292.11	Drug-induced psychotic disorder with delusions
292.2	Pathological drug intoxication
304.00	Drug dependence, opioid type dependence, unspecified
304.91	Unspecified drug dependence, continuous
724.5	Backache, unspecified

A. 292.2, 724.5
B. 292.11, 292.2, 304.91
C. 292.0, 304.00, 724.5
D. 292.11, 304.91, 724.5

REFERENCE: Brown, p 117
Schraffenberger, p 115-117

152. Acute epileptic twilight state with delirium

293.0	Delirium due to conditions classified elsewhere (epileptic twilight state)
293.1	Subacute delirium
294.0	Amnestic disorder in conditions classified elsewhere
345.00	Generalized nonconvulsive epilepsy without mention of intractable epilepsy
780.02	Transient alteration of awareness

A. 293.0
B. 780.02
C. 293.1
D. 294.0, 345.00

REFERENCE: Brown, p 136

153. Sally has been diagnosed with panic attacks and is prescribed Xanax. She has been taking the medication as prescribed by her physician for 3 days and is now having hallucinations. Her physician advises her to stop taking the medication and her symptoms abate. Her doctor determines that the hallucinations were due to the Xanax.

292.12	Drug-induced psychotic disorder with hallucinations
300.01	Panic disorder without agoraphobia
E939.4	Benzodiazepine-based tranquilizers

A. 292.12, E939.4, 300.01
B. 292.12
C. E939.4, 292.12
D. 300.01, 292.12

REFERENCE: Brown, p 365-368
Schraffenberger, p 111, 298

154. Lou has profound mental retardation due to mongolism.

317	Mild mental retardation
318.0	Moderate mental retardation
318.2	Profound mental retardation
758.0	Down's syndrome
759.0	Anomalies of spleen

A. 318.2, 758.0
B. 318.0, 759.0
C. 758.0, 318.2
D. 317, 758.0

REFERENCE:　　Lovaasen and Schwerdtfeger, p 545-546
　　　　　　　　Schraffenberger, p 111

Diseases of the Nervous System and Sense Organs

155. Mark has a long history of epilepsy. He is brought to the emergency department and is admitted with intractable epileptic seizures. Mark's epilepsy is the result of a head injury he suffered several years ago.

345.11	Generalized convulsive epilepsy with intractable epilepsy
345.10	Generalized convulsive epilepsy, without mention of intractable epilepsy
345.3	Grand mal status
345.91	Epilepsy, unspecified, with intractable epilepsy
780.39	Other convulsions
907.0	Late effect of intracranial injury without mention of skull fracture

A. 780.39, 907.0
B. 345.91, 907.0
C. 345.3
D. 345.10, 780.39

REFERENCE:　　Brown, p 49-50, 136
　　　　　　　　Schraffenberger, p 125-126

156. Jeff was in a car accident when he was 25 years old and suffered a spinal cord injury. As a result, he is a paraplegic and has neurogenic bladder. Jeff also has chronic ulcers of the buttocks. He is being seen for evaluation of his paraplegia.

344.1	Paraplegia
344.60	Cauda equina syndrome without mention of neurogenic bladder
596.53	Paralysis of bladder
596.54	Neurogenic bladder, not otherwise specified
707.00	Chronic pressure ulcer of skin, unspecified site
707.8	Chronic ulcer of other specified sites
907.2	Late effect of spinal cord injury

A. 344.1, 907.2, 596.54, 707.8
B. 344.60, 596.53, 707.00, 907.2
C. 344.1, 596.53, 907.2
D. 344.1, 596.54, 707.8

REFERENCE:　　Brown, p 50, 354

157. Josephine has developed senile cataracts in both eyes. She is admitted for right extracapsular cataract extraction with synchronous lens insertion.

366.10	Senile cataract, unspecified
366.9	Unspecified cataract
13.59	Other extracapsular extraction of lens
13.71	Insertion of intraocular lens prosthesis at time of cataract extraction, one stage

A. 366.9, 13.71
B. 366.10, 13.59, 13.71

C. 366.9, 13.59, 13.71
D. 366.10, 13.59

REFERENCE: Brown, p 142
Schraffenberger, p 128

158. Diabetic macular or retinal edema

250.50	Diabetes mellitus with ophthalmic manifestation, type II or unspecified type, not stated as uncontrolled
250.51	Diabetes mellitus with ophthalmic manifestation, type I (juvenile type), not stated as uncontrolled
362.01	Background diabetic retinopathy
362.02	Proliferative diabetic retinopathy
362.07	Diabetic macular edema

A. 250.51, 362.07, 262.02
B. 362.07, 250.51, 362.02

C. 250.50, 362.07, 362.01
D. 362.05, 362.07, 250.50

REFERENCE: Schraffenberger, p 96-99

159. Bilateral sensorineural conductive hearing loss

389.20	Mixed hearing loss, unspecified
389.21	Mixed hearing loss, unilateral
389.22	Mixed hearing loss, bilateral
389.9	Unspecified hearing loss

A. 389.22
B. 389.21

C. 389.9
D. 389.20

REFERENCE: Schraffenberger, p 129

Diseases of the Circulatory System

160. Madeline is diagnosed with bilateral carotid stenosis. She is being admitted for a bilateral endarterectomy. Madeline is also treated for Parkinson's disease and glaucoma.

332.0	Paralysis agitans (Parkinson's disease)
365.9	Unspecified glaucoma
433.30	Occlusion and stenosis of precerebral arteries, multiple and bilateral, without mention of cerebral infarction
38.12	Endarterectomy, other vessels of head and neck

A. 433.30, 38.12
B. 433.30, 38.12, 38.12

C. 433.30, 332.0, 365.9, 38.12
D. 433.30, 332.0, 365.9, 38.12, 38.12

REFERENCE: Brown, p 134, 143, 284-285
Schraffenberger, p 152

161. Bleeding prolapsed internal hemorrhoids and chronic constipation. Patient is admitted for rubber band ligation of the internal hemorrhoids.

455.1	Internal thrombosed hemorrhoids
455.2	Internal hemorrhoids with other complication
564.09	Other constipation
49.44	Destruction of hemorrhoids by cryotherapy
49.45	Ligation of hemorrhoids
49.46	Excision of hemorrhoids

A. 455.1, 564.09, 49.44   C. 455.2, 564.09 49.45
B. 455.1, 49.45   D. 455.1, 455.2, 49.45

REFERENCE: Schraffenberger, p 134, 176

162. Frank has been diagnosed with sick sinus syndrome and is being admitted for dual chamber pacemaker and leads insertion. Frank also has type II diabetes on oral medication as well as insulin regimen. Surgery is carried out without complication.

250.00	Diabetes mellitus without mention of complication, type II or unspecified type, not stated as uncontrolled
250.01	Diabetes mellitus without mention of complication, type I (juvenile type), not stated as uncontrolled
427.81	Sinoatrial node dysfunction
V58.67	Long-term (current) use of insulin
37.70	Initial insertion of lead (electrode), not otherwise specified
37.71	Initial insertion of transvenous lead (electrode) into ventricle
37.72	Initial insertion of transvenous leads (electrode) into atrium and ventricle
37.82	Initial insertion of single-chamber device, rate responsive
37.83	Initial insertion of dual chamber device

A. 427.81, 250.00, V58.67, 37.72, 37.83   C. 427.81, 37.70, 37.83
B. 427.81, 250.01, 37.71, 37.83   D. 427.81, 250.00, 250.01, 37.72, 37.83

REFERENCE: Brown, p101-102, 298

163. Patient is treated for congestive heart failure with pleural effusion. A therapeutic thoracentesis is performed.

428.0	Congestive heart failure, unspecified
511.9	Unspecified pleural effusion
34.04	Insertion of intercostal catheter for drainage
34.91	Thoracentesis

A. 511.9, 34.91   C. 428.0, 511.9
B. 428.0, 34.04   D. 428.0, 511.9, 34.91

REFERENCE: Brown, p 157, 281-282
                        Schraffenberger, p 148-149

164. Patient presents to the emergency room complaining of a severe headache. Work-up revealed a ruptured berry aneurysm.

430	Subarachnoid hemorrhage
437.3	Cerebral aneurysm, nonruptured
784.0	Headache

A. 430

B. 784.0

C. 784.0, 430

D. 437.3

REFERENCE: Brown, p 284-285

Diseases of the Respiratory System

165. Joseph has had cough, fever, and painful respirations for 2 days. He also has congestive heart failure and COPD. Joseph presents to the emergency department with severe shortness of breath, using accessory muscles to assist with breathing. Upon examination, Joseph is diagnosed with acute respiratory failure, congestive heart failure, pneumonia, and exacerbation of COPD. Joseph is intubated and placed on mechanical ventilation. He is weaned from the ventilator on the third day of admission. Two days later, he again goes into respiratory failure, requiring reintubation and placement on the ventilator. Fortunately, he is able to breath on his own the following day, so was extubated.

428.0	Congestive heart failure, unspecified
486	Pneumonia, organism unspecified
491.21	Obstructive chronic bronchitis with (acute) exacerbation
496	Chronic airway obstruction, not elsewhere classified
518.81	Acute respiratory failure
96.04	Insertion of endotracheal tube
96.71	Continuous invasive mechanical ventilation for less than 96 consecutive hours
96.72	Continuous invasive mechanical ventilation for 96 consecutive hours or more

A. 428.0, 486, 496, 518.81, 96.04, 96.71

B. 518.81, 428.0, 491.21, 96.04, 96.71

C. 486, 428.0, 518.81, 491.21, 96.04, 96.72

D. 518.81, 486, 428.0, 491.21, 96.04, 96.71, 96.04, 96.71

REFERENCE: Bowie and Schaffer, p 181
Brown, p157-159, 162-163, 281-282
Schraffenberger, p 148, 165, 168-171

166. Ronald is admitted for stenosis of his tracheostomy. He is a quadriplegic, C1-C4 secondary to spinal cord injury suffered in a diving accident. He has chronic respiratory failure and is maintained on mechanical ventilation. He undergoes revision of his tracheostomy.

344.00	Quadriplegia, unspecified
344.01	Quadriplegia, C1-C4, complete
518.83	Chronic respiratory failure
519.02	Mechanical complication of tracheostomy
519.09	Other complications of tracheostomy
907.2	Late effect of spinal cord injury
V46.11	Dependence on respirator status
31.74	Revision of tracheostomy
31.79	Other repair and plastic operations on trachea
96.71	Continuous invasive mechanical ventilation for less than 96 consecutive hours
96.72	Continuous invasive mechanical ventilation for 96 consecutive hours or more

A. 518.83, 519.09, 907.2, 31.74
B. 344.01, 518.83, 519.02, 31.79, V46.11
C. 519.02, 344.01, 518.83, 907.2, V46.11, 31.74, 96.72
D. 519.02, 518.83, 907.2, 31.74

REFERENCE: Brown, p157-159, 162-163
              Schraffenberger, p 125, 163, 168-171

167. Jennifer presents to the emergency department with severe chest pain and shortness of breath. Chest x-ray revealed a spontaneous pneumothorax. Jennifer also has acute bronchitis. The emergency department physician inserts a chest tube and Jennifer is admitted.

466.0	Acute bronchitis
491.20	Obstructive chronic bronchitis without exacerbation
491.21	Obstructive chronic bronchitis with (acute) exacerbation
512.0	Spontaneous tension pneumothorax
512.1	Iatrogenic pneumothorax
512.8	Other spontaneous pneumothorax
34.01	Incision of chest wall
34.04	Insertion of intercostal catheter for drainage

A. 512.8, 466.0, 34.04   C. 466.0, 491.21, 512.1, 34.04
B. 512.0, 491.21, 34.01   D. 491.20, 466.0, 512.8, 34.01

REFERENCE: Schraffenberger, p 163

168. Dale is admitted with emphysematous nodules. He undergoes, without complication, a wedge resection of the right upper lobe. Dale developed atelectasis post-operatively that required monitoring with portable chest x-rays and extended his length of stay.

492.8	Other emphysema
518.0	Pulmonary collapse (Atelectasis)
518.89	Other diseases of lung, not elsewhere classified
997.3	Respiratory complications
32.29	Other local excision or destruction of tissue of lung
32.3	Segmental resection of lung

A. 518.89, 997.3, 32.3
B. 997.3, 518.0, 518.89, 32.29
C. 492.8, 997.3, 518.0, 32.29
D. 518.89, 518.0, 32.29

REFERENCE: Brown, p 156-157
               Schraffenberger, p 163, 168-171, 288-289

169. Agnes is admitted with cough, fever, and dysphagia. Chest x-ray shows infiltrates in both lower lobes. Sputum culture is positive for Staph aureus. Swallow study indicates that Agnes aspirates. Physician documents aspiration pneumonia and Staph aureus pneumonia. As a coder, you would assign codes for the following and with correct sequencing order.
A. Staph aureus pneumonia, dysphagia
B. Staph aureus pneumonia, aspiration pneumonia
C. Aspiration pneumonia, dysphagia
D. Aspiration pneumonia, Staph aureus pneumonia, dysphagia

REFERENCE: Bowie and Schaffer, p 180
               Brown, p 149-151
               Schraffenberger, p 166

170. This patient has pneumonia. She also has acute exacerbation of COPD.

486	Pneumonia, organism unspecified
491.20	Obstructive chronic bronchitis, without exacerbation
491.21	Obstructive chronic bronchitis, with (acute) exacerbation

A. 491.21
B. 486, 491.21
C. 491.20, 486
D. 486

REFERENCE: Brown, p 149, 154
               Schraffenberger, p 165, 168

171. Acute and chronic maxillary sinusitis. Maxillary sinusectomy performed.

461.0	Acute maxillary sinusitis
461.2	Acute ethmoidal sinusitis
473.0	Chronic maxillary sinusitis
22.62	Excision of lesion of maxillary sinus with other approach

A. 461.0, 22.62
B. 473.0, 22.62
C. 461.0, 473.0, 22.62
D. 461.2, 22.62

REFERENCE: Schraffenberger, p 163

Diseases of the Digestive System

172. Grace has been having abdominal pain for several weeks and has been vomiting blood for 2 days. Her physician performs an esophagogastroduodenoscopy and biopsies a lesion in the duodenum. The pathology report indicates Grace has acute and chronic gastritis.

532.00	Acute duodenal ulcer with hemorrhage without mention of obstruction
535.01	Acute gastritis with hemorrhage
535.11	Chronic (atrophic) gastritis with hemorrhage
789.00	Abdominal pain, unspecified site
45.13	Esophagogastroduodenoscopy
45.16	Esophagogastroduodenoscopy (EGD) with closed biopsy

A. 532.00, 789.00, 45.13
B. 535.01, 789.00, 45.16
C. 535.01, 535.11, 789.00. 45.13
D. 535.01, 535.11, 45.16

REFERENCE: Brown, p 167

173. Mary presents to the emergency department with complaints of chest pain. Myocardial infarction is ruled out, however gastrointestinal studies indicate Mary is suffering from gastroesophageal reflux disease (GERD). Mary is given medication to relieve her symptoms and instructed to follow up with her physician.

410.91	Acute myocardial infarction, unspecified site, initial episode of care
530.81	Gastroesophageal reflux (GERD)
786.50	Chest pain, unspecified

A. 530.81
B. 786.50
C. 530.81, 410.91
D. 410.91, 786.50

REFERENCE: Brown, p 168
Lovaasen and Schwerdtfeger, p 516

174. Crystal has been vomiting for 24 hours with complaint of right lower quadrant pain. Examination is suspicious for acute appendicitis. Crystal is taken to surgery and laparoscopic appendectomy is carried out. Pathological diagnosis is consistent with acute appendicitis. Crystal developed post-operative paralytic ileus.

540.0	Acute appendicitis with generalized peritonitis
540.9	Acute appendicitis, without mention of peritonitis
560.1	Paralytic ileus
997.4	Digestive system complications, not elsewhere classified
47.01	Laparoscopic appendectomy
47.09	Other appendectomy
47.11	Laparoscopic incidental appendectomy

A. 540.0, 997.4, 47.11
B. 540.0, 997.4, 47.09
C. 540.9, 997.4, 560.1, 47.01
D. 997.4, 560.1, 540.9, 47.09

REFERENCE: Brown, p 176
Lovaasen and Schwerdtfeger, p 519

175. Admission for intestinal obstruction due to adhesions. Peripheral vascular disease and chronic urinary tract infections, both conditions treated with oral medication.

443.9	Peripheral vascular disease, unspecified
560.81	Intestinal or peritoneal adhesions with obstruction (postoperative) (post infection)
560.89	Other specified intestinal obstruction
560.9	Unspecified intestinal obstruction
599.0	Urinary tract infection, site not specified

   A.   560.81, 443.9, 599.0   C.   560.9, 443.9, 599.0
   B.   560.9   D.   560.89, 443.9, 599.0

REFERENCE: Brown, p 174, 181

176. This patient has chronic diarrhea associated with Crohn's disease. She also has protein-calorie malnutrition. She is admitted for bowel resection of the diseased colon.

263.9	Unspecified protein-calorie malnutrition
555.1	Regional enteritis, large intestine (Crohn's disease)
556.9	Ulcerative colitis, unspecified
787.91	Diarrhea
45.79	Other and unspecified partial excision of large intestine
45.94	Large-to-large intestinal anastomosis

   A.   556.9, 263.9, 45.79, 45.94   C.   555.1, 787.91, 263.9, 45.79
   B.   555.1, 263.9, 45.79   D.   556.9, 263.9, 45.79, 45.94

REFERENCE: Schraffenberger, p 96, 178

177. Hepatic coma with ascites due to Laennec's cirrhosis

571.2	Alcoholic cirrhosis of liver (Laennec's cirrhosis)
572.2	Hepatic coma
789.59	Other ascites

   A.   572.2, 571.2, 789.59   C.   789.59, 572.2
   B.   571.2, 789.59   D.   789.59, 572.2, 571.2

REFERENCE: Schraffenberger, p 176

Diseases of the Genitourinary System

178. Infertility secondary to pelvic peritoneal adhesions. Surgery performed is laparoscopic lysis of adhesions.

614.6	Pelvic peritoneal adhesions, female (post-operative) (post-infection)
628.2	Infertility, female, of tubal origin
54.21	Laparoscopy
65.81	Laparoscopic lysis of adhesions of ovary and fallopian tube

   A.   628.2, 614.6, 65.81   C.   614.6, 65.81, 54.21
   B.   628.2, 54.21, 65.81   D.   614.6, 54.21

REFERENCE: Brown, p 174

179. Chronic pelvic inflammatory disease with dysmenorrhea. Patient undergoes a diagnostic laparoscopy.

614.4	Chronic or unspecified parametritis and pelvic cellulitis
625.3	Dysmenorrhea
54.21	Laparoscopy
54.4	Excision or destruction of peritoneal tissue

A. 625.3, 54.21
B. 614.4, 54.4
C. 625.3, 614.4, 54.21
D. 614.4, 625.3, 54.21

REFERENCE: Schraffenberger, p 191

180. Chronic interstitial cystitis; cystoscopy with biopsy performed

595.1	Chronic interstitial cystitis
595.2	Other chronic cystitis
599.0	Urinary tract infection, site not specified
57.32	Other cystoscopy
57.33	Closed (transurethral) biopsy of bladder

A. 599.0, 57.32
B. 595.1, 57.33 .
C. 595.2, 57.32, 57.33
D. 595.1, 599.0, 57.32

REFERENCE: Brown, p 181

181. Fibrocystic disease of the breast; needle biopsy of breast

610.1	Diffuse cystic mastopathy (fibrocystic disease of breast)
610.2	Fibroadenosis of breast
610.3	Fibrosclerosis of breast
610.9	Benign mammary dysplasia, unspecified
85.11	Closed (percutaneous) (needle) biopsy of breast
8512	Open biopsy of breast

A. 610.1, 85.11
B. 610.3, 85.12
C. 610.2, 85.11
D. 610.9, 85.12

REFERENCE: Brown, p 192

Obstetrics

182. Intrauterine pregnancy, twins, 33 weeks. Premature rupture of membranes. Spontaneous delivery of premature twins, vertex presentation, both live born.

644.21	Early onset of delivery, delivered, with or without mention of antepartum condition
644.22	Early onset of delivery, delivered, with mention of postpartum complication
644.23	Early onset of delivery, antepartum condition or complication
651.01	Twin pregnancy, delivered, with or without mention of antepartum condition
651.02	Twin pregnancy, delivered, with mention of postpartum complication
658.11	Premature rupture of membranes, delivered, with or without mention of antepartum condition
659.11	Failed medical or unspecified induction, delivered, with or without mention of antepartum condition
V27.2	Outcome of delivery, twins, both liveborn
73.59	Other manually assisted delivery

A. 644.21, 658.11, 651.01, V27.2, 73.59
B. 644.22, 659.11, V27.2
C. 644.23, 658.11, 651.02, 73.59
D. 658.11, 651.01, V27.2, 73.59

REFERENCE: Brown, p221-227
Schraffenberger, p 198, 201, 212-213

183. A pregnant patient was admitted to the hospital with uncontrolled diabetes mellitus. She is a type I diabetic and was brought under control. The following code was assigned:

648.03	Other current conditions in the mother classifiable elsewhere but complicating pregnancy, childbirth or the puerperium, diabetes mellitus, antepartum condition or complication

Which of the following describe why the coding is in error?
A. The incorrect fifth digit was used.
B. The condition should have been coded as gestational diabetes because she is pregnant.
C. An additional code describing the diabetes mellitus should be used.
D. Only the code for the diabetes mellitus should be used.

REFERENCE: Brown, p105-106, 227-228
Schraffenberger, p 209-210

Skin

184. Max is 80% bald. He is admitted for a hair transplant, which he undergoes without complication. Max is also treated for congestive heart failure and hypertension for which he is on medication.

401.9	Essential hypertension, unspecified
402.91	Hypertensive heart disease unspecified as to malignant or benign, with heart failure, unspecified
428.0	Congestive heart failure, unspecified
704.00	Alopecia, unspecified
704.8	Other specified diseases of hair and hair follicles
86.64	Hair transplant

A. 704.00, 402.91, 86.64
B. 704.8, 401.9, 428.0, 86.64
C. 704.00, 401.9, 428.0, 86.64
D. 704.8, 402.91, 86.64

REFERENCE: Brown, p 229, 281-282
                      Schraffenberger, p 136-138, 148-149, 219

185. Melissa is status post mastectomy due to breast cancer. There has been no recurrence of the disease. She is admitted for insertion of unilateral breast implant.

174.9	Malignant neoplasm of breast (female), unspecified
V10.3	Personal history of malignant neoplasm of breast
V45.71	Acquired absence of breast and nipple
V51.0	Encounter for breast reconstruction following mastectomy
V58.42	Aftercare following surgery neoplasm
85.53	Unilateral breast implant
85.54	Bilateral breast implant

A. V51.0, V10.3, 85.54
B. V58.42, V51.0, V45.71, V10.3, 85.53
C. V45.71, 174.9, 85.53
D. V51.0, V45.71, V10.3, 85.53

REFERENCE: Brown, p 70, 75-76

186. Roscoe is 57-years old and has been diagnosed with gynecomastia. Roscoe also is on medication for temporal arteritis. Roscoe is admitted and bilateral mammectomy is performed. Roscoe's intravenous catheter infiltrates and he develops cellulitis at the IV site in the arm. This condition requires additional treatment.

446.5	Giant cell arteritis
611.1	Hypertrophy of breast
682.3	Other cellulitis and abscess upper arm and forearm
999.39	Infection following other infusion, injection, transfusion, or vaccination
85.34	Other unilateral subcutaneous mammectomy
85.36	Other bilateral subcutaneous mammectomy

A. 611.1, 85.36, 85.36
B. 611.1, 999.39, 446.5, 85.36
C. 611.1, 999.39, 682.3, 446.5, 85.36
D. 611.1, 682.3, 446.5, 85.34

REFERENCE: Brown, p 381-382
                Schraffenberger, p 190-191, 290

187. Brandon has an infected ingrown toenail that his physician removes.

681.11	Onychia and paronychia of toe
703.0	Ingrowing nail
77.89	Other partial ostectomy, other site
86.23	Removal of nail, nail bed, or nail fold
86.27	Debridement of nail, nail bed, or nail fold

A. 703.0, 86.23
B. 681.11, 86.23
C. 681.11, 86.27
D. 703.0, 86.23, 77.89

REFERENCE: Schraffenberger, p 219

Musculoskeletal

188. Julia is an 80-year-old female with osteoporosis. She presents to the emergency department complaining of severe back pain. X-rays revealed pathological compression fractures of several vertebrae.

721.90	Spondylosis of unspecified site without mention of myelopathy
733.00	Osteoporosis, unspecified
733.13	Pathological fracture of vertebrae
805.8	Fracture of vertebral column without mention of spinal cord injury, unspecified, closed

A. 733.13, 733.00
B. 805.8, 733.00
C. 721.90, 733.13
D. 733.00, 733.13

REFERENCE: Brown, p 210-211, 345
                Lovaasen and Schwerdtfeger, p 437-438
                Schraffenberger, p 229-230

189. Scott has a deformity of his left ring finger, due to an old tendon injury. He is admitted and undergoes a transfer of the flexor tendon from the distal phalanx to the middle phalanx.

727.82	Calcium deposits in tendon and bursa
736.20	Unspecified deformity of finger (acquired)
834.02	Closed dislocation of finger, interphalangeal (joint), hand
905.8	Late effect of tendon injury
82.55	Other change in hand muscle or tendon length
82.56	Other hand tendon transfer or transportation

A. 727.82, 82.56   C. 834.02, 82.55
B. 736.20, 905.8, 82.56   D. 727.82, 82.55

REFERENCE: Schraffenberger, p 229

190. Sara has Dupuytren's contracture of the right middle finger. She has an incision and division of the palmar fascia.

728.6	Contracture of palmar fascia (Dupuytren's contracture)
728.71	Plantar fascial fibromatosis
728.86	Necrotizing fasciaitis
82.12	Fasciotomy of hand
82.19	Other division of soft tissue of hand

A. 728.6, 82.12   C. 728.6, 82.19
B. 728.71, 82.19   D. 728.86, 82.12

REFERENCE: Schraffenberger, p 228

191. Cheryl has had chronic worsening pain of her left knee from rheumatoid arthritis. She has decided to undergo a total knee replacement as recommended by her physician. The surgery goes well; however, she develops a urinary tract infection that requires an additional day of stay in the hospital.

599.0	Urinary tract infection, site not specified
714.0	Rheumatoid arthritis
714.31	Polyarticular juvenile rheumatoid arthritis, acute
715.96	Osteoarthritis, unspecified whether generalized or localized, low leg
81.53	Revision of hip replacement, not otherwise specified
81.54	Total knee replacement

A. 715.96, 599.0, 81.54   C. 714.31, 81.53
B. 714.0, 599.0, 81.54   D. 714.31, 81.54

REFERENCE: Brown, p 181, 207-208, 210-211
               Schraffenberger, p 188-189, 227

Injury and Poisoning

192. A patient who is HIV positive and currently asymptomatic is admitted with a compound fracture of the tibia. The patient was treated previously for pneumocystis carinii pneumonia. Given the following codes, which is the correct coding and sequencing?

042	Human Immunodeficiency Virus (HIV) disease
136.3	Pneumocystosis (pneumonia due to *Pneumocystis carinii*)
V08	Asymptomatic HIV infection status
823.80	Fracture of tibia alone, unspecified part, closed
823.90	Fracture of tibia alone, unspecified part, open

   A. 823.90, V08   C. 823.80, V08, 136.3
   B. 823.90, 042   D. 823.80, 042

REFERENCE: Brown, p 97-98
                        Schraffenberger, p 70-73, 259-261

193. The diagnosis reads "first-, second-, and third-degree burns of the right arm." You would code
   A. the first degree only.   C. the third degree only.
   B. the second degree only.   D. each degree of burn separately.

REFERENCE: Brown, 359-360
                        Lovaasen and Schwerdtfeger, p 479-480
                        Schraffenberger, p 269-270

V Codes

194. Patient is admitted for elective cholecystectomy for treatment of chronic cholecystitis with cholelithiasis. Prior to administration of general anesthesia, patient suffers cerebral thrombosis. Surgery is subsequently canceled. Code and sequence the coding from the following codes.

434.00	Cerebral thrombosis, without mention of cerebral infarction
574.10	Calculus of gallbladder with other cholecystitis without mention of obstruction
V64.1	Surgical or other procedure not carried out because of contraindication
997.02	Iatrogenic cerebrovascular infarction or hemorrhage
51.22	Cholecystectomy

   A. 997.02, 574.10, 51.22   C. 997.02, 434.00, V64.1
   B. 574.10, 434.00, V64.1   D. 434.00, V64.1

REFERENCE: Brown, p 60-61
                        Schraffenberger, p 152, 179, 331-332

And Just A Few More Coding Questions for Practice

195. A physician lists the final diagnosis as diarrhea and constipation due to either irritable bowel syndrome or diverticulitis. The following codes are assigned:

562.10	Diverticulosis of colon without mention of hemorrhage
562.11	Diverticulitis of colon without mention of hemorrhage
564.00	Constipation, unspecified
564.1	Irritable bowel syndrome
787.91	Diarrhea

A. 564.1, 562.11
B. 562.10, 564.1
C. 564.00, 787.91, 564.1, 562.11
D. 564.1, 562.10, 564.00, 787.91

REFERENCE: Brown, 22-23
Schraffenberger, p 176, 248-249

196. When an open biopsy is followed by a more extensive definitive procedure the coder reports
A. the open biopsy.
B. the extensive definitive procedure and the open biopsy.
C. no procedures.
D. the extensive definitive procedure.

REFERENCE: Brown, p 58-59
Schraffenberger, p 42

197. In ICD-9-CM, when an exploratory laparotomy is performed followed by a therapeutic procedure, the coder reports
A. therapeutic procedure first, exploratory laparotomy second.
B. exploratory laparotomy, therapeutic procedure, closure of wound.
C. exploratory laparotomy first, therapeutic procedure second.
D. therapeutic procedure only.

REFERENCE: Brown, p56
Schraffenberger, p 37-38

198. Codes from category 655, known or suspected fetal abnormality affecting the mother, should
A. be assigned if the fetal conditions are documented.
B. be assigned at the discretion of the physician.
C. be assigned when they affect the management of the mother.
D. never be assigned.

REFERENCE: Brown, p 227-228
Schraffenberger, p 198

199. There are a limited number of late effect codes in ICD-9-CM. When coding a residual condition where there is no applicable late effect code, one should code
A. the residual condition followed by its cause.
B. the cause followed by the residual condition.
C. only the residual condition.
D. only the cause of the residual condition.

REFERENCE: Brown, p 49-50
Schraffenberger, p 305-309

200. A patient is admitted for a total hip replacement because of rheumatoid arthritis. Following admission, but prior to surgery, the patient develops congestive heart failure, which necessitates transfer to ICU. The hip replacement is canceled and the patient is treated for the heart failure. What is the principal diagnosis?
    A.   congestive heart failure   C.   hip replacement
    B.   rheumatoid arthritis   D.   canceled surgical procedure

REFERENCE: Brown, p 60-61
                  Schraffenberger, p 40

201. According to the UHDDS guidelines, the principal procedure is performed for-_____ rather than for _____.
    A.   diagnostic or exploratory purposes; definitive treatment
    B.   exploratory purposes; complications
    C.   definitive treatment; diagnostic or exploratory purposes
    D.   complications; definitive treatment

REFERENCE: Schraffenberger, p 49

202. A diabetic patient is admitted to the hospital with acute gastrointestinal hemorrhage due to ulcer disease. In this case, the diabetes would be
    A.   the principal diagnosis.
    B.   a comorbid condition.
    C.   a complication.
    D.   irrelevant and not coded.

REFERENCE: Brown, p 21-22
                  Schraffenberger, p 49

203. Which of the following are considered late effects regardless of time?
    A.   congenital defect
    B.   nonunion, malunion, scarring
    C.   fracture, burn
    D.   poisoning

REFERENCE: Brown, p 354

204. When a patient is admitted in respiratory failure due to a chronic nonrespiratory condition,
    A.   the respiratory failure is the principal diagnosis.
    B.   the chronic nonrespiratory problem is the principal diagnosis.
    C.   only the respiratory failure is coded.
    D.   only the chronic nonrespiratory condition is coded.

REFERENCE: Brown, p 157-159
                  Schraffenberger, p 168-171

205. When Robert was discharged, his physician listed his diagnoses as congestive heart failure with acute pulmonary edema. You're coding Robert's record and you will code
    A.   the CHF only.
    B.   the edema only.
    C.   both the CHF and the edema; sequence the CHF first.
    D.   both the CHF and the edema; sequence the edema first.

REFERENCE: Brown, p 21, 25

206. A patient was admitted with severe abdominal pain, elevated temperature, and nausea. The physical examination indicated possible cholecystitis. Acute and chronic pancreatitis secondary to alcoholism was recorded on the face sheet as the final diagnosis. The principal diagnosis is
    A. alcoholism.
    B. abdominal pain.
    C. cholecystitis.
    D. acute pancreatitis.

REFERENCE: Brown, p 21, 24

207. A patient was admitted to the hospital with hemiplegia and aphasia. The hemiplegia and aphasia were resolved before discharge and the patient was diagnosed with cerebral thrombosis. What is the correct coding and sequencing?
    A. hemiplegia; aphasia
    B. cerebral thrombosis
    C. cerebral thrombosis; hemiplegia; aphasia
    D. hemiplegia; cerebral thrombosis; aphasia

REFERENCE: Brown, p 21-22, 284-285

Use this information to answer questions #208-210:

Present on admission (POA) guidelines were established to identify and report diagnoses that are present at the time of a patient's admission. The reporting options for each ICD-9-CM code are:
    A. Y=Yes
    B. N=No
    C. U=Unknown
    D. W=clinically undetermined
    E. Unreported/Not Used (Exempt from POA) reporting

208. The physician explicitly documents that a condition is not present at the time of admission.
    A. Y=Yes
    B. N=No
    C. U=Unknown
    D. W=clinically undetermined
    E. Unreported/Not Used (Exempt from POA) reporting

REFERENCE: Lovaasen and Schwerdtfeger, p 90-93

209. The physician documents that the patient has diabetes that was diagnosed prior to admission.
    A. Y=Yes
    B. N=No
    C. U=Unknown
    D. W=clinically undetermined
    E. Unreported/Not Used (Exempt from POA) reporting

REFERENCE: Lovaasen and Schwerdtfeger, p 90-93

210. The medical record documentation is unclear as to whether the condition was present on admission.
    A. Y=Yes
    B. N=No
    C. U=Unknown
    D. W=clinically undetermined
    E. Unreported/Not Used (Exempt from POA) reporting

REFERENCE::   Lovaasen and Schwerdtfeger, p 90-93

Answer Key for ICD-9-CM Coding

1.	D	46.	A	
2.	B	47.	C	
3.	A	48.	B	
4.	C	49.	A	
5.	D	50.	D	
6.	C	51.	C	
7.	D	52.	A	
8.	C	53.	C	
9.	A	54.	B	The physician should be asked if the blood loss should be added as a discharge diagnosis.
10.	B			
11.	C			
12.	B	55.	A	
13.	A	56.	C	
14.	D	57.	D	
15.	B	58.	A	
16.	A	59.	C	
17.	C	60.	A	
18.	B	61.	A	
19.	D	62.	C	
20.	B	63.	B	
21.	A	Pain is a symptom that is integral to the sickle cell crisis and therefore is not coded.	64.	D
		65.	B	
		66.	D	
22.	C	67.	B	
23.	B	68.	D	
24.	D	69.	A	
25.	D	70.	B	
26.	B	71.	A	
27.	A	72.	C	
28.	C	73.	B	
29.	B	74.	D	
30.	D	75.	C	
31.	C	76.	A	
32.	B	77.	C	
33.	A	78.	B	
34.	C	79.	C	
35.	B	80.	D	
36.	D	81.	B	Newborn V-code is not assigned by the receiving facility when a newborn is transferred.
37.	A			
38.	C			
39.	D	82.	C	
40.	A	83.	A	
41.	B	84.	B	
42.	A	85.	D	
43.	D	86.	C	
44.	A	87.	A	
45.	B	88.	D	

Answer Key for ICD-9-CM Coding

89. C	
90. A	
91. C	
92. B	
93. A	
94. C	
95. D	
96. C	
97. B	
98. A	
99. D	
100. C	
101. A	
102. D	
103. C	
104. B	
105. A	
106. C	
107. D	
108. C	
109. D	
110. A	
111. A	
112. B	
113. D	
114. C	
115. B	
116. A	
117. A	
118. D	
119. C	
120. D	
121. A	
122. B	
123. D	Fatigue and flulike symptoms/signs of hepatitis would not be coded.
124. A	
125. D	
126. A	
127. A	
128. C	
129. A	
130. C	
131. B	
132. C	
133. D	SSS would not be reported as a current condition because the pacemaker would have taken care of this condition.

134. A	
135. B	
136. C	The coder cannot assume a causal relationship between the diabetes and conditions that are usually related to the diabetes unless a physician confirms this relationship.
137. A	
138. C	The physician should be queried as to whether the diabetes was uncontrolled.
139. A	
140. C	
141. A	
142. D	
143. B	
144. A	
145. B	
146. C	
147. A	
148. C	
149. A	
150. D	
151. C	
152. A	
153. A	
154. A.	
155. B	
156. A	
157. B	
158. C	
159. A	
160. D	
161. C	
162. A	
163. D	
164. A	
165. D	COPD (496) is a general term. It will present as chronic obstructive bronchitis.
166. C	
167. A	

Answer Key for ICD-9-CM Coding

168. C   The atelectasis is coded because it required monitoring and extended his length of stay.

169. D
170. B
171. C   The alphabetic index is misleading and directs the coder to use one code for acute and chronic sinusitis. The Tabular List, however, directs the coder to use two separate codes.

172. D
173. A
174. C   The note under category 997 instructs the coder to "use additional code to identify complication."

175. A
176. B
177. A
178. A
179. D
180. B
181. A
182. A
183. C
184. C
185. B
186. C
187. A
188. A
189. B
190. A
191. B
192. B   A "compound" fracture is considered an "open" fracture.
193. C   Code the highest degree burn ONLY of the same site.
194. B
195. C
196. B
197. D
198. C
199. C
200. B
201. C
202. B
203. B
204. A
205. A

206. D
207. B
208. B
209. A
210. C

REFERENCES

Bowie, M., & Schaffer, R. (2006). *Understanding ICD-9-CM: A worktest*. Clifton Park, NY: Thomson Delmar Learning.

Brown, F. (2009). *ICD-9-CM coding handbook with answers*. Chicago: American Hospital Association (AHA).

Channel Publishing, Ltd. (2009). *The educational annotation of ICD-9-CM*. Reno: Channel Publishing, Ltd.

Eid, D. (2008) *Applying coding concepts: Encoder workbook*. Clifton Park, NY: Thomson Delmar Learning.

Ingenix (2008). *ICD-9-CM Expert for hospitals, Vol. 1, 2 and 3*. St. Louis: Ingenix.

Lovaasen, K., & Schwerdtfeger, J. (2009). *ICD-9-CM coding: Theory and practice*. St. Louis: Saunders Elsevier.

Schraffenberger, L. A. (2009). *Basic ICD-9-CM coding*. Chicago: American Health Information Management Association (AHIMA).

IX. CPT Coding

2009 Current Procedural Terminology © 2008 American Medical Association. ALL RIGHTS RESERVED

Lisa Delhomme, MHA, RHIA

Evaluation and Management

1. Patient is admitted to the hospital with acute abdominal pain. The attending medical physician requests a surgical consult. The consultant agrees to see the patient and conducts a comprehensive history and physical examination. The physician ordered lab work to rule out pancreatitis, along with an ultrasound of the gallbladder and abdominal x-ray. Due to the various diagnosis possibilities and the tests reviewed, a moderate medical decision was made.
   A. 99244
   B. 99222
   C. 99254
   D. 99204

   REFERENCE: Buck, p 55-57
                Frisch, p 82-85
                Green, p 387-389
                Johnson and McHugh, p
                Smith, p 199

2. An established patient returns to the physician's office for follow-up on his hypertension and diabetes. The physician takes the blood pressure and references the patient's last three glucose tests. The patient is still running above normal glucose levels, so the physician decides to adjust the patient's insulin. An expanded history was taken and a physical examination was performed.
   A. 99213
   B. 99232
   C. 99202
   D. 99214

   REFERENCE: Buck, p 50
                Frisch, p 53-55
                Johnson and McHugh, p 127-128
                Smith, p 198

3. Patient arrives in the emergency room via a medical helicopter. The patient has sustained multiple life-threatening injuries due to a multiple car accident. The patient goes into cardiac arrest 10 minutes after arrival. An hour and 30 minutes of critical care time is spent trying to stabilize the patient.
   A. 99285; 99288; 99291
   B. 99291; 99292
   C. 99291; 99292; 99285
   D. 99282

   REFERENCE: Buck, p 62-63
                Frisch, p 27-29
                Green, p 392-393
                Johnson and McHugh, p 170-171
                Smith, p 200-201

4. The physician provided services to a new patient who was in a rest home for an ulcerative sore on the hip. A problem-focused history and physical examination were performed and a straightforward medical decision was made.
   A. 99304
   B. 99325
   C. 99324
   D. 99334

   REFERENCE: Buck, p 67
                Johnson and McHugh, p 17
                Smith, p 202

5. A doctor provides critical care services in the emergency department for a patient in respiratory failure. He initiates ventilator management and spends an hour and ten minutes providing critical care for this patient.
   A. 99281, 99291, 99292, 94002
   B. 99291, 99292, 94002
   C. 99291, 94002
   D. 99291

REFERENCE: Buck, p 62-63
　　　　　　　Green, p 392
　　　　　　　Johnson and McHugh, p 170-174
　　　　　　　Smith, p 200-201

6. Services were provided to a patient in the emergency room after the patient twisted her ankle stepping down from a curb. The emergency room physician ordered x-rays of the ankle, which came back negative for a fracture. A problem-focused history and physical examination were performed and ankle strapping was applied. A prescription for pain was given to the patient. Code the emergency room visit only.
   A. 99201　　　　　　　　　　　C. 99281
   B. 99282　　　　　　　　　　　D. 99211

REFERENCE: Buck, p 60-61
　　　　　　　Frisch, p 71-72
　　　　　　　Johnson and McHugh, p 168
　　　　　　　Smith, p 200

7. An established patient was seen in her primary physician's office. The patient fell at home and came to the physician's office for an examination. Due to a possible concussion, the patient was sent to the hospital to be admitted as an observation patient. A detailed history and examination were performed and the medical decision was low complexity. The patient stayed overnight and was discharged the next afternoon.
   A. 99214; 99234　　　　　　　C. 99218
   B. 99214; 99218; 99217　　　　D. 99218; 99217

REFERENCE: CPT Book, 2009
　　　　　　　Buck, p 51-52
　　　　　　　Frisch, p 69-71Smith, p 198
　　　　　　　Johnson and McHugh, p 162-163

8. An out-of-town patient presents to a walk-in clinic to have a prescription refilled for a nonsteroidal anti-inflammatory drug. The physician performs a problem-focused history and physical examination with a straightforward decision.
   A. 99211　　　　　　　　　　　C. 99212
   B. 99201　　　　　　　　　　　D. 99202

REFERENCE: Buck, p 48-49
　　　　　　　Frisch, p 49-51
　　　　　　　Johnson and McHugh, p 126-124
　　　　　　　Smith, p 198

9. An office consultation is performed for a post-menopausal woman who is complaining of spotting in the past 6 months with right lower quadrant tenderness. A detailed history and physical were performed with a low-complexity medical decision.
   - A. 99242
   - B. 99243
   - C. 99253
   - D. 99254

REFERENCE: Buck, p 55-57
                Frisch, p 77-81
                Green, p 387-388
                Johnson and McHugh, p 167-168
                Smith, p 199

Anesthesia

10. Upper abdominal ventral hernia repair
    - A. 00832
    - B. 00750
    - C. 00752
    - D. 00830

REFERENCE: Buck, p 82-92
                Johnson and McHugh, p 196-197
                Smith, p 229-230

11. Total hip replacement
    - A. 01210
    - B. 01402
    - C. 01230
    - D. 01214

REFERENCE: Buck, p 82-92
                Smith, p 229-23012.

12. Vaginal hysterectomy
    - A. 00846
    - B. 00944
    - C. 00840
    - D. 01963

REFERENCE: Buck, p 82-92
                Smith, p 229-230

13. Placement of vascular shunt in forearm
    - A. 01844
    - B. 01850
    - C. 00532
    - D. 01840

REFERENCE: Buck, p 82-92
                Smith, p 229-230

14. Decortication of left lung
    - A. 01638-LT
    - B. 00542-LT
    - C. 00546-LT
    - D. 00500-LT

REFERENCE: Buck, p 82-92
                Smith, p 229-230

15. Total shoulder replacement
    A. 01760
    B. 01630
    C. 01402
    D. 01638

REFERENCE: Buck, p 82-92
              Smith, p 229-230

16. Cesarean section
    A. 00840
    B. 01961
    C. 00940
    D. 01960

REFERENCE: Buck, p 82-92
              Smith, p 229-230

17. Procedures on bony pelvis
    A. 00400
    B. 01170
    C. 01120
    D. 01190

REFERENCE: Buck, p 82-92
              Smith, p 229-230

18. Corneal transplant
    A. 00144
    B. 00140
    C. 00147
    D. 00190

REFERENCE: Buck, p 82-92
              Smith, p 229-230

Surgery—Integumentary System

19. Patient presents to the hospital for skin grafts due to previous third-degree burns. The burn eschar of the back was removed. Once the eschar was removed, the defect size measured 10 cm x 10 cm. A skin graft from a donor bank was placed onto the defect and sewn into place as a temporary wound closure.
    A. 15170, 15002
    B. 15300
    C. 15002, 15200
    D. 15002, 15300

REFERENCE: Buck, p 146-148
              Smith, p 66-68

20. Patient presents to the operating room for excision of a 4.5 cm malignant melanoma of the left forearm. A 6 cm x 6 cm rotation flap was created for closure.
    A. 14021
    B. 11606; 14020
    C. 14300
    D. 11606; 15100

REFERENCE: Buck, p 137-138, 149-151
              Smith, p 66

21. Female patient has a percutaneous needle biopsy of the left breast lesion in the lower outer quadrant. Following the biopsy frozen section results, the physician followed this with an excisional removal of the same lesion.
    A. 19100; 19125   C. 19120-LT
    B. 19100; 19120-LT   D. 19100; 19120; 19120

REFERENCE: Buck, p 158-159
              Green, p 495
              Smith, p 73-74

22. Patient presents to the emergency room with lacerations of right lower leg that involved the fascia. Lacerations measured 5.0 cm and 2.7 cm.
    A. 11406; 11403   C. 12032; 12031
    B. 12034   D. 12032

REFERENCE: Buck, p 141-145
              Smith, p 60-61

23. 10 sq cm epidermal autograft to the face from the back
    A. 15110   C. 15110, 15115
    B. 15115   D. 15120

REFERENCE: CPT Book, 2009

24. Nonhuman graft for temporary wound closure. Patient has a 5 cm defect on the scalp.
    A. 15335   C. 15420
    B. 15400   D. 15430

REFERENCE: CPT Book, 2009
              Green, p 485
              Smith, p 68

25. Patient is admitted for a blepharoplasty of the left lower eyelid and a repair for a tarsal strip of the left upper lid.
    A. 67917-E1; 15822-E2   C. 67917-E1
    B. 67917-E1; 15820-E2   D. 67917-E1; 15823-E2

REFERENCE: CPT Assistant, January 2005, p 46

26. Patient presents to the emergency room with lacerations sustained in an automobile accident. Repairs of the 3.3 cm skin laceration of the left leg that involved the fascia, 2.5 cm and 3.0 cm lacerations of the left arm involving the fascia, and 2.7 cm of the left foot, which required simple sutures, were performed. Sterile dressings were applied.
    A. 12032; 12032-51; 12031-51; 12002-51   C. 12034, 12002-51
    B. 12002, 12002-51   D. 13150; 12032-51, 12032-51, 12001-51

REFERENCE: Buck, p 141-145
              Green, p 483-484
              Smith, p 60-61

27. Patient presents to the operating room for excision of three lesions. The 1.5 cm and 2.0 cm lesions of the back were excised with one excision. The 0.5 cm lesion of the hand was excised. The pathology report identified both back lesions as squamous cell carcinoma. The hand lesion was identified as seborrheic keratosis.
   A. 11604; 11420
   B. 11402; 11420; 11403
   C. 11403; 11642; 11462
   D. 11602; 11402

REFERENCE: Buck, p 137-138
             CPT Assistant, Nov. 2002, p 5-6, 8
             Green, p 477-479
             Smith, p 55-56

28. Patient presents to the radiology department where a fine-needle aspiration of the breast is performed utilizing computer tomography.
   A. 19120; 77012
   B. 19102
   C. 19125
   D. 10022, 77012

REFERENCE: CPT Assistant, November 2002, p 2-3
             Buck, p 129

29. Patient presents to the operating room where a 3.2 cm malignant lesion of the shoulder was excised and repaired with simple sutures. A 2.0 cm benign lesion of the cheek was excised and was repaired with a rotation skin graft.
   A. 11604; 11442; 14040; 12001
   B. 14040; 11604
   C. 15002; 15120
   D. 17264; 17000; 12001

REFERENCE: CPT Assistant, November 2002, p 5-8
             CPT Assistant, August 2002, p 5
             CPT Assistant, July 1999, p 3-4
             Buck, p 137-138, 146
             Smith, p 55-57, 66

30. Patient was admitted to the hospital for removal of excessive tissue due to massive weight loss. Liposuction of the abdomen and bilateral thighs was performed.
   A. 15830
   B. 15830; 15833; 15833
   C. 15877; 15879-50
   D. 15839

REFERENCE: Buck, p 151

Surgery—Musculoskeletal

31. Patient presents to the hospital with ulcer of the right foot. Patient is taken to the operating room where a revision of the right metatarsal head is performed.
   A. 28104-RT
   B. 28111-RT
   C. 28288-RT
   D. 28899-RT

REFERENCE: CPT Book, 2009

32. Patient presents to the emergency room following a fall. X-rays were ordered for the lower leg and results showed a fracture of the proximal left tibia. The emergency room physician performed a closed manipulation of the fracture with skeletal traction.
    A. 27532-LT
    B. 27536-LT
    C. 27530-LT
    D. 27524-LT

REFERENCE: Buck, p 165-168
              Smith, p 78

33. Trauma patient was rushed to the operating room with multiple injuries. Open reduction with internal fixation of intertrochanteric femoral fracture; open reduction of the tibial and fibula shaft with internal fixation was performed.
    A. 27245; 27759
    B. 20690
    C. 27248; 27756
    D. 27244; 27758

REFERENCE: Buck, p 165-168
              Smith, p 78

34. Open IandD of a deep abscess of the cervical spine
    A. 22010
    B. 22015
    C. 10060
    D. 10140

REFERENCE: CPT Book, 2009

35. Patient presents to the emergency room following an assault. Examination of the patient reveals blunt trauma to the face. Radiology reports that the patient suffers from a fracture to the frontal skull and a blow-out fracture of the orbital floor. Patient is admitted and taken to the operating room where a periorbital approach to the orbital fracture is employed and an implant is inserted.
    A. 21407; 21275
    B. 21387; 61330
    C. 21390
    D. 61340; 21401

REFERENCE: Buck, p 165-168
              Smith, p 78

36. Patient presents with a traumatic partial amputation of the second, third, and fourth fingers on the right hand. Patient was taken to the operating room where completion of the amputation of three fingers was performed with direct closure.
    A. 26910-F6; 26910-F7; 26910-F8
    B. 26843-RT
    C. 26951-F6; 26951-F7; 26951-F8
    D. 26550-RT

REFERENCE: CPT Book, 2009

37. Patient is brought to the emergency room following a shark attack. The paramedics have the patient's amputated foot. The patient is taken directly to the operating room to reattach the patient's foot.
    A. 28800
    B. 28200; 28208
    C. 28110
    D. 20838

REFERENCE: CPT Book, 2009

38. Patient presents to the hospital with a right index trigger finger. Release of the trigger finger was performed.
    A. 26060-F7
    B. 26055-F6
    C. 26170-F6
    D. 26110

REFERENCE: CPT Book, 2009

39. Patient had been diagnosed with a bunion. Patient was taken to the operating room where a simple resection of the base of the proximal phalanx along with the medial eminence was performed. Kirschner wire was placed to hold the joint in place.
    A. 28292
    B. 28290
    C. 28293
    D. 28298

REFERENCE: CPT Assistant, December 1995, p 5-7
             CPT Book, 2009

Surgery—Respiratory

40. Patient has a bronchoscopy with endobronchial biopsies of three sites.
    A. 31625; 31625; 31625
    B. 31625
    C. 31622; 31625
    D. 31622; 31625; 31625; 31625

REFERENCE: CPT Assistant, June 2004, p 11
             Smith, p 92

41. Patient presents to the surgical unit and undergoes unilateral endoscopy, partial ethmoidectomy, and maxillary antrostomy.
    A. 31254; 31256-51
    B. 31201; 31225-51
    C. 31290; 31267-51
    D. 31233; 31231-51

REFERENCE: Buck, p 188-189
             CPT Assistant, January 1997, p 4-6
             Smith, p 86-87

42. Patient has been diagnosed with metastatic laryngeal carcinoma. Patient underwent subtotal supraglottic laryngectomy with radical neck dissection.
    A. 31540
    B. 31367
    C. 31365
    D. 31368

REFERENCE: Buck, p 196-197
             Green, p 536-537

43. Patient was involved in an accident and has been sent to the hospital. During transport the patient develops breathing problems and, upon arrival at the hospital, an emergency transtracheal tracheostomy was performed. Following various x-rays, the patient was diagnosed with traumatic pneumothorax and a thoracentesis with insertion of tube was performed.
    A. 31603; 31612
    B. 31610; 32421
    C. 31603; 32422
    D. 31603; 32421

REFERENCE: Buck, p 198-202

44. Patient with laryngeal cancer has a tracheoesophageal fistula created and has a voicebox inserted.
   A. 31611   C. 31395
   B. 31580   D. 31502

REFERENCE: CPT Book, 2009

45. Upper lobectomy of the right lung with repair of the bronchus
   A. 32480   C. 32320
   B. 32486   D. 32480, 32501

REFERENCE: Buck, p 202-204
                     Green, p 540

46. Patient with a deviated nasal septum that was repaired by septoplasty
   A. 30400   C. 30520
   B. 30620   D. 30630

REFERENCE: Buck, p 193

47. Lye burn of the larynx repaired by laryngoplasty
   A. 31588   C. 31360
   B. 16020   D. 31540

REFERENCE: CPT Book, 2009

48. Bronchoscopy with multiple transbronchial right upper and right lower lobe lung biopsy with fluoroscopic guidance
   A. 31628-RT; 76000-RT   C. 32405-RT
   B. 31717-RT; 31632-RT   D. 31628-RT; 31632-RT

REFERENCE: CPT Assistant, March 1999, p 3
                     Buck, p 188
                     Green, p 538-539
                     Smith, p 92

49. Patient has recurrent spontaneous pneumothorax which has resulted in a chemical pleurodesis by thoracoscopy.
   A. 32650   C. 32605
   B. 32310; 32601   D. 32960

REFERENCE: Buck, p 188

50. Laryngoscopic stripping of vocal cords for leukoplakia of the vocal cords
   A. 31535   C. 31541
   B. 31540   D. 31570

REFERENCE: Smith, p 90
                     Buck, p 188-189

Surgery—Cardiovascular System

51. Patient returns to the operating room following open-heart bypass for exploration of blood vessel to control postoperative bleeding in the chest.
    A. 35820   C. 35761
    B. 20101   D. 35905

REFERENCE: CPT Book, 2009

52. Patient undergoes construction of apical aortic conduit with an insertion of a single-ventricle ventricular assist device.
    A. 33400   C. 33977
    B. 33975   D. 33975; 33404

REFERENCE: CPT Assistant, January 2004, p 28

53. Patient presents to the operating room where a CABG x 3 is performed using the mammary artery and two sections of the saphenous vein.
    A. 33534; 33511   C. 33535
    B. 33534; 33518; 33511   D. 33533; 33518

REFERENCE: Buck, p 217
              Green, p 565
              Smith, p 96

54. Patient complains of recurrent syncope following carotid thromboendarterectomy. Patient returns 2 weeks after initial surgery and undergoes repeat carotid thromboendarterectomy.
    A. 33510   C. 35201
    B. 35301   D. 35301; 35390

REFERENCE: CPT Assistant, Winter 1993, p 3

55. Patient is admitted with alcohol cirrhosis and has a TIPS procedure performed.
    A. 35476; 36011; 36481   C. 37182
    B. 37183   D. 37140

REFERENCE: CPT Assistant, December 2003, p 1-3

56. Eighty-year-old patient has carcinoma and presents to the operating room for placement of a tunneled implantable centrally inserted venous access port.
    A. 36558   C. 36561
    B. 36571   D. 36481

REFERENCE: CPT Assistant, February 1999, p 1-5
              CPT Assistant, November 1999, p 19-20
              Green, p 583-585
              Smith, p 103-105

57. Patient presents to the operating room and undergoes an endovascular repair of an infrarenal abdominal aortic aneurysm utilizing a unibody bifurcated prosthesis.
    A. 34800; 34813
    B. 34802
    C. 34804
    D. 35081

REFERENCE: CPT Assistant, September 2002, p 4;
              CPT Assistant, February 2003, p 2-4, 16
              Buck, p 223-224
              Green, p 572-574

58. The physician punctures the left common femoral to examine the right common iliac.
    A. 36245
    B. 36246
    C. 36247
    D. 36140

REFERENCE: CPT Book, 2009

59. Patient has a history of PVD for many years and experiences chest pains. The patient underwent Doppler evaluation which showed a common femoral DVT. Patient is now admitted for thromboendartectomy.
    A. 35371
    B. 35372
    C. 35456
    D. 35256

REFERENCE: CPT Book, 2009

60. Patient presents to the hospital with a diagnosis of femoral artery atherosclerotic disease. The patient is taken to the operating room and undergoes an aortofemoral popliteal bypass.
    A. 35551
    B. 35651
    C. 35556
    D. 35656

REFERENCE: CPT Book, 2009

Surgery—Hemic and Lymphatic Systems, Mediastinum, and Diaphragm

61. Patient has breast carcinoma and is now undergoing sentinel node biopsy. Patient was injected for sentinel node identification and two deep axillary lymph nodes showed up intensely. These two lymph nodes were completely excised. Path report was positive for metastatic carcinoma.
    A. 38525; 38790
    B. 38589
    C. 38308; 38790
    D. 38525; 38792

REFERENCE: CPT Assistant, November, 1998 p 15-16
              CPT Assistant, July 1999, p 6-12
              Buck, p 316-317
              Green, p 593-594

62. Patient has a history of hiatal hernia for many years, which has progressively gotten worse. The decision to repair the hernia was made and the patient was sent to the operating room where the repair took place via the thorax and abdomen.
    A. 39545
    B. 39530
    C. 39502
    D. 39503

REFERENCE: Buck, p 306-307

63. Patient has a bone marrow aspiration of the iliac crest and of the tibia.
    A. 38220, 38220-59   C. 38230
    B. 38221   D. 38220

REFERENCE: CPT Assistant, January 2004, p 26
               Buck, p 316

64. Trauma patient is rushed to the operating room with multiple injuries. The patient had his spleen removed due to massive rupture with repair of lacerated diaphragm.
    A. 38115; 39501   C. 38102; 39540
    B. 38120; 39599   D. 38100; 39501

REFERENCE: Buck, p 309, 316

65. Laparoscopic retroperitoneal lymph node biopsy
    A. 38570   C. 49323
    B. 38780   D. 38589

REFERENCE: Buck, p 316-317

66. Excision of mediastinal cyst
    A. 11400   C. 17000
    B. 39200   D. 39400

REFERENCE: Buck, p 308-309

67. Patient diagnosed with cystic hygroma of the axilla, which was excised.
    A. 38555   C. 38550
    B. 11400   D. 38300

REFERENCE: CPT Book, 2009

68. Laparoscopy with multiple biopsies of retroperitoneal lymph nodes
    A. 38570   C. 38570-22
    B. 38571   D. 38572

REFERENCE: CPT Book, 2009

69. Cannulation of the thoracic duct
    A. 38794   C. 36260
    B. 36810   D. 38999

REFERENCE: CPT Book, 2009

70. Patient has been on the bone marrow transplant recipient list for 3 months. A perfect match was made and the patient came in and received peripheral stem cell transplant.
    A. 38242   C. 38241
    B. 38230   D. 38240

REFERENCE: Green, p 592-593
               Buck, p 316

Surgery—Digestive System

71. Laparoscopic gastric banding
    A. 43842
    B. 43843
    C. 43770
    D. 43771

REFERENCE: CPT Book, 2009

72. Patient presents with a history of upper abdominal pain. Cholangiogram was negative and patient was sent to the hospital for ERCP. During the procedure the sphincter was incised and a stent was placed for drainage.
    A. 43260; 43262; 43624
    B. 43262; 43269
    C. 43267
    D. 43262; 43268

REFERENCE: CPT Assistant, Spring 1994, p 5-7

73. Patient presents to the emergency room with right lower abdominal pains. Emergency room physician suspects possible appendicitis. Patient was taken to the operating room where a laparoscopic appendectomy was performed. Pathology report was negative for appendicitis.
    A. 44950
    B. 44950; 49320
    C. 44970
    D. 44901

REFERENCE: CPT Book, 2009

74. Morbidly obese patient comes in for vertical banding of the stomach.
    A. 43848
    B. 43659
    C. 43842
    D. 43999

REFERENCE: CPT Assistant, May 1998, p 5-6

75. Patient underwent anoscopy followed by colonoscopy. The physician examined to colon to 60 cm.
    A. 46600; 45378
    B. 46600; 45378-59
    C. 45378
    D. 45999

REFERENCE: Buck, p 301, 304
              Green, p 614-615
              Smith, p 109, 111-112

76. Injection snoreplasty for treatment of palatal snoring.
    A. 42299
    B. 42145
    C. 42999
    D. 40899

REFERENCE: CPT Assistant, December 2004, p 19

77. Patient arrives to the hospital and has a Nissen fundoplasty done endoscopically.
    A. 43410
    B. 43415
    C. 43502
    D. 43280

REFERENCE: CPT Book, 2009

78. Young child presents with cleft lip and cleft palate. This is the first attempt of repair, which includes major revision of the cleft palate and unilateral cleft lip repair.
    A. 42200; 40701
    B. 42225; 40700
    C. 42220; 40720
    D. 42215; 40700

REFERENCE: CPT Book, 2009

79. Patient has a history of chronic alcohol abuse with portal hypertension. Patient has been vomiting blood for the past 3 days and presented to his physician's office. Patient was sent to the hospital for evaluation and an EGD was performed. Biopsy findings showed gastritis, esophagitis and bleeding esophageal varices, which were injected with sclerosing solution.
    A. 43235; 43244; 43204
    B. 43239; 43244
    C. 43239; 43243
    D. 43239; 43243; 43204

REFERENCE: Buck, p 299
              Green, p 614-616
              Smith, p 109

Surgery—Urinary System

80. Patient is admitted for contact laser vaporization of the prostate. The physician performed a TURP and transurethral resection of the bladder neck at the same time.
    A. 52648
    B. 52648; 52450; 52500
    C. 52450; 53500
    D. 52648; 52450

REFERENCE: CPT Assistant, July 2005, p 15

81. Patient comes to the hospital with a history of right flank pain. Urine tests are negative. Radiology examination reveals that the patient has renal cysts. Patient is now admitted for laparoscopic ablation of the cysts.
    A. 50541
    B. 50390
    C. 50280
    D. 50920

REFERENCE: CPT Assistant, November 1999, p 25
              CPT Assistant, May 2000, p 4
              CPT Assistant, October 2001, p 8
              CPT Assistant, January, 2003, p 19

82. Patient has extensive bladder cancer. She underwent a complete cystectomy with bilateral pelvic lymphadenectomy and creation of ureteroileal conduit.
    A. 51575; 50820
    B. 50825; 51570; 38770
    C. 51595
    D. 51550; 38770

REFERENCE: CPT Book, 2009

83. Patient presents to the hospital with right ureteral calculus. Patient is taken to the operating room where a cystoscopy with ureteroscopy is performed to remove the calculus.
    A. 52353
    B. 52310
    C. 51065
    D. 52352

REFERENCE: Buck, p 289
              Green, p 638-640

84. Female with 6 months of stress incontinence. Outpatient therapies are not working and the patient decides to have the problem fixed. Laparoscopic urethral suspension was completed.
    A. 51992
    B. 51990
    C. 51840
    D. 51845

REFERENCE: CPT Assistant, November 1999, p 26
              CPT Assistant, May 2000, p 4
              CPT Changes: An Insider's View, 2000

85. Patient has ovarian vein syndrome and has ureterolysis performed.
    A. 58679
    B. 58660
    C. 52351
    D. 50722

REFERENCE: Buck, p 285

86. Male patient has been diagnosed with benign prostatic hypertrophy and undergoes a transurethral destruction of the prostate by radiofrequency thermotherapy.
    A. 52648
    B. 53852
    C. 52601
    D. 53850

REFERENCE: CPT Assistant, November 1997, p 20
              CPT Assistant, April 2001, p 4

87. Nephrectomy with resection of 1/2 of the ureter.
    A. 50220
    B. 50234
    C. 50230; 50650
    D. 50546

REFERENCE: Buck, p 284-285

88. Male with urinary incontinence. Sling procedure was performed 6 months ago and now the patient has returned for a revision of the sling procedure.
    A. 53449
    B. 53442
    C. 53440
    D. 53431

REFERENCE: CPT Book, 2009

89. Excision of 2.5 cm bladder tumor with cystoscopy.
    A. 51550
    B. 51530
    C. 52235
    D. 51060

REFERENCE: Buck, p 286- 290

90. Closure of ureterocutaneous fistula
    A. 50930
    B. 50920
    C. 57310
    D. 50520

REFERENCE: CPT Book, 2009

Surgery—Male Genital System

91. Removal of nephrostomy tube with fluoroscopic guidance
    A. 50387
    B. 50389
    C. 99212
    D. 99213

REFERENCE: CPT Book, 2009

92. Patient has been diagnosed with prostate cancer. Patient arrived in the operating room where a therapeutic orchiectomy is performed.
    A. 54560
    B. 54530
    C. 55899
    D. 54520

REFERENCE: CPT Assistant, October 2001, p 8

93. Patient undergoes laparoscopic orchiopexy for intra-abdominal testes.
    A. 54650
    B. 54699
    C. 54692
    D. 55899

REFERENCE: CPT Assistant, November 1999, p 27
           CPT Assistant, May 2000, p 4
           CPT Assistant, October 2001, p 8

94. Scrotal wall abscess drainage
    A. 55100
    B. 55150
    C. 54700
    D. 55110

REFERENCE: CPT Book, 2009

95. Hydrocelectomy of spermatic cord
    A. 55500
    B. 55000
    C. 55041
    D. 55520

REFERENCE: CPT Assistant, October 2001, p 8

96. Patient has been followed by his primary care physician for elevated PSA. Patient underwent prostate needle biopsy in the physician office 2 weeks ago and final pathology was positive for carcinoma. Patient is admitted for prostatectomy. Frozen section of the prostate and one lymph node is positive for prostate cancer with metastatic disease to the lymph node. Prostatectomy became a radical perineal with bilateral pelvic lymphadenectomy.
    A. 55845
    B. 55815
    C. 55815; 38562
    D. 38770

REFERENCE: Smith, p 130-131

97. Male presented to operating room for sterilization by bilateral vasectomy.
   A. 55200
   B. 55400
   C. 55250
   D. 55450

REFERENCE: CPT Assistant, June 1998, p 10
             CPT Assistant, July 1998, p 10

98. Laser destruction of penile condylomas
   A. 54057
   B. 17106
   C. 17270
   D. 54055

REFERENCE: CPT Book, 2009
             Smith, p 130

99. First-stage repair for hypospadias with skin flaps
   A. 54300
   B. 54308; 14040
   C. 54322
   D. 54304

REFERENCE: CPT Book, 2009

100. Priapism operation with spongiosum shunt
   A. 54450
   B. 54352
   C. 54430
   D. 55899

REFERENCE: CPT Book, 2009

Surgery—Female Genital System

101. Patient was admitted to the hospital with sharp pelvic pains. A pelvic ultrasound was ordered and the results showed a possible ovarian cyst. The patient was taken to the operating room where a laparoscopic destruction of two corpus luteum cysts was performed.
   A. 49321
   B. 58925
   C. 58561
   D. 58662

REFERENCE: Buck, p 256-257

102. Patient was admitted with a cystocele and rectocele. An anterior colporrhaphy was performed.
   A. 57250
   B. 57260
   C. 57240
   D. 57110

REFERENCE: Buck, p 250

103. Patient has a Bartholin's gland cyst that was marsupialized.
   A. 54640
   B. 10060
   C. 58999
   D. 56440

REFERENCE: CPT Book, 2009

104. Patient is at a fertility clinic and undergoes intrauterine embryo transplant.
    A. 58679   C. 58323
    B. 58322   D. 58974

REFERENCE: CPT Book, 2009

105. Patient has been diagnosed with carcinoma of the vagina and she has a radical vaginectomy with complete removal of the vaginal wall.
    A. 57107   C. 58150
    B. 57110   D. 57111

REFERENCE: Buck, p 249-250

106. Patient has been diagnosed with uterine fibroids and undergoes a total abdominal hysterectomy with bilateral salpingo-oophorectomy.
    A. 58200   C. 58262
    B. 58150   D. 58150; 58720

REFERENCE: Buck, p 253
              McHugh,p 370-371
              Smith, p 136

107. Hysteroscopy with D&C and polypectomy
    A. 58563   C. 58120; 58100; 58555
    B. 58558   D. 58558; 58120

REFERENCE: Buck, p 254-256
              Green, p 661
              Smith, p 135

108. Laparoscopic tubal ligation utilizing Endoloop
    A. 58670   C. 58671
    B. 58615   D. 58611

REFERENCE: Buck, p 256-257
              Green, p 662

109. Laser destruction extensive herpetic lesions of the vulva
    A. 17106   C. 56515
    B. 17004   D. 56501

REFERENCE: CPT Book, 2009

110. Patient undergoes hysteroscopy with excision uterine fibroids
    A. 58545   C. 58561
    B. 58140   D. 58140; 49320

REFERENCE: Buck, p 254-256
              Smith, p 135

Surgery—Maternity Care and Delivery

111. Attempted vaginal delivery in a previous cesarean section patient, which resulted in a repeat cesarean section.
    A. 59409
    B. 59612
    C. 59620
    D. 59514

REFERENCE: Buck, p 259-260
              Green, p 666
              Smith, p 136

112. Patient is admitted to the hospital following an ultrasound at 25 weeks which revealed fetal pleural effusion. A fetal thoracentesis was performed.
    A. 59074
    B. 32421
    C. 32422
    D. 76815

REFERENCE: CPT Assistant, May 2004, p 3-4

113. Patient in late stages of labor arrives at the hospital. Her OB physician is not able to make the delivery and the house physician delivers the baby vaginally. Primary care physician resumes care after delivery. Code the delivery.
    A. 59409
    B. 59612
    C. 59620
    D. 59400

REFERENCE: Buck, p 259-260

114. Patient is 24 weeks' pregnant and arrives in the emergency room following an automobile accident. No fetal movement or heartbeat noted. Patient is taken to the OB ward where prostaglandin is given to induce abortion.
    A. 59200
    B. 59855
    C. 59821
    D. 59410

REFERENCE: Green, p 666
              Buck, p 262

115. Patient is 6 weeks' pregnant and complains of left-sided abdominal pains. Patient is suspected of having an ectopic pregnancy. Patient has a laparoscopic salpingectomy with removal of the ectopic tubal pregnancy.
    A. 59120
    B. 59200
    C. 59121
    D. 59151

REFERENCE: CPT Book, 2009

116. Cesarean delivery with antepartum and postpartum care
    A. 59610
    B. 59514
    C. 59400
    D. 59510

REFERENCE: Buck, p 259-260
              Smith, p 136

117. A pregnant patient has an incompetent cervix which was repaired using a vaginal cerclage.
    A. 57700
    B. 57531
    C. 59320
    D. 53902

REFERENCE: CPT Book, 2009

118. A DandC is performed for postpartum hemorrhage.
    A. 59160
    B. 58120
    C. 58558
    D. 58578

REFERENCE: Buck, p 261

119. Hysterotomy for hydatidifom mole and tubal ligation
    A. 58285; 58600
    B. 58150; 58605
    C. 51900; 58605
    D. 59100; 58611

REFERENCE: CPT Book, 2009

120. D and C performed for patient with diagnosis of incomplete abortion at 8 weeks.
    A. 59812
    B. 59820
    C. 58120
    D. 59160

REFERENCE: Buck, p 262

Surgery—Endocrine System

121. Patient comes in for a percutaneous needle biopsy of the thyroid gland.
    A. 60000
    B. 60270
    C. 60699
    D. 60100

REFERENCE: CPT Assistant, June 1997, p 5

122. Laparoscopic adrenalectomy, complete
    A. 60650
    B. 60650-50
    C. 60659
    D. 60540

REFERENCE: CPT Book, 2009

123. Left carotid artery excision for tumor of carotid body
    A. 60650
    B. 60600
    C. 60605
    D. 60699

REFERENCE: Buck, p 317

124. Patient undergoes total thyroidectomy with parathyroid autotransplantation.
    A. 60240; 60512
    B. 60520; 60500
    C. 60260; 60512
    D. 60650; 60500

REFERENCE: Buck, p 317- 318

125. Unilateral partial thyroidectomy
   A. 60252   C. 60220
   B. 60210   D. 60520

REFERENCE: Buck, p 317-318

Surgery—Nervous System

126. Patient comes in through the emergency room with a wound that was caused by an electric saw. Patient is taken to the operating room where two ulna nerves are sutured.
   A. 64837   C. 64836; 64837
   B. 64892; 69990 D. 64856; 64859

REFERENCE: Buck, p 324

127. Laminectomy and excision of intradural lumbar lesion
   A. 63272   C. 63282
   B. 63267   D. 63252

REFERENCE: CPT Book, 2009

128. Patient comes in for steroid injection for lumbar herniated disk. Marcaine and Aristocort were injected into the L2-L3 space.
   A. 64520   C. 62311
   B. 64483   D. 64714

REFERENCE: CPT Assistant, September 1997, p 10
              Smith, p 141-142

129. Patient with Parkinson's disease is admitted for insertion of a brain neurostimulator pulse generator with one electrode array.
   A. 61885   C. 61888
   B. 61850; 61863 D. 61867; 61870

REFERENCE: CPT Assistant, April 2001, p 8-9
              CPT Assistant, June 2000, p 4, 12

130. Patient has rhinorrhea which requires repair of the CSF leak with craniotomy.
   A. 63707   C. 62100
   B. 63709   D. 62010

REFERENCE: CPT Book, 2009

131. Patient has metastatic brain lesions. Patient undergoes stereotactic radiosurgery gamma knife of two lesions.
   A. 61533   C. 61796; 61797
   B. 61500   D. 61796

REFERENCE: CPT Book, 2009

132. Patient has right sacroiliac joint dysfunction and requires a right S2-S3 paravertebral facet joint anesthetic nerve block.
    A. 62311   C. 64483
    B. 64475   D. 64520

REFERENCE: CPT Assistant, November 1999, p 33, 37
              CPT Assistant, February 2000, p 4
              CPT Assistant, September 2004, p 3
              Smith, p 141-142

133. Patient requires repair of a 6 cm meningocele.
    A. 63700   C. 63180
    B. 63709   D. 63702

REFERENCE: CPT Book, 2009

134. Patient comes in through the emergency room with a laceration of the posterior tibial nerve. Patient is taken to the operating room where the nerve requires transposition and suture.
    A. 64856   C. 64840; 64874
    B. 64831; 64832; 64876   D. 64834; 64859; 64872

REFERENCE: Buck, p 324

Surgery—Eye and Ocular Adnexa

135. Patient returns to the physician's office complaining of obscured vision. Patient has had cataract surgery 6 months prior. Patient requires laser discission of secondary cataract.
    A. 66821   C. 67835
    B. 64831   D. 66830

REFERENCE: Smith, p 146-147

136. Patient undergoes enucleation of left eye and muscles were reattached to an implant.
    A. 65135-LT   C. 65730-LT
    B. 65105-LT   D. 65103-LT

REFERENCE: CPT Book, 2009

137. Patient suffers from strabismus and requires surgery. Recession of the lateral rectus (horizontal) muscle with adjustable sutures was performed.
    A. 67340; 67500   C. 67332; 67334
    B. 67314; 67320   D. 67311; 67335

REFERENCE: CPT Book, 2009
              CPT Assistant, Summer 1993, p 20
              CPT Assistant, March 1997, p 5
              CPT Assistant, November 1998, p 1
              CPT Assistant, September 2002, p 10
              Smith, p 149

138. Radial keratotomy
   A. 92070   C. 65767
   B. 65855   D. 65771

REFERENCE: Green, p 686

139. Correction of trichiasis by incision of lid margin
   A. 67840   C. 67835
   B. 67830   D. 67850

REFERENCE: CPT Book, 2009

140. Patient undergoes ocular resurfacing construction utilizing stem cell allograft from a cadaver.
   A. 67320   C. 68371
   B. 66999   D. 65781

REFERENCE: CPT Assistant, May 2004, p 9-11

141. Aphakia penetrating corneal transplant
   A. 65755   C. 65750
   B. 65730   D. 65765

REFERENCE: CPT Book, 2009

142. Lagophthalmos correction with implantation using gold weight
   A. 67912   C. 67901
   B. 67911   D. 67121

REFERENCE: CPT Assistant, May 2004, p 12

143. Lacrimal fistula closure
   A. 68760   C. 68700
   B. 68761   D. 68770

REFERENCE: CPT Book, 2009

Surgery—Auditory

144. Patient comes into the office for removal of impacted earwax.
   A. 69210   C. 69222
   B. 69200   D. 69000

REFERENCE: Buck, p 331
              Green, p 691

145. Patient with a traumatic rupture of the eardrum. Repaired with tympanoplasty with incision of the mastoid. Repair of ossicular chain not required.
   A. 69641   C. 69642
   B. 69646   D. 69635

REFERENCE: CPT Book, 2009

146. Patient came in for excision of a middle ear lesion.
    A. 11440   C. 69552
    B. 69540   D. 69535

REFERENCE: CPT Book, 2009

147. Patient with chronic otitis media requiring eustachian tube catheterization
    A. 69400   C. 69421
    B. 69424   D. 69405

REFERENCE: CPT Book, 2009

148. Modified radical mastoidectomy
    A. 69511   C. 69635
    B. 69505   D. 69641

REFERENCE: CPT Book, 2009

149. Decompression internal auditory canal
    A. 69979   C. 69970
    B. 69915   D. 69960

REFERENCE: CPT Book, 2009

150. Myringoplasty
    A. 69620   C. 69610
    B. 69635   D. 69420

REFERENCE: CPT Assistant, March 2001, p 10

151. Insertion of cochlear device inner ear
    A. 69711   C. 69930
    B. 69949   D. 69960; 69990

REFERENCE: CPT Book, 2009

152. Patient with Bell's palsy requiring a total facial nerve decompression
    A. 64742   C. 69955
    B. 64771   D. 64864

REFERENCE: CPT Book, 2009

153. Drainage of simple external ear abscess
    A. 69000   C. 10060
    B. 69100   D. 69020

REFERENCE: CPT Assistant, October 1997, p 11
              CPT Assistant, October 1999, p 10

Radiology

154. Administration of initial oral radionuclide therapy for hyperthyroidism
     A. 78015
     B. 77402
     C. 78099
     D. 79005

REFERENCE: Buck, p 363-364

155. Patient comes into the outpatient department at the local hospital for an MRI of the cervical spine with contrast. Patient is status post automobile accident.
     A. 72156
     B. 72142
     C. 72149
     D. 72126

REFERENCE: Buck, p 351-352
              Smith, p 162-163

156. Obstetric patient comes in for a pelvimetery with placental placement.
     A. 74710
     B. 76946
     C. 76805
     D. 76825

REFERENCE: CPT Book, 2009

157. Patient comes into his physician's office complaining of wrist pain. Physician sends the patient to the hospital for an arthrography. Code the complete procedure.
     A. 73115
     B. 73100
     C. 73110
     D. 25246; 73115

REFERENCE: Buck, p 351-352

158. Patient has carcinoma of the breast and undergoes proton beam delivery of radiation to the breast with a single port.
     A. 77523
     B. 77432
     C. 77520
     D. 77402

REFERENCE: Buck, p 361

159. CT scan of the head with contrast
     A. 70460
     B. 70542
     C. 70551
     D. 70470

REFERENCE: Buck, p 351-352
              Smith, p 162-163

160. Patient undergoes x-ray of the foot with three views.
     A. 73620
     B. 73610
     C. 73630
     D. 27648; 73615

REFERENCE: Buck, p 351-352
              Smith, p 162-163

161. Radiologist provides fluoroscopic guidance for facet joint injection.
     A. 71023
     B. 77002
     C. 76001
     D. 77003

REFERENCE: CPT Book, 2009

162. Pregnant female comes in for a complete fetal and maternal evaluation via ultrasound.
    A. 76856   C. 76811
    B. 76805   D. 76810

REFERENCE: Buck, p 355-357

163. Ultrasonic guidance for the needle biopsy of the liver. Code the complete procedure.
    A. 47000; 76942   C. 47000; 76999
    B. 47000; 76937   D. 47000; 77002

REFERENCE: Buck, p 350-352

Pathology and Laboratory

164. What code is used for a culture of embryos less than 4 days?
    A. 89251   C. 89268
    B. 89272   D. 89250

REFERENCE: CPT Assistant,, April 2004, p 2
              CPT Assistant, May 2004, p 16
              CPT Assistant, June 2004, p 9

165. Basic metabolic panel (calcium, total) and total bilirubin
    A. 80048; 82247   C. 80100
    B. 80053   D. 82239; 80400; 80051

REFERENCE: Buck, p 371-372
              Green, p 762
              Smith, p 174

166. Huhner test and semen analysis
    A. 89325   C. 89310
    B. 89258   D. 89300

REFERENCE: CPT Assistant, November 1997, p 36
              CPT Assistant, July 1998, p 10
              CPT Assistant, October 1998, p 1
              CPT Assistant, April 2004, p 3

167. Chlamydia culture
    A. 87110   C. 87118
    B. 87106   D. 87109; 87168

REFERENCE: Buck, p 377
              Green, p 770-771

168. Partial thromboplastin time utilizing whole blood
    A. 85732   C. 85245
    B. 85730   D. 85246

REFERENCE: Buck, p 376
              Green, p 766
              Smith, p 175

169. Pathologist bills for gross and microscopic examination of medial meniscus.
    A. 88300
    B. 88302; 88311
    C. 88325
    D. 88304

REFERENCE: Buck, p 378-379
                Smith, p 175

170. Cytopathology of cervical Pap smear with automated thin-layer preparation utilizing computer screening and manual rescreening under physician supervision.
    A. 88175
    B. 88148
    C. 88160; 88141
    D. 88161

REFERENCE: Buck, p 378-379
                CPT Assistant, July 2003, p 9
                CPT Assistant, March 2004, p 4

171. Pathologist performs a postmortem examination including brain of an adult. Tissue is being sent to the lab for microscopic examination.
    A. 88309
    B. 88025
    C. 88099
    D. 88028

REFERENCE: Buck, p 378-379
                Smith, p 175

172. Clotting factor VII
    A. 85220
    B. 85240
    C. 85362
    D. 85230

REFERENCE: Buck, p 376
                Green, p 766
                Smith, p 175

Medicine Section

173. IV push of one anti-neoplastic drug
    A. 96401
    B. 96409
    C. 96411
    D. 96413

REFERENCE: Buck, p 401-402
                Smith, p 223

174. One-half hour of IV chemotherapy by infusion followed by IV push of a different drug
    A. 96413
    B. 96413; 96411
    C. 96413; 96409
    D. 96409; 96411

REFERENCE: Buck, p 401-402
                Smith, p 223

175. Caloric vestibular test using air
    A. 92543; 92700
    B. 92543; 92543
    C. 92700
    D. 92543

REFERENCE: CPT Assistant, November 2004, p 10

176. Patient presents to the emergency room with chest pains. The patient is admitted as a 23-hour observation. The cardiologist orders cardiac workup and the patient undergoes left heart catheterization via the left femoral artery with visualization of the coronary arteries and left ventriculography. The physician interprets the report. Code the heart catheterization.

    A. 36245; 93514; 93545; 93540; 93555
    B. 93524; 93545; 93542; 93555; 93556
    C. 93510; 93545; 93543; 93555; 93556
    D. 93511; 93539; 93541; 93545; 93555

REFERENCE: Buck, p 232-235
                  Green, p 806-809
                  Smith, p 218-221

177. Mother brings her 1-year-old in for the influenza split virus vaccine. Physician discusses merits of the vaccine with the mother.

    A. 90658; 90472   C. 90703
    B. 90657; 90465   D. 90657

REFERENCE: Buck, p 385-387
                  CPT Assistant, April 2005, p 2-3
                  Green, p 790
                  Smith, p 210

178. Patient with hematochromatosis had a therapeutic phlebotomy performed on an outpatient basis.

    A. 99195   C. 36514
    B. 36522   D. 99199

REFERENCE: CPT Assistant, June 1996, p 10

179. A physician performs a PTCA with drug-eluting stent placement in the left anterior descending artery and angioplasty only in the right coronary artery.

    A. 92996; 92980   C.   93510; 92980; 92981
    B. 92980-LD; 92984-RC   D. 92982; 92996; 92981

REFERENCE: CPT Assistant, April 2005, p 14
                  Smith, p 216-217

180. Transesophageal echocardiography (TEE) with probe placement, image, and interpretation and report.

    A. 93307   C. 93312; 93313; 93314
    B. 93303; 93325   D. 93312

REFERENCE: CPT Assistant, December 1997, p 5
                  CPT Assistant, January 2000, p 10

181. Which code listed below would be used to report an esophageal electrogram during an EPS?

    A. 93600   C. 93612
    B. 93615   D. 93616

REFERENCE: CPT Assistant, April 2004, p 9
                  Smith, p 221

182. Cardioversion of cardiac arrhythmia by external forces
  A. 92961
  B. 92950
  C. 92960
  D. 92970

REFERENCE: CPT Assistant, Summer 1993, p 13
             CPT Assistant, November 1999, p 49
             CPT Assistant, June 2000, p 5
             CPT Assistant, November 2000, p 9
             CPT Assistant, July 2001, p 11

183. Osteopathic manipulative treatment to three body regions.
  A. 98926
  B. 98941
  C. 97110
  D. 97012

REFERENCE: Buck, p 404
             Green, p 821

184. Patient presents to the Respiratory Therapy Department and undergoes a pulmonary stress test. CO_2 production with O_2 uptake with recordings was also performed.
  A. 94450
  B. 94620
  C. 94002
  D. 94621

REFERENCE: CPT Assistant, November 1998, p 35
             CPT Assistant, January 1999, p 8
             CPT Assistant, August 2002, p 10

185. IV infusion of chemotherapy for 3 hours
  A. 96422, 96423, 96423
  B. 96409, 96411
  C. 96413, 96415, 96415
  D. 96413, 96413, 96413

REFERENCE: Buck, p 401-402
             Smith, p 223

For the following questions, you will be utilizing the codes provided for the scenarios. You will need to code appropriate ICD-9-CM and CPT-4 codes.

186. Patient presents to the hospital for debridement of a diabetic ulcer of the left ankle. The patient has a history of recurrent ulcers. Medication taken by the patient includes Diabeta and the patient was covered in the hospital with insulin sliding scales. The ulcer was debrided down to the bone.

250.70	Diabetes with peripheral circulatory disorders, type II, or unspecified
250.71	Diabetes with peripheral circulatory disorders, type I
250.80	Diabetes with other specified manifestations, type II, or unspecified
250.81	Diabetes with other specified manifestations, type I
707.06	Decubitus ulcer, ankle
707.09	Decubitus ulcer other site
11043	Debridement, skin, subcutaneous tissue and muscle
11044	Debridement, skin, subcutaneous tissue, muscle and bone

  A. 250.81, 707.06, 11044
  B. 250.71, 11043
  C. 250.80, 707.06, 11044
  D. 250.81, 250.70, 707.09, 11044

REFERENCE: Buck, p 130
             Brown, p 101-105

187. Patient presents to the emergency room following a fall from a tree. X-rays were ordered for the left upper arm which showed a fracture of the humerus shaft. The emergency room physician performed a closed reduction of the fracture and placed the patient in a long arm spica cast. Code the diagnoses and procedures, excluding the x-ray.

812.21	Fracture humerus, shaft, closed
812.31	Fracture, humerus, shaft, open
E884.9	Other fall from one level to another
24500	Closed treatment of humeral shaft fracture; without manipulation
24505	Closed treatment of humeral shaft fracture; with manipulation, with or without skeletal traction
24515	Open treatment of humeral shaft fracture with plate/screws, with or without cerclage
29065	Application, cast; shoulder to hand (long arm)
LT	Left side

A. 812.21, E884.9, 24505-LT
B. 812.21, 24515-LT

C. 812.21, E884.9, 24505-LT, 29065
D. 812.31, 24500-LT

REFERENCE: Buck, p 165-168
Smith, p 78-79
Brown, p 343-344

188. Patient was admitted with hemoptysis and underwent a bronchoscopy with transbronchial lung biopsy. Following the bronchoscopy the patient was taken to the operating room where a left lower lobe lobectomy was performed without complications. Pathology reported large cell carcinoma of the left lower lobe.

162.5	Malignant neoplasm of the lower lobe of the lung
162.8	Malignant neoplasm of other parts of bronchus or lung
162.9	Malignant neoplasm of the bronchus and lung, unspecified
31625	Bronchoscopy with biopsy, with or without fluoroscopic guidance
31628	Bronchoscopy with transbronchial lung biopsy, with or without fluoroscopic guidance
32405	Biopsy, lung or mediastinum, percutaneous needle
32440	Removal of lung, total pneumonectomy
32480	Removal of lung, other than total pneumonectomy, single lobe (lobectomy)
32484	Removal of lung, other than total pneumonectomy, single segment (segmentectomy)

A. 162.9, 31625
B. 162.5, 31628, 32480

C. 162.9, 32405, 32484
D. 162.8, 32440

REFERENCE: Green, p 540
Smith, p 92
CPT Assistant, June 2001, p 10
CPT Assistant, September 2004, p 9
CPT Assistant, June 2002, p 10

189. Patient was admitted for right upper quadrant pain. Workup included various x-rays that showed cholelithiasis. Patient was taken to the operating room where a laparoscopic cholecystectomy was performed. During the procedure, the physician was unable to visualize through the ports and an open cholecystectomy was elected to be performed. Intraoperative cholangiogram was performed. Pathology report states acute and chronic cholecystitis with cholelithiasis.

574.00	Calculus of gallbladder with acute cholecystitis without obstruction
574.10	Calculus of gallbladder with other cholecystitis without obstruction
789.01	Abdominal pain of the right upper quadrant
V64.41	Laparoscopic procedure converted to open procedure
47605	Cholecystectomy with cholangiography
47563	Laparoscopy, surgical; cholecystectomy with cholangiography

A. 789.01, 574.10, 47563
B. 789.01, 574.00, 574.10, 47563, 47605
C. 574.00, 574.10, V64.41, 47605
D. 574.00, 47563, 47605

REFERENCE: Brown, p 171
             Buck, p 306
             Hazelwood and Venable, p 181-182

190. Patient came to the hospital from a local nursing home for a PEG tube placement via EGD. Patient had neurogenic dysphagia and dominant hemiplegia due to prior CVA.

436	Acute, but ill-defined, cerebrovascular disease
438.21	Late effect of CVA with hemiplegia affecting dominant side
438.81	Late effect of CVA with apraxia
438.82	Late effect of CVA with dysphagia
787.29	Dysphagia, neurogenic
43219	Esophagoscopy, rigid or flexible with insertion of plastic tube or stent
43246	Upper gastrointestinal endoscopy of esophagus, stomach, and either the duodenum and/or jejunum with directed placement of percutaneous gastrostomy tube
44372	Small intestine endoscopy, enteroscopy beyond second portion of duodenum with placement of percutaneous jejunostomy tube

A. 438.81, 43219
B. 438.82, 438.21, 787.29, 43246

C. 436, 787.29, , 44372
D. 436, 43246

REFERENCE: Buck, p 299-302
             Brown, p 284-286
             Hazelwood and Venable, p 153-154
             Smith, p 109

191. Patient presents to the emergency room complaining of right forearm/elbow pain after racquetball last night. Patient states that he did not fall, but overworked his arm. Past medical history is negative and the physical examination reveals the patient is unable to supinate. A four-1view x-ray of the right elbow is performed and is negative. The physician signs the patient out with right elbow sprain. Prescription of Motrin is given to the patient.

841.2	Sprain of radiohumeral joint
841.8	Sprain of other specified sites of the elbow and forearm
841.9	Sprain of unspecified site of the elbow and forearm
E927.2	Excessive physical exertion from prolonged activity
E928.9	Unspecified accident
73040	X-ray of shoulder, arthrography radiological supervision and interpretation
73070	X-ray of elbow, two views
73080	X-ray of elbow, complete, minimum of three views
99281	E/M visit to emergency room—problem-focused history, problem-focused exam, straightforward medical decision.
99282	E/M visit to emergency room—expanded problem-focused history, expanded problem-focused exam, medical decision of low complexity

A. 841.8, 73080
B. 841.9, E928.9, 99281, 73070

C. 841.2, 73080, 99282, 73040
D. 841.9, E927.2, 99281, 73080

REFERENCE: CPT Book, 2009
Brown, p 335-337
Smith, p 162-163, 200

192. A physician orders a lipid panel on a 54-year-old male with hypercholesterolemia, hypertension, and a family history of heart disease. The lab employee in his office performs and reports the total cholesterol and HDL cholesterol only.

272.0	Pure hypercholesterolemia
401.9	Essential hypertension, unspecified
402.90	Hypertensive heart disease, unspecified, without heart failure
V17.49	Family history of other cardiovascular disease
80061	Lipid panel; This panel must include the following: Cholesterol, serum, total (82465); Lipoprotein, direct measurement, high density cholesterol (HDL cholesterol) (83718); Triglycerides (84478)
82465	Cholesterol, serum or whole blood, total
83718	Lipoprotein, direct measurement; high density cholesterol (HDL cholesterol)
84478	Triglycerides
52	Reduced services

A. 272.0, 80061-52
B. 272.0, 401.9, V17.49, 80061-52
C. 272.0, 401.9, V17.49, 82465, 83718
D. 272.0, 402.90, 82465, 83718

REFERENCE: Buck, p 372
Green, p 762
Smith, p 174

193. Chronic nontraumatic rotator cuff tear. Arthroscopic subacromial decompression with mini-open rotator cuff repair.

726.10	Disorders of bursae and tendons in shoulder region, unspecified
727.61	Complete rupture of rotator cuff, nontraumatic
840.4	Sprains and strains of rotator cuff (capsule)
23410	Repair of ruptured musculotendinous cuff (e.g., rotator cuff); open, acute
23412	Repair of ruptured musculotendinous cuff (e.g. rotator cuff) open; chronic
29821	Arthroscopy, shoulder, surgical; synovectomy, complete
29823	Arthroscopy, shoulder, surgical; debridement, extensive
29826	Arthroscopy, shoulder, surgical; decompression of subacromial space with partial acromioplasty, with or without coracoacromial release
29827	Arthroscopy, shoulder, surgical; with rotator cuff repair

A. 840.4, 726.10, 29823　　　　C. 840.4, 29826, 29821
B. 727.61, 29826, 23412　　　　D. 727.61, 23410

REFERENCE:　Buck, 181-182
　　　　　　　Smith, p 82

194. The patient is on vacation and presents to a physician's office with a lacerated finger. The physician repairs the laceration and gives a prescription for pain control and has the patient follow up with his primary physician when he returns home. The physician fills out the superbill as a problem-focused history and examination with straightforward medical decision making. Also checked is a laceration repair for a 1.5 cm finger wound.

99201	New patient office visit with a problem-focused history, problem-focused examination and straightforward medical decision making
99212	Established patient office visit with a problem-focused history, problem-focused examination and straightforward medical decision making
12001	Simple repair of superficial wounds of scalp, neck, axillae, external genitalia, trunk and/or extremities (including hands and feet); 2.5 cm or less
13131	Repair, complex, forehead, cheeks, chin, mouth, neck, axillae, genitalia, hands and/or feet; 1.1 cm to 2.5 cm

A. 99212; 13131　　　　C. 99212; 12001
B. 12001　　　　　　　　D. 99201; 12001

REFERENCE:　Buck, p 48-50, 141-145
　　　　　　　Green, p 380, 483-484
　　　　　　　Smith, p 60-61, 180

195. A 69-year-old established female patient presents to the office with chronic obstructive lung disease, congestive heart failure, and hypertension. The physician conducts a comprehensive history and physical examination and makes a medical decision of moderate complexity. Physician admits the patient from the office to the hospital for acute exacerbation of CHF.

428.0	Congestive heart failure, unspecified
402.91	Hypertensive heart disease, with congestive heart failure
401.9	Essential hypertension, unspecified
401.1	Essential hypertension, benign
496	Chronic obstructive pulmonary disease
99212	Established office visit for problem-focused history and exam, straightforward medical decision making
99214	Established office visit for a detailed history and exam, moderate medical decision making
99222	Initial hospital care for comprehensive history and exam, moderate medical decision making
99223	Initial hospital care for comprehensive history and exam, high medical decision making

A. 402.91; 496; 99214
B. 428.0; 496; 401.1; 99223
C. 428.0; 496; 401.9; 99222
D. 402.91; 496; 401.1; 99212

REFERENCE: Buck, p 52
Brown, p 288-289
Green, p 380-381
Smith, p 198

196. Established 42-year-old patient comes into your office to obtain vaccines required for his trip to Sri Lanka. The nurse injects intramuscularly the following vaccines: hepatitis A and B vaccines, cholera vaccine, and yellow fever vaccine. As the coding specialist, what would you report on the CMS 1500 form?
A. office visit, hepatitis A and B vaccine, cholera vaccine and yellow fever vaccine
B. office visit, intramuscular injection; HCPCS Level II codes
C. office visit; administration of two or more single vaccines; vaccine products for hepatitis A and B, cholera, and yellow fever
D. Administration of two or more single vaccines; vaccine products for hepatitis A and B, cholera, and yellow fever.

REFERENCE: Buck, p 385-387
Green, p 790
Smith, p 210

197. Patient presents to the operating room where the physician performed, using imaging guidance, a percutaneous breast biopsy utilizing a rotating biopsy device.

19000	Puncture aspiration of cyst of breast
19103	Biopsy of breast; percutaneous, automated vacuum assisted or rotating biopsy device, using imaging guidance
19120	Excision of cyst, fibroadenoma, or other benign or malignant tumor, aberrant breast tissue, duct lesion, nipple or areolar lesion (except 19300), open, male or female, one or more lesions
19125	Excision of breast lesion identified by preoperative placement of radiological marker, open; single lesion
19295	Image guided placement, metallic localization clip, percutaneous, during breast biopsy (List separately in addition to code for primary procedure)

A. 19103
B. 19125; 19295

C. 19120
D. 19000

REFERENCE: CPT Assistant, Jan 2001, page 10-11
Buck, p 158
Green, p 494
Smith, p 73-74

198. Facelift utilizing the SMAS flap technique

15788	Chemical peel, facial; epidermal
15825	Rhytidectomy; neck with platysmal tightening (platysmal flap, P-flap)
15828	Rhytidectomy; cheek, chin, and neck
15829	Rhytidectomy; superficial musculoaponeurotic system (SMAS) flap

A. 15825
B. 15788

C. 15829
D. 15828

REFERENCE: Buck, p 151

199. Patient presents to the operating room for a secondary Achilles tendon repair.

27599	Unlisted procedure, femur or knee
27650	Repair, primary, open or percutaneous, ruptured Achilles tendon
27654	Repair, secondary, Achilles tendon, with or without graft
27698	Repair, secondary, disrupted ligament, ankle, collateral (e.g., Watson-Jones procedure)

A. 27599
B. 27654

C. 27650
D. 27698

REFERENCE: CPT Book, 2009

200. Tracheostoma revision with flap rotation

31613	Tracheostoma revision; simple, without flap rotation
31614	Tracheostoma revision; complex, with flap rotation
31750	Tracheoplasty; cervical
31830	Revision of tracheostomy scar

A. 31830   C. 31614
B. 31750   D. 31613

REFERENCE: Buck, p 198-200

201. Patient complains of frequent temporal headaches and the physician suspects temporal arteritis. Patient underwent temporal artery biopsy.

784.0	Headache
446.5	Temporal arteritis
37600	Ligation; external carotid artery
37609	Ligation or biopsy, temporal artery
37615	Ligation, major artery (e.g., post-traumatic, rupture); neck

A. 784.0; 37615   C. 446.5; 37600
B. 784.0; 37609   D. 446.5; 37609

REFERENCE: CPT Book, 2009

202. Blood transfusion of three units of packed red blood cells

36430	Transfusion, blood or blood components
36455	Exchange transfusion; blood, other than newborn
36460	Transfusion, intrauterine, fetal

A. 36430   C. 36460
B. 36430; 36430; 36430   D. 36455

REFERENCE: CPT Book, 2009

203. Two-year-old patient returns to the hospital for cleft palate repair where a secondary lengthening procedure takes place.

40720	Plastic repair of cleft lip/nasal deformity; secondary, by recreation of defect and reclosure
42145	Palatopharyngoplasty
42220	Palatoplasty for cleft palate; secondary lengthening procedure
42226	Lengthening of palate, and pharyngeal flap

A. 40720   C. 42226
B. 42220   D. 42145

REFERENCE: CPT Book, 2009

204. Tonsillectomy on a 14-year-old

42820	Tonsillectomy and adenoidectomy; under age 12
42821	Tonsillectomy and adenoidectomy; age 12 or over
42825	Tonsillectomy, primary or secondary; under age 12
42826	Tonsillectomy, primary or secondary; age 12 or over

A. 42820
B. 42821
C. 42825
D. 42826

REFERENCE: Buck, p 298
Green, p 612

205. Laparoscopic repair of umbilical hernia

49580	Repair umbilical hernia, under age 5 years, reducible
49585	Repair umbilical hernia, age 5 years or over, reducible
49562	Laparoscopy, surgical, repair, ventral, umbilical, spigelian or epigastric hernia (includes mesh insertion when performed); reducible
49564	Laparoscopy, surgical, repair, incisional hernia (includes mesh insertion when performed); reducible

A. 49580
B. 49564
C. 49585
D. 49562

REFERENCE: CPT Book, 2009

206. Excision of simple internal and external hemorrhoids

46221	Hemorrhoidectomy, by simple ligature (e.g., rubber band)
46255	Hemorrhoidectomy, internal and external, simple
46260	Hemorrhoidectomy, internal and external, complex or extensive
46945	Ligation of internal hemorrhoids; single procedure

A. 46255
B. 46945
C. 46221
D. 46260

REFERENCE: CPT Book, 2009

207. Ureterolithotomy completed laparoscopically

50600	Ureterotomy with exploration or drainage (separate procedure)
50945	Laparoscopy, surgical ureterolithotomy
52325	Cystourethroscopy; with fragmentation of ureteral calculus
52352	Cystourethroscopy, with urethroscopy and/or pyeloscopy; with removal or manipulation of calculus (ureteral catheterization is included)

A. 52352
B. 52325
C. 50600
D. 50945

REFERENCE: CPT Assistant, November 1999, p 26
CPT Assistant, May 2000, p 4
CPT Assistant, October 2001, p 8

208. Patient undergoes partial nephrectomy for carcinoma of the kidney.

50220	Nephrectomy, including partial ureterectomy, any open approach including rib resection
50234	Nephrectomy with total ureterectomy and bladder cuff; through same incision
50240	Nephrectomy, partial
50340	Recipient nephrectomy (separate procedure)

A. 50234
B. 50220

C. 50340
D. 50240

REFERENCE: Buck, p 279-282

209. Patient presents to the operating room for fulguration of bladder tumors. The cystoscope was inserted and entered the urethra which was normal. Bladder tumors measuring approximately 1.5 cm were removed.

50957	Ureteral endoscopy through established ureterostomy, with or without irrigation, instillation, or ureteropyelography, exclusive of radiologic service; with fulguration and/or incision, with or without biopsy
51530	Cystotomy; for excision of bladder tumor
52214	Cystourethroscopy, with fulguration of trigone, bladder neck, prostatic fossa, urethra, or periurethral glands
52234	Cystourethroscopy, with fulguration (including cryosurgery or laser surgery) and/or resection of small bladder tumor(s) (0.5 up to 2.0 cm)

A. 52234
B. 50957

C. 52214
D. 51530

REFERENCE: Buck, p 289-290
            Smith, p 124

210. Excision of Cowper's gland

53220	Excision or fulguration of carcinoma of urethra
53250	Excision of bulbourethral gland (Cowper's gland)
53260	Excision or fulguration; urethral polyp(s), distal urethra
53450	Urethromeatoplasty, with mucosal advancement

A. 53250
B. 53450

C. 53260
D. 53220

REFERENCE: CPT Book, 2009

211. Placement of double-J stent

52320	Cystourethroscopy (including ureteral catheterization); with removal of ureteral calculus
52330	Cystourethroscopy; with manipulation, without removal of ureteral calculus
52332	Cystourethroscopy with insertion of indwelling ureteral stent (e.g. Gibbons or double-J type)
52341	Cystourethroscopy, with treatment of ureteral stricture (e.g. balloon dilation, laser electrocautery, and incision)

A. 52341
B. 52320

C. 52330; 52332
D. 52332

REFERENCE: Buck, p 289-290
             Smith, p 124

212. Closure of traumatic kidney injury.

13100	Repair, complex trunk, 1.1 cm to 2.5 cm
50400	Pyeloplasty (Foley Y-pyeloplasty), plastic operation on renal pelvis, with or without plastic operation on ureter, nephropexy, nephrostomy, pyelostomy or ureteral splinting; simple
50500	Nephrorrhaphy, suture of kidney wound or injury
50520	Closure of nephrocutaneous or pyelocutaneous fistula

A. 50520
B. 13100

C. 50500
D. 50400

REFERENCE: CPT Book, 2009

213. Litholapaxy, 3.0 cm calculus

50590	Lithotripsy, extracorporeal shock wave
52317	Litholapaxy, simple or small (less than 2.5 cm)
52318	Litholapaxy, complicated or large (over 2.5 cm)
52353	Cystourethroscopy, with ureteroscopy and/or pyeloscopy; with lithotripsy

A. 52353
B. 50590

C. 52318
D. 52317

REFERENCE: CPT Book, 2009

214. Patient presented to the operating room where an incision was made in the epigastric region for a repair of ureterovisceral fistula.

50520	Closure of nephrocutaneous or pyelocutaneous fistula
50525	Closure of nephrovisceral fistula, including visceral repair; abdominal approach
50526	Closure of nephrovisceral fistula including visceral repair; thoracic approach
50930	Closure of ureterovisceral fistula (including visceral repair)

A. 50526
B. 50930

C. 50520
D. 50525

REFERENCE: CPT Book, 2009

215. Amniocentesis

57530	Trachelectomy, amputation of cervix (separate procedure)
57550	Excision of cervical stump, vaginal approach
59000	Amniocentesis, diagnostic
59200	Insertion of cervical dilator (separate procedure)

A. 59000   C. 57550
B. 59200   D. 57530

REFERENCE: Buck, p 260

216. Excision of thyroid adenoma

60100	Biopsy thyroid, percutaneous core needle
60200	Excision of cyst or adenoma of thyroid, or transection of isthmus
60210	Partial thyroid lobectomy, unilateral; with or without isthmusectomy
60280	Excision of thyroglossal duct cyst or sinus

A. 60210   C. 60280
B. 60200   D. 60100

REFERENCE: CPT Book, 2009

217. Patient is admitted to the hospital with facial droop and left-sided paralysis. CT scan of the brain shows subdural hematoma. Burr holes were performed to evacuate the hematoma.

432.1	Subdural hematoma
852.20	Subdural hemorrhage following injury without mention of open intra-cranial wound, unspecified state of unconsciousness
61150	Burr hole(s) or trephine; with drainage of brain abscess or cyst
61154	Burr hole(s) with evacuation and/or drainage of hematoma, extradural or subdural
61156	Burr hole(s); with aspiration of hematoma or cyst, intracerebral
61314	Craniectomy or craniotomy for evacuation of hematoma, infratentorial; extradural or subdural

A. 852.20; 61156   C. 432.1; 61154
B. 432.1; 61314   D. 852.20; 61150

REFERENCE: Buck, p 319
              Brown, 342-343

218. Spinal tap

62268	Percutaneous aspiration, spinal cord or syrinx
62270	Spinal puncture, lumbar diagnostic
62272	Spinal puncture, therapeutic, for drainage of cerebrospinal fluid (by needle or catheter)
64999	Unlisted procedure, nervous system

A. 62272   C. 62268
B. 64999   D. 62270

REFERENCE: Buck, p 322-323

219. Injection of anesthesia for nerve block of the brachial plexus

64413	Injection, anesthetic agent; cervical plexus
64415	Injection, anesthetic agent; brachial plexus, single
64510	Injection, anesthetic agent; stellate ganglion (cervical sympathetic)
64530	Injection, anesthetic agent; celiac plexus, with or without radiologic monitoring

A. 64415
B. 64413

C. 64530
D. 64510

REFERENCE: Buck, p 324

220. Repair of retinal detachment with vitrectomy

67040	Vitrectomy, mechanical, pars plana approach; with endolaser panretinal photocoagulation
67105	Repair of retinal detachment, one or more sessions; photocoagulation, with or without drainage of subretinal fluid
67108	Repair of retinal detachment; with vitrectomy, any method, with or without air or gas tamponade, focal endolaser photocoagulation, cryotherapy, drainage of subretinal fluid, scleral buckling, and/or removal of lens by same technique
67112	Repair of retinal detachment; by scleral buckling or vitrectomy, on patient having previous ipsilateral retinal detachment repair(s) using scleral buckling or vitrectomy techniques

A. 67112
B. 67105

C. 67108
D. 67040

REFERENCE: CPT Assistant, October 2002, p 8

221. SPECT bone imaging

77080	Dual energy x-ray absorptiometry (DXA), bone density study, one or more sites; axial skeleton (e.g. hips, pelvis, spine)
76977	Ultrasound bone density measurement and interpretation, peripheral site(s), any method
78300	Bone and/or joint imaging; limited area
78320	Bone and/or joint imaging; tomographic (SPECT)

A. 76977
B. 78320

C. 77080
D. 76977

REFERENCE: CPT Book, 2009
CPT Assistant, June 2003, p 11

222. Vitamin B$_{12}$

82180	Ascorbic acid (vitamin C, blood)
82607	Cyanocobalamin (vitamin B12)
84590	Vitamin A
84591	Vitamin, not otherwise specified

A. 84590　　　　　　　　　C. 84591
B. 82180　　　　　　　　　D. 82607

REFERENCE:　Green, p 766-767
　　　　　　　Smith, p 175

223. Hepatitis C antibody.

86803	Hepatitis C antibody
86804	Hepatitis C antibody; confirmatory test (e.g., immunoblot)
87520	Infectious agent detection by nucleic acid (DNA or RNA); hepatitis C, direct probe technique
87522	Infectious agent detection by nucleic acid (DNA or RNA); hepatitis C, quantification

A. 86804　　　　　　　　　C. 87522
B. 86803　　　　　　　　　D. 87520

REFERENCE:　Buck, p 376
　　　　　　　Green, p 768

224. Creatinine clearance.

82550	Creatine kinase (CK), (CPK); total
82565	Creatinine; blood
82575	Creatinine; clearance
82585	Cryofibrinogen

A. 82550　　　　　　　　　C. 82575
B. 82565　　　　　　　　　D. 82585

REFERENCE:　Buck, p 375
　　　　　　　Green, p 766-767
　　　　　　　Smith, p 175

225. Comprehensive electrophysiologic evaluation (EPS) with induction of arrhythmia.

93618	Induction of arrhythmia by electrical pacing
93619	Comprehensive electrophysiologic evaluation with right atrial pacing and recording, right ventricular pacing and recording, His bundle recording, including insertion and repositioning of multiple electrode catheters, without induction or attempted induction of arrhythmia
93620	Comprehensive electrophysiologic evaluation including insertion and repositioning of multiple electrode catheters with induction or attempted induction of arrhythmia; with right atrial pacing and recording, right ventricular pacing and recording, His bundle recording
+93623	Programmed stimulation and pacing after intravenous drug infusion (List separately in addition to code for primary procedure.)
93640	Electrophysiologic evaluation of single- or dual-chamber pacing cardioverter-defibrillator leads including defibrillation threshold evaluation (induction of arrhythmia, evaluation of sensing and pacing for arrhythmia termination) at time of initial implantation or replacement

A. 93618; 93620
B. 93620

C. 93640; 93623
D. 93619; 93620

REFERENCE: CPT Assistant, Summer 1994, p 12
CPT Assistant, August 1997, p 9
CPT Assistant, October 1997, p 10
CPT Assistant, July 1998, p 10

226. Patient presents to the hospital for a two-view chest x-ray for a cough. The radiology report comes back negative. What would be the correct codes to report to the insurance company?

786.2	Cough
786.3	Hemoptysis
V72.5	Radiology examination, not elsewhere classified
71010	Radiologic examination, chest; single view, frontal
71020	Radiologic examination, chest, two views, frontal and lateral
71035	Radiologic examination, chest, special views

A. V72.5; 71020
B. 786.2; 71020

C. V72.5; 71035
D. 786.2; 786.3, 71010

REFERENCE: Schraffenberger, p 497
CPT Book, 2009

227. Patient presents to the hospital for a three-view x-ray of the right shoulder. The diagnosis is shoulder pain and the radiology report states the patient has a dislocated shoulder. What would be the correct codes to report to the insurance company?

719.41	Shoulder pain
831.00	Closed dislocation shoulder, unspecified
831.01	Closed dislocation shoulder, anterior
73020	Radiologic examination, shoulder; one view
73030	Radiologic examination, shoulder; complete, minimum of two views
73060	Radiologic examination; humerus, minimum of two views
RT	Right side

A. 831.00; 73060-RT

B. 719.41; 73020-RT

C. 831.01; 73030-RT

D. 831.00; 73030-RT

REFERENCE: Brown, p 81-82
                        CPT Book, 2009

And now a few more CPT visits to code with your CPT book

228. A 32-year-old patient has a colonoscopy with removal of three polyps by snare. Moderate sedation was used and provided by the physician. The intraservice time was 30 minutes
   A. 45385; 45385-51; 45385-51
   B. 45385; 99144
   C. 45385
   D. 45385, 45385-51, 45385-51, 99144

REFERENCE: CPT Assistant, February 2006, p 9-10
   CPT Book, 2009

229. High-energy ESW of the lateral humeral epicondyle using general anesthesia
   A. 0019T
   B. 0101T
   C. 0102T
   D. 28890

REFERENCE: CPT Assistant, March 2006 p 2

230. Laparoscopic gastric restrictive procedure and placement of adjustable gastric band
   A. 43770
   B. 43800
   C. 43845
   D. 43846

REFERENCE: CPT Assistant, April 2006, p 2

231. Laparoscopic takedown of the splenic flexure and a partial colectomy with anastomosis
   A. 44204, 44213
   B. 44204
   C. 44213
   D. 44204, 44213

REFERENCE: CPT Assistant, April 2006, p 19

232. Laparoscopic submucosal removal of non-neoplastic lesion of the vocal cord with graft reconstruction. An operating microscope was used.
   A. 31546, 69990
   B. 31546, 20926
   C. 31546
   D. 31546, 20926-51

REFERENCE: CPT Assistant, May 2006, p 16-17

233. Laparoscopic removal and replacement of both a gastric band and the subcutaneous port components
   A. 43774, 43659
   B. 43659
   C. 43773
   D. 43848

REFERENCE: CPT Assistant, June 2006, p 16

Answer Key for CPT-4 Coding

1. C
2. A
3. B
4. C
5. D
6. C
7. D
8. B
9. B
10. C
11. D
12. B
13. A
14. B
15. D
16. B
17. C
18. A
19. D
20. C
21. C
22. B
23. B
24. C
25. B
26. C
27. A
28. D
29. B
30. C
31. D
32. A
33. D
34. A   Codes 10060 and 10140 are used for I&Ds of superficial abscesses.
35. C
36. C
37. D
38. B
39. A
40. B
41. A
42. D
43. C
44. A
45. D
46. C
47. A
48. D
49. A

50. B
51. A
52. B
53. D
54. B
55. C
56. C
57. C
58. A
59. A
60. B
61. D
62. B
63. A
64. D
65. A
66. B
67. C
68. A
69. A
70. D
71. C
72. D   Radiology codes would be used for the supervision and interpretation.
73. C
74. C
75. C
76. A
77. D
78. D
79. C
80. A
81. A
82. C
83. D
84. B
85. D
86. B
87. A
88. B
89. C
90. B
91. B
92. D
93. C
94. A
95. A
96. B

Answer Key for CPT-4 Coding

97.	C	148.	B
98.	A	149.	D
99.	D	150.	A
100.	C	151.	C
101.	D	152.	C
102.	C	153.	A
103.	D	154.	D
104.	D	155.	B
105.	D	156.	A
106.	B	157.	D
107.	B	158.	C
108.	C	159.	A
109.	C	160.	C
110.	C	161.	D
111.	C	162.	C
112.	A	163.	A
113.	A	164.	D
114.	B	165.	A
115.	D	166.	D
116.	D	167.	A
117.	C	168.	B
118.	A	169.	D
119.	D	170.	A
120.	A	171.	B
121.	D	172.	D
122.	A	173.	B
123.	C	174.	B
124.	A	175.	C

175. C — Code 92543 is for use when an irrigation substance is used.

125.	B	176.	C
126.	C	177.	B
127.	A	178.	A
128.	C	179.	B

179. B — Physicians use codes 92980 or 92981 for placement of drug eluting stents. Hospitals report placement of drug eluting stents with HCPCS Level II codes (G0290 or G0291).

129.	A	180.	D
130.	C	181.	B
131.	C	182.	C
132.	B	183.	A
133.	D	184.	D
134.	C	185.	C
135.	A	186.	C
136.	B	187.	A

187. A — Casting is included in the surgical procedure.

137.	D	188.	B
138.	D	189.	C
139.	B	190.	B
140.	D	191.	D
141.	C		
142.	A		
143.	D		
144.	A		
145.	D		
146.	B		
147.	D		

Answer Key for CPT-4 Coding

192. C   In order to use the code for the panel, every test must have been performed.

193. B   Code both the arthroscopic procedure and the open procedure. Both need to be reported because there were two separate procedures.

194. D

195. C   According to CPT guidelines, when a patient is admitted to the hospital on the same day as an office visit, the office visit is not billable. Code rules do not allow the use of 402.91 because the scenario given does not state that the patient has hypertensive heart disease.

196. D   According to the CPT coding guidelines for vaccines, only a separate identifiable Evaluation and Management code may be billed in addition to the vaccine. In this scenario, the patient was seen only for his vaccines. This guideline immediately eliminates all the other answers.

197. A
198. C
199 B
200. C
201. B
202. A   Report this code only once no matter how many units were given.

203. B
204. D
205. D

206. A
207. D
208. D
209. A
210. A
211. D
212. C
213. C
214. B
215. A
216. B
217. C   Codes starting with 852 are considered to be traumatic injuries. No injury was stated in the case, so 432.1, non-traumatic subdural hematoma, would be the appropriate code.

218. D
219. A
220. C
221. B
222. D
223. B
224. C
225. B
226. B
227. D
228. C   CPT designates certain procedures as including moderate sedation; therefore moderate sedation is included in the code for the removal of polyps.

229. C
230. A
231. D
232. C
233. B

REFERENCES

American Medical Association. *CPT Assistant.* Chicago: American Medical Association (AMA).

American Medical Association. (2009). *Physician's current procedural terminology (CPT) 2009, professional edition.* Chicago: American Medical Association (AMA).

Brown, F. (2009). *ICD-9-CM coding handbook 2009 with nswers.* Chicago: American Hospital Association (AHA).

Buck, C. J. (2007). *Step-by-step medical coding, 2007 edition.* St. Louis: Saunders Elsevier.

Frisch, B. (2007). *Correct coding for Medicare compliance and reimbursement.* New York: Thompson Delmar Learning.

Green, M. (2007). *3-2-1 code It.* New York: Thompson Delmar Learning.

Hazelwood, A., & Venable, C. (2009). *ICD-9-CM coding and reimbursement for physician services.* Chicago: American Health Information Management Association (AHIMA).

Johnson, S. L., and McHugh, C. S. (2006) *Understanding Medical Coding: "a comprehensive guide* (2nd ed.) New York: Thompson Delmar Learning.

Schraffenberger, L. A. (2009). *Basic ICD-9-CM coding.* Chicago: American Health Information Management Association (AHIMA).

Smith, G. (2008). *Basic CPT/HCPCS coding, 2008 edition.* Chicago: American Health Information Management Association (AHIMA).

X. Informatics and Information Systems

Nanette B. Sayles, EdD, RHIA, CCS, CHP, FAHIMA

Special Note

The Information Technology and Systems domains are very different for the RHIA and RHIT Examinations. Questions with only an RHIA competency begin at question 56. We advise that RHIT students also study these questions. It is always better to know more than less.

1. Dr. Brown insists on the new EHR assisting physicians in their decision-making process by using a technology that brings available information to the attention of the physician. This is called
   A. push technology.
   B. pull technology.
   C. workflow.
   D. tactical decision making.

REFERENCE: Johns, 2006, p 829

2. Your new release of information system has part of the computing on the workstation and part on the file server. What type of technology is being used?
   A. Internet
   B. client server
   C. LAN
   D. operating system

REFERENCE: Eichenwald-Maki and Petterson, p 29-30, 288
               Marreel and McLellan, p 8, 191
               Abdelhak, p 246-247
               Johns, 2006, p 768-769

3. Dr. Smith is entering a medication order in a CPOE. A window pops up and says,

> Patient is on beta-blocker, which is a contraindication for this medication. Do you want to order this medication? Yes or NO.

   This is an example of a(n)
   A. reminder.
   B. alert.
   C. allergy.
   D. structured entry.

REFERENCE: Eichenwald-Maki and Petterson, p 128, 130, 131-133, 287
               Marreel and McLellan, p 16
               Amatayakul, p 208

4. Barbara is being seen at a physician's office that she has never been to before. This physician practice is independently owned. She did not have to request copies of her medical records, but the physician has everything that she needs. The physician must be part of a(n)
   A. integrated health network.
   B. corporation.
   C. regional health information organization.
   D. electronic health record.

REFERENCE: Eichenwald-Maki and Petterson, 5-7
               McWay, p 39, 181-183
               Marreel and McLellan, p 39, 181-182
               Johns, 2006, p 124-126
               LaTour and Eichenwald-Maki, p 218

5. What types of software provide a front-end structure/interface that presents information in a familiar format leading to a natural style of interaction through the use of icons and a mouse?
   A. graphical user interface
   B. fiber optics
   C. assembly level language
   D. machine language

REFERENCE: Marreel and McLellan, p 196
              Abdelhak, p 120
              Johns, 2006, p 760
              LaTour and Eichenwald-Maki, p 548
              McWay, p 171

6. With data exchange standards, the ability to transfer data from one system to another system is called (page 137, 153)
   A. electronic data interchange.
   B. messaging standards.
   C. interfaces.
   D. interoperability.

REFERENCE: Eichenwald-Maki and Petterson, p 3
              Marreel and McLellan, p 75-76, 199
              Johns, 2006, p 974
              LaTour and Eichenwald-Maki, p 220

7. The technique used to identify patterns in data using fuzzy logic or neural networks is called
   A. genetic algorithms.
   B. data mining.
   C. online analytical processing.
   D. clinical data repository.

REFERENCE: McWay, p 176
              Marreel and McLellan, p 191
              Green and Bowie, p 248

8. Review the simplistic screen below. This is an example of how _____ data can be entered.

   ☐ Cardiac exam WNL

   ☐ Cardiac exam abnormal

      ☐ Murmur   ☐ Arrhythmia   ☐ Other

   A. unstructured
   B. structured
   C. nomenclature
   D. template

REFERENCE: Eichenwald-Maki and Petterson, p 35-37, 108
              Amatayakul, p 148

9. As database administrator, you have just added a foreign key to one of your tables. Why did you do this?

   A. the data element refers to ethnicity
   B. to indicate that it is a primary key in another table
   C. to ensure that each row is unique
   D. to separate two tables

REFERENCE: Johns, 2006, p 763
              LaTour and Eichenwald-Maki, p 114

10. The health care facility is testing all parts of the system, including volume, data flow, and screen design. This is called
    A. stress testing.
    B. acceptance testing.
    C. rigorous testing.
    D. final testing.

REFERENCE: LaTour and Eichenwald-Maki, p 235

11. You just used a scheduling system to schedule an appendectomy for Dr. Smith. The system automatically looked up how long it takes Dr. Smith to perform the surgery. It contacted the patient's insurance company to confirm that the procedure is covered by the patient's policy and notified materials management of the supplies that would be needed that day. This is an example of how _____ could work.
    A. reminders
    B. alerts
    C. OLAP
    D. clinical guidelines

REFERENCE: McWay, p 176
               Green and Bowie, p 248
               Amatayakul, p 217
               LaTour and Eichenwald-Maki, p 581

12. One of the problems facing National Health Information Network is:
    A. lack of interest in the electronic health record.
    B. intraoperability.
    C. lack of HIM professionals.
    D. multiple types of data collected.

REFERENCE: Eichenwald-Maki and Petterson, 5-7,
               McWay, p 175
               LaTour and Eichenwald-Maki, p 47

13. You have been hired to work with a computer-assisted coding initiative. The technology that you will be working with is:
    A. electronic data interchange
    B. intraoperability
    C. message standards
    D. natural language processing

REFERENCE: Eichenwald-Maki and Petterson, p 160
               McWay, p 132
               LaTour and Eichenwald-Maki, p 128
               Johns, 2006, p 803-804

14. Mary is designing a computer screen that will be used to collect patient demographic information. What input design should be utilized for the state field?
    A. icon
    B. dialog box
    C. menu
    D. free form text

REFERENCE: Eichenwald-Maki and Petterson, 33-35
               Abdelhak, p 332
               McWay, p 110

15. The hospital needs information system A to share information with information system B. The ability to exchange data between these two systems is known as
    A. electronic data interchange.
    B. interoperability.
    C. messaging standards.
    D. data exchange.

REFERENCE: McWay, p 181
               Eichenwald-Maki and Petterson, p 3

16. Which of the following tests how well new systems being implemented work with existing systems?
   A. volume test
   B. system test
   C. unit test
   D. integration test

REFERENCE: McWay, p 318-319
               Abdelhak, p 337

17. You are working with a database that is created from multiple databases being stored in a single database. This is a(n)
   A. electronic health record.
   B. personal health record.
   C. clinical data repository.
   D. health information exchange.

REFERENCE: McWay, p 175
               Marreel and McLellan, p 175
               Green and Bowie, p 95

18. At our integrated delivery system, the hospital and clinic have separate networks. There are times when they need to share information across the network. This can be accomplished with a
   A. gateway.
   B. hub.
   C. router.
   D. bridge.

REFERENCE: Marreel and McLellan, p 206
               Amatayakul, p 180
               Glandon, Smaltz, and Slovensky, p 154

19. The data on your hard drive was erased by a corrupted file that had been attached to an e-mail message. If you had _____ software, maybe this would not have happened.
   A. productivity
   B. utility
   C. virus
   D. encryption

REFERENCE: McWay, p 321
               Marreel and McLellan, p 156-157
               Johns, 2002, p 162

20. Your organization has many information systems from several different vendors. These systems need to share common information such as patient name and medical record number. Some data elements, such as service, may be stored differently in the different systems. You should consider using a(n)
   A. ASP.
   B. network.
   C. Internet.
   D. interface engine.

REFERENCE: Marreel and McLellan, p 198
               Amatayakul, p 258

21. You have just inserted data contained in a spreadsheet into your word processed document. This is an example of a(n) _____ system.
   A. integrated
   B. interfaced
   C. mapped
   D. graphical user interface

REFERENCE: Glandon, Smaltz, Slovensky, p 144
               McWay, p 171
               Marreel and McLellan, p 74-75

22. Dr. Smith goes to Hollywood Hospital's website and logs in. He sees a list of patients currently in the hospital, test results, and more. Ms. Brown, a patient of Dr. Smith who is having surgery next week, logs onto the same website and only sees the date and time of her preoperative visit. This is an example of:
   A. web portal
   B. single sign-on technology
   C. application service provider
   D. intranet

REFERENCE: LaTour and Eichenwald-Maki, p 58
McWay, p 321

23. Patient care can be improved through the use of technology. Which of the following is an example of how this happens?
   A. elimination of illegible orders
   B. scanning of medical record image
   C. redundant testing
   D. voice recognition

REFERENCE: McWay, p 328
Green and Bowie, p 83
Eichenwald-Maki and Petterson, p 144-146

24. In the RFP, you have asked for information regarding the amount of time that a vendor has been in business and the number of installations of the product under consideration. If you want to review this information, you would go to the _____ section.
   A. functional specifications.
   B. organizational profile.
   C. vendor information.
   D. licensing and contractual details.

REFERENCE: McWay, p 344
Marreel and McLellan, p 109-110
Amatayakul, p 262
Murphy, p 135
Abdelhak, p 349

25. Your facility has the technology in place for physicians to log on to your website and enter a password. Once they have successfully logged into the system, they are able to view information that is not available to the general public. Which of the following are the physicians utilizing?
   A. intranet
   B. extranet
   C. Internet
   D. clinical information system

REFERENCE: McWay, p 321
Abdelhak, p 291

26. One of the ways that an EHR is distinguished from a clinical data repository is that the EHR
   A. has clinical decision support capabilities.
   B. has data from multiple information systems.
   C. can have digital images.
   D. aggregates data.

REFERENCE: McWay p 175 and 327
Green and Bowie, p 95

27. What type of database model does this simple diagram depict?

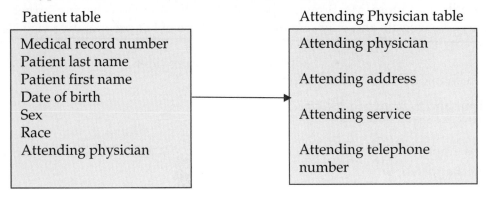

Patient table   Attending Physician table

Medical record number
Patient last name
Patient first name
Date of birth
Sex
Race
Attending physician

Attending physician

Attending address

Attending service

Attending telephone
number

    A. hierarchical   C. relational
    B. network   D. object oriented

REFERENCE: Marreel and McLellan, p 83, 205
                    Abdelhak, p 276
                    LaTour and Eichenwald-Maki, p 111
                    McWay, p 170

28. The network topology that our system uses paused to prevent data from colliding with other network traffic. This is
    A. FDDI.   C. Ethernet.
    B. token ring.   D. ATM.

REFERENCE: Marreel and McLellan, p 194
                    Amatayakul, p 178

29. What HIM health record function would best benefit from the use of bar coding?
    A. correspondence/ROI control   C. record location/tracking
    B. record completion   D. transcription

REFERENCE: Green and Bowie, p 209, 211
                    Abdelhak, p 238
                    LaTour and Eichenwald-Maki, p 51

30. In order for the EHR and other systems to be interoperable, the systems must meet certain
    A. rules.   C. standards.
    B. guidelines.   D. alerts.

REFERENCE: McWay, p 317
                    Marreel and McLellan, p, 75-76

31. You are developing a list of functions needed by users of a release of information system. You are also evaluating the current system to see what opportunities there are to improve the system. Which stage of the system developmental life cycle stages are you in?
    A. analysis   C. design
    B. implementation   D. obsolescence

REFERENCE: Marreel and McLellan, p 62-64, 317-319
                    McWay, p 317-319
                    Johns, 2006, p 751
                    LaTour and Eichenwald-Maki, p 133

32. Your Community Hospital utilizes a WAN that transports data across the Internet by using a private tunnel. This is a
  A. WLAN.   C. VPN.
  B. LAN.   D. FDDI.

REFERENCE: Marreel and McLellan, p 319
                Amatayakul, p 176
                Glandon, Smaltz, and Slovensky, p 147
                McWay, p 319

33. Dr. Smith wants to see the latest test results first. Dr. Brown wants to see the nurse's notes first. The different user views can be available by use of by a
  A. subschema.   C. data dictionary.
  B. schema.   D. GUI.

REFERENCE: Johns, 2002, p 208

34. You need a system that will provide information on your census, update your master patient index, and distribute demographic data. What type of system would you purchase?
  A. ADT   C. clinical information system
  B. executive information system   D. financial information system

REFERENCE: Green and Bowie, p 227-230
                Marreel and McLellan, p 8, 187
                Abdelhak, p 283-284

35. As HIM Department Director, you are on the implementation team for the new MPI. You have been assigned the responsibility of looking at every data element stored in the system and establishing criteria for the use of each. An example of what you are doing is below:

Name	Last name
Description	This field is for the patient's last name
Number of characters	30
Alphanumeric	Alpha
Acceptable characters	a-z
Responsible person	HIM Director
Used in reports	admissions list, discharge list, transfer list, health record number list, UB-92, CMS-1500

You are responsible for the
  A. data flow diagram.   C. data dictionary.
  B. decision tree.   D. rules based algorithms.

REFERENCE: Eichenwald-Maki and Petterson, p 27
                Marreel and McLellan, p 79-81, 191
                McWay, p 170
                Green and Bowie, p 240, 243
                Amatayakul, 163
                Johns, 2006, p 764

36. WORM technology is useful in storing medical information on optical disks or platters because
  A. it does not require that information be digitally scanned into the computer.
  B. records may be modified as needed to update the patient's medical record.
  C. the write-once, read-many feature permanently stores information without the ability to alter or modify the original documentation.
  D. only authorized personnel are allowed to make changes in the medical record.

REFERENCE: Abdelhak, p 257

37. A common language used in data definition language and data manipulation language is:
   A. unified modeling language
   B. metadata
   C. HTML
   D. SQL

REFERENCE: McWay, p 171
Marreel and McLellan, p 207
LaTour and Eichenwald-Maki, p 111

38. Your new optical disk system has the ability to automatically route charts that need coding, analyzing, and other processing to the appropriate person. What is this technology called?
   A. workflow
   B. data flow
   C. routing
   D. integration

REFERENCE: Abdelhak, p 257-258
LaTour and Eichenwald-Maki, p 652, 654

39. Differentiate between the physical and logical data models.
   A. The physical data model shows how the logical model will be created and the logical data model shows the technology plan to be used.
   B. The logical data model shows what the system should do and the physical data model shows how the logical data model will be created.
   C. The logical data model uses DFDs and the physical data model uses entity relationship models.
   D. The physical data model uses DFDs and the logical uses entity relationship model.

REFERENCE: Amatayakul, p 118
LaTour and Eichenwald-Maki, p 112

40. The administrator has asked us to develop a patient satisfaction database internally. This database will be used to collect data that can be used to improve our services. He does not want this to be a long, drawn-out process. Which of the following could speed up this process?
   A. RFI
   B. RFP
   C. prototyping
   D. functional requirements

REFERENCE: Johns, 2002, p 140

41. Cynthia wants to retrieve a list of patients from the new electronic document management system. She wants a list of patients admitted to the hospital by Dr. Smith. Which of the following would explain why she cannot generate this list?
   A. improper scanning
   B. the necessary indexing to retrieve this list was not done
   C. the data is stored on optical disk so it not readily available
   D. the COLD technology has not downloaded the lab reports

REFERENCE: McWay, p 115-117, 197
Mahoney, p 28
Abdelhak, p 26-257

42. A Web site that uses links to provide easy access to information of interest to the users is called a(n)
   A. intranet.
   B. internet.
   C. extranet.
   D. portal.

REFERENCE: McWay, p 321

43. The EHR system implementation team is using simulated patients and simulated patient information to add progress notes, nurses' notes, etc., to the EHR prior to implementation. Which phase is the team involved in?
   A. conversion
   B. testing
   C. analysis
   D. site preparation

REFERENCE: McWay, p 317-319
               Abdelhak, p 365
               LaTour and Eichenwald-Maki, p 135
               Johns, 2006, p 814

44. You are interested in performing some data analysis on patients with cardiac problems. You have downloaded the data that you need on the cardiology patients from the data warehouse into a smaller database that you can work with. You are using a
   A. data mart.
   B. clinical data repository.
   C. specialized data warehouse.
   D. executive information system.

REFERENCE: McWay, p 176
               Amatayakul, p 165
               Johns, 2002, p 230-231
               LaTour and Eichenwald-Maki, p 62
               Abdelhak, p 299-300

45. The laboratory system was installed 3 years ago. It is running well and meeting the needs of the department. Which stage of the IS life cycle is the lab system in?
   A. initiation
   B. development
   C. implementation
   D. operations (maintenance)

REFERENCE: McWay, p 317-319
               Marreel and McLellan, p 62-64, 317-319
               LaTour and Eichenwald-Maki, p 310
               Johns, 2006, p 755
               Abdelhak, p 310-312

46. Your facility is developing a new information system. Your department is viewing the product as it develops and providing feedback that is used to update the system. This process is called
   A. prototyping.
   B. data flow diagramming.
   C. diagramming entity relationships.
   D. updating the data dictionary.

REFERENCE: Murphy, p 371
               Johns, 2002, p 140
               Abdelhak, p 314-315

47. An example of a system analysis tool is
   A. a data model..
   B. SQL.
   C. a Gantt chart.
   D. a PERT chart.

REFERENCE: McWay, p 173
               LaTour and Eichenwald-Maki, p 84-85, 112-113, 669-670
               Abdelhak, p 314-315

48. As a systems analyst, Mark acts as:
   A. database administrator.
   B. Web master.
   C. liaison between end users and technical support staff.
   D. network administrator.

REFERENCE: LaTour and Eichenwald-Maki, 2006, p 138

49. The CEO needs to make a decision about the future of the health care facility. To make this decision, he utilizes an information system that queries a database containing data from a number of different information systems. What type of system is being used?
    A. EHR
    B. results reporting
    C. financial information system
    D. executive information system

REFERENCE: Abdelhak, p 284
              LaTour and Eichenwald-Maki, p 577

System Evaluation: Chart Location System							
Requirement	Priority	System A	System B	System C	System A Weighted	System B Weighted	System C Weighted
Ad hoc reporting	2	1	3	2	2	6	4
Check out chart	3	3	3	3	9	9	9
Mass check out of chart	3	3	3	3	9	9	9
Unlimited locations	1	2	2	1	2	2	1
Password security	2	2	3	2	4	6	4
User friendly	3	3	2	3	9	6	9
Check in chart	3	1	3	3	3	9	9
Total					38	47	45

50. The EHR system selection committee evaluated three systems on a scale of 1-3 with a score of 3 being the best. The priority is ranked on a scale of 1-3 with 3 being the highest. Based on the evaluation above, which of the following systems should be purchased?
    A. system A
    B. system B
    C. system C
    D. none of the above

REFERENCE: Abdelhak, p 349-350

51. You are performing the final review of the RFP that is to be sent out to prospective vendors. Upon review, you see content that should not be included in the operational requirement section of the document, so you delete this information. Which of the following would you delete?
    A. response time
    B. data architecture
    C. data conversion
    D. data analysis tools

REFERENCE: McWay, p 344-345
              Marreel and McLellan, p 90-100
              Amatayakul, p 262

52. Dr. Smith needs something small and lightweight to use for dictating reports and entering data on the go. You suggest he use
    A. a laptop utilizing wireless technology.
    B. a VPN.
    C. voice recognition.
    D. a PDA.

REFERENCE: McWay, p 316
              Johns, 2006, p 129
              LaTour and Eichenwald-Maki, p 65

53. Maria has received a request to update a patient's insurance number. She accesses the _____ and updates the system. What system is she using?
   A. executive information system
   B. clinical decision support system
   C. admission-discharge-transfer system
   D. laboratory information system

REFERENCE: Green and Bowie, p 227-230
               Marreel and McLellan, p 8, 187
               Johns, 2006, p 803-804
               Abdelhak, p 283-284

54. You are developing a plan that shows the fields that a database will contain, the operations that the database will exhibit, and the types of relationships. You are developing the
   A. data model.   C. database manager.
   B. database design.   D. data dictionary.

REFERENCE: McWay, p 171
               LaTour and Eichenwald-Maki, p 112

55. To enter the results of a CBC into the computer system, you would use a:
   A. laboratory system   C. pharmacy system
   B. radiology system   D. order entry/results reporting system

REFERENCE: Green and Bowie, p 156, 158-159
               Marreel and McLellan, p 14-15, 187
               Johns, 2006, p 801

The following questions represent advanced competencies.

56. You are developing your Information Systems Strategic Plan. Which of the following should be your basis for the plan?
   A. business plan   C. consultant's recommendations
   B. previous IS strategic plan   D. previous IS budgets

REFERENCE: McWay, p 249-250
               Tan, p 223
               LaTour and Eichenwald-Maki, p 130

57. Your hospital is working toward the implementation of an electronic health record. In the meantime you are using an electronic document management system. The EDMS is an example of a(n):
   A. EHR   C. knowledge-based system
   B. bridge technology   D. clinical decision support system

REFERENCE: LaTour and Eichenwald-Maki, p 213

58. You are implementing a new information system. You have to deal with issues related to other existing systems such as lack of integrations and differences in how data are stored. These existing systems are called:
   A. hospital information systems   C. legacy systems
   B. practice management system   D. continuity of care record

REFERENCE: Marreel and McLellan, p 200
               LaTour and Eichenwald-Maki, p 216-217

59. Mary has recommended using an infrared wireless network for the new clinical information system. This system will allow the hospital and physicians to communicate no matter where the physician's office is located. You tell Mary that that this is not feasible because
    A. the bandwidth is not wide enough.
    B. you can only operate 200 feet away.
    C. infrared is not a type of wireless network.
    D. infrared requires a line of sight.

REFERENCE: LaTour and Eichenwald-Maki, p 65

60. During systems analysis you use a tool that shows relations between data. You are using a(n)
    A. data dictionary.
    C. flowchart.
    B. data flow diagram.
    D. entity relationship diagram.

REFERENCE: Abdelhak, p 322
                 LaTour and Eichenwald-Maki, p 112
                 Johns, 2002, p 133-134, 376
                 McWay, p 171-172

61. The physician will be called automatically when a lab result is at the panic level. This is an example of a
    A. data-driven rule.
    C. clinical guideline.
    B. database.
    D. reminder.

REFERENCE: Murphy, p 338

62. Your administrator has asked for the name of a standard that will allow different computer applications to communicate. Which of the following standards would you give him?
    A. Joint Commission
    C. HL-7
    B. IOM CPR definition
    D. ASC X12

REFERENCE: Marreel and McLellan, p 75-76
                 McWay, p 174-175
                 Eichenwald-Maki and Petterson, p 2, 6, 52-53
                 Abdelhak, p 39
                 Johns, 2006, p 133
                 LaTour and Eichenwald-Maki, p 160

63. Webster Medical Center is installing a computerized provider order-entry system. Currently we are training the staff and testing the system. We must be in the
    A. design phase.
    C. maintenance phase.
    B. implementation phase.
    D. analysis phase.

REFERENCE: McWay, p 317-319
                 Eichenwald-Maki and Petterson, p 21-22
                 Johns, 2006, p 755, 776-777
                 LaTour and Eichenwald-Maki (2006), p 132

64. The steps from project identification to implementation and support of an information system are called
    A. systems analysis.
    C. project management.
    B. information system life cycle.
    D. data model.

REFERENCE: McWay, p 317-319
                 Marreel and McLellan, p 62-64, 317-319

65. The hospital is undergoing the development of an information system strategic plan. The part of the process where changes in the community, legislation, and other factors are monitored is called
   A.   health information exchange.
   B.   alerts.
   C.   environmental scanning.
   D.   critical path analysis.

REFERENCE: McWay, p 249-250
             Glandon, Smaltz, and Slovensky, p 124-125

66. Your transcription system utilizes disk mirroring. This is an example of a technology called
   A.   RAID.
   B.   HL-7.
   C.   DASD.
   D.   CPOE.

REFERENCE: Amatayakul, p 175

67. You are developing an entity relationship diagram. In the entity of patient shown here, which of the attributes is the primary key?

Patient
Last name
First name
Middle initial
Street address
City
State
Zip
Medical record number
Date of birth

   A.   last name
   B.   combination of last and first name
   C.   street address
   D.   medical record number

REFERENCE: McWay, p 171-172
             LaTour and Eichenwald-Maki, p 113

68. A preliminary step prior to issuing a formal RFP, which allows the facility to narrow down the field of potential vendors for procurement of a new hospital-wide computer system, would be to
   A.   select the system to be purchased.
   B.   create a Gantt chart to monitor project progress.
   C.   issue a request for information (RFI) to potential vendors.
   D.   initiate contract negotiations.

REFERENCE: McWay, p 344
             Marreel and McLellan, p 88-90
             LaTour and Eichenwald-Maki, p 134
             Johns, 2006, p 810-812

69. Administration has asked the clinical provider order-entry task force to select the method of implementation that will reduce risk to the hospital. What method should they choose?
    A. Implement all modules across the entire organization.
    B. Implement one module in one unit while running the current system in parallel.
    C. Implement all modules across the entire organization while running the current system in parallel.
    D. Implement one module in one unit while shutting down the existing system.

REFERENCE: Abdelhak, p 337
                Johns, 2006, p 814-815

70. Which type of system would be utilized to help the CEO of a facility in determining whether or not to expand the radiation therapy services?
    A. clinical information system   C. ambulatory care system
    B. strategic decision support system   D. enterprise system

REFERENCE: Marreel and McLellan, p 39-48
                McWay, p 249-251
                Abdelhak, p 284
                Johns, 2006, p 805
                LaTour and Eichenwald-Maki, p 544-545

71. You recently installed a new computer system and you just learned that the vendor does not have the right to use one portion of the system. Another company owns the rights to the information contained in this portion of the system. What clause in your contract would you review to see if you are protected from being sued by the other company?
    A. warranties   C. support
    B. indemnification   D. force majeure

REFERENCE: Marreel and McLellan, p 103
                McWay, p 344
                Abdelhak, p 536

72. A RHIO is a(n)
    A. group of organizations that share clinical services.
    B. application service provider.
    C. group of national organizations that share clinical information.
    D. group of organizations in a geographic region that shares clinical information.
REFERENCE: Mon, p 56
                Eichenwald-Maki and Petterson, p 5
                LaTour and Eichenwald, p 48
                McWay, p 181

73. You are selecting the database model for your new information system's database. You have chosen the one that is structurally independent, is easy to use and manage, and has a strong database management system. What have you chosen?
    A. network   C. hierarchical
    B. relational   D. bus

REFERENCE: Marreel and McLellan, p 83
                LaTour and Eichenwald-Maki, p 112
                Johns, 2006, p 762-764
                McWay, p 170

74. As Director of Health Information Services, you are negotiating a contract to purchase a new computerized dictation system that will be used across three satellite ambulatory clinics. What element is most critical in the contract negotiation to ensure use of the software in multiple environments?

    A. delivery terms   C. price and payment terms

    B. scope and term of warranties   D. license grant

REFERENCE: Abdelhak, p 352

75. The most secure model of signatures used in information systems is

    A. digital signature.

    B. electronic signature.

    C. digitized signature.

    D. there is no difference in the level of security between these models.

REFERENCE: McWay, p 328-329

                      LaTour and Eichenwald-Maki, p 228

76. Your facility is implementing a new document management system. This system will require the storage of large amounts of data. Which of the following storage devices would you recommend?

    A. external hard drive   C. file server

    B. CDs   D, redundant arrays of independent disks

REFERENCE: LaTour and Eichenwald-Maki, p 224

Task	Mandatory	Desired
Add new patient	X	
Assign medical record number	X	
Barcodes for data entry		X
Delete patient	X	
Admit patient	X	
Discharge patient	X	
Transfer patient	X	

77. The table above presents an example of

    A. the systems standards.   C. the functional specifications.

    B. a RFI.   D. a systems design.

REFERENCE: Abdelhak, p 344

                      McWay, p 345

                      Marreel and McLellan, p 93

                      LaTour and Eichenwald-Maki, p 134

78. Mary is scheduled to program the interfaces in June. John will develop the training plan in July. Robert will test the system in July. Mark will be on sick leave during August and he has to write the documentation before he leaves. In order to make sure that the staff needed is available during these time periods, what process should be utilized?

    A. systems analysis   C. resource allocation

    B. implementation   D. Gantt chart

REFERENCE: Marreel and McLellan, p 126-132

                      Abdelhak, p 309

79. You are developing an entity-relationship diagram. The entity that you are currently working on is "patient". Which of the following would be the primary key for the entity patient?
   A. last name
   B. address
   C. attending physician number
   D. health record number

REFERENCE: McWay, p 171-172
                Johns, 2002, p 168

80. An acute care facility is installing a new computer system in the chart-tracking area. During implementation, the current existing system will continue to operate while bringing up the new system, allowing a comparison of the outputs from both systems for accuracy over a 1-month period. This process describes what type of conversion?
   A. history processing
   B. direct conversion
   C. phased-in conversion
   D. parallel conversion

REFERENCE: Tan, p 278-279

81. John had a car accident on I-65 in Birmingham while traveling from Michigan to Mobile. John is vague on his medical history. Which of the following could BEST help the physicians in the ER give him quality care?

   A. personal health record
   B. RHIO
   C. EHR
   D. data warehouse

REFERENCE: AHIMA e-HIM Personal Health Record Work Group, p 64A
                McWay, p 181

82. The diagram below demonstrates which of the following relationships?

   A. one to one
   B. many to many
   C. one to many
   D. one and only one

REFERENCE: Abdelhak, p 322
                Johns, 2002, p 134, 149-150

83. There was an unexpected hardware failure for our EHR. It is expected to be up and operational in three hours. Until then, which of the following plans would you need to initiate?
   A. information system strategic plan
   B. implementation plan
   C. business continuity plan
   D. project planning

REFERENCE: Glandon, Smaltz and Slovensky, p 191
                McWay, p 402-403
                Krager and Krager

84. You are the HIM Director at the hospital in Columbus, Georgia. Your administrator wants to partner with a hospital across the river in Phoenix City, Alabama. This partnership would involve the use of telemedicine. What issue should you vocalize?
   A. the needed technology is not available
   B. telemedicine is only useful for rural facilities
   C. physicians are licensed by the state
   D. Joint Commission does not approve of telemedicine

REFERENCE: Abdelhak, p 292-293

85. Mountaintop Hospital has decided to use the "best of breed" philosophy. Because of this, they need a(n) _____ to manage the sharing of data.
    A. DBMS
    B. RFP
    C. consultant
    D. interface engine

REFERENCE: Marreel and McLellan, p 198
               Amatayakul, p 258

86. The HIM supervisor is evaluating software that would utilize electronic logging and monitoring of requests for copies of patient information. What department function is this most useful for?
    A. correspondence/ROI control
    B. record completion
    C. record location/tracking
    D. transcription

REFERENCE: Green and Bowie, p 285-286

87. Byron is helping his supervisor solve a computer problem. He said that it is a primary storage problem. He must mean that it deals with
    A. RAM.
    B. CD.
    C. imaging.
    D. Magnetic storage.

REFERENCE: Glandon, Smaltz, and Slovensky, p 138

88. Installation of a new electronic document management system is scheduled for the HIM department. The department director calls a meeting of the HIM supervisors to coordinate plans for training the HIM staff. What key factors must be taken into consideration as part of the training preparation process?
    A. the total storage capacity and price of the new system
    B. collecting the results of the RFP responses and vendor selection process used during the selection process
    C. presentation content and scheduling to accommodate all employee shifts
    D. scheduling training times and locations for all physicians and hospital personnel who will use the system

REFERENCE: Abdelhak, p 364
               LaTour and Eichenwald-Maki, p 713

89. Your assignment is to collect and analyze some data. Which type of software package will you use?
    A. word processing
    B. e-mail
    C. database
    D. spreadsheet

REFERENCE: LaTour and Eichenwald-Maki, p 429

90. The laboratory system was installed 3 years ago. It is running well and meeting the needs of the department. Which stage of the IS life cycle is the laboratory system in?
    A. initiation
    B. development
    C. implementation
    D. operation

REFERENCE: Marreel and McLellan, p 62-64, 317-319
               McWay, p 317-319
               Abdelhak, p 310
               LaTour and Eichenwald-Maki, p 136

91. The new information system that your facility just purchased requires having software loaded on a server and also requires having software loaded on each individual workstation. This type of architecture is called
    A. peer network.
    C. client server.
    B. file server.
    D. dumb terminals.

REFERENCE: Marreel and McLellan, p 8, 191
Glandon, Smaltz, and Slovensky, p 149
LaTour and Eichenwald-Maki, p 217

92. Your department must send information electronically to the state health department every day. Currently this is taking a significant amount of time. What technology can be used to automatically send this information without human intervention?
    A. electronic data interchange
    C. Internet
    B. LAN
    D. network interface card

REFERENCE: Marreel and McLellan, p 4, 55-60
Glandon, Smaltz, and Slovensky, p 159
LaTour and Eichenwald-Maki, p 53
Johns, 2006, p 306
McWay, p 174

93. The CIO has given you a list of critical success factors developed for the EHR that your facility is developing. Which of the following would you expect to see on this list?
    A. implement e-prescribing
    C. utilize thin clients
    B. get buy-in from the key players
    D. utilize encryption

REFERENCE: Amatayakul, p 143-146
Johns (2002), p 108

94. Your hospital has been having financial difficulty. They desperately need to implement a new information system because their current one is about to crash, but they just do not have the funds to outlay for hardware, software, and a long implementation. They just read about a project where the software and hardware resides at the vendor's data center facility. The hospital uses a VPN to access the database that also resides at the vendor's data center. They are seriously considering this model because the implementation time would be short and the upfront costs are low when compared to an onsite installation. Which of the following are they considering?
    A. Internet
    C. e-commerce
    B. application service provider
    D. e-health

REFERENCE: LaTour and Eichenwald-Maki, p 134
Sheridan, p 38

95. You have had a problem with duplicate medical record numbers in your facility's MPI. Now you are joining a health information exchange, so you will need to clean up your database and prevent the duplicates from happening again. If you want to find near matches as well as identical matches in your MPI, you should implement a _____ algorithm.
    A. probabilistic
    C. fuzzy
    B. deterministic
    D. none of the above

REFERENCE: McWay, p 115-116, 176
Gudea, p 51

96. Juan has been asked to investigate e-health companies. Which of the following would NOT be included in his investigation?
    A. Health Data: a company that stores patient identifiable health information online
    B. HealthInfo: a company that provides medical references to patients
    C. Physician Services: a company that provides medical references to physicians
    D. Café Services: a company that provides cafeteria services to the hospital

REFERENCE: Fuller, p 50
               McWay, p 325-326

97. If your network was graphed, it would show a hub in the middle with nodes surrounding it. What type of network is it and why would you choose it?
    A. star, ease of adding computers   C. bus, ease of adding computers
    B. ring, operates over high distance   D. ring, does not go down much

REFERENCE: Glandon, Smaltz, and Slovensky, p 158

98. You just learned that you will be storing the same data in two places in the database. What kind of problem do you have?
    A. data quality   C. normalization
    B. schema   D. knowledge management

REFERENCE: LaTour and Eichenwald-Maki, p 553

99. The ADT system is undergoing testing, training, and programming. Therefore this system must be in the _____ stage of the information life cycle
    A. implementation.   C. initiation.
    B. obsolescence.   D. maintenance.

REFERENCE: Marreel and McLellan, p 62-64, 317-319
               McWay, p 317-319
               Abdelhak, p 310
               Johns, 2006, p 812-814
               LaTour and Eichenwald, p 135

100. The new computer hardware arrived and the technical staff was not able to install it because there was not enough space in the computer room. Which of the following implementation steps was not properly executed?
    A. system evaluation   C. site preparation
    B. conversion   D. user preparation

REFERENCE: Abdelhak, p 336

101. You are considering three vendors for your new encoder. Your facility wants to purchase the system from a stable company. After reviewing the vendor profile information below, which of the vendors would you eliminate from consideration?

Topic	Vendor A	Vendor B	Vendor C
Number of years in business	2	10	3
Number of installations	72	135	5
Number of installation staff	3	4	1
Age of product	2	6	3
Financial standing	Good	Excellent	Fair

   A. Vendor A
   B. Vendor B
   C. Vendor C
   D. cannot eliminate any of the vendors

REFERENCE: Marreel and McLellan, p 101-106
               McWay, p 344-345
               LaTour and Eichenwald-Maki, p 134
               Johns, 2006, p 810-812

102. Outsourcing information systems results in which of the following?
   A. increased accessibility of competent IT staff
   B. reduced equipment investment
   C. reduction in time to implement
   D. all of the above

REFERENCE: McWay, p 36
               LaTour and Eichenwald-Maki, p 137, 651

Answer Key for Informatics and Information Systems

1. A		38. A	
2. B		39. B	
3. B		40. C	
4. C		41. B	
5. A		42. D	
6. D		43. B	
7. B		44. A	
8. B		45. D	
9. B		46. A	
10. A		47. A	
11. C	OLAP is used to analyze data, determine relationships, look for trends, and conduct "what if" analysis. In the scenario, it would need to determine how long Dr. Smith takes to perform the surgery, determine the instruments and supplies that would be needed, obtain information from the insurance company, and determine if the surgery is covered.	48. C	
		49. D	
		50. B	
		51. C	
		52. D	
		53. C	
		54. A	
		55. A	
		56. A	
		57. C	
		58. C	
12. B		59. D	
13. D		60. D	
14. C		61. A	
15. B		62. C	
16. D		63. B	
17. C		64. B	
18. C		65. C	
19. C		66. A	
20. D		67. D	
21. A		68. C	
22. A		69. B	
23. A		70. B	
24. C		71. A	
25. B		72. D	
26. A		73. B	
27. C		74. D	
28. C		75. A	
29. C		76. D	
30. C		77. C	
31. A		78. C	
32. C		79. D	
33. A		80. D	
34. A		81. D	
35. C		82. A	
36. C		83. C	
37. D		84. C	

Answer Key for Informatics and Information Systems

85. D Although the facility may benefit from the services of a consultant and they will need a DBMS to manage the database for the new systems, it is the interface engine that will be needed to manage communication between the various systems.

86. A
87. A
88. C
89. D
90. D

91. C
92. A
93. B
94. B
95. A
96. D
97. A
98. C
99. A
100. C
101. C
102. A

REFERENCES

Abdelhak, M., Grostick, S., Hanken, M. A., & Jacobs, E. (2007). *Health information: management of a strategic resource* (3rd ed.). Philadelphia: W. B. Saunders.

Amatayakul, M. K. (2006). *Electronic health records: A practical guide for professionals and organizations* (3rd ed.). Chicago: American Health Information Management Association.

American Health Information Management Association: AHIMA e-HIM Personal Health Record Work Group. (2005). The role of the personal health record in the EHR. *Journal of AHIMA, 76*(8), 64A-64D. Chicago: American Health Information Management Association (AHIMA).

Fuller, S. (2000). To "E" or not to "E": HIM and the dawn of e-health. *Journal of AHIMA, 71*(4), 50-53. Chicago: American Health Information Management Association (AHIMA).

Glandon, G., Smaltz, D., & Slovensky, D. (2008). *Information systems for healthcare management.* Chicago: Health Administration Press.

Eichenwald-Maki, S., & Petterson, B. (2008). *Using the electronic health record.* Clifton Park, NY: Thomson Delmar Learning.

Graham, D. (2000). Implementing an electronic imaging system. *Journal of AHIMA, 71*(2), 20-23. Chicago: American Health Information Management Association (AHIMA).

Green, M. A., & Bowie, M. J. (2004). *Essentials of health information management.* Clifton Park, NY: Thomson Delmar Learning.

Gudea, S. (2005). Deterministic, probabilistic, or fuzzy? A primer on the search algorithms that drive MPI quality. *Journal of AHIMA, 76*(8), 5-54. Chicago: American Health Information Management Association (AHIMA).

Johns, M. L. (2006). *Health information management technology: An applied approach* (2nd ed.). Chicago: American Health Information Management Association.

Johns, M. L. (2002). *Information management for health professional* (2nd ed.). Clifton Park, NY: Thomson Delmar Learning.

Krager, D., & Krager, C. (2008). *HIPAA for health care professionals.* New York: Delmar Cengage Learning.

LaTour, K., & Eichenwald-Maki, S. (2006). *Health information management: Concepts, principles, and practice* (2nd ed.). Chicago: American Health Information Management Association (AHIMA).

Mahoney, M. E. (1997). Document imaging and workflow technology in health care today. *Journal of AHIMA, 68*(4), 28-36. Chicago: American Health Information Management Association (AHIMA).

Marreel, R. , & McLellan, J. (1999). *Information management in health care.* New York. Thomson Delmar Learning.

McWay, D. (2008). *Today's health information management: An integrated approach.* Chicago: Thomson Delmar Learning.

Mon, D. (2005). An update on the NHIN and RHIOs. *Journal of AHIMA, 76*(6), 56-57, 59. Chicago: American Health Information Management Association (AHIMA).

Murphy, G. F., Hanken, M. A., & Waters, K. (1999). *Electronic health records: Changing the vision.* Philadelphia: W. B. Saunders.

Peters, Jr., R. M. (2000). XML: Defining the transition from paper to digital record. *Journal of AHIMA, 71*(1), 34-38. Chicago: American Health Information Management Association (AHIMA).

Seals, M. (2000). The use of XML in health care information management. *Journal of Health care Information Management, 14*(2), 85-95. Chicago: American Health Information Management Association (AHIMA).

Sheridan, C. (2001). Do you need an ASP ASAP? *Journal of AHIMA*, 72(8), 38-42. Chicago: American Health Information Management Association (AHIMA).

Tan, J. K. (2001). *Health management information systems, methods and practical applications* (2nd ed.). Gaithersburg, MD: Aspen Publishers.

Waegemann, C. P., & Tessier, C. (2002) Documentation goes wireless: A look at mobile health care computing devices. *Journal of AHIMA*, 73(8), 36-39. Chicago: American Health Information Management Association (AHIMA).

XI. Health Information Privacy and Security

Nanette B. Sayles, EdD, RHIA, CCS, CHPS, FAHIMA

1. You are the Chief Privacy Officer for Premier Medical Center. Which of the following are you responsible for?
   A. backing up data
   B. developing a plan for reporting privacy complaints
   C. writing policies on protecting hardware
   D. writing policies on encryption standards

REFERENCE: Hjort (2001), p 64B
               Johns, p 733
               Krager and Krager, p 11-12, 41
               McWay, p 36, 57

2. Which of the following situations violate a patient's privacy?
   A. The hospital sends patients who are scheduled for deliveries information on free childbirth classes.
   B. The physician on the quality improvement committee reviews medical records for potential quality problems.
   C. The hospital provides patient names and addresses to a pharmaceutical company to be used in a mass mailing of free drug samples.
   D. The hospital uses aggregate data to determine whether or not to add a new operating room suite.

REFERENCE: Amatayakul (2001b), p 16B
               Krager and Krager, p 39
               Green and Bowie, p 283

3. Margaret has signed an authorization to release information regarding her ER visit for a fractured finger to her attorney. Specifically, she says to release the ER history and physical, x-rays, and any procedure notes for finger fracture. Which of the following violates her privacy?
   A. release of face sheet used in ER as a history
   B. x-ray of chest
   C. x-ray of finger
   D. documentation of suturing of finger

REFERENCE: Hughes, 2002b, p 56A
               Krager and Krager, p 34, 41
               McWay, p 62

4. Mary processed a request for information and mailed it out last week. Today, the requestor, an attorney, called and said that all of the requested information was not provided. Mary pulls the documentation, including the authorization and what was sent. She believes that she sent everything that was required. She confirms this with her supervisor. The requestor still believes that some extra documentation is required. Given the above information, which of the following statements is true?
   A. Mary is not required to release the extra documentation because the facility has the right to interpret a request and apply the minimum standard rule.
   B. Mary is required to release the extra documentation because the requestor knows what is needed.
   C. Mary is required to release the extra documentation because, in the customer service program for the facility, the customer is always right.
   D. Mary is not required to release the additional information because her administrator agrees with her.

REFERENCE: Hughes (2002b), p 56A
              Johns, p 712-713
              McWay, p 62
              Krager and Krager, p 34-35, 41

5. You are writing a new policy for tracking the release of identifiable patient information. Which of the following will be included in the list of disclosures to track?
   A. release for patient care
   B. release to the patient
   C. release to attorney with patient consent
   D. release made to law enforcement agencies

REFERENCE: Dougherty, p 72E
              McWay, p 389
              Green and Bowie, p 285-287

6. Physical safeguards include:

   1. tools to monitor access
   2. tools to control access to computer systems
   3. fire protection
   4. tools preventing unauthorized access to data

   A. 1 and 2 only   C. 2 and 3 only
   B. 1 and 3 only   D. 2 and 4 only

REFERENCE: Hartley and Jones, p 106-107
              McWay, p 322-324
              Green, p 270
              Krager and Krager, p 92-93

7. You are looking at your policies, procedures, training program, etc., and comparing them to the HIPAA regulations. You are conducting a
   A. policy assessment.
   B. risk assessment.
   C. compliance audit.
   D. none of the above

REFERENCE: Hjort (2001) p 64A
             McWay, p 252-253
             Krager and Krager, p 86-87, 105
             Green and Bowie, p 84-85

8. The notice of privacy practices says: "Your medical record may be used for quality reviews." The reason this statement is on the notice is
   A. the verbiage is required by HIPAA.
   B. it is an example of health care operations.
   C. it is the purpose of the medical record.
   D. the covered entity cannot use the medical record unless this is specifically documented in the notice.

REFERENCE: Hughes, 2002a, p 64I
             McWay, p 60
             Krager and Krager, p 31, 35
             Green and Bowie, p 265

9. Kyle, the HIM Director, has received a request to amend a patient's medical record. The appropriate action for him to take is
   A. make the modification.
   B. file the request in the chart.
   C. route the request to the physician who wrote the note in question.
   D. return the notice to the patient.

REFERENCE: Thieleman, p 46
             Krager and Krager, p 44-45
             McWay, p 263
             Green and Bowie, p 84-85

10. Dr. Brown has just approved the patient's request to amend the medical record. Dr. Brown has routed the request with his approval to the HIM Department. What should the HIM Department do?
   A. File the request where the erroneous information is located.
   B. File the request where the erroneous information is located and send a copy of the amendment to anyone who has a copy of the erroneous information.
   C. File in the front of the chart.
   D. File the request where the erroneous information is located and send a copy of the amendment to anyone who has a copy of the erroneous information plus anyone the patient requests.

REFERENCE: Thieleman, p 44
             Green and Bowie, p 84-85

11. State law says that the hospital must keep a record of disclosures for 10 years. HIPAA says 6 years. What should the hospital do to comply with the conflicting laws?
    A. Keep it the 10 years required by the state because it is stricter than HIPAA.
    B. Keep it 6 years because HIPAA is a federal law that preempts state laws.
    C. Keep it 10 years if you are a state hospital, 6 years if you are not a state hospital.
    D. Keep it 6 years if you are a federal hospital, 6 years if you are not a federal hospital.

REFERENCE: Hughes (2002c), p 68, 70
                     McWay, p 12-13
                     Green and Bowie, p 196-197

12. Patricia is processing a request for medical records. The record contains an operative note and a discharge summary from another hospital. The records are going to another physician for patient care. What should Patricia do?
    A. Notify the requestor that redisclosure is illegal and so he must get the operative and discharge summary records from the original source hospital.
    B. Include the documents from the other hospital.
    C. Redisclose when necessary for patient care.
    D. Redisclose when allowed by law.

REFERENCE: Hughes, 2001b, p 72B
                     Krager and Krager, p 127-128

13. Ralph has asked for a list of disclosures of his medical record. He seems surprised not to see his physician, Dr. Emory, on it. What do you tell him?
    A. Dr. Emory has not viewed the medical record.
    B. Disclosures used for treatment are not recorded.
    C. You will run the report again to make sure you ran the report correctly.
    D. Go talk to Dr. Emory.

REFERENCE: Hughes, 2002c, p 68
                     McWay, p 389
                     Green and Bowie, p 285-287

14. Contingency planning includes which of the following processes?
    A. data quality   C. disaster planning
    B. systems analysis   D. hiring practices

REFERENCE: Johns, p 858-859
                     Hartley and Jones, p 146-147, 152
                     Green and Bowie, p 268-269
                     McWay, p 252-254
                     Krager and Krager, p 91-92

15. Your transcription system is set up to back up your hard drive every 5 minutes. The backup is on the hard drive of another computer. This computer is located in the room next door to the primary computer. What should be done to improve the backup process?

    A. Place the backup on an optical disk.
    B. Back up on a daily basis.
    C. Back up on a diskette.
    D. Move backup computer to an office 100 miles away.

REFERENCE: Abdelhak, p 242

16. Crystal has received a copy of some documents from her medical record. In the request, she had specifically requested the discharge summary, history and physical, operative report, pathology report, laboratory results, and x-ray reports. The records that she received only included the discharge summary and history and physical. The enclosed letter said that the other documents were not enclosed because of the minimum necessary rule. What should the director tell Crystal when she calls?
    A. The clerk was appropriate in what was sent.
    B. The operative report should have been included too.
    C. The operative report and pathology report should have been included.
    D. All of the requested information should have been sent because the patient is an exception to the minimum necessary rule.

REFERENCE: Hughes (2002B), p 56
               Krager and Krager, p 32-33
               McWay, p 62, 84,
               Green and Bowie, p 283-284

17. Choosing to be in the directory means which of the following?
    A. friends and family can find out what room you are in
    B. your condition can be released to any caller in specific terms
    C. your condition can be released to the public
    D. no information can be released

REFERENCE: Roach, p 172
               Krager and Krager, p 35-36 40, 124-125

18. Which of the following techniques would a facility employ for access control?

       1. automatic logoff
       2. passwords
       3. token
       4. unique user identification

    A. 1 and 4   C. 2 and 4 only
    B. 1 and 2 only   D. all of the above

REFERENCE: Hartley and Jones, p 157
               McWay, p 173, 323
               Krager and Krager, p 96-98
               McWay, p 389
               Green and Bowie, p 270-271

19. Which of the following statements is true about the Privacy Act of 1974?
    A. It applies to all organizations who maintain health care data in any form.
    B. It applies to all health care organizations.
    C. It applies to the federal government.
    D. It applies to federal government except for the Veterans Health Administration.

REFERENCE: LaTour and Eichenwald-Maki, p 250
               Green and Bowie, p 273

20. Brad Thomas is a former patient at Alabama General Hospital. He came to the HIM Department today and asked for a list of people who have requested his medical records over the past 10 years. He also wants to know what was released. Which is the appropriate response to Brad's request?
    A. Give him what he requested.
    B. Give him the information on records released over the past 6 years.
    C. Do not give him any information.
    D. Give him his medical record and let him find out who requested information for himself.

REFERENCE: Dougherty, p 72E
               Johns, p 712-713
               McWay, p 389
               Green and Bowie, p 263, 285-287

21. As Privacy Officer of Florida Beach Hospital, you are reviewing the following new policy for approval and implementation.

> _Policy_: _Due to recent legislation, Florida Beach Hospital will track release of confidential patient identifiable information in the following circumstances as required by law:_
> _Employers_
> _Attorneys_
> _Patients_
> _External researchers_

    Based on the HIPAA accounting of disclosure rules, what problem with the policy do you have?
    A. You do not have to track release to employers because it is exempted from legislation.
    B. You do not have to track release to attorneys because it is exempted from legislation.
    C. You do not have to track release to patients because it is exempted from legislation.
    D. You do not have to track release to external researchers because it is exempted from legislation.

REFERENCE: Dougherty, 72E
               McWay, p 389
               Green and Bowie, p 285-287

22. Encryption, access control, emergency access to records, and biometrics are examples of
    A. transmission security.
    B. technical security.
    C. a security incident.
    D. telecommunications.

REFERENCE: Roach, p 469-471
               McWay, p 323
               LaTour and Eichenwald-Maki, p 225
               Krager and Krager, p 96-100
               Green and Bowie, p 271
               Abdelhak, p 297

23. Intentional threats to security could include
    A. a natural disaster (flood).
    B. equipment failure (software failure).
    C. human error (data entry error).
    D. data theft (unauthorized downloading of files).

REFERENCE: Johns, p 853-854

24. Which of the following would be a business associate?
    A. release of information company
    B. bulk food service provider
    C. childbirth class instructor
    D. marketing consultant

REFERENCE: Johns, p 703-704
               McWay, p 56
               Krager and Krager, p 42

25. Which of the following statements demonstrates a violation of protected health information?
    A. "Yes, Mr. Smith is in room 222. I will transfer your call."
    B. Physician's office staff calls centralized scheduling and says, "Dr. Smith wants to perform a bunionectomy on Mary Jones next Tuesday."
    C. "Mary, at work yesterday I saw that Susan had a hysterectomy."
    D. Dr. Jones tells a nurse on the floor to give Ms. Brown Demerol for her pain.

REFERENCE: Roach, p 45
               Johns, p 701-702
               McWay, p 59-60
               Krager and Krager, p 19, 29-30

26. Which of the following is an example of health care operations?
    A. sending bill to insurance company
    B. providing copy of record to Department of Homeland Security for national security purposes
    C. sharing record with hospital attorney defining facility in malpractice case
    D. providing record to physician for patient care

REFERENCE: Abdelhak, p 517
               LaTour and Eichenwald-Maki, p 257
               Krager and Krager, p 34-35
               Green and Bowie, p 265

27. The IRB has approved Dr. Grant's research with the stipulation that only a limited data set is provided. Which of the following would be a violation of the requirement to remove direct identifiers?
    A. street address   C. admission date
    B. discharge disposition   D. diagnosis

REFERENCE: Hughes (2002d), p 66
               McWay, p 180, 233
               Krager and Krager, p 37

28. You are evaluating what makes up the designated record set for Birmingham Medical Center. Which of the following would be included?
    A. quality reports
    B. psychotherapy notes
    C. discharge summary
    D. information compiled for use in civil hearing

REFERENCE: Amatayakul and Waymack, p 16A
               LaTour and Eichenwald-Maki, p 253
               Krager and Krager, p 31

29. You have been asked to provide examples of technical security measures. Which of the following would you add to your list of examples?
    A. locked doors
    B. automatic logout
    C. minimum necessary
    D. training

REFERENCE: Johns, p 867-869
               McWay, p 322-323
               Krager and Krager, p 90-100
               Green and Bowie, p 270-271

30. You have been given the responsibility of deciding which access control to use. Which of the following is one of your options?
    A. audit trail
    B. biometrics
    C. authentication
    D. mitigations

REFERENCE: Fuller, p 40
               Abdelhak, p 294
               Green and Bowie, p 270
               McWay, p 222-223
               Krager and Krager, p 96-97

31. Ms. Thomas was a patient at your facility. She has been told that there are some records that she cannot have access to. These records are most likely
    A. psychotherapy notes.
    B. alcohol and drug records.
    C. AIDS records.
    D. mental health assessment.

REFERENCE: Hughes (2001a), p 90
               Johns, p 706
               Krager and Krager, p 38-39
               Green and Bowie, p 268, 283-284

32. Your organization is sending confidential patient information across the Internet using technology that will transform the original data into unintelligible code that can be re-created by authorized users. This technique is called
    A. a firewall.
    B. validity processing.
    C. a call-back process.
    D. data encryption.

REFERENCE: Abdelhak, p 297
               McWay, p 321
               Krager and Krager, p 99-100
               Green and Bowie, p 286

33. Ms. Hall has requested that Dr. Moore amend her medical record. He emphatically refused. What type of documentation is required, if any?
    A. no documentation is required
    B. documentation of request and refusal
    C. documentation of request
    D. none of the above

REFERENCE: Amatayakul (2001b), p 16C
               Krager and Krager, p 32-33
               McWay, p 62, 85,
               Green and Bowie, p 84-85

34. Which of the following should record destruction program include?
    A. the method of destruction
    B. name of person responsible for destruction
    C. cite of laws followed
    D. requirement of daily destruction

REFERENCE: LaTour and Eichenwald-Maki, p 203-204
               Abdelhak, p 241
               McWay, p 112-115
               Green and Bowie, p 98-100

35. In the event of corrupted, lost, or damaged electronic data, one method of disaster recovery planning is to
    A. create regular backups that are stored in a safe location off premises.
    B. establish passwords and audit trails.
    C. make duplicate copies of all paper records and store them in an off-site location.
    D. submit all electronic records to a health information exchange.

REFERENCE: Abdelhak, p 242-243
               McWay, p 322
               Krager and Krager, p 92-95

36. The administrator states that he should not have to participate in privacy and security training. How should you respond?
    A. "All employees are required to participate in the training, including top administration."
    B. "I will record that in my files."
    C. "Did you read the privacy rules?"
    D. "You are correct. There is no reason for you to participate in the training."

REFERENCE: Krager and Krager, p 90
               Johns (2002b), p 230
               Hartley and Jones, p 118
               McWay, p 322-323

37. The surgeon comes out to speak to a patient's family. He tells them that the patient came through the surgery fine. The mass was benign and they could see the patient in an hour. He talks low so that the other people in the waiting room will not hear but someone walked by and heard. This is called a(n)
    A. privacy breach.   C. incidental disclosure.
    B. violation of policy.   D. privacy incident.

REFERENCE: Johns (2007), p 727
               Krager and Krager, p 19, 36

38. The HIPAA rule does not require specific technologies to be used but rather provides direction on the outcome. The term used to describe this philosophy is
    A. technology free.
    B. technology neutral.
    C. administrative rules.
    D. generic technology.

REFERENCE: Roach, p 460
               Krager and Krager, p 101

39. The patient has asked that all bills and other communications from the physician office go through a post office box rather than the home address. Which statement is true?
    A. The facility should honor the request since it is reasonable.
    B. HIPAA mandates that the home address is always used.
    C. The facility does not have to honor this since it is unreasonable.
    D. This is prevented by the Privacy Act of 1974.

REFERENCE: LaTour and Eichenwald-Maki, p 253-254
                Roach, p 230

40. Marjorie has filed a request asking to be notified before any of her medical records are released to anyone outside of the health care facility. You receive a request from an insurance company. There is a patient authorization attached. What do you do?
    A. Release the chart because you want to get paid.
    B. Release the chart because the patient has consented.
    C. Notify patient and follow her instructions.
    D. Notify patient and release chart as per authorization.

REFERENCE: Amatayakul (2001b) p 16B
                Johns, p 714
                LaTour and Eichenwald-Maki, p 253

41. The hospital has received a request for an amendment. How long does the facility have in order to accept or deny the request?
    A. 30 days   C. 14 days
    B. 60 days   D. 10 days

REFERENCE: Roach, p 233
                McWay, p 63
                Krager and Krager, p 23-24, 44
                Green and Bowie, p 84-85, 263

42. You work for a 60-bed hospital in a rural community. You are conducting research on what you need to do to comply with HIPAA. You are afraid that you will have to implement all of the steps that your friend at a 900-bed teaching hospital is implementing at his facility. You continue reading and learn that you only have to implement what is prudent and reasonable for your facility. This is called
    A. scalable.   C. technology neutral.
    B. risk assessment.   D. access control.

REFERENCE: U.S. Department of Health and Human Services (2001), p 2
                Krager and Krager, p 87
                McWay, p 57

43. Rachel, a nurse, can write progress notes in the patient's electronic health record. Vera, a coder, can view the progress notes but is not authorized to write a progress note. What controls this?
    A. authentication   C. biometrics
    B. two-factor authentications   D. based access control

REFERENCE: Abdelhak, p 295
                McWay, p 173
                Krager and Krager, p 88-89

44. Alisa has trouble remembering her password. She is trying to come up with a solution that will help her remember. She reads the policies on passwords. Based on the policy, she chooses which of the following options
    A. the word "password" for her password
    B. his daughter's name for her password
    C. to write the complex password on the last page of her calendar
    D. a combination of letters and numbers

REFERENCE: Amatayakul and Walsh, p 16C
              Johns, p 850
              McWay, p 321
              Krager and Krager, p 88-89, 97

45. A patient asked for an amendment to her medical record. The hospital has denied the request. According to HIPAA, this can be done if
    A. the facility created the documentation.
    B. it is part of the designated record set.
    C. it is accurate and complete.
    D. it is part of the medical record.

REFERENCE: Roach, p 234
              Krager and Krager, p 32-33, 44-45
              McWay, p 62, 85, 263
              Green and Bowie, p 84-85

The following questions represent advanced competencies

46. Nicole is developing an agreement that will be used between the hospital and the health care clearing house. This agreement will require the two parties to protect the privacy of data exchanged. This is called a
    A. business associate agreement.   C. trading partner agreement.
    B. business contract.   D. none of the above

REFERENCE: Amatayakul (2001a), p 16B
              Johns, p 703-704
              Krager and Krager, p 42, 92, 100
              McWay, p 56

47. The computer system containing the electronic health record was located in a room that was flooded. As a result, the system is inoperable. Which of the following would be implemented?
    A. SWOT analysis
    B. information systems strategic planning
    C. request for proposal
    D. business continuity processing

REFERENCE: Johns, p 858-859
              Green and Bowie, p 268-269
              McWay, p 252-254
              Krager and Krager, p 91-92

48. You are walking around the facility to identify any privacy and security issues. You walk onto the 6W nursing unit and stand in a public area to look for possible violations. From where you are standing, you see that anyone can watch the nurse entering confidential patient information. You make a note of this. What are you doing?
    A. conducting a gap analysis
    B. conducting a risk assessment
    C. monitoring audit trail
    D. none of the above

REFERENCE: Hjort (2001), p 64A
                Krager and Krager, p 86-87, 104-105
                McWay, p 252

49. You are walking around the facility to identify any privacy and security issues. You walk onto the 6W nursing unit and are able to watch the nurse entering confidential patient information. How can you best improve the privacy of the patient's health information?
    A. Ask the nurse to type the data at another computer.
    B. Turn the computer screen so that the public cannot see it.
    C. Give the nurse additional training.
    D. none of the above

REFERENCE: Amatayakul (2002a), p 16C
                Krager and Krager, p 86-87, 104-105
                McWay, p 252

50. In conducting an environmental risk assessment, which of the following would be considered in the assessment?
    A. placement of water pipes in the facility
    B. verifying that virus checking software is in place
    C. use of single sign-on technology
    D. authentication

REFERENCE: Dennis, p 18
                McWay, p 253

51. Which of the following documents is subject to the HIPAA security rule?
    A. document faxed to the facility
    B. copy of discharge summary
    C. paper medical record
    D. scanned operative report stored on CD

REFERENCE: Roach, p 459
                McWay, p 57
                Krager, and Krager, p 6, 84-85

52. The privacy and security rules are part of the HIPAA
    A. Administrative Simplification.
    B. Transactions and Code sets.
    C. Insurance Portability.
    D. Identifiers.

REFERENCE: Dennis, p 69-72, 74
                Krager and Krager, p 2-6
                McWay, p 56-57

53. As Chief Privacy Officer, you have been asked why you are conducting a risk assessment. Which reason would you give?
    A. get rid of problem staff
    B. change organizational culture
    C. prevent breach of confidentiality
    D. none of the above

REFERENCE: Dennis p 36
               McWay, p 252-253
               Krager and Krager, p 86-87, 105
               Green and Bowie, p 84-85

54. You have decided that the current method of tracking release of confidential information is no longer appropriate for your facility's needs. You have decided that it is necessary to purchase a computerized tracking system. The administrator is supportive of the purchase but has asked for a formal justification of the system. Which of the following is NOT a reason to purchase the system?
    A. Everyone in the facility who releases information can enter information into a common database.
    B. A report can be printed upon demand.
    C. The system would restrict the release to the HIM department.
    D. You do not have to track down manual entries.

REFERENCE: Dougherty, p 72F

55. A covered entity:
    A. is exempt from the HIPAA privacy and security rules..
    B. includes all healthcare providers.
    C. includes healthcare providers who perform specified actions electronically.
    D. must utilize business associates.

REFERENCE: McWay, p 56
               Roach, p 141-142
               LaTour and Eichenwald-Maki, p 252
               Krager and Krager, p 10-11, 13

56. You have been given the responsibility of developing the plan to be used in the event that the ADT system goes down and your facility has to revert to manual backup processes. Which of the following should be considered?
    A. Print everything in the ADT.
    B. Ask patients to memorize their medical record number.
    C. Use the same number for the patient account number and medical record number.
    D. Use an MPI card system or maintain a paper or microfilm copy of an alphabetic MPI listing.

REFERENCE: Abdelhak, p 230
               McWay, p 322

57. Protected health information includes
    A. only electronic individually identifiable health information.
    B. only paper individually identifiable health information.
    C. individually identifiable health information in any format stored by a health care provider.
    D. individually identifiable health information in any format stored by a health care provider or business associate.

REFERENCE: LaTour and Eichenwald-Maki, p 252
                McWay, p 57
                Roach, p 105
                Green and Bowie, p 263
                Krager and Krager, p 6-8, 28-29

58. The enforcement of the HIPAA privacy rule has been delegated to the
    A. Office of Civil Rights.   C. Joint Commission.
    B. CMS.   D. states.

REFERENCE: McWay, p 57
                Krager and Krager, p 28, 45-46

59. On the day that a new employee is hired, he requests that no one in the department have access to his EHR. You tell the employee that you will
    A. send a memo to everyone in the department informing them of his request for confidentiality.
    B. increase the level of confidentiality on his record.
    C. examine his record yourself to determine who else currently has access to it.
    D. delete his record from the system.

REFERENCE: Johns, p 714
                LaTour and Eichenwald-Maki, p 253

60. Surf Side Hospital has conducted extensive privacy training for their employees. They trust their employees because it is a small community. There have not been any breaches in the past. They feel that monitoring compliance through an audit trail is not necessary. In this circumstance would it be reasonable to forgo keeping an audit trail?
    A. yes, since it is a small community
    B. no
    C. yes, if there is a hotline where violations can be reported
    D. yes, if employees are well trained

REFERENCE: Fuller, p 40
                Krager and Krager, p 90, 98, 105

61. Differentiate between authentication and authorization.
    A. Authentication is confirming that you are able to log into the system; authorization is determining what you can do.
    B. Authentication is determining what you can do; authorization is confirming that you are able to log into the system.
    C. Authentication is confirming that you are able to log into the system; authorization is identifying what a user did in the system.
    D. Authentication is determining what you can do and authorization is identifying what a user did in the system.

REFERENCE: Miller and Gregory, p 28-29
               McWay, p 103
               Krager and Krager, p 30-31, 99

62. Mark is an HIM employee who utilizes six different information systems as part of his job. Each of these has a different password. In order to keep up with the password for each system, Mark has written them all on paper and taped it to the back of his wife's picture on his desk. What technology could be used to eliminate this problem for Mark and other employees in the same situation?
    A. role-based access   C. SSO
    B. user-based access   D. DAC

REFERENCE: Miller and Gregory, p 40
               Krager and Krager, p 88-89, 97

63. Cindy, Tiffany, and LaShaundra are all nurses at Desert Sands Health Care. They all have access to the same functions in the information system. It is likely that this facility is using
    A. user-based access.   C. DAC.
    B. role-based access.   D. MAC.

REFERENCE: Miller and Gregory, p 49
               Krager and Krager 88-89, 105

64. You will be choosing the type of encryption to be used for the new EHR. What are your choices?
    A. symmetric and conventional   C. symmetric and asymmetric
    B. asymmetric and public key   D. public key and integrity

REFERENCE: Stallings, p 651

65. If HIPAA and state law conflicts, which prevails:

    A. HIPAA always
    B. state law always
    C. whichever is more protective of the patient's privacy
    D. HIPAA unless the state law is weaker

REFERENCE: LaTour and Eichenwald-Maki, p 252
               Stallings, p 662
               Abdelhak, p 515
               McWay, p 58

66. Sarah is the director of HIM at a Brandon Community Hospital. This is a small hospital that does not have an alcohol or drug abuse unit, nor does it treat patients of this type. Last night in the ER a patient came in who was diagnosed with acute alcoholism and was transferred to another facility for treatment. Does Brandon Community Hospital have to follow the regulations on the confidentiality of alcohol and drug abuse patients?
    A. yes, if the patient was in withdrawal and any treatment was provided to him
    B. yes, since they treated the patient
    C. no, since they do not have a program and there is no staff whose primary function is to treat these patients
    D. no, since they immediately transferred the patient from the emergency room

REFERENCE: Abdelhak, p 515-517

67. De-identified information can be released
    A. only with patient consent.
    B. only with IRB approval.
    C. without patient consent.
    D. for public health purposes only.

REFERENCE: McWay, p 60, 180, 233
               Krager and Krager, p 37-39

68. You are a researcher at the local university hospital. You will need to access patient information without patient authorization to conduct your research. Which of the following statements is true?

    A. You cannot gain any information without patient consent.
    B. You can obtain the information if the institutional review board waives the requirement for patient authorization.
    C. You can access anything that you need as long as you sign a statement saying that you will only use it for the purpose described on the form.
    D. You can access the information if you call the patients personally and get their written permission.

REFERENCE: Abdelhak, p 521-522
               Johns, p 725-726
               LaTour and Eichenwald-Maki, p 479-480, 527
               McWay, p 60, 180, 233
               Krager and Krager, p 37-39

69. The term "de-identified" indicates
    A. the patient's name has been removed.
    B. the patient's name and medical record number have been removed.
    C. the patient's name, medical record number, and social security number have been removed
    D. all of the HIPAA specified patient identifiers have been removed.

REFERENCE: Amatayakul (2007), p 385
                Johns, p 704-706
                Abdelhak, p 521-523
                LaTour and Eichenwald-Maki, p 479, 526
                McWay, p 60, 180, 233
                Krager and Krager, p 37-39

70. An employee utilizes the patient's name and Social Security number to obtain a credit card. This is an example of
    A. theft.
    B. de-identified information.
    C. limited data set.
    D. security incident.

REFERENCE: McWay, p 63
                Krager and Krager, p 29-30, 44-45

71. Your system just crashed. Fortunately you have established a site that holds computer processors that can be converted to meet our needs quickly. This is a
    A. hot site.   C. redundant site.
    B. cold site.   D. backup site

REFERENCE: NIST, chap. 11, p 5

72. The purpose of the notice of privacy practices is to
    A. notify the patient of uses of PHI.   C. report incidents to the OIG.
    B. notify patient of audits.   D. notify researchers of allowable data use.

REFERENCE: McWay, p 60
                Krager and Krager, p 43

73. The purpose of the new security awareness program is(are)
    A. to help staff realize the importance of security.
    B. remind users of procedures.
    C. lock down PHI.
    D. both A and B

REFERENCE: NIST, chap. 13, p 10
                Krager and Krager, p 90
                McWay, p 60

74. When addressing physical security, which of the following should be taken into consideration?
    A. natural threats   C. damaging nearby activities
    B. human-made threats   D. all of the above

REFERENCE: NIST, chap. 15, p 1
                McWay, p 323
                Krager and Krager, p 92-95

75. According to HIPAA, covered entities may include marketing in a newsletter that is sent to a wide range of individuals.
    A. true
    B. true if there is an opt-out procedure identified
    C. false
    D. false if services marketed do not apply to the individual

REFERENCE: Hughes (2002d), p 64
               Krager and Krager, p 38-39

76. Would an entity that conducts the sale or dispensing of a drug, device, equipment, or other item in accordance with a prescription be a covered entity?
    A. yes
    B. no

REFERENCE: Krager and Krager, p 10-11

77. Which of the following situations would require a business associate agreement?
    A. company to whom transcription is outsourced
    B. company who contracts to paint the nursing units
    C. company who is auditing accounts payable
    D. architects who are planning the renovations of the nursing units

REFERENCE: Sullivan, p 92
               McWay, p 56
               Krager and Krager, p 42
               Johns, p 703-704, 869-870

78. Miles has asked you to explain the rights that he has via HIPAA privacy standards. Which of the following is one of his HIPAA-given rights?
    A. He can review his bill.
    B. He can ask to be contacted at an alternative site.
    C. He can discuss financial arrangements with business office staff.
    D. He can ask a patient advocate to sit in on all appointments at the facility.

REFERENCE: U.S. Office of Civil Rights (n.d.), p 1-2
               LaTour and Eichenwald, p 253-254
               McWay, p 57

79. The following is a sentence from the notice of privacy practices. What problem do you identify?

The party of the first part vows to mitigate breaches should a security incident occur.

    A. None, because that is the responsibility of a covered entity.
    B. None, because that is the responsibility of a business associate.
    C. It is not the responsibility of a covered entity.
    D. It is not written in plain English.

REFERENCE: U.S. Department of Health and Human Services Office for Civil Rights (2003), p 32
               Krager and Krager, p 31

80. HIPAA workforce security requires
    A. a criminal background check.
    B. a two-factor authentication.
    C. that access to PHI be appropriate.
    D. the use of card keys.

REFERENCE: Roach, p 463
                Krager and Krager, p 88-89
                McWay, p 323

81. Which of the following is a true statement regarding psychotherapy notes?
    A. Patients have open access to psychotherapy notes.
    B. Psychotherapy notes are never intended to be shared with anyone.
    C. Psychotherapy notes cannot be used in defending oneself in a court case.
    D. Psychotherapy notes are to be destroyed after one year because of their confidential nature

REFERENCE: U.S. Department of Health and Human Services Office for Civil Rights (2003), p 35
                LaTour and Eichenwald-Maki, p 257
                Johns, p 706
                Krager and Krager, p 16, 38-39
                Green and Bowie, p 268

82. Richard has asked to view his medical record. The record is stored off-site. How long does the facility have to provide this record to him?
    A. 30 days
    B. 60 days
    C. 14 days
    D. 10 days

REFERENCE: U.S. Department of Health and Human Services Office for Civil Rights (2003), p 35

83. A patient authorizes Hospital A to send a copy of a discharge summary for the latest hospitalization to Hospital B. Hospital B uses the discharge summary in the patient's care and files it in the medical record. When Hospital B receives a request for records, a copy of Hospital A's discharge summary is sent. This is an example of:
    A. a privacy violation
    B. redisclosure
    C. satisfactory assurance
    D. inappropriate release

REFERENCE: Servais, p 345-349
                Krager and Krager, p 127-128
                Green and Bowie, p 284-285
                Abdelhak, p 525-526

84. You have to decide which type of firewall that you want to use in your facility. Which of the following is one of your options?
    A. packet filter
    B. secure socket layer
    C. CCOW
    D. denial of service

REFERENCE: Abdelhak, p 296-297

85. Don has requested an accounting of disclosure. Which of the following would be on the list?
    A. his previous request
    B. the nurses involved in his care
    C. the attorney request of March 2003
    D. none of the above

REFERENCE: Dougherty, p 72E
                LaTour and Eichenwald-Maki, p 253
                Johns, p 712
                McWay, p 389
                Green and Bowie, p 285-287

86. Juan comes out to speak to a patient's family. He tells them that the patient came through surgery fine. The mass was benign and they could see the patient in an hour. He talks low so that other people will not hear, but someone walked by and heard. This is
    A. a HIPAA violation because another patient overheard.
    B. an incidental disclosure.
    C. a HIPAA violation because he shared this with the patient's family who is actively involved.
    D. acceptable if the patient who overheard was asked to keep his or her mouth shut.

REFERENCE: Hjort (2003b), p 2
               Johns (2007), p 727
               Krager and Krager, p 19, 36

87. Which of the following situations requires compliance with the minimum necessary rule?
    A. patient requests records
    B. patient authorization received
    C. sharing information with consulting physician for patient care
    D. coroner identifying a body

REFERENCE: Hjort (2003b), p 1
               Johns, p 701-702
               LaTour and Eichenwald-Maki, p 259
               McWay, p 62
               Krager and Krager, p 34-35, 41
               Abdelhak, p 517

88. Which of the following set(s) is an appropriate use of the emergency access procedure?
    A. A patient is crashing. The attending physician is not in the hospital, so a physician who is available helps the patient.
    B. One of the nurses is at lunch. The nurse covering for her needs patient information.
    C. The coder who usually codes the emergency room charts is out sick and the charts are left on a desk in the ER admitting area.
    D. A and B

REFERENCE: HIMSS, 7.3
               Krager and Krager, p 89, 105
               Green and Bowie, p 268, 271

89. Today is August 30, 2008. When can the training records for the HIPAA privacy training being conducted today be destroyed?
    A. August 30, 2013   C. August 30, 2016
    B. August 30, 2014   D. August 30, 2018

REFERENCE: Hjort (2002), p 60 A-G
               Krager and Krager, p 90

90. We have just become aware that an employee, looked up his own medical record. Which of the following actions should be taken?
    A. Notify his or her supervisor because this is a minor incident and therefore not subject to the incident response procedure.
    B. Follow the incident response procedure.
    C. Terminate the employee on the spot.
    D. Notify OCR.

REFERENCE: HIMSS, p 6.0, 6.1
               LaTour and Eichenwald-Maki, p 865

91. Choosing to be in the directory means which of the following?
    A. Friends and family can find out what room you are in.
    B. Your condition can be released in general terms.
    C. Your friends can be told your specific condition.
    D. both A and B

REFERENCE: Rhodes, p 640
               Johns, p 722
               Krager and Krager, p 35-36, 40, 124-125

92. In which of the following circumstances would a data use agreement be required?
    A. The hospital is contracting with a new release of information company.
    B. The IRB is approving the release of a limited data set to researchers.
    C. The hospital needs to destroy records on the imaging system.
    D. The hospital needs to destroy records more than 10 years old.

REFERENCE: Amatayakul (2002b), p 24C

93. A data use agreement allows the organization receiving the data to
    A. use the non-PHI data any way they want.
    B. use PHI data any way they want.
    C. use data only within the bounds of the agreement.
    D. conduct business for the organization.

REFERENCE: U.S. Department of Health and Human Services Office for Civil Rights (2003)., p 31

94. The following data elements are in a limited data set file being released. Which data element is in the file in error, in that it is PHI?
    A. zip code   C. vehicle identification number
    B. city   D. chargemaster item number

REFERENCE: U.S. Department of Health and Human Services Office for Civil Rights (2003)., p 31
               Krager and Krager, p 37
               McWay, p 180, 233

95. Margot has just gone through some computer training. One of the issues covered was how to prevent viruses from being spread. Actions that she, a computer user, should take include all of the following EXCEPT
    A. do not e-mail a file to anyone else in the organization if a virus has been identified.
    B. do not download shareware on her computer.
    C. do not share diskettes between computers.
    D. update the virus protection on at least a daily basis.

REFERENCE: HIMSS, 5.2

96. Which of the following is an example of mitigation?
    A. providing copy of notice of privacy practices
    B. giving a discount on services
    C. sending out billing notices
    D. picking up records mailed to the wrong site

REFERENCE: Burrington-Brown, p 64B

97. Treatment, payment, and health care operations
    A. are allowed usages of PHI.
    B. are not discussed in the notice of privacy practices.
    C. are a concept of the Privacy Act of 1974.
    D. require patient consent.

REFERENCE: LaTour and Eichenwald-Maki, p 256
                Krager and Krager, p 31
                Green and Bowie, p 265-268
                McWay, p 60

98. When is a data use agreement required?
    A. when a complaint has been issued
    B. when a limited data set is used
    C. when a notice of disclosure is requested
    D. when information is provided to a business associate

REFERENCE: Roach, p 109-110
                McWay, p 180, 233

99. An exception to the minimum necessary rule can be made when:
    A. releasing PHI to patients.
    B. fulfilling the purpose of a request for information.
    C. providing information to business associates.
    D. requesting information form other covered entities.

REFERENCE: Roach, p 146
                McWay, p 62, 84
                McWay, p 62-63, 84-85
                Krager and Krager, p 33-35, 41

100. An organization that is a covered entity, performs functions that are covered and noncovered by
     HIPAA, and specifies the portion of the organization that will be subject to HIPAA is called a(n)
     A. hybrid entity.
     B. affiliated covered entity.
     C. organized health care arrangement.
     D. business associate.

REFERENCE: Roach, p 149

Health Information Privacy and Security

ANSWER   EXPLANATION

1. B

2. C   The release of childbirth information is acceptable because it is related to the reason for admission. The mass mailing of samples violates giving out confidential information to outside agencies.

3. B   The chest x-ray has no bearing on the finger fracture.

4. A

5. D

6. A

7. B

8. B

9. C   The person who recorded the documentation in question should be the one who authorizes the change. While these references may not explicitly state this, it does state that the form should have a place for the provider's signature and comments.

10. D

11. A

12. B

13. B

14. C

15. D

16. D

17. A

18. B

19. C

20. B

21. C

22. B

23. D   Natural disasters, equipment failure, and human error are usually unintentional threats to security. Data theft is intentional.

24. A

25. C

26. C

27. A

28. C

29. B

30. B

31. A

32. D

33. B

34. A

35. A

36. A

37. C

38. B

39. A

40. D   Once the provider agrees the request cannot be violated except in emergency care. The patient should be notified even though you have patient authorization.

41. A

42. A

43. D

44. D

45. C

46. A

47. D

48. B

49. B

50. A

51. D

52. D

53. C

54. C

55. C

56. D

57. D

58. A

59. B

60. B   The audit is not required; however, it is good practice and is therefore strongly recommended.

61. A

62. C

63. B

64. C

65. C

66. C

Health Information Privacy and Security

ANSWER EXPLANATION

67. C

68. B

69. D

70. A

71. B

72. A

73. D

74. D

75. B

76. A

77. A

78. B

79. D The Notice of Privacy must be written in plain English so that it can be understood.

80. C

81. B

82. B

83. B

84. B

85. D

86. B

87. D

88. D

89. B

90. B

91. D

92. B

93. C

94. D

95. D Although virus software should be updated at least daily, it is not typically done by the user.

96. D

97. A

98. B

99. A

100. A

REFERENCES

Abdelhak, M., Grostick, S., Hanken, M. A., & Jacobs, E. (2004). *Health information: Management of a strategic resource* (2nd ed.). Philadelphia: W.B. Saunders.

Amatayakul, M. (2001a). HIPAA on the job series: Five steps to reading the HIPAA rules. *Journal of AHIMA, 72*(8), 16A-C.

Amatayakul, M. (2001b). HIPAA on the job series: Managing individual rights requirements under HIPAA privacy. *Journal of AHIMA, 72*(6), 16A-D.

Amatayakul, M. (2002a). HIPAA on the job: A reasonable approach to physical security. *Journal of AHIMA, 73*(4), 16A-C.

Amatayakul, M. (2002b). United under HIPAA: A comparison of arrangements and agreements. *Journal of AHIMA, 73*(8), 24A-D.

Amatayakul, M. (2007). *Electronic health records a practical guide for professionals and organizations* (3rd ed). Chicago, American Health Information Management Association.

Amatayakul, M., & Walsh, T. Selecting strong passwords (HIPPA on the job series). *Journal of AHIMA 72, 40.9 (2001)16A-D.*

Amatayakul, M., & Waymack, P. (2002). What's your designated record set? *Journal of AHIMA, 73*(6), 16A-C.

Burrington-Brown, J. (2003). AHIMA practice brief: Handling complaints and mitigation. *Journal of AHIMA, 74*(10), *64A-C.*

Cassidy, B. S. (2000). HIPAA on the job: Understanding chain of trust and business partner agreements. *Journal of AHIMA, 71*(9), 16A-C.

Cassidy, B. S. (2001). HIPAA on the job: The next challenge: Employee training on privacy, security. *Journal of AHIMA, 72*(1), 16A-C.

Dennis, J. C. (2000). *Privacy and confidentiality of health information.* San Francisco: Jossey-Bass.

Dougherty, M. (2001). Practice brief: Accounting and tracking disclosure of protected health information. *Journal of AHIMA, 72*(10), 72E-H.

Fuller, S. (1999). Implementing HIPAA security standards—are you ready? *Journal of AHIMA, 70*(9), 38-44.

Green, M. A., & Bowie, M.J. (2004). *Essentials of health information management.* Clifton Park, NY: Thomson Delmar Learning.

Hartley, C. P., & Jones III, E .D. (2004). *HIPAA plain and simple: A compliance guide for health care professionals.* Chicago: American Medical Association.

HIMSS (2003). HIMSS CPRI Toolkit.
Retrieved on October 1, 2006, from http://www.himss.org
http://www.himss.org/ASP/topics_cpriToolkit.asp?faid=78andtid=4
http://www.himss.org/ASP/topics_cpriToolkit.asp?faid=78andtid=4#toolkit

Hjort, B. (2001). AHIMA practice brief: A HIPAA privacy checklist. *Journal of AHIMA, 72*(6), 64A-C.

Hjort, B. (2002). Privacy and security training. *Journal of AHIMA, 73*(4), 60A-G.

Hjort, B. (2003a). Practice brief: Security audits. Retrieved November 9, 2005, from http://ahima.org http://library.ahima.org

Hjort, B. (2003b). Practice brief: Understanding the minimum necessary standard. Retrieved September 9, 2005, from http://ahima.org http://library.ahima.org

Hughes, G. (2001a). Managing exceptions to HIPAA's patient access rule. *Journal of AHIMA, 72*(9), 90-92.

Hughes, G. (2001b). Practice briefs: Redisclosure of PHI. *Journal of AHIMA, 72*(8), 72A, 72B.

Hughes, G. (2002a). Practice briefs: Notice of information practices (updated). Journal of AHIMA, 72(5), 64I-M.

Hughes, G. (2002b). Practice brief: Understanding the minimum necessary standard. *Journal of AHIMA, 73*(1), 56A-B.

Hughes, G. (2002c). Simple steps to tracking disclosures. *Journal of AHIMA, 73*(7), 2002, 68-70.

Hughes, G. (2002d). Understanding the privacy rule's amendments. *Journal of AHIMA, 73*(10), 64-66.

Johns, M. L. (2006). *Health information technology: An applied approach* (2nd ed.). Chicago: American Health Information Management Association.

Krager, D., Krager, C. (2008). *HIPAA for health care professionals.* New York: Delmar Cengage Learning.

LaTour, K. M., & Eichenwald-Maki, S. (2006). *Health information management: Concepts, principles, and practice* (2nd ed.). Chicago: American Health Information Management Association.

McWay, D. (2008). *Today's health information management: An integrated approach.* Chicago: Thomson Delmar.

Miller, L., & Gregory, P. (2002). *CISSP for dummies.* New York: Wiley Publishing.

National Institute of Standards and Technology (NIST). (2005). Special Publication 800-12: An Introduction to Computer Security - The NIST Handbook. Printed from http://csrc.nist.gov/publications/nistpubs/800-12/800-12-html, on August 1, 2005.

Rhodes, H. (2001). Practice brief: Patient anonymity (updated). *Journal of AHIMA, 72*(5), 64O-R.

Roach, M. (2001). HIPAA compliance questions for business partner agreements. *Journal of AHIMA, 72*(2), 45-51.

Roach, W, R. Hoban, B. Broccolo, A. Roth, & T. Blanchard. (2006). *Medical records and the law.* Sudbury, MA: Jones and Bartlett.

Servais, C., Olderman, N., & Trahan, K. (2008) *The legal health record*. Chicago: American Health Information Management Association.

Stallings, W. (2000). *Data and computer communication* (6th ed). Upper Saddle River, NJ: Prentice-Hall.

Sullivan, T. (2002). Mind your business associate access: Six steps.
Journal of AHIMA, 73(9), 92, 94, 96.

Thieleman, W. (2002). A patient friendly approach to the record amendment process.
Journal of AHIMA, 73(5), 46-47.

Train for HIPAA. (n.d.) Glossary.
Retrieved March 8, 2007 from http://www.trainforhipaa.com/resources/glossary.html

U.S. Department of Health and Human Services (2001). HHS fact sheet: Protecting the privacy of patient's health information.
Retrieved March 8, 2007 from: http://www.hhs.gov/news/press/2002pres/privacy.html

U.S. Department of Health and Human Services Office for Civil Rights (2003). *Standards for Privacy of Individually Identifiable Health Information Security Standards for the Protection of Electronic Protected Health Information General Administrative Requirements Including, Civil Money Penalties: Procedures for Investigations, Imposition of Penalties, and Hearings Regulation Text* (Unofficial Version) (45 CFR Parts 160 and 164)
December 28, 2000 as amended: May 31, 2002, August 14, 2002, February 20, 2003, and April 17, 2003.
Retrieved March 8, 2007 from http://www.hhs.gov/ocr/combinedregtext.pdf

U.S. Office of Civil Rights (n.d.). Your health information privacy rights.
Retrieved September 9, 2005 from http://www.hhs.gov/ocr/hipaa/consumer_rights.pdf

XII. Health Law

Barbara W. Mosley, PhD, RHIA

CASE STUDY #1

Dr. Roberts, an orthopedic surgeon, and Nurse Parrish, head nurse on the orthopedic surgery unit, have had an acrimonious working relationship for years. While making rounds on the unit, Dr. Roberts discovered that the physical therapy evaluation he had ordered for one of his patients had not been performed and became outraged. Even though he did not have proof, Dr. Roberts placed the blame for the missed evaluation with Nurse Parrish. Dr. Roberts wrote in the patient's medical record that Nurse Parrish failed to properly order the physical therapy evaluation because she was incompetent and could not be trusted to carry out even the simplest order. After having read Dr. Roberts' note, Nurse Parrish countered by making a disparaging remark about Dr. Roberts to the medical personnel at the nurses' station. Nurse Parrish stated that Dr. Roberts was the one who was incompetent and was responsible for the needless suffering of countless patients over the years.

1. Referring to Case Study #1, the written statement by Dr. Roberts about Nurse Parrish's professional competence in the patient's medical record can constitute
   A. libel.   C. perjury.
   B. slander.   D. defamation.

REFERENCE: LaTour and Eichenwald, p 246
              McWay, p 94
              McWay (2003), p 52-53
              Pozgar, p 47, 530
              Roach, p 401

2. Referring to Case Study #1, the oral statement by Nurse Parrish about Dr. Roberts's professional practices at the nurses' station can constitute
   A. libel.   C. perjury.
   B. slander.   D. defamation.

REFERENCE: LaTour and Eichenwald, p 246
              McWay, p 54
              McWay (2003), p 52-53
              Pozgar, p 47, 532
              Roach, p 401

3. Referring to Case Study #1, what should Dr. Roberts be reminded of regarding his notation in the patient's chart about Nurse Parrish?
   A. It is against the law to mention names of persons who are not actively attending to his patient.
   B. His action violates the 1974 Privacy Act.
   C. The medical record must not be used as a battleground against another professional.
   D. He should erase his note about Nurse Parrish because it is malicious.

REFERENCE: Pozgar, p 304, 310
              Roach, p 291-292

4. Rules and principles determined by legislative bodies constitute which type of law?
    A. statutory law   C. common law
    B. administrative law   D. case law

REFERENCE: Green and Bowie, p 257
               LaTour and Eichenwald and Eichenwald, p 242, 947
               McWay, p 46
               McWay (2003), p 8
               Pozgar, p 17, 532
               Roach, p 6-7

5. Which of the following elements of negligence must be present in order to recover damages?
    A. duty of care; breach of duty of care; value attached to injury is greater than a certain value
        (ordinarily $1,000); provisions of the HIPAA Privacy Rule have been met
    B. duty of care; breach of the duty of care; suffered an injury; value attached to injury is greater
        than a certain value (ordinarily $1,000)
    C. duty of care; breach of duty of care; suffered an injury; defendant's conduct caused the
        plaintiff harm
    D. breach of duty of care; suffered an injury; value attached to injury is greater than a certain
        value (ordinarily $1,000); provision of HIPAA Privacy Rule have been met

REFERENCE: LaTour and Eichenwald, p 245
               Green and Bowie, p 257
               McWay, p 56
               McWay (2003), p 44-48
               Pozgar, p 33

6. When the physician failed to give the patient the lips of the famous actress she requested, the
    physician engaged in which of the following?
    A. slander.   C. libel.
    B. a breach of contract.   D. invasion of privacy.

REFERENCE: McWay, p 54
               McWay (2003), p 55
               LaTour and Eichenwald, p 247-248

7. Laws that limit the period during which legal action may be brought against another party are
    known as
    A. case law.   C. statutes of limitations.
    B. summons.   D. common law.

REFERENCE: Green and Bowie, p 257
               McWay, p 112
               McWay (2003), p 55-57
               Pozgar, p 132-133
               Roach, p 43-44
               LaTour and Eichenwald, p 247, 946

8. The protection of a patient's health information is addressed in each of the following EXCEPT
   A. Health Insurance Portability and Accountability Act.
   B. Privacy Act.
   C. Drug Abuse and Treatment Act.
   D. U.S. Patriot Act.

REFERENCE: Green and Bowie, p 272-273
LaTour and Eichenwald and Eichenwald, p 249-251
McWay (2003), p 90-101; 151-152
Pozgar, p 26, 300
Roach, p 104-105

9. In a court of law, Attorney A, the attorney for Sun City Hospital, introduces the medical record from the hospital as evidence. However, Attorney B, the attorney for the defendant, objects on the grounds that the medical record is subject to the hearsay rule which prohibits its admission as evidence. Attorney B's objection is overridden. Why?
   A. The medical record does not belong to the hospital; therefore, the hospital has no right to release the medical record as evidence.
   B. It would violate physician-patient privilege, even though the patient signed a proper release of information form.
   C. The doctrine of res ipsa loquitur prevails; therefore, reference to the medical record is moot.
   D. The medical record may be admitted as business records or as an explicit exception to hearsay rule.

REFERENCE: Green and Bowie, p 260-261
McWay (2003), p 136
Pozgar, p 122-125
Roach, p 383-384
Servais, p 4-5

10. Medical record information may be exempt from the Freedom of Information Act requirements if the request for information meets the test of being an unwarranted invasion of personal privacy. Which of the following is NOT one of the conditions of the test?
    A. The information must be contained in a personal, medical, or similar file.
    B. The information is generated from federally funded research conducted by a private health care organization.
    C. Disclosure of the information constitutes an invasion of personal privacy.
    D. The severity of the invasion must outweigh the public's interest in disclosure.

REFERENCE: LaTour and Eichenwald, p 250-251
McWay (2003), p 120
Roach, p 123-127

11. The doctrine that the decisions of the court should stand as precedents for future guidance is
    A. res ipsa loquitur.   C. stare decisis.
    B. respondeat superior.   D. statute of limitations.

REFERENCE: Green and Bowie, p 257
McWay (2003), p 11
Pozgar, p 9, 532

12. The body of law founded on custom, natural justice and reason, and sanctioned by usage and judicial decision is known as
   A. common law.
   B. lien law.
   C. constitutional law.
   D. statutory law.

REFERENCE: Green and Bowie, p 255-256
               LaTour and Eichenwald and Eichenwald, p 241, 916
               McWay (2003), p 10
               Pozgar, p 14, 528
               Roach, p 10, 545

CASE STUDY #2

You are the Director of the Health Information Management Department for Bayshore Hospital. A former patient of the hospital, Barbara Masters, is suing the hospital for negligent care of an infected decubitus ulcer. You are asked by Barbara's attorney to provide sworn verbal testimony and/or written answers to questions.

13. Referring to Case Study #2, Barbara Masters is the _____ in this case.
   A. appellant
   B. appellee
   C. defendant
   D. plaintiff

REFERENCE: Green and Bowie, p 255
               LaTour and Eichenwald-Maki, p 243
               McWay, p 52
               McWay (2003), p 25
               Pozgar, p 108, 531

14. Referring to Case Study #2, Bayshore Hospital is the _____ in this case.
   A. appellant
   B. appellee
   C. defendant
   D. plaintiff

REFERENCE: Green and Bowie, p 255
               LaTour and Eichenwald-Maki, p 243
               McWay, p 52
               McWay (2003), p 25
               Pozgar, p 108, 528

15. Referring to Case Study #2, the sworn verbal testimony you are asked to provide is called a(n)
   A. interrogatory.
   B. deposition.
   C. physical and mental examination.
   D. court order.

REFERENCE: Green and Bowie, p 255
               McWay (2003), p 26
               Pozgar, p 111, 528
               LaTour and Eichenwald-Maki, p 243

16. Referring to Case Study #2, the written answers to questions you have been asked to provide are known as a(n)
    A. interrogatory.
    B. deposition.
    C. physical and mental examination.
    D. court order.

REFERENCE: Green and Bowie, p 255
               LaTour and Eichenwald-Maki, p 243
               McWay (2003), p 26-28
               Roach, p 375

17. Referring to Case Study #2, you are involved in what phase of the lawsuit?
    A. pretrial conference   C. discovery
    B. trial   D. appeal

REFERENCE: Pozgar, p 110-111, 529
               Green and Bowie, p 255
               McWay (2003), p 26-27
               Roach, p 374-375
               LaTour and Eichenwald-Maki, p 243

18. Which of the following claims of negligence fits into the category of res ipsa loquitur?
    A. incorrect administration of anesthesia
    B. failure to refer patient to a specialist
    C. leaving a foreign body inside a patient
    D. improper use of x-rays

REFERENCE: Green and Bowie, p 257
               McWay, p 55
               McWay (2003), p 48-49
               Pozgar, p 117-118, 281, 532
               LaTour and Eichenwald-Maki, p 247

19. The failure to obtain the written consent of the patient before performing a surgical procedure may constitute
    A. battery.   C. libel.
    B. contempt.   D. malpractice.

REFERENCE: Green and Bowie, p 274
               LaTour and Eichenwald-Maki, p 245
               McWay, p 54
               McWay (2003), p 52
               Pozgar, p 44, 527

20. The fee paid for reimbursement for expenses incurred from providing health information whether for subpoena or reproduction by healthcare providers is determined by the
    A. American Health Information Management Association.
    B. hospitals and lawyers.
    C. statute or court rules.
    D. plaintiff and defendant lawyers.

REFERENCE: McWay (2003), p 102

21. Who determines the retention period for health records?
    A. state and federal governments
    B. medical staff
    C. city and state governments
    D. commercial storage vendors

REFERENCE: Servais, p 350-354
               Green and Bowie, p 97
               LaTour and Eichenwald-Maki, p 202, 206, 251
               McWay, 49
               McWay (2003), p 76-77
               Pozgar, p 303
               Roach, p 40-41

22. The extent to which the HIPAA privacy rule may regulate an individual's rights of access is not meant to preempt other existing federal laws and regulations. This means that if an individual's rights of access
    A. is less under another existing federal law, HIPAA must follow the directions of that law.
    B. is refused by a federal facility, HIPAA must also refuse the individual of the access.
    C. is greater under another applicable federal law, the individual should be afforded the greater access.
    D. is greater under another existing federal law, HIPAA can obstruct freedoms of the other federal law when using electronic health records.

REFERENCE: Servais, p 119

CASE STUDY #3

A 73-year-old male was admitted to the Sunset Nursing Facility with senility, cataracts, and S/P cerebrovascular accident with right-side hemiplegia. On his second day at the facility, the resident was discovered to have extensive thermal burns on his buttocks and legs by one of the facility's attendants.

23. Referring to Case Study #3, the resident's family brought legal action against the nursing facility for
    A. medical abandonment.   C. assault and battery.
    B. vicarious liability.   D. negligence.

REFERENCE: Green and Bowie, p 257
               LaTour and Eichenwald-Maki, p 244-245, 936
               McWay, p 55
               McWay (2003), p 45-46
               Pozgar, p 33-37, 225, 531

24. Referring to Case Study #3, which of the following can the attorney of the resident's family also use as a basis for the lawsuit and why?
    A. The doctrine of res ipsa loquitur because it allows the plaintiff to shift the burden of proof to the defendant because direct evidence is available.
    B. The doctrine of charitable immunity because the nursing facility is a private institution and is shielded from liability for any torts committed on its property.
    C. The Good Samaritan Statutes because they protect the Director of Nursing, an employee of the nursing facility, who was not present when the injury occurred.
    D. The failure to warn theory because the doctor did not inform the resident's family that the resident was in danger at the nursing facility.

REFERENCE: Green and Bowie, p 257
               McWay, p 55
               McWay (2003), p 48
               Pozgar, p 117-118, 532

25. In a negligence or malpractice case, all of the following elements must be present in order to shift the burden of proof onto the defendant EXCEPT the
    A. event would not normally have occurred in the absence of negligence.
    B. health care facility does not have a risk management program.
    C. defendant had exclusive control over the instrumentality that caused the injury.
    D. plaintiff did not contribute to the injury.

REFERENCE: Green and Bowie, p 255
               McWay, p 55
               McWay (2003), p 44; 48

26. When a healthcare facility fails to investigate the qualifications of a physician hired to work as an independent contractor in the emergency room and is accused of negligence, the healthcare facility can be held liable under
    A. respondeat superior.   C. contributory negligence.
    B. corporate negligence.   D. general negligence.

REFERENCE: McWay (2003), p 50-51
               Pozgar, p 150-152

27. What source or document is considered the "supreme law of the land"?
    A. Bill of Rights
    B. Supreme Court decisions
    C. presidential power
    D. Constitution of the United States

REFERENCE: LaTour and Eichenwald-Maki, p 241
               McWay, p 55
               McWay (2003), p 5
               Pozgar, p 17

28. Hospitals that destroy their own medical records must have a policy that
    A. ensures records are destroyed and confidentiality is protected.
    B. notifies the physicians when the records of their patients are destroyed.
    C. states that all records are destroyed annually.
    D. ensures that the type of equipment to be used for destruction of records is properly maintained.

REFERENCE: Green and Bowie, p 98-99
               LaTour and Eichenwald-Maki, p 203
               McWay, p 112-113, 115
               McWay (2003), p 79
               Roach, p 49-50

29. A written authorization from the patient releasing copies of his or her medical records is required by all of the following EXCEPT
    A. the patient's attorney.
    B. a physician requesting copies from another physician.
    C. an insurance company.
    D. the hospital attorney for the facility where the patient is treated.

REFERENCE: Green and Bowie, 281
               LaTour and Eichenwald-Maki, p 256-257
               McWay (2003), p 101-102

30. The medical record is generally accepted as being the property of the
    A. patient's guardian.   C. institution.
    B. court.   D. patient.

REFERENCE: Green and Bowie, p 75-76
               LaTour and Eichenwald-Maki, p 251-252
               McWay, p 61
               McWay (2003), p 90
               Servais, p 54
               Pozgar, p 299

31. The ownership of the information contained in the physical medical/health record is considered to belong to the
    A. patient.   C. physician.
    B. hospital.   D. insurance company.

REFERENCE: Green and Bowie, p 75-76
               LaTour and Eichenwald-Maki, p 251-252
               McWay (2003), p 90; 100
               Pozgar, p 299

32. When developing a record retention policy, the HIM professionals should consider all of the following EXCEPT
   A. current storage space.
   B. uses of and need for information.
   C. all applicable statutes and regulations.
   D. the thickness of the records.

REFERENCE: Green and Bowie, p 96-97
               LaTour and Eichenwald-Maki, p 202, 251
               McWay, p 112-113
               McWay (2003), p 77-78
               Servais, p 350-353
               Pozgar, p 303

33. If the patient record is involved in litigation and the physician requests to make a change to that record, what should the HIM professional do?
   A. Refer request to legal counsel.
   B. Allow the change to occur.
   C. Notify the patient.
   D. Say the record is unavailable.

REFERENCE: Green and Bowie, 84-85
               Servais, p 30-32

34. One of the greatest threats to the confidentiality of health data is
   A. when medical information is reviewed as a part of quality assurance activities.
   B. disclosure of information for purposes not authorized in writing by the patient.
   C. lack of written authorization by the patient.
   D. when medical information is used for research or education.

REFERENCE: Green and Bowie, p 261
               LaTour and Eichenwald-Maki, p 273-274
               Servais, p 52-55
               McWay, p 59-60
               McWay (2003), p 116-121

35. HIM professionals are bound to protect the confidentiality of patient information under the
   A. Patient Bill of Rights.
   B. AHIMA's Code of Ethics.
   C. Hippocratic oath.
   D. JCAHO standards.

REFERENCE: Green and Bowie, p 337-338
               LaTour and Eichenwald-Maki, p 274
               McWay, p 83

36. Upon learning that a court order violates state law, the HIM professional should
   A. call the judge issuing the court order.
   B. call the opposing attorney.
   C. call the legal counsel for the health care institution.
   D. ignore the court order.

REFERENCE: Servais, p 60-62
               McWay, p 65-66
               McWay (2003), p 144
               Roach, p 323-324

37. What type of testimony is inappropriate for a health information manager serving as custodian of the record when he or she is called to be a witness in court?
    A. whether the record is in the practitioner's possession
    B. title and position held in the health care facility
    C. whether the medical record was made in the usual course of business
    D. interpretation of documentation in the record

REFERENCE: McWay (2003), p 136-137
                Servais, p 4-5, 208

38. In order to determine which information should be considered confidential, a health information manager should consider and answer yes to all the following questions EXCEPT:
    A. Is there a patient-provider relationship?
    B. Is the information needed to treat or diagnose the patient?
    C. Was the information in question exchanged through the professional relationship?
    D. Is there a need for all health care providers to access the patient information?

REFERENCE: Green and Bowie, p 261
                McWay, p 59-60
                Servais, p 7, 53-55

Case Study #4

William is a 16-year-old male who lives at home with his parents and works part-time as a dishwasher at one of the local restaurants. While emptying the dishwasher, William is severely scalded and rendered unconscious. He is taken to the emergency room of the local acute care hospital for emergency treatment.

39. Referring to Case Study #4, given the emergency of the situation, who should the health care provider, seek consent from in order to provide treatment to William?
    A. the employer
    B. the parents
    C. the patient
    D. no consent is needed for emergency care

REFERENCE: Pozgar, p 328
                Roach, p 89-91
                LaTour and Eichenwald-Maki, p 257
                McWay (2003), p 125-127

40. Referring to Case Study #4, in order to release information to his employer, the hospital must receive a
    A. consent signed by the patient.
    B. court order.
    C. consent signed by the doctor.
    D. consent signed by the patient's parent.

REFERENCE: LaTour and Eichenwald-Maki, p 256-258
                McWay, p 61-62
                McWay (2003), p 99
                Pozgar, p 182

41. A valid authorization for the disclosure of health information should not be
    A. dated prior to discharge of the patient.
    B. in writing.
    C. addressed to the health care provider.
    D. signed by the patient.

REFERENCE: LaTour and Eichenwald-Maki, p 255-256
               McWay (2003), p 96-100
               Pozgar, p 325

42. Internal disclosures of patient information for patient care purposes should be granted
    A. to legal counsel.
    B. on a need to know basis.
    C. to any physician on staff.
    D. to a family member who is an employee.

REFERENCE: Green and Bowie, p 124, 126
               LaTour and Eichenwald-Maki, p 257
               McWay, p 62
               McWay (2003), p 99; 102

43. According to AHIMA's Position on Transmission of Health Information, the health information manager should engage in all of the following to ensure that information is properly sent via facsimile transmission EXCEPT
    A. to always follow up by sending the original record by mail.
    B. to pre-program into the machine the number of destination sites.
    C. encrypt the data if public channels are used for electronic transmittal.
    D. as the sender contact the recipient prior to and after transmission.

REFERENCE: McWay (2003), p 100
               Roach, p 492-495
               Servais, p 263-264

44. All of the following need a proper authorization to access a patient's health information EXCEPT
    A. local and state law enforcement officers.
    B. IRS agents.
    C. medical examiners or coroners.
    D. FBI agents.

REFERENCE: Green and Bowie, p 278
               LaTour and Eichenwald-Maki, p 259

45. One best practice to follow in order to establish safeguards for the security and confidentiality of a patient's information when a person makes a request for his or her records in person, is to
    A. ask the requester for identification and the request in writing.
    B. refuse the request.
    C. refer the requester to the facility's attorney.
    D. charge an exorbitant fee.

REFERENCE: Roach, p 239-241

46. Which of the following acts was passed to stimulate the development of standards to facilitate electronic maintenance and transmission of health information?
    A. Health Insurance for the Aged
    B. Health Insurance Portability and Accountability Act
    C. Conditions of Participation
    D. Hospital Survey and Construction Act

REFERENCE: Green and Bowie, p 11, 312
               LaTour and Eichenwald-Maki, p 250
               McWay, p 360
               McWay, p 218
               Pozgar, p 26

47. The premise that charitable institutions could be held blameless for their negligent acts is known as
    A. doctrine of respondeat superior.
    B. doctrine of res ipsa loquitur.
    C. doctrine of charitable immunity.
    D. negligence factor.

REFERENCE: McWay (2003), p 57
               Pozgar, p 153, 528
               Roach, p 10-11

48. Under traditional rules of evidence, a medical/health record is considered _____ and is _____ into evidence.
    A. hearsay; admissible   C. reliable; admissible
    B. hearsay; inadmissible   D. reliable; inadmissible

REFERENCE: Green and Bowie, p 260-261
               LaTour and Eichenwald-Maki, p 261
               McWay (2003), p 136
               Roach, 383-385

49. The hospital has a policy that states, "Original medical records may be removed from the Medical Record Department jurisdiction only by court order." Which situation would be a violation of the policy?
    A. A physician wishes to have the record sent to the physician lounge in the OR suite for final signatures.
    B. The Risk Manger requests the record for review by physicians at a quality assurance meeting.
    C. A lawyer has subpoenaed the record for deposition.
    D. The physician has been sued and wants to study the original record at home prior to his deposition.

REFERENCE: LaTour and Eichenwald-Maki, p 263
               Green and Bowie, p 260-261, 268

50. Who is legally responsible for obtaining the patient's informed consent for surgery?
    A. the admissions clerk
    B. the surgeon performing the surgery
    C. the nurse
    D. medical record personnel

REFERENCE: Green and Bowie, p 119, 122
              McWay, p 64-65
              Pozgar, p 180
              Roach, p 74

51. With regard to confidentiality, when HIM functions are outsourced (i.e., record copying, microfilming, or transcription), the HIM professional should confirm that the outside contractor's
    A. costs are not prohibitive, thus compromising confidentiality.
    B. hours of operation permit easy access by all health care providers.
    C. is contractually bound to handle confidential information appropriately.
    D. is located in an easy to find place.

REFERENCE: Green and Bowie, p 36
              McWay (2003), p 107

52. A 21-year-old employee of National Services was treated in an acute care hospital for an illness unrelated to work. A representative from the personnel department of National Services calls to request information regarding the employee's diagnosis. What would be the appropriate course of action?
    A. Request that the personnel office send an authorization for release of information that is signed and dated by the patient.
    B. Require parental consent.
    C. Release the information because the employer is paying the patient's bill.
    D. Call the patient to obtain verbal permission.

REFERENCE: Green and Bowie, p 281
              LaTour and Eichenwald-Maki, p 255-256
              McWay (2003), p 102

53. Darling v. Charleston Community Memorial Hospital is considered one of the benchmark cases in health care because it was with this case that the doctrine of _____ was eliminated for nonprofit hospitals.
    A. charitable immunity
    B. corporate negligence
    C. professional negligence
    D. contributory negligence

REFERENCE: Green and Bowie, p 257
              McWay (2003), p 177
              Pozgar, 150-151

54. All of the following are elements of a contract EXCEPT
    A. offer/communication.   C. price/consideration.
    B. duty.   D. acceptance.

REFERENCE: LaTour and Eichenwald-Maki, p 247-248
              Pozgar, p 87-88

55. A valid authorization for release of information contains
    A. the name, agency, or institution to which the information is to be provided.
    B. the name of the hospital or provider who is releasing the medical information.
    C. the date and signature of the patient or the patient's authorized representative.
    D. all of the above

REFERENCE: LaTour and Eichenwald-Maki, p 255-256
              McWay, p 61-63
              McWay (2003), p 96-100

56. Release of information without the patient's authorization is permissible in which of the following circumstances?
    A. release to an attorney
    B. release to third-party payers
    C. release to state workers' compensation agencies
    D. release to insurance companies

REFERENCE: Green and Bowie, p 280
              LaTour and Eichenwald-Maki, p 257
              McWay (2003), p 102

57. Who decides whether all or portions of the medical record will be received in evidence in a court of law?
    A. presiding judge/court   C. clerk of the court
    B. subpoenaing attorney   D. defendant

REFERENCE: LaTour and Eichenwald-Maki, p 261
              McWay (2003), p 15
              Servais, p 4

58. Which of the following health care systems have to comply with the requirements of the Freedom of Information Act?
    A. private hospitals   C. veteran's hospitals
    B. physicians' offices   D. single day surgery clinics

REFERENCE: LaTour and Eichenwald-Maki, p 250
              McWay (2003), p 100
              Roach, p 123

59. Which of the following measures should a health care facility incorporate into its institution-wide security plan to protect the confidentiality of the patient record?
    A. verification of employee identification
    B. locked access to data processing and record areas
    C. use unique computer passwords, key cares, or biometric identification
    D. all of the above

REFERENCE: Green and Bowie, p 272
              LaTour and Eichenwald-Maki, p 263
              McWay (2003), p 221
              Roach, p 239-24
              Servais, p 42-46

60. A signed consent for release of information dated December 1, 2005, is received with a request for the chart from the patient's admission of 12/5/2005. Indicate the appropriate response from the options below.
    A. Request another authorization that is dated closer, but prior to, the admission date.
    B. Request another authorization dated after the discharge date.
    C. Release the requested information.
    D. Call the patient for a verbal authorization.

REFERENCE: McWay (2003), p 97-98

61. Willful disregard of a subpoena is considered
    A. breach of contract.
    B. abuse of process.
    C. contributory negligence.
    D. contempt of court.

REFERENCE: McWay, p 65
               McWay (2003), p 139
               Pozgar, p 115-116
               Roach, p 322

62. HIM personnel charged with the responsibility of bringing a medical record to court would ordinarily do so in answer to a
    A. personal subpoena.   C. subpoena duces tecum.
    B. deposition.   D. judgment.

REFERENCE: Green and Bowie, p 278
               McWay, p 65
               McWay (2003), p 139
               Pozgar, p 115-116
               Roach, p 317
               Servais, p 36, 60, 63

63. HIPAA requires that certain covered entities provide every patient a Notice of Privacy Practices that sets forth all of the following EXCEPT
    A. covered entities provide every patient with its annual business report.
    B. how covered entities may use and disclose PHI.
    C. patient's rights regarding the covered entities' uses and disclosures.
    D. covered entities' obligations for protecting the patient's PHI.

REFERENCE: LaTour and Eichenwald-Maki, p 252
               Green and Bowie, p, 263-267
               McWay, p 60
               McWay (2003), p 90-96
               Roach, p 219

64. A record that has been requested by subpoena duces tecum is currently located at an off-site microfilm company. By contacting the microfilm provider, you learn that the microfilm is ready and the original copy of the record still exists. What legal requirement would compel you to produce the original record for the court?
    A. best evidence rule   C. motion to quash
    B. hearsay rule   D. subpoena instanter

REFERENCE: Roach, p 487-488

65. Which resource is the most valuable to monitor Medicare changes?
    A. Journal of AHIMA
    B. HIM peers
    C. Federal Register
    D. Medical Records Briefing

REFERENCE: Green and Bowie, p 29, 255
               LaTour and Eichenwald-Maki, p 242
               McWay, p 293
               McWay (2003), p 9

66. As a general rule, a person making a report in good faith and under statutory command (e.g., on child abuse, communicable diseases, births, deaths, etc.) is
    A. not protected from liability claims.
    B. subject to penalties imposed by federal law.
    C. subject to penalties imposed by state law.
    D. protected.

REFERENCE: Green and Bowie, p 277
               McWay (2003), p 106
               Pozgar, p 335
               Roach, p 247-248

67. According to AHIMA and AHA guidelines, which of the following would be an acceptable authorization for release of information from the medical record of an adult, mentally competent patient hospitalized from 4/16/2007 to 5/10/2007? An authorization dated
    A. 7/10/2007 and presented 7/15/2007
    B. 5/09/2007 and presented 1/15/2008
    C. 3/10/2007 and presented 5/15/2007
    D. 2/15/2007 and presented 1/10/2008

REFERENCE: Green and Bowie, p 122, 124-125,
               McWay, p 62
               McWay (2003), p 96-98

68. Which would be the better "best practice" for handling fax transmission of a physician's orders?
    A. Treat faxed orders like verbal orders and require authentication of the orders by appropriate medical staff within the required time period.
    B. Faxed orders should be placed on the patient's chart immediately upon receipt after the head nurse signs the orders.
    C. Wait 24 hours before placing faxed orders on the patient's chart to ensure that the orders are legitimate.
    D. Faxed orders should never be accepted.

REFERENCE: Green and Bowie, p 81
               Roach, p 494

69. The Darling v. Charleston Community Memorial Hospital case established the following doctrine for hospitals to observe and changed the way hospitals dealt with liability.
    A. doctrine of respondeat superior
    B. doctrine of continuing wrong
    C. doctrine of res ipsa loiter
    D. doctrine of corporate negligence

REFERENCE: Green and Bowie, p 257
               McWay (2003), p 50-51
               Pozgar, p 150

70. HIM professionals have a duty to maintain health information that complies with
   A. state statutes.
   B. federal statutes.
   C. accreditation standards.
   D. all of the above.

REFERENCE: Green and Bowie, p 260-261
               LaTour and Eichenwald-Maki, p 251
               McWay, p 102-103
               McWay (2003), p 67-70
               Roach, p 40-41
               Servais, p 7-9

71. In general, which of the following statements is correct?
   A. When federal and state laws conflict, valid federal laws supersede state laws.
   B. When federal and state laws conflict, valid state laws supersede federal laws.
   C. When federal and state laws conflict, valid local laws supersede federal and state laws.
   D. When federal and state laws conflict, valid corporate policies supersede federal and state laws.

REFERENCE: McWay, p 58
               McWay (2003), p 95-96

72. Which of the following statements is correct regarding HIPAA preemption analysis?
   A. If the state law that recognizes a patient's right to health care information privacy is more stringent than the HIPAA federal rule, then the state law prevails.
   B. State law regarding a patient's right to health care information privacy can never prevail over the HIPAA federal rule.
   C. If a state law that recognizes a patient's right to health care information privacy is more stringent than the HIPAA federal rule, then the courts must decide which shall prevail.
   D. Even if the state law that recognizes a patient's right to health care information privacy is more stringent than the HIPAA federal rule, the HIPAA federal rule will still prevail.

REFERENCE: Green and Bowie, p 276-277
               LaTour and Eichenwald-Maki, p 352
               McWay, p 58
               McWay (2003), p 95-96
               Roach, p 100-101

73. The minimum record retention period for patients who are minors is
   A. age of majority.
   B. age of majority plus the statute of limitations.
   C. 5 years past treatment.
   D. 2 years past treatment.

REFERENCE: Green and Bowie, p 96
               LaTour and Eichenwald-Maki, p 206
               McWay, p 112-113
               McWay (2003), p 77
               Roach, p 43-44
               Servais, p 350

74. The Privacy Act of 1974 permits patients to request amendments to their medical record in which type of facility?
    A. private proprietary health care facility
    B. mental health and chemical dependency facility
    C. university-based teaching facility
    D. Department of Defense health care facility

REFERENCE: Green and Bowie, p 273-274
               LaTour and Eichenwald-Maki, p 253
               McWay (2003), p 100-101
               Pozgar, p 121-122

75. What advice should be given to a physician who has just informed you that she just discovered that a significant portion of a discharge summary she dictated last month was left out?
    A. Squeeze in the information omitted by writing in available spaces such as the top, bottom, and side margins.
    B. Dictate the portion omitted with the heading "Discharge Summary—Addendum" and make a reference to the addendum with a note that is dated and signed on the initial Discharge Summary (e.g., "9/1/08—See Addendum to Discharge Summary"— Signature).
    C. Redictate the discharge summary and replace the old one with the new one.
    D. Inform the physician that nothing can be done about the situation.

REFERENCE: Green and Bowie, p 84-85
               McWay (2003), p 73-74
               Roach, p 70
               Servais, p 30-32

76. While performing routine quantitative analysis of a record, a medical record employee finds an incident report in the record. The employee brings this to the attention of her supervisor. Which best practice should the supervisor follow to deal with this situation?
    A. remove the incident report and send it to the patient.
    B. tell the employee to leave the report in the record.
    C. remove the incident report and have nursing personnel transfer all documentation from the report to the medical record.
    D. refer this record to the Risk Manager for further review and removal of the incident report.

REFERENCE: Green and Bowie, p 88
               LaTour and Eichenwald-Maki, p 266
               McWay, p 110
               McWay (2003), p 181-182
               Pozgar, p 339
               Roach, p 393

77. Which of the following is considered confidential information if the patient is seeking treatment in a substance abuse facility?
    A. patient's name   C.   patient's diagnosis
    B. patient's address   D.   all of the above

REFERENCE: Green and Bowie, p 272, 284-285
               McWay (2003), p 152-153
               Pozgar, p 300

78. In electronic health records, authentication may be achieved by
    A. handwritten signature.
    B. digital signature.
    C. verbal statement.
    D. all the above.

REFERENCE: Green and Bowie, p 26, 82, 268
               LaTour p 74; 228
               McWay, p 321
               McWay (2003), p 214-215
               Servais, p 34-35, 269

79. It is common practice to forgo patient authorization for the release of information when the
    A. patient is an employee.
    B. patient is a physician.
    C. patient has a direct transfer from the hospital to a long-term care facility.
    D. patient is incompetent.

REFERENCE: LaTour and Eichenwald-Maki, p 253; 256-257

80. Many states have recognized a minor's right to seek treatment without parental consent in all of the following situations EXCEPT a(n)
    A. minor seeking treatment for breast reduction.
    B. minor seeking treatment for a sexually transmitted disease.
    C. minor seeking treatment for alcohol and substance abuse.
    D. emancipated minor seeking treatment for breast enlargement.

REFERENCE: McWay (2003), p 123-124
               Pozgar, p 328
               Roach, p 89-90

81. When a record custodian brings the medical record to court in response to a subpoena duces tecum, it is her responsibility to
    A. identify the record in her official capacity as custodian.
    B. present the case favorably for the patient involved.
    C. leave the original record in the possession of the plaintiff's attorney.
    D. explain details of the medical treatment given to the patient.

REFERENCE: McWay, p 65
               McWay (2003), p 137
               Servais, p 36, 60, 63

82. When substituting a photocopy of the original record in response to legal process, which of the following can be helpful in convincing the court to accept the photocopy as a true and exact copy of the original?
    A. certificate of authentication
    B. consent from the patient
    C. consent from the hospital administrator
    D. correspondence from the attending physician

REFERENCE: Servais, p 6-7, 58-56

83. Which of the following should be required to sign a confidentiality statement before having access to patients' medical information?
    A. nursing students
    B. medical students
    C. HIM students
    D. all of the above

REFERENCE: Green and Bowie, p 44
               Pozgar, p 292

84. All of the following have laws and regulations addressing medical records EXCEPT
    A. accrediting agencies.
    B. corporate law.
    C. state laws.
    D. federal laws.

REFERENCE: Green and Bowie, p 255
                Servais, p 7-8

85. The proper method for correcting a documentation error in a medical record is for the author to
    A. draw an "X" through the incorrect documentation.
    B. draw a single line through the incorrect information, date and initial the change.
    C. white it out, date and initial the change.
    D. remove the form from the chart and add a revised form.

REFERENCE: Green and Bowie, p 84-85
                McWay (2003), p 73-75
                Roach, p 70
                Pozgar, p 310
                Servais, p 30-32, 113-114

86. All of the following are sources for the rules and regulations that define the legal aspects of medical records EXCEPT
    A. institutional policies.
    B. laws.
    C. paralegals.
    D. regulations, governmental and nongovernmental.

REFERENCE: Green and Bowie, p 255
                McWay, p 47-49
                McWay (2003), p 67-70
                Servais, p 7-8

87. To be admitted into court as evidence, medical records or health information are introduced as
    A. torts or contracts.
    B. privileged information.
    C. records or exceptions to hearsay rule.
    D. product liability.

REFERENCE: Green and Bowie, p 260-261
                LaTour and Eichenwald-Maki, p 261
                McWay (2003), p 135-136
                Roach, p 383-386
                Servais, p 4 -5, 123-130

88. A health care organization's compliance plans should not only focus on regulatory compliance, but also have a
    A. strong personnel component that reduces the rapid turnover of nursing personnel.
    B. coding compliance program that prevents fraudulent coding and billing.
    C. component that increases the security of medical records.
    D. substantial program that increases the availability of clinical data.

REFERENCE: Green and Bowie, p 313
                LaTour and Eichenwald-Maki, p 90; 390
                Mc Way, p 69, 133
                McWay (2003), p 242
                Pozgar, p 341-342
                Servais, p 224-228

89. Written consent from the patient is required for which of the following in order to learn a patient's HIV status?
    A. insurance companies
    B. emergency medical personnel
    C. spouse or needle partner
    D. health care workers

REFERENCE: Green and Bowie, p 281-283
                      McWay, p 90
                      Pozgar, p 380
                      Roach, p 352-362

90. The Uniform Business Records as Evidence Act addresses
    A. medical records maintained on health care workers.
    B. insurance documents.
    C. medical and lab reports in health care facilities.
    D. admissibility of record reproductions.

REFERENCE: Green and Bowie, p 260
                      Roach, p 494-495
                      Servais, p 4-5

91. The ideal consent for medical treatment obtained by the physician is
    A. expressed.   C. implied.
    B. informed.   D. verbal.

REFERENCE: Green and Bowie, p 119-, 122
                      McWay, p 64-65
                      McWay (2003), p 127
                      Roach, p 78-81
                      Pozgar, p 180

92. Which of the following is an example of the breach of confidentiality?
    A. a nurse speaking with the physician in the patient's room
    B. staff members discussing patients in the elevator
    C. the admission clerk verifying over the phone that the patient is in-house
    D. the hospital operator paging code blue in room 3 north

REFERENCE: Pozgar, p 52-53
                      LaTour and Eichenwald-Maki, p 246
                      Roach, p 406-408

93. Which of the following would be an inappropriate procedure for the custodian of the medical record to perform prior to taking a medical record from a health care facility to court?
    A. Number each page of the record in ink.
    B. Document in the file folder the total number of pages in the record.
    C. Remove any information that might prove detrimental to the hospital or physician.
    D. Prepare an itemized list of sheets contained in the medical record.

REFERENCE: LaTour and Eichenwald-Maki, p 261
                      McWay (2003), p 135-137
                      Pozgar, p 292, 304

94. Which of the following agencies is empowered to implement the law governing Medicare and Medicaid?
    A. Centers for Medicare and Medicaid Services (CMS) formerly known as Health Care Financing Administration (HCFA)
    B. Joint Commission
    C. Institutes of Health
    D. Department of Health and Human Services

REFERENCE: Green and Bowie, p 68-69
                        LaTour and Eichenwald-Maki, p 346
                        McWay, p 50, 69
                        McWay (2003) 10
                        Pozgar, p 24-25

95. Consent forms may be challenged on all the following grounds EXCEPT
    A. wording was too technical.
    B. the treating physician obtained the patient's signature.
    C. it's written in a language that the patient could not understand.
    D. the signature was not voluntary.

REFERENCE: Green and Bowie, p 119, 122, 124
                        Roach, p 97

96. Mandatory reporting requirements for vital statistics generally
    A. do not require authorization by the patient.
    B. require authorization by the physician.
    C. require authorization by the payer.
    D. do not apply to health care facilities.

REFERENCE: Green and Bowie, p 277
                        McWay, p 61-62
                        McWay (2003), p 106
                        Pozgar, p 335

97. The responsibility of obtaining an informed consent for a surgical or invasive procedure rests with the
    A. patient.   C. physician.
    B. nurse.   D. hospital.

REFERENCE: Green and Bowie, p 119, 122, 124
                        McWay, p 64
                        Pozgar, p 315
                        Roach, p 91-94

98. Courts have released adoption records based upon
    A. the request of the adoptee.
    B. the request of the biological parent(s).
    C. the Freedom of Information Act.
    D. a court order for good cause.

REFERENCE: Roach, p 301
                        McWay (2003), p 107

99. The legislation that required all federally funded facilities to inform patients of their rights under state law to accept or refuse medical treatment is known as
    A. advance directives.
    B. living wills.
    C. Patient Self-Determination Act.
    D. durable power of attorney.

REFERENCE: Green and Bowie, p 119
McWay, p 65
McWay (2003), p 124-125
Roach, p 97
Pozgar, p 325

100. An oral consent is binding if it
    A. can be proven or corroborated.
    B. has the signature of the patient.
    C. does not cause confusion.
    D. occurs only at the time of admission.

REFERENCE: Pozgar, p 325

Answer Key for Health Law

1.	A	35.	B	69.	D
2.	B	36.	C	70.	D
3.	C	37.	D	71.	A
4.	A	38.	D	72.	A
5.	C	39.	D	73.	B
6.	B	40.	D	74.	D
7.	C	41.	A	75.	B
8.	D	42.	B	76.	D
9.	D	43.	A	77.	D
10.	B	44.	C	78.	B
11.	C	45.	A	79.	C
12.	A	46.	B	80.	A
13.	D	47.	C	81.	A
14.	C	48.	B	82.	A
15.	B	49.	D	83.	D
16.	A	50.	B	84.	B
17.	C	51.	C	85.	B
18.	C	52.	A	86.	C
19.	A	53.	A	87.	C
20.	C	54.	B	88.	B
21.	A	55.	D	89.	A
22.	C	56.	C	90.	D
23.	D	57.	A	91.	B
24.	A	58.	C	92.	B
25.	B	59.	D	93.	C
26.	B	60.	B	94.	A
27.	D	61.	D	95.	B
28.	A	62.	C	96.	A
29.	D	63.	A	97.	C
30.	C	64.	A	98.	D
31.	A	65.	C	99.	C
32.	D	66.	D	100.	A
33.	A	67.	A		
34.	B	68.	A		

REFERENCES

Green, M. A., & Bowie, M. J. (2005). *Essentials of health information management: Principles and practices.* Clifton Park, NY: Delmar Cengage Learning.

LaTour, K., & Eichenwald-Maki, S. (2006). *Health information management: Concepts, principles, and practice* (3rd ed.). Chicago: American Health Information Management Association (AHIMA).

McWay, D. C. (2008). *Today's health information management: An integrated approach.* Clifton Park, NY: Delmar Cengage Learning.

McWay, D. C. (2003). *Legal aspects of health information management* (2nd ed.). Clifton Park, NY: Delmar Cengage Learning.

Pozgar, G. D. (2004). *Legal aspects of health care administration* (9th ed.). Gaithersburg, MD: Aspen Publications.

Roach, W. H. (2006). *Medical records and the law* (4th ed.). Gaithersburg, MD: Aspen Publications.

Servais, C. E. (2008). *The legal health record.* Chicago: American Health Information Management Association (AHIMA).

XIII. Health Statistics and Research

Kathy C. Trawick, EdD, RHIA

As noted in the main Introduction section, you will be able to access the statistical formulas on the computer to use during the exam. You may not find them in any set location—be prepared to look around for them a little.

Although some questions are included from the Commonly Computed Rates and Percentages for Hospital Inpatients, you will often be asked to interpret everyday data and/or solve questions that have more to do with common sense and good math skills than with memorized formulas. To help you distinguish among the types of questions you might expect, and to make sure you realistically evaluate your skills in this area, this chapter has been divided into four sections:
1. Statistical basics
2. Commonly computed rates
3. Data display and interpretation
4. Research and financial statistics

According to the breakdown of content for both the RHIA and RHIT exams, the health statistics questions have been included in domain II: Health Statistics, Biomedical Research, and Quality Management; subdomain A: Health Care Statistics and Research. This section not only covers statistics and research, but also may also include data collection, interpretation, and presentation. You should also be prepared to analyze and interpret statistical charts and graphs. Some questions will refer to a graphical representation of data when asking for the answer. Refer to the specific details of these items in the domain and subdomain competencies found in the Certification Guide. You will want to work with statistical formulas from this chapter, from your formal courses, and previous textbooks until you get your speed up. Sometimes the length of time it takes in calculating formulas and mathematical computations can make or break you on the entire examination as far as your testing time. Thus, increasing your speed by practicing formulas can really help you at exam time.

Most answers in this section should be rounded to the first decimal point. On the national examination, let the answers provided in the test be your guide, or follow the examination instructions in order to round correctly.

Don't let the word problems throw you off. Some of these are quite long; look for the pertinent data. Don't panic—approach word problems just as you did in your formal classes. You will have most of the formulas provided for you on the exam. For problems that you may not have a formula for, try the memory device of: "what did happen divided by what could have happened." Here, the "what did happen" is always the numerator (top number) and the "what could have happened" is always the denominator (bottom number).

We suggest that on exam day you take along an extra battery-powered calculator. Solar-powered calculators could be tricky depending on the lighting in the exam room. Don't take chances. It pays to be prepared for a little Murphy's law.

We recommend that you review the textbooks listed at the back of this chapter as you study for this section of your exam.

Health Statistics Definitions and Formulas

There are a number of important things to think about when you tackle census and occupancy statistics. First, remember when it comes to occupancy, beds and bassinets are counted separately. This means newborn discharges are separated from the discharges of adults and children. Next, remember not to be fooled by beds set up temporarily to meet unusual admission needs; all occupancy statistics should be calculated based on approved, permanent beds only. The common rates used for census and occupancy statistics are as follows:

Census Statistics

Daily Inpatient Census	Total number of patients treated during a 24-hour period
Inpatient Service Day	Services received by one inpatient in one 24-hour period
Total Inpatient Service Days	Sum of all inpatient service days for each of the days in the period
FORMULA: Average Daily Census	$\dfrac{\text{Total inpatient service days for a period (excluding newborns)}}{\text{Total number of days in the period}}$

Length of Stay

Length of Stay (LOS)	Number of calendar days from admission to discharge
Total Length of Stay	Sum of the days stay of any group of inpatients discharged during a specific period of time
FORMULA: Average LOS	$\dfrac{\text{Total length of stay (discharge days)}}{\text{Total number of discharges}}$

Bed Count

Inpatient Bed Count	Number of available hospital beds, both occupied and vacant, on any given day
Inpatient Bed Count Day	Counts the presence of one inpatient bed (occupied or vacant) that is set up and staffed for use in one 24-hour period
Total Inpatient Bed Count Day	Sum of inpatient bed count days for each of the days in a period

Percentage of Occupancy

FORMULA:	$\dfrac{\text{Total number of inpatient service days for a period} \times 100}{\text{Total inpatient bed count days} \times \text{number of days in the period}}$

Bed Turnover Rate

Direct Formula:
$$\frac{\text{Total number of discharges for a period}}{\text{Average bed count for the same period}}$$

Indirect Formula:
$$\frac{\text{Percentage of occupancy} \times \text{Days in the period} \times 100}{\text{Average length of stay}}$$

NOTE: The indirect formula must be used in cases where the bed count changes during the period in question.

Death (Mortality) Rates

Anesthesia Death Rate	$\dfrac{\text{Total number of deaths caused by an anesthetic agent} \times 100}{\text{Total number of anesthetics administered}}$
Fetal Death Rate (Stillbirth Rate)	$\dfrac{\text{Total number of intermediate and late fetal deaths} \times 100}{\text{Total number of births (plus intermediate and late fetal deaths)}}$
Gross Hospital Death Rate	$\dfrac{\text{Total number of inpatient deaths (including newborns)} \times 100}{\text{Total number of discharges (including deaths and newborns)}}$
Net Hospital Death Rate	$\dfrac{\text{Number of inpatient deaths (including NB) minus deaths} < 48 \text{ hours of admission} \times 100}{\text{Total discharges (including deaths and NB. minus deaths} < 48 \text{ hours)}}$
Maternal Death Rate	$\dfrac{\text{Total number of maternal deaths for a period} \times 100}{\text{Total number of obstetrical discharges}}$
Neonatal Death Rate (Infant Mortality Rate)	$\dfrac{\text{Total number of newborn (NB. deaths for a period} \times 100}{\text{Total number of newborn (NB. discharges}}$
Post-operative Death Rate	$\dfrac{\text{Number of deaths within 10 days of surgery} \times 100}{\text{Total number of patients operated on}}$

Autopsy Rates

Newborn (NB) Autopsy Rate	$\dfrac{\text{Number of autopsies on NB deaths} \times 100}{\text{Total number of NB deaths}}$
Fetal Autopsy Rate	$\dfrac{\text{Number of autopsies on intermediate and late fetal deaths} \times 100}{\text{Total number of intermediate and late fetal deaths}}$
Gross Autopsy Rate	$\dfrac{\text{Total inpatient autopsies for a period} \times 100}{\text{Total inpatient deaths for the period}}$
Net Autopsy Rate	$\dfrac{\text{Total inpatient autopsies for a period} \times 100}{\text{Total inpatient deaths minus unautopsied coroner's or medical examiner's cases for the period}}$
Hospital Autopsy Rate (Adjusted)	$\dfrac{\text{Total hospital autopsies} \times 100}{\text{Number of deaths of hospital patients whose bodies are available for hospital autopsy}}$

The hospital patients whose bodies after death are available for hospital autopsy include:

Inpatients, unless the bodies are removed from the hospital by legal authorities. However, in any such case, if the hospital pathologist or delegated physician of the medical staff performs an autopsy while acting as an agent for the coroner, the autopsy is included in the numerator and the death in the denominator.

Other hospital patients (including hospital home care patients, outpatients, and previous hospital patients who have died elsewhere) whose bodies have been made available for the performance of hospital autopsies.

Infection (Morbidity) Rates

Total Hospital (Morbidity) Infection Rate	$\dfrac{\text{Total number of hospital infections} \times 100}{\text{Total number of discharges}}$
Nosocomial Infection Rate	$\dfrac{\text{Number of hospital acquired infections} \times 100}{\text{Total number of discharges (including deaths)}}$
Community-acquired Infection Rate	$\dfrac{\text{Number of community-acquired infections} \times 100}{\text{Total number of discharges}}$
Post-operative Infection Rate	$\dfrac{\text{Number of post-operative infections for a period (within 10 days postop)} \times 100}{\text{Total number of operations performed}}$

Other Rates

Cesarean Section Rate	$\dfrac{\text{Total number of Cesarean sections performed in a period} \times 100}{\text{Total number of deliveries in the period}}$
Consultation Rate	$\dfrac{\text{Total number of consultations for a period} \times 100}{\text{Total number of discharges for the period}}$
Delinquent Medical Record Rate	$\dfrac{\text{Total number of delinquent records} \times 100}{\text{Average number of discharges during a completion period}}$
Incomplete Medical Record Rate	$\dfrac{\text{Total number of incomplete records} \times 100}{\text{Total number of discharges during the completion period}}$
Percentage of Medicare Patients	$\dfrac{\text{Total number of Medicare discharges} \times 100}{\text{Total number of adult and children discharges}}$
Percentage of Medicare Discharge Days	$\dfrac{\text{Total number of Medicare discharge days} \times 100}{\text{Total number of discharge days for adults and children}}$
Re-Admission Rate	$\dfrac{\text{Number of re-admissions for a period} \times 100}{\text{Number of total admissions (including readmissions)}}$

Generic Formula for Percentage Rates	$\dfrac{\text{Total number of times events actually happened} \times 100}{\text{Total number of times events could have happened}}$
Mean	Add all the available values and divide the sum by the total number of values involved. Example: Average length of stay or average daily inpatient census.
Median	The midpoint of an ordered series of numbers arranged in numerical order from highest to lowest or vice versa.
Mode	The most frequently recurring value in a set of numbers is the mode.

Section I—Math and Statistical Basics

The basics include mathematical and statistical terminology as well as the measures of central tendency and variations around those measures. It is unlikely that you will get instructions for calculating the measures of central tendency, so they are supplied along with the statistical formulas at the beginning of this chapter.

1. Sandy Beach Hospital reports 1652 discharges for September. The infection control report documents 21 nosocomial infections and 27 community-acquired infections for the same month. What is the community-acquired infection rate?
    A. 1.3
    B. 1.4
    C. 1.6
    D. 2.9

    REFERENCE: Koch, p 179
                   Johns, p 468

2. Physicians at South Seas Clinic are expected to see six patients per hour, on average. The physicians with the highest productivity each week are exempted from on-call responsibilities for the weekend. Which physician will get the weekend off this week?

SOUTH SEAS CLINIC PHYSICIAN PRODUCTIVITY Week 1 January 2009		
PHYSICIAN NAME	NUMBER OF HOURS WORKED	NUMBER OF PATIENTS SEEN
Robinson	32	185
Beasley	30	161
Hiltz	35	200
Wolf	26	157

    A. Robinson
    B. Beasley
    C. Hiltz
    D. Wolf

    REFERENCE: Koch, p 56-57
                   Abdelhak, p 373
                   McWay, p 192
                   Johns, p 911
                   LaTour and Eichenwald-Maki, p 659

3. If there are 150,000 medical records and the Health Information Department receives 3,545 requests for records in a week, what percentage of the records are requested weekly?
    A. 2.4%
    B. 3.5%
    C. 4.6%
    D. 5.1%

    REFERENCE: Horton, p 14
                   Koch, p 48
                   McWay, p 192
                   Abdelhak, p 373
                   Johns, p 431
                   LaTour and Eichenwald-Maki, p 402

4. You are conducting a study on the pain associated with a specific illness. For the purpose of your study, you classify pain level as follows:

CODE	PAIN LEVEL (as described by the patient)
01	None
02	Little or Minimal
03	Moderate
04	Heavy
05	Severe

This data is best described as
  A. discrete.
  B. continuous.
  C. nominal.
  D. ordinal.

REFERENCE: McWay, p 199-201
               Abdelhak p 384-385
               Horton, p 162
               Koch p 12-13

5. You are choosing restaurants where you might eat while you are in Chicago at the AHIMA Leadership conference. You have collected the following information about four possible lunch restaurants that are all located within easy walking distance of the meeting site. The data is displayed below:

RESTAURANT NAME	MEAN LUNCH COST	STANDARD DEVIATION
Bon Appetite	$8.00	0.75
Mario's	$7.50	1
Au Courant	$9.00	1.25
The Windy City Grill	$7.50	1.5

You want to stay within the reimbursement rate allowed by your Component State Association, so it is important to you that you have at least a 95% chance of eating a lunch that costs no more than $10.00. Therefore, when lunchtime comes you head to
  A. Bon Appetite or Mario's.
  B. Mario's or Au Courant.
  C. Au Courant or The Windy City Grill.
  D. The Windy City Grill or Bon Appetite.

REFERENCE: McWay, p 194-195
               Koch, p 246-247
               Abdelhak, p 474
               Horton, p 151
               Johns, p 440

6. Organizations collect statistics to increase their knowledge of a specified population. The knowledge doesn't come automatically – it is developed in the following sequence:
  A. data → facts → information → knowledge.
  B. data → information → facts → knowledge.
  C. facts → data → information → knowledge.
  D. facts → information → data → knowledge.

REFERENCE: Horton, p 2
               Johns, p 25

Questions number 7 and 8 are based on the study and data below.

The coding supervisor at Bayside Hospital regularly has her coders recode records from the previous week in an effort to improve and monitor coding consistency. The supervisor has collected the data displayed below on four coders.

Coder	Records Under Review	Same Code on Self-Coding Review	Same Code on Peer Coding Review
Coder A	28	22	20
Coder B	18	16	16
Coder C	45	42	43
Coder D	17	15	16

7. The data in the column on the far right were collected when the coders traded records for recoding. This is a common practice used to check
   A. interrater reliability.
   B. intrarater reliability.
   C. interrater validity.
   D. intrarater validity.

REFERENCE: McWay, p 231
               Abdelhak, p 411-414
               Johns, p 421
               Shi, p 299

8. The coder with the highest overall accuracy rating will get the day after Thanksgiving off. Which coder will get to spend the day after Thanksgiving shopping rather than coding?
   A. Coder A
   B. Coder B
   C. Coder C
   D. Coder D

REFERENCE: Abdelhak p 373
               Johns, p 421
               Koch, p 48
               Horton, p 208

9. Phyllis saw Dr. Holland during a scheduled office visit. Dr. Holland prescribed a new medication; Jean called Dr. Holland with a question about her medication. Dr. Holland returned the telephone call and answered Jean's question; Howard was seen by Dr. Holland in the hospital emergency department after having a reaction to his medication; the pharmacy got telephone approval from Dr. Horton for a refill on Jackson's prescription. Which of these interactions fit the definition of a patient encounter?
   A. Phyllis, Jean, Howard, and Jackson
   B. Jackson, Howard, and Jean
   C. Jean, Phyllis, and Howard
   D. Phyllis and Howard

REFERENCE: Horton, p 4
               LaTour and Eichenwald-Maki, p 416
               Abdelhak, p 133

10. A small portion of the form you are using for a research study is reproduced below.

| Male | 1 |
| Female | 2 |

This is an example of

A. ordinal data.
B. ranked data.

C. nominal data.
D. discrete data.

REFERENCE: McWay, p 199-201
Abdelhak, p 384-385
Horton, p 162
Koch, p 12-13
LaTour and Eichenwald-Maki, p 401

11. You have made a list of the advantages and disadvantages of a measure of central tendency:

ADVANTAGES	DISADVANTAGES
Easy to obtain and interpret	May not be descriptive of the distribution
Not sensitive to extreme observations in the frequency distribution	May not be unique
Easy to communicate and explain to others	Does not provide information about the entire distribution

The measure of central tendency you are describing is the

A. mean.
B. median.

C. range.
D. mode.

REFERENCE: McWay, p 194
Horton, p 142
Koch, p 234-243
Abdelhak, p 389-391
Johns, p 434
LaTour and Eichenwald-Maki, p 432

The following data were collected in your physician office practice from one morning's visits. Use the data for questions 12, 13, and 14.

Office Visit ID Number	Minutes with the Physician	Physician
508-123	5	Robinson
508-124	9	Robinson
508-125	8	Beasley
508-126	12	Wolf
508-127	6	Beasley
508-128	7	Beasley
508-129	5	Wolf
508-130	10	Baumstark
508-131	7	Baumstark
508-132	9	Robinson
508-133	11	Wolf

12. The median number of minutes with the physician (considering all physicians) is
   A. 7 minutes.
   B. 8 minutes.
   C. 8.4 minutes.
   D. 9 minutes.

REFERENCE: McWay, p 194
                 Abdelhak, p 390
                 Koch, p 236-237
                 Johns, p 436
                 Horton, p 144

13. The mean number of minutes with the physician (considering all physicians) is
   A. 7 minutes.
   B. 8 minutes.
   C. 8.4 minutes.
   D. 9 minutes.

REFERENCE: McWay, p 194
                 Abdelhak, p 389
                 Koch, p 234-236
                 Johns, p 435
                 Horton, p 143

14. Which physician spent the longest average time with patients on that day?
   A. Beasley
   B. Wolf
   C. Baumstark
   D. Robinson

REFERENCE: Abdelhak, p 389-391
                 Koch, p 234-236
                 Johns, p 435

Use this portion of yesterday's discharges printout below to answer questions 15 and 16.

Patient #	Admit Date	Service	Physician ID	Room #	LOS
12-32-21	1/02/08	MED	212	44-A	13
12-32-22	1/02/08	SURG	218	32	13
12-32-85	1/14/08	PEDS	214	23-B	1
11-99-94	1/12/08	MED	212	46-A	3
10-93-23	1/10/08	MED	212	45	5
12-35-94	1/11/08	SURG	218	33	4
10-85-14	1/01/08	PEDS	214	23-A	14

15. Without even performing any complex calculations, you can get a quick, simple measure of dispersion in the LOS for yesterday's discharges by computing the
   A. range of the data set.
   B. mean of the data set.
   C. variance of the data set.
   D. coefficient of variation of the data set.

REFERENCE: Koch, p 216, 243
                 Abdelhak, p 389-391
                 Johns, p 434
                 Horton, p 148

16. Looking more closely at the LOS for these patients. When you calculate the standard deviation on the data, you would expect
    A. a large standard deviation because the dispersion is large.
    B. a small standard deviation because the dispersion is small.
    C. a large standard deviation because the dispersion is small.
    D. a small standard deviation because the dispersion is large.

REFERENCE: Koch, p 246-247
                    McWay, p 194-195
                    Abdelhak, p 391-392
                    Johns, p 440
                    Horton, p 151

17. Farside Hospital collected the following data on patients discharged on January 1, 2008. Which measure of central tendency would be most affected by Mallory's extremely long LOS?

Patient Name	Length of Stay
Ben	1
Josh	2
Emma	3
Bryan	4
Mallory	29
Taylor	2
Matthew	3
Aiden	2
Trevor	4
Tyler	2

    A. variance
    B. median
    C. mean
    D. mode

REFERENCE: McWay, p 194
                    Horton, p 143
                    Koch, p 234-243
                    Johns, p 435
                    LaTour and Eichenwald-Maki, p 432
                    Abdelhak, p 389-391

18. The major purpose of random assignment in a clinical trial is to
    A. reduce selection bias in allocation of treatment.
    B. help ensure that study subjects are representative of the general population.
    C. facilitate double-blinding.
    D. ensure that the study groups are comparable on baseline characteristics.

REFERENCE: Abdelhak, p 426-427
                    LaTour and Eichenwald-Maki, p 452
                    McWay, p 227
                    Shi, p 155-157

19. Patients in the pediatrics ward were studied to determine their favorite color. The survey results are listed below. The results of the favorite color study are reported in a

REPORTED FAVORITE COLOR OF PEDIATRIC PATIENTS HAPPY VALLEY HOSPITAL JANUARY 18, 2008	
FAVORITE COLOR	NUMBER OF RESPONDENTS
RED	12
GREEN	14
BLUE	22
YELLOW	18
ORANGE	16

A. percentage.
B. ratio.
C. frequency distribution.
D. systematic fashion.

REFERENCE: Shi, p 359-360
McWay, p 203
Koch, p 213-237
Horton, p 167
Johns, p 434
Abdelhak, p 373-386

20. All of the following items mean the same thing, with one exception:
A. inpatient service day.
B. daily inpatient census.
C. daily census.
D. inpatient census.

REFERENCE: Koch, p 67-69
McWay, p 198-199
Abdelhak, p 382
Horton, p 25
LaTour and Eichenwald-Maki, p 404

21. Pasadena Bay Hospital reports an average LOS in February of 3.7 days with a standard deviation of 20. This tells us that
A. most patients had a LOS of 3 to 4 days.
B. there was a small variation in the LOS.
C. patients at Pasadena Bay stay longer than average.
D. there was a large variation in the LOS.

REFERENCE: McWay, p 198
Abdelhak, p 391-392
Koch, p 246-247
Johns, p 440
LaTour and Eichenwald-Maki, p 434
Horton, p 151

22. Jason collected data on the length of stay (LOS) for 10 patients and then determined the median LOS as follows:

1	
2	
4	
3	
1	← median
3	
2	
4	
2	
8	

What is wrong with Jason's determination of the median?
A. There is nothing wrong with Jason's determination of the median.
B. Jason forgot to put the numbers in sequential order before determining the median.
C. It is not possible to determine the median on such a small number of data points.
D. It is not possible to determine the median on an even number of data points.

REFERENCE: McWay, p 194
              Koch, p 236-237
              Horton, p 144
              Johns, p 436
              Abdelhak, p 389-391

Section II—Commonly Computed Rates and Percentages for Hospital Inpatients

23. All Women's Hospital reports the following statistics:

Single births	
Vaginal	40
c-section	0
Twin births	
Twins - vaginal	12 (6 sets)
Twins - c-section	8 (4 sets)
Other multiple births	0
Intermediate fetal deaths	
Vaginal	5
c-section	0
Late fetal deaths	
Vaginal	2
c-section	0

How many deliveries occurred?
A. 50
B. 57
C. 60
D. 67

REFERENCE: Horton, p 104
Koch, p 140

24. The inpatient census at midnight is 67. Two patients were admitted in the morning; 1 died two hours later; the second patient was transferred to another facility that same afternoon. The inpatient service days for that day will be
A. 65.
B. 67.
C. 68.
D. 69.

REFERENCE: Abdelhak, p 382
Horton, p 25
Koch, p 68-69
Johns, p 454
LaTour and Eichenwald-Maki p 404

25. Bayside Hospital has 275 adult beds, 30 pediatric beds, and 40 bassinets. In a nonleap year, inpatient service days were 75,860 for adults, 7,100 for pediatrics, and 11,800 for newborns. What was the average daily census for the year?
A. 227
B. 208
C. 207
D. 259

REFERENCE: Abdelhak p 382-383
Horton, p 34
Koch p 75-76
Johns, p 455
LaTour and Eichenwald-Maki, p 404

26. In order to derive the total inpatient service days for any given day, you would need to
    A. subtract intra-hospital transfers from the inpatient census.
    B. add same-day admits and discharges to the inpatient census.
    C. add intra-hospital transfers to the inpatient census.
    D. subtract same day admits and discharges from the inpatient census.

REFERENCE: McWay, p 198
              Abdelhak, p 382
              Horton, p 25
              Koch, p 69-705
              Johns, p 454
              LaTour and Eichenwald-Maki, p 404

27. Mr. McDonaldson was admitted to your hospital at 10:45 PM on January 1, 2008. He died at 4:22 AM on January 3, 2008. How many inpatient service days did Mr. McDonaldson receive?
    A. 1   C. 3
    B. 2   D. 4

REFERENCE: McWay, p 198
              Abdelhak, p 382
              Horton, p 25
              Koch, p 68-69
              Johns, p 454
              LaTour, p 404

28. A patient admitted to the hospital on January 24 and discharged on February 9 has a length of stay of
    A. 16 days.   C. 17 days.
    B. 15 days.   D. 14 days.

REFERENCE: McWay, p 198
              Abdelhak, p 382
              Horton, p 42
              Koch, p 103-104
              Johns, p 457

Use the data in the table below to answer questions 29 and 30.

Royal Palm Hospital has 500 beds and 55 bassinets. In February of a nonleap year, it reported the following statistics:

Inpatient service days:	
Adult and pediatric	12,345
Newborn	553
Discharges:	
Adult and pediatric	1,351
Newborn	77
Discharge days:	
Adult and pediatric	9,457
Newborn	231

29. What was the percentage of occupancy for adults and pediatrics in February?
    A. 84.8%   C. 79.6%
    B. 88.2%   D. 80.5%

REFERENCE: McWay, p 199
              Abdelhak, p 383
              Koch, p 87-88
              Johns, p 457
              Horton, p 42

30. What was the average length of stay at Royal Palm Hospital in February?
    A. 6.8 days   C. 9 days
    B. 7 days   D. 9.1 days

REFERENCE: McWay, p 198
              Abdelhak, p 382-383
              Koch, p 106-107
              Johns, p 459
              Horton, p 52

31. You are responsible for calculating and reporting average length of stay (ALOS) for your hospital each month. This month, there were 92 discharges and the total discharge days equal 875. One of the patients discharged this month had a total of 428 discharge days, so the ALOS is distorted by this unusually long stay. In this situation, you should report an ALOS of
    A. 9.51 days; no further information is necessary.
    B. 9.61 days and make a note that the one patient with an unusually long LOS was subtracted prior to making the calculation.
    C. 4.86 days and make a note that one unusually long LOS was subtracted prior to making the calculation.
    D. 4.91 days and make a note that the data on one patient with an unusually long LOS was subtracted prior to making the calculation.

REFERENCE: McWay, p 198
              Horton p 52
              Johns, p 459
              Abdelhak, p 382-383
              Koch, p 106-112

32. A hospital reported the following statistics during a nonleap year. Calculate the percentage of occupancy for the entire year.

Time Period	Bed Count	Inpatient Service Days
January 1–May 31	200	28,690
June 1–October 15	250	27,400
October 16–December 31	275	19,250

    A. 85.2%   C. 90.0%
    B. 88%   D. 91.2%

REFERENCE: McWay, p 199
              Abdelhak, p 383
              Koch, p 87-94
              Johns, p 457
              Horton, p 42
              LaTour and Eichenwald-Maki, p 405

33. Styles Hospital has 200 beds and 20 bassinets. In a nonleap year, Styles Hospital admitted 16,437 adults and children; 16,570 adults and children were discharged. There were 1,764 live births and 1,798 newborns discharged. The bed turnover rate for Styles Hospital that year was

Total nu of discharges including death
Bed count.

A. 82.2.
C. 82.9.
B. 82.7.
D. 93.5.

REFERENCE: Koch, p 185-187
Abdelhak, p 383
Horton, p 47
LaTour and Eichenwald-Maki, p 406

34. Sea Crest Hospital has 200 beds and 20 bassinets. There was a sudden spurt in the birth rate in the town in November—the hospital set up five additional bassinets for the entire month. Total bed count days for Sea Crest Hospital in a nonleap year would be

A. 73,000.
C. 80,450.
B. 80,300.
D. 80,455.

REFERENCE: Koch, p 89-94
Horton, p 44
Abdelhak, p 382-383
Johns, p 457
LaTour and Eichenwald-Maki, p 405

35. Use the statistics provided in the table to compute the fetal death rate at All Women's Hospital for March.

All Women's Hospital March Statistics	
Live births	225
Intermediate and late fetal deaths	5
Early fetal deaths	4
Newborn discharges	235

A. 4.0%
C. 2.2%
B. 1.78%
D. 1.77%

REFERENCE: Abdelhak, p 376
Koch, p 147-149
Johns, p 463
Horton, p 76
LaTour and Eichenwald-Maki, p 409

The following obstetrical statistics were collected for the month of October. Use the data in the table below to answer questions 36 and 37:

DELIVERED		TOTAL	DELIVERED BY C-SECTION
Live			
	Single infant	50	15
	Twins	3 sets	1 set
Dead			
	Early fetal	1	0
	Late fetal	1	1

Counted as delivery

3 sets → 2 × 3
6 children

36. The number of births in the facility in October is
    A. 53.   C. 56.
    B. 55.   D. 58.

REFERENCE: Koch, p 209
                Johns, p 442

37. The number of deliveries in the facility in October is
    A. 53   C. 56
    B. 55   D. 58

REFERENCE: Koch, p 140
                Johns, p 442
                Horton, p 166

38. Happy Valley Hospital recorded six fetal deaths during the last year; details are listed below:

Fetal Death Information		
ID	WEIGHT	GESTATIONAL AGE
A	526 g	22 weeks
B	405 g	18 weeks
C	817 g	26 weeks
D	1023 g	30 weeks
E	629 g	24 weeks
F	1113 g	29 weeks

    How should these deaths be counted in the hospital death rates?
    A. All the deaths except B will be included in the gross death rate.
    B. Deaths D and F will be included in the gross death rate.
    C. Deaths C, D, and F will be included in the gross death rate.
    D. None of these deaths will be included in the gross death rate.

REFERENCE: Abdelhak, p 374
                Koch, p 119-120
                LaTour and Eichenwald-Maki, p 409
                Johns, p 462
                Horton, p 64

39. William Rumple was pronounced dead on arrival (DOA). The hospital pathologist performed an autopsy on Mr. Rumple's body. This statistical event would be counted in the
    A. net death rate.   C. net autopsy rate.
    B. gross death rate.   D. hospital autopsy rate.

REFERENCE: Horton, p 86
                Koch, p 120-121, 164-167
                Johns, p 464
                LaTour and Eichenwald-Maki, p 411
                Abdelhak, p 374-379

Happy Valley Hospital discharged 6069 adults/children and 545 newborns last year. A total of 1648 adults/children and 1279 newborns were seen in the emergency department. Information on the deaths at Happy Valley last year is listed below. Use the data to answer the next two questions.

INPATIENT DEATHS		
Adult/child	245 < 48 hrs	105 > 48 hrs
Newborn	8 < 48 hrs	3 > 48 hrs

OUTPATIENT (ED) DEATHS		
Adult/child	2	
Newborn	0	

FETAL DEATHS		
Early	1	
Intermediate	3	
Late	2	

40. What was the gross (hospital) death rate at Happy Valley Hospital last year?
    A. 3.8%   C. 5.5%
    B. 5.4%   D. 5.6%

REFERENCE: Koch, p 120
                Horton, p 64
                Johns, p 462
                LaTour and Eichenwald-Maki, p 409
                Abdelhak, p 374

41. What was the net death rate at Happy Valley Hospital last year?
    A. 1.6%   C. 1.8%
    B. 1.7%   D. 1.9%

REFERENCE: Abdelhak p 375
                Koch, p 120-121
                LaTour and Eichenwald-Maki, p 409
                Johns, p 462
                Horton, p 67

42. During the month of September, Superior Health Care Center had 1,382 inpatient discharges, including 48 deaths. There were 38 deaths over 48 hours. Statistics also show 4 fetal deaths, 3 DOAs, and 4 inpatient coroner's cases. Which of the following calculations is correct to figure the net death rate?
    A. (48 × 100)/(1382 - 10)   C. (1382 × 100)/(48 - 10)
    B. (48-10 × 100)/(1382-10)   D. (1382 - 10) × 100/(48 - 10)

REFERENCE: Abdelhak, p 375
                Horton, p 67
                Koch, p 120-121
                Johns, p 462
                LaTour and Eichenwald-Maki, p 409

43. The best form/graph for demonstrating trends over time would be
    A. frequency polygon.
    B. line graph.
    C. pie chart.
    D. histogram.

REFERENCE: McWay, p 201
              Horton, p 174
              Koch, p 274-278

44. Joseph Woodley has been on a third floor nursing unit since October of 2007 and was finally discharged to a nursing home in December of 2008. When the average length of stay is calculated for the year 2008, this very long length of stay will
    A. have little impact on the average length of stay.
    B. result in a special cause variation in the average length of stay.
    C. result in a small variation in the average length of stay.
    D. result in a common cause variation in the average length of stay.

REFERENCE: Koch, p 240
              Johns, p 459
              Horton, p 52
              LaTour and Eichenwald-Maki, p 406
              Abdelhak, p 391-392

45. Still thinking about Mr. Woodley and his long stay, if you were to graph the LOS for the facility in 2008, which of the following graphs would you expect to see?

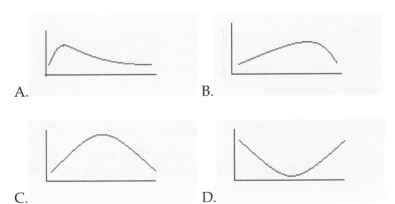

A.   B.

C.   D.

REFERENCE: Horton, p 171
              Koch, p 240
              LaTour and Eichenwald-Maki, p 423
              Abdelhak, p 391-392

46. The New Beginnings Maternity Center recorded the following statistics in December:

FETAL DEATHS:	
EARLY	240
INTERMEDIATE	40
LATE	32
BIRTHS	980
DELIVERIES	994
NEWBORN DISCHARGES	1008

40+32 x100.
──────────────
980 + 40+32

= 7200.

What was the fetal death rate at New Beginnings Maternity Center in December?
A. 6.8%
B. 7.3%
C. 7.4%
D. 31.8%

REFERENCE: Johns, p 463
Horton, p 76
LaTour and Eichenwald-Maki, p 409
Abdelhak, p 376
Koch, p 147-149

47. The statistics reported for a 300-bed hospital for 1 year were 20,932 discharges with 136,651 discharge days and 3,699 consultations performed. What was the consultation rate for the year?
A. 16.5%
B. 17.0%
C. 17.7%
D. 18.0%

REFERENCE: Horton, p 104
Koch, p 182-184
Johns, p 469

Section III—Data Display

You have already practiced reading tables in many of the preceding questions. Data display—the selection, interpretation, and construction of data—is an important part of HIM practice. Therefore, a number of data display questions should be expected. Examples of these kinds of questions follow.

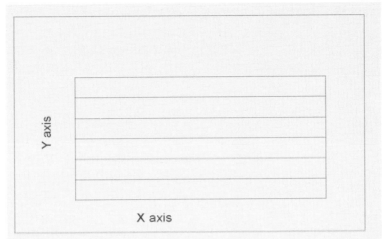

48. Look at the graph grid displayed above. If you want to follow accepted principles for graph construction, you'll follow the three-quarter-high rule. That means the
   A. height of the graph should be three-fourths the length of the graph.
   B. length of the graph should be three-fourths the height of the graph.
   C. height of the graph should display three-fourths of the data in the graph.
   D. length of the graph should display three-fourths of the data in the graph.

REFERENCE: Johns, p 434
               Horton, p 171
               LaTour and Eichenwald-Maki, p 423

49. You are preparing data from a series of weight loss studies for display. The data collected during the study is as follows:

POUNDS LOST	NUMBER IN GROUP A WITH THIS WEIGHT LOSS	NUMBER IN GROUP B WITH THIS WEIGHT LOSS
7.5 TO 9.4	1	2
9.5 TO 11.4	3	2
11.5 TO 13.4	6	5
13.5 TO 15.4	5	4
15.5 TO 17.4	8	7
17.5 TO 19.4	2	3

If you want to allow the reader to compare the results of Group A with those of Group B on one graphic display, your best choice would be to construct a
   A. bar chart.   C. histogram.
   B. line graph.   D. frequency polygon.

REFERENCE: McWay, p 203
               Horton, p 174
               Koch, p 264-266
               Johns, p 450
               LaTour and Eichenwald-Maki, p 426
               Abdelhak, p 386

50. A distribution is said to be positively skewed when the mean is
  A. bimodal.
  B. multimodal.
  C. shifted to the left.
  D. shifted to the right.

REFERENCE: Koch, p 239-240
                Horton, p 155
                LaTour and Eichenwald-Maki, p 431

51. You want to graph the number of patients admitted to three different medical staff services on each day of the last month. Because you have a large number of observations (one for each day of the month) and you want to be able to compare the observations for each of the three services on one data display, your best choice is a
  A. table.
  B. bar chart.
  C. line graph.
  D. histogram.

REFERENCE: McWay, p 201-203
                Johns, p 444
                Horton, p 171
                LaTour and Eichenwald-Maki, p 423
                Koch, p 274-278

52. You have just constructed the chart displayed below:

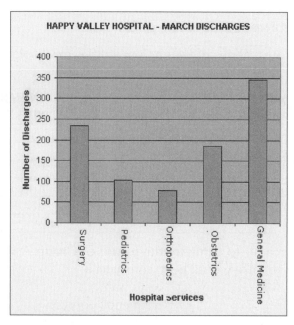

The names of the hospital services are hard to read. The best way to deal with this problem would be to
  A. construct a line graph instead of a bar chart.
  B. use a column chart instead of a bar chart.
  C. plot your primary variable along the × axis.
  D. divide the data into two charts.

REFERENCE: Koch, p 264-268
                Horton, p 171
                Johns, p 444
                LaTour and Eichenwald-Maki, p 423

53. The data display below is a

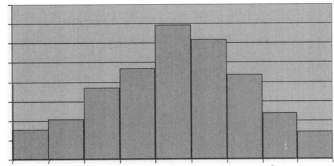

    A. bar chart, which is commonly used to display continuous data.
    B. bar chart, which is commonly used to display discrete data.
    C. histogram, which is commonly used to display continuous data.
    D. histogram, which is commonly used to display discrete data.

REFERENCE: McWay, p 203
                 Horton, p 171-174
                 Koch, p 264-286
                 Johns, p 446-450
                 LaTour and Eichenwald-Maki, p 423-425

54. The data display below is a

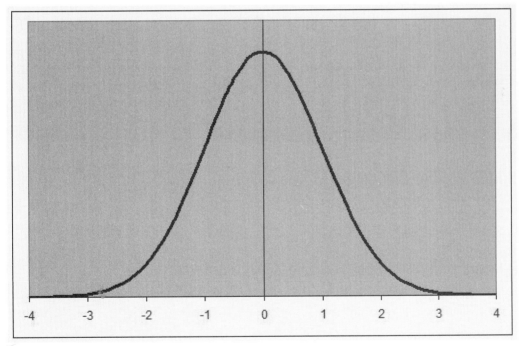

    A. normal distribution or curve.
    B. positive skewed curve.
    C. negative skewed curve.
    D. heterogenous curve.
    E. none of the above.

REFERENCE: McWay, p 208
                 Koch, p. 238-241

Shi, p 359

55. What conclusion can you make from the pie graph below?

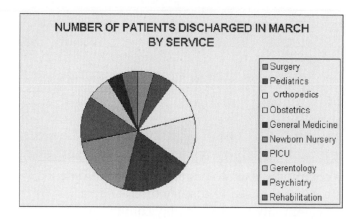

A. A pie graph should not be used because there are too many categories for effective display.
B. A pie graph should not be used, because the data are representational instead of quantitative.
C. A pie graph should not be used, because the data are qualitative instead of quantitative.
D. A pie graph is a good choice and is often used to display this kind of data.

REFERENCE: McWay, p 201, 203
            Horton, p 174
            Koch, p 273-274
            Abdelhak, p 386-388
            Johns, p 446
            LaTour, and Eichenwald-Maki, p 424

56. You are trying to improve communications with your staff by posting graphs of significant statistics on the employee bulletin board. You recently calculated the percentage of time employees spend on each of six major tasks. Because you would like the employees to appreciate each task as a percentage of their whole day, you will post these figures using a
A. line graph.   C. scatter diagram.
B. bar graph.   D. pie graph.

REFERENCE: McWay, p 201, 203
            Abdelhak, p 386-388
            Horton, p 174
            Koch, p 264-286
            Johns, p 446
            LaTour and Eichenwald-Maki, p 424

57. The graph below can best be described as

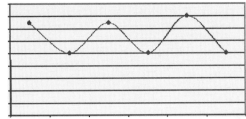

A. sequential.
B. multimodal.
C. substitutional.
D. erratic.

REFERENCE: Koch, p 328-241
Horton, p 156

58. Looking at the data represented in the scatter diagram below, you would conclude that there is

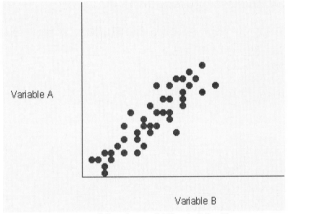

A. no correlation between Variable A and Variable B.
B. a positive correlation between Variable A and Variable B.
C. a negative correlation between Variable A and Variable B.
D. a cause and effect relationship between Variable A and Variable B.

REFERENCE: McWay, p 203-204
LaTour and Eichenwald-Maki, p 424
Horton, p 181
Johns, p 578

59. The data displayed in the histogram below could best be described as

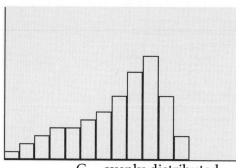

A. negatively skewed.   C. evenly distributed.
B. positively skewed.   D. normally distributed.

REFERENCE: Horton, p 174
              Koch, p 238-241
              Johns, p 450
              LaTour and Eichenwald-Maki, p 426

60. You want to construct a data display for a frequency distribution. You will use a
   A. frequency polygon or histogram.
   B. frequency polygon or bar chart.
   C. line graph or histogram.
   D. line graph or bar chart.

REFERENCE: McWay, p 203
              Horton, p 151
              Abdelhak, p 386
              Johns, p 440

61. Look at the graph below. It is an example of a

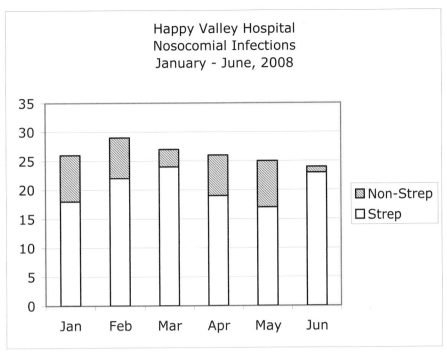

A. stacked bar chart; it is well constructed.
B. histogram; it is well constructed.
C. comparison bar chart; it is not well constructed.
D. frequency polygon; it is not well constructed.

REFERENCE: McWay, p 201
               Koch, p 264-286
               Abdelhak, p 386
               Johns, p 446

Use the historical graph below to answer questions 62 and 63.

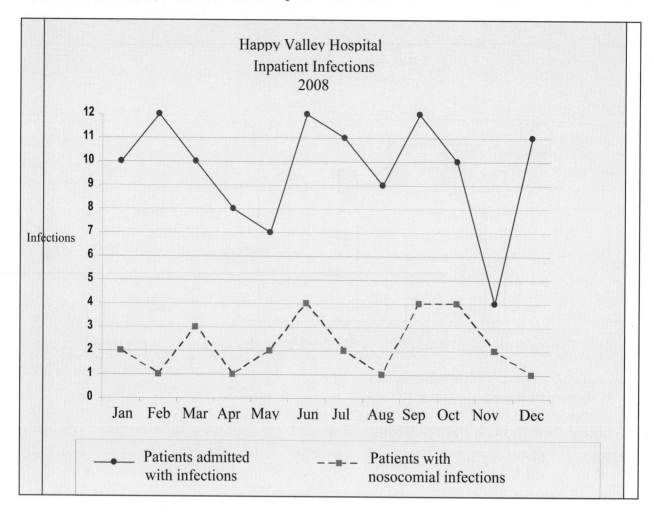

62. The total number of infections at Happy Valley Hospital during the first quarter (JAN-MAR) of 2008 was
    A. 6.
    B. 12.
    C. 22.
    D. 38.

REFERENCE: McWay, p 203,205
                    Abdelhak, p 386-389
                    Koch p, 263-278
                    Johns, p 448
                    Horton, p 174

63. Look again at the graph you used for the last question. From this graph, you can assume that more people
    A. were admitted to the facility with infections than without infections.
    B. were admitted to the facility with infections than is typical for U.S. hospitals.
    C. were admitted to the facility with infections than acquired infections in the hospital.
    D. acquired infections in the hospital than were admitted with infections.

REFERENCE: McWay, p 203, 205
                    Abdelhak, p 386-889
                    Koch, p 263-278

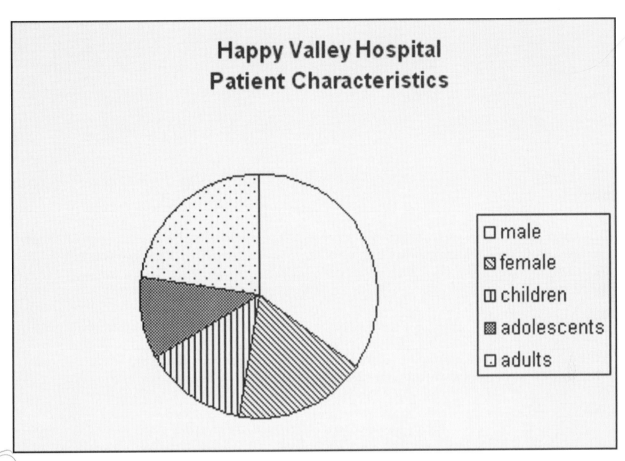

Happy Valley Hospital
Patient Characteristics

□ male
☒ female
▥ children
▨ adolescents
□ adults

64. What is the biggest problem with the pie graph displayed above?
   A. There is not enough variation in the patterns to clearly distinguish between females and children.
   B. The total males and females do not equal the total children, adolescents, and adults.
   C. There are no definitions for children, adolescents, and adults.
   D. There is more than one variable displayed on the chart.

REFERENCE: McWay, p 201-203
               Horton, p 174
               Koch, p 273-274

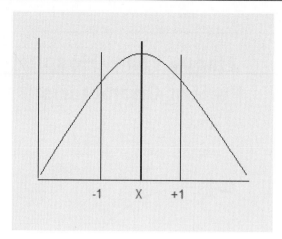

65. The chart above shows a normal distribution. What percentage of the cases fall within the two lines showing the standard distribution between -1 and +1 on either side of the mean?
    A. 68%   C. 95%
    B. 75%   D. 99%

REFERENCE: Horton, p 151-154
                  Koch, p 238-241

66. A transcription supervisor collected the data displayed below. What kind of data display is it? And, how many errors are attributed to skipped words?

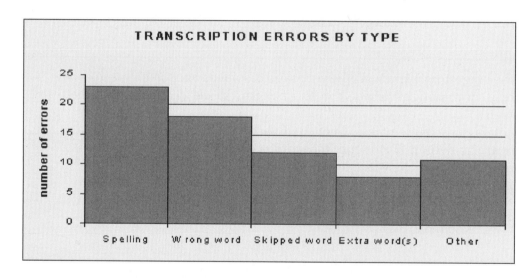

    A. This is a Pareto diagram; twelve (12) errors were due to skipped words.
    B. This is a bar chart; eighteen (18) errors were due to skipped words.
    C. This is a Pareto diagram; eighteen (18) errors were due to skipped words.
    D. This is a bar chart; twelve (12) errors were due to skipped words.

REFERENCE: McWay, p 148-149, 274
                  Johns, p 576

Section IV—Research, Financial Statistics, Etc.

You will use your statistics skills for a number of HIM functions. As usual, you must be prepared for that nebulous category we call "other." For these questions, use your basic problem-solving skills along with the terminology you learned in your statistics class. Many of these questions deal primarily with research and budgeting matters, so they are typically considered more appropriate for the RHIA than the RHIT. The RHIA questions are listed last and are so labeled.

67. The time period of a facility's Institutional Review Board (IRB) or Independent Ethics Committee (IEC) registration with the Department of Health and Human Services (HHS) is
    A. 6 months.
    B. 1 year.
    C. 2 years.
    D. 3 years.

REFERENCE: Health and Human Services Web site: http://www.hhs.gov/ohrp/

68. Harry H. Potter was admitted to your hospital to receive a second round of chemotherapy for an invasive tumor. Four days after admission, Harry complained of a sore throat and developed a fever. Harry's throat culture was positive for strep. His strep throat will be
    A. added to the denominator of the hospital's nosocomial infection rate.
    B. added to the numerator of the hospital's community-acquired infection rate.
    C. considered separately because Harry H. Potter is immune suppressed from chemotherapy.
    D. added to the numerator of the hospital's nosocomial infection rate.

REFERENCE: McWay, p199
               Abdelhak, p 379-381
               Koch, p 18-182
               Johns, p 468
               LaTour and Eichenwald-Maki, p 413

69. Twelve new cases of a certain disease occurred during the month of August. If 4,000 persons were at risk during August, then the
    A. prevalence was 3 per 1,000 persons.
    B. prevalence was 6 per 1,000 persons.
    C. incidence was 3 per 1,000 persons.
    D. incidence was 6 per 1,000 persons.

REFERENCE: McWay, p 198-199
               Abdelhak, p 381
               Johns, p 478
               Koch, p 205
               LaTour and Eichenwald-Maki, p 420

70. The primary difference between an experimental (randomized) clinical trial and other observational study designs in epidemiology is that in an experimental trial, the
    A. study is prospective.
    B. investigator determines who is and who is not exposed.
    C. study is case controlled.
    D. study and control maps are selected on the basis of exposure to the suspected causal factor.

REFERENCE: Abdelhak: p. 426-427
               McWay, p 243-344
               Shi, p 166-167, 182-186

71. The ability to obtain the same results from different studies using different methodologies and different populations is
   A. reliability.
   B. validity.
   C. confidence.
   D. specificity.

REFERENCE: McWay, p 231
               Sui, p 291, 297-300
               Abdelhak, p 349-350
               Johns, p 421
               LaTour and Eichenwald-Maki, p 301

72. You have been conducting productivity studies on your coders and find that 20% of their time is devoted to querying physicians about missing or unclear diagnoses. Assuming your coders work a 7-hour day, how many minutes do they spend per day querying physicians?
   A. 21
   B. 56
   C. 84
   D. 140

REFERENCE: Koch, p 56-57
               Abdelhak, p 373
               Johns, p 910
               Horton, p 112

Use these data to calculate answers questions 73 and 74.
Rocky Top Hospital collected the data displayed below concerning their four highest volume MS-DRGs.

MS-DRG A		MS-DRG B		MS-DRG C		MS-DRG D	
CMS WEIGHT	NUMBER PATIENTS WITH THIS MS-DRG	CMS WEIGHT	NUMBER PATIENTS WITH THIS MS-DRG	CMS WEIGHT	NUMBER PATIENTS WITH THIS MS-DRG	CMS WEIGHT	NUMBER PATIENTS WITH THIS MS-DRG
2.023	323	0.987	489	1.925	402	1.243	386

73. The MS-DRG that generated the most revenue for Rocky Top Hospital is
   A. MS-DRG A.
   B. MS-DRG B.
   C. MS-DRG C.
   D. MS-DRG D.

REFERENCE: McWay, p 130-132, 135-136, 209, 357
               Johns, p 278
               Horton, p 128

74. CMS has increased the weight for MS-DRG A by 14%, increased the weight for MS-DRG B by 20%, and decreased the weight for MS-DRG D by 10%. Given these new weights, which MS-DRG generated the most revenue for Rocky Top Hospital?
   A. MS-DRG A
   B. MS-DRG B
   C. MS-DRG C
   D. MS-DRG D

REFERENCE: Johns, p 278
               Horton, p 128

Use these data to answer questions 75 and 76:

Sea Side Clinic (SSC) provides episode of care service for four insurance companies. Data on services provided and reimbursement received are provided below.

COMPANY	UNITS OF SERVICE A	REIMBURSEMENT FOR SERVICE A	UNITS OF SERVICE B	REIMBURSEMENT FOR SERVICE B	TOTAL REIMBURSEMENT
Lifecare	259	31,196.55	812	163,577.40	194,773.95
Get Well	786	100,859.52	465	96,929.25	197,788.77
SureHealth	462	54,631.50	509	107,093.60	161,725.10
Be Healthy	219	26,991.75	417	89,425.65	116,417.40

75. It would be most profitable for Sea Side Clinic to increase episode of care service with
   A. Lifecare.
   B. Get Well.
   C. SureHealth.
   D. BeHealthy.

REFERENCE: Koch, p 234-237
               Johns, p 434
               Horton, p 143
               LaTour and Eichenwald-Maki, p 432

76. The most profitable insurance company for the units of services Sea Side Clinic performs is
   A. service A with Lifecare.
   B. service B with GetWell.
   C. service A with SureHealth.
   D. service B with BeHealthy.

REFERENCE: Koch, p 234-237
               Johns, p 434
               Horton, p 143
               LaTour and Eichenwald-Maki, p 432

Use these statistics to calculate answers to questions 77 and 78.

The physicians at Sunset Shore Clinic reported the following statistics last Tuesday.

PHYSICIAN	SERVICE A	SERVICE B	SERVICE C
Truba	10	18	14
Wooley	14	22	9
Howe	18	5	6
Masters	12	20	7

77. The physician who performed the highest number of services overall last Tuesday was Doctor
   A. Truba.
   B. Wooley.
   C. Howe.
   D. Masters.

REFERENCE: Koch, p 257-260
               Johns, p 443
               LaTour and Eichenwald-Maki, p 422
               Horton, p 166

78. It takes twice as long to perform Service C, so the doctors decided Service C should count as two services for the purpose of calculating workload. If Service C counts twice as much as Service A or Service B, then the physician who provides the most services was Doctor
    A. Truba.
    B. Wooley.
    C. Howe.
    D. Masters.

REFERENCE: Koch, p 257-260
                Johns, p 443
                LaTour and Eichenwald-Maki, p 422
                Horton, p 166

The following questions begin advanced competencies:

79. Your facility conducted a study of patient satisfaction, but you question the reliability of the questionnaire you used. The high degree of patient satisfaction expressed on the questionnaire just doesn't match the large number of complaints you have been receiving. You decide to try switching to an investigative strategy that will give you an immediate opportunity to review patient responses and correct errors. You have decided to use
    A. samples.
    B. interviews.
    C. observations.
    D. questionnaires.

REFERENCE: LaTour and Eichenwald-Maki, p 454
                Horton, p 208

The American Health Information Management Association conducted a study on job stress and job satisfaction in HIM professionals with more than 5 years of experience. The data they collected is displayed below. The next five questions will be based on this study and the data collected for it.

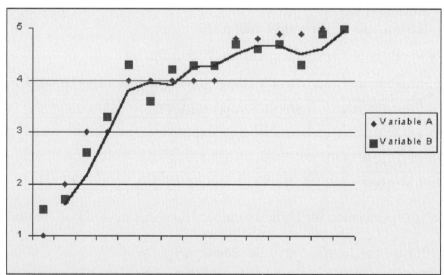

80. The researchers at AHIMA started by assuming there was no relationship between job stress and job satisfaction. This statement is generally called the
    A. study statement.
    B. false assumption.
    C. null hypothesis.
    D. correlation statement.

REFERENCE: McWay, p 195
                Abdelhak, p 392-393
                Horton, p 195
                LaTour and Eichenwald-Maki, p 460

81. Based on the data display, you can assume there is
    A. a positive relationship between variable A and variable B.
    B. a negative relationship between variable A and variable B.
    C. a causal relationship between variable A and variable B.
    D. no assumptions can be made based on the data display.

REFERENCE: LaTour and Eichenwald-Maki, p 428
              Horton, p 181
              Johns, p 578
              McWay, p 203-208
              Koch, p 2247-248

Very Dissatisfied	Somewhat Dissatisfied	Neutral	Somewhat Satisfied	Very Satisfied
1	2	3	4	5

82. The researchers at AHIMA had professionals with 5 or more years HIM experience rate their stress on a scale of 1 to 5, as shown in the chart above. Job satisfaction and job stress are both continuous variables. If the AHIMA researchers want to assess both the direction and degree of the relationship between these two continuous variables, they may choose to compute the
    A. variable correlation coefficient.
    B. Pearson correlation coefficient.
    C. continuous correlation coefficient.
    D. Danbury correlation coefficient.

REFERENCE: Abdelhak, p
              McWay, p 208-209
              Shi, p 366-367

83. There were some HIM professionals who refused to participate in the job stress/job satisfaction study. This is of great concern to the AHIMA researchers, who worry about the introduction of
    A. recall bias.   C. interviewer bias.
    B. selection bias.   D. nonresponse bias.

REFERENCE: Abdelhak, p 414-415
              LaTour and Eichenwald-Maki, p 466
              Shi, p 382

84. A researcher has repeated the same study 10 times. Each time the study is repeated, the p value decreases. As the p value approaches zero, the
    A. size of the sample increases.
    B. value of the study decreases.
    C. chance that the results are due to a sampling error decreases.
    D. chance that the results are due to a sampling error increases.

REFERENCE: Abdelhak, p 393-394
              Horton, p 465

85. You and your colleague are designing a study to try to determine the ideal mean cost for a discretionary service. You will market your service to a very large population. Your colleague thinks you will get the best data if you take lots of small samples. You think the data will be more reliable if you take one or two very large samples.
   A. Your colleague is right—the mean of multiple samples will yield more reliable results.
   B. You are right—the means of a few large samples will yield more reliable results.
   C. You are equally correct—there is little difference in the reliability of these sampling methods.
   D. You are equally wrong—unless you use stratified sampling, you cannot expect reliable results.

REFERENCE: Abdelhak, p 399-400
               LaTour and Eichenwald-Maki, p 465
               Horton, p 211
               Shi, p 279-280, 282-284

86. You are conducting a patient satisfaction survey in your outpatient clinic using interviewers who administer a questionnaire. Because you typically see about 300 people per day in the clinic, you decide to have the interviewers administer the questionnaire on every tenth patient. You are using
   A. systematic sampling.   C. variable sampling.
   B. stratified sampling.   D. convenience sampling.

REFERENCE: Abdelhak, p 399-400
               Horton, p 209
               LaTour and Eichenwald-Maki, p 464
               Shi, p 272-274

87. The people of Treasure Island Beach have been struck with a rash that seems to be infecting almost everyone in town. The staff of the hospital is working to design a study of this mysterious disease. They decide to do a cross-sectional study because cross-sectional or prevalence studies are known for
   A. quickly identifying cause and effect relationships that can serve as a basis for treatment.
   B. concurrently describing characteristics and health outcomes at one specific point in time.
   C. providing the information necessary to test for the most effective treatment of an illness or condition.
   D. supplying entire populations with therapeutic interventions on an epidemiologically sound basis.

REFERENCE: Abdelhak, p 414-417
               LaTour and Eichenwald-Maki, p 453
               Koch, p 205
               McWay, p 198-199
               Shi, p 61,

88. You are planning a prospective study to try to prove a cause and effect relationship between dipping snuff and throat cancer. First, you identify subjects who regularly dip snuff and who are free of any signs of throat cancer. Next, you need to identify subjects who
   A. dip snuff regularly and who currently have throat cancer.
   B. dip snuff regularly and who currently have significant signs of throat cancer.
   C. do not dip snuff and who currently have significant signs of throat cancer.
   D. do not dip snuff and who are free of any signs of throat cancer.

REFERENCE: Abdelhak, p 424-425
               LaTour and Eichenwald-Maki, p 530
               McWay, p 227
               Shi, p 15-16, 371-374

89. Your administrator is concerned about the snuff study (see previous question #88). The administrator would like to consider using a case control study model rather than the prospective one you are planning. One of the biggest reasons the administrator is promoting the case control model is because case control is
   A. more likely to be free of design errors than a prospective study.
   B. the best way to analytically test the hypothesis of cause and effect.
   C. more likely to decrease recall bias errors than prospective studies.
   D. less expensive than prospective studies because it uses existing records.

REFERENCE: Abdelhak, p 424-425
               LaTour and Eichenwald-Maki, p 530
               McWay, p 228

90. You point out to your administrator that the study model generally accepted to be the best method to determine the magnitude of risk in the population with the characteristic or suspected risk factor is the
   A. descriptive study design.   C. prospective study design.
   B. analytic study design.   D. case control study design.

REFERENCE: Abdelhak, p 415-425
               LaTour and Eichenwald-Maki, p 530
               McWay, p 227

91. Investigator A claims his results are statistically significant at the 10% level. Investigator B argues that significance should be announced only if the results are statistically significant at the 5% level. From this we can conclude
   A. if investigator A has significant results at the 10% level, they will never be significant at the 5% level.
   B. it will be more difficult for investigator A to reject statistical null hypotheses if he always works at the 10% level compared with investigator B who works at the 5% level.
   C. if investigator A has significant results at the 10% level, they will also be significant at the 5% level.
   D. it will be less difficult for investigator A to reject statistical null hypotheses if he always works at the 10% level compared with investigator B who works at the 5% level.

REFERENCE: Abdelhak, p 393-394
               McWay, p 95
               Shi, p 371

92. John Parker surveyed members of AHIMA's student COP regarding the relationship between clinical experiences and job opportunities. All respondents were seniors in HIA programs and each one expected to graduate and take the national exam within the next 6 months. Fifteen of the eighteen respondents indicated at least one clinical rotation had resulted in a job offer. Based on this information, Parker expects to be offered a job during senior clinical rotations. John is basing this expectation on
    A. scientific inquiry.
    B. empiricism.
    C. inductive reasoning.
    D. deductive reasoning.

REFERENCE: LaTour and Eichenwald-Maki, p 442
               Shi, p 6, 35
               McWay, p 190

Use the formula below as a resource to answer questions 93 and 94:

FORMULA FOR CALCULATING SAMPLE SIZE

$$n = \frac{Np\,(1-p)}{(N-1)\,\dfrac{(B^2)}{4} + (p)\,(1-p)}$$

93. If population size (N) = 1200 and the proportion of subjects needed (p) = 0.5 and the acceptable amount of error (B) = 0.05, then sample size (n) =
    A. 200.
    B. 300.
    C. 400.
    D. 600.

REFERENCE: LaTour and Eichenwald-Maki, p 465-466
               Abdelhak, p 399-400
               Sui, p 279- 280, 282-283

94. After the researchers see the number of subjects they will have to interview, they re-examine their criteria. The researchers could decrease the number of subjects while having the least impact on the reliability of the study by
    A. increasing p and decreasing B.
    B. increasing p or decreasing B.
    C. decreasing p and increasing B.
    D. decreasing p or increasing B.

REFERENCE: LaTour and Eichenwald-Maki, p 465
               Abdelhak, p 399-400
               Shi, p 279-280, 282-283

95. Which statistical analysis would be the best technique to use on the following problem?

A study compared the effects of retesting on the scores of students who failed a writing test. Students who did not pass on their first attempt were allowed to retest. Results showed that students had higher mean scores at retest whether they attended additional training before retesting or not.

    A. descriptive stats
    B. ANOVA
    C. regression
    D. T test

REFERENCE: Abdelhak, p 331-336
               Horton, p 197-199
               McWay, p 195-196

96. The name given to the error committed when the null hypothesis is rejected and it is actually true is: The name give in
   A. type II error.
   B. selection bias.
   C. type I error.
   D. alternative hypothesis.

REFERENCE: Abdelhak, p. 393
                      McWay, p 212

97. The OB/GYN Department reported the following information to the Quality Management/Statistics Committee:

CASE NUMBER	BRIEF DESCRIPTION
101-43-26	A 32-year-old female was admitted through the ED following an automobile accident. She spontaneously delivered a 720 g fetus that showed no sign of life.
101-44-23	A 22-year-old female was admitted in labor. Following an uneventful course, she delivered a 7 pound 4 ounce term male. The child developed sudden and unexpected respiratory distress. All attempts at resuscitation failed; the baby was pronounced dead less than 2 hours after delivery.
101-48-69	A 19-year-old female spontaneously delivered a 475 g fetus following a fall down the stairs at home.
101-56-29	A 28-year-old female was admitted for a late-term therapeutic abortion. The procedure was completed without complication; product of conception weighed 728 g.

When the committee considers these adverse outcomes from the OB/GYN Department, which of the cases will be included in the numerator of the facility's fetal death rate?

   A. 101-43-26
   B. 101-43-26 and 101-44-23
   C. 101-43-26 and 101-48-69
   D. 101-43-26 and 101-56-29

REFERENCE: Horton, p 76
                      Koch, p 147-149
                      LaTour, and Eichenwald-Maki, p 409
                      Johns, p 463
                      Abdelhak, p 376

98. Which of the cases listed above will have an impact on the facility's gross death rate?
   A. 101-43-26
   B. 101-44-23
   C. 101-48-69
   D. 101-56-29

REFERENCE: Horton, p 64
                      Koch, p 120
                      LaTour and Eichenwald-Maki, p 409
                      Johns, p 462
                      Abdelhak, p 374

99. A major disadvantage of cross-sectional studies is that
    A. the time sequence of exposure and disease is usually not known.
    B. they are usually more expensive and can take a long time to complete.
    C. prevalence rates cannot be calculated.
    D. they cannot provide information on both exposure and disease status in the same individual.

REFERENCE: Abdelhak, p 415
               LaTour and Eichenwald-Maki, p 530
               Shi, p 75, 131, 191

100. A study found that liver cancer rates per 100,000 males among cigarette smokers and nonsmokers
     in a major U.S. city were 48.0 and 25.4, respectively. The relative risk of developing liver cancer
     for male smokers compared to nonsmokers is
     A. 1.89.   C. 22.6.
     B. 15.6.   D. 48.0.

REFERENCE: Abdelhak, p 423-425
               LaTour, and Eichenwald-Maki, p 532
               McWay, p 241
               Shi, p 371-373

Answer Key for Health Statistics and Research

ANSWER   EXPLANATION

1. C $(27 \times 100) / 1{,}652 = 1.6\%$
2. D   Calculate the answer as follows:

PHYSICIAN NAME	NUMBER OF HOURS WORKED	NUMBER OF PATIENTS SEEN	NUMBER OF PATIENTS SEEN PER HOUR WORKED
Robinson	32	185	185/32 = 5.78
Beasley	30	161	161/30 = 5.37
Hiltz	35	200	200/35 = 5.71
Wolf	**26**	**157**	**157/26 = 6.04**

3. A   3545 requested records × 100 / 150,000 total records = 354500/150,000 = 2.36 = 2.4%.
4. D
5. A   CALCULATIONS: 95% of the observations fall within two standard deviations of the mean, so the cost of a lunch at Bon Appetite will be between $6.50 [8 - (2 × 0.75)] and $9.50 [8 + (2 × 0.75)].

        Lunch at Mario's will be between $5.50 [7.5 - (2 × 1)] and $9.50 [7.5 + (2 × 1)].
        Lunch at Au Courant will cost too much [$9 + (2 × 1.25) = $11.50].
        As will the Windy City Grill [$7.50 (2 × 1.5) = $10.50].

6. B
7. A
8. C   Calculations:

	Records Under Review	Same Code on Self Coding Review	Intrarater Reliability Percentage	Same Code on Peer Coding Review	Interrater Reliability Percentage	Mean Reliability Percentage
Coder A	28	22	78.57	20	71.43	75.00
Coder B	18	16	88.89	16	88.89	88.89
Coder C	45	42	93.33	43	95.56	94.44
Coder D	17	15	88.24	16	94.12	91.18

9. D
10. C
11. D
12. B
13. B   Calculation: 5+9+8+12+6+7+5+10+7+9+11 = 89/11 = 8.09
14. B   Calculate the mean time each physician spent with patients as follows:

PHYSICIAN	TIMES WITH PATIENTS	AVERAGE (MEAN) TIME WITH PATIENTS
Beasley	8,6,7	7
Robinson	5,9,9	7.7
Baumstark	10,7	8.5
Wolf	**12,5,11**	**9.3**

Answer Key for Health Statistics and Research

ANSWER   EXPLANATION

15. A
16. A
17. C
18. A
19. C
20. D

21. D

22. B
23. B $40 + 10 + 5 + 2 = 57$
24. D $67 + 2 = 69$ admissions/discharges same day
(transfers to other facilities and deaths are forms of discharge)
25. A $(75,860 + 7,100) / 365 = 227$
(Note: average daily census includes adult and pediatrics, but NOT newborns.)

26. B
27. B   The day of admission is counted as an inpatient service day, but the day of discharge is not.
28. A   March 24 through March 31 = 8 days. April 1 through April 8 = 8 days. So $8 + 8 = 16$
29. B $(12,345 \times 100) / (500X28) = 88.2\%$
30. B   9,457 discharge days/1,351 discharges = 7 days. (Count the day of admission but not discharge.)
31. D   Only two answers, A and D, are correctly calculated. Should you choose to include the unusually long LOS, you should make a note to avoid confusing readers, which makes the answer "A" a poor choice. Should you choose to eliminate the potentially confusing LOS, you must subtract both the patient from the total discharges and the discharge days from the total discharge days.
32. B $\frac{(28,690 + 27,400 + 19,250) \times 100}{(151 \times 200) + (137 \times 250) + (77 \times 275)} = 88.0 = 88\%$
33. C   Use the direct method, bed turnover

    16,570 adult and peds discharges/200 adult and peds beds = 82.85 = 82.9%
34. A   200 beds × 365 days in a non leap year = 73,000 (note: bassinets are excluded)
35. C $\frac{(5 \times 100)}{(225 + 5)} = 2.2\%$
36. C   50 + (3 sets of twins × 2 births per set) = 56 births
37. B   Multiple births are one delivery; fetal deaths are counted as deliveries

    $50 + 3 + 1 + 1 = 55$
38. D
39. D
40. C   Calculations: 361 total inpatient deaths × 100/6614 total discharges = 5.45 = 5.5%

    Fetal deaths and outpatient deaths are not included in this calculation.

Answer Key for Health Statistics and Research

ANSWER   EXPLANATION

41. B Calculations:

(108 total inpatient deaths > 48 hours) × 100   = $\underline{10800}$

(6614 total discharges – 253 deaths < 48 hours) =   6361   =1.697 = 1.7%

42. B 48 - 38 deaths over 48 hours = 10 deaths less than 48 hours. $\underline{(48-10)\ (100)}$

(1382-10)

43. B

44. B

45. B LOS would increase through the year and drop when patient is discharged.

46. A (72 intermediate and late fetal deaths × 100)   =   7200 = 6.8%

(980 births + 72 intermediate and late fetal deaths)   1052

47. C (3,699 X100) / 20,932 = 17.7%

48. A

49. C

50. D

51. C

52. B

53. C

54. A

55. A

56. D

57. B

58. B

59. A

60. A

61. A

62. D

63. C

64. D

65. A

66. A

67. D The Institutional Review Board (IRB) or Independent Ethics Committee (IEC) registration is effective for 3 years and must be renewed at the end of that period of time to remain effective. If the information on record with the Office for Human Research Protections (OHRP) for the IRB/IEC registration needs to be changed, those changes should be submitted within 90 days of the change. All updates of the IRB/IEC registration using the electronic system automatically renew the IRB/IEC registration for another 3 years. Complete updates (the Federal Wide Assurance [FWA] is fully completed) submitted in hard copy renew an FWA for another 3 years, while limited updates (the FWA is partially completed) submitted in hard copy will not change the FWA expiration date.

For additional information you may want to visit:

http://www.hhs.gov/ohrp/humansubjects/assurance/renwirb.htm.

Answer Key for Health Statistics and Research

ANSWER   EXPLANATION

68. D

69. C

70. B

71. A

72. C 7 hours per day × 60 minutes per hour = 420 minutes per day. 20% of 420 = 84

73. C Calculations:
- MS-DRG A = 2.023 × 323 = 653.43
- MS-DRG B = 0.987 × 489 = 482.64
- MS-DRG C = 1.925 × 402 = 773.85
- MS-DRG D = 1.243 × 386 = 479.80

74. C Calculations:
- MS-DRG A = 2.023 × 0.14 = 0.283; 0.283 + 2.023 = 2.306 × 323 = 744.84
- MS-DRG B = 0.987 × 0.20 = 0.197; 0.987 + 0.197 = 1.184 × 489 = 578.98
- MS-DRG C = 1.925 × 402 = 773.85
- MS-DRG D = 1.243 × 0.10 = 0.124; 1.243 − 0.124 = 1.119 × 386 = 431.93

75. D Arrive at the answer by calculating the reimbursement per unit for each service and averaging those answers, as shown below:

INSURANCE COMPANY	UNITS OF SERVICE A	REIMBURSE-MENT FOR SERVICE A	REIMBURSE-MENT PER UNIT FOR SERVICE A	UNITS OF SERVICE B	REIMBURSE-MENT FOR SERVICE B	REIMBURSE-MENT PER UNIT FOR SERVICE B	TOTAL REIMBURSE MENT	AVERAGE REIMBURSE-MENT PER UNIT OF SERVICE
Lifecare	259	31,196.55	**120.45**	812	163,577.40	**201.45**	194,773.95	**160.95**
Get Well	786	100,859.52	**128.32**	465	96,929.25	**208.45**	197,788.77	**168.39**
SureHealth	462	54,631.50	**118.25**	509	107,093.60	**210.40**	161,725.10	**164.33**
Be Healthy	219	26,991.75	**123.25**	417	89,425.65	**214.45**	116,417.40	**168.85**

76. D Reference the table above.

77. B Calculate by adding total services:

PHYSICIAN	SERVICE A	SERVICE B	SERVICE C	TOTAL SERVICES
Truba	10	22	10	42
Wooley	**14**	**22**	**9**	**45**
Howe	18	5	6	29
Masters	12	20	7	39

78. A Double Service C in the table above.

79. B

80. C

81. A

82. C

83. D

84. C

Answer Key for Health Statistics and Research

ANSWER	EXPLANATION
85. B	
86. A	
87. B	
88. D	
89. D	
90. C	
91. B	
92. C	
93. B	

$$n = \frac{(1200)\,(.5)\,(1-.5)}{\dfrac{(1200-1)\,(.05^2) + (.5)\,(1-.5)}{4}}$$

$$n = \frac{300}{(1199)\,(.000625) + .25}$$

$$n = \frac{300}{.749 + .25} = \frac{300}{1} = 300$$

94. D

95. D

96. C

97. A

98. B

99. A

100. A   RR= risk exposed divided by risk not exposed = 48 divided by 25.4 = 1.89

REFERENCES

Abdelhak, M., Grostick, S., Hanken, M. A., & Jacobs, E. (Eds.) (2007). *Health information: Management of a strategic resource* (3rd ed.). St. Louis, MO: Saunders Elsevier Publishing.

Horton, L. (2007). *Calculating and reporting health care statistics* (2nd ed.). Chicago: American Health Information Management Association (AHIMA).

Johns, M. L. (2006). *Health information management technology: An applied approach* (2nd ed.). Chicago: American Health Information Management Association (AHIMA).

Koch, G. (2008). *Basic allied health statistics and analysis* (3rd ed.). Clifton Park, NY: Thomson Delmar Learning.

LaTour, K., & Eichenwald-Maki, S. (2006). *Health information management: Concepts, principles, and practice* (2nd ed.). Chicago: American Health Information Management Association (AHIMA).

McWay, D. C. (2008). *Today's health information management: An integrated approach.* Clifton Park, NY: Thomson Delmar Learning.

Shi, L. (2008). *Health services research methods* (2nd ed.). Clifton Park, NY: Thomson Delmar Learning.

XIV. Quality and Performance Improvement

Robert L. Garrie, MPA, RHIA

1. What process assists a health care facility in continuously looking at the ways that problems develop and seeking ways to prevent problems from happening in the future?
    A. risk management
    B. quality control
    C. utilization management
    D. performance improvement

    REFERENCE: McWay, p. 143, 157
                          Abdelhak, p 438, 447, 460, 462
                          Shaw, p 3-4
                          Johns, p 555
                          LaTour and Eichenwald, p 490, 670

2. The primary source document used in quality assessment monitoring is the
    A. admission and discharge register.
    B. procedure index.
    C. medical record.
    D. diagnosis index.

    REFERENCE: McWay, p. 143
                          Abdelhak, p 97, 126
                          Shaw, p 332-333
                          Johns, p 398
                          LaTour and Eichenwald, p 288, 496

3. The Blood Usage Review Committee has a quality monitor established to review all blood transfusion reaction cases. The HIM Director will be working with the committee to identify and abstract patient outcome information for committee evaluation. What data should be collected?
    A. effects of transfusion reaction (e.g., rash, death, etc.)
    B. type and cross-match accuracy
    C. justification for the transfusion
    D. all of the above

    REFERENCE: Shaw, p 183-184
                          LaTour and Eichenwald, p 508

4. As supervisor of the record completion function of the HIM department, you are asked for record completion statistics for specific physicians who are being evaluated for reappointment to the medical staff. Which of the following information elements would you report for each physician?
    A. physician education and training
    B. number of delinquent records
    C. state licensure expiration date
    D. prior physician malpractice claims history

    REFERENCE: McWay, p. 21-22
                          Abdelhak, p 468-469
                          Shaw, p 275-278
                          LaTour and Eichenwald, p 196

5. The HIM department is asked to pull records for review by the Quality Improvement Organization (QIO). The QIO reviewers analyze records to ensure that health care services are
    A. rendered according to appropriate professional standards.
    B. medically necessary.
    C. performed in the most efficient, effective, and economical manner.
    D. all of the above

    REFERENCE: McWay, p. 160
                          Abdelhak, p 70-71, 438
                          Johns, p 34
                          LaTour and Eichenwald, p 16, 25, 495
                          Shaw, p 314

6. The coding supervisor is responsible for reviewing a random sample of each coder's work and reporting on the error rate for each coder. A check sheet is used to collect the number of charts reviewed, the number of errors for each coder, and the type of errors. What types of graphs or charts could be used to report the information gathered?

A. bar charts

B. Pareto charts

C. histograms

D. all of the above

REFERENCE: McWay, p. 149-151

Abdelhak, p 386, 452-453

Cofer and Greeley, p 53-55, 62, 68, 71

Shaw, p 57-59

Johns, p 446, 450, 576

LaTour and Eichenwald, p 674-675

7. Clinical privileges are granted to the physician for an interval specified in the medical staff bylaws, but not longer than

A. 6 months.

B. 1 year.

C. 2 years.

D. 3 years.

REFERENCE: Shaw, p 277

LaTour and Eichenwald, p 506

8. In compiling statistics to report the specific cause of death for all open-heart surgery cases, the quality coordinator assists in documenting

A. patient care outcomes.

B. utilization of hospital resources.

C. delineation of physician privileges.

D. compliance with OSHA standards.

REFERENCE: McWay, p. 153

Abdelhak, p 442

Shaw, p 182-183

LaTour and Eichenwald, p 19, 533

Johns, p 508

9. Requirements for monitoring the quality and appropriateness of inpatient services to Medicare beneficiaries and federally funded patients are outlined in the

A. Peer Review Improvement Act.

B. QIO Scope of Work.

C. Manual of National Health care Policy.

D. National Practitioner Data Bank.

REFERENCE: McWay, p. 160

Abdelhak, p 70-71, 438

LaTour and Eichenwald, p 510

10. What quality indicator would prove useful in tracking customer satisfaction in the correspondence/release of information function?
    A. the number of medical record personnel required to perform the function
    B. the amount of overtime necessary to stay current
    C. the number of charts pulled for correspondence requests
    D. the turnaround time from the date a request is received to the date the information is provided to the requester

REFERENCE: Cofer and Greeley, p 24-25
                   Shaw, p 82-87
                   LaTour and Eichenwald, p 657-658, 667

11. Most health care facilities use this type of screening criteria for utilization review purposes to determine the need for inpatient services and justification for continued stay.
    A. severity of illness/intensity of service criteria (SI/IS)
    B. critical pathways
    C. Joint Commission defined and developed criteria
    D. HEDIS measures

REFERENCE: Abdelhak, p 463-465
                   Shaw, p 113-114, 122-123
                   Johns, p 521-522
                   LaTour and Eichenwald, p 503-504

12. The process of comparing the outcomes of HIM abstracting functions at your facility with those of comparable departments of superior performance in other health care facilities to help improve accuracy and quality is referred to as
    A. focused review.   C. peer review.
    B. benchmarking.   D. occurrence screening.

REFERENCE: McWay, p. 148
                   Abdelhak, p 446-447, 613
                   Shaw, p 16
                   Johns, p 481
                   LaTour and Eichenwald, p 491, 679

13. With the passage of Medicare (Title XVIII of the Social Security Act) in 1965, which of the following functions became mandatory?
    A. quality improvement   C. quality assessment
    B. risk management   D. utilization review

REFERENCE: McWay, p. 160
                   Abdelhak, p 462
                   Shaw, p xxv-xxvi
                   Johns, p 521, 607
                   LaTour and Eichenwald, p 509

14. An ophthalmologist has requested permission to perform specialized laser procedures within the hospital. His request is evaluated by the Credentials Committee through a process to determine the specific procedures and services this physician can perform. This is known as
A. discharge planning.
B. medical staff evaluation.
C. delineation of privileges.
D. reappointment.

REFERENCE:　　McWay, p. 21
　　　　　　　　Abdelhak, p 23, 467
　　　　　　　　Shaw, p 276-277
　　　　　　　　LaTour and Eichenwald, p 506
　　　　　　　　Johns, p 515, 733-734

15. Major responsibilities of the Risk Manager generally include
A. loss prevention and reduction.
B. liability claims management.
C. participating in safety and security programs.
D. all of the above

REFERENCE:　　McWay, p. 158
　　　　　　　　Abdelhak, p 460-461
　　　　　　　　Shaw, p 152-157, 164, 166-168
　　　　　　　　LaTour and Eichenwald, p 511
　　　　　　　　Johns, p 528-531

16. Needlesticks, patient or employee falls, medication errors, or any event not consistent with routine patient care activities would require risk reporting documentation in the form of an
A. operative report.
B. emergency room report.
C. incident report.
D. insurance claim.

REFERENCE:　　McWay, p. 110, 158
　　　　　　　　Abdelhak, p 455 -456
　　　　　　　　Shaw, p 154-157, 160-163
　　　　　　　　LaTour and Eichenwald, p 266, 512
　　　　　　　　Johns, p 529

17. The responsibility for performing quality monitoring and evaluation activities in a departmentalized hospital is delegated to the
A. director of utilization management.
B. chairman of the board of trustees.
C. clinical chairpersons of medical staff committees or ancillary department directors.
D. chief executive officer.

REFERENCE:　　Shaw, p 300, 302, 306
　　　　　　　　LaTour and Eichenwald, p 505, 514

18. What criterion is critical in selecting performance indicators for a medical record department?
A. The indicators must include the most important aspects of performance.
B. Indicators must correlate with Deming's 14 points.
C. Identify at least 25 indicators that are reflective of all department functions.
D. Select only indicators that reflect positively on the department.

REFERENCE:　　Shaw, p 6
　　　　　　　　LaTour and Eichenwald, p 657-659
　　　　　　　　Johns, p 555

19. In the Act phase of the PDSA method, what step can assist in implementing change in a department?
   A. incorporating changes into a policy statement or new standard
   B. distributing new policies and procedures to people affected by the changes and explaining the rationale for the changes
   C. informing all affected parties about the changes
   D. all of the above

Plan do check act

REFERENCE:　　McWay, p. 143, 153
　　　　　　　　Abdelhak, p 447
　　　　　　　　Cofer and Greeley, p 79-84
　　　　　　　　LaTour and Eichenwald, p 671-672
　　　　　　　　Johns, p 569-570

20. What feature distinguishes the Nominal Group Technique (NGT) from brainstorming?
   A. NGT can be accomplished by mail.
   B. NGT uses a visual device like a flip chart to keep track of responses.
   C. NGT draws responses from a large group of people.
   D. NGT determines the importance of responses through a rating system.

REFERENCE:　　McWay, p. 148
　　　　　　　　Abdelhak, p 450
　　　　　　　　Cofer and Greeley, p 37-38
　　　　　　　　Shaw, p 19-21
　　　　　　　　LaTour and Eichenwald, p 673
　　　　　　　　Johns, p 573-574

21. The policy and procedure manual no longer reflects current practices. This situation is a risk management issue because
   A. supervisory time and effort will be wasted to correct the manual.
   B. training of new personnel will not be standardized.
   C. broad and permissive policy statements cannot commit the organization to a course of action.
   D. the manual represents the normal course of business.

REFERENCE:　　Pozgar, p 117
　　　　　　　　Shaw, p 157

22. The medical malpractice crisis of the 1970s prompted development of what type of programs in health care facilities?
   A. utilization management　　　　C. quality improvement programs
   B. financial analysis programs　　D. risk management

REFERENCE:　　McWay, p. 158
　　　　　　　　Abdelhak, p 461
　　　　　　　　LaTour and Eichenwald, p 511
　　　　　　　　Johns, p 528

23. The best protection against injuries and ensuing financial liability is
   A. risk reporting.　　　　　　　C. occurrence screening.
   B. risk settlement.　　　　　　　D. risk prevention.

REFERENCE:　　McWay, p. 158
　　　　　　　　Abdelhak, p 461
　　　　　　　　LaTour and Eichenwald, p 511
　　　　　　　　Shaw, p 154-155
　　　　　　　　Johns, p 529

24. The effective coordination of utilization review, quality assessment functions, and risk management activities can help eliminate
    A. antitrust violations.
    B. occurrence screening.
    C. duplicate record review.
    D. incident reporting.

REFERENCE: Abdelhak, p 412

25. The Utilization Review Coordinator reviews inpatient records at regular intervals to justify necessity and appropriateness of care to warrant further hospitalization. Which of the following utilization review activities is being performed?
    A. admission review
    B. pre-admission
    C. retrospective review
    D. continued stay review

REFERENCE: McWay, p. 161
               Abdelhak, p. 463
               LaTour and Eichenwald, p 509-510
               Johns, p 522

26. The Joint Commission recently surveyed an acute care hospital. The hospital just received the survey report and the accreditation decision. Which of the following categories should the hospital leaders address first?
    A. Requirements for Improvement
    B. Grid Elements
    C. Written Progress Reports
    D. Triennial Exception Rules

REFERENCE: Joint Commission, p AAP-1, GL-20
               Shaw, p 7, 322

27. What feature is a trademark of an effective PI program?
    A. a one-time cure-all for a facility's problems
    B. an unmanageable project that is too expensive
    C. a cost-containment effort
    D. a continuous cycle of improvement projects over time

REFERENCE: McWay, p. 157
               Cofer and Greeley, p 8-9
               Shaw, p 4-5
               LaTour and Eichenwald, p 671
               Johns, p 555

28. What QI tool uses criteria to weigh different alternatives? This display would assist in viewing all relevant information at the same time.
    A. the PDSA method
    B. a decision matrix
    C. a flowchart
    D. a customer satisfaction survey

REFERENCE: Abdelhak, p 451
               Cofer and Greeley, p 57-59
               LaTour and Eichenwald, p 612

29. Strictly from a quality standpoint, which of the following organizations was a forerunner of the evaluation of medical care?
    A. Joint Commission on Accreditation of Health care Organizations (Joint Commission)
    B. Peer Review Organizations (PRO)
    C. Professional Standards Review Organization (PSRO)
    D. Health Care Financing Administration (HCFA)

REFERENCE: McWay, p. 142
                Abdelhak, p 7, 14 Shaw, p xxiv
                LaTour and Eichenwald, p 491-492
                Johns, p 508

30. Surgical case review includes all the following EXCEPT
    A. determination of surgical justification based on clinical indication(s) in cases where no tissue has been removed.
    B. cases with elements missing in the preoperative anesthesia consultation.
    C. cases where there is a significant discrepancy between preoperative, postoperative, and pathological diagnoses.
    D. cases with serious surgical complications or surgical mortalities.

REFERENCE: LaTour and Eichenwald, p 508

31. Joint Commission requires that medical record review be performed to evaluate adequacy, accuracy, completeness, and quality of documentation
    A. annually.   C. on an ongoing basis.
    B. every 2 years.   D. quarterly.

REFERENCE: Joint Commission, p IM-14
                Medical Records Briefing, July 1997, p 3
                Shaw, p 6-7
                LaTour and Eichenwald, p 507
                Johns, p 351

32. Which of the following established legal liability for hospitals in 1965?
    A. P.L. 92-603
    B. Health Care Financing Administration (HCFA)
    C. Joint Commission on Accreditation of Health care Organizations (Joint Commission)
    D. Darling v. Charleston Community Memorial Hospital

REFERENCE: Abdelhak, p 506
                LaTour and Eichenwald, p 494
                Johns, p 528

33. The Credentials Committee of the medical staff reviews information about applicants for staff membership and makes recommendations for staff appointment and reappointment to the
    A. QI/UR Committee.
    B. Medical Record Committee.
    C. facility's governing body.
    D. Director of Health Information Management Services.

REFERENCE: McWay, p. 22
                Abdelhak, p 466
                Shaw, p 278
                LaTour and Eichenwald, p 505
                Johns, p 515, 733-734

34. Reporting the number of incomplete charts over a 6-month period using a run or line chart will prove valuable in the following two ways:
    A. The run or line chart data can show how much and how far service goes.
    B. Over time, the data can reveal trends and point out areas for improvement.
    C. The data in the run or line chart can indicate the level of customer satisfaction related to transcription errors.
    D. Over time, the data can reveal an increase in office morale and productivity.

REFERENCE: McWay, p 149, 151, 201-202
              Abdelhak, p 452-453, 453f
              Cofer and Greeley, p 70-71
              LaTour and Eichenwald, p 675-676
              Johns, p 580

35. As a HIM coding supervisor, you are asked to compare the current coding process with a proposed concurrent coding process. What visual tool would be the best to identify all the logical steps and sequence of each procedure?
    A. decision matrix   C. flowchart
    B. cause and effect diagram   D. run chart

REFERENCE: McWay, p. 273
              Abdelhak, p 450-451, 618
              Cofer and Greeley, p 45-49
              Shaw, p 138, 144-145
              LaTour and Eichenwald, p 653, 673
              Johns, p 575

36. Physicians who are members of the Surgery Committee meet to review surgical cases referred for quality issues and deviations from standard care norms. This type of review in which a physician's record is reviewed by his or her professional colleagues is known as
    A. concurrent review.   C. incident screening.
    B. clinical pertinence review. D. peer review.

REFERENCE: Abdelhak, p 407
              Shaw, p 306
              LaTour and Eichenwald, p 25, 507-508
              Johns, p 625

37. Patient mortality, infection and complication rates, adherence to living will requirements, adequate pain control, and other documentation that describe end results of care or a measurable change in the patient's health are examples of
    A. outcome measures.   C. sentinel events.
    B. threshold level.   D. incident reports.

REFERENCE: McWay, p. 153
              Abdelhak, p 442
              Shaw, p 14, 85
              LaTour and Eichenwald, p 497, 938
              Johns, p 508

38. In quality review activities, departments are directed to focus on clinical processes that are
    A. high volume.   C. problem prone.
    B. high risk.   D. all of the above

REFERENCE: Shaw, p 15
              LaTour and Eichenwald, p 513

2

98.

McWay

39. The HIM department frequently experiences a backlog in loose report filing. A quality improvement team is assembled to identify the outcome variables and the major or root causes. What visual QI tool is helpful to report the findings?
A. PDCA method
B. run chart
C. fishbone (cause and effect) diagram
D. scatter diagram

REFERENCE: McWay, p. 148
Abdelhak, p 451
Cofer and Greeley, p 50-52
Shaw, p 169-170
LaTour and Eichenwald, p 673
Johns, p 575

40. What action(s) would assist the manager of a medical record department in improving customer perception of the quality of services provided by the department?
A. Establish a 2-week turnaround time for all dictated reports.
B. Refuse to fax patient information to protect confidentiality.
C. Have physicians and hospital staff retrieve their own medical records.
D. Identify specific customer needs in order to design value-added services.

REFERENCE: Cofer and Greeley, p 25
Shaw, p 85-87
LaTour and Eichenwald, p 667

41. As based in case law decisions and the Joint Commission standards, who is ultimately responsible to ensure quality and appropriateness of patient care in a health care facility?
A. chief executive officer
B. medical staff
C. governing body or board of trustees
D. hospital attorney

REFERENCE: McWay, 17-18
Abdelhak, p 21-22
Shaw, p 300
LaTour and Eichenwald, p 493
Johns, p 734, 885

42. The quality improvement team for the HIM department meets to generate ideas to address physician complaints about missing dictation reports. What QI tool would prove useful in discussing various recommendations for solving this problem?
A. flowchart
B. scatter diagram
C. check sheet
D. brainstorming

REFERENCE: McWay, p. 148
Abdelhak, p 450
Cofer and Greeley, p 34
Shaw, p 19-20
LaTour and Eichenwald, p 672
Johns, p 573, 575, 578

43. A histogram is a valuable tool for representing
   A. the solution to a problem.
   B. priorities in problem solving.
   C. a frequency distribution with continuous-interval data.
   D. the root causes of a problem.

REFERENCE: McWay, p. 149
               Abdelhak, p 386, 452
               Cofer and Greeley, p 64-69
               Shaw, p 57-58
               LaTour and Eichenwald, p 675
               Johns, p 450, 579

44. Eighty (80) requests for records to be pulled for the emergency room were processed in January. From the histogram provided, what was the most frequent amount of time taken to process a request?

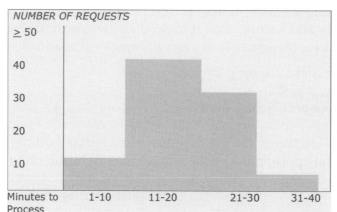

   A. 1-10 minutes   C. 21-30 minutes
   B. 11-20 minutes   D. 31-40 minutes

REFERENCE: McWay, p. 149
               Abdelhak, p 386
               Cofer and Greeley, p 64-69
               Shaw, p 57-58
               LaTour and Eichenwald, p 675
               Johns, p 450, 579

45. Which quality management theorist focused on zero defects as the goal of performance improvement efforts?
   A. Kaizen   C. Peters
   B. Crosby   D. Deming

REFERENCE: Cofer and Greeley, p 12-13
               Johns, p 674

46. As Director of the HIM department, you are asked to chair a committee that will recommend a pharmacy information system. The information has been collected, and you bring your committee together to prioritize their suggestions. This method of working with information is known as
   A. force field analysis.   C. nominal group process.
   B. Delphi process.   D. correlation analysis.

REFERENCE: McWay, p 148, 273

47. The following performance tool is used to provide structure by classifying information into smaller groups. What is the name of this chart/diagram?

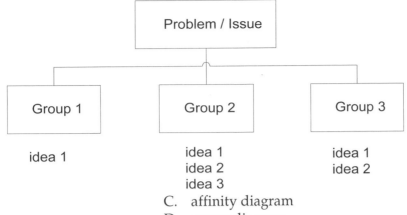

A. flowchart
B. matrix

C. affinity diagram
D. arrow diagram

REFERENCE: McWay, p. 148
              Abdelhak, p 450
              Shaw, p 20
              LaTour and Eichenwald, p 673
              Johns, p 574

48. Which quality management theorist believed that merit raises, formal evaluations, and quotas established through benchmarking hinder worker productivity and growth?
A. Brian Joiner
B. Philip Crosby

C. Joseph Juran
D. W. Edwards Deming

REFERENCE: Cofer and Greeley, p 8-11
              Johns, p 563-567
              Shaw, p xxvii
              LaTour and Eichenwald, p 605

49. As head of the Performance Improvement Department, you are asked to evaluate patient satisfaction and offer recommendations for action. The following performance tool is used to graphically display the results. What is the name of this chart?

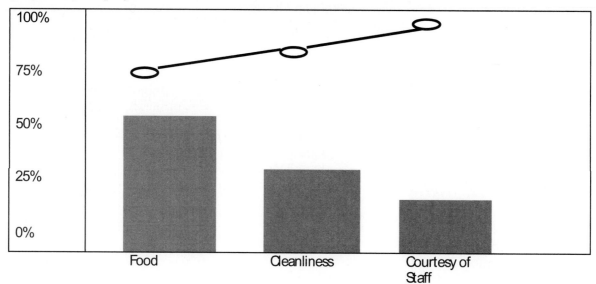

A. Pareto chart
B. line chart
C. bar chart
D. run chart

REFERENCE: McWay, p. 148
Abdelhak, p 453
Cofer and Greeley, p 60-63
Shaw, p 58-59
LaTour and Eichenwald, p 674
Johns, p 576

50. Based on the previous graphic chart, which two areas should you recommend be acted upon first in order to address 80% of the patients' complaints?

A. food and cleanliness
B. food and courtesy of staff
C. cleanliness and courtesy of staff
D. not enough information to determine

REFERENCE: McWay, p. 148
Shaw, p 58-59
LaTour and Eichenwald, p 674
Johns, p 576

51. As Director of the HIM department, it is your responsibility to reduce the turnaround time for your organization's accounts receivable balance. The following performance improvement tool was used to add weights in order to prioritize ideas. What is it called?

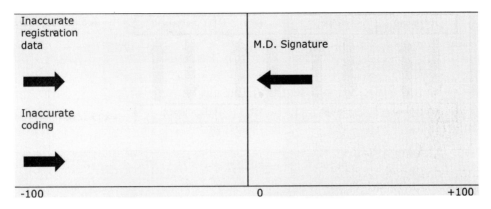

A. fishbone diagram
B. precision matrix

C. flowchart
D. force field analysis

REFERENCE: McWay, p. 273
               Abdelhak, p 452
               Cofer and Greeley, p 127-129
               LaTour and Eichenwald, p 674
               Johns, p 577

52. Which of the following processes is mandatory for health care facilities?
A. accreditation
B. certification

C. AHA registration
D. licensure

REFERENCE: McWay, p 17
               Abdelhak, p 12
               Shaw, p 312
               LaTour and Eichenwald, p 32
               Johns, p 628-629

53. A surgeon left a clamp in a patient, resulting in a return to the operating room. In an integrated organizational quality management model, all of the following entities would receive data about the investigation EXCEPT the
A. Tissue Committee.
B. Credentials Committee.

C. Risk Management Program.
D. Pharmacy and Therapeutics Committee.

REFERENCE: Shaw, p 210
               LaTour and Eichenwald, p 508

54. P.L. 92-603 provided for the establishment of
A. PSROs.
B. Joint Commission as a governmental organization.
C. PROs.
D. ACSs.

REFERENCE: McWay, p. 160
               LaTour and Eichenwald, p 15
               Johns, p 607

55. An indicator about the placement and number of fire extinguishers would be which type?
    A. process
    B. outcome
    C. structure
    D. regulation

REFERENCE: Abdelhak, p 442
Shaw, p 14
LaTour and Eichenwald, p 496
Johns, p 555-556

56.) An indicator about the institution's death rate would be which type?
    A. process
    B. outcome
    C. structure
    D. regulation

REFERENCE: McWay, p 153
Abdelhak, p 442
Shaw, p 14
LaTour and Eichenwald, p 496
Johns, p 555-556

57. HEDIS gathers data in the following area:
    A. measures of access (e.g., at least one visit to a provider within three years).
    B. measures of quality (e.g., cholesterol screenings).
    C. measures of financial performance (e.g., cost per member).
    D. all of the above

REFERENCE: McWay, p. 179-180
Abdelhak, p. 692-693
Shaw, p 187
Johns, p 171
LaTour and Eichenwald, p 539-540

58. If administrators of a home health agency wanted to measure the outcomes of adult patients receiving their agency's services, which tool would they use?
    A. OASIS
    B. HEDIS
    C. ORYX
    D. QAI

REFERENCE: McWay, p. 177
Abdelhak, p 137-138
LaTour and Eichenwald, p 153-154, 368
Johns, p 169
Shaw, p 190

59. To comply with ORYX, a nursing home administrator would need to
    A. implement RUGS appropriateness screening.
    B. collect performance measure data that apply to the residents.
    C. conduct ongoing open record review.
    D. submit MDS data directly to the Joint Commission.

REFERENCE: McWay, p 154
Shaw, p 48
LaTour and Eichenwald, p 496-499
Johns, p 172, 508

60. Continuous quality improvement is best described by the following statements EXCEPT:
  A. Corrective action targets clinicians more so than processes.
  B. Standards are defined, measured, and systematically applied.
  C. Monitoring is ongoing with periodic feedback.
  D. All personnel support quality improvement efforts, including top management and the governing body.

REFERENCE: McWay, p 142
Abdelhak p 441-442
Shaw, p 4-8
LaTour and Eichenwald, p 670-672
Johns, p 557-560

61. Which of the following is a disadvantage of retrospective data collection?
  A. Data are all available.
  B. Fewer data collectors are required.
  C. Deficiencies in documentation can effect reimbursement.
  D. Reviewer bias is reduced.

REFERENCE: McWay, p 104-106, 152

62. According to current theory in the quality management field, should concurrent data collection or retrospective data collection be utilized?
  A. Concurrent and retrospective data collection methods are both necessary in order to effect meaningful interventions and contain costs.
  B. Concurrent data collection methods alone are meaningful because they emulate health practitioner training.
  C. Concurrent data collection methods alone are meaningful because interventions must always be immediate.
  D. Retrospective data collection methods alone are appropriate in the reimbursement realities of this decade.

REFERENCE: McWay, p 104-106, 152

63. You are determining the sample size for a quality study. Which of the following factors should you consider first?
  A. cost
  B. personnel
  C. size of the target population
  D. confidentiality of the record

REFERENCE: Shi, p 279-286
Abdelhak, p. 399-400
LaTour and Eichenwald, p 465

64. The Anesthesia Department is adding a new indicator to its plan. The Chief Anesthesiologist has come to you, the Director of Quality Management, to help her design a data collection methodology. The two of you are now considering who will be doing the data collection. All of the following are factors in your deliberations EXCEPT
  A. quality management organizational model of the institution.
  B. Joint Commission standards and required characteristics.
  C. the location of data.
  D. the expertise of the staff.

REFERENCE: McWay, p 143
Shaw, p 48

65. The manager of the utilization review department wants to monitor and evaluate the prevention of inappropriate admissions. When would the manager need to collect data?
    A. prospectively
    B. concurrently
    C. retrospectively
    D. long-term care review

REFERENCE: McWay, p 227
               Abdelhak, p 463
               LaTour and Eichenwald, p 509
               Johns, p 522

66. The manager of the Quality Department is listing various sources of data. Which of the following data sources would be an example of an external source?
    A. emergency room logs
    B. incident reports
    C. patient registration and admission, discharge, transfer (ADT) information
    D. quality improvement organization information

REFERENCE: McWay, p. 142, 160
               Abdelhak, p 438
               Shaw, p 48
               Johns, p 559

67. The primary advantage of concurrent quality data collection is that
    A. multiple chart reviews eliminate collector bias.
    B. patient care problems can be remedied immediately.
    C. practitioners receive immediate feedback about patient processes and outcomes.
    D. staffing is decreased.

REFERENCE: McWay, p 104, 161,

SUMMARY OF SELECTED BLOOD PRODUCT REVIEW

Monitoring Element	Packed Red Blood Cells		Fresh Frozen Plasma		Platelets	
(N = 295)	(N = 256)		(N = 29)		(N = 10)	
	Met N (%)	Unmet N (%)	Met N (%)	Unmet N (%)	Met N (%)	Unmet N (%)
Indications	232 (91%)	24 (9%)	7 (24%)	22 (76%)	10 (100%)	0 (0%)

68. Refer to the table Summary of Selected Blood Product Review. Which blood component or derivative had the most units reviewed?
    A. packed red blood cells
    B. fresh frozen plasma
    C. platelets
    D. unable to determine from the table

REFERENCE: McWay, p 192-193, 218
               Shi, p 358-360
               Abdelhak, p 384, 386
               Shaw, p 51
               LaTour and Eichenwald, p 402, 422-423, 432
               Johns, p 434-438

69. Refer to the table Summary of Selected Blood Product Review. The table was first produced during which quality improvement function?
   A. pharmacy and therapeutics function
   B. drug usage evaluation
   C. medical record review
   D. blood usage review

REFERENCE: LaTour and Eichenwald, p 508

70. Refer to the table Summary of Selected Blood Product Review. What percent of the fresh frozen plasma units met indications?
   A. 7%   C. 22%
   B. 24%   D. 76%

REFERENCE: McWay, p 192-193, 218
               Shi, p 358-360
               Abdelhak, p 384, 386
               Shaw, p 51, 114
               LaTour and Eichenwald, p 402, 422-423, 432
               Johns, p 435

71. Refer to the table Summary of Selected Blood Product Review. Based on the results reported in the table, which blood component or derivative should first be the topic of an in-depth study?
   A. packed red blood cells   C. platelets
   B. fresh frozen plasma   D. unable to determine from the table

REFERENCE: Abdelhak, p 384, 386, 452
               LaTour and Eichenwald, p 508
               Shaw, p 57

CASE STUDY #1

Upon employment at your facility, all new employees read, demonstrate understanding, and sign Confidentiality Statements. Disclosure of confidential information is grounds for immediate dismissal. Each year, during the annual performance evaluation, every employee again reads, demonstrates understanding, and signs the Confidentiality Statement.

You are the Director of the Quality Department. Your department has found that the femoral-popliteal bypass failure rate of one of your vascular surgeons, Dr. Z, is twice that of the national average. Members of the surgery department have reviewed that vascular surgeon's performance both by reading the medical records and by watching videos of her surgery. The Surgery Department and the Executive Committee have decided to deny reappointment for this surgeon.

Lucille X, the mother of one of your quality coordinators, has severe peripheral vascular disease. She was admitted to your facility and had an angiogram. The angiogram shows that she should have a femoral-popliteal bypass. She had told you that she would be in your facility and asked you to visit her. You are now fulfilling that promise and are also bringing her flowers. While pausing to knock on her door, you hear your employee, Mary G, vehemently state to her mother, "Mom, Dr. Z is a quack; half of her bypass surgeries fail. You must have Dr. DoGood!"

72. Referring to Case Study #1, what do you do as Director of the Quality Department?
    A. Seek the advice of the facility's legal counsel.
    B. Immediately dismiss Mary G upon her arrival back in the department.
    C. Walk into Lucille's room and state that Dr. Z is a fine surgeon and also advise Mary G to lower her voice.
    D. Upon Mary G's arrival back in the department, give her a written warning.

REFERENCE: McWay, p 79, 81-84, 94
                 McWay (2003), p 52-53
                 Abdelhak, p 521, 534-536
                 Johns, p 652-653
                 LaTour and Eichenwald, p 265, 514

73. Referring to Case Study #1, are the meeting minutes about the decisions regarding Dr. Z of the Department of Surgery and of the Executive Committee admissible in court?
    A. Yes, federal amendments to the Medicare Act require release of peer review.
    B. Yes, state laws allow discovery of medical review committee records.
    C. No, the federal Freedom of Information Act and state "sunshine laws" protect peer review.
    D. No, under state laws, records of medical review committees are not subject to introduction into evidence.

REFERENCE: Abdelhak, p 534-536
                 Shaw, p 403-404
                 LaTour and Eichenwald, p 265

CASE STUDY #2

You are helping the Nursing Department to write indicators, to determine appropriate formulas for ratios and to determine data collection time frames. One important aspect of care is the documentation of education of patients. More specifically, the nursing department would like to assess its documentation of education on colostomy care for patients with new colostomies.

74. Referring to Case Study #2, what would be the most cost-effective and appropriate data collection time frame?
    A. prospectively   C. retrospectively
    B. concurrently   D. long-term care review

REFERENCE: McWay, p 152
                 LaTour and Eichenwald, p 265

75. Referring to Case Study #2, which of the following ratios would you recommend?
    A. number of records with documentation of colostomy-care teaching
        total number of patients on surgery unit
    B. number of records with documentation of teaching
        total number of discharges
    C. number of records with documentation of colostomy-care teaching
        total number of patients with new colostomy
    D. number of records reviewed with documentation of colostomy-care teaching
        total number of records reviewed

REFERENCE: McWay, p 198-200
                 Abdelhak, p 373
                 Johns, p 432-433
                 LaTour and Eichenwald, p 402
                 Shaw, p 113-114

76. A culture and sensitivity report was returned to the inpatient unit of Brian Hospital. The sensitivity showed bacterial resistance to the current antibiotic the patient was receiving. The patient continued on the same antibiotic without improvement. A generic quality screen identified this case for review. At a minimum, which committee should review this case?
   A. Surgical Case Review
   B. Safety Committee
   C. Information Management Committee
   D. Pharmacy and Therapeutics Committee

REFERENCE: Shaw, p 210
               LaTour and Eichenwald, p 508

77. The outpatient coding staff has been working to improve coding accuracy. The standard for the number of cases that must be coded has been raised four times in the past year. The staff states that "the more cases that must be coded, the greater the error rate will be for the corresponding time period." The department keeps statistics on both the numbers of cases coded and the corresponding error rate. What is the best QI tool for testing the coding staff's theory?
   A. control chart   C. run chart
   B. Pareto chart   D. scatter diagram

REFERENCE: McWay, p. 149-151
               Cofer and Greeley, p 87-91
               LaTour and Eichenwald, p 674-677
               Johns, p 578

78. The health information reception desk is experiencing a huge influx of phone calls on Monday, Tuesday, and Wednesday mornings. This is creating a problem in getting requested patient information out within an acceptable time frame. The reception staff work group has agreed to start recording the reason for the phone calls for the next 4 weeks. They want to focus on solving the response-time problem by reducing the turnaround time for the largest category of phone calls. Which QI tool best supports this goal?
   A. control chart   C. run chart
   B. Pareto chart   D. scatter diagram

REFERENCE: McWay, p. 148-151
               Abdelhak, p 453
               Cofer and Greeley, p 87-91
               Shaw, p 58-59
               LaTour and Eichenwald, p 674
               Johns, p 576

79. The board of directors of a 400-bed women's hospital receives a report of key quality indicator results on a periodic basis. The report always includes the quarterly cesarean section rate and has for many years. This recent period they have seen a rise in the rate and want to know if this is significant. What is the best QI tool for this purpose?
   A. control chart   C. run chart
   B. Pareto chart   D. scatter diagram

REFERENCE: McWay, p. 148-151
               Abdelhak, p 453
               Cofer and Greeley, p 87-91
               Johns, p 580-581
               LaTour and Eichenwald, p 676
               Shaw, p 610

80. What is the best tool for differentiating between common cause variation and special cause variation?
A. control chart
B. Pareto chart
C. run chart
D. scatter diagram

REFERENCE: McWay, p. 211-212
              Abdelhak, p. 453-454
              Johns, p 580-581
              LaTour and Eichenwald, p 676
              Shaw, p 61
              Joint Commission, p PI-15

81. Which department will most likely be responsible for taking corrective action regarding the following quality indicator?

> QUALITY INDICATOR:
> Ninety-five percent (95%) of physician appointments/reappointments will be completed within 90 days of receipt of all required materials.

A. Admitting
B. Business Office
C. Health Information Department
D. Medical Staff Office

REFERENCE: Abdelhak, p. 443, 467-468
              Shaw, p 276-278
              LaTour and Eichenwald, p 505-507

82. Which department will most likely be responsible for taking corrective action regarding the following quality indicator?

> QUALITY INDICATOR:
> The number of DRG validation changes made by the PRO will not exceed 2%.

A. Admitting
B. Business Office
C. Health Information Department
D. Medical Staff Office

REFERENCE: Abdelhak, p 442, 659

83. All of the following are among Joint Commission's initial core measure sets for hospitals EXCEPT
A. acute myocardial infarction.
B. diabetes.
C. pneumonia.
D. surgical procedures and complications.

REFERENCE: Joint Commission, p M-3
              Shaw, p 182-183, 186-187
              LaTour and Eichenwald, p 498

84. Which department will most likely be responsible for taking corrective action regarding the following quality indicator?

> QUALITY INDICATOR:
> Number of insurance claims requiring resubmission due to errors (not related to coding) will not exceed 3%.

A. Admitting
B. Business Office
C. Health Information Department
D. Medical Staff Office

REFERENCE: Abdelhak, p 657

85. All of the following data would appear on a "public accountability report card" EXCEPT
    A. average cost of bypass surgery.
    B. average number of clinicians in the operating room during bypass surgery.
    C. customer satisfaction rating for the hospital providing bypass surgery.
    D. complication and death rate for bypass surgery.

REFERENCE: Abdelhak, p 440

86. Historic accomplishments impacting quality in medical care include all EXCEPT
    A. ensuring competent practitioners.
    B. Darling v. Charleston Community Hospital.
    C. implementation of OTRA.
    D. medical education reform (Flexner report findings).

REFERENCE: McWay, p. 142
                 Abdelhak, p 7-8, 438-439
                 LaTour and Eichenwald, p 491, 494
                 Johns, p 502-503

87. An accreditation agency counterpart to the Joint Commission for managed care organizations is the
    A. AHRQ.   C. IOM.
    B. AHCPR.   D. NCQA.

REFERENCE: McWay, p. 48
                 Abdelhak, p 14, 439
                 Shaw, p 187
                 LaTour and Eichenwald, p 539
                 Johns, p 510

88. Quality requirements of providers participating in the Medicare program are found in all EXCEPT the
    A. Conditions of Participation.   C. ORYX.
    B. Federal Register.   D. QIO regulations governing work scope.

REFERENCE: Abdelhak, p 438
                 Shaw, p 182
                 LaTour and Eichenwald, p 494-495
                 Johns, p 511-514

89. Which data bank is a result of HIPAA legislation?
    A. Fraud and Abuse Data Bank
    B. Health care Integrity and Protection Data Bank
    C. National Practitioner Data Bank
    D. Privacy Information Breach Data Bank

REFERENCE: McWay, p. 58-59
                 Abdelhak, p 468
                 Johns, p 609
                 LaTour and Eichenwald, p 296-297

90. The following "sentinel events" must be available for Joint Commission review EXCEPT
A. infant abduction.
B. petechiae due to adverse drug reaction.
C. rape.
D. surgery on wrong patient or wrong body part.

REFERENCE: McWay, p. 159
              Abdelhak, p. 456, 459
              Joint Commission, p SE-2
              Shaw, p 155
              LaTour and Eichenwald, p 512-513
              Johns, p 535

91. Using the information in the table below, calculate the average percentage of patients for the entire year who waited longer than an acceptable amount of waiting time. (The sample size for each month's data is 100.)

Year 2008 Month	Percent Patients with Unacceptable Waiting Time
January	5%
February	4%
March	3%
April	5%
May	3%
June	10%
July	5%
August	2%
September	1%
October	2%
November	1%
December	3%

A. 3.1%
B. 3.6%
C. 3.7%
D. 4.0%

REFERENCE: McWay, p. 194
              Abdelhak, 389-390
              Shaw, p 61-62
              LaTour and Eichenwald, p 432
              Johns, p 435

92. Which of the following is incorrect about the use of control charts?
A. Control charts can be used to measure key processes over time.
B. The upper and lower control limits are always ± 2 standard deviations.
C. The lower control limits are always ± 2 standard deviations.
D. The upper control limits are always ± 1.8 standard deviations.

REFERENCE: McWay, p 149, 151, 211-212
              Shaw, p 61

93. The average percent of patients exceeding acceptable waiting time was 3.7% (see table for question number 91). The calculated UCL is 9.4. When you plot the upper and lower limits, what would you suggest as the reason for the June variation?
   A. common cause variation
   B. root cause variation
   C. special cause variation
   D. unable to determine with the data given

REFERENCE: McWay, p 211-212
               Abdelhak, p. 453-454
               Joint Commission, p PI-15
               Shaw, p 61

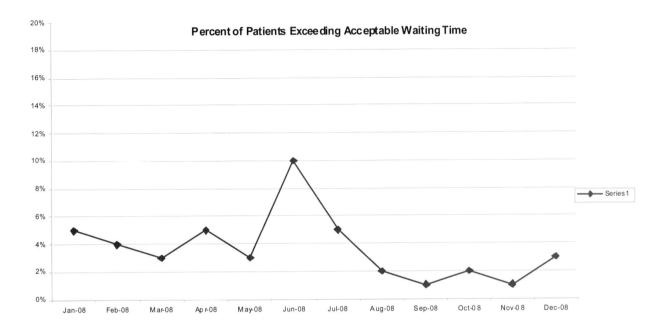

94. Adding the UCL (upper control limit) and LCL (lower control limit) to the chart above (from question 93) creates a
   A. control chart.
   B. frequency distribution.
   C. run chart.
   D. variation graph.

REFERENCE: McWay, p. 149, 211-212
               Abdelhak, p 452-454
               Shaw, p 61
               Johns, p 580-581
               LaTour and Eichenwald, p 676

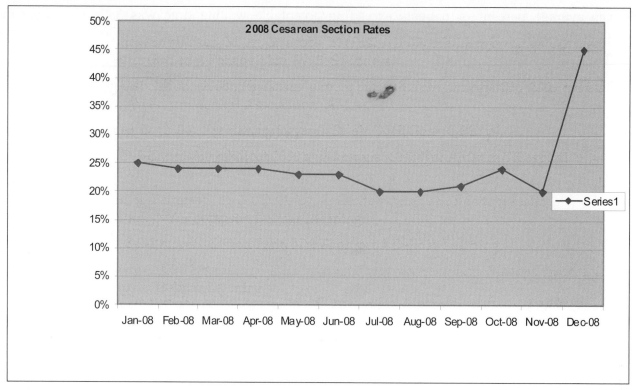

95. You are the Quality Coordinator for the medical staff. Analyze the chart above and determine the steps to be taken next.
    A. Plot control limits, check indicator threshold, and take December charts to OB/GYN Committee if threshold exceeded.
    B. Plot control limits and take December charts to OB/GYN Committee if December data point exceeds UCL.
    C. Plot control limits, pull charts for December, and do a focused review screening.
    D. Plot control limits and refer to Medical Executive Committee for variation review.

REFERENCE: McWay, p. 211-212
              Abdelhak, p 386, 453-454
              Johns, p 580-581
              LaTour and Eichenwald, p 676
              Shaw, p 61

Answer Key for Quality and Performance Improvement

1. D		49. A	
2. C		50. A	
3. D		51. D	
4. B		52. D	
5. D		53. D	
6. D		54. A	
7. C		55. C	
8. A		56. B	
9. B		57. D	
10. D		58. A	
11. A	Definition: HEDIS is Health Plan Employer Data and Information Set	59. B	
		60. A	
12. B		61. C	
13. D		62. A	
14. C		63. C	
15. D		64. B	
16. C		65. A	
17. C		66. D	
18. A		67. B	
19. D		68. A	
20. D		69. D	
21. D		70. B	
22. D		71. B	
23. D		72. B	
24. C		73. D	
25. D		74. C	
26. A		75. C	Number of times an event occurred divided by number of times the event could have occurred
27. D			
28. B			
29. A		76. D	
30. B		77. D	
31. C		78. B	
32. D		79. A	
33. C		80. A	
34. B		81. D	
35. C		82. C	
36. D		83. B	
37. A		84. B	
38. D		85. B	
39. C		86. C	
40. D		87. D	
41. C		88. C	
42. D		89. B	
43. C		90. B	
44. B			
45. B			
46. C			
47. C			
48. D			

Answer Key for Quality and Performance Improvement

91. C (5 + 4 + 3 + 5 + 3 + 10 + 5 + 2 + 1 + 2 +
       1 + 3) ÷ 12 = 3.66 = 3.7
92. D
93. C Data points that lie outside the upper
       or lower control limits may signal
       special cause variation.
94. A
95. A

REFERENCES

Abdelhak, M., Grostick, S., Hanken, M. A., & Jacobs, E. (2007). *Health information: Management of a strategic resource* (3rd ed.). Philadelphia: W. B. Saunders.

Cofer, J. I., & Greeley, H. P. (1996). *Quality improvement techniques for medical records.* Marblehead, MA: Opus Communications.

Johns, M. L. (2006). *Health information management technology: An applied approach* (2nd ed.). Chicago: American Health Information Management Association (AHIMA).

Joint Commission on Accreditation of Health care Organizations. (2005). *Hospital accreditation standards.* Oak Brook Terrace, IL: Joint Commission on Accreditation of Health care Organizations (Joint Commission).

LaTour, K., & Eichenwald-Maki, S. (2006). *Health information management: Concepts, principles, and practice* (2nd ed.). Chicago: American Health Information Management Association (AHIMA).

McWay, D. (2008). *Today's health information management: An integrated approach.* Clifton Park, NY: Thomson-Delmar Learning.

Medical records briefing.(July 1997). Marblehead, MA: HCPro (formerly Opus Communications).

Pozgar, G.D. (2006). *Legal aspects of health care administration* (9th ed.). Sudbury, MA: Jones and Bartlett.

Shaw, P. (2006). *Quality and performance improvement in health care: A tool for programmed learning* (3rd ed.). Chicago: American Health Information Management Association (AHIMA)

XV. Organization and Management

Carol Venable, MPH, RHIA, FAHIMA

Anita Hazelwood, MLS, RHIA, FAHIMA

1. The manager of a Health Information Department has many training and development methods available for the departmental and nondepartmental staff. Consider the following situation. The department's working hours are 8:00 AM to 6:00 PM. After 6:00 PM, if a record is needed in the emergency room for a possible readmission, the ER clerk has access to the HID in order to retrieve the record. On the occasions when the ER clerk has retrieved a record, she has left the department open, the records have been pulled and not replaced, and it appears as if the clerk was viewing records unnecessarily. What would be the best training or development method for the ER clerk in order to rectify this situation?
   A. receive training by an ER coworker
   B. receive training by an expert in record documentation
   C. attend an outside workshop or seminar
   D. receive training by the supervisor of files

REFERENCE: LaTour and Eichenwald-Maki, p 706-707
              McWay, p 290

2. Strong lateral relationships within a facility are most likely when
   A. vertical relationships are less than adequate.
   B. individual departments cooperate together to achieve organizational goals.
   C. individual departments are only interested in their internal goals.
   D. individual departments avoid one another.

REFERENCE: LaTour and Eichenwald-Maki, p 606-607

3. The Director of the Health Information Services Department has asked that the supervisor of coding institute a method to monitor the accuracy of coding. What method would be the most effective approach?
   A. Perform a 100% review of one of the employees' work each day.
   B. Review a sample of each employee's work annually.
   C. Review a random sample of each employee's work monthly.
   D. Have each employee check each other's work and report any problems to the supervisor.

REFERENCE: McWay, p 264-265
              LaTour and Eichenwald-Maki, p 657-658

4. You are the Coding Supervisor and wish to know the amount of time eight employees had spent coding this month. You have the following productivity log. What percentage of time was spent on coding?

Productivity Log January			
# of Employees	Charts Coded	Standard	Hours Worked
8	725	12 minutes per chart	1,280

   A. 14.7%   C. 8.8%
   B. 6.8%   D. 11.3%

REFERENCE   McWay, p 264-265
             Shortell and Kaluzny, p 419

5. The Director of Health Information Services has asked the supervisor over files to determine productivity standards for the file clerks. In initiating this process, the supervisor has determined that the best way to institute work standards is to
   A. determine which employee can work the fastest.
   B. perform time and motion studies.
   C. improve employee morale.
   D. develop standards based on professional standards and industry benchmarks.

REFERENCE: McWay, 264-265
               Shortell and Kaluzny, p 419

6. A new health information management clerk has been on staff for 2 days. She has thus far analyzed charts incorrectly, sent out confidential information improperly, and used the copy machine inappropriately. Evaluate this situation and determine the best resolution.
   A. Review the job description and job procedure with clerk and follow up with an in-service.
   B. Review the job procedure with the clerk and have the analysis supervisor monitor her progress.
   C. Review the job description and job procedure with the clerk and follow up with a merit evaluation.
   D. Review job procedures with the clerk and follow up with an in-service.

REFERENCE: McWay, p 264-265
               LaTour and Eichenwald-Maki, p 695

7. "Qualified employees should be given priority when vacancies within the organization occur" is an example of
   A. a policy of the organization.
   B. an objective for the organization.
   C. a rule for the organization.
   D. a procedure for the organization.

REFERENCE: McWay, p 252, 260-261
               LaTour and Eichenwald-Maki, p 695

8. A rule is helpful to both managers and the employees in the decision-making process. A rule
   A. allows judgments to be made.
   B. requires interpretation.
   C. pre-decides issues.
   D. provides the necessary details.

REFERENCE: McWay, p 21, 45
               Liebler, p 110

9. Which of the following statements describes a method?
   A. Medical records requested by the emergency room will be retrieved and delivered within 30 minutes.
   B. Multiple-page discharge summaries are stapled together in the left-hand corner.
   C. Transcription turnaround time is established as 24 hours following completion of dictation by the physician.
   D. Only HIM personnel have access to the medical record filing area.

REFERENCE: McWay, p 21, 45, 230
               Liebler, p 109-110

10. The supervisor of retention and retrieval was receiving frequent complaints from the file clerks regarding the discharge clerk's job performance. The file clerks stated it was becoming difficult to maintain their productivity levels because the discharge clerk was not processing the requisition slips in a timely manner. In order to get a clearer understanding of the situation, the supervisor asked the file clerks and the discharge clerk to complete a task list for a 2-week period. The supervisor is constructing a
    A. flow process chart.
    B. movement diagram.
    C. work distribution chart.
    D. procedure flowchart.

REFERENCE: McWay, p 260
               LaTour and Eichenwald-Maki, p 649

11. In a filing system containing a total of 1,255 records, 48 records are identified as misfiles. What is the percentage of filing accuracy for this area?
    A. 26.14%   C. 3.82%
    B. 74%   D. 96%

REFERENCE: McWay, p 264-265
               LaTour and Eichenwald-Maki, p 657-658, 692

12. The standard for record retrieval is 200 work units per month. Based on the table below, what is the variance from standard for the month of May?

May Productivity Report—Chart Retrieval			
Week 1	Week 2	Week 3	Week 4
30	40	25	35

    A. 75%   C. 53%
    B. 65%   D. 15%

REFERENCE: Shortell and Laluzny, p 419
               McWay, p 264-265

13. Ms. Wolf, supervisor of coding and abstracting, would like to determine the coders' accuracy. Which type of management tool would provide her with the information she needs?
    A. a stopwatch study
    B. an audit
    C. an employee-reported log
    D. a time log

REFERENCE: McWay, p 264-265
               LaTour and Eichenwald-Maki, p 659-660

14. After a work sampling study was completed, it was found that 20% of a coder's time was devoted to pulling records for physicians with missing diagnoses. How many minutes of a 7-hour day are taken up with this activity?
    A. 140   C. 21
    B. 84   D. 56

REFERENCE: McWay, p 264-265
               LaTour and Eichenwald-Maki, p 659-660

15. Written documents that assist an organization in achieving its objectives and carrying out its mission statement are known as
    A. strategic plans.
    B. game plans.
    C. tactical plans.
    D. operational plans.

REFERENCE: McWay, p 249
              Shortell and Kaluzny, p 460-461

16. Anna Kathryn is attending budget training for new supervisors. The representative from Finance explains that _____ costs will vary in direct proportion to changes in the volume of care provided.
    A. fixed
    B. periodic
    C. variable
    D. semi-variable

REFERENCE: McLean, p 129

17. The organizing process determines how the work in a particular department will be divided and accomplished. In order to be in the best position to organize the work effectively, the manager must first engage in which management function?
    A. staffing
    C. planning
    B. directing
    D. controlling

REFERENCE: McWay, p 254, 277, 349
              LaTour and Eichenwald-Maki, p 606-607

18. The director of a Health Information Department has discovered that the department's policy regarding the usage of the copy machine has been consistently abused by the majority of the staff. To put an end to this inappropriate use of the copy machine, the director should institute a department
    A. method.
    B. rule.
    C. objective.
    D. procedure.

REFERENCE: McWay, p 21, 45
              Liebler, p 110

19. The average number of transcribed lines per month at Bent Tree Hospital is 142,500. The daily production standard is 950 lines per day. With 20 workdays in the month, calculate the minimum number of FTEs needed for this volume.
    A. 13
    B. 8
    C. 6
    D. 7.5

REFERENCE: LaTour and Eichenwald-Maki, p 650

20. The supervisor of release of information in a Health Information Department is preparing a work distribution chart in the hopes of identifying some problem areas. Although the work distribution chart can provide the supervisor with a great deal of information concerning the work performed by her staff, it will not indicate
    A. if a task is divided among employees disproportionately.
    B. the solution to a specific problem area.
    C. if the skills of each employee are utilized appropriately.
    D. the appropriate method of work division.

REFERENCE: McWay, p 260
              LaTour and Eichenwald-Maki, p 649

21. Emma Grace is a transcriptionist. Her productivity level, as determined by line count per day, has dropped significantly over the past 2 weeks. As a result, there is a backlog in transcription of history and physical reports and surgical reports. Several doctors and the operating room supervisor have complained. An appropriate initial course of action for the Supervisor of Transcription is to
    A. counsel the transcriptionist privately.
    B. fire the transcriptionist immediately.
    C. refer the matter to the Human Resources Department.
    D. suspend the transcriptionist without pay for 3 days.

REFERENCE: McWay, p 301-302
            LaTour and Eichenwald-Maki, p 698

22. The Director of the Health Information Services Department has determined that an in-service for department supervisors on improving productivity levels in their respective areas is needed. As an outcome of this in-service, the director would like the supervisors to understand that when setting productivity levels, a supervisor must
    A. tailor any training needs to each individual employee to achieve the productivity levels.
    B. direct training needs to the most efficient employee within the department in order to achieve the productivity levels.
    C. determine the productivity standards for each area and job function.
    D. consider only quantity and not quality.

REFERENCE: McWay, p 300
            LaTour and Eichenwald-Maki, p 664-665, 692-693

23. The coding supervisor reviewed the productivity logs of four newly hired coders after their first month. The report below illustrates each coder's output. Based on analysis of this report, which employee will require additional assistance in order to meet the coding standards?

PRODUCTIVITY REPORT Coding Standard: 20 charts per day				
Coder	Week 1	Week 2	Week 3	Week 4
1	90	100	95	100
2	100	105	105	95
3	70	75	90	85
4	85	85	90	100

    A. Coder 1
    B. Coder 2
    C. Coder 3
    D. Coder 4

REFERENCE: McWay, p 300
            Shortell and Kaluzny, p 419

24. Which of the following statements best describes the scalar or chain of command principle?
    A. Effective organization is made up of people who perform the work assigned.
    B. There is a clear flow of authority from superior to subordinate throughout the organization.
    C. The objectives of a business or a group of functions within the business must be clearly defined and understood.
    D. The number of subordinates under the immediate supervision of the supervisor should be limited.

REFERENCE: Shortall and Kaluzny, p 253-284
              McWay, p 255-258
              LaTour and Eichenwald-Maki, p 602

The following questions represent advanced competencies.

IMPLEMENTATION PROCESS OF A HID COMPUTER SYSTEM

25. Based on the Gantt chart shown above, which planned activities can be done simultaneously?
    A. Activities 1 and 2
    B. Activities 3 and 4
    C. Activities 1, 3, and 4
    D. Activities 2 and 3

REFERENCE: McWay, p 254
              LaTour and Eichenwald-Maki, p 601-602

26. In order to improve efficiency and productivity, which of the following sequence of steps is the most effective?
    A. Break down the work into component activities, assign personnel, and delegate authority.
    B. Delegate authority, assign personnel, and define individual job duties.
    C. Know the objective; assign personnel and group activities into proper organizational units.
    D. Know the objective; break down the work into component activities, and group activities into proper organizational units.

REFERENCE: McWay, p 255
              Shortell and Kaluzny, p 419

The following questions represent advanced competencies.

27. Amelia Claire is a CNA and an RHIA who is a clinical documentation trainer for a large health system. The results of a quality improvement study indicated that an informed consent was not obtained for 25% of the surgical procedures performed. Brooke had discussed the problem with the director of the Health Information Department and they have decided to begin corrective action by providing an in-service. The most important participants that should attend this in-service are
    A. nurses and unit clerks.
    B. medical record and quality improvement personnel.
    C. physicians and residents.
    D. administrators.

REFERENCE: McWay, p 265
               LaTour and Eichenwald-Maki, p 712-714

28. The Director of Health Information Services has recently received approval to purchase the necessary equipment to place all inactive records on optical disc. The director plans to redo the department layout to accommodate the equipment and to ensure that the equipment is placed in the most appropriate area of the department. Which of the following tools will best assist the director with this new layout?
    A. proximity chart   C. Gantt chart
    B. frequency chart   D. replacement chart

REFERENCE: Abdelhak, p 638-639

29. One of your first tasks as the new Manager of Health Information Services is to review the department policy and procedure manual. You have determined that several policy statements are incongruent with appropriate current employee practices. Proper management conventions require
    A. leaving the policy as written in the manual.
    B. contacting the hospital attorney to decide what action to take.
    C. enforcing the existing policy.
    D. revising the policy appropriately and documenting the date of the change.

REFERENCE: McWay, p 252
               LaTour and Eichenwald-Maki, p 691-693

30. Elizabeth Hoke is the Chief Executive Officer (CEO) at Anywhere Medical Center. At the beginning of each fiscal year, she begins a formal planning cycle. Her annual planning process should begin with which of the following?
    A. revising the institutional mission
    B. developing strategic plans
    C. establishing the annual organizational objectives
    D. developing strategic goals

REFERENCE: McWay, p 251-252
               LaTour and Eichenwald-Maki, p 606

31. Which of the following statements is false in regard to departmental reengineering?
    A. It is mainly done to reduce departmental costs.
    B. It is intended to make small or minor changes in order to improve a function or process.
    C. It is intended to improve departmental productivity.
    D. It is intended to ensure satisfied customers.

REFERENCE: McWay, p 676-677
               LaTour and Eichenwald-Maki, p 677

32. In preparing a capital budget request, the first priority will be to document
    A.   the specific type of equipment requested.
    B.   where the new equipment will be located.
    C.   the need for the new equipment.
    D.   the cost of the new equipment.

REFERENCE: McWay, p 341
              McLean, p 152

33. Based on the information displayed in the decision matrix below, which vendor would you recommend for the purchase of a copy machine?

Criteria	Weight	Vendor A Rating	Vendor B Rating	Vendor C Rating	Vendor D Rating
Quality	5	4	3	3	3
Speed	4	3	1	3	2
Service	2	3	3	5	2

    A.   Vendor A   C.   Vendor C
    B.   Vendor B   D.   Vendor D

REFERENCE: McWay, p 261-262, 318
              LaTour and Eichenwald-Maki, p 611-612

34. As the Director of the Health Information Department, you are preparing a request for approval for the purchase of an encoding system. Because this is considered a capital request, you are required to submit the cost-benefit ratio. The software and license costs $6,000, hardware maintenance is $1,500, and the training of two employees will cost $500. It is expected that the encoding system will increase reimbursement by $10,000. The cost-benefit ratio is
    A.   0.8.   C.   1.25.
    B.   1.7.   D.   1.33.

REFERENCE: McWay, p 337
              Abdelhak p 339-341

35. What two types of budgets are often prepared by managers of health information departments?
    A.   capital budget and the finance budget
    B.   capital budget and the revenue and expense budget
    C.   profit and loss budget and the finance budget
    D.   finance budget and the revenue and expense budget

REFERENCE: McLean, p 151-152

36. Mary and Sue are both employed as medical transcriptionists at ABC Hospital. They are able to set their own work hours provided the department is covered by one of them during regular office hours. This kind of work arrangement is referred to as:
    A.   compressed work week.   C.   flex time.
    B.   job sharing.   D.   telecommuting.

REFERENCE: LaTour and Eichenwald-Maki, p 650-651

37. The most important consideration in planning the office layout for a Health Information Services department is the
    A. number of employees.
    B. cost.
    C. types of furniture to be purchased.
    D. workflow.

REFERENCE: LaTour and Eichenwald-Maki, p 652-656

38. Allison has conducted a timely performance evaluation for one of her employees and awarded the employee a 4% merit increase. She is currently completing the paperwork to submit to Human Resources. If the employee's hourly salary is presently $7.10, what will the hourly salary be with this increase?
    A. $7.33
    B. $7.38
    C. $7.80
    D. $7.54

REFERENCE: Abdelhak, p 666

39. The span of control in an organization refers to the
    A. number of supervisors for each functional area.
    B. amount of space assigned to one supervisor.
    C. amount of work expected of an employee.
    D. number of people who report to one supervisor.

REFERENCE: LaTour and Eichenwald-Maki, p 607

40. A work environment that is not ergonomically sound could lead to
    A. injuries.
    B. conflict among departments.
    C. employee arguments.
    D. increases in department equipment budgets.

REFERENCE: McWay, p 260
               LaTour and Eichenwald-Maki, p 656-657

41. Jessica is the leader of a project team working on the definition of the women's health service line. Several departments are so enthusiastic about the progress that they ask for additions to the project. This is not uncommon, and is known as
    A. add-ons.
    B. scope creep.
    C. effort expansion.
    D. deliverable increase.

REFERENCE: McWay, p 318
               LaTour and Eichenwald-Maki, p 771

42. The transcription production for February was 225,333 lines. The total work hours for all transcriptionists for the same period was 2,000. The average hourly cost was $13.50. Determine the cost per line for operating this service for this month.
    A. $1.20
    B. $0.24
    C. $2.40
    D. $0.12

REFERENCE: Abdelhak, p 611

43. Based on the budget illustrated below, what is the monthly budget variance percent for supplies?

HEALTH INFORMATION DEPARTMENT MONTHLY BUDGET JANUARY		
Items	Budget	Actual
Supplies	495	675
Travel	300	150
Rental Equipment	1,250	1,250
Service Contracts	900	1,130

A. 13.6%
B. 36%

C. 26.6%
D. 11.9%

REFERENCE: McWay, p 342
McLean, p 156-157

44. The most realistic approach that could encourage increased productivity in the tedious record file/retrieval area is to
   A. shorten the workday by 1 hour.
   B. vary and rotate the work assigned to each file clerk.
   C. have all the file clerks work on a part-time basis.
   D. arrange for all the file clerks to have flex time.

REFERENCE: McWay, p 265-2666
LaTour and Eichenwald-Maki, p 694-695

45. The HIM Department of a local hospital will experience a 20% increase in the number of discharges processed per day as the result of a merger with a smaller facility. This 20% increase is projected as 120 additional records per day. The standard time for coding a record is 15 minutes. Compute the number of FTEs required to handle this increased volume in coding based on an 8-hour day.
   A. 3.75
   B. 2.8

   C. 6.5
   D. 5.25

REFERENCE: LaTour and Eichenwald-Maki, p 657-658

46. Cheryl is the Director of the Health Information Services Department and Suzanne is the Assistant Director. Cheryl notices one of Suzanne's subordinates leaving the department for an unscheduled break. When the employee returns, Cheryl immediately asks the employee to step into her office and begins discussing the unauthorized break. Which organizational principle is this director violating?
   A. organizational function
   B. grievance procedure

   C. span of control
   D. unity of command

REFERENCE: LaTour and Eichenwald-Maki, p 684

47. As the Director of Health Information Services, you manage the department with the assistance of four supervisors. One day you observe a coder coding charts from the face sheet without reviewing the record for additional documentation. The most appropriate course of action would be to

 A. discuss your concerns with the Supervisor of Coding and direct her to address this issue immediately.
 B. discuss the problem with the CFO.
 C. discuss the matter directly with the coder and instruct him to review the entire record for correct assignment of codes.
 D. do nothing because the coding area is extremely productive.

REFERENCE: LaTour and Eichenwald-Maki, p 684

48. During the month of May there were 800 discharge abstracts processed at a cost of $0.90 per abstract for a total of $720.00. In June, 732 discharge abstracts were processed for a total cost of $658.80. This type of cost is known as

 A. semi-variable.   B. adjustable rate.
 C. fixed.   D. variable.

REFERENCE: McLean, p 129
              McWay, p 342

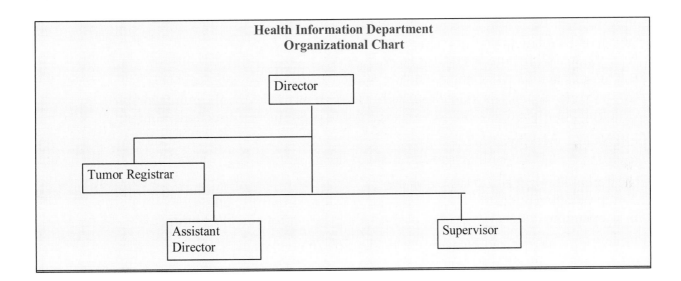

49. Which statement is an inaccurate description of the organization chart shown above?
 A. The director has authority over others in the department.
 B. The director has subordinates.
 C. The assistant director and the supervisor have a lateral relationship.
 D. The tumor registrar has authority over the assistant director.

REFERENCE: McWay, p 256-258
              LaTour and Eichenwald-Maki, p 685-686

50. The Director of a Health Information Department has received the quarterly variance budget report. The report indicates the "overtime" category is unfavorable. The director is required to justify this overtime expense. Which of the following would be considered an acceptable explanation for this expenditure? Overtime is unfavorable this quarter due to
    A. the annual purging of inactive files.
    B. a chronic backlog in transcription.
    C. a decrease in admissions this quarter.
    D. a lack of supervision in the file area.

REFERENCE: McWay, p 265, 342
              LaTour and Eichenwald-Maki, p 761-762

51. The director of a Health Information Department has asked the department supervisors to review and revise all job descriptions. Missie Harris, the supervisor over coding and analysis, has determined that the job description for the senior coders must be revised. Ms. Harris' decision to revise the job description is probably due to a change in the
    A. number of coders.
    B. recruitment practices for coders.
    C. scope of coding responsibilities.
    D. method in which the coders' performance is evaluated.

REFERENCE: McWay, p 263-265, 300-301
              LaTour and Eichenwald-Maki, p 691-692

52. Which of the following is false in regard to budget variances?
    A. Variances are often calculated on the monthly budget report.
    B. Permanent budget variances do not resolve during the current fiscal year.
    C. A variance analysis identifies whether the variance is favorable or unfavorable.
    D. Temporary budget variances are expected to continue in subsequent months.

REFERENCE: McWay, p 265, 342
              LaTour and Eichenwald-Maki, p 761

53. The expense budget is also known as the
    A. production budget.   C. contract budget.
    B. operating budget.   D. profit and loss budget.

REFERENCE: LaTour and Eichenwald-Maki, p 760-761

54. The Supervisor of a Health Information Department has aspirations of becoming the HID director. She works very long hours so that she can address all department issues herself rather than relying on her staff to assist her. Which type of management skills is she in need of improving in order to attain her goal of department director?
    A. delegating skills   C. motivating skills
    B. leadership skills   D. political skills

REFERENCE: McWay, p 262-263
              LaTour and Eichenwald-Maki, p 696-697, 727-728

55. The supervisor over release of information has requested a meeting with her superior, the Director of Health Information Services. She begins the meeting by describing how overwhelmed she is feeling. She is extremely behind in her work and she doesn't know what she can do to change the situation. In advising the supervisor, the director suggests that perhaps she should begin addressing her problem by attending a management workshop. Which of the following workshop topics is more likely to help the supervisor with her problem?
   A. "Leadership Styles for Women Managers and Supervisors"
   B. "The Nature of Delegation"
   C. "Understanding Your Employee"
   D. "Writing Skills for the Release of Information Supervisor"

REFERENCE: McWay, p 262-263
             LaTour and Eichenwald-Maki, p 696-697, 727-728

56. The Director of the Health Information Services Department is developing a plan to convert their existing filing system to a terminal digit filing system. The tool that is most useful to the director in displaying the steps and completion schedule for each phase of the conversion is a
   A. work distribution chart.   C. procedure flowchart.
   B. Gantt chart.   D. flow process chart.

REFERENCE: McWay, p148, 254, 271
             LaTour and Eichenwald-Maki, p 136, 601-602

57. Mr. Beasley determined that the rate of absenteeism with three of his employees was 15%. He felt that this was unacceptable and decided that there were two different ways he could handle this situation. He evaluated these alternatives and thought the best thing to do would be to suspend all three for 2 days. Once he implemented this idea, he analyzed the consequences. How would you label this process?
   A. decision making   B. planning
   C. crisis management   D. communicating

REFERENCE: McWay, p 85-87, 261-262
             LaTour and Eichenwald-Maki, p 611-612

58. The Project Manager is responsible for all of the following functions, EXCEPT:
   A. approval of the budget for the project.   B. creation of project plan.
   C. recruitment of project team.   D. recommending plan revisions.

REFERENCE: McWay, p 271
             LaTour and Eichenwald-Maki, p 774-775

59. A basic concept of office layout and workflow is that the
   A. paper and employee move to a predetermined location.
   B. employee moves to the paper.
   C. office layout and workflow should be revised frequently.
   D. paper moves to the employee.

REFERENCE: LaTour and Eichenwald-Maki, p 652-654

60. Which of the following tasks is the most appropriate for the Health Information Services Director to delegate to the Supervisor of Record Processing and Statistics?
    A. formulating a record retention policy for the entire facility
    B. reviewing monthly statistical reports to verify accuracy
    C. interviewing applicants for the position of Tumor Registrar
    D. completing a performance rating on the Assistant Director of the department

REFERENCE: McWay, p 35-36
              LaTour and Eichenwald-Maki, p 726-727

61. When interviewing a prospective employee, which of the following questions is inappropriate to ask?
    A. "Can you type?"
    B. "Where may we contact you?"
    C. "What language other than English can you speak or write?"
    D. "Do you own a home?"

REFERENCE: LaTour and Eichenwald-Maki, p 694

62. If the budgeted payroll expense was $24,300 and the actual payroll expense was $25,800, what is the percentage of cost variance?
    A. 6.0%   C. 6.17%
    B. 0.58%   D. 6.7%

REFERENCE: McLean, p 156-157

63. Which of the following actions illustrates the use of a participative management style?
    A. discussing suggested approaches of improving productivity and performance with employees
    B. basing decisions on information found in the manual of operations
    C. providing supervision only when requested by employees
    D. micromanaging all aspects and functions performed in the department

REFERENCE: McWay, p 269
              LaTour and Eichenwald-Maki, p 726-727

64. In deciding to purchase or lease a new dictation system, the Director of HI Services calculated the payback period and rate of return on the investment. The hospital's required payback period is 3 years with a required rate of return of 20%. If the equipment costs $32,000 and generates $8,000 per year in savings, what would the payback period for this equipment be?
    A. 2 years   C. 3 years
    B. 5 years   D. 4 years

REFERENCE: McWay, p 334
              LaTour and Eichenwald-Maki, p 764-765

65. The Director of a Health Information Department prepared a document in which the following information could be obtained: job title, reporting line, span of control, and routes of promotion. The document she was preparing was a(n)
    A. job description.   C. work distribution chart.
    B. organizational chart.   D. job procedure.

REFERENCE: McWay, p 256-258
              LaTour and Eichenwald-Maki, p 684-686

66. The Director of the Health Information Department had to resign immediately due a family crisis requiring her to leave the country. Her superior, the Administrator of Support Services, must appoint an Acting Director as soon as possible, but is questioning who might be the best individual for this temporary role. What tool would assist the administrator with this decision?
    A. staffing table
    B. replacement chart
    C. proximity chart
    D. frequency chart

REFERENCE: Abdelhak p. 575

67. The file section supervisor, is preparing the staffing budget for the coming fiscal year. Presently the staff is filing approximately 500 charts per day. By the time the fiscal year begins, this is expected to increase to 650 charts per day. Currently it takes 9 FTEs to file 500 charts. The supervisor should project a FTE increase for the coming year's budget of
    A. 13%.
    B. 76%.
    C. 23%.
    D. 55%.

REFERENCE: Shortell and Kaluzny, p 419

68. Lizzie O'Leary, Director of the Health Information Services Department, is writing a memo about a recent problem the department has had with a contracted copy service when she is notified of an emergency, hospital-wide department-head meeting. Because it is necessary that the memo be completed by the end of the day, it is most appropriate for the director to delegate its completion to the supervisor of
    A. storage and retrieval.
    B. transcription.
    C. coding and abstracting.
    D. release of information.

REFERENCE: McWay, p 259, 262-263, 336
                LaTour and Eichenwald-Maki, p 696-697, 727-728

69. Of the following, which is NOT considered justification to approve overtime? Overtime is not justified
    A. for unpredictable fluctuations in volume.
    B. when there is unusually high absenteeism.
    C. when there is a temporary change of work methods.
    D. for employees who want to supplement their wages.

REFERENCE: LaTour and Eichenwald-Maki, p 760-762

70. A job analysis includes the
    A. summation of the qualifications needed in a worker for a specific job.
    B. collection of data to determine the content of a job.
    C. title of the job and summary of the basic tasks making up a job.
    D. goals to be achieved by a worker over a specified period of time.

REFERENCE: McWay, p 258
             Abdelhak, p 676-678

71. The Director of the Health Information Services Department is preparing the department's budget for the coming year. She has included the costs for the coding staff to attend at least two workshops in the budget. What portion of the department's budget will the cost of the workshops be allocated to?
    A. staffing budget
    B. revenue budget
    C. personnel budget
    D. expense budget

REFERENCE: McLean, p 152

72. The manager of a transcription agency is preparing December's staffing schedule. Because this month has several holidays, there are more requests for vacation and personal days than usual. Additionally, it is apparent to the supervisor that she will not be able to approve all requests for time off. It will be best for the supervisor to construct the schedule by
    A. processing requests based on seniority.
    B. granting requests on a first-come basis.
    C. adhering to the hospital and department policy regarding requests for time off.
    D. not approving any time off, thus eliminating any conflicts.

REFERENCE: McWay, p 252
LaTour and Eichenwald-Maki, p 691, 649-650

73. The supervisor over the file section has discovered an enormous backlog of loose lab reports. The first step that the supervisor should take in attempting to resolve this matter is to
    A. analyze possible courses of action.
    B. gather relevant data regarding the problem.
    C. identify and clarify the problem.
    D. choose the best course of action.

REFERENCE: McWay, p 262
LaTour and Eichenwald-Maki, p 611-612

74. New equipment has just been purchased for a Health Information Services Department. Prior to its arrival and placement in the department, it is important for the manager to adhere to the rules and regulations governed by
    A. FDA.   C. CMS
    B. OSHA.   D. SSA.

REFERENCE: McWay, p 260, 297
LaTour and Eichenwald-Maki, p 652-657

75. The best source for obtaining data for a job analysis is the
    A. department director.   C. the person who performs the job.
    B. supervisor of the job.   D. procedures manual.

REFERENCE: McWay, p 258
Abdelhak, p 676-678

76. John Doe is an information specialist in the Department of Information Technology. He has been asked to assist with the Joint Commission survey process, which accounts for approximately 75% of his time. He also receives project assignments from the HIM director, his immediate supervisor, as well as the overall project manager. This refers to what type of authority relationship?
    A. functional   C. matrix
    B. parallel   D. divisional

REFERENCE: Shortell and Kaluzny, p 330-333

77. The department director is responsible for budget costs that are controllable. Which of the following costs would be out of the director's control?
    A. equipment purchases
    B. fringe benefit cost per employee
    C. supply requisitions
    D. overtime authorizations

REFERENCE: McWay, p 339-342
LaTour and Eichenwald-Maki, p 760-761

78. Kim Khoury is planning a luncheon for the team members and stakeholders on the CPOE implementation to celebrate reaching a major milestone. Which of the following is true?
    A. Acknowledging accomplishments and milestones motivates teams.
    B. Budgets rarely permit these extra expenses.
    C. Celebrations are only appropriate at the close of a project.
    D. Professionals are self-motivated, making celebrations unnecessary.

REFERENCE: McWay, p 266
              Marreel and McLellan
              LaTour and Eichenwald-Maki, p 783

79. Beth Huber, Director of Health Information, has been selected to participate in a strategic planning retreat for her health system. In preparation, she refreshes her understanding of strategic planning. Which of the following will likely be included in the retreat?
    A. improvement of existing programs and services
    B. opportunities to review internal structures and systems
    C. enhancing customer and patient satisfaction
    D. focus on the organization's fit with the external environment

REFERENCE: McWay, p 249-251
              LaTour and Eichenwald-Maki, p 786-789, 793-794

80. The project definition justifies the need for the new project. What would you expect to see in the project justification?
    A. project scope, resources needed, and amount of time required
    B. project scope, resources needed, and developing the solution
    C. resources needed, amount of time required, and preparing supporting documentation for the system chosen
    D. amount of time required, alternative analysis, and implementation review

REFERENCE: McWay, p 270-271, 318-319
              LaTour and Eichenwald-Maki, p 775

81. Roberta Little Eagle is the new HIM supervisor at a large South Dakota reservation clinic. In order to become familiar with the specific steps currently used in record processing, she uses which graphic tool?
    A. force field analysis   C. fishbone analysis
    B. histogram   D. flowchart
REFERENCE: McWay, p 263
            LaTour and Eichenwald-Maki, p 652-653, 670-671, 691-692

82. Megan is the new Director of Health Information at Blue Ridge Rehabilitation Associates, a large multi-specialty clinic. Her initial assessment of the department's functioning is that there is considerable duplication of effort. To collect information on the systems used in the current functions and to analyze and improve the process, she chose to use a
    A. work process flowchart.   C. decision tree.
    B. systems diagram.   D. Pareto chart.

REFERENCE: McWay, p 260-261, 263

83. Which of the following would NOT be a scientific method of establishing standards?
    A.   stopwatch studies
    B.   work sampling
    C.   personal experience
    D.   time-log studies

REFERENCE: McWay, p 264-265
                LaTour and Eichenwald-Maki, p 657-660

84. Lucy Ann manages a claims review unit for an insurance company. Her staff keys a high volume of data daily. She scheduled a staff PT to do the annual ergonomics presentation to help prevent repetitive strain injuries. All of the following would be included EXCEPT
    A.   using a footrest.
    B.   wrists should be elevated.
    C.   monitor placed directly in front and elevated.
    D.   lumbar support provided.

REFERENCE: Marreel and McLellan, p 171-177
                LaTour and Eichenwald-Maki, p 756-757

85. North Ridge Hospital is preparing to open as a new 250-bed acute care hospital. This facility is located in a growing area of the city and is projected to have 85% occupancy within 3 years. To determine the number of employees needed in the HIM department, the director must first
    A.   determine employee salary ranges.
    B.   develop a departmental organizational chart.
    C.   collect data from hospitals that are of comparable size.
    D.   identify the departmental functions to be performed.

REFERENCE: McWay, p 252
                LaTour and Eichenwald-Maki, p 691

86. A national HIM publication routinely requests that practitioners submit statistics from their facility regarding department functions. These are then summarized and published in graphic form, providing a tool for which of the following activities?
    A.   benchmarking
    B.   work standards
    C.   job evaluation
    D.   job redesign

REFERENCE: McWay, p 148, 153, 157
                LaTour and Eichenwald-Maki, p 659-660

Answer Key for Organization and Management
  ANSWER   EXPLANATION

NOTE: Explanations are provided for those questions that require mathematical calculations and questions which are not clearly explained in the references that are sited.

1. D

2. B   The reference pages indicated do not answer the question directly. The references relate to discussions of the organizational structure and design. Based on that information, assumptions regarding organizational relationships (vertical, lateral, matrix, etc.) can be made.

3. C

4. D   Remember to convert the hours to minutes.
       725×12 minutes = 8,700 minutes
       1,280 hours $\times$ 60 minutes = 76,800 minutes
       8,700 minutes on coding/76,800 minutes worked = 11.3% spent on coding

5. D

6. B   This is clearly a problem of not understanding the procedures of the tasks; therefore reviewing the job description probably won't be of much help. This rules out answers A and C. This also does not seem to be a problem that would require an in-service, thereby ruling out answer D. Therefore, the best solution is to review the procedures with her and have the analysis clerk monitor her progress to ensure that she fully understands the procedures.

7. A

8. C

9. B   Answers A and C describe a standard. Answer D describes a rule.

10. C

11. D   1,255 - 48 = 1207; 1207 / 1255 = .96 $\times$ 100 = 96%

12. B   Formula: Total actual work units $\times$ 100/ Standard work units = variance percent $(30 + 40 + 25 + 35) \times 100 = 13,000$; 13,000/200 = 65%

13. B

14. B   The hours must first be converted to minutes.
        7 hours $\times$ 60 = 420 minutes
        420 minutes $\times$ .20 = 84 minutes

15. A

16. C

17. C

18. B

19. D $950 \times 20 = 19,000$; 142,500/19,000 = 7.5 FTEs

20. B

21. A

Answer Key for Organization and Management
ANSWER   EXPLANATION

22. C

23. C   20 charts x 5 days = 100 per week x 4 weeks = 400
         A standard of 400 charts coded over 4 weeks per coder.
         Coder 3 has coded only 320 charts over the 4 weeks.

24. B

25. D

26. D

27. C   It is the physician's responsibility to ensure that a patient has consented to a surgical
         procedure.

28. A

29. D

30. C   Although a CEO is involved in all of the options given, only the organizational objectives are
         completed annually. The mission statement is reviewed to ensure that the organizational
         objectives are consistent with it, but it is not revised annually. Strategic goals and objectives
         are completed on a long-term basis, not annually.

31. B

32. C

33. A   In order to determine which vendor to choose, each vendor's scores are added. The vendor
         that scores the highest for all three criteria is chosen. Calculations: Multiply the weight for
         each criterion by the rating. After this is done, each column is totaled. Vendor A scores 38;
         Vendor B, 25; Vendor C, 37; Vendor D, 27.

34. C   Costs = $6,000 + $1,500 + $500 = $8,000.
         Benefits = $10,000. (That's the increase in reimbursement.)
         10,000/8,000 = 1.25. Benefits/Costs Ratio = 1.25 (This also known as the cost-benefit figure.)
         In other words, for every dollar invested in the encoding system, it will have a return of $1.25
         after one year.

35. B

36. C

37. D

38. B $7.10 \times .04 = .284 + $7.10 = $7.384

39. D

40. A

41. B

42. D   2,000 \times $13.50 = $27,000; $27,000/225,333 = .1198, rounded to 0.12

43. B   The formula for budget variance percent is actual minus budget divided by budget.
         675 - 495 = 180
         (180 \times 100)/495 = 36\%

Answer Key for Organization and Management
  ANSWER   EXPLANATION

44. B

45. A   To determine the number of employees needed for a specific job, first determine how much time the work requires. In this case, we know we will have an additional 120 records per day and each record will average about 15 minutes. To figure the amount of total time, multiply $120 \times 15 = 1,800$ minutes. Compute this to hours by dividing by 60 (60 minutes in an hour): $1,800/60 = 30$ hours. Based on the 8-hour day, divide 30 hours by 8 = 3.75 FTEs.

46. D

47. A

48. D

49. D

50. A

51. C

52. D

53. B

54. A

55. B

56. B   A Gantt chart is a scheduling tool.

57. A

58. A

59. D

60. B

61. D   One must be familiar with the various labor laws to ensure that an interviewee is not asked questions that could be considered discriminating or illegal.

62. C $25,800 - 24,300 = 1,500; 1,500/24,300 = .0617 \times 100 = 6.17\%$

63. A

64. D   Formula: initial investment/annual cash flow = payback period $32,000/$8,000 = 4 years

65. B

66. B

67. C   Currently, each FTE files 55.5 charts ($500/9 = 55.5$).
   - Since there will be 150 more charts per day needing filing ($150/55.5 = 2.70$), you will need 2.70 FTEs for filing the extra charts.
   - Add current 9 FTE to the 2.70 FTE increase needed = 11.7 FTE.
   - Divide by the increase of 2.7 FTE by the 11.7 total FTE needed to get the percentage increase in FTE. ($2.7/11.7 = 23\%$ increase).

   For an anticipated increase from 500 to 650 you will need to increase your filing FTE staff by 23%.

Answer Key for Organization and Management

	ANSWER	EXPLANATION
68.	D	
69.	D	
70.	B	
71.	D	
72.	C	
73.	C	
74.	B	
75.	C	
76.	C	
77.	B	
78.	A	
79.	D	
80.	A	
81.	D	
82.	A	
83.	C	Personal experience is subjective. A, B, and D rely on objective measurement of job performance.
84.	B	Wrists should be in a neutral position.
85.	D	
86.	A	

REFERENCES

Abdelhak, M., Grostick, S., Hanken, M. A., & Jacobs, E. (2004). *Health information: management of a strategic resource* (2nd ed.). Philadelphia: W. B. Saunders.

LaTour, K., & Eichenwald-Maki, S. (2006). *Health information management: Concepts, principles, and practice* (2nd ed.). Chicago: American Health Information Management Association (AHIMA).

Liebler, J. G., & McConnell, C.R. (2004). *Management principles for health professionals.* Sudbury, MA: Jones and Bartlett (acquired from Aspen).

McLean, R. (2003). *Financial management in health care organizations.* Clifton Park, NY: Thomson Delmar Learning.

McWay, D. (2008). *Today's health information management: An integrated approach.* Chicago: Thomson Delmar.

Shortell, S., & Kaluzny, A. (2006). *Health care management: Organization design and behavior.* Clifton Park, NY: Thomson Delmar Learning

XVI. Human Resources

Mary Teslow, MLIS, RHIA

Use the following information to answer questions 1–3:

The training staff in the Human Resources Department is proposing a computer-based training program for 200 employees and needs to prepare a budget for the time and cost of the training.
- The training program will be 30 minutes in length.
- The employees can take the training online at any time.
- There are 200 employees to be trained.
- The rate of pay for 50 of the employees is $15.50 per hour.
- The rate of pay for 50 employees is $12.00 per hour.
- The rate of pay for the other 100 employees is $18.00.

1. How many employee clock hours will be needed to complete the training?
   A. 200 hours
   B. 150 hours
   C. 100 hours
   D. 50 hours

REFERENCE: Horton, p 120–122
               Koch, p 55-56
               Liebler and McConnell, p 311–317

2. When submitting the cost of training, how much should the training staff request in the budget for doing the computer-based training?
   A. $3,175.00
   B. $1,975.00
   C. $1,887.50
   D. $1,587.50

REFERENCE: Horton, p 120–122
               Koch, p 55-56
               Liebler and McConnell, p 311–317

3. What would be the average cost for training an employee?
   A. $ 7.94
   B. $ 9.00
   C. $15.50
   D. $15.87

REFERENCE: Horton, p 120–122
               Koch, p 55-56
               Liebler and McConnell, p 311–317

4. At Great Plains Regional Hospital, record processing takes approximately 18 minutes. If there are 15,620 discharges for the month, how many personnel hours are needed for this volume of work?
   A. 2,891
   B. 4,686
   C. 5,496
   D. 3,394

REFERENCE: Abdelhak, p 57-575, 664
               Koch, p 55-56
               Davis and LaCour, p 110–114
               Horton, p 120–122
               Johns, p 909
               LaTour and Eichenwald-Maki, p 658
               Liebler and McConnell, p 315
               McConnell, p 344–345

5. Coastal Hospital is a covered entity under HIPAA. In order to comply with the requirements, they must train their workforce on policies and procedures with respect to protected health information (PHI). Which of the following levels of the workforce would be exempt from training?
    A. HIM staff because they have already received training in release of information
    B. staff physicians because they have taken the Hippocratic Oath
    C. administrative staff because they do not perform hands-on care
    D. none of the above

REFERENCE: Hjort, p 60 A-G
                Green, p 268
                Johns, p 865
                McWay, p 323-324

6. Mallory, the coding supervisor, must determine the number of full-time employees (FTEs) needed to code 600 discharges per week. It takes an average of 20 minutes to code each record and each coder will work 40 hours per week. How many coders are needed?
    A. 6.0   C. 12.0
    B. 5.0   D. 4.5

REFERENCE: Abdelhak, p 664
                Koch, p 55-56
                Johns, p 909
                LaTour and Eichenwald-Maki, p 658
                McConnell, p 344–345
                Liebler and McConnell, p 315

7. Under the Americans with Disabilities Act (ADA), prior to employment, it is illegal to require a
    A. math aptitude test.   C. coding proficiency test.
    B. typing skill test.   D. pre-employment physical exam.

REFERENCE: Abdelhak, p 563-565
                McWay, p 295-297

8. Jason, an HIM educator, plans to lecture on department design and the legislative act or agency that was created to ensure that workers have a safe and healthy work environment. He will describe which of the following?
    A. OSHA   C. Taft-Hartley Law
    B. Wagner Act   D. Labor Management Relations Act

REFERENCE: Abdelhak, p 566
                Davis and LaCour, p 380
                Johns, p 533
                LaTour and Eichenwald-Maki, p 690
                McWay, p 293, 297-298

9. Dana, the transcription supervisor, has prepared an evaluation for one of her employees. As the evaluation is reviewed by the HIM director, he notes that the employee received an overall rating of "needs improvement." After reading the comments, the director asks Dana to document specific performance improvement recommendations. Dana is unable to do so because she is basing her assessment on her memory of incidents that have occurred over the past year. The director suggests that Dana reassess the employee's evaluation because, ideally, performance appraisals should occur
A. at the end of the 90 day probationary period.
B. when the employee needs counseling.
C. on a continuous basis.
D. once a year.

REFERENCE: Abdelhak, p 589-590
McWay, p 300-304
Davis and LaCour, p 370–371
LaTour and Eichenwald-Maki, p 698
Shortell and Kaluzny, p 430-431

10. A local union is conducting an organizing campaign at Pacific Health Systems. The Human Resources department is providing training to management staff. The training indicates that managers can do which of the following during the union campaign?
A. state that a strike is inevitable if the union wins
B. promise regular wage increases
C. question employees about their union activity
D. state opposition to the union

REFERENCE: Abdelhak, p 567-569
McWay, p 298-299
McConnell, p 567–570

11. Kari works 40 hours per week at Rocky Mountain Radiology Associates, which pays time-and-a-half for overtime and double-time for holidays. During the past week, Kari took 6 hours of unpaid personal leave, and worked an 8-hour holiday. How many hours will Kari be paid for?
A. 34   C. 42
B. 50   D. 48

REFERENCE: McConnell, p 448–451
Koch, p 55-56

12. Yanique is a new supervisor at Park Ridge Pavilion, a mental health facility. She discovers that one of her employees has shared her password with a co-worker. This action violates policies and procedures and is the first occasion of difficulty with this employee. Disciplinary action should be taken by
A. waiting for another occurrence to act.
B. referring the action to Human Resources.
C. asking for guidance from Human Resources and then acting.
D. immediately dismissing the employee.

REFERENCE: Abdelhak, 592-594
Liebler, p 479
McWay, p 302-303

13. Postage charges for Health Information Services have increased over the last quarter. As the Director, you have seen mail envelopes that have been meter-stamped that did not appear to be official hospital business. The best course of action is to
    A. remove the postage meter from the department.
    B. keep a watchful eye to see who is using the postage meter improperly.
    C. call a department meeting and issue employee warnings.
    D. put one person in charge of the meter.

REFERENCE: LaTour and Eichenwald-Maki, p 758
               McConnell, p 58–59
               McWay, p 363-365

14. The HIPAA Privacy and Security Rule requires that training be documented. What methods of documenting training efforts need to be used?
    A. retention of training aids and handouts
    B. meeting handouts and minutes
    C. training content, training dates, and attendee names
    D. signed confidentiality statements

REFERENCE: Hjort, p 60A-G
               Johns, p 733

15. Holly is the day supervisor who works from 7:00 AM to 4:00 PM. Kim is the evening supervisor who works from 2:00 PM to 11:00 PM. Suni is a transcriptionist who works from 10:00 AM to 7:00 PM which overlaps the day and evening shifts. Suni asked Holly, the day supervisor, if she could leave early for personal reasons. Holly said she could leave early if Kim, the evening supervisor, agrees. This situation violates which theory of management?
    A. span of control   C. specialization of labor
    B. formal theory of authority   D. unity of command

REFERENCE: Davis and LaCour, p 346
               McConnell, p 56–57

16. You are preparing a training program for specific functional areas of the department (e.g. coding, transcription, etc.). Which of the following is the primary factor to consider in developing an effective training program?
    A. credentials of the employees
    B. objectives of each functional area
    C. cost of training the employees
    D. number of employees to be trained

REFERENCE: Abdelhak, p 598-599
               McWay, p 286-290
               Davis and LaCour 392, 399–400
               LaTour and Eichenwald-Maki, p 710–712

17. Grace Holt, RHIA, is the HIM Department Manager. She is reviewing interviewing techniques with Maria Hernandez, RHIT, as she prepares to interview for a new analyst. Grace recommends that Maria should
    A. ask questions that encourage a "yes" or "no" response.
    B. interrupt occasionally to seek clarification.
    C. talk down to the applicant.
    D. phrase questions so the expected answer is encouraged.

REFERENCE: Abdelhak, p 582-583
                Davis and LaCour, p 378–379
                Johns, p 894–895
                McConnell, p 135–136
                McWay, p 284-286

18. Your job description states that as Assistant Director of the Health Information Management Department, you will supervise day-to-day operations for the record processing, transcription, and release of information areas. What principle of management is described?
    A. specialization   C. span of control
    B. centralized authority   D. delegation

REFERENCE: Davis and LaCour 346
                LaTour and Eichenwald-Maki, p 606–607
                Liebler and McConnell, p 169–171
                McConnell, p 57

19. Bonnie's work performance has diminished over the last 2 weeks. In addition, she has uncharacteristic mood swings and has exhibited difficulty concentrating. She is also having difficulties with tardiness and attendance. As her supervisor, you meet with Bonnie to discuss your concerns. She reveals that she is struggling financially. What action should you take?
    A. Tell her that as long as she can perform her job acceptably, her personal life is none of your concern.
    B. Put her on probation.
    C. Refer her to the Employee Assistance Program.
    D. Terminate her.

REFERENCE: Abdelhak, p 592
                McWay, p 301-302
                McConnell, p 238–239

20. Nancy arrives for work Monday through Friday any time between 7:00 and 9:00 AM, is on the job until at least 3:00 PM, and then may leave any time between 3:00 and 6:00 PM. Nancy's schedule is an example of
    A. the 8/80 work week.
    B. the staggered work hours program.
    C. variable work schedule.
    D. flex time.

REFERENCE: Abdelhak, p 558
                LaTour and Eichenwald-Maki, p 650, 699–700, 723–724

21. Based on the following statistics from Utah Home Health, calculate the absenteeism rate.

Month: January	
Number of employees	20
Number of workdays	22
Total work days lost	25

    A. 0.44%   C. 5.8%
    B. 5.68%   D. 0.568%

REFERENCE: Horton, p 17
                     McWay, p 198

22. As an HIM supervisor at Bayview Hospital, you supervise five employees. One of your employees reports that a co-worker has returned from lunch on numerous occasions with the smell of alcohol on his breath. What is the best approach in handling this problem?
    A. Confront the employee and place him on suspension for 1 week.
    B. Terminate the employee immediately.
    C. Ignore the report because it is hearsay.
    D. Handle the situation the same as you would any other disease that affects an employee's work.

REFERENCE: Abdelhak, p 592
                     McWay, p 301-303
                     McConnell, p 237–239

23. Gary's primary concern is job continuity and adequate health insurance for his large family. What level of Maslow's hierarchy of needs does Gary operate from?
    A. physiological   C. esteem
    B. self-actualization   D. safety

REFERENCE: LaTour and Eichenwald-Maki, p 603
                     Liebler and McConnell, p 370
                     McWay, p 265-266
                     Shortell and Kaluzny, p 85-88
                     McConnell, p 175–178

24. Employers may be able to demonstrate that age is a reasonable requirement for a position. Such an exception to the Age Discrimination in Employment Act (ADEA) is called a
    A. job description essential.
    B. bona fide occupational qualification.
    C. essential element for employment.
    D. there is no such exception to ADEA.

REFERENCE: Abdelhak, p 553
                     McWay, p 295
                     McConnell, p. 134–135

25. Julian supervises the department's coding section. He notices that the coding technician is working 30 additional minutes each day before clocking in at her scheduled starting time. After discussing her timecard with her, he discovers she is starting work early in order to check the unbilled account report. Under which act are you required to pay her for all hours worked?

A. ERISA
B. Fair Labor Standards Act
C. National Labor Relations Act
D. Equal Pay Act

REFERENCE: Abdelhak, p 567
LaTour and Eichenwald-Maki, p 697
McWay, p 446-451
McConnell, p 446–451

26. Heartland Health System has set hiring goals and taken steps to guarantee equal employment opportunities for protected groups' members (e.g., American Indians, women, blacks, etc.). It is complying with

A. Affirmative Action.
B. Equal Pay Act.
C. Minority Hiring Act.
D. Civil Rights Act.

REFERENCE: Abdelhak, p 562-563
McWay, p 307
Davis and LaCour, p 380
McConnell, p 453–454

27. Arizona Health System has numerous semiretired staff. The Human Resources Department has provided training regarding the Age Discrimination in Employment Act (ADEA), emphasizing that it protects employees and applicants between what ages?

A. 50 and 75
B. 45 and 99
C. 62 and 85
D. 40 and 70

REFERENCE: Abdelhak, p 565-566
McWay, p 295
McConnell, p 452–453

28. The general New Employee Orientation training at Mid-Atlantic Mental Health would most likely cover which of the following HIPAA components?

A. marketing issues
B. business associate agreements
C. physical/workstation security
D. job-specific training (e.g., patient's right to amend record)

REFERENCE: Hjort, p 60A-G.
Johns, p 732–733

29. Kristen combined her HIM and legal education and is now a Risk Manager. An employee has a complaint that may be considered a grievance. She should listen to the employee and then

A. put the complaint aside to see if other employees complain about the same issue.
B. deal with the issue as if it were a bona fide grievance.
C. deal with the complaint only if the employee seldom complains.
D. ignore the complaint until it is in writing.

REFERENCE: Abdelhak, p 593-594
McWay, p 302-303
Johns, p 900
LaTour and Eichenwald-Maki, p 699

30. The Human Resources Department provides training for new supervisors. It includes discussion of the Equal Pay Act, which was passed to eliminate discrimination based on which of the following?
    A. merit of the employee
    B. seniority of the employee
    C. employee gender
    D. personal productivity, such as in a incentive compensation system

REFERENCE: Abdelhak, p 567
               McWay, p 302-303
               Davis and LaCour, p 379–380
               McConnell, p 452

31. The transcription area has an opening for a transcriptionist with demonstrated skill in medical and surgical reports. Which of the following types of tests should be administered?
    A. performance   C. intelligence
    B. aptitude   D. stress

REFERENCE: Abdelhak, p 581-582
               Davis and LaCour, p 378–379
               McWay, p 285
               LaTour and Eichenwald-Maki, p 693–694
               McConnell, p 126

32. As manager of record processing, you supervise a 55-year-old employee who has worked as a correspondence clerk for many years. Her performance has gradually diminished and has become unsatisfactory. This employee is not interested in further education or in learning a new job. What method would most likely prove to be INEFFECTIVE in assisting this employee in improving her performance?
    A. threatening to fire the employee
    B. asking the employee to cross-train with other employees
    C. delegation of special assignments
    D. consulting the employee on various filing problems

REFERENCE: Abdelhak, p 590
               McWay, p 3030-304
               LaTour and Eichenwald-Maki, p 698
               McConnell, p 214–216

33. As the HIM clerical supervisor, Debbie is concerned that some employees are not utilizing their talents and skills effectively. Which of the following should Debbie consider first?
    A. revising job descriptions
    B. performing a job analysis
    C. observing the workers more closely
    D. giving the employees additional responsibilities

REFERENCE: Abdelhak, p 576-578
               Liebler and McConnell, p 195–196
               McWay, p 303-304
               Johns, p 898-902
               McConnell, p 190–191

34. As the manager of the billing department, Jessica has heard from her employees that rumors have been circulating throughout the hospital concerning centralization and layoffs. At a meeting with the CFO, all departments were asked to cut back 15%. What should Jessica tell her employees?
    A. nothing, as it would only depress them.
    B. that no one in the HIM department will be laid off
    C. share with employees the facts as she knows them from the meeting
    D. tell one employee who likes to spread rumors so employees will learn of the information from each other

REFERENCE: Abdelhak, p 584
                McWay, p 268
                LaTour and Eichenwald-Maki, p 614–615, 695–696, 640–641
                McConnell, p 301–302

35. Lindsay has combined her HIM education with a master's degree in Human Resources, and is training a new supervisor to interview a candidate for a credentialed position for handling subpoenas in the release of information section. Which of the following is the LEAST appropriate question?
    A. Do you have transportation for attendance at depositions and court?
    B. Please share an experience where you had to determine applicable state law.
    C. Please provide a copy of your most recent CE certificate and AHIMA membership.
    D. Do you have family responsibilities that would keep you from remaining at a trial?

REFERENCE: Liebler and McConnell, p. 124–127
                McWay, p 284-286

36. Carlos has noted increased complaints by employees of headaches and fatigue. Which of the following factors should he consider?
    A. room temperature   C. lighting
    B. humidity   D. air quality

REFERENCE: Abdelhak, p 644
                McWay, p 13
                LaTour and Eichenwald-Maki, p 654–657

37. Which of the following describes the act that requires employers to make reasonable accommodations in the workplace for individuals to perform essential job functions?
    A. Age Discrimination Act   C. Rehabilitation Act
    B. Americans with Disabilities Act D. Equal Opportunity Employment Act

REFERENCE: Abdelhak, p 564-565
                Liebler and McConnell, 139–140, 486–487
                McWay, p 295-297
                McConnell, p 453–454

38. Eva Pulaski supervises the electronic document management (EDM) section. She is preparing a report that includes a graphic that displays data over time and provides an excellent visualization of trends. It is called a(n)
    A. Pareto chart.
    B. correlation analysis.
    C. run or line chart.
    D. scatter diagram.

REFERENCE: Abdelhak, p 452
               Johns, 546
               Koch, p 247-278
               McWay, p 149, 151, 201
               LaTour and Eichenwald-Maki, p 675–676
               Liebler and McConnell, p 284

39. Amanda, the Coding Supervisor at Mission Medical Center, wants to increase the problem-solving skills among the coders. Which of the following approaches is likely to have the best and most long-lasting results?
    A. hiring a consultant to assess the coding area
    B. developing a coding work team
    C. taking a field trip to a neighboring facility known for quality coding
    D. request that Human Resources conduct a training session on program solving

REFERENCE: LaTour and Eichenwald-Maki, p 726–728
               McWay, p 304-305
               Liebler and McConnell, p 358–360

40. Natalie was an orientation counselor in college and knows that a well-designed program can help those new to a setting feel comfortable. As a new manager, she continues her commitment and contributes to new employee orientation. Which of the following statements about orientation programs is NOT true?
    A. A good orientation program can substitute for a job-specific departmental training.
    B. The most meaningful training program includes a "show and tell" format by peers.
    C. The orientation assists the employee in learning about the workplace culture.
    D. Proper training can enhance employee satisfaction.

REFERENCE: Abdelhak, p 584
               LaTour and Eichenwald-Maki, p 708–710
               McWay, p 286-290

41. Gina is the HIPAA Privacy and Security Officer and primary trainer for a regional health system. In determining how a person in a position in a department uses health information, she must certainly review the
    A. past performance evaluations of persons in the position.
    B. position or job description.
    C. facility policy on protecting health information.
    D. facility policy and procedure on documenting training.

REFERENCE: Hjort, p 60A-G.
               McWay, p 259, 300
               LaTour and Eichenwald-Maki, p 691–692

42. Mary Ellen Smith has been an excellent biller for the past 5 years of employment. Lately, you have noticed that she has the highest error rate and the lowest productivity rate of the entire billing section. She also seems to be distracted and unhappy. You have a conversation with her and she confides that she is having many "personal problems" that are causing her enormous stress. As her supervisor, you
   A. accept this explanation and determine that it is probably a temporary situation.
   B. issue a verbal warning to Mary Ellen to shape up.
   C. issue a written warning with a date to review her progress.
   D. refer her to the EAP.

REFERENCE: Abdelhak, p 572
                McWay, p 301-302
                McConnell, p 238–239
                Johns, 898–902

43. Melissa is an RHIA who has just been hired as systems analysts in Information Technology. At Orientation she receives her Employee Handbook. All of the following information about the Employee Handbook is true, EXCEPT:
   A. it provides a contractual obligation to continued employment.
   B. it provides policies and procedures developed by management.
   C. a receipt must be documented in writing.
   D. it must be reviewed periodically by legal counsel to avoid legal risk.

REFERENCE: Abdelhak, p 578-579

44. Fareeda's method improvement objectives are to use an organized approach to determine how to accomplish a task with less effort in less time or at a lower cost while maintaining or improving the quality of the outcome. Frequently, methods improvement is referred to as
   A. benchmarking.   C. work simplification.
   B. work distribution.   D. data quality improvement.

REFERENCE: Abdelhak, p 614-615
                McWay, p 263

45. Katie understands that employee turnover is expensive and stressful on staff. The best defense against employee dissatisfaction is
   A. the employee handbook.
   B. open and honest communication.
   C. written policies and procedures.
   D. weekly departmental meetings.

REFERENCE: McWay, p 268
                LaTour and Eichenwald-Maki, p 614–616, 694–695
                Liebler and McConnell, p 373
                McConnell, p 146–148

46. Southwest Home Care utilizes a discipline system that provides for stronger penalties for each successive repeat offense. You are most likely using
   A. corrective discipline.
   C. progressive discipline.
   B. preventive discipline.
   D. terminating discipline.

REFERENCE: Abdelhak, p 592-594
               Johns, 745
               LaTour and Eichenwald-Maki, p 698
               Liebler and McConnell, p 454–455
               McConnell, p 214–219
               McWay, p 302

47. When interviewing a candidate, which of the following questions is inappropriate to ask?
   A. "Can you type?"
   B. "Where may we contact you?"
   C. "What language other than English can you speak or write?"
   D. "Do you own a home?"

REFERENCE: Abdelhak, p 582-583
               McWay, p 285
               LaTour and Eichenwald-Maki, p 694

48. You work in a unionized organization and have filed a grievance. Which of the following will most likely take place?
   A. You can be terminated for registering a grievance.
   B. The grievance procedure regulations stipulated in the union contract will be followed.
   C. Follow facility policies and procedures for prompt and fair action on any grievance.
   D. The time from complaint to resolution should be no longer than 90 days.

REFERENCE: Abdelhak, p 594
               McWay, p 298-299, 302-303
               LaTour and Eichenwald-Maki, p 699
               Johns, 900

49. According to Frederick Herzberg, challenging work, recognition of workers and their accomplishments, and employee self-improvement are examples of
   A. maintenance factors.
   C. motivators.
   B. needs.
   D. hygienic factors.

REFERENCE: Liebler and McConnell, p 370
               McConnell, p 177–179
               McWay, p 266

50. Your department's productivity and morale have been steadily deteriorating, while absenteeism and turnover are increasing. As you go through the department, you notice that there are some questionable jokes pinned on the department corkboard. The source of the problems you are experiencing in the department could likely be
   A. cutbacks in staffing.
   B. a need for job enrichment.
   C. boredom.
   D. sexual harassment in the workplace.

REFERENCE: Abdelhak, p 564
               McWay, p 294

51. One of your new employees has just completed orientation, receiving basic HIPAA training. You are now providing more specific training related to her job. She asks whether the information she provided during the hiring process, as well as benefits claims, are also protected under HIPAA. Which of the following can you assure her that the Human Resources Department protects?
    A. all personal health information (PHI)
    B. benefits enrollment
    C. Employee Assistance Program contacts
    D. OSHA information

REFERENCE: Abdelhak, p 515-516
               LaTour and Eichenwald-Maki, p 699
               McConnell, p 272, 469–470
               McWay, p 299

52. The management assumption that work and the opportunity to utilize skills, knowledge, and talents are basic human needs was presented in McGregor's
    A. Theory X.   C. Delphi Process.
    B. Theory Y.   D. Managerial Grid Model.

REFERENCE: LaTour and Eichenwald-Maki, p 603–604
               Liebler and McConnell, 527–528
               McWay, p 269

53. Emma Miller, RHIA, interviewed one applicant for the position of inpatient coder and subsequently hired the applicant. During the 20-minute interview, she told the applicant about the department and hospital and what the job entailed. Much to Emma's disappointment, this newly hired employee did not work out. What went wrong?
    A. Emma asked too many questions during the interview.
    B. Emma should not have told the applicant anything about the hospital because that is the responsibility of Human Resources.
    C. Emma failed to interview enough applicants.
    D. Emma did not allow enough time for the interview.

REFERENCE: Abdelhak, p 582-583
               Davis and LaCour, p 378–379
               Johns, 694–695
               LaTour and Eichenwald-Maki, p 693–694
               McConnell, p 129–130

54. Carrie Ann provides a dynamic and effective orientation to the HIM Department. It includes all of the following EXCEPT
    A. the role and function of the department.
    B. facility emergency procedures.
    C. department policies, procedures, and rules.
    D. the organization of the department.

REFERENCE: Abdelhak, p 584
               LaTour and Eichenwald-Maki, p 695–710
               McWay, p 286-290

55. Which of the following is the LEAST effective way to discipline an employee?
    A. written warning
    B. oral reprimand
    C. punishment by cutting work hours and pay
    D. constructive criticism

REFERENCE: Abdelhak, p 592-594
                      McWay, p 302-303
                      LaTour and Eichenwald-Maki, p 698
                      Liebler and McConnell, p 453–456
                      McConnell, p 214–219

56. Elizabeth is the manager of the state cancer registry. In developing a training "to do list," she is reviewing the staff and what general training and specialized training topics would be necessary. What tool would be most helpful in organizing this information?
    A. Gantt chart to show who gets trained when
    B. spreadsheet with grids identifying who needs what type of training
    C. a "train-the-trainers" training manual to help in consistency in training
    D. documentation of previous orientation training to see what has already been covered

REFERENCE: Hjort, p 60A-G.
                      LaTour and Eichenwald-Maki, p 707–709, 712–714, 730–731

The following questions represent advanced competencies.

57. To ensure consistency of coverage among trainers, you may want to develop
    A. training manuals.
    B. meeting handouts and minutes.
    C. signed confidentiality statements acknowledging receipt and understanding of any training attended.
    D. ongoing training to keep the issues in front of the workforce.

REFERENCE: Hjort, p 60A-G.

58. Mark Beck is a new graduate preparing for an interview. In school, he had the opportunity to role-play a technique which requires applicants to give specific examples of how they have performed a specific task or handled a specific problem in the past. This technique is becoming more popular, and is known as:
    A. audition interview.   C. structured interview.
    B. behavioral interview.   D. targeted interview.

REFERENCE: Abdelhak, p 582-583
                      LaTour and Eichenwald-Maki, p 694
                      McConnell, p 135–136

59. Amy Chan, RHIT, is Manager of Health Information at Golden Gate Home Care. She is the elected leader of the documentation team, and is preparing to call a meeting. Which of the following is NOT an advantage of committee meetings?
    A. Group judgment improves decision making.
    B. Group process stimulates creativity.
    C. Committees enhance acceptance.
    D. Committees are economical.

REFERENCE: Liebler and McConnell, p 331–335
                      McConnell, p 320–321

60. Human Resources uses a systematic procedure to determine the relative worth of a position to the organization. When this approach is used, compensation for the position is most likely based on
    A. job evaluation.   C. job survey.
    B. job planning.   D. job ranking.

REFERENCE: McWay, p 259
    LaTour and Eichenwald-Maki, p 697
    Liebler and McConnell, p 195

61. After receiving completed requisitions to fill positions within the Health Information Management Department, the Human Resources Department can be most effective in recruiting qualified applicants with the assistance of
    A. a departmental organizational chart.
    B. current job descriptions.
    C. salary schedules.
    D. employee benefits handbook.

REFERENCE: Abdelhak, p 589–591
    Davis and LaCour, p 364–365, 371–372
    Johns, 734–735
    LaTour and Eichenwald-Maki, p 691–691, 697
    Liebler and McConnell, p 100,194–198
    McWay, p 259, 300
    McConnell, p 253–254

62. Which appraisal method places the employees into a set of ordered groups (e.g., top 10%, above average 20%, middle 40%) on the basis of a global measure?
    A. critical incident method
    B. behaviorally anchored ranking scales
    C. Management by Objectives
    D. forced ranking

REFERENCE: Abdelhak, p 586-589
    McConnell, p 189–191

63. Ashley supervises a group of very young employees who have low responsibility and little experience. Which leadership style will likely be most effective?
    A. directing   C. participating
    B. coaching   D. delegating

REFERENCE: Shortell and Kaluzny, p 132-135
    Abdelhak, p 546-548
    Liebler and McConnell, p 451
    McConnell, p 26–27

64. A union is engaged in an organizing campaign in a hospital facility. Which activity should management personnel AVOID during this time?
    A. telling employees that they are free to join or not to join any organization without threat to their status with the facility
    B. telling employees of the disadvantages that may result from belonging to a union
    C. promising employees a pay increase or promotion if they vote against the union
    D. telling employees the benefits they presently enjoy

REFERENCE: Abdelhak, p 567-569
    McConnell, p 567–569

65. Kimberly Wolf wants a Mercedes and the position of Vice President of Information Services. She feels that achieving these goals will provide her with a sense of achievement, prestige, and reputation in the eyes of others. What level of Maslow's hierarchy of needs is she operating at?
    A. esteem
    B. safety
    C. self-actualization
    D. basic physiological

REFERENCE: LaTour and Eichenwald-Maki, p 603
                Liebler and McConnell, p 370
                McWay, p 265-266
                McConnell, p 175–179

66. Research findings on productivity improvement show all of the following EXCEPT
    A. productivity increases when employees are rewarded for extra output.
    B. productivity increases as it becomes the primary goal of management.
    C. productivity goes up when it is measured.
    D. productivity increases when the office environment is re-engineered.

REFERENCE: Abdelhak, p 613
                McWay, p 269

67. Sheena is an RHIA who continued her education and has a master's degree in Public Health. She is the Director of Health Information for the large County Health Department. In seeking the most reliable reference for a job applicant, which of the following would be preferred?
    A. a telephone reference from a personal friend of the applicant
    B. a written reference from a former supervisor of the applicant
    C. a telephone reference from a former supervisor of the applicant
    D. a written reference from the Human Resources Department of the applicant's former employer

REFERENCE: Abdelhak, p 581
                McWay, p 284-285
                LaTour and Eichenwald-Maki, p 694
                McConnell, p 137–138

68. In your new position as Director of Health Information Services, you have noticed that department supervisors arbitrarily allow employees to make up missed time due to absences. You decide that you need a policy to reinforce the attendance policy and cut down on tardiness and absences. Which policy statement would support your overall departmental goals?
    A. Make-up time is allowed only with approval from the director.
    B. Sick days can be used in lieu of time missed due to tardiness or absences.
    C. No make-up time for absences and tardiness is allowed.
    D. Changes in work schedules must be approved in advance and depend upon departmental operations.

REFERENCE: Abdelhak, p 636-637
                McWay, p 252
                LaTour and Eichenwald-Maki, p 649–650
                McConnell, p 211

69. As HIM Director, you receive a call from the CEO informing you that she has received a complaint from a patient. The patient reports that one of the coders in your department revealed the patient's diagnosis to the patient's neighbor. What action is recommended?
   A. Gather all the facts prior to meeting with the employee.
   B. Give the employee a written warning.
   C. Terminate the employee immediately for violation of the confidentiality policy.
   D. Immediately call a departmental meeting to discuss the importance of maintaining confidentiality.

REFERENCE: McWay, p 301-303
               Abdelhak, p 592-594
               Davis and LaCour, p 277
               McConnell, p 211

70. When analyzing discipline problems, which of the following should be considered?
   A. the prior performance of the employee in question
   B. the frequency of the problem
   C. the seriousness of the problem
   D. all of the above

REFERENCE: Abdelhak, p 592-594
               McWay, p 302-303
               LaTour and Eichenwald-Maki, p 698–699
               Liebler and McConnell, p 453–456
               McConnell, p 212–213

71. Michael is a new manager at Tri-County Health Systems. Human Resources has recently provided training for and implemented a new performance appraisal system which includes input from managers, peers, and staff. This approach is typically known as
   A. 360-degree evaluation.   C. holistic appraisal.
   B. group appraisal.   D. multi-factor evaluation.

REFERENCE: LaTour and Eichenwald-Maki, p 698
               McWay, p 301

72. Chris and Amy, two coders on your team, have come to you complaining that Jane, the discharge clerk, is deliberately holding back charts, causing a coding backlog. You are not sure Jane is really the cause of this problem because Chris and Amy have a history of blaming others for their work-related delays. To determine if Jane is truly a "problem employee" it would be best to first
   A. determine the source of the conflict.
   B. discretely ask other employees if they are having similar problems with Jane.
   C. request assistance from the Human Resources Department.
   D. observe Jane's interaction with others.

REFERENCE: Abdelhak, p 592-594
               LaTour and Eichenwald-Maki, p 698–699
               McWay, p 267-268

73. One of the most common rater biases that affect an employee's evaluation is the halo effect. The halo effect suggests that the supervisor
    A. rates everyone as average.
    B. is too lenient or too strict in rating employee performance.
    C. rates the employee on the basis of a strong like or dislike of the person.
    D. bases the employee evaluation on his behavior in the most recent period rather than the entire evaluation period.

REFERENCE: Abdelhak, p 585-589
              McConnell, p 195

74. Summer is the document imaging manager. She has had a meeting with the scanning clerks. They are complaining that the pay rate for their position is too low in their facility. What would be the best way to deal with this complaint?
    A. Submit a request for merit raises for all scanning clerks.
    B. Work with the Human Resources Department on a job evaluation and current wage and salary survey.
    C. Explain to the scanning clerks that health care cost containment means little money for raises.
    D. Ignore the complaint.

REFERENCE: Abdelhak, p 596-598
              LaTour and Eichenwald-Maki, p 697
              McWay, p 259
              McConnell, p 250

75. The teaching method selected by an instructor influences the student's ability to understand the material. Instructor-led classrooms work best when
    A. in-depth training and interaction are desired.
    B. there are three shifts of employees to train.
    C. you want to minimize the cost for training.
    D. employees from all departments must be trained.

REFERENCE: Hjort, p 60A-G.
              LaTour and Eichenwald-Maki, p 718–722

76. Which of the following scenarios best describes job enrichment as a motivational technique?
    A. Anna is a good clerical worker. In addition to her regular job duties, her supervisor has assigned her to special projects and committee assignments.
    B. Becky prefers to work where she can be active and have personal contacts. The supervisor rotates her through all clerical jobs in the department so that she can have variety in her work.
    C. Cheryl's job keeps her fully occupied all day. In fact, she frequently has to rush to get the work completed daily. Cheryl's supervisor decides to remove some responsibility from her job so she has less stress.
    D. Derek has worked in the department for several years. His supervisor decided to combine several jobs and add other tasks to enable Derek to use his knowledge and skills gained in school. With these increased responsibilities he is increasing his chances of being promoted.

REFERENCE: McConnell, p 183–184
              McWay, p 266-267
              Shortell and Kaluzny, p 115

77. HIM professionals increasingly participate on project teams. Tuckman has developed a model describing predictable stages. Which of the following reflects the stage where teams may experience disequilibrium?
   A. forming
   B. storming
   C. norming
   D. performing

REFERENCE: Liebler and McConnell, p. 352–354
               Shortell and Kaluzny, 189
               Umiker, p 119–120

78. There is an opening for a coder in a 150-bed acute care hospital. The position requires someone who can code from a wide variety of medical records using both ICD and CPT. Of the following candidates interviewing for this position, which would be the most appropriate to hire?
   A. a high school graduate who has applied for entry into the 2-year community college RHIT program
   B. a recent graduate of a 4-year HIM program, RHIA eligible, who hopes to become a department manager within 1 year
   C. a graduate of a 2-year community college HIT program, RHIT eligible, with 1 year of outpatient coding experience
   D. a RHIA with 5 years of supervisory experience in medical records who recently moved to this city and can find no other available position as a supervisor at this time

REFERENCE: Abdelhak, p 582-583
               McWay, p 285
               Johns, p 738–739
               LaTour and Eichenwald-Maki, p 693–694

79. Tina, the Coding Supervisor at Upstate Hospital, has heard rumors that the Health Information Management Department at her facility is starting a coding training program. Rumor also has it that the Department Director, Rose, is trying to recruit the coding supervisor from a neighboring hospital to head up the training position. Tina makes the following statement to the assistant director: "I'm obviously not good enough for the training position. Perhaps I should resign." As the Assistant Director, how should you respond?
   A. Ignore Tina's statement.
   B. Refer Tina to the Employee Assistance Program.
   C. Assist Tina in developing her career goals.
   D. Guarantee Tina that she will be considered for the position.

REFERENCE: Abdelhak, p 598-600
               McWay, p 290-291, 303-304
               Johns, p 900–902
               LaTour and Eichenwald-Maki, p 726–727
               Liebler and McConnell, p 242–245

80. Jon is a recent graduate who is considering accepting a position as Trauma Registrar at a large metropolitan medical center while he prepares to apply to graduate school. In making the decision, he considers the offer of $15 per hour for a 40-hour week, benefits of 27.5% of his salary, and tuition waivers of 6 credits per year at $145. He calculated that the total compensation would be
   A. $40, 650.00
   B. $39,563.25.
   C. $38,599.00
   D. $31,030.00

REFERENCE: Koch, p 55-56

81. Your organization's employees consist of a mixture of women and men. The women are of all ages, some are single mothers, others are married women with no children, and still others are women who care for older parents at home. The men also have varying personal lifestyles. You are working with Human Resources to provide a benefit program that allows your employees to choose from an array of benefits based on their own needs or lifestyle. You want to offer them a(n)

A. prepaid benefit plan. C. flexible benefit plan.
B. cafeteria benefit plan. D. employee-driven benefit plan.

REFERENCE: Abdelhak, p 558

82. Samantha is the evening discharge analysis clerk. As the evening supervisor, you personally trained her regarding the correct job procedures and policies. Within the last 2 months, Samantha has received an oral and written warning for failure to follow job procedures. Your facility utilizes a progressive discipline system. What is the next appropriate step?

A. demotion
B. suspension
C. oral reprimand from the evening supervisor
D. written warning from the director of the department

REFERENCE: Abdelhak, p 592-594
McWay, p 302-303
LaTour and Eichenwald-Maki, p 698
McConnell, p 215–219
Liebler and McConnell, p 415–416

83. In your department employee performance is rated using a continuous scale range of unsatisfactory through average to outstanding. Some other departments use a discrete system in which the supervisor assigns "does not meet standards," "meets standards," and "exceeds standards." Both systems being used are

A. rating scales. C. critical incident methods.
B. checklists. D. ranking methods.

REFERENCE: McWay, p 300-301
Abdelhak, p 586-588
McConnell, p 189–192

84. Virginia is the Record Processing Coordinator, which is a lead position. She has an excellent work record and is able to assist in most work areas of the department. She knows that she could easily get another job within the hospital for the asking. Recently she has been arriving late and has been uncooperative in dealing with others. As her immediate supervisor, what is the BEST first step in dealing with this situation?

A. Institute progressive discipline.
B. Ignore the situation and hope she will improve because she is a good employee.
C. Counsel her by encouraging self-analysis and problem-solving processes.
D. Suggest that she transfer to another department.

REFERENCE: Abdelhak, p 599-600
McWay, p 301-304
LaTour and Eichenwald-Maki, p 726–727
McConnell, p 222–223
Johns, p 900–902

85. Health care is known for rapid change. Cherelle understands the importance of change management and being a positive change agent. Which of the following approaches would be LEAST likely to support her approach?
    A. being available to listen to staff
    B. holding on to the vision
    C. measuring and celebrating success
    D. easing up on delegating

REFERENCE: Johns, p 916
               McWay, p 270
               LaTour and Eichenwald-Maki, p 637–642
               Liebler and McConnell, p 27–30

86. Mercedes, supervisor of the HIM analysts, determined that the outpatient surgery center had record analysts who were doing comparable jobs. The outpatient analysts were ranked two job grades above the HIM analysts. What document could she revise to reflect the actual skills, knowledge, and responsibilities in order to have the HIM analysis position re-evaluated?
    A. needs assessment
    B. job description/job specifications
    C. wage and salary survey
    D. department policy and procedures

REFERENCE: Abdelhak, p 598
               McWay, p 259
               Johns, p 734–735
               LaTour and Eichenwald-Maki, p 697
               Liebler and McConnell, 194–198

87. Rita Mizner, MBA, RHIA, is Director of Information Services for Mt. Sinai Medical Center. She is well respected for a management style that empowers her staff. All of the following are characteristics of effective delegation, EXCEPT
    A. explaining exactly what needs to be done.
    B. agreeing on performance standards.
    C. providing necessary resources.
    D. retaining authority to make key decisions.

REFERENCE: McWay, p 262-263
               LaTour and Eichenwald-Maki, p 726–727
               McConnell, p 65–72

88. Jordan is an RHIA who works at a large academic medical center. Her $37,540 salary is paid 60% from research grants as clinical trial coordinator, and 40% by HIM as a database manager. The hospital's fringe benefit rate is 23%. How much must the HIM director include in the budget (rounded to the nearest dollar) to cover Jordan's database management role?
    A. $15,016
    B. $18,470
    C. $22,524
    D. $27.705

REFERENCE: Koch, p 55-56

89. Christina is a pharmacy tech and has recently earned her RHIA. She is interviewing to become a representative of an international pharmaceutical firm. She would work from home, login to the corporate Web site several times a day, and make calls on various pharmacies in her territory. She would visit headquarters about once a quarter. This proposed work arrangement can best be described as
    A. flex time.
    B. outsourcing.
    C. consulting
    D. telecommuting.

REFERENCE: LaTour and Eichenwald-Maki, p 650–651
               Liebler and McConnell, p 188–190

90. Which of the following employees is exempt under the Fair Labor Standards Act?
    A. an RHIA who performs record analysis and coding 90% of the time and who supervises three employees
    B. an RHIT who manages the Health Information Services department and is involved with planning and decision-making activities 90% of the time
    C. the department secretary who spends 100% of her time performing clerical duties for the Director of Health Information Services
    D. a file clerk who spends 100% of the time on filing activities

REFERENCE: Abdelhak, p 567
               Davis and LaCour, p 379–380
               McConnell, p 446–448
               McWay, p 298

91. C. J. is employed as a regional coding consultant by a corporate hospital chain. In the organization chart, this position would be
    A. shown as a line position.
    B. shown as a staff position.
    C. not shown, because it is a consulting position.
    D. not shown, because this function is outsourced.

REFERENCE: Liebler and McConnell, p 172–174
               McConnell, p 51–52

92. Juan is director at a medical center that includes a daycare center and has several employees who have young children. He knows that it's important to be familiar with the provisions of the Family Medical Leave Act (FMLA), which includes all the following provisions EXCEPT:
    A. ensures any job the employee is qualified for upon return.
    B. both men and women qualify under the FMLA.
    C. covers leave to care for a spouse, child, or parent.
    D. provides up to 12 weeks of unpaid leave annually.

REFERENCE: Abdelhak, p 558-567
               McWay, p 92
               Liebler and McConnell, p 487
               McWay, p 298

93. Ty Ngynn is Assistant Director in Information Services. He has made an appointment with the Director of Human Resources to discuss his recent trip to the state HIM meeting with his Director, Wendy Richards. During the trip, Wendy repeatedly asked Ty to her room, suggesting they work on new plans for the department. When Ty declined, Wendy suggested it might not be worthwhile for him to attend future state meetings. The HR Director should
    A. explain that off-site events are outside the scope of the HR Department.
    B. provide Ty with additional training on resisting unwanted advances.
    C. take the complaint seriously and begin a sexual harassment investigation.
    D. explain that it's the Director's right to select who attends professional meetings.

REFERENCE:　　Abdelhak, p 564
　　　　　　　　Liebler and McConnell, p 287–288
　　　　　　　　McWay, p 294

94. Which of the following types of members is best for a committee?
    A. individuals of equal rank and authority
    B. a diverse group with widely varied rank and authority
    C. a blend of managers and entry level staff
    D. There is no clear benefit to one form or another.

REFERENCE:　　Liebler and McConnell, p. 339

95. As a new RHIA and coding manager, how likely is it that you will participate on committees?
    A. Infrequently until you are promoted to a higher position
    B. You should expect committee participation to be a regular part of your job.
    C. Occasionally, mostly with your staff
    D. It depends on whether your organization chooses to use the committee structure.

REFERENCE:　　Liebler and McConnell, p. 327–328
　　　　　　　　Umiker p 446

96. Inner City Hospital needs occasional help in coding to remain current. Rena, the coding manager, is seeking an individual who is available evenings and weekends and will be responsible for his or her own actions. While networking at a regional meeting, Rena explains that she is looking for which of the following?
    A. a consultant
    B. a statutory employee
    C. a part-time employee
    D. an independent contractor

REFERENCE:　　Abdelhak, p 536
　　　　　　　　Umiker p 446

97. Juan owns a record storage and destruction business in Texas. Under the Immigration Reform and Control Act, he knows all of the following apply EXCEPT:
    A. may not hire undocumented workers.
    B. must give preference to U.S. citizens.
    C. may not discriminate against non-citizens.
    D. must have I-9 documentation.

REFERENCE:　　Abdelhak, p 566
　　　　　　　　Umiker p 446

Answer Key for Human Resources

ANSWER   EXPLANATION

NOTE: Explanations are provided for those questions that require mathematical calculations and questions that are not clearly explained in the references that are cited.

1.   C $200 \times 30/60 = 100$ hours total

2.   D   50 employees × $15.50 per hour × ½ hour   =   387.50
            50 employees × $12.00 per hour × ½ hour   =   300.00
            100 employees × $18.00 per hour × ½ hour   =   900.00
            $387.50 +$300.00 + $900.00   = $1,587.50

3.   A   Calculate by time: $1,587.50 total cost for training/100 hours needed to train = $15.88 per hour/2 to get cost for ½ hour of training = 7.938 =$7.94
                                OR
            Calculate by employee: $1,587.50/200 employees = 7.938 =$7.94

4.   B   To determine the number of hours needed to perform a volume of work or "service units," in this case discharges (15,620) are multiplied by the "time standard" (18 minutes) and then divided by the number of minutes per hour (60).
            $(15,620 \times 18) = 281,160$ divided by 60 = 4,686.

5.   D   All members of the workforce must be trained on policies and procedures with respect to private health information as appropriate for their job function.

6.   B   To determine the number of employees needed for a specific position, you must first determine how much time is being spent on work currently being done. The "service units," in this case discharges (600), are multiplied by the "time factor," 20 minutes. (600 × 20 = 12,000 minutes) Because this problem's time factor is in minutes, you must also compute the number of available minutes per week. The "actual hours" in this case, 40 hours, is multiplied by 60 (60 minutes per hour) (40 × 60 = 2400). The earned time, 12,000 minutes, is then divided by the actual minutes, 2400, to determine the number of employees needed to perform a specific job duty. So, 12,000 divided by 2400 = 5.

7.   D

8.   A

9.   C   Dana should be assessing employee performance on an ongoing basis. Without proper documentation, an evaluation of "needs improvement" will be difficult to justify.

10.   D

11.   C   Kari took 6 hours unpaid leave (40 - 6 = 34), but worked a holiday at double-time (8 × 2 = 16). Because 8 hours of the holiday are already figured in the work week, add an additional 8 hours for holiday pay. So, 34 + 8 = 42.

12.   C

13.   D   Although putting one person in charge of the meter may not stop the abuse of the postage meter, it is the best first course of action to take. Answers A and C are too drastic, and answer B is not efficient use of a manager's time.

14.   C You are required to document the training content, dates, and attendees.

15.   D

16.   B

17.   B

18.   C

19.   C

20.   D

Answer Key for Human Resources

ANSWER EXPLANATION

21. B To calculate the absenteeism rate, use the following formula as suggested by the U.S. Department of Labor:

$$\frac{\text{Worker-days lost during period} \times 100}{(\text{Avg. number of workers}) (\text{Number of days in period})} \qquad \frac{(25 \times 100)}{(20 \times 22)} = 5.68\%$$

22. D

23. D

24. B

25. B

26. A

27. D

28. C Physical/workstation security training would be appropriate for all employees in general orientation training. A and B are higher level functions that would not be performed by all new employees. D. Job-specific training would be better suited to training in the department in which the employee will work.

29. B

30. C

31. A

32. A

33. B

34. C Managers should not attempt to "water down" information, even if it is bad news. Fueling the grapevine can also lead to additional misinformation. Managers should make every effort to communicate factual information to their employees in a calm and timely manner.

35. D

36. D Although all of these environmental conditions can contribute to the employees' well-being, air pollution, such as stale or dusty air, is a known contributor to headaches and fatigue.

37. B

38. C

39. B

40. A

41. B A well-written job description includes what health information and how that information is used in a position. The job description would be the document Gina would review for choosing appropriate training levels for staff members in different positions.

42. D

43. A

44. C

45. B Weekly department meetings, having an employee handbook, and written policies and procedures are all part of the necessary open and honest communication.

46. C

47. D

Answer Key for Human Resources

ANSWER   EXPLANATION

48.   B   It is illegal for an organization to fire an employee for filing a grievance. The union contract stipulates the policy and procedures for resolving grievances. You would need to refer to the union contract for any specific time boundaries.

49.   C

50.   D   Cutbacks in staffing, the need for job enrichment, and boredom could account for some of the problems in the department, but having potentially offensive jokes would certainly lead to an investigation of possible sexual harassment in the department.

51.   A

52.   B   Theory "Y" can be recalled as answering "yes" to the question: Do employees fundamentally want to do a good job and contribute to the organization?

53.   C

54.   B   In the department orientation, the new employee should also be oriented to the location of various facilities (restrooms, cafeteria) and to the general position tasks to be performed. In addition to the department orientation, there is usually a facility-wide orientation meeting for all new hires. The facility emergency procedures are usually covered at this facility-wide orientation meeting.

55.   C   The objective of discipline is to correct the inappropriate behavior.

56.   B   A spreadsheet with grids identifying who needs what type of training would help in defining the department privacy and security training plan.

57.   A   Training manuals would help ensure consistency of coverage of the materials among trainers. B and C serve to help in documenting the training that was given. D. In addition to initial training, the security rule requires ongoing training/reminders.

58.   B

59.   D   Employee salary expense is significant.

60.   A

61.   B   Job descriptions should be reviewed and updated before beginning the hiring process.

62.   D

63.   A   Directing or telling is associated with the low maturity level and/or low experience level of a group.

64.   C

65.   A

66.   D

67.   C   Just be sure to follow appropriate labor practices.

68.   D

69.   A   Even though a serious incident such as this could result in termination of an employee, it is important to gather all the facts prior to meeting with the employee to substantiate any claims.

70.   D

71.   A

72.   A

73.   C

74.   B   A common and easy solution to this problem is to ignore the complaint, although this won't solve the problem; it will only prolong it. If the clerks complain that their job rate is too low, a job evaluation seeks to determine the position's relative worth to maintain pay equity within the organization and a wage and salary survey helps in determining the market value of the position.

Answer Key for Human Resources

ANSWER   EXPLANATION

75.   B   In-depth training and interaction are best obtained in instructor-led classroom style of training. B, C, and D are disadvantages of instructor-led training. Instructor-led training becomes expensive and time intensive when scheduling and training many shifts of employees from all departments.

76.   A   Job enrichment involves assigning more challenging tasks and responsibilities without combining jobs, which is called job enlargement. Switching job tasks among employees is called job rotation. All of these are attempts to diversify work and motivate employees. Redesigning a job by removing responsibility, however, would probably not be a motivational factor.

77.   B

78.   C

79.   C

80.   A   Calculation: $15.00 × 2,080 hours per year = $31,200 × 27.5% = $8,580
Tuition waiver = 6 credits at $145 = $870.
Therefore, $31,200, + $8,580 + $870 = $40,650

81.   B

82.   B

83.   A

84.   C

85.   D

86.   B

87.   D   To be effective, authority needs to be delegated along with responsibility.

88.   B   Calculations: $37,540 × 123% = $46,174.20.
HIM pays 40% or $46,174.20 × .40 = $18,469.68, rounded to $18,470

89.   D

90.   B

91.   B

92.   A

93.   C

94.   A

95.   C

96.   D

97.   B

REFERENCES

Abdelhak, M., Grostick, S., Hanken, M. A., & Jacobs, E. (Eds.). (2007). *Health information: Management of a strategic resource* (3rd ed.). Philadelphia: W. B. Saunders.

Davis, N., & LaCour, M. (2004). *Introduction to health information technology.* Philadelphia: W. B. Saunders.

Hjort, B. (updated November 2003). AHIMA Practice Brief: HIPAA Privacy and Security Training. *Journal of AHIMA, 73,* no.4 (2002): 60A-G. Chicago: American Health Information Management Association (AHIMA).

Horton, L. (2006) *Calculating and reporting health care statistics* (2nd ed.). Chicago: American Health Information Management Association (AHIMA).

Johns, M. L. (2006). *Health information technology: An applied approach* (2nd ed.). Chicago: American Health Information Management Association (AHIMA).

Koch, P. G. (2008). *Basic allied health statistics and analysis* (3rd ed.). Clifton Park, NY: Delmar Cengage Learning.

LaTour, K., & Eichenwald-Maki, S. (2006). *Health information management: Concepts, principles and practice* (2nd ed.). Chicago: American Health Information Management Association (AHIMA).

Liebler, J. G., & McConnell, C. R. (2004). *Management principles for health professionals.* Sudbury, MA: Jones and Bartlett Publishers.

McConnell, C. *The effective health care supervisor* (6th ed.). Sudbury, MA: Jones and Bartlett.

McWay, D. C. (2008). *Today's health information management, an integrated approach.* Clifton Park, NY: Delmar Cengage Learning.

Shortell, S. M. & Kaluzny, A. D. (2006). *Health care management, organizational design and behavior* (5th Ed). Clifton Park, NY: Delmar Cengage Learning.

XVII. Mock Examination

Debra W. Cook, MAEd, RHIA
Sheila Carlon, Ph.D, RHIA, FAHIMA

NOTE: If you are taking the mock for the RHIT examination, you may choose to complete the first 150 questions. The mock for the RHIA examination has 180 questions to complete. In timing your speed at answering questions, allow about 1.35 minutes per question. For example, if you are taking the entire mock exam in one sitting, you should allow about 4 hours and 3 minutes (180 questions X 1.35 minutes for a total of 243 minutes = 4 hours and 3 minutes).

1. Each month, the staff of the clinic with the lowest overall waiting time is awarded a free dessert in the Gulfside Health care Center cafeteria. Take a look at the information listed below:

GULFSIDE HEALTH CARE CENTER AVERAGE CLINIC WAITING TIME BY TIME BLOCK DECEMBER 2007				
TIME BLOCK	PEDIATRICS	OBSTETRICS	CARDIOLOGY	ORTHOPEDICS
8:00-11:00	12	18	10	9
11:01-2:00	8	10	8	14
2:01-5:00	10	7	7	12

The winner will be selected based on
A. demonstrative pedantic data.
B. comparative aggregate data.
C. objective individual data.
D. duplicate thematic data.

REFERENCE: McWay (2008), p 226
Abdelhak, p 443
LaTour and Eichenwald-Maki, p 288

2. A union campaign is being conducted at your facility. As a department manager, it is appropriate for you to tell employees
A. a strike is inevitable if the union wins.
B. wages will increase if the union is defeated.
C. you need the names of those involved in union activities.
D. you are opposed to the union.

REFERENCE: Abdelhak, p 567-569
Pozgar, p 442-445

3. You work at All Paper Hospital, a small facility with no computerized health information capacity. There are ongoing problems because many departments collect the same data, creating space problems and issues with data discrepancies. You are exhausted with all this data
A. overload.
B. similarity.
C. transparency.
D. redundancy.

REFERENCE: Johns, (2002), p 204

4. Employing the SOAP style of progress notes, choose the "assessment" statement from the following:
A. patient states low back pain with sciatica is as severe as it was on admission.
B. patient moving about very cautiously, appears to be in pain.
C. adjust pain medication; begin physical therapy tomorrow.
D. sciatica unimproved with hot pack therapy.

REFERENCE: Abdelhak, p 115
Green and Bowie, p 90-92
LaTour and Eichenwald-Maki, p 186
Eichenwald-Maki and Petterson, p 48
McWay, p 103

5. In preparation for an EHR, you are conducting a total facility inventory of all forms currently used. You must name each form for bar coding and indexing. The unnamed document in front of you includes a checklist for assessing an obstetric patient's lochia, fundus, and perineum. The document type you give to this form is
   A. prenatal record.
   B. labor record.
   C. delivery room record.
   D. postpartum record.

REFERENCE: Abdelhak, p 111
                Green and Bowie, p 174

SAMPLE MS-DRG REPORT		
MS-DRG IDENTIFIER	RELATIVE WEIGHT	NUMBER OF PATIENTS WITH THIS MS-DRG
A	1.234	12
B	3.122	10
C	2.165	19
D	5.118	16

6. Based on the MS-DRG report above, what is the case-mix index for this facility?
   A. 0.204193
   B. 2.965807
   C. 11.639
   D. 57

REFERENCE: Koch, p 49-50
                Horton, p 128-129, 133

7. The special form or view that plays the central role in planning and providing care at nursing, psychiatric, and rehabilitation facilities is the
   A. interdisciplinary patient care plan.
   B. medical history and review of systems.
   C. interval summary.
   D. problem list.

REFERENCE: Peden, p 339
                Abdelhak, p 107
                LaTour and Eichenwald-Maki, p 185
                Johns, p 83

8. Four patients were discharged from Happy Time Hospital yesterday. A final progress note is an appropriate discharge summary for
   A. Howard, who died within 24 hours after his admission for a second heart attack in 2 weeks.
   B. Jackson, who had no co-morbidities or complications during this admission for replacement of a pacemaker battery.
   C. Fieldstone, who was admitted just 15 days following a heart attack for the acute onset of chest pain.
   D. Babson, who delivered a healthy 8-pound boy without complications for either mother or child.

REFERENCE: Abdelhak, p 109
                Green and Bowie, p 134
                LaTour and Eichenwald-Maki, p 183

Use the information in the tables below to answer the next two questions:

Make Me Better Clinic (MMBC) provides well child visits and childhood immunizations for four insurance companies. Data on the services they provided and the reimbursement they received from the four companies are listed in the two tables below:

Table 1

INSURANCE COMPANY	NUMBER OF WELL CHILD VISITS	REIMBURSEMENT FROM PAYER FOR WELL CHILD VISITS
Lifecare	259	$ 31,196.55
Getwell	786	$100,859.52
SureHealth	462	$ 54,631.50
BeHealthy	219	$ 26,991.75

Table 2

INSURANCE COMPANY	NUMBER OF IMMUNIZATIONS	REIMBURSEMENT FROM PAYER FOR EACH IMMUNIZATION
Lifecare	412	5.28
Getwell	1465	6.18
SureHealth	609	5.88
BeHealthy	417	5.08

9. MMBC receives the best reimbursement for well child visits from
   A. Lifecare.
   B. Getwell.
   C. SureHealth.
   D. BeHealthy.

REFERENCE: Math Calculation

10. Most of the children who are seen at MMBC will have a well child visit and two immunizations. If you factor in the reimbursement for two immunizations with each well child visit, which insurance company benefits MMBC most?
   A. Lifecare
   B. Getwell
   C. SureHealth
   D. BeHealthy

REFERENCE: Math Calculation

11. You are calculating the fee schedule payment amount for physician services covered under Medicare Part B. You already have the relative value unit figure. The only other information you need is
   A. the facility's case-mix index.
   B. a national conversion factor.
   C. the facility's base rate.
   D. MS-DRG relative weights.

REFERENCE: Johns, p 279-280
                Green, p 849
                Green and Rowell, p 292

VALLEY VIEW HOSPITAL FOUR HIGHEST MS-DRGs							
MS-DRG A		MS-DRG B		MS-DRG C		MS-DRG D	
CMS WEIGHT	NUMBER OF PATIENTS WITH MS-DRG A	CMS WEIGHT	NUMBER OF PATIENTS WITH MS-DRG B	CMS WEIGHT	NUMBER OF PATIENTS WITH MS-DRG C	CMS WEIGHT	NUMBER OF PATIENTS WITH MS-DRG D
2.023	323	0.987	489	1.925	402	1.243	386

12. Valley View Hospital collected the data displayed above concerning their four highest volume MS-DRGs. Which MS-DRG generated the most revenue for the hospital?
    A. MS-DRG A
    B. MS-DRG B
    C. MS-DRG C
    D. MS-DRG D

REFERENCE: Abdelhak, p 660
                Johns, p 275-278
                LaTour and Eichenwald-Maki, p 363-364

13. In reviewing a health record for coding purposes, the coder notes that the patient was put on Keflex postsurgery. There is no mention of a postoperative complication in the attending physician's discharge summary. Before querying the doctor, the coder will seek to confirm the infection by reviewing the
    A. lab report.
    B. nurses' notes.
    C. operative report.
    D. pathology report.

REFERENCE: Johns, p 60
                Green, p 11-12
                Green and Bowie, p 158

14. Stan works in an acute care general hospital, Fran works for a skilled nursing facility, Ann is employed at an assisted living facility, and Dan works for a home care provider. Which people are employed in facilities that may seek Joint Commission accreditation?
    A. Stan, Fran, and Ann
    B. Fran, Ann, and Dan
    C. Ann, Dan, and Stan
    D. Dan, Stan, and Fran

REFERENCE: Abdelhak, p 14
                Johns, p 599
                LaTour and Eichenwald-Maki, p 19
                McWay, p 7, 102, 180, 354

15. Happy Valley Clinic allows patients to communicate by e-mail to ask questions regarding their treatment and request appointment changes. E-mails and text messages are
    A. considered health care business records and are subject to the same regulations as records created in face-to-face patient encounters.
    B. considered proof of patient contact and should be summarized in a progress note in the patient record.
    C. generally maintained in a facility's electronic mail system until the next face-to-face patient encounter.
    D. not typically maintained or documented as patient encounters.

REFERENCE: McWay (2003), p 226-227
                Eichenwald-Maki and Petterson, p 142-143

16. The proposed National Health care Information Network (NHIN) dimensions are graphically depicted in the diagram below, with Roman numerals added to allow for the identification of specific areas. Where would information concerning a patient's health insurance be located on this chart?

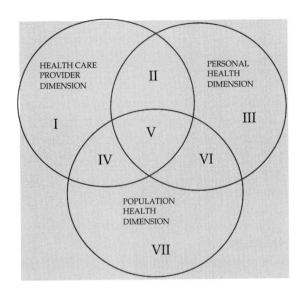

A. I

B. II

C. III

D. V

REFERENCE: LaTour and Eichenwald-Maki, p 157
                Johns, p 127

17. As a new HIM manager at an acute care facility, you have been asked to update the facility's policy for physician's verbal orders in accordance with state law and regulations. Your first area of investigation is the qualifications of those individuals in your facility who have been authorized to record verbal orders. For this information, you will consult the
   A. policy and procedure manual.
   B. hospital's Quality Management Plan.
   C. data dictionary.
   D. hospital bylaws, rules, and regulations.

REFERENCE: Green and Bowie, p 20-23
                Johns, p 92, 620
                McWay, 20-23

18. Parker is a type I diabetic with hypertension that is currently controlled with medication. Parker was admitted through the ED for an emergency appendectomy. Following surgery, the patient developed an infection at the wound site that was treated with antibiotics. When making decisions about sequencing the codes for this case, the coder should rely on definitions found in the
   A. UHDDS.
   B. Coding Clinic.
   C. CMS Coding Guidelines.
   D. Federal Register.

REFERENCE: Green and Bowie, p 118, 244
                Green, p 204-211

19. Parker is a type I diabetic with hypertension that is currently controlled with medication. Parker was admitted through the ED for an emergency appendectomy. Following surgery, the patient developed an infection at the wound site that was treated with antibiotics. Parker's principal diagnosis is the
    A. complications of hypertension
    B. co-morbidity of the wound infection
    C. co-morbidity of type 1 diabetes
    D. acute appendicitis

REFERENCE: UHDDS
               Green, p 204-212
               Green and Bowie, p 118

20. Dr. Reed tried to explain wound care to Baker prior to discharge, but Baker (who is 104 and moderately senile) just couldn't seem to understand or remember what the doctor said. So, Dr. Reed explained Baker's aftercare to his daughter. Dr. Reed should document discharge instructions
    A. in the discharge summary.
    B. on a patient instructions form signed by Dr. Reed and Baker and filed in Baker's medical record.
    C. in the discharge summary and on a patient instructions form signed by Dr. Reed and Baker and filed in Baker's medical record.
    D. in the discharge summary and on a patient instructions form signed by Dr. Reed and Baker's daughter and filed in Baker's medical record.

REFERENCE: Abdelhak, p 109
               Johns, p 68
               Green and Bowie, p 133-134

21. The physician has documented the final diagnoses as acute myocardial infarction, COPD, CHF, hypertension, atrial fibrillation and status-post cholecystectomy. The following conditions should be reported

401.1	Hypertension, benign
401.9	Hypertension, unspecified
402.91	Hypertension, heart disease, unspecified, with heart failure
410.91	Acute myocardial infarction, unspecified site, initial episode of care
427.31	Atrial fibrillation
428.0	Congestive heart failure, unspecified
496	Chronic obstructive pulmonary disease
V45.79	Acquired absence of gallbladder

    A. 410.9, 496, 402.91, 427.31, V45.79
    B. 410.91, 496, 428.0, 401.9, 427.31
    C. 410.91, 496, 428.0, 401.9, 427.31, V45.79
    D. 410.91, 496, 428.0, 401.1, 427.31

REFERENCE: Schraffenberger, p 141-144, 148-149, 168
               Brown, p 275-277

22. A patient is 6 weeks post-mastectomy for carcinoma of the breast. She is admitted for chemotherapy. What is the correct sequencing of the codes?

174.9	Malignant neoplasm of the breast
V10.3	Personal history of malignant neoplasm of breast
V58.1	Encounter for other and unspecified procedure and aftercare, antineoplastic chemotherapy
V58.11	Encounter for antineoplastic chemotherapy
V67.00	Follow-up exam after surgery
V67.09	Unspecified follow-up examination

A. V58.11, 174.9
B. V58.1, V10.3
C. V67.09, V58.1
D. V10.3, V67.00

REFERENCE: Bowie & Schaffer (2006), p 106-108
Frisch, 144, 153
Green, p 131-133
Johnson & McHugh, p 56-58
Lovaasen and Schwerdtfeger, p 356

23. Which of the following is coded as an adverse effect in ICD-9-CM?
A. tinnitus due to allergic reaction after administration of ear drops
B. mental retardation due to intracranial abscess
C. rejection of transplanted kidney
D. nonfunctioning pacemaker due to defective soldering

REFERENCE: Frisch, p 149-150
Green, p 160-162
Johnson & McHugh, p 68-70
Lovaasen and Schwerdtfeger, p 483

24. You have been assigned to code the cases listed below. Which one will you appropriately assign to Category 402, Hypertensive Heart Disease?

- Mallory: left heart failure with benign hypertension
- Emma: congestive heart failure; hypertension
- Taylor: hypertensive cardiovascular disease with congestive heart failure
- Trevor: cardiomegaly with hypertension

A. Mallory
B. Emma
C. Taylor
D. Trevor

REFERENCE: Green, p 138-141
Schraffenberger, p 137-140
Brown, p 282

25. If the same condition is described as both acute and chronic and separate subentries exist in the ICD-9-CM alphabetic index at the same indentation level
    A. they should both be coded, acute sequenced first.
    B. they should both be coded, chronic sequenced first.
    C. only the acute condition should be coded.
    D. only the chronic condition should be coded.

REFERENCE: Bowie & Schaffer (2006), p 54
                        Brown, p 47
                        Frisch, p 133
                        Green, p 105
                        Johnson & McHugh, p 75
                        Schraffenberger, p 442

26. A patient is admitted for a total hip replacement because of rheumatoid arthritis. Following admission, but prior to surgery, the patient develops congestive heart failure which necessitates transfer to ICU. The hip replacement is canceled and the patient is treated for the heart failure. What is the principal diagnosis?
    A. congestive heart failure
    B. rheumatoid arthritis
    C. hip replacement
    D. canceled surgical procedure

REFERENCE: Green, p 111-112
                        Brown, p 60-61
                        Schraffenberger, p 40-41

27. Which of the following would be coded as a poisoning?
    A. Coumadin intoxication due to a cumulative effect
    B. idiosyncratic reaction to Artane
    C. interaction between Aldomet and a vasodilating agent
    D. reaction between Coumadin and an over-the-counter medication

REFERENCE: Schraffenberger, p 283-285
                        Brown, p 365-370
                        Green, p 160-162, 165-166

28. Which of the following diagnoses or procedures would prevent the normal delivery code, 650, from being assigned?
    A. occiput presentation
    B. single liveborn
    C. episiotomy
    D. low forceps

REFERENCE: Bowie & Schaffer (2006), p 216
                        Brown, p 224-225
                        Green, p 147
                        Johnson & McHugh, p 49
                        Schraffenberger, p 206-207

29. Which of the following are considered late effects regardless of time?
    A. congenital defect
    B. nonunion
    C. nonhealing fracture
    D. poisoning

REFERENCE: Bowie & Shaffer (2006), p 57-59
                        Brown, p 49-50, 354
                        Green, p 106, 159
                        Johnson & McHugh, p 72-73
                        Schraffenberger, p 306-307

30. Four people were seen in your emergency department yesterday. Which one will be coded as a poisoning?

- Josh was diagnosed with digitalis intoxication.

- Ben had an allergic reaction to a dye administered for a pyelogram.

- Bryan developed syncope after taking Contac pills with a double scotch.

- Matthew had an idiosyncratic reaction between two properly administered prescription drugs.

A. Josh
B. Ben
C. Bryan
D. Matthew

REFERENCE: Brown, p 365-368
               Eid, p 262-263
               Frisch, p 149-150
               Green, p 160-165
               Johnson & McHugh, p 68-69
               Schraffenberger, p 283-284

31. Patient is admitted for elective cholecystectomy for treatment of chronic cholecystitis with cholelithiasis. Prior to administration of general anesthesia, patient suffers cerebral thrombosis. Surgery is subsequently canceled. Code and sequence the coding from the following codes.

434.00	Cerebral thrombosis without cerebral infarction
574.10	Chronic cholecystitis with cholelithiasis
V64.1	Surgery cancelled, contraindication
997.02	Iatrogenic cerebrovascular infarction or hemorrhage
51.22	Cholecystectomy, total

A. 997.02, 574.10, 51.22
B. 574.10, 434.00, V64.1
C. 997.02, 434.00, V64.1
D. 434.00, V64.1

REFERENCE: Bowie & Shaffer (2006), p 307
               Brown, p 60-61
               Green, p 208
               Johnson & McHugh, p 24
               Schraffenberger, p 40-41

32. A coworker complained of the sudden onset of chest pain and was admitted. A myocardial infarction was ruled out. You would code
A. the myocardial infarction as if it were an established condition.
B. both the infarction and the chest pain and sequence the infarction first.
C. as an impending myocardial infarction.
D. only the chest pain.

REFERENCE: Bowie & Schaffer (2006), p 59, 61
               Green, p 30-31
               Johnson & McHugh, p 213, 574-575
               Lovaasen and Schwerdtfeger, p 86

33. A physician lists the final diagnosis as diarrhea and constipation due to either irritable bowel syndrome or diverticulitis. The following codes are assigned:

562.11	Diverticulitis of colon without hemorrhage
564.00	Constipation
564.1	Irritable colon
787.91	Diarrhea

A. 564.1, 562.11
B. 562.11, 564.1

C. 564.00, 787.91, 564.1, 562.11
D. 564.1, 562.11, 564.00, 787.91

REFERENCE: Schraffenberger, p 53
Brown, p 23-24 81-82
Green, p 208

34. The health information practitioner had two patient records, each with a final diagnosis of fracture of the pelvis. Patient A had a single break in the pelvic ring; patient B had severe multiple fractures of the pelvis and a possible pulmonary embolus. Although the principal diagnosis is the same, what method can be used to further recognize the patient who is at a higher risk?
A. SNDO codes
B. HCPCS codes

C. severity of illness system
D. resource utilization groups (RUGS)

REFERENCE: LaTour and Eichenwald-Maki, p 363-365, 413, 503-504
Green, p 198-200

35. In your state, it is legal for minors to seek medical treatment for a sexually transmitted disease without parental consent. When this occurs, who would be expected to authorize the release of the medical information documented in this episode of care to the patient's insurers?
A. the patient
B. a court-appointed guardian on behalf of the patient
C. the custodial parent of the patient
D. the patient's doctor on behalf of the patient

REFERENCE: LaTour and Eichenwald-Maki, p 256
McWay (2003), p 123-124

36. A patient was diagnosed with a left choanal polyp and was taken to the ambulatory surgery suite where a left Caldwell-Luc operation was performed. The CPT index should be referenced under which of the following entries?
A. Operation, Intestine, Polyp excision
B. Operation, Colon, Polyp excision
C. Removal, Polyp, Larynx
D. Sinus, Maxillary, Polyp excision

REFERENCE: Green, p 455-461

37. The patient had a thrombectomy, without catheter, of the peroneal artery, by leg incision.

34203	Embolectomy or thrombectomy, with or without catheter; popliteal-tibio-peroneal artery, by leg incision
35226	Repair blood vessel, direct; lower extremity
35302	Thromboendarterectomy, including patch graft if performed; superficial femoral artery
37799	Unlisted procedure, vascular surgery

A. 34203
B. 37799
C. 35302
D. 35226

REFERENCE: Bowie & Schaffer (2008), p 172-173
Eid, p 97
Green, p 571-572
Johnson & McHugh, p 301

38. Patient was seen for excision of two interdigital neuroma from the left foot.

28080	Excision, interdigital (Morton) neuroma, single, each
64774	Excision of neuroma; cutaneous nerve, surgically identifiable
64776	Excision of neuroma; digital nerve, one or both, same digit

A. 64774
B. 64776
C. 28080
D. 28080, 28080

REFERENCE: CPT Book, 2009

39. Patient was seen in the Emergency Department with lacerations on the left arm. Two lacerations, one 7 cm and one 9 cm, were closed with layered sutures.

12002	Simple repair of superficial wounds of scalp, neck, axillae, external genitalia, trunk and/or extremities (including hands and feet); 2.6 cm to 7.5 cm
12004	Simple repair of superficial wounds of scalp, neck, axillae, external genitalia, trunk and/or extremities (including hands and feet); 7.6 cm to 12.5 cm
12035	Layer closure of wounds of scalp, axillae, trunk and/or extremities (excluding hands and feet); 12.6 cm to 20.0 cm
12045	Layer closure of wounds of neck, hands, feet and/or external genitalia; 12.6 cm to 20.0 cm

A. 12045
B. 12035
C. 12002, 12004
D. 12004

REFERENCE: Bowie & Schaffer (2008), 100-102
Green, p 482-484
Johnson & McHugh, p 214, 226-228
Smith, p 60-61

40. Office visit for 43-year-old male, new patient, with no complaints. Patient is applying for life insurance and requests a physical examination. A detailed health and family history was obtained and a basic physical was done. Physician completed life insurance physical form at patient's request. Blood and urine were collected.

99381	Initial comprehensive preventive medicine evaluation and management of an individual including an age and gender appropriate history, examination, counseling/anticipatory guidance/risk factor reduction interventions, and the ordering of appropriate immunization(s), laboratory/diagnostic procedures, new patient; infant (age under 1 year)
99386	Initial comprehensive preventive medicine evaluation and management of an individual including a comprehensive history, a comprehensive examination, counseling/anticipatory guidance/risk factor reduction interventions, and the ordering of appropriate immunization(s), laboratory/diagnostic procedures, new patient; 40-64 years
99396	Periodic comprehensive preventive medicine re-evaluation and management of an individual including an age and gender appropriate history, examination, counseling/anticipatory guidance/risk factor reduction interventions, and the ordering of appropriate immunization(s), laboratory/diagnostic procedures, established patient; 40-64 years
99450	Basic life and/or disability examination that includes completion of a medical history following a life insurance pro forma

A. 99450   C. 99396
B. 99386   D. 99381

REFERENCE: Bowie & Schaffer (2008), p 74-75CPT Book (2009), p 32
Green, p 402
Johnson & McHugh, p 180

41. Patient was seen today for regular hemodialysis. No problems reported, tolerated procedure well.

90935	Hemodialysis procedure with single physician evaluation
90937	Hemodialysis procedure requiring repeated evaluations(s) with or without substantial revision of dialysis prescription
90945	Dialysis procedure other than hemodialysis (e.g., peritoneal dialysis, hemofiltration, or other continuous renal replacement therapies), with single physician evaluation
+99354	Prolonged physician service in the office or other outpatient setting requiring direct (face-to-face) contact beyond the usual service (e.g., prolonged care and treatment of an acute asthmatic patient in an outpatient setting); first hour (List separately in addition to code for office or other outpatient Evaluation and Management service.)

A. 90937   C. 90945
B. +99354   D. 90935

REFERENCE: Bowie & Schaffer (2008), p 346-349
Green, p 798
Johnson & McHugh, p 414-415
Smith, p 214

42. An established patient was seen by the physician in the office for DTaP vaccine and HiB.

90471	Immunization administration (includes percutaneous, intradermal, subcutaneous, intramuscular injections); one vaccine (single or combination vaccine/toxoid)
+90472	Immunization administration (includes percutaneous, intradermal, subcutaneous, or intramuscular injections); each additional vaccine (single or combination vaccine/toxoid) (List separately in addition to code for primary procedure)
90700	Diphtheria, tetanus toxoids, and acellular pertussis vaccine (DTaP), when administered to individuals younger than 7 years, for intramuscular use
90720	Diphtheria, tetanus toxoids, and whole cell pertussis vaccine and Hemophilus influenza B vaccine (DTP-Hib), for intramuscular use
90721	Diphtheria, tetanus toxoids, and acellular pertussis vaccine and Hemophilus influenza B vaccine (DtaP-Hib), for intramuscular use
90748	Hepatitis B and Hemophilus influenza b vaccine (HepB-Hib), for intramuscular use
99211	Office or other outpatient visit for the evaluation and management of an established patient, which may not require the presence of a physician. Usually, the presenting problem(s) are minimal. Typically, 5 minutes are spent performing or supervising these services.

A. 90471, +90472, 90721
B. 90720, 90471

C. 90700, 90748, 99211
D. 90471, 90721

REFERENCE: Bowie & Schaffer, p 342
CPT Book (2009), p 386-387
Eid, p 184-185
Green, p 789-791
Johnson and McHugh, p 411,413
Smith, p 21043.

43. A patient with lung cancer and bone metastasis is seen for complex treatment planning by a radiation oncologist.

77263	Therapeutic radiology treatment planning; complex
77290	Therapeutic radiology simulation-aided field setting; complex
77315	Teletherapy, isodose plan (whether hand or computer calculated); complex (mantle or inverted Y, tangential ports, the use of wedges, compensators, complex blocking, rotational beam, or special beam considerations)
77334	Treatment devices, design and construction; complex (irregular blocks, special shields, compensators, wedges, molds, or casts)

A. 77315
B. 77263

C. 77290
D. 77334

REFERENCE: Bowie & Schaffer, p 327-328
CPT Book (2009), p 328-329
Eid, p 163
Green, p 736-739
Johnson & McHugh, p 391
Smith, p 157–159

44. A 4-year-old had a repair of an incarcerated inguinal hernia. This is the first time this child had been treated for this condition.

49496	Repair initial inguinal hernia full-term infant, under age 6 months, or preterm infant over 50 weeks' postconception age and under 6 months at the time of surgery, with or without hydrocelectomy; incarcerated or strangulated
49501	Repair initial inguinal hernia, age 6 months to under 5 years, with or without hydrocelectomy; incarcerated or strangulated
49521	Repair recurrent inguinal hernia, any age; incarcerated or strangulated
49553	Repair initial femoral hernia, any age; incarcerated or strangulated

A. 49553   C. 49521
B. 49496   D. 49501

REFERENCE: Bowie & Schaffer, p 226
                Green, p 631-632
                Johnson & McHugh, p196-197
                Smith, p 117-118

45. A quantitative drug assay was performed for a patient to determine digoxin level.

80050	General health panel
80101	Drug screen, qualitative; single drug class method (e.g., immunoassay, enzyme assay), each drug class
80162	Digoxin (therapeutic drug assay, quantitative examination)
80166	Doxepin (therapeutic drug assay, quantitative examination)

A. 80101   C. 80166
B. 80050   D. 80162

REFERENCE: Bowie & Schaffer (2008), p 235-236
                Green, p 764-766
                Johnson & McHugh, p 401-402
                Smith, p 173

46. Provide the CPT code for anesthesia services for the transvenous insertion of a pacemaker.

00530	Anesthesia for permanent transvenous pacemaker insertion
00560	Anesthesia for procedures on heart, pericardial sac, and great vessels of chest; without pump oxygenator
33202	Insertion of epicardial electrode(s); open incision
33206	Insertion or replacement of permanent pacemaker with transvenous electrode(s); atrial

A. 00560   C. 00530
B. 33202, 00530   D. 33206, 00560

REFERENCE: Bowie & Schaffer (2008), p 81-822
                Green, p 415, 419, 421-422, 434, 438
                Johnson & McHugh, p 182-183

47. The transcriptionists have collected data on the number and types of problems with the dictation equipment. The best tool to display the data they collected is a

A. flowchart.
B. Pareto chart.
C. Gantt chart.
D. PERT chart.

REFERENCE: McWay, p 148-149
               LaTour and Eichenwald-Maki, p 674
               Brassard, p 95

48. Based on the information below, what was the net death rate at Seaside Hospital in January?

SEASIDE HOSPITAL SELECTED STATISTICS-JANUARY 2008				
Admissions	Discharged to Home	Discharge Transfers	Deaths <48 hours	Deaths >48 hours
280	212	28	8	6

A. 2.4%
B. 2.8%
C. 3.8%
D. 5.8%

REFERENCE: Koch, p 120-121
               Horton, p 67-68
               LaTour and Eichenwald-Maki, p 409
               Johns, p 462-464

49. The formula used to calculate the percentage of ambulatory care visits made with same day appointments is

A. $\dfrac{\text{number of patients seen with same day appointments for a period} \times 100}{\text{number of patients seen with advance appointments for the same period}}$

B. $\dfrac{\text{number of patients seen with advance appointments for a period} \times 100}{\text{number of patients seen with same day appointments for the same period}}$

C. $\dfrac{\text{number of patients seen with same day appointments for a period} \times 100}{\text{number of patients seen in the same period}}$

D. $\dfrac{\text{number of patients seen with advance appointments for a period} \times 100}{\text{number of patients seen in the same period}}$

REFERENCE: McWay, p 192
               Koch, p 178
               LaTour and Eichenwald-Maki, p 329
               Horton, p 14-15, 17
               Johns, p 432-433

50. A HIM Department Budget Report for May shows a payroll budget of $25,000 and an actual payroll expense of $22,345. The percentage of budget variance for the month is

A. $2,655.
B. 11%.
C. $265.
D. 0.9%.

REFERENCE: LaTour and Eichenwald-Maki, p 761-762

51. Your large office practice has decided to try an e-health initiative. They have established a practice Web site and encourage patients to submit questions electronically instead of calling the advice nurse. After an initial surge in interest, very few patients use the service. The Web site is attractive and easy to navigate. Questions submitted via the site are answered by the nursing staff within 2 working days. You suspect few patients use the service because
    A. most of your patients are too old to be Internet savvy.
    B. the turnaround time is too long to replace the advice nurse.
    C. the nurses may be using language that is too technical for patients.
    D. most patients just prefer the personal touch they get on the phone.

REFERENCE: LaTour and Eichenwald-Maki, p 71

52. Your facility is engaged in a research project concerning patients newly diagnosed with type II diabetes. The researchers notice older patients have a longer length of stay than younger patients. They have seen a
    A. positive correlation between age and length of stay.
    B. negative correlation between age and length of stay.
    C. causal relationship between age and length of stay.
    D. homologous relationship between age and length of stay.

REFERENCE: McWay, p 203-206
                LaTour and Eichenwald-Maki, p 427-428
                Johns, p 578
                Brassard, p 44-46
                Koch, p 248
                Shi, p 13

53. Johnston City was set upon by a swarm of killer bees. All 5,000 residents are at risk of a bee attack. If 25 residents were attacked by the bees, the incidence of bee attacks
    A. is 5 in 1,000.   C. is 25 in 1,000.
    B. is 5 in 5,000.   D. cannot be determined at this time.

REFERENCE: Koch, p 205
                McWay, p 227-228
                Abdelhak, p 381
                LaTour and Eichenwald-Maki, p 420-421
                Sui, p 61

54. A 335-bed hospital opened a new wing on June 1 of a nonleap year, increasing its bed count to 350 beds. The total bed count days for the year at the hospital was
    A. 122,275.
    B. 125,485.
    C. 127,750.
    D. The answer cannot be calculated with the information provided.

REFERENCE: Koch, p 86
                Johns, p 457
                LaTour and Eichenwald-Maki, p 405

55. A patient who was admitted to the hospital on January 14 and discharged on March 2 in a nonleap year has a length of stay of
A. 45 days.
B. 46 days.
C. 47 days.
D. 48 days.

REFERENCE: Koch, p 102
                      LaTour and Eichenwald-Maki, p 406-407
                      Johns, p 459-460

56. Release of information has increased its use of part-time prn clerical support in order to respond to increased requests for release of information. The budget variance report will reflect
A. the increase in the cost of part-time clerical support for ROI, but not the increase in revenue from this area.
B. the increase in revenue from increased volume in ROI, but not the increased costs of part-time clerical support.
C. both the increases in revenue and increased costs for clerical support in ROI.
D. neither the increased costs nor increased revenue, as temporary changes are rarely reflected on variance reports.

REFERENCE: Abdelhak, p 664
                      LaTour and Eichenwald-Maki, p 761-762

57. You are heading a research study that includes a patient questionnaire. Five of the questions will be answered using the following scale:

1	Strongly disagree
2	Disagree
3	No opinion
4	Agree
5	Strongly agree

You would like to display the study in your report. If you'd like to include responses to all five questions on one display, you should use a
A. stacked bar graph.
B. pie chart.
C. frequency table.
D. frequency polygon.

REFERENCE: Abdelhak, p 384
                      LaTour and Eichenwald-Maki, p 422-428
                      Shi, p 359-360

58. Your HMO manager has requested a report on the number of patient visits per year for preschool children. Which of the age groupings below will you use for your report?

A. 0–1 year
    1–2 years
    2–3 years
    3–4 years
    4–5 years

B. < 12   months
    12–24   months
    25–37   months
    38–50   months
    51–63   months

C. >12   months
    12–24   months
    25–37   months
    38–50   months
    < 51   months

D. 0–2 years
    3–4 years
    5   years

REFERENCE: Koch, p 260
              LaTour and Eichenwald-Maki, p 422-423
              Johns, p 443-444

59 . Collins Family Hospital had a bed count of 150 for the first 6 months of the year. On June 1, it added 15 beds when it opened a new wing. If you are given the average length of stay for the year, can you calculate the annual bed turnover rate? How?
A. Yes, using the direct method.
B. Yes, using the indirect method.
C. Yes, using the Joint Commission method.
D. No, there is insufficient data to complete the calculation.

REFERENCE: Koch, p 185-186
              Abdelhak, p 383
              LaTour and Eichenwald-Maki, p 405-406
              Horton, p 47-48

60. You are heading a research study that includes a patient questionnaire. Five of the questions will be answered using the following scale:

1	Strongly disagree
2	Disagree
3	No opinion
4	Agree
5	Strongly agree

The data collected using this scale is called
A. cardinal data.
B. ordinal data.
C. nominal data.
D. continuous data.

REFERENCE: McWay, p 201
              Koch, p 13
              Abdelhak, p 384
              LaTour and Eichenwald-Maki, p 401
              Horton, p 207, 112
              Sui, p 293

61. Three people applied for a job: Ted is 84, Fred is 62, and Joe is 38. None of the applicants were offered the job. Given some of the remarks made during the interview, all three men felt they were not hired because they might have been considered too old. They went to an attorney to inquire into filing suit under the Federal Age Discrimination in Employment Act. The attorney said
    A. Ted may have a case, but Fred and Joe are too young to qualify under the Act.
    B. Ted and Fred may have a case, but Joe is too young to qualify under the Act.
    C. Fred and Joe may have a case, but Ted is too old to qualify under the Act.
    D. Fred may have a case, but Joe is too young and Ted is too old to qualify under the Act.

REFERENCE: Pozgar, p 438
               Abdelhak, p 565-566

62. The patient's family asked the attending physician to keep the patient in the hospital for a few days more until they could make arrangements for the patient's home care. Because the patient no longer meets criteria for continued stay, if the physician complies with the family's request, this would be considered
    A. the best utilization of the hospital's resources.
    B. an inappropriate use of hospital resources.
    C. a compassionate use of the hospital's resources.
    D. appropriate, provided it is limited to a few days.

REFERENCE: Abdelhak, p 462-463
               LaTour and Eichenwald-Maki, p 509-510
               Johns, p 521-526

63. The state is considering the closure of the Arcadia Hospital. In reviewing the hospital statistics, which indicator will best help state officials determine whether closure is warranted?
    A. daily census   C. inpatient service days
    B. percentage of occupancy   D. average length of stay

REFERENCE: LaTour and Eichenwald-Maki, p 405
               Johns, p 457
               Koch, p 84

64. The census taken at midnight on August 1 showed 99 patients remaining in the hospital. On August 2, four patients were admitted, there was one fetal death, one DOA, and seven patients were discharged. One of these patients was admitted in the morning and remained only 8 hours. How many inpatient service days were rendered on August 2?
    A. 94   C. 96
    B. 95   D. 97

REFERENCE: Abdelhak, p 382
               Koch, p 64-67
               LaTour and Eichenwald-Maki, p 404
               Johns, p 452-453

65. You are implementing a quality improvement plan that utilizes the PDSA cycle. If you correctly implement PDSA, which phase of the project will take the most of your time?
    A. P   C. S
    B. D   D. A

REFERENCE: Johns, p 569-570
               LaTour and Eichenwald-Maki, p 671-672
               McWay, p 143

66. A run or line chart would be most useful for collecting data on
    A. waiting time in the Pediatrics Clinic.
    B. patient satisfaction with the food.
    C. delays in scheduling elective surgical procedures.
    D. medication errors and their causes.

REFERENCE: Koch, p 274-275
               McWay, 149, 151, 201
               LaTour and Eichenwald-Maki, p 675-676
               Johns, p 580

Number of Visits and Wait Times in the ER

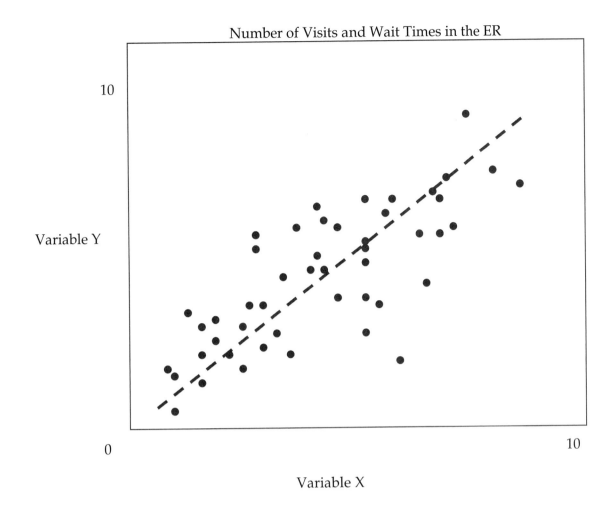

67. The ER staff has collected the data on the number of visits and wait times in the ER and has displayed the data on the chart shown. Based on this information, what kind of correlation do you see between the number of visits (Variable X) and the wait times (Variable Y)?
   A. a positive correlation between Variable X and Variable Y
   B. a negative correlation between Variable X and Variable Y
   C. a conjunctive correlation between Variable X and Variable Y
   D. a causative correlation between Variable X and Variable Y

REFERENCE: McWay, p 203-204
               LaTour and Eichenwald-Maki, p 674-675
               Johns, p 578
               Brassard, p145
               Koch, p 247-248

68. Because Fred is recovering nicely, he asks Dr. Jones if he can go home for the weekend. Dr. Jones approves a two-night leave of absence (LOA). Chances are Fred is a patient in
    A. an acute care facility; his LOA will decrease the month's average daily inpatient census.
    B. a long-term care facility; his LOA will increase the month's percentage of occupancy.
    C. an acute care facility; his LOA will increase the month's total discharge days.
    D. a long-term care facility; his LOA will decrease the month's total inpatient service days.

REFERENCE: Horton, p 25, 57
               Koch, p 111-112

69. Community Hospital reported an average LOS in December of 3.7 days with a standard deviation of 23. This information indicates that
    A. there was a small variation in the LOS at Community Hospital.
    B. there was a large variation in the LOS at Community Hospital.
    C. most of the patients at Community Hospital stay 3 to 4 days.
    D. patients stay longer at Community than at most hospitals.

REFERENCE: McWay, p 198
               LaTour and Eichenwald-Maki, p 434
               Koch, p 246-247

70. Four HIT students are working on a LOS project at their clinical site. To describe the variability of the data, Smithson suggests using range because it is the most exact; Donaldson wants to use the mean because it is easy to calculate; Franklin recommends variance because it is the most popular measure of variability; and Howell proposes the use of standard deviation because it is the most easily understood. Who made the best suggestion?
    A. Smithson   C. Franklin
    B. Donaldson   D. Howell

REFERENCE: McWay, p 194-195
               Koch, p 246
               LaTour and Eichenwald-Maki, p 434
               Johns, p 440

71. Sun City reported 12 cases of chronic heart disease in a population of 8,000 in 2004. In 2008, Sun City reported there were still 12 cases of chronic heart disease, but its population had decreased to 6,000. This represents an increase in the
    A. prevalence of chronic heart disease in Sun City.
    B. incidence of chronic heart disease in Sun City.
    C. reliability of reporting chronic heart disease in Sun City.
    D. occurrence of chronic heart disease in Sun City.

REFERENCE: McWay, p 198-199
               Koch, p 145-146205
               LaTour and Eichenwald-Maki, p 420-421
               Sui, p 61

72. Community Hospital Administration decided to change the number of adult and children beds from 300 to 375 effective July 1. The total number of inpatient service days for adults and children for the year was 111,963. What was the percentage of occupancy rate for adults and children for the entire year?

    A. 0.9%
    B. 45.4%
    C. 90.8%
    D. 91.0%

REFERENCE: LaTour and Eichenwald-Maki, p 405-406
               Horton, p 47-48
               Koch, p 91-92

73. When checking the census data at South Beach Women's Center, you see that just yesterday, there were four sets of triplets, five sets of twins and eight single births. Yesterday, South Beach Women's Center had

    A. 17 deliveries.
    B. 25 deliveries.
    C. 30 deliveries.
    D. 39 deliveries.

REFERENCE: Koch, p 140
               Horton, p 102

74. In preparing the retention schedule for health records, the most concrete guidance in determining when records may be destroyed will be

    A. the average readmission rate for the facility.
    B. the available options for inactive records.
    C. the statute of limitations in your state.
    D. Joint Commission and AOA standards regarding minimum retention periods.

REFERENCE: McWay (2003), p 75-76
               LaTour and Eichenwald-Maki, p 202
               Johns, p 683-684
               Pozgar, p 303-304
               Roach, p 40-48

The Credentialing Committee reviewed Dr. Hernandez's application for renewal of his medical staff privileges. They noted that Dr. Hernandez had a high incidence of nosocomial infections after hip replacement surgery. The committee recommended renewal of Dr. Hernandez's general medical staff privileges, but suspended his permission to perform hip replacement surgery until he completed an AMA-approved course on infection control and successfully demonstrated improved technique to the department chair.

75. The Credentialing Committee discovered the problems with Dr. Hernandez's hip replacements by

    A. sampling and reviewing Dr. Hernandez's patient records.
    B. reviewing Dr. Hernandez's quality profile.
    C. querying the National Physician Data Bank.
    D. interviewing the Chief of Surgery.

REFERENCE: Abdelhak p 467-468
               LaTour and Eichenwald-Maki p 505-507

76. You are starting your new job as the sole HIM professional at a small psychiatric practice. The practice uses DSM for billing purposes. You find this "theoretically" reasonable because DSM
    A. is a widely used and accepted classification system.
    B. codes are also valid ICD-9-CM codes.
    C. codes are also valid CPT codes.
    D. is the industry standard for psychiatric billing systems.

REFERENCE: Green and Bowie, p 297
               LaTour and Eichenwald-Maki, p 312

77. As the Information Security Officer at your facility, you have been asked to provide examples of the physical safeguards used to manage data security measures throughout the organization. Which of the following would you provide?
    A. audit controls   C. chain-of-trust partner agreements
    B. entity authentication   D. workstation use and location

REFERENCE: Green and Bowie, p 270-271
               LaTour and Eichenwald-Maki, p 226
               McWay, p 323
               Marreel and McLellan, p 161-163

78. The MS-DRG weight in a particular case is 2.0671 and the hospital's payment rate is $3,027. How much would the hospital receive as reimbursement in this case?
    A. $3,027.00   C. $6,257.11
    B. $5,094.10   D. $ 960.00

REFERENCE: Johns, p 277-278
               Abdelhak, p 660

79. A patient's husband slipped and fell in your HIM reception area and now he is suing the facility. You have to prepare detailed written answers to a long list of questions and send them to your hospital attorney. You will spend the afternoon working on
    A. affidavits.   C. interrogatories.
    B. allocutions.   D. depositions.

REFERENCE: McWay (2003), p 27
               LaTour and Eichenwald-Maki, p 243
               Pozgar, p 527
               Abdelhak, p 507

Use the information on errors in indexing of scanned material that you have collected and presented in the table below to answer the next two questions.

TYPE OF MATERIAL	NUMBER SCANNED	NUMBER INDEXING ERRORS
CONSULTATION REPORTS	2879	431
LAB SLIPS	15242	458
CORRESPONDENCE	1426	114
OTHER	6271	313

80. If you want to begin with the type of material that has the highest error rate, you will start by working on problems with
    A. consultation reports.
    B. lab slips.
    C. correspondence.
    D. other.

REFERENCE: Koch, p 48
               Abdelhak, p 373

81. Referring again to the data collected on scanning errors, if you want to work on the type of material with the highest volume, you will work on problems with
    A. consultation reports.
    B. lab slips.
    C. correspondence.
    D. other.

REFERENCE: Koch, p 48
               Abdelhak, p 373

82. You are providing an educational session to new hires at your hospital. You tell the new employees that hospital records may be used as evidence in court even though hearsay laws bar the use of most evidence that does not represent personal knowledge of the witness. That's because the hospital record
    A. is written rather than spoken.
    B. was kept in the regular course of business.
    C. has not been tampered with in any way.
    D. is accurate and complete.

REFERENCE: McWay (2003), p 156
               Abdelhak, p 514
               LaTour and Eichenwald-Maki, p 261
               Pozgar, p 295
               Roach, p 383-387

83. Which of the following responsibilities would you expect to find on the job description of a facility's Information Security Officer, but NOT on the job description of Chief Privacy Officer?
    A. cooperate with the Office of Civil Rights in compliance investigations
    B. conduct audit trails to monitor inappropriate access to system information
    C. oversee the patient's right to inspect, amend, and restrict access to protected health information
    D. monitor the facility's business associate agreements

REFERENCE: McWay, p 36, 57-61, 324
               Green and Bowie, p 42, 270
               LaTour and Eichenwald-Maki, p 137-138
               Johns, p 818-820

84. Sally is a HIM professional with many years of experience. Unlike some of her colleagues, Sally loves the challenge of adapting to change. She is happy that HIPAA empowers the Secretary of DHHS to adopt standards for electronically maintained health information. Sally hopes the standardization under HIPAA will make it easier to design safeguards for electronic data, to protect against unauthorized access,
    A. to make and use copies of the data, and to guard against unauthorized data integration.
    B. to protect electronic records from corruption, and to prosecute hackers under federal law.
    C. to prevent the corruption of electronically stored data, and to protect the integrity of the information itself.
    D. to submit revisions of claims as they are denied, and to track third-party payers.

REFERENCE: McWay, p 57, 322-324
               Abdelhak, p 512
               LaTour and Eichenwald-Maki, p 252-260
               Johns, p 700-703

85. An 11-year-old female is brought to the emergency room with a compound, comminuted fracture of the right tibia and fibula. Her mother was very seriously injured in the same accident and is unconscious. What should be done?
    A. Nothing until consent can be obtained from the nearest relative.
    B. The mother can be treated under implied consent, but not the child.
    C. The hospital should quickly seek a court-appointed guardian for the child.
    D. Both patients can be treated under implied consent.

REFERENCE: McWay (2003), 122-127
               Pozgar, p 328
               Roach, p 76-77
               Johns, p 62

86. A pharmacist at your facility was caught running a drug ring. The pharmacist filled orders of valuable medications with cheap outdated ones purchased on the Internet, then sold the good drugs for profit. Patients have been injured and the lawsuits are starting. Unfortunately, your facility is going to be held responsible for the pharmacist's negligent acts under the doctrine of
    A. adjudicus res.   C. respondeat superior.
    B. res ipsa loquitur.   D. stare decisis.

REFERENCE: McWay (2003), 49-50
               Pozgar, p 90, 147-150

87. A clerk brings you a question about a request for information. The patient was treated for meningitis at age 3 (15 years ago). The patient is now 18. The patient's attorney is requesting information on the admission. You tell the clerk the information is
    A. no longer available because your facility retains information for 10 years after the last patient visit.
    B. available, but the attorney will have to obtain a court order before you will release it.
    C. available, but the patient's parents will have to sign a consent for you to release it.
    D. available and the patient may sign a consent to release the information in the record.

REFERENCE: McWay (2003), p 96-100
               Abdelhak, p 442-444
               LaTour and Eichenwald-Maki, p 255-256

88. A patient has written to request a copy of his own record. When the clerk checked the record, it was noted that the patient was last admitted to the psychiatric unit of the facility. You advise the clerk to
    A. comply with the request immediately.
    B. contact the patient's attending physician before complying.
    C. ignore the request and advise you if it is repeated.
    D. ask the patient to send the required fee prior to the release.

REFERENCE: Green and Bowie, p 283-284
               Abdelhak, p 525
               LaTour and Eichenwald-Maki, p 280-281
               Johns, p 75

89. Your HIS Department receives an authorization for Sara May's medical history to be sent to her attorney, but the expiration date noted on the authorization has passed. What action is appropriate according to HIPAA privacy rules?
    A. Do not honor because the authorization is invalid.
    B. Contact the patient to get permission to respond.
    C. Contact the attending physician for permission to respond.
    D. Honor the authorization since the patient obviously approves of the release.

REFERENCE: McWay (2003), p 97-98
               Hughes (AHIMA)

90. Codes act as a primary means of communication with third-party payers. You look forward to the day that you will use
    A. ICD-9-CM procedure codes for inpatients and HCPCS or CPT procedure codes for outpatients.
    B. ICD-9-CM procedure codes for outpatients and HCPCS or CPT procedure codes for inpatients.
    C. ICD-9-CM procedure codes for all patients, regardless of setting.
    D. one universal procedure coding system for all patients, regardless of setting.

REFERENCE: Green and Bowie, p 293
               Abdelhak, p 202
               McWay, p 128, 132

91. As the Information Security Officer at your facility, you have been asked to provide examples of technical security safeguards adopted as a result of HIPAA legislation. Which of the following would you provide?
    A. audit controls
    B. evidence of security awareness training
    C. surge protectors
    D. workstation use and location

REFERENCE: McWay, p 323
               Green and Bowie, p 270-271
               Johns, p 867-869
               LaTour and Eichenwald-Maki, p 227
               Eichenwald and Petterson, p 38

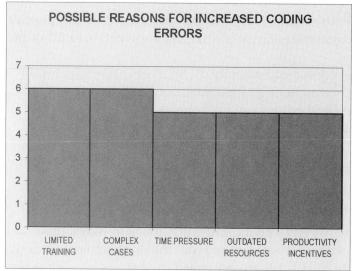

92. After your coders helped you rank the reasons for coding errors in the order of their importance, you then plotted the results on the chart above. The results of your work surprise you because
    A. you expected the coders to put more emphasis on time pressure.
    B. you thought limited training was the primary reason for the errors.
    C. the rankings show surprising disagreement on the issue.
    D. the results appear to violate the Pareto principle.

REFERENCE: McWay, p 148-149, 274
                Brassard, 95
                LaTour and Eichenwald-Maki, p 674

93. Joanie Howell presents to Dr. Franklin requesting rhinoplasty. Because Howell is covered by Medicare, Dr. Franklin must provide Howell with
    A. a Notice of Exclusion, because rhinoplasty is not a Medicare covered service.
    B. an Advance Beneficiary Notice, because rhinoplasty is not a Medicare covered service.
    C. a Notice of Exclusion, because Howell's rhinoplasty may not be medically necessary.
    D. an Advance Beneficiary Notice, because Howell's rhinoplasty may not be medically necessary.

REFERENCE: Green and Rowell, p 125, 252-253, 328-329, 441-443
                LaTour and Eichenwald-Maki, p 383-385
                Johns, p 308-310

94. A 19-year-old former patient faxes a request to your facility requesting the release of his medical records of all episodes of care to the Army. The release of information clerk should
    A. send the records as requested.
    B. inform the young man that specific reports must be identified in his request.
    C. send a letter informing him that faxed requests are not accepted.
    D. deny the request.

REFERENCE: McWay (2003), p 96-100
                Abdelhak, p 524
                LaTour and Eichenwald-Maki, p 252-254

95. A 16-year-old male was treated at your facility for a closed head injury. The patient's 18-year-old wife accompanied him to the hospital and signed the consent for admission and treatment because of the patient's incapacity at the time. The patient has requested that copies of his medical records be sent to his attorney. Who should sign the authorization to release the records?
    A. the patient
    B. either of the patient's parents
    C. the patient's parent or legal guardian
    D. the patient's wife

REFERENCE: McWay (2003), p 96-100
               Abdelhak, p 524
               LaTour and Eichenwald-Maki, p 252-254

96. A 75- year-old patient was admitted for repair of a hiatal hernia, which was performed on the first day of admission. While recovering, the patient fell out of bed and sustained a fractured femur which was surgically reduced. Further complications included severe angina for which a cardiac catheterization and PTCA were performed. The principal procedure is
    A. femur reduction.   C. catheterization.
    B. herniorrhaphy.   D. PTCA.

REFERENCE: Green, p 204-205, 208-210
               Green and Bowie, p 118
               Green and Rowell, p 127-128
               Brown, p 21-27

97. Sally had three babies in 4 years and she considered that more than enough. During her hospitalization for her third delivery, Sally had a sterilization procedure performed. When the record is coded, the V-code for sterilization, V25.2 is
    A. not used.
    B. used and sequenced as the principal diagnosis.
    C. used and sequenced as a secondary diagnosis.
    D. the only code used.

REFERENCE: Schraffenberger, p 319
               Brown, p 236

98. A transcription unit has been asked to tally the number of times they have to leave sections of a report blank for various reasons (poor dictation technique, background noise, etc.). The quality improvement tool most likely to help collect this data would be
    A. force field analysis.   C. flowchart.
    B. decision matrix.   D. check sheet.

REFERENCE: LaTour and Eichenwald-Maki, p 674-675
               Brassard, p 31

99. Your facility is part of a community health information network and you belong to a committee charged with the responsibility of encouraging the uniform collection and reporting of data. Among your recommendations is the adoption of a common
    A. data set.
    B. forms design.
    C. record format.
    D. data quality monitoring system.

REFERENCE: McWay, p 176-181
              Abdelhak, p 99
              LaTour and Eichenwald-Maki, p 150
              Johns, p 160
              Eichenwald-Maki and Petterson, p 6-7

100. The Chief of Staff, Chief of Medicine, President of the Governing Body, and most departmental managers have already completed CQI training. Unfortunately, the hospital administrator has not been to training, refuses to get involved with CQI, and refuses to let the administrative departmental staff get training.
    A. This level of involvement is enough to meet Joint Commission standards.
    B. The Joint Commission only expects involvement from clinical staff.
    C. This will not do because it violates Joint Commission standards and CQI philosophy.
    D. If you can talk him into training his staff, you can let him skip the training.

REFERENCE: McWay, p 142-144
              LaTour and Eichenwald-Maki, p 513-514
              Johns, p 565-566

Use the table below for the next three questions.

RECORD COMPLETION INFORMATION FOR DECEMBER 2008				
INCOMPLETE RECORDS	DELINQUENT RECORDS	AVERAGE MONTHLY DISCHARGES	AVERAGE MONTHLY OPERATIVE PROCEDURES	DELINQUENT OPERATIVE REPORTS
604	304	845	526	14

101. The delinquent rate
    A. cannot be determined.
    B. is 36%.
    C. is 50%.
    D. is 71%.

REFERENCE: Abdelhak, p 124-126
              Green and Bowie, p 83-84
              LaTour and Eichenwald-Maki, p 195-196, 402

102. The percentage of records delinquent due to the absence of an operative report
    A. is 1.7%.
    B. is 2.7%.
    C. is 4.6%.
    D. cannot be determined from the information given.

REFERENCE: Abdelhak, p 124-126
              Green and Bowie, p 83-84
              LaTour and Eichenwald-Maki, p 195-196, 402

103. Referring to the record completion data for December, you would be most concerned with the
    A. overall number of incomplete records.
    B. percentage of incomplete records.
    C. percentage of delinquent operative reports.
    D. percentage of delinquent records.

REFERENCE: Green and Bowie, p 83-84
               Abdelhak, p 124-126
               LaTour and Eichenwald-Maki, p 195-196

104. You and the statistician, Dr. Cline, are working to determine sample size. You are discussing which sampling method you will use. There are 1,200 possible records and you need 100 records for the study. Dr. Cline suggests you select every twelfth record until sample size is achieved. This makes sense to you. It takes less time and is less subject to error than other sampling methods. The two of you agree to use
    A. random sampling.   C. systematic sampling.
    B. simple sampling.   D. stratified random sampling.

REFERENCE: Koch, p 11
               Shi, p 272-274
               Abdelhak, p 399
               Horton, p 209-212
               LaTour and Eichenwald-Maki, p 450-452

105. The difference between an Institutional Review Board (IRB) and a hospital's Ethics Committee is that
    A. the IRB focuses on patient care only, and the Ethics Committee addresses both patient care and business practices.
    B. the Ethics Committee reviews ethics complaints, and the IRB focuses on developing policies and procedures.
    C. the IRB deals with the ethical treatment of human research subjects, and the Ethics Committee covers a wide range of issues.
    D. the IRB is made up entirely of patient care providers, and the Ethics Committee is multidisciplinary.

REFERENCE: McWay, p 84, 231-232
             Koch, p 250
             Johns, p 487

106. In order to alter the facility's health record format to achieve a record that is strictly chronological, the committee would recommend a(n)
    A. integrated medical record.   C. problem-oriented medical record.
    B. universal chart order.   D. source-oriented medical record.

REFERENCE: Green and Bowie, p 91-92
             Abdelhak, p 115
             LaTour and Eichenwald-Maki, p 186
             Johns, p 41, 93

107. You are considering the classification of two patients discharged from your hospital yesterday. Both patients had a length of stay that was increased due to co-morbidities and/or complications described below:

- Fred's hospitalization for gallbladder surgery was extended because Fred is a brittle diabetic. True to form, Fred's blood glucose dropped to alarming levels and his hospital stay was extended until it was back under control.
- Ted is also a diabetic, but his sugar is typically well controlled. After Ted's surgery, the physician prescribed a broad-spectrum antibiotic prophylactically. Ted had a severe reaction to the medication and had to spend an additional night in the hospital.

The best way to describe these two cases would be to say that:
A. Both Fred and Ted have concomitant chronic co-morbidities; Fred also had a nosocomial complication.
B. Both Fred and Ted have concomitant chronic co-morbidities; Ted also had an iatrogenic complication.
C. Fred had a concomitant chronic co-morbidity; Ted had a concomitant complication.
D. Fred had a concomitant chronic complication; Ted had a concomitant co-morbidity.

REFERENCE: Green and Bowie, p 118
Green and Rowell, p 128
Green, p 210

108. Your facility would like to improve physician documentation in order to allow improved coding. As coding supervisor, you have found it very effective to provide the physicians with
A. a copy of the facility coding guidelines, along with written information on improved documentation.
B. the UHDDS and information on where each data element is collected and/or verified in your facility.
C. regular in-service presentations on documentation, including its importance and tips for improvement.
D. feedback on specific instances when improved documentation would improve coding.

REFERENCE: Green, p 13-14
Abdelhak, p 183-184

109. A piece of objective data collected upon initial assessment of the patient is the
A. review of systems.   C. chief complaint.
B. history of present illness.   D. vital signs.

REFERENCE: Green and Bowie, p 91, 137-138
Abdelhak, p 105-106
LaTour and Eichenwald-Maki, p 177-178, 186

110. The use of computer key signatures requires the same administrative controls as
A. rubber stamp signatures.   C. signatures made by interns and residents.
B. computer passwords.   D. use of faxed signatures.

REFERENCE: Green and Bowie, p 177-178
Abdelhak, p 178
LaTour and Eichenwald-Maki, p 196-197

111. A number of key elements for your facility's computerized patient record are still input by clerical staff from handwritten data entry sheets. You are concerned about the transfer of data. If the vital signs stored in the database are not what were originally recorded, the impact on patient care could be severe. You are concerned about the
   A. stability of the data.
   B. validity of the data.
   C. legitimacy of the data.
   D. reliability of the data.

REFERENCE: Green and Bowie, p 127
              McWay, p 143
              Koch, p 249
              Abdelhak, p 411-412
              LaTour and Eichenwald-Maki, p 301
              Johns, p 421

112. ORYX is a program that was developed by
   A. CMS to track Medicare costs.
   B. Joint Commission to link patient outcomes to accreditation.
   C. NIH to track communicable diseases.
   D. AMA to allow for rapid CPT updates

REFERENCE: McWay, p 157-158, 180
              Green and Bowie, p 244
              LaTour and Eichenwald-Maki, 2nd edition p 155
              Johns, p 172

113. In preparation for conversion to a computerized patient record, a committee at your facility is defining each of the data elements in a patient record to determine which elements should be required and to set parameters for each element. The committee is working on the data
   A. edits.
   B. reasonableness.
   C. dictionary.
   D. feasibility.

REFERENCE: McWay, p 170
              Green and Bowie, p 243
              Eichenwald-Maki and Peterson, p 37-38
              Abdelhak, p 495-499
              Johns, p 762-765
              Johns (2002), p 219-220
              LaTour and Eichenwald-Maki, p 115-117

114. An effective means of protecting the security of computerized health information would be to
   A. require all facility employees to change their passwords at least once a month.
   B. write detailed procedures for the entry of data into the computerized information system.
   C. install a system that would require fingerprint scanning and recognition for data access.
   D. develop clear policies on data security that are supported by the top management of the facility.

REFERENCE: McWay, p 322-323
              Johns (2002), p 333-334
              Johns, p 865-866
              Marreel and McLellan, p 155, 163

115. In reviewing the policies on release of information in respect to the privacy rules, you note that it is still acceptable to allow release of protected health information without patient permission to
   A.   the patient's spouse.
   B.   a health care provider interested in the case.
   C.   the quality assurance committee for review purposes.
   D.   a third-party payer with a direct interest in the case.

REFERENCE: McWay (2003), p 96-100
             LaTour and Eichenwald-Maki, p 253-254

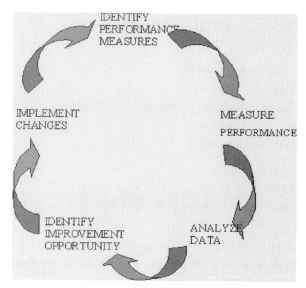

116. Your facility has been working to develop a strong performance improvement model and they have come up with the model shown above. They ask if you see anything missing from the model. You tell them they
   A.   are missing a step requiring regular employee input into the process.
   B.   are missing a step requiring reporting to the board of directors.
   C.   are missing a step requiring ongoing monitoring and reassessment.
   D.   aren't missing any steps; the model is a good one.

REFERENCE: Shaw, p 8-9
             McWay, p 152

117. Part of your job description is to educate physicians regarding proper documentation policies and standards. You are the
   A.   Information Security Manager.   C.   Health Information Manager.
   B.   Clinical Data Specialist.   D.   Risk Manager.

REFERENCE: Green and Bowie, p 101-102
             Johns, p 652

118. Your hospital has purchased a number of outpatient facilities. You have been assigned to chair an interdisciplinary committee that will write record retention policies for the new corporation. You begin by telling the committee their primary consideration when making retention decisions must be

A. space considerations.
B. statutory requirements.
C. provider preferences.
D. professional standards.

REFERENCE: McWay (2003), 75-78
McWay, p 112-113
Abdelhak, p 512
Johns, p 695
LaTour and Eichenwald-Maki, p 202-203

119. The Health Department is considering a big newspaper advertising campaign to promote their family planning services. You suggest they first conduct an external analysis to determine the type of advertising most of the people in your target group rely on when making health care choices. You are suggesting the Health Department first engage in a(n)

A. SWOT analysis.
B. gap analysis.
C. utilization analysis.
D. allocation analysis.

REFERENCE: Johns (2002), p 107

120. Your facility is storing scanned records for long-term storage on optical disk. The Risk Management Committee's Disaster Task Force has recommended that copies of the disks be stored at a facility across town. The administrator is concerned that records may be altered on the disks stored off-site. You tell the administrator

A. this is a legitimate concern; it should be addressed in the contract written with the storage facility.
B. this is not a concern because WORM technology makes it impossible to alter the documents.
C. this is a legitimate concern; perhaps the committee should consider storing duplicates in two locations in this facility.
D. this is not a concern; there is really no need to make and store duplicate disks as they are difficult to damage.

REFERENCE: LaTour and Eichenwald-Maki, p 205
Abdelhak, p 257

121.Your Pharmacy and Therapeutics Committee has asked you to find out more about a computerized order entry system that calculates drug dosages based on patient parameters (weight, age, etc.) and even suggests the best drug given the patient's diagnosis and current treatment. The committee is asking for information on a(n)

A. application system.
B. expert system.
C. ordering system.
D. practice parameters system.

REFERENCE: Marreel and McLellan, p 16
Eichenwald-Maki and Petterson, p126-133
Abdelhak, p 284
LaTour and Eichenwald-Maki, p 544-545
Johns (2002), p 33-34
Johns, p 749, 835

122. A portion of a deficiency slip is reproduced below. This patient was discharged yesterday. Your greatest concern regarding deficiencies on this record would be the missing

Physician: Hunter, J. T.				
Missing Signatures			Missing Reports	
X	History			Diagnoses/Procedure
	Physical			History
	Consultative Report			Physical
X	Operative Report			Consultation Report
	Discharge Summary		X	Operative Report
	X-ray Report			Discharge Summary
	Other			X-Ray Report
				Others

A. signature on the physical exam.
B. signature on the discharge summary.
C. diagnoses and procedures.
D. operative report.

REFERENCE: Green and Bowie, p 153
Abdelhak, p 124-126
Johns, p 66

123. A record documentation requirement shared by BOTH acute care and emergency departments is
A. condition on discharge.
B. time and means of arrival.
C. known advance directive.
D. problem list.

REFERENCE: Green and Bowie, p 130
Johns, p 68, 79

124. Annual costs for the only Release of Information Clerk at Happy Valley Hospital (salary and benefits) are $36,429. The monthly cost for the copier used solely for ROI is $89 (supplies and repairs). It costs the department $0.95 on average for ROI mailings (envelopes and postage). Happy Valley filled 687 requests for ROI last month. The cost per request for release of information last month was
A. $4.42.
B. $4.55.
C. $4.63.
D. $5.50.

REFERENCE: Horton, p 114-116

125. The decision makers in the HIM department have decided to use the decision analysis matrix method to select coding software. Use of this method will help ensure
A. all alternatives/vendors are evaluated subjectively.
B. the personalities of individual vendors will not influence the decision.
C. consistent criteria are used to evaluate the alternatives/vendors.
D. the level of software support will be considered in the decision.

REFERENCE: Abdelhak, p 619-620
McWay, p 157-158, 318

126. Many of the departments in your facility create and modify forms often. A major key to forms control in this setting is
    A. consistent formatting of each page of each form.
    B. capturing every data item required by UHDDS.
    C. giving each form or view an identifiable name, number, and revision date.
    D. providing instructions when necessary for appropriate data fields.

REFERENCE: Green and Bowie, p 184,186
             McWay, p 109-110
             Abdelhak, p 121-122
             LaTour and Eichenwald-Maki, p 198
             Johns, p 369

127. Which of the following names would be filed first alphabetically?
    A. Lovette, Thomas
    B. Lovette, Lyle
    C. Lovett, T.J. (Senior)
    D. Lovett, William

REFERENCE: Green and Bowie, p 198
             Abdelhak, p 224
             Johns, p 341

128. In a terminal digit filing system, with all records in the system, which record numbers fall directly before and after the record number 25-31-99?
    A. 24-31-98 and 26-31-00
    B. 25-30-98 and 26-32-99
    C. 24-30-99 and 26-32-00
    D. 24-31-99 and 26-31-99

REFERENCE: Green and Bowie, p 201-202
             Abdelhak, p 225
             LaTour and Eichenwald-Maki, p 200-201
             Johns, p 342

129. As the HIM Director at the Pediatric Clinic, you have just contracted with a firm that will scan your retired paper records to disk. You tell the administrator you would like to have retired records currently on microfilm scanned to disk, too. The administrator would like to keep those records on roll film to save the cost of the extra scanning. You tell the administrator you don't recommend this because
    A. roll microfilm is an outdated medium that is no longer accepted in most courts.
    B. agencies with more than four rolls of microfilm must store them in fire-safe cabinets.
    C. keeping the old film will require maintaining an old reader-printer for access.
    D. roll microfilm is such an old technology that the clinic should be ashamed to use it.

REFERENCE: Green and Bowie, p 97-99
             LaTour and Eichenwald-Maki, p 204-206
             Abdelhak, p 249-250
             Johns, p 348

130. Which patient numbering system(s) always assign(s) the next new number in the system to link a new or readmitted patient to his or her health history?
    A. unit numbering system
    B. both unit and serial numbering systems
    C. both serial and serial-unit numbering systems
    D. terminal digit numbering system

REFERENCE: Green and Bowie, p 195
             LaTour and Eichenwald-Maki, p 199-200
             Abdelhak, p 221
             Johns, p 339-340

131. A supervisor reviews a job to determine the required content, skills, knowledge, abilities, and responsibilities for the position. The tasks are grouped and lines of responsibility and authority are defined. The supervisor is writing a job
    A. description.   C. process.
    B. analysis.   D. detail.

REFERENCE: McWay, p 300
             Abdelhak, p 578
             LaTour and Eichenwald-Maki, p 691-692

132. The emergency department staff has complained that the clerical staff in your department is delaying stat reports. You decide to meet with your staff and develop a cause and effect diagram to determine possible reasons for the delay. You have explained the issue to your staff and have set up a blank cause and effect diagram. The next step is to
    A. discuss the importance of prompt delivery of stat reports.
    B. determine whether there are internal conflicts in the area.
    C. brainstorm possible reasons for delays in delivering the reports.
    D. design a new system that will support prompt report delivery.

REFERENCE: McWay, p 274
             Abdelhak, p 450
             LaTour and Eichenwald-Maki, p 673-674
             Johns, p 575

133. As your meeting with the clerical staff on the stat report continues, one clerk suggests a possible reason for the delays is a lack of training concerning the nature of stat reports. On the cause and effect diagram, this would most appropriately be listed under
    A. personnel.   C. materials.
    B. equipment.   D. methods.

REFERENCE: McWay, p 274
             Abdelhak, p 451-452
             LaTour and Eichenwald-Maki, p 673-674
             Johns, p 575

134. You stop by an office to meet a friend for lunch. Looking on the desk, you see the grid below: Your friend is trying to

	Rule 1	Rule 2	Rule 3	Rule 4
Condition 1				
Condition 1				
Condition 1				
Condition 1				
Action1				
Action 2				
Action 3				
Action 4				

A. plan a conversion.
B. design a system.
C. analyze a workflow.
D. make a decision.

REFERENCE: Abdelhak, p 620
LaTour and Eichenwald-Maki, p 611-612
McWay, p 86-87, 262

135. The performance standard for coders is 28–33 workload units per day. Workload units are calculated as follows:

Inpatient record = 1 workload unit
Outpatient surgical procedure records = 0.75 workload units
Outpatient observation/emergency records = 0.50 workload units

One week's productivity information is listed below:

HAPPY VALLEY HOSPITAL CODING PRODUCTIVITY WEEK ENDING December 27, 2008			
EMPLOYEE NUMBER	INPATIENT	OUTPATIENT PROCEDURE	EMERGENCY OR OBSERVATION
425	120	35	16
426	48	89	95
427	80	92	4
428	65	109	16

What percentage of the coders is meeting the productivity standards?
A. 100%
B. 75%
C. 50%
D. 25%

REFERENCE: Abdelhak, p 611-613
McWay, p 209-214

136. The coding supervisor tends to deal with issues as they come up, prioritizing only when problems are pressing or appear to be important to upper management. This crisis manager is particularly weak in which management function?
    A. planning
    B. organizing
    C. controlling
    D. budgeting

REFERENCE: McWay, p 249
             Abdelhak, p 573-574
             LaTour and Eichenwald-Maki, p 786-789

137. As a new HIM manager, you recognize that employee development is a necessary investment for the long-term survival and growth of the organization. Your goal is to design and implement a staff development program for your employees, so one of your first steps is to
    A. implement training programs that emphasize teamwork.
    B. establish a budget for all hospital employee training.
    C. survey the HIM employees to assess their need for new skills or knowledge.
    D. establish HIPAA training programs hospital-wide.

REFERENCE: McWay, p 290, 303-304
             Abdelhak, p 598-599_____

138. Now that the EHR has been fully implemented, you are ready to move old records to basement storage. You are ordering shelving for those old paper files. You have 18,000 records, they average three per filing inch. The shelf units you have selected have six shelves that will hold 34 inches per shelf. You will have to plan for a 20% expansion rate to accommodate miscellaneous paper records over the next 10 years. How many shelving units should you order?
    A. 30
    B. 31
    C. 35
    D. 36

REFERENCE: Green and Bowie, p 205-208
             LaTour and Eichenwald-Maki, p 202

139. Postage charges in the Health Information Department have increased during the last quarter. The department director has seen metered envelopes in the mail bin that do not appear to be those used for departmental business. The best course of action for the director would be to
    A. remove the postage meter from the department.
    B. keep a watchful eye on the meter and who uses it.
    C. issue employee warnings at the next departmental meeting.
    D. assign responsibility for the postage meter to one employee.

REFERENCE: LaTour and Eichenwald-Maki, p 608-609
             McWay, p 299-300

140. A clerk's work performance has diminished dramatically during the past 2 weeks. The supervisor initiates a discussion with the clerk, during which the clerk reveals that he recently accepted that he has an alcohol addiction. The clerk states an intention to quit drinking completely. The supervisor should
    A. terminate the clerk if it can be proved alcohol was used on the job.
    B. suspend the clerk if alcohol has diminished the clerk's job performance.
    C. give the clerk a leave of absence until these problems can be resolved.
    D. refer the clerk to the facility's Employee Assistance Program.

REFERENCE: McWay, p 302
             Abdelhak, p 592
             LaTour and Eichenwald-Maki, p 698

141. Everyone in the Health Information Department has been working overtime to complete a major record conversion. The supervisor will have to plan for overtime pay for all personnel who are not
    A. hourly employees.
    B. salaried exempt employees.
    C. salaried nonexempt employees.
    D. temporary employees.

REFERENCE: McWay, p 298
             Abdelhak, p 567
             LaTour and Eichenwald-Maki, p 697

142. If a time standard is determined from sample observations to be 2.50 minutes per record for coding emergency room records, what is the daily standard for the number of records coded when a 15% fatigue factor is allowed? The coder works 7.5 hours per day.
    A. 153 records per day
    B. 180 records per day
    C. 192 records per day
    D. 200 records per day

REFERENCE: McWay, p 264
             Horton, p 119-120

143. The correspondence section of your department receives an average of 50 requests per day for release of information. It takes an average of 30 minutes to fulfill each request. Using 6.5 productive hours per day as your standard, calculate the staffing needs for the correspondence section.
    A. 3.8 FTE
    B. 2.5 FTE
    C. 3 FTE
    D. 4 FTE

REFERENCE: Koch, p 55
             Horton, p 114-115

144. Your hospital takes advantage of the 8/80 exemption for health care facilities. Assuming that no employee worked more than 8 hours in a day, which of the employees listed in the table below will be paid overtime this pay period?

EMPLOYEE NUMBER	SCHEDULED HOURS PER WEEK	ACTUAL HOURS THIS WEEK	ACTUAL HOURS LAST WEEK
101	40	42	40
102	40	38	42
103	30	40	40
104	20	22	24
105	40	40	48

    A. employees 101 and 105
    B. employees 101, 102, and 105
    C. employees 101, 104, and 105
    D. employees 101, 103, 104, and 105

REFERENCE: Abdelhak, p 567
             Pozgar, p 436-437
             LaTour and Eichenwald-Maki, p 697

145. During the work sampling of a file clerk's activity, it is noted that the employee is speaking on the telephone during 76 of 300 observations. How much of the employee's time is spent on the phone if the employee works 7 hours a day?
    A. 1.77 hours
    B. 3.28%
    C. 3.94 hours
    D. 9.2%

REFERENCE: Koch, p 52-54
             Horton, p 112-113, 119-120

146. You are conducting an educational session on benchmarking. You tell your audience that the key to benchmarking is to use the comparison to
   A. implement your QI process.
   B. make recommendations for improvement.
   C. improve your department's processes.
   D. compare your department with another.

REFERENCE: McWay, p 148, 153, 157
               LaTour and Eichenwald-Maki, p 491
               Abdelhak, p 446-447

147. In conducting an educational session for your staff about implementing a benchmarking program, you tell your staff that when an organization uses benchmarking, it is important to compare your facility's outcomes to
   A. nationally known facilities.
   B. larger facilities.
   C. facilities within your corporation.
   D. facilities with superior performance.

REFERENCE: McWay, p 148, 153, 157
               Abdelhak, p 446-447
               LaTour and Eichenwald-Maki, p 491

148. You supervise five clerical employees who will be moving when a new wing of your facility is completed. When you meet with the architect to plan their space, you will ask for
   A. 200 square feet of space for your clerical staff.
   B. 250 square feet of space for your clerical staff.
   C. 300 square feet of space for your clerical staff.
   D. 350 square feet of space for your clerical staff.

REFERENCE: Abdelhak, p 644

149. How long will it take to complete the project described below?

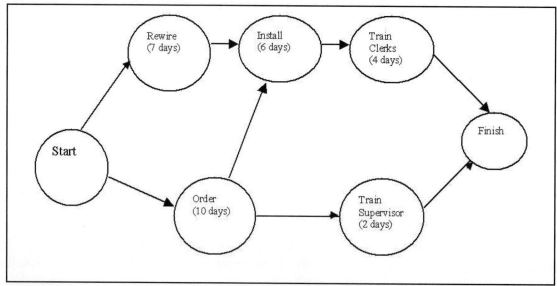

   A.   12 days   C.   20 days
   B.   17 days   D.   29 days

REFERENCE: McWay, p 254
               Abdelhak, p 632-633

150. The file clerks in your department's main file area report they are able to locate 400 out of 450 requested records during the past month. There are a total of 4,500 records in the main file. What is the area's accuracy rate?
    A. 1.1%
    B. 8.9%
    C. 10.0%
    D. 88.9%

REFERENCE: Calculation

END OF MOCK EXAMINATION FOR THE RHIT MOCK EXAMINATION

CONTINUE AND COMPLETE THE FINAL 30 QUESTIONS FOR THE RHIA MOCK EXAMINATION

151. Encoding software was installed at your hospital 2 years ago. The coders are well trained on it and like using it. It functions well and only requires ICD code updates yearly. In terms of the Information Systems Life Cycle phases, the coding system is likely in the
    A. design phase.
    B. implementation phase.
    C. operation and maintenance phase.
    D. obsolescence or decline phase.

REFERENCE: McWay, p 317-318
             Abdelhak, p 310

152. A clerical-level employee reports an incident in which the clerk felt the first-line supervisor discriminated on the basis of the clerk's gender. The best action for you to take at this time is to
    A. thoroughly investigate the matter and document your findings.
    B. talk with the first-line supervisor to determine what happened.
    C. ask the other clerical level staff if they have had similar experiences.
    D. ask the clerk to provide objective evidence of the discrimination.

REFERENCE: Abdelhak, p 593
             LaTour and Eichenwald-Maki, p 698-700

153. A section of a job description states that the incumbent will handle day-to-day operations in the transcription and release of information areas. This section defines the
    A. skills required to perform the job.
    B. time required for each function.
    C. authority associated with the job.
    D. scope of responsibility in the job.

REFERENCE: McWay, p 259, 300-301
             Abdelhak, p 578
             LaTour and Eichenwald-Maki, p 691-692

154. There are 15 employees in your department. There were 21 working days last month. There were a total of 12 lost workdays last month due to absenteeism of all types. The absenteeism rate for your department last month was
    A. 21%.
    B. 57%.
    C. 4%.
    D. 5%.

REFERENCE: Calculation

155. You have been the supervisor in quality management at Happy Valley Hospital for almost a year now and your appraisal is right around the corner. Your director has asked the members of your staff and the physicians on the committees you service to complete forms that will provide input into the appraisal process. In addition, you have been asked to formally assess your own progress in this new position. It is time consuming and more than a little intimidating, but you suppose it will provide you with some good insights into the quality of your work. Because you are, after all, the supervisor in QM, it is only fair that you participate fully in your facility's commitment to
A. participative evaluation.
B. 360-degree evaluation.
C. conductive evaluation.
D. managed evaluation.

REFERENCE: McWay, p 300-301
             Abdelhak p 585
             Johns, p 898

156. You are a new supervisor in the HIM department and find it difficult to deal with performance issues. Laney, an employee in the Release of Information section. has been late several times this month. She has already been given a verbal warning. She was late again today. According to the progressive discipline process, your next step will be to
A. reinforce the institution's policies.
B. reissue the verbal warning.
C. suspend the employee.
D. issue a written warning.

REFERENCE: McWay, p 302
             Abdelhak, p 592-594
             LaTour and Eichenwald-Maki, p 698

157. The CFO of your facility asks you to prepare a budget for the fiscal year based on the past volume and type of healthcare services compared to anticipated needs for the services. This process is an example of using the "_____" budgeting method.
A. rolling budget
B. fixed budget
C. statistics budget
D. zero-based budget

REFERENCE: McWay, p 341

158. The committee that is preparing your acute care hospital for an electronic health record is planning for an imaging system for record archiving in the immediate future. They are looking for a solution for data interfacing or integration of the imaging system into other computer systems. You recommend
A. data dictionary guidelines.
B. Health Level 7 standards.
C. Regional Health Information Organization guidelines.
D. Joint Commission standards.

REFERENCE: McWay, p 174
             LaTour and Eichenwald-Maki, p 160-162
             Abdelhak, p 156
             Marreel and McLellan, p 76
             Eichenwald-Maki and Petterson, p 2

159. Your facility has decided to purchase an integrated patient information system. Your part in the initial work plan is to develop system specifications that will ultimately be sent out to vendors who will potentially submit a bid on your system. You are working on the systems specs that will become part of the
   A. CPR.
   B. IRB.
   C. RFP.
   D. CRS.

REFERENCE: McWay, p 344-345
             Abdelhak p 343
             LaTour and Eichenwald-Maki, p 134
             Johns (2002), p 235-241
             Marreel and McLellan, p 90-101

160. Reference checks are conducted on potential employees to help assess the applicant's fit with the position and also to
   A. confirm the accuracy of information provided on the application.
   B. uncover skills the applicant may have neglected to report.
   C. get another opinion on the applicant's emotional stability.
   D. alert the past employer that the applicant is job hunting.

REFERENCE: McWay, p 284-285
             Abdelhak, p 581
             LaTour and Eichenwald-Maki, p 694

161. Your facility is preparing to invest in a new document imaging system in preparation for the move to an EHR. The Information Technology Department recommends that a system be purchased rather than developed in house and begins to put together a Request for Proposal. After reviewing the strategic plan for the facility, the next step in the process is to
   A. complete an analysis of user needs.
   C. identify interfaces.
   B. solicit possible vendors.
   D. develop training components.

REFERENCE: McWay, p 318-319
             LaTour and Eichenwald-Maki, p 134
             Abdelhak, p 344
             Marreel and McLellan, p 161-164

162. When the National Health care Information Network is fully implemented, plans are to allow for electronic communication among providers using
   A. Large mainframe technology with router connections to individual providers.
   B. distributed technology using existing LANs connected by fiber optic cable lines.
   C. Internet technology that emphasizes data security and confidentiality.
   D. distributed technology using WANs and telephone-based communication.

REFERENCE: McWay, p 175
             Eichenwald-Maki and Petterson, p 5, 65-66
             Johns (2002), p 173
             LaTour and Eichenwald-Maki, p 156

Diabetic patients participated in a study to determine the effectiveness of a new drug, Glucodown. The drug was taken at bedtime. The drug company expected patients taking Glucodown to have a normal early morning fasting blood sugar level. The null hypothesis for the study follows:

There will be no difference in fasting early morning blood sugar levels between patients taking Glucodown and patients taking a placebo.

Half the patients were given Glucodown. Half were given a placebo.

Early morning fasting blood sugar levels are reported below:

Patient	STUDY GROUP (patients receiving Glucodown)					CONTROL GROUP (patients receiving placebo)				
	1	2	3	4	5	6	7	8	9	10
Day 1	102	89	114	95	114	143	160	128	128	106
Day 2	100	83	112	98	99	147	165	111	125	110
Day 3	106	84	103	99	95	139	156	106	115	111
Day 4	100	86	114	102	98	150	168	110	128	114
Day 5	98	88	109	98	91	142	159	102	122	110

163. Based on this information, you would expect the researchers to
    A. accept the null hypothesis.
    B. reject the null hypothesis.
    C. restate the null hypothesis.
    D. draw no conclusions.

REFERENCE: McWay, p 195
             LaTour and Eichenwald-Maki, p 460

164. The researchers in the previous question wonder if there is any relationship between patient age and average fasting blood sugar. The best data display tool the researchers could use to look for a possible relationship would be a
    A. Pareto diagram.
    B. line graph.
    C. scatter diagram.
    D. cause and effect diagram.

REFERENCE: McWay, p 149-150, 152
             LaTour and Eichenwald-Maki, p 674-675
             Johns, p 578-579
             Brassard, p 44-46

165. You have been asked to reduce your department's operating budget by 20%. In order to do so, you will have to effect reductions in your largest budget line. You will have to make cuts in
    A. equipment.
    B. personnel.
    C. supplies.
    D. contracts.

REFERENCE: Abdelhak, p 664
             LaTour and Eichenwald-Maki, p 761

166. Take a look at the comparison of the two life cycles below:

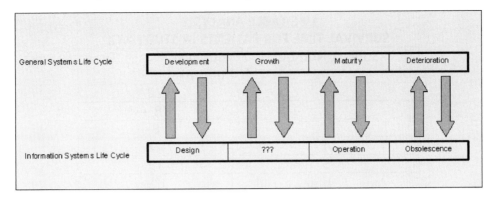

Look at the cell in the Information Systems Life Cycle that is filled with question marks. Which of the following should replace those question marks to make a complete, correct comparison?

A. growth
B. installation
C. implementation
D. reevaluation

REFERENCE: McWay, p 317-319
LaTour and Eichenwald-Maki, p 133-136

167. You are the coding supervisor at a large inpatient facility. Recently, there has been an increase in coding errors. You have a meeting with your coders to discuss possible reasons for the problem. The group agrees on the reasons listed below:

POSSIBLE REASONS FOR INCREASED CODING ERRORS
Limited training opportunities
Case complexity
Time pressure
Outdated resources
Productivity incentives

Having determined a good list of possible reasons for the increase in coding errors, you would like to have your coders help you determine where you should place your problem resolution efforts first. Your best bet for achieving consensus is to use

A. brainstorming.
B. nominal group technique.
C. force field analysis.
D. affinity grouping.

REFERENCE: McWay, p 148, 273
LaTour and Eichenwald-Maki, p 673
Abdelhak, p 450

168. In your job as Chief Security Officer, you are evaluating software programs that will support your policy on sound terminal controls within your facility. One of the features you include in your request for information to vendors is

A. time-out feature.
B. encryption.
C. voice recognition feature.
D. unique identifier for log-on.

REFERENCE: Marreel and McLellan, p 6-7, 164
Johns, p 224
LaTour and Eichenwald-Maki, p 226

LIFE TABLE ANALYSIS SURVIVAL TIME FOR PATIENTS IN STUDY XYZ	
Subject Number	Survival Time (months)
1	22
2	18 +
3	8
4	12
5	19
6	11+
7	14
8	6
+ censored observations	

169. The plus sign beside survival time for subjects two (2) and six (6) in the table above indicate observations on these subjects were censored. This means the subjects
    A. entered the study at an advanced stage of the subject's illness.
    B. have one or more risk factors in addition to the subject's illness.
    C. withdrew from the study alive or were lost to follow-up.
    D. died prior to the end of the study, regardless of cause.

REFERENCE: Abdelhak, p 429

170. As the Project Manager for the upcoming HER implementation, you ask one of your assistants to develop a work breakdown structure (WBS). Critical to implementations and project success, the WBS
    A. lists steps needed to complete the project.
    B. determines dependencies among project tasks.
    C. describes project responsibilities.
    D. defines the project's critical path.

REFERENCE: Abdelhak, p 630
          LaTour and Eichenwald-Maki, p 776

171. As the HIM manager in charge of your department's budget, you are mandated to report on variances of more than 6% either positive or negative to your Chief Financial Officer and include the reasons for the variance and any action plans necessary. Based on the table below for the December variance report, what category would you be required to report on to the CFO?

Variance Report for December			
Description	December Budget	December Actual	Variance
Office Supplies	5,120	5,550	(430)
Contract Services	8,500	8,340	160
Travel	3,500	3,700	(200)
Education	2,500	2,400	100

    A. office supplies   C. travel
    B. contract services   D. education

REFERENCE: McWay, p 342
          Abdelhak, p 664
          LaTour and Eichenwald-Maki, p 760

172. Evidence-based management and decision-making is an emerging model now used to make more informed decisions. The primise of this model is
    A. using intuition based on previous experience.
    B. using a decision tree that branches to alternatives.
    C. using the best clinical and research practices available.
    D. using an alternative that meets minimum requirements.

REFERENCE: McWay, p 145
             LaTour and Eichenwald-Maki, p 611

Beginning Date:	December 2008		Date:		October	2008	
Document Imaging Implementation							
Activity	**Assigned:**	**October**	**November**	**December**	**9-Jan**	**9-Feb**
Kickoff	Team	→				
RFP	PM	→				
SysAnal	PM	→				
Design	ITS		→			
RFPeval	Team			→		
Select Ven	Team			→		
Purchase	CFO/ITS				→	
Build Sys	ITS				→	
Implement	Team					→

173. As a member of the project team for document imaging implementation, you were asked to provide the information in the grid above. This is an example of a(an)
    A. PERT diagram.   C. PMBOK chart.
    B. Gantt chart.   D. work flow diagram.

REFERENCE: McWay, p 254
             Marreel and McLellan, p 150
             Abdelhak, p 601
             LaTour and Eichenwald-Maki, p 601

174. Carson surveyed members of AHIMA's student CoP regarding the relationship between clinical experiences and job opportunities. All respondents were seniors in HIA programs and each one expected to graduate and take the national exam within the next 6 months. Fifteen of the eighteen respondents indicated at least one clinical rotation had resulted in a job offer. Based on this information, Carson expects to be offered a job during senior clinical rotations. Carson is basing this expectation on
    A. scientific inquiry.   C. inductive reasoning.
    B. empiricism.   D. deductive reasoning.

REFERENCE: LaTour and Eichenwald-Maki, p 442

175. Investigator A claims his results are statistically significant at the 10% level. Investigator B argues that significance should be announced only if the results are statistically significant at the 5% level. From this we can conclude
    A. if investigator A has significant results at the 10% level, they will never be significant at the 5% level.
    B. it will be more difficult for investigator A to reject the statistical null hypotheses if he always works at the 10% level compared with investigator B who works at the 5% level.
    C. if investigator A has significant results at the 10% level, they will also be significant at the 5% level.
    D. it will be less difficult for investigator A to reject the statistical null hypotheses if he always works at the 10% level compared with investigator B, who works at the 5% level.

REFERENCE: McWay, p 195
             Abdelhak, p 393
             LaTour and Eichenwald-Maki, p 460

176. A researcher at your facility has submitted his study to the IRB for approval. As a member of the IRB Review Committee, you note that his research is investigating lung cancer occurrence in women who smoke. His timeframe for the study is January through December of 2008. In this study, the independent variable in this case is:
    A. the study timeframe.   C. women who do not smoke.
    B. women who smoke.   D. cancer occurrence.

REFERENCE: Shi, p 11-12
             LaTour and Eichenwald-Maki, p 452
             Abdelhak, p 406

177. Your HIM department is moving to a new location, and in order to arrange your employees and functions for optimal work flow efficiency and to decide which employees need to be placed close to each other, the tool you decide to use is a
    A. data flow diagram.   C. proximity chart.
    B. PERT chart.   D. flow process chart.

REFERENCE: LaTour and Eichenwald-Maki, p 669
             Abdelhak, p 661

178. A p value of less than 0.05 is what researchers commonly use to reject the null hypothesis. A small p value may place interpretation of the results of the study at risk for a
    A. sampling error.   C. type 1 (a) error.
    B. stratification error.   D. type 2 (b) error.

REFERENCE: Abdelhak, p 393
             LaTour and Eichenwald-Maki, p 460

179. Which of the following employees would be considered exempt under the Fair Labor Standards Act?
    A. the head of the Department of Health Information Services who is involved in decision making and planning 90% of the time
    B. the coding supervisor who has responsibility for three employees and performs analysis and coding 80% of the time
    C. the departmental secretary who is responsible for performing a variety of clerical and administrative tasks
    D. the sole employee in the physician's workroom who has responsibility for maintaining and tracking medical record deficiencies

REFERENCE: McWay, p 298
             Abdelhak, p 567
             Pozgar, p 436-437

180. In order to prevent the accidental introduction of a virus into your facility's local area network, your facility has a policy that strictly prohibits
    A. doing personal work on the computer system, even during personal time.
    B. sharing disks from one workstation to another within the facility.
    C. downloading executable files from electronic bulletin boards.
    D. sending or receiving e-mail from addresses that have not been authorized.

REFERENCES: Abdelhak, p 297

END OF RHIA MOCK EXAMINATION

Answer Key for the Mock Examination

ANSWER   EXPLANATION

1. B
2. D
3. D
4. D
5. D
6. B   CALCULATION: $\dfrac{169.051 \text{ total relative weight}}{57 \text{ total patients seen}} = 2.965807$
7. A
8. D
9. B   CALCULATIONS:

INSURANCE COMPANY	NUMBER OF WELL CHILD VISITS	REIMBURSEMENT FROM PAYER FOR WELL CHILD VISITS	REIMBURSEMENT FROM PAYER FOR ONE WELL CHILD VISIT (TOTAL REIMBURSEMENT/ NUMBER OF VISITS)
Lifecare	259	$31,196.55	$120.45
Getwell	786	$100,859.52	$128.32
SureHealth	462	$54,631.50	$118.25
BeHealthy	219	$26,991.75	$123.25

10. B   CALCULATIONS:

INSURANCE COMPANY	REIMBURSEMENT FOR ONE WELL CHILD VISIT	REIMBURSEMENT FOR TWO IMMUNIZATIONS [(TOTAL REIMBURSEMENT/NUMBER OF IMMUNIZATIONS) x2]	TOTAL REIMBURSEMENT FOR ONE AVERAGE VISIT (REIMBURSEMENT FOR ONE WELL CHILD VISIT + REIMBURSEMENT FOR TWO IMMUNIZATIONS)
Lifecare	$120.45	$10.56	$131.01
Getwell	$128.32	$12.36	$140.68
SureHealth	$118.25	$11.76	$130.01
BeHealthy	$123.25	$10.16	$133.41

11. B
12. C   CALCULATIONS: MS-DRG A $2.023 \times 323 = 653.43$
                                         MS-DRG B $0.987 \times 489 = 485.65$
                                         MS-DRG C   **$1.925 \times 402 = 773.85$**
                                           MS-DRG D $1.243 \times 386 = 479.80$
13. A
14. D
15. A
16. B
17. D
18. A
19. D
20. D

Answer Key for the Mock Examination

ANSWER   EXPLANATION

21. B   The category V45.7X, acquired absence of organ, is intended to be used for patient care where the absence of an organ affects treatment.
22. A
23. A
24. C
25. A
26. B
27. D
28. D
29. B
30. C
31. B
32. D
33. C
34. C
35. A
36. D   A choanal polyp is a nasal polyp that extends into the pharynx.
37. A
38. D   Look up in CPT codebook index under foot, neuroma.
39. B
40. A
41. D
42. D
43. B
44. D
45. D
46. C
47. B
48. A   Calculation: $\frac{(6 \times 100)}{(212 + 28+6)} = 2.4\%$

49. C
50. B   Calculation: $2,655 x 100 divided by $25,000 = 10.6 = 11%
51. B
52. A
53. A
54. B   Calculation: (335 × 151) + (350 × 214) = 125,485
55. C   Calculation: 31-14 +28 + 2 = 47 days
56. A
57. C
58. B
59. D
60. B
61. D
62. B
63. B

Answer Key for the Mock Examination

ANSWER   EXPLANATION

64. D   Calculation: Remaining at midnight 8/1   99
                           Admissions   +4
                           Discharges   -7
                           In and Out Same Day   +1
                           Inpatient Service Days 8/2   97
       Fetal Deaths and DOA have no impact on inpatient service days.
65. A
66. A
67. A
68. D
69. B
70. D
71. A
72. C   Calculation: $$\frac{(111{,}963 \times 100)}{(300 \times 181) + (375 \times 184)} = 90.8\%$$
73. A   Multiple births are still considered one delivery for statistical purposes.
74. C
75. B
76. B
77. D
78. C   Calculation: $\$3{,}027 \times 2.0671 = \$6{,}257.11$
79. C
80. A   Calculation: $(431 \times 100)/2{,}879 = 14.97\%$
                           $(458 \times 100)/1{,}5242 = 3\%$
                           $(114 \times 100)/1{,}426 = 8\%$
                           $(313 \times 100)/6{,}271 = 5\%$
       The highest percentage of error is in consultation reports.
81. B   The highest volume (number) of errors is in lab slips.
82. B
83. B
84. C
85. D
86. C
87. D
88. B
89. A
90. D
91. A
92. D
93. D
94. A
95. A
96. B

Answer Key for the Mock Examination

ANSWER	EXPLANATION
97. C	
98. D	
99. A	
100. C	It is the responsibility of organizational leaders to participate in the QI process.
101. B	Calculation: (304 × 100)/845=36%
102. B	Calculation: (14 × 100)/526=2.7%
103. C	
104. C	
105. C	
106. A	
107. B	
108. D	
109. D	
110. A	
111. B	
112. B	
113. C	
114. D	
115. C	
116. C	
117. C	
118. B	
119. B	
120. B	
121. B	
122. D	
123. A	B. Time and means of arrival are required on ED records only; C. Evidence of known advance directives is required on inpatient records only; D. Problem list is required on ambulatory records by the third visit.
124. D	CALCULATIONS: • $36,429 annual labor costs/12 = $3,035.75 cost per month • $3,035.75 + $89 copier cost = $3,124.75 monthly costs/687 • ROI last month = 4.548 or $4.55 unit cost (not counting mailing) • $4.55 + 0.95 average mailing cost = $5.50 per ROI
125. C	
126. C	
127. C	
128. D	
129. C	
130. C	
131. A	
132. C	
133. A	
134. D	

Answer Key for the Mock Examination

ANSWER   EXPLANATION

135. A   employee # 425: 120+(35 × .75)+(16 × .5) = 154.25
                    154.25/5 = 30.85 average work units per day
                employee # 426: 48+(89 × .75)+(95 × .5) = 162.25
                    162.25/5 = 32.45 average work units per day
                employee # 427: 80+(92 × .75)+(4 × .5) = 151
                    151/5 = 30.2 average work units per day
                employee # 428: 65+(109 × .75)+(16 × .5) = 154.75
                    154.75 = 30.95 average work units per day

136. A
137. C
138. D   Calculation: (You can only purchase whole shelf units.)
                34 × 3 = 102 records per shelf
                102 × 6 = 612 records per filing unit
                18,000 × .20 = 3,600 records for projected expansion
                18,000 + 3,600 = 21,600 total records
                21,600/612 = 35.29 = 36 total filing units needed

139. D
140. D
141. B
142. A   Calculation: 7.5 hours × 60 minutes per hour = 450 minutes per day
                450 × 15% = 67.5   450-67.5 = 382.5   382.5/2.5 = 153
143. A   Calculation: 50 × 30 = 1500   1500/60 = 25   25/6.5 = 3.8
144. A   Although employees 103 and 104 worked more hours than scheduled, they still did not
                work overtime using the 8/80 rules.
145. A   Calculation: 76/300 = 0.253   0.253 × 7 hours = 1.77 hours
146. C
147. D
148. C   Generally, allow 60 sq. ft. per employee.
149. C
150. D   Calculation: (400 × 100)/450 = 88.9%
151. C
152. A
153. D
154. C   Calculation: (12 × 100) / (15 × 21) = 3.80=4%
155. B
156. D
157. C
158. B
159. C
160. A
161. A
162. C
163. B
164. C
165. B
166. C

Answer Key for the Mock Examination

ANSWER   EXPLANATION

167. B
168. A
169. C
170. A
171. C
172. C
173. B
174. C
175. B
176. B
177. C
178. D
179. A
180. C

REFERENCES

Abdelhak, M., Grostick, S., Hanken, M. A., & Jacobs, E. (Eds.). (2007). *Health information: Management of a strategic resource* (3rd ed.). Philadelphia: W. B. Saunders.

American Medical Association. (2008). *Physicians' current procedural terminology: CPT 2009, professional edition*. Chicago: American Medical Association (AMA).

Brassard, M., & Ritter, D. (2004). *The memory jogger II*. Salem, NH: Goal/QPC.

Brown, F. (2008). *ICD-9-CM coding handbook 2009 with answers*. Chicago: American Hospital Association (AHA).

Eichenwald-Maki, S., & Petterson, B. (2008). *Using the electronic health record in the health care provider practice*. Clifton Park, NY: Thompson Delmar Learning.

Green, M. A. (2005). *3-2-1 code it!*. Clifton Park, NY: Thompson Delmar Learning.

Green, M. A., & Bowie (2005). *Essentials of health information management: Principles and practice*. Clifton Park, NY: Thompson Delmar Learning.

Green, M. A., & Rowell J. C. (2008). *Understanding health insurance: A guide to billing and reimbursement*. (9th ed.). Clifton Park, NY: Thompson Delmar Learning.

Horton, L. (2006) *Calculating and reporting health care statistics* (2nd ed.). Chicago: American Health Information Management Association (AHIMA).

Hughes, G. (2002). AHIMA Practice brief: Required content for Authorizations to disclose (updated). Chicago: American Health Information Management Association (AHIMA). Available online at http://AHIMA.org.

Koch, G. (2008). *Basic allied health statistics and analysis* (3rd ed.). Clifton Park, NY: Thomson Delmar Learning.

Johns, M. (2002). *Information management for health professions* (2nd ed.). Clifton Park, NY: Thompson Delmar Learning.

Johns, M. L. (2006). *Health information technology: An applied approach* (2nd ed.). Chicago: American Health Information Management Association (AHIMA).
[NOTE: All references to this book have been listed as "Johns".]

LaTour, K., & Eichenwald-Maki, S. (2006). *Health information management: Concepts, principles and practice* (2nd ed.). Chicago: American Health Information Management Association (AHIMA).

McWay, D. C. (2008). *Today's health information management: An integrated approach*. Clifton Park, NY: Delmar Cengage Learning.

McWay, D. C. (2003). *Legal aspects of health information management* (2nd ed.). Clifton Park, NY: Delmar Cengage Learning.

Marreel, R. D., & McLellan, J. M. (1999). *Information management in health care*. Clifton Park, NY: Thompson Delmar Learning.

Pozgar, G. D. (2006). *Legal aspects of health care administration* (9th ed.). Sudbury, MA: Jones and Bartlett.

Roach, W. H. (2006). *Medical records and the law* (4th ed.). Gaithersburg, MD: Aspen Publications.

Schraffenberger, L. A. (2009). *Basic ICD-9-CM coding*. Chicago: American Health Information Management Association (AHIMA).

Shaw, P. (2006). *Quality and performance improvement in health care: A tool for programmed learning* (3rd ed.). Chicago: American Health Information Management Association (AHIMA).

Shi, L. (2008). *Health services research methods* (2nd ed.). Clifton Park, NY: Thomson Delmar Learning.

Sources for the ICD-9-CM code book with October 2008 updates:

American Medical Association. *AMA ICD-9-CM: Physician, international classification of diseases: Clinical modification.* Chicago: American Medical Association (AMA).

Channel Publishing, Ltd. *The educational annotation of ICD-9-CM.* Reno: Channel Publishing, Ltd.

INGENIX. *2009 ICD-9-CM Expert for hospitals, Vol. 1, 2 and 3.* St. Louis: Author.

EVALUATION FORM FOR THE BOOK

As we have learned through quality improvement concepts, there is always the opportunity to do something better. Therefore, if you have suggestions for improving the book and CD-ROM, please let us know. We invite your input and feedback.

Please rate each of the following aspects of this book on a scale of 1 to 5, where: **5 is excellent, 4 is above average, 3 is average, 2 is below average, and 1 is poor.**

Depth/completeness of coverage	5	4	3	2	1
Organization of material	5	4	3	2	1
Study tips	5	4	3	2	1
Appropriate level of writing	5	4	3	2	1
Cover design and attractiveness	5	4	3	2	1
Overall design and layout of book	5	4	3	2	1
Overall satisfaction with book	5	4	3	2	1

Would you recommend this book and CD-ROM to future graduates studying for the national examinations?

RHIA	☐	Yes	☐	No
RHIT	☐	Yes	☐	No

What can we do to make this book better for you to use? _____
_____
_____
_____
_____

Please attach additional comments if you have further suggestions.   Thank you!

Attention: Patricia J. Schnering
c/o Cengage Delmar Learning
Executive Woods
5 Maxwell Drive
Clifton Park, NY 12065

Email your comments and questions to the author at: PJSPRG@AOL.COM